Global Flood Hazard: Mapping, Forecasting and Risk Assessment

Global Flood Hazard: Mapping, Forecasting and Risk Assessment

Edited by Flynn Hayes

SYRAWOOD
PUBLISHING HOUSE
New York

Published by Syrawood Publishing House,
750 Third Avenue, 9th Floor,
New York, NY 10017, USA
www.syrawoodpublishinghouse.com

Global Flood Hazard: Mapping, Forecasting and Risk Assessment
Edited by Flynn Hayes

International Standard Book Number: 978-1-64740-130-6 (Hardback)

Cataloging-in-Publication Data

Global flood hazard : mapping, forecasting and risk assessment / edited by Flynn Hayes.
p. cm.
Includes bibliographical references and index.
ISBN 978-1-64740-130-6
1. Floods. 2. Flood forecasting. 3. Flood damage prevention. 4. Floodplains--Monitoring.
5. Flood control. I. Hayes, Flynn.
GB1399 .G56 2022
551.489--dc23

TABLE OF CONTENTS

PREFACE

The world is advancing at a fast pace like never before. Therefore, the need is to keep up with the latest developments. This book was an idea that came to fruition when the specialists in the area realized the need to coordinate together and document essential themes in the subject. That's when I was requested to be the editor. Editing this book has been an honour as it brings together diverse authors researching on different streams of the field. The book collates essential materials contributed by veterans in the area which can be utilized by students and researchers alike.

An overflow of water that primarily submerges the dry land is known as flood. Floods are of primary concern in the field of agriculture, civil engineering and public health. It can occur due to upslope factors, downslope factors and sometimes by coincidence. Flooding is the result of an overflow of water from water bodies, due to the gathering of rainwater, or when the river flow rate exceeds the capacity of the river channel. Floods often cause damage to homes and businesses. Loss of life, damage to buildings, bridges, roadways, and canals are some primary effects of the flood. The secondary effects can result in economic hardship due to a temporary decline in tourism, rebuilding costs, food shortages, etc. Flood forecasting is an important element of flood warning. It uses forecasted precipitation and streamflow data to forecast flow rates and water levels. Planting vegetation to retain extra water, construction of floodways, dams, diversion canals, flood plains, coastal defenses, temporary perimeter barriers are few examples of flood control methods that are used to reduce or prevent the damaging effects of flood waters. This book contains some path-breaking studies on floods. It presents researches and studies performed by experts across the globe. Those in search of information to further their knowledge will be greatly assisted by this book.

Each chapter is a sole-standing publication that reflects each author's interpretation. Thus, the book displays a multi-facetted picture of our current understanding of application, resources and aspects of the field. I would like to thank the contributors of this book and my family for their endless support.

Editor

1

A physical approach on flood risk vulnerability of buildings

B. Mazzorana[1], **S. Simoni**[2], **C. Scherer**[3], **B. Gems**[4], **S. Fuchs**[5], **and M. Keiler**[6]

[1]Department of Hydraulic Engineering, Autonomous Province of Bolzano, Bolzano, Italy
[2]Mountain-eering S.r.l., Bolzano, Italy
[3]Obrist & Partner Engineering, Caldaro, Italy
[4]Institute for Infrastructure Engineering, University of Innsbruck, Innsbruck, Austria
[5]Institute of Mountain Risk Engineering, University of Natural Resources and Life Sciences, Vienna, Austria
[6]Institute of Geography, University of Bern, Bern, Switzerland

Correspondence to: B. Mazzorana (bruno.mazzorana@provinz.bz.it)

Abstract. The design of efficient hydrological risk mitigation strategies and their subsequent implementation relies on a careful vulnerability analysis of the elements exposed. Recently, extensive research efforts were undertaken to develop and refine empirical relationships linking the structural vulnerability of buildings to the impact forces of the hazard processes. These empirical vulnerability functions allow estimating the expected direct losses as a result of the hazard scenario based on spatially explicit representation of the process patterns and the elements at risk classified into defined typological categories. However, due to the underlying empiricism of such vulnerability functions, the physics of the damage-generating mechanisms for a well-defined element at risk with its peculiar geometry and structural characteristics remain unveiled, and, as such, the applicability of the empirical approach for planning hazard-proof residential buildings is limited. Therefore, we propose a conceptual assessment scheme to close this gap. This assessment scheme encompasses distinct analytical steps: modelling (a) the process intensity, (b) the impact on the element at risk exposed and (c) the physical response of the building envelope. Furthermore, these results provide the input data for the subsequent damage evaluation and economic damage valuation. This dynamic assessment supports all relevant planning activities with respect to a minimisation of losses, and can be implemented in the operational risk assessment procedure.

1 Introduction

In European mountain regions, losses due to mountain hazards are still considerable high even if there is an ongoing debate on the overall increasing or decreasing trend (Fuchs, 2009; Gall et al., 2009). The concept of risk had been introduced in order to manage the resulting challenges, with respect to temporal and spatial dynamics of social (de Vries, 2007, Cutter and Finch, 2008) and engineering dimensions (Kienholz et al., 2004; Fuchs et al., 2013). Despite a relatively long tradition of the application of the risk concept in the European Alps (Kienholz et al., 2004), there still is a particular gap in the assessment of vulnerability (Fuchs et al., 2012a).

Scholars with various scientific backgrounds have a different understanding on the definition of vulnerability (Fuchs, 2009; Hufschmidt, 2011). Social scientists often focus on the characteristics of people or communities in terms of their capacity to anticipate, cope with, resist, and recover from the impact of a hazard (Wisner, 2004). In contrast, engineers and natural scientists define vulnerability as the degree of loss to an element at risk as a result of the impact of a hazard with a given frequency and magnitude (Fell et al., 2008), regularly assessed based on empirical data or modelled scenarios. As a consequence, there is neither a common definition for vulnerability nor a standardized methodology for an integrative vulnerability assessment available (Fuchs et al., 2007; Papathoma-Köhle et al., 2011), the only available concepts remain fragmentary with respect to a practical implementation (Birkmann et al., 2013). However, the different dimensions of vulnerability such as physical (structural), social, economic, or institutional vulnerability, although maybe differently defined, are connected to each other. Structural or physical vulnerability is hereby seen as a prerequisite or starting point, resulting in physical loss and may influence the other dimensions of vulnerability (Fuchs, 2009; Papathoma-Köhle et al., 2011; Kappes et al., 2012a, b).

Recently, the physical vulnerability of buildings exposed to torrent processes has been studied comprehensively in different mountain regions of Europe facing both the aim to compute vulnerability functions for use in operational risk assessment (Fuchs et al., 2007; Papathoma-Köhle et al., 2012; Totschnig and Fuchs, 2013) and to implement local structural mitigation measures (Holub and Fuchs, 2008; Holub et al., 2012, Hawkesbury–Nepean Floodplain Management Steering Committee, 2006). Despite these efforts, considerable research gaps still remain open: while the first studies combined empirical loss data with information on one process parameter (deposition height) resulting in damage-loss functions, the latter studies were solely focused from a practical perspective on the reduction of structural vulnerability of individual buildings. Quan Luna et al. (2011) added a further step: Based on intensity information derived by numerical modelling back-analyzing the Selvetta debris-flow event, they presented vulnerability curves for the following independent variables: flow height [m], kinematic viscosity [$m^2\,s^{-1}$] and impact pressure [kPa].

The empirical vulnerability functions allow for an estimation of expected direct losses as a result of considered hazard scenarios which are based on a spatially explicit representation of process patterns and elements at risk categorized into defined typological classes. However, due to the underlying empiricism of such vulnerability functions, the transferability to other building types is limited (Papathoma-Köhle et al., 2011). The physics of the damage-generating mechanisms remains unveiled and restricts the applicability of the empirical approach for planning hazard-adapted buildings. In fact, as outlined by Fuchs (2009) and confirmed by Totschnig and Fuchs (2013), the analysis of empirical data from torrent processes has shown that the vulnerability of buildings affected by medium hazard intensities (e.g. 1.00–1.50 m deposition height for torrent processes) critically depends on the patterns of material intrusion through openings such as doors, wells and windows. This points out that in addition to the intensity of the physical impact and the structural response of the considered element at risk also the geometry characterizing the individual building has to be carefully considered in vulnerability analyses (Totschnig et al., 2011; Jakob et al., 2012; Jakob, 2013).

Moreover, previous studies have shown that spatial patterns in vulnerability of buildings exposed to torrent processes exist (Fuchs et al., 2012b) which cannot be satisfactorily explained only by the spatial and temporal process dynamics on the torrential fans. Therefore, a deeper insight into the mechanisms causing losses is necessary as a basis of any subsequent engineering design of feasible and economically efficient risk mitigation strategies (Mazzorana et al., 2012a, b; Mazzorana and Fuchs, 2010). Since in Alpine regions – due to an increasing scarceness of funding available – public investments for natural hazard risk mitigation may decrease significantly, envisaged solutions must be convincing, both from a technical and economic viewpoint (Fuchs, 2013), and also be sustainable from an ecological perspective. This holds also for mainly private capital investments in terms of local structural protection strategies aiming at reducing the physical vulnerability of endangered buildings (Holub and Fuchs, 2009; Holub et al., 2012; Mazzorana et al., 2012b).

From a purely theoretical perspective rigorous approaches to vulnerability computations for structures can be derived from physical and numerical analyses of the fluid–structure–soil interaction with free surface flows. With respect to fluid–structure coupling, Walhorn et al. (2005) presented a monolithic model for fluid–structure interaction problems involving free surface using a space–time finite element discretization. They implemented a strong coupling algorithm and a time adaptable space–time finite element formulation to enforce conservation of momentum and mechanical energy at the fluid–structure interface. Moreover, they obtained an enhanced tracking of the fluid–solid interface through a refined level set method. However, reliable results have been provided so far only for simple geometrical configurations (e.g. single flexure elements impacted by a fluid flow) and the geomechanical processes have been neglected. Similar arguments hold for challenges involving the coupling between fluid flow and soil mechanics. Although front-end solutions for particular case studies have been obtained, so far there is a particular gap for the specific domain of mountain hazard risk management.

Therefore, we propose to treat the complex fluid–structure–soil interaction by decoupling it considering the following distinct analytical steps:

a. For a comprehensive physically based concept of vulnerability evaluation, a very detailed representation of the impacting hazard process is necessary with respect to both space and time.

b. To quantify the resulting impacts on the building envelope and to detect possible liquid and solid material intrusion pathways, the geometrical structure of buildings has to be analysed with respect to the time-varying flow field of the impacting process and, if geomechanical actions may interfere, with respect to the residual bearing capacity of the soil layers the construction is situated.

c. Once quantified the time-varying impact spectrum, the physical response (i.e. resistance) of the building structure has to be evaluated, mainly from a structural analysis perspective (statics, elastostatics and dynamics) and from a building physics viewpoint. The analytical step (c) should result in a comparison of the stresses and strains on structural elements focusing on admissible values providing the short term effects for their structural integrity.

Moreover, the physical processes taking place on and through the building envelope which may exhibit long-lasting consequences (e.g. material intrusion and moisture transfer and accumulation, wetting and drying of the outer and inner layers of the building) should be described. The basic product of this analytic step is the damage susceptibility profile containing the results of a set of ultimate limit state, serviceability limit state, durability limit state and no material intrusion verifications. Furthermore, these results provide the input data for the subsequent damage evaluation and economic damage valuation.

Subsequently, based upon the derived response (in terms of a damage susceptibility profile of the considered building structure), scenarios reflecting the post-impact status of the considered residential building, along with the consequences in terms of damage for the electrical heating and hydraulic system as well as other values, have to be considered. For potential damage analysis Mazzorana and Fuchs (2010) developed a structured procedure to elicit and integrate expert knowledge. Papathoma-Köhle et al. (2012) provides an approach for economic damage estimation and Gallerani et al. (2011) discuss the most probable reinstatement value to restore the full functionalities of the original building. In Fig. 1 the steps of a physically based assessment procedure are shown in a workflow.

Following the workflow presented in Fig. 1 our contribution in this paper is directed at unveiling the sequences of significant loss generation mechanisms, both methodologically and computationally. We will derive simplified computational schemes to perform structural analyses for specific impact spectrums (e.g. negligible geomechanical actions) and check whether potential material intrusion into the element at risk might take place. Finally we will discuss the added value of the presented methodological approach for the planning of both functionally and economically efficient local structural measures as a complement to conventional mitigation strategies. By evaluating the potential damages, the scope of application of vulnerability assessments is expanded beyond its classical role as a decision-support tool and is closely linked to the core of the planning process.

2 Method

2.1 Overview

In this section we address in detail the first three steps of the necessary five analytic steps to accurately assess the physical vulnerability of the built environment:

a. Process modelling, which leads to a spatially explicit and time-varying quantification of the process related primitive variables expressing its intensities;

b. Impact modelling, which leads to the time-varying representation of the actions and effects the building structure is subjected to structural and physical response modelling;

c. Structural and physical response modelling, which consists in a verification of a well-defined set of limit states (i.e. ultimate, serviceability limit states) as well as the verification of non-intrusion conditions for the liquid and solid process volumes.

The remaining two steps, damage modelling and the economic loss valuation, have been extensively covered e.g. in Mazzorana et al. (2012b, c, 2013).

A prerequisite for the above listed methodological steps is to define for each considered element at risk a suitable control volume and convenient control sections where the process intensities and magnitudes have to be traduced into defined loading configurations (i.e. actions). Hence, we define a control volume of minimum extent of parallelepiped form entirely containing the considered element at risk (compare Fig. 2).

To account for geomechanics, it is necessary to define additional control sections extending beyond the previously defined control volume. This is done by encompassing the building and the entire elevation profile and extending it to the stream cross sections subjected to relevant incision processes (compare Fig. 2). Taking a local coordinate system x', y', z' for the considered element at risk, $p = 1, \ldots, P$ control sections A_p are identified by the vertical planes of the parallelepiped control volume. The control sections containing the elevation profiles for geomechanical analysis are variably oriented vertical planes symbolized by $A_{r,z'}$ (where the intersection between r and the base area of the building is a nonempty set).

2.2 Process modelling

2.2.1 Fluid flow process

Relevant fluid flow processes in this context are floods, fluvial sediment transport, debris floods and debris flows (Pierson and Costa, 1987; Slaymaker, 1988). Moreover, large wood (LW) is increasingly recognized as one of the main problems for risk assessment in Alpine streams (Mazzorana et al., 2011), mostly because of the LW potential to (1) trigger more severe flood inundations due to dam-break surges downstream of temporary wood dams (Mao and Comiti, 2010), (2) clog bridges and narrow sections (Diehl, 1997; Comiti et al., 2008), and (3) increase the destructive power of debris flows (Ishikawa, 1990).

As outlined by Armanini et al. (2009) debris flows can be interpreted as rapid massive sediment motions that occur in relatively small and steep catchments. Large amounts of sediment can become unstable in particular geomorphological situations and under extreme meteorological conditions

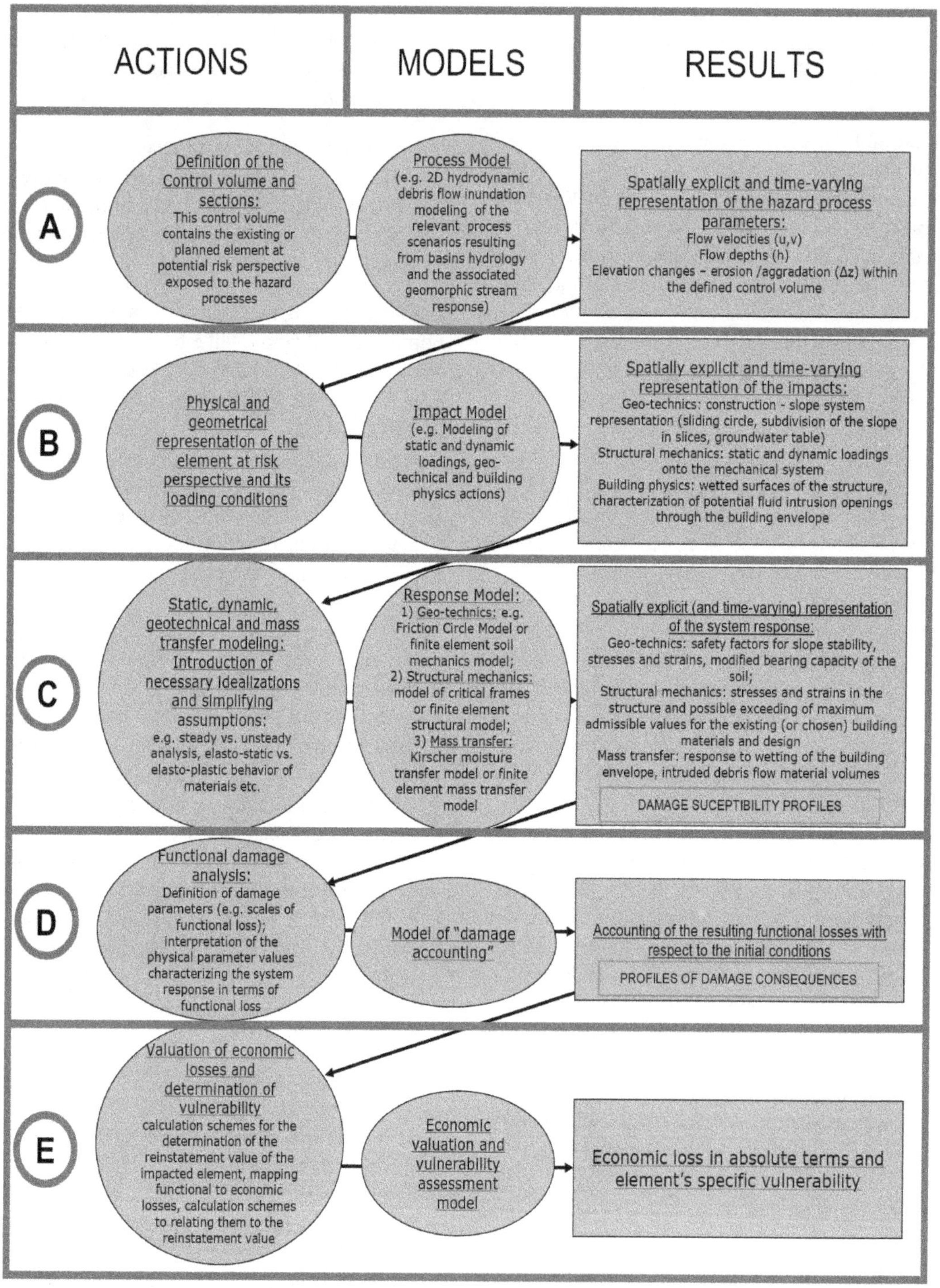

Figure 1. Overview of the physically based vulnerability assessment procedure, analytic steps A through E. Please note steps D and E are not explicitly addressed in this paper, for details refer to Mazzorana et al. (2012c).

(intense rainfalls) and flow by gravity as a dense mixture of water and sediments (Iverson, 1997).

Mathematically, debris flows can be described as a two-phase fluid composed by an interstitial liquid (water) and by granular matter (sediments) that constitutes the solid phase and has proper rheological properties (Pitman and Le, 2005; Rosatti et al., 2013). In the particular, accurate computational modelling approaches have been recently proposed either in a 1-D or in a 2-D setting (e.g. Rosatti and Fraccarollo, 2006; Rosatti et al., 2013), considering the very relevant case of

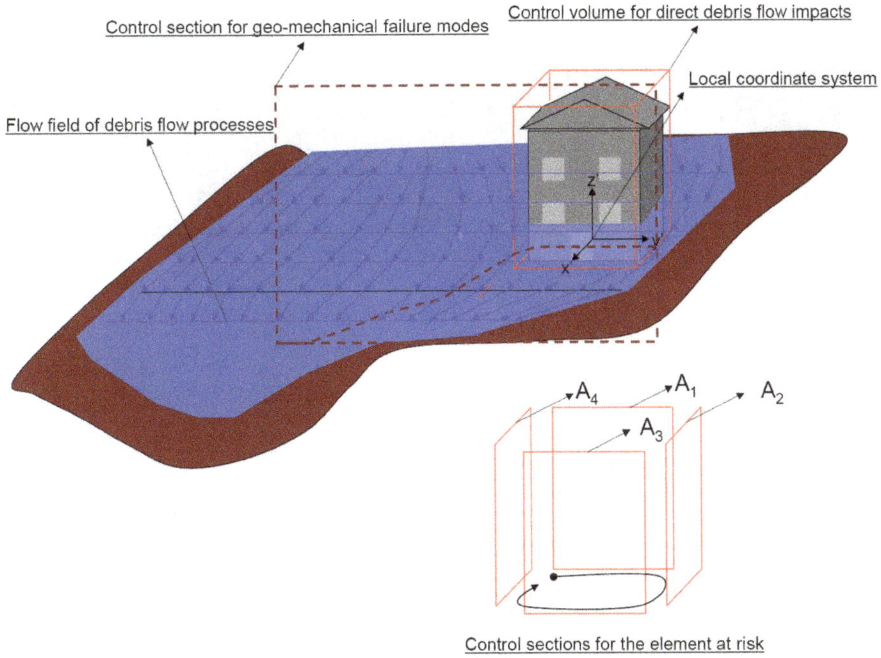

Figure 2. System of control volume and control sections adopted for representing the loading configuration for the considered element at risk. The lateral plains of the control volume identify the control sections through which the debris-flow mass may enter or leave the control volume.

flows of water–sediments mixture without cohesive properties and, hence, with negligible fractions of clay and silt. Whereas plastic stresses may play a significant role due to significant fractions of clay and silt additional research efforts are still needed to computationally implement the most advanced rheological findings.

2-D modelling approaches are required for process representation accurate in space and time for allowing a technically sound and physically based vulnerability assessment of endangered buildings. Prior to this analytic step, a detailed process routing along the stream network where the sediment volumes are mobilized and along which the water and sediment fluxes are transferred is necessary (Hübl et al., 2003). With respect to the preliminary process routing step, a comprehensive methodology has recently been proposed by Mazzorana et al. (2012a). Endowed with reliable process scenarios in terms of both liquid and solid discharges at critical nodes (e.g. apexes of alluvial fans), the subsequent step consists in representing the process propagation in space and time in those areas where the assets at risk are located. Regarding the debris-flow simulation process in the endangered area, the two-dimensional simulation model over mobile bed – TRENT 2-D – developed by Armanini et al. (2009) and substantially enhanced by Rosatti et al. (2013) has been applied. In this model the system of partial differential equations derived from the mass and momentum conservation principles is hyperbolic and characterized by a non-conservative nature. The details about the mathematical model and the associated finite-volume, explicit Godunov-type numerical approach are documented in Rosatti et al. (2013). Applying this approach for each cell of the computational domain and for each time step values for the transposed vector of primitive physical variables, $\boldsymbol{W}$, can be extracted by the following:

As previously stated $\boldsymbol{W} = (h_{\mathrm{DF}}, u, v, z_{\mathrm{b}})^T$ is the transposed vector of primitive physical variables, where h_{DF} is the flow depth, u, v are the depth-averaged velocities in x and y direction respectively, and $z_{\mathrm{b}} = h_{\mathrm{D}} + h_{\mathrm{S}}$ is the elevation of the mobile bed, which consists of the thickness of the pre-existing soil layer h_{S} above a datum and the thickness of the deposit h_{D}. Rigorously, the thickness of the pre-existing soil layer can diminish if erosion of the soil stratum takes place.

Since the subsequent analytic step is the quantification of the impacts on the endangered building under consideration, first the values of the primitive variables for the computational cells have to be calculated for each cell along the above-defined control sections for each time step within the event duration, namely $\boldsymbol{W}_{A_{\mathrm{p}}}(t_k)$, with $k = 1, \ldots, K$, where K is the total number of considered time steps. Second, the evolution of the bed elevation profiles $\mathbf{Z} = (z_{\mathrm{b},1}, \ldots, z_{\mathrm{b,R}})^T$ in the vertical planes $A_{r,z'}$, which identify the cross sections for geotechnical analysis (where the subscript $r = 1, \ldots, R$ identifies the computational cells along $\boldsymbol{r}$), have to be computed.

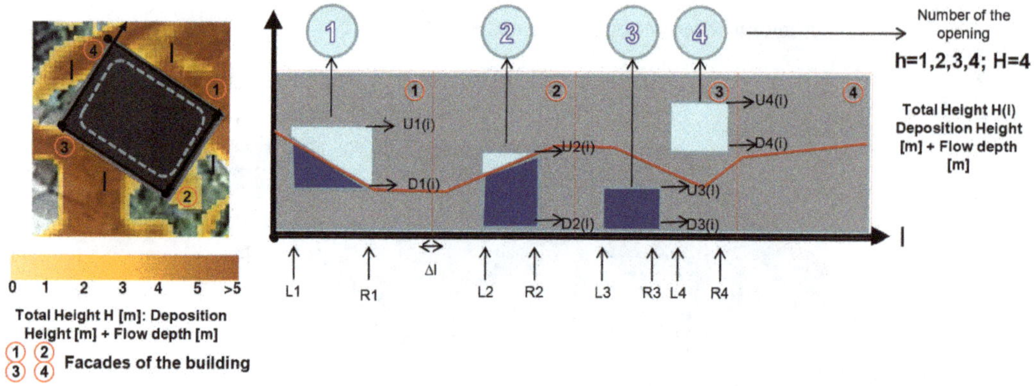

Figure 3. Definition sketch for the determination of potential material intrusion and building physics consequences.

2.2.2 Geomechanical process

The 2-D soil-structure models for each $A_{r,z'}$ might be represented differently depending on the chosen geomechanical analysis approach. In more simple cases of slope stability computations the slip circle method with its slice-based discretization is commonly used, whereas in more complex cases modern stability computation techniques are based on a finite element analysis with peculiar finite element discretization approaches (Plaxis, 2011).

2.3 Impact modelling

2.3.1 Preliminary considerations

According to Fig. 1 and following the digressions of the previous subsection we characterize the impact from a fluid dynamics perspective, from a building physics point of view and from a geomechanical perspective. Concerning the impacts deriving from fluid dynamic actions we first set the analytic focus on determining the loads on the envelope of the building and in a second stage, if material intrusion is relevant, additional loading configurations have to be considered.

As a preliminary step the structural and geometrical idealizations have to be defined:

a. For the purposes of structural analysis the considered building can be idealized in a variety of ways depending on the necessary level of sophistication required to represent its structural and physical characteristics. As a general procedure, suitable for different degrees of complexity, we suggest the application of matrix methods and finite element methods, each one endowed with particular discretization approaches (e.g. Steinke, 2012).

b. For the purposes of material intrusion analysis and for building physics considerations we ideally approach the envelope of the building in clockwise sense along a coordinate l, with $0 \leq l \leq L$, traced along the perimeter of the base area of the building, as shown in Fig. 3. The openings are enumerated progressively with h, $h = 1, \ldots, H$ and their geometry is tracked with the functions, $U(l)$ and $D(l)$, identifying their upper and lower cord between L_h and R_h along the coordinate l, respectively. The maximum elevation of the envelope of the building along l is given by $E(l)$.

2.3.2 Fluid flow impacts relevant for structural and physical response analysis

The main aim is the representation of the direct static and dynamic loadings (actions) exerted by the debris-flow impact on the building's envelope in terms of pressure distributions (pressures in $[\mathrm{N\,m^{-2}}]$). Considering a vertical wall impacted by a debris flow it has to be determined whether the debris-flow surge approaches the element at risk as confined or unconfined flow, and distinct impact mechanisms have to be considered.

In case of an unconfined flow behaviour which can be considered as an external flow with respect to the element at risk, the assumed dynamic pressure exerted on the wall is (Holub et al., 2012):

$$q_\mathrm{p} = \frac{1}{2} \cdot C_\mathrm{f} \cdot \rho_\mathrm{df} \cdot \upsilon^2, \tag{1}$$

where C_f is the drag coefficient which depends on the shape of the obstacle and the flow characteristics of the debris-flow mixture, ρ_df is the density of the debris-flow mixture and υ is the depth-averaged velocity component orthogonal to the projected area of the obstacle on a plane normal to the flow direction. In case of almost confined flow situations which typically occur if incised flow paths develop on the debris cone and the element at risk is located along such a flow path, Holub et al. (2012) suggest the following expression to account for the dynamic pressure:

$$q_\mathrm{p} = \rho_\mathrm{df} \cdot \upsilon^2. \tag{2}$$

Regarding the special case of totally confined debris-flow impacts on a vertical wall, we refer to the debris-flow impact

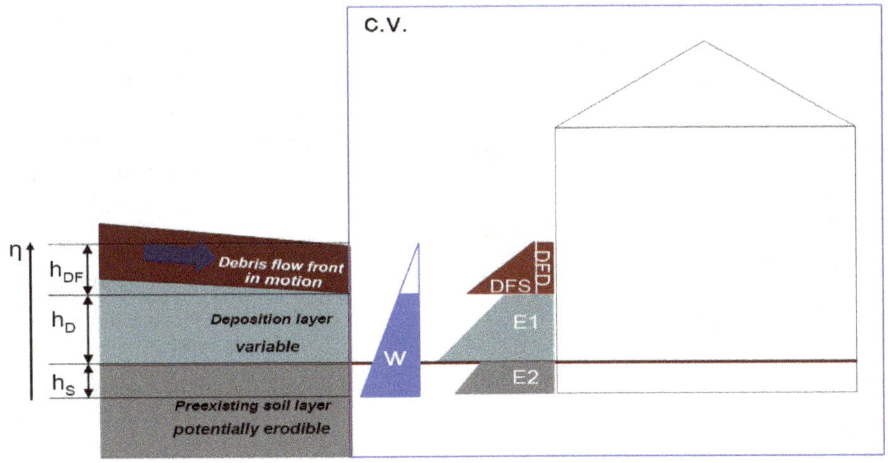

Figure 4. Qualitative scheme of the debris-flow process configuration and the resulting pressure distribution on the exposed portion of the building.

theory of Armanini et al. (2011). Whereas the latter impact case is typical for check dams impacted by almost canalized debris flows, it is rather the exception on alluvial fans where debris flows propagate and deposit. Hence, acknowledging that further experimental evidence is needed to refine the debris-flow impact assessments for the former flow cases, we adopt Eqs. (1) or (2) to assess the dynamic debris-flow impact pressure.

We assume that the pressure distribution on the building envelope is caused by the impact of a debris-flow front, accounting for both dynamic and static components, symbolized with DFS and DFD respectively, passing over saturated strata of debris-flow deposits (e.g. aggradations formed during the event duration preceding the main surge) and the soil layer and which exert both earth and hydrostatic pressure on the building envelope (E1, E2 and W, compare Fig. 4).

Taking the process model results as a basis, we can deduce for each control section A_p the structure of the pressure distribution for each computational time step t_k as follows: indicating with h_{DF}, h_D, h_S the flow depth of the front, the overall thickness of the deposits and of the soil stratum above the building basement level, and adopting the notations p_{DFT}, p_{DFD}, p_{DFS}, $p_{S',D'}$, $p_{S,S}$, and p_W to identify the total debris-flow pressure, the constant value of the dynamic debris-flow pressure, the static debris-flow pressure, the deposit earth pressure at $\eta = h_S + h_D$ (in consideration of the weight of the overflowing surge), the soil earth pressure at $\eta = 0$ and the hydrostatic pressure at $\eta = 0$ (building basement level), the pressure distribution $p(\eta)$ can be formalized as follows:

$$p(\eta) = \begin{cases} p_{SS} - \frac{p_{SS} - p_{S'D'}}{h_S + h_D} \cdot \eta + p_W - \frac{p_W}{h_S + h_D + h_{DF}} \cdot \eta \\ \quad \text{for } 0 \le \eta < h_S + h_D \\ p_{DFT} - \frac{p_{DFS}}{h_{DF}} \cdot \eta + \frac{p_{DFS}}{h_{DF}} \cdot (h_S + h_D) \\ \quad \text{for } h_S + h_D \le \eta < h_S + h_D + h_{DF} \end{cases} \tag{3}$$

with

$$p_{DFD} = \frac{1}{2} \cdot C_f \cdot \rho_{df} \cdot \upsilon^2,$$
$$p_{DFS} = \rho_{df} \cdot g \cdot h_{DF},$$
$$p_{DFT} = \rho_{df} \cdot g \cdot h_{DF} + \frac{1}{2} \cdot C_f \cdot \rho_{df} \cdot \upsilon^2,$$
$$p_{S'D'} = \gamma_{DF} \cdot h_{DF} \cdot K_{ah_D},$$
$$p_{SS} = p_{S'D'} + (\gamma_S - \gamma_W) \cdot (h_D + h_S) \cdot K_{ah_D},$$

and

$$p_W = \gamma_W \cdot (h_D + h_S + h_{DF}).$$

In Eq. (3), K_{ah_D} is the active earth pressure coefficients of the deposition stratum (including the pre-existing soil layer), g is the acceleration of gravity, ρ_{df} and γ_{df} are the density and the specific weight of the debris flow, υ is the local velocity of the debris flow evaluated in normal and inwardly oriented direction with respect to the perimeter of the considered building.

For the computation of the area of the openings subjected to material intrusion we evaluate for each computational time point t_k with reference to the definition sketch shown in Fig. 3:

$$\text{Diff}(l, t_k) = H(l, t_k) - D_h(l) \text{ if } D_h(l) < H(l, t_k) \le U_h(l);$$
$$\text{Diff}(l, t_k) = U(l) - D_h(l) \text{ if } H(l, t_k) > U_h(l) \text{ and}$$
$$\text{Diff}(l, t_k) = 0 \text{ if } H(l, t_k) \le D_h(l), \text{ where}$$
$$H(l, t_k) = h_{DF}(l, t_k) + z_b(l, t_k).$$

The wetted area of the considered opening h is therefore

$$O_h(t_k) = \int_{L_h}^{R_h} \text{Diff}(l, t_k)\,\mathrm{d}l. \tag{4}$$

The total area available for potential material intrusion is given by the sum of the wetted parts of all openings $h = 1, \ldots, H$:

$$\mathrm{TO_H}(t_k) = \sum_{h=1}^{\mathrm{H}} O_h(t_k). \tag{5}$$

To evaluate the area of wetted envelope of the building we proceed analogously, by computing first:

$$\mathrm{DIFF}(l, t_k) = H(l, t_k) \text{ if } H(l, t_k) \leq E(l),$$

where $E(l)$ is the maximum elevation of the envelope at l and

$$\mathrm{DIFF}(l, t_k) = E(l) \text{ if } H(l, t_k) > E(l).$$

The wetted area of the building envelope is therefore:

$$\mathrm{WE}(t_k) = \left[\int_0^L \mathrm{DIFF}(l, t_k)\,\mathrm{d}l\right] - \mathrm{TO_H}(t_k). \tag{6}$$

2.3.3 Geomechanical impacts relevant for structural response analysis

Depending on the results of the analysis of the geomechanical processes (compare Sect. 2.2.2) the associated impacts relevant for structural response analysis are modelled by assuming a lowered bearing capacity of the soil supporting the building.

2.4 Structural and physical response analysis

The set of norms EN 1990 (Eurocode 0: Basis of Structural Design), EN 1991 (Eurocode 1: Actions on Structures) and the specific design codes EN 1992 to EN 1999 inspired our concept of structural response analysis and the physical response analysis concept is analogously set up.

In particular EN 1990 is based on the limit state concept used in conjunction with the partial safety factor method. In this context limit states are intended as states beyond which the structure no longer fulfils relevant design criteria. Two different types of limit states are considered, namely ultimate limit state and serviceability limit state (compare Gulvanessian, 2009). As stated in EN 1990 it has to be verified, based on the application of load models and structural models, that no limit state is exceeded when the design values for actions, material properties and geometrical data are used. Here (a) the ultimate limit states (ULS) and (b) the serviceability limit states (SLS) are briefly illustrated in their essential aspects.

a. Ultimate limit states – ULS: the exceeding of these limit states may result in a structural collapse or other forms of structural failures. They are related to the safety of people and/or the safety of the structure. In this context EN 1990 prescribes the following set of verifications:

   - ECU: loss of static equilibrium of the entire structure or of specific parts, all considered as rigid bodies. In this case small deviation of the value and the spatial distribution of the considered action type (e.g. dead weight of the structural parts) are relevant, whereas the strength of construction materials or the building ground are of no influence;
   - STR: failure or excessive deformation of the structure or its parts including the foundation, piles. Here the bearing capacity and the strength of materials are relevant;
   - GEO: failure or excessive deformation of the building ground, whereas the bearing capacity of the soil (or rock) is decisive;
   - FAT: failure of the structure as a consequence of fatigue.

   All the above-reported verifications consist in a comparison between the design values for the effects of the actions on the building of interest and the design values for the corresponding resistances, namely

   $$\mathrm{ECU}: \; E_{\mathrm{d,dst}} \leq R_{\mathrm{d,stb}}, \tag{7}$$

   where $E_{\mathrm{d,dst}}$ is the design value of the effects of the destabilizing actions, $R_{\mathrm{d,stb}}$ is the design value of the effects of the stabilizing actions,

   $$\mathrm{STR\ or\ GEO}: \; E_{\mathrm{d}} \leq R_{\mathrm{d}}, \tag{8}$$

   where E_{d} is the design value of the effects of actions and R_{d} is the design value of the corresponding resistances.

   This verification approach is based on the partial factor method which incorporates a semi-probabilistic safety concept (compare Feix and Walkner, 2012 for details); a representation is provided in Fig. 5.

   The ultimate limit states have to be verified for particular design situations representing the sets of physical conditions reflecting the real conditions occurring during the construction and use of the structure. The reference design situation for natural hazard impact is that of an accidental situation.

b. Serviceability limit states – SLS: these limit states correspond to a situation if defined conditions are no longer met and specified service requirements for a structure or a structural element are needed (compare Gulvanessian et al., 2004). The design situations to be considered in this case are structural function of the entire building or of a portion, the comfort of people and the appearance of the building. To assess these limit states the following criteria can be adopted: limitation of strain, deformations, crack widths and oscillations. These types of assessments consist in a comparison between the design

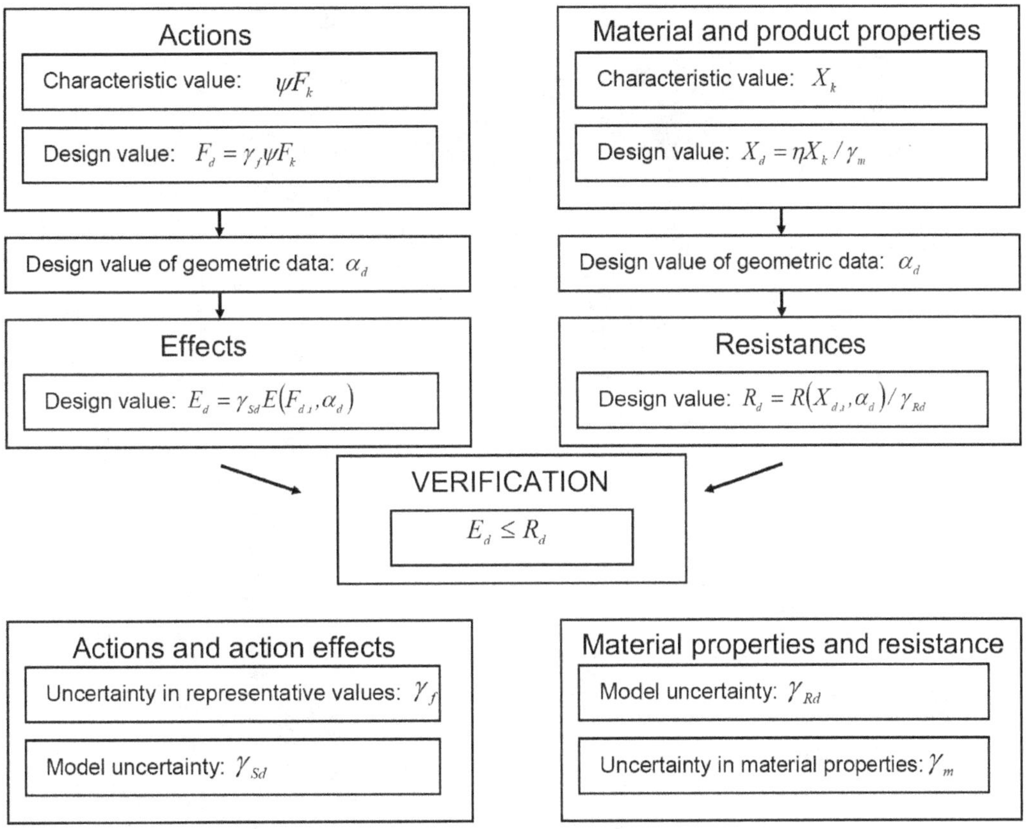

Figure 5. Verification scheme by the partial factor method (after Gulvanessian et al., 2004).

values of the effect – E_d – and of the upper limit of the considered serviceability design criteria – C_d:

$$E_\mathrm{d} \leq C_\mathrm{d}. \tag{9}$$

For complex structural settings it is convenient to use the finite element method – FEM. For specific details about modelling aspects and algorithms employed, the reader is referred to the well-established literature (compare for example Zienkiewicz et al., 2005).

c. No material intrusion limit state – NLS: analogue to the design basics outlined above and in agreement with the methodological approaches outlined in the previous subsections, we add a supplementary limit state, the no intrusion (permeability) limit state. This state is defined as the requirement of that the openings should not be exposed to wetting throughout the event duration and is formalized as follows:

$$\mathrm{TO_H}(t_k) = \sum_{h=1}^{\mathrm{H}} O_h(t_k) = 0 \quad \forall t_k. \tag{10}$$

The limit states formalized above (compare Eqs. 7 to 10) can be used to define a damage susceptibility profile for the considered building.

The damage susceptibility profile contains the verification for the relevant design situations and for all time steps t_k of the ULS, the SLS and the NLS. Since the relevance of both ULS and NLS is indisputable for the generation of direct damages, these limit states are considered in our analytic setup.

Once the damage susceptibility profile is comprehensively elaborated for the building of interest, including also the ad hoc defined no material intrusion and no wetting damage verification (Eq. 10), it is necessary to infer the possible profile of damage consequences, whose elaboration is essentially based on expert opinions elicited and structured through appropriated scenario development techniques (compare Mazzorana et al., 2012a). The proposed analytic setup allows for a comprehensive description of the damage response behaviour of the building envelope. Since the flow process through the building is not simulated, an expert based derivation of stochastic event trees might be helpful in hypothesizing the full range of possible damage consequences of the considered building. In this case, however, subjective probability assignments are necessary. For a comprehensive treatment of rigorous elicitation methods for subjective probabilities we refer to Wakker (2010). Consequently, the economic damage can be calculated (Papathoma-Köhle et al., 2012).

The damage susceptibility profile represents the ideal starting point of the planning process aiming at providing optimal object protection, since the final aim of the planning efforts is to verify that the building under consideration is hazard-adapted.

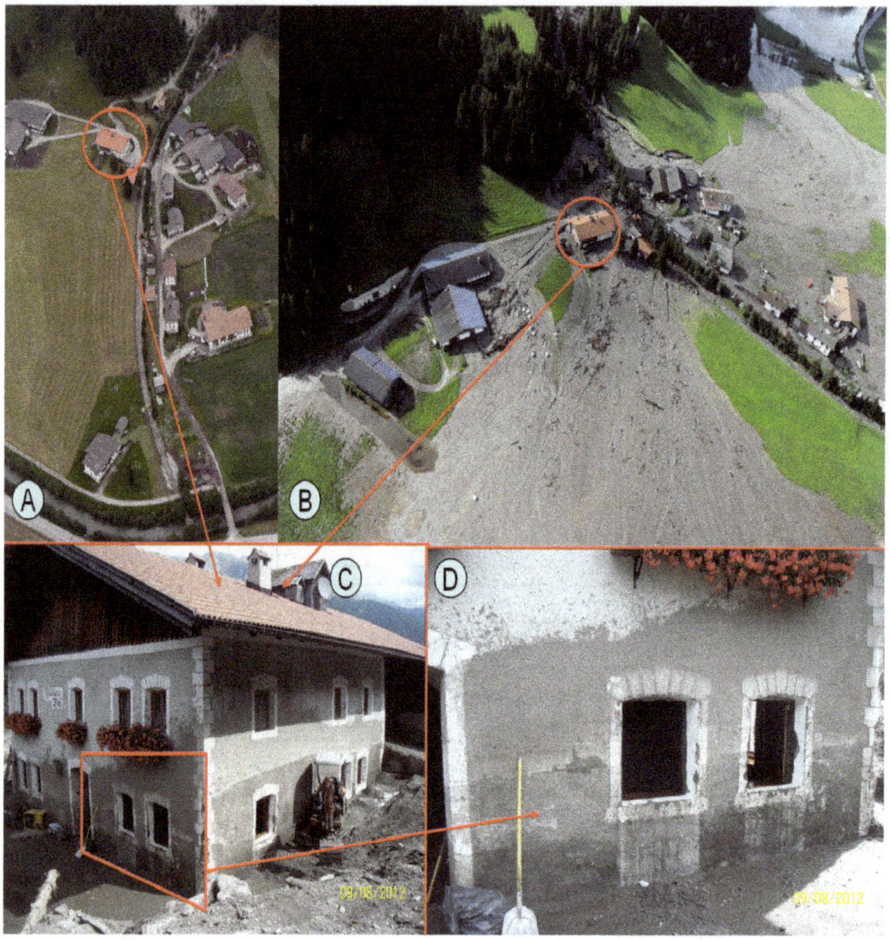

Figure 6. Location on the debris cone and details about the damage process for the selected residential building example. **(a)** Configuration of the settlement area and detailed location of the example building (pre-event situation); **(b)** depositional process patterns on the debris cone and location of the example building; **(c)** and **(d)** detailed views on the impact mechanisms and the damage processes for the considered building.

3 Application to a case study

In this section we present a practical application of the analytic steps outlined in Sect. 2, taking as an example a residential building, which is located on the debris cone of the Grossberg torrent, Italian Alps. In the 1970s a trapezoidal channel was built in the fan area to prevent damages on houses and crops. The channel cross section (5.6 m^2) was designed for a liquid discharge 45 $m^3\,s^{-1}$; additionally a large slit dam with an available retention volume of 19 000 m^3 was built in 2009 at the fan apex to protect the downstream village. On 4 August 2012, an event occurred with a debris volume of 53 000 m^3 and seriously damaged several residential buildings in the debris cone area (see Fig. 6). Following the analytic structure employed in Sect. 2 we first set up a validated process model for this debris-flow event, than we derive the relevant impacts on the buildings envelope and successively we proceed by modelling the structural and physical response.

3.1 Process modelling

With respect to the full procedure outlined in the previous sections it is admissible to restrict the investigation to the analysis of the fluid flow processes since geomechanical processes can be neglected for the specific case.

By means of two-dimensional debris-flow simulation model over mobile bed – TRENT 2-D – (Armanini et al., 2009; Rosatti et al., 2013) the event of 4 August 2012 was reconstructed by using the detailed event documentation data.

3.1.1 Process analysis

A convective storm hit the Pfitsch valley on 4 August 2012; cumulated rainfall in 6.25 h reached 45 mm. Using the intensity–duration–frequency curve for the area provided by the Hydraulic Engineering Department of the Autonomous Province of Bolzano the storm can be classified approximately as a 300-year return-period event. The storm

Figure 7. Overview of the triggering areas and the main erosion and deposition phenomena.

originated in the western part of the Province (Passer valley) and moved in north-west direction, towards the Upper Isarco valley where roughly 30 debris and mudflows were triggered. Triggering conditions have been exacerbated by abundant precipitations, occurred during the previous month, leading to a partial saturation of the soil (total cumulated rainfall in July was 230 mm in Vipiteno). Figure 7 shows triggering areas scattered over the steep landscape.

The watershed of the Gossbergbach is characterized by an area of $10\,\mathrm{km}^2$, ranging from 1420 to 3130 m a.s.l. The steepness of the valley side and the availability of sediments enhanced the process. Figure 8a and b display the steepness of the channel in the proximity of the slit dam and the tendency towards debris-flow initiation, according to Cavalli and Marchi (2006). Red dots indicate channel sections where the ratio between the contributing area and the local slope can cause soil failure.

Hydrological and hydrodynamics modelling was undertaken with the purpose of quantifying static and dynamic loadings exerted by the debris-flow impact on the target building and their evolution in time. In particular, flow velocities (for each control section), flow height and deposit thickness for this specific event are identified. The computational 2-D domain was chosen with the purpose of focusing on the spreading of the debris flow along the fan, i.e. downstream the slit dam. The rational for this was the knowledge of the total volume deposited on the fan. The volume was measured through intensive field campaigns carried out by the Hydraulic Engineering Department few days after the event.

Hydrological and hydrodynamics modelling was undertaken with the purpose of quantifying static and dynamic loading impact of the debris flow on the target building and their evolution in space and time. In particular, for this specific event, flow velocities, flow heights, and deposit thickness were computed and compared to measured values. Patterns of deposits were measured by intensive field surveys carried out by the Hydraulic Engineering Department of Bolzano few days after the event and used for model calibration. The computational 2-D domain was chosen with the purpose of focusing on the spreading of the debris flow along the fan, i.e. downstream the slit dam. An additional rational for this choice was that the patterns of deposition and the total volume deposited an the fan were known. The total volume was estimated to be $53\,000\,\mathrm{m}^3$ Boundary conditions were given in terms of liquid and solid hydrograph; the liquid hydrograph was derived using a back-analysis approach aiming at reproducing field observations, i.e. the event duration (roughly 6 h, compare Fig. 9) and the total amount of transported sediment (i.e. flow transport capacity). The liquid boundary condition was computed using a geomorphic, semi-distributed hydrological model (Rigon et al., 2011) which accounts for different resident times characterizing various portions of the watershed. The rainfall input to the model was derived from measured rainfall data. Solid inflow boundary conditions were calculated on the gradient basis of the stream, the average characteristics of the transported sediments (internal friction angle, d_{50}), and the liquid hydrograph.

3.1.2 Results of process analysis

Results are displayed in Fig. 10c in terms of deposition thickness. Figure 10a and b offer a comparison with the observed event. Considerations on the maximum local velocities may additionally help to validate the modelling results. As shown

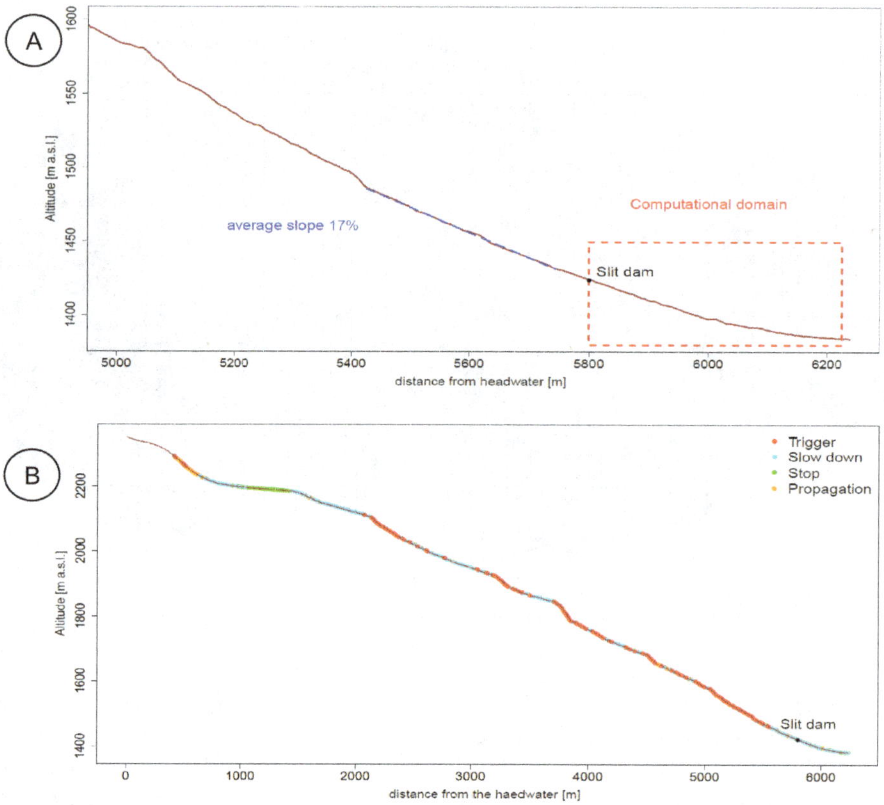

Figure 8. (a) Channel slope upstream and downstream the slit dam. The computational domain is represented with a red dashed line; **(b)** triggering (red) points along the channel profile according to Cavalli and Marchi (2006). Light blue points, close to the slit dam, represent decreasing velocity area.

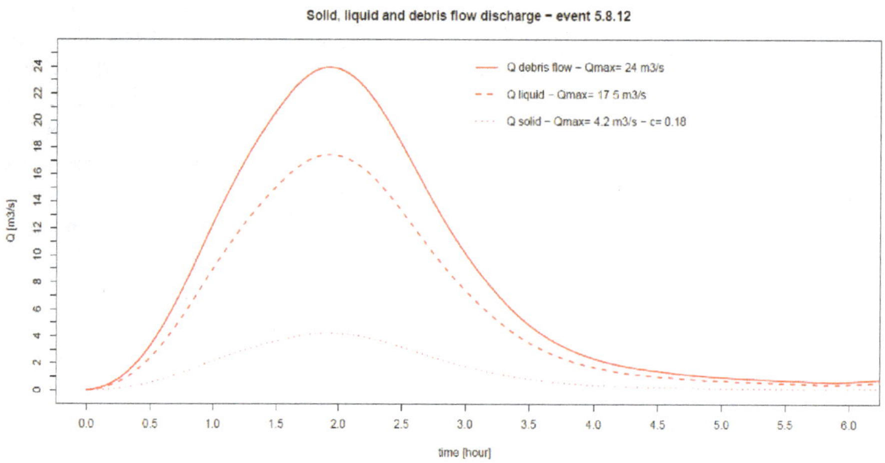

Figure 9. Boundary condition: input liquid, solid and mixture hydrograph.

in Table 1 the maximum local velocities in the immediate surroundings of the selected residential building are considerably large ($2\,\mathrm{m}^3\,\mathrm{s}^{-1}$). Although deposition took place as the net result of the transport process (max. 1 m), relevant amounts of solid material were transported further as it is proved by the large deposition lobe downstream of the considered building.

For the subsequent fluid flow impact, the process simulation output of the primitive physical variables (i.e. debris-flow depths, velocities in x and y direction and thicknesses of the deposition layer) on the four vertical control sections containing the considered residential building are relevant. We considered $K = 3$ representative time steps to mirror

Table 1. Arrays of the values $\mathbf{W} = (h_{DF}, v_n, h_D)^T$ for each control section A_p, with $p = 1, 2, 3$.

Point ID	Control section	Prog coord	h_{DF} [m]	h_D [m]	v_n [m s^{-1}]
0	3	0	0.14	0.00	0.424
1	3	1	0.14	0.00	0.394
2	3	2	0.15	0.00	0.288
3	3	3	0.14	0.00	0.223
4	3	4	0.12	0.00	0.313
5	3	5	0.12	0.10	0.204
6	3	6	0.11	0.17	0.278
7	3	7	0.11	0.21	0.161
8	3	8	0.11	0.29	0.246
9	3	9	0.11	0.38	0.153
10	3	10	0.10	0.44	0.212
11	3	11	0.09	0.53	0.180
12	3	12	0.09	0.60	0.102
13	3	13	0.09	0.60	0.102
14	3	14	0.09	0.65	0.066
15	3	15	0.08	0.64	0.106
16	3	16	0.09	0.70	0.014
17	3	17	0.08	0.64	0.015
18	3	18	0.07	0.57	0.008
19	3	19	0.07	0.55	0.122
20	1	0	0.00	0.00	0.000
21	1	1	0.00	0.00	0.000
22	1	2	0.00	0.00	0.000
23	1	3	0.00	0.00	0.000
24	1	4	0.00	0.00	0.000
25	1	5	0.00	0.00	0.000
26	1	6	0.00	0.00	0.000
27	1	7	0.00	0.00	0.000
28	1	8	0.00	0.00	0.000
29	1	9	0.00	0.00	0.000
30	1	10	0.02	0.00	0.126
31	1	11	0.01	0.00	0.161
32	1	12	0.02	0.00	0.160
33	1	13	0.00	0.00	0.000
34	1	14	0.07	0.00	0.423
35	1	15	0.09	0.00	0.502
36	1	16	0.09	0.00	0.411
37	1	17	0.15	0.00	0.872
38	1	18	0.17	0.00	1.044
39	1	19	0.29	0.00	1.984
40	1	19	0.29	0.00	1.984
41	2	0	0.29	0.00	1.114
42	2	1	0.32	0.00	0.897
43	2	2	0.27	0.00	0.956
44	2	3	0.24	0.00	1.181
45	2	4	0.25	0.00	0.925
46	2	5	0.22	0.00	0.899
47	2	6	0.19	0.00	0.667
48	2	7	0.16	0.00	0.618
49	2	8	0.12	0.00	0.344
50	2	9	0.13	0.00	0.541
51	2	10	0.11	0.00	0.479
52	2	11	0.08	0.06	0.220

Table 1. Continued.

Point ID	Control section	Prog coord	h_{DF} [m]	h_D [m]	v_n [m s^{-1}]
53	2	12	0.07	0.08	0.272
54	2	13	0.05	0.15	0.157
55	2	14	0.04	0.21	0.288
56	2	15	0.04	0.21	0.288
57	2	16	0.04	0.22	0.407
58	2	17	0.03	0.37	0.340
59	2	18	0.02	0.53	0.403
60	2	19	0.02	0.59	0.415
61	2	20	0.02	0.59	0.415
62	2	21	0.01	0.69	0.391
63	2	22	0.01	0.77	0.347
64	2	23	0.01	0.75	0.345
65	2	24	0.01	0.80	0.326
66	2	25	0.01	0.70	0.358
67	2	26	0.01	0.64	0.415
68	2	27	0.02	0.63	0.496
69	2	27	0.02	0.63	0.496

appropriately the dynamics of the debris-flow event (compare Fig. 11).

According to Fig. 11 one may note that the building side 1 is exposed to the debris flow mainly in the initial part of the depositional event; the building side 2 is mostly exposed in the medium time range of depositional event, and the building side 3 is exposed for the entire event duration only in its upper part. This specific pattern of debris-flow propagation is due to the deflection effect exerted by an agricultural building located further upstream.

As an example we report in Table 1 for the time step $k = 2 \rightarrow t_k = 7200$ s the values of the primitive variables $\mathbf{W} = (h_{DF}, v_n, h_D)^T$, where v_n is the flow velocity normal to the control section, h_{DF} is the debris-flow depth and $h_D = z_b$ is the thickness of the deposition layer.

Figure 12 depicts the map of maximum flow velocities (Fig. 12a) and shows as a comparison a detailed view (Fig. 12b) of the mud marks up to the second floor of the building envelope, suggesting that the dynamics of the process was characterized by high kinetic energies.

A complete process analysis should include, as outlined in Sect. 2.2, a detailed analysis of the geomechanical processes possible inducing a destabilization of the building considered. The relevance of such influences, however, can be categorically excluded in the analyzed case study, since no erosion patterns, inducing even the slightest changes in slope stability, could be detected throughout the event duration. Hence, we will assume for this case study, also concerning the subsequent impact modelling, the complete absence of significant geomechanical actions.

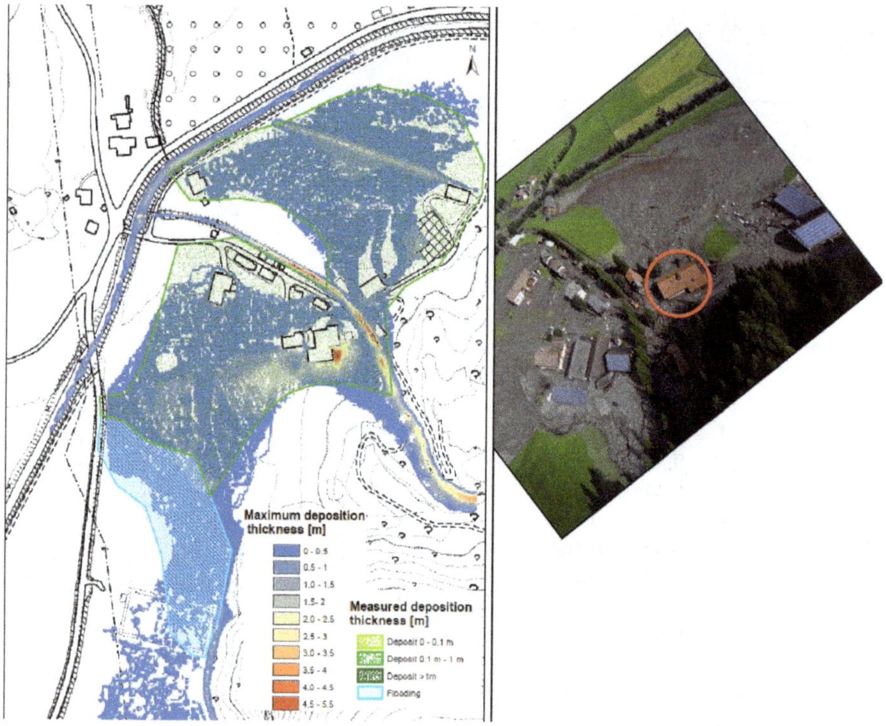

Figure 10. Left panel: comparison between simulated and measured deposition thickness. Right panel: debris-flow deposition patterns.

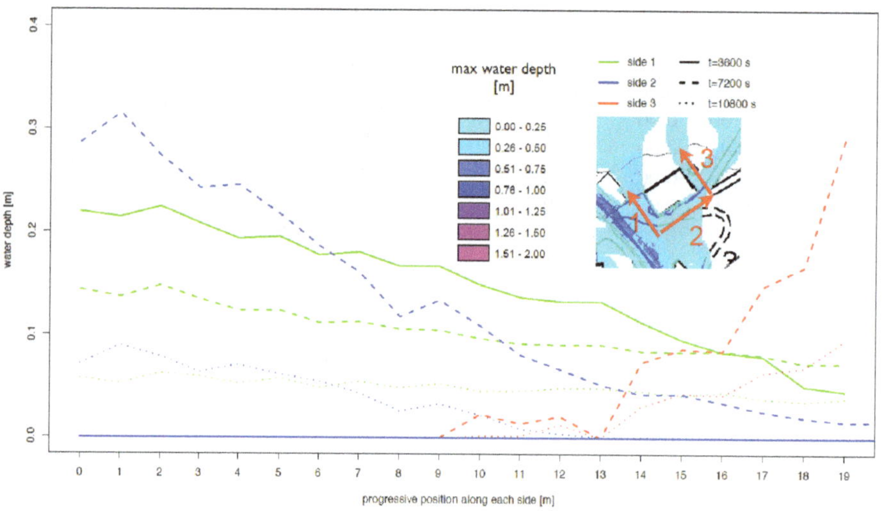

Figure 11. Water depths as a function of time as all positions along the three impacted sides of the building.

3.2 Impact modelling

According to Sect. 2.3.2, and specifically to the analytic expressions (Eqs. 3 and 4) the pressure distribution on the building envelope has been determined for the vertical planes normal to the envelope's walls located at each progressive coordinate (compare third column in Table 1). In Fig. 13 a specific pressure distribution for the time step $k=2 \rightarrow t_k=7200\,\mathrm{s}$ is shown as an example, corresponding to a specific vertical plane. Note that in this case both the velocity of the impacting debris-flow surge ($v_\mathrm{n}=0.21\,\mathrm{m\,s^{-1}}$) and the thickness of the position layer ($h_\mathrm{D}+h_\mathrm{S}=0.44\,\mathrm{m}$) are > 0.

In Fig. 14 the maximum impact pressures at the building envelope perimeter are presented for the considered time step, $k=2 \rightarrow t_k=720\,0\mathrm{s}$.

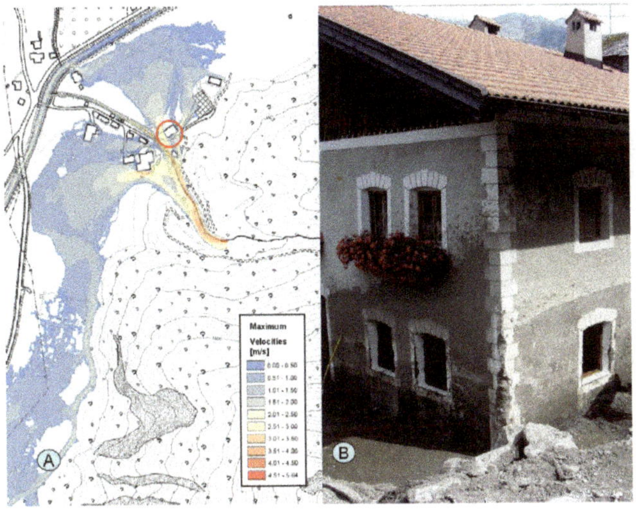

Figure 12. **(a)** Flow velocities and **(b)** mud marks reaching the second floor of the building envelope.

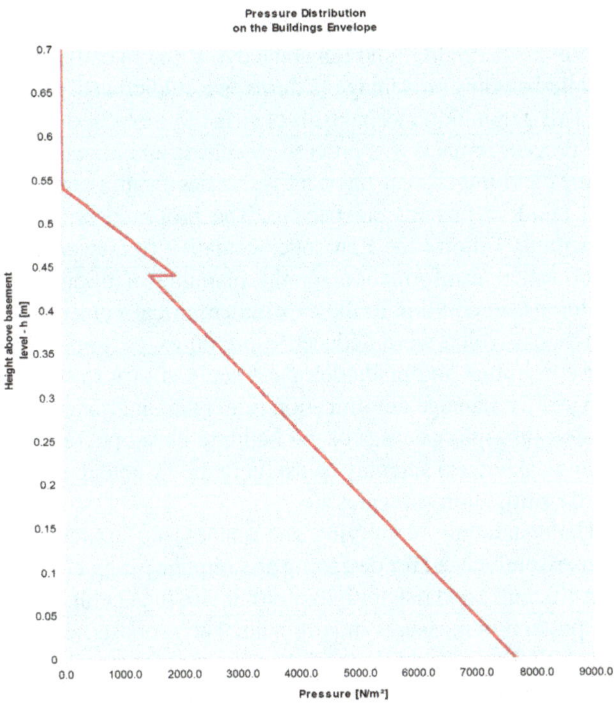

Figure 13. Pressure distribution on a selected vertical plane. The discontinuity in the pressure distribution in the upper part (layer approximately > 0.44 m) results from the boundary between debris-flow material in motion and deposited volumes.

Functional to the analysis of potential intrusion of solid material in the interior volumes of the building we quantified according to Eqs. (5) and (6), regarding the three selected time steps, the exposure to wetting and the potential permeability of the building envelope (compare Table 2).

Figure 14. Representation of maximum pressure values in $\mathrm{N\,m^{-2}}$ on the building envelope.

Table 2. Overall exposure to wetting and potential permeability for the selected time steps.

Time step k	Overall exposure to wetting – WE (t_k) – in m^2 where	Overall potential permeability – $TO_H(t_k)$ – in m^2 where
$k = 1 \rightarrow t_k = 3600\,s$	3.63	1.45
$k = 2 \rightarrow t_k = 7200\,s$	10.00	4.36
$k = 3 \rightarrow t_k = 10\,800\,s$	7.79	3.58

3.3 Structural and physical response analysis

For the purposes of the present case study the structural analysis is restricted to the verification of one specific ultimate limit state deemed as relevant, namely STR (compare Sect. 2.4), implying failure or excessive deformation of the structure. As already stated, the reference design situation for natural hazard impact is that of an accidental situation, corresponding for each specific vertical plane to a loading spectrum similar to the example shown in Fig. 13.

With reference to the impacts of time step $k = 2 \rightarrow t_k = 7200\,s$ the resulting loading configuration for the entire building is shown in Fig. 15. The distributed loading configurations are converted into their work-equivalent nodal loads, since a finite element analysis using the software Sismicad 12.1 (Concrete Srl, 2012) is performed.

The relevant results of the Finite Element Analysis for each finite element of the building model (compare definition sketch in Fig. 16) are the shear forces (V_O and V_Z) shown in Fig. 17, the tensile stresses (F_{OO} and F_{ZZ}) and shear stress component – F_{OZ} – represented in Fig. 18, and the bending moments (M_{OO} and M_{ZZ}) and torque – M_{OZ} – visualized in Fig. 19.

For the computed stress resultants the building structure proved to be verified with respect to the ultimate limit state STR. Whereas simple exposure to wetting is not critical for

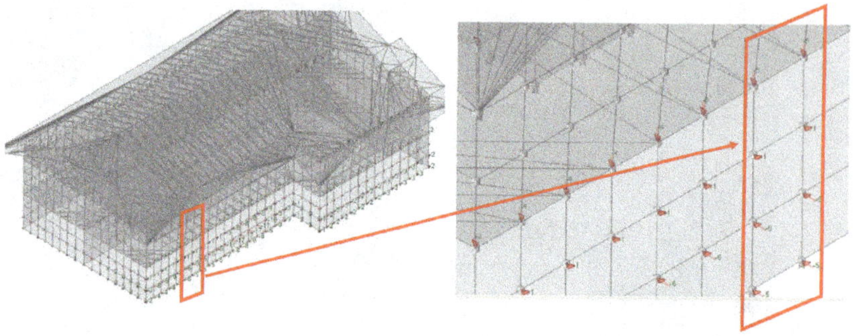

Figure 15. Work-equivalent nodal loads for the finite element structure with reference to the impacts of time step $k = 2 \rightarrow t_k = 7200$ s.

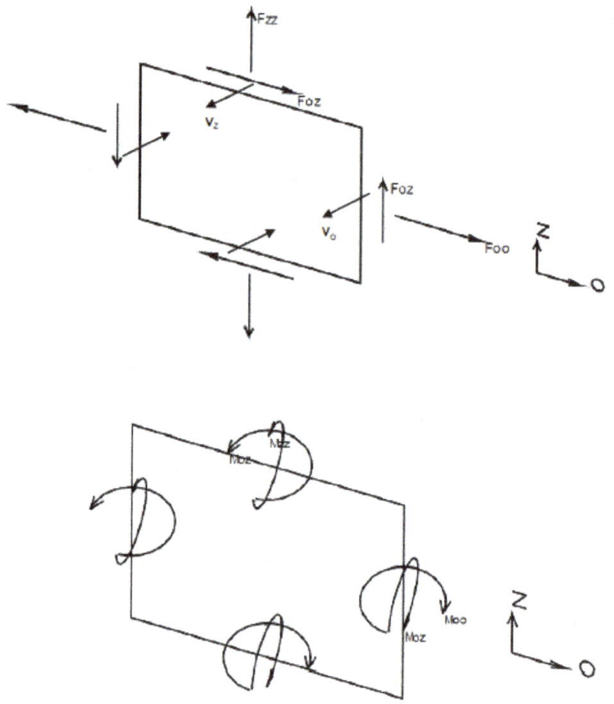

Figure 16. Definition sketch – stress resultants for each finite element.

the considered building, the no-intrusion limit state could not be verified for all openings of the building in the first floor (compare Eq. 10 and Table 2). The resulting damage susceptibility profile (i.e. structural stability, but permeability to debris-flow material intrusion) captures in its essentials the weak points which characterize the physical vulnerability of such building typologies exposed to similar ranges of debris-flow intensities.

It has to be noted that in the debris-flow case the process of moisture transport to the building walls is limited and the associated effects can be neglected.

4 Discussion and conclusion

The presented study extended earlier works on the deduction of empirical loss functions for buildings located on Alpine torrent fans. Taking an engineering perspective, and therefore neglecting any social implications, we presented a method to quantify vulnerability of buildings exposed to torrent processes. Starting with an overview on recent empirical studies on vulnerability, and acknowledging the overall gap in detailed studies on damage patterns, we studied analytically the loss generation mechanisms of structures exposed to hazard process impacts (i.e. process modelling and impact modelling) and the critical physical responses from a structural and building physics perspective. The proposed procedure coherently follows the Eurocode normative framework, and is of valuable information for the planning of flood-prone buildings. In addition to the existing empirical vulnerability functions, which were deduced using an ex-post approach, our conceptual and methodological setup allows to identify triggers for damage amplification (e.g. potential material intrusion through openings of the building envelope, or structural weaknesses) and may be useful in the ex-ante definition of risk mitigation strategies.

Understanding, identifying and quantifying vulnerability is an essential need for designing and implementing effective and efficient flood risk mitigation strategies in general and local protection measures in particular. The proposed damage susceptibility concept is a useful entry point for the planning process. It highlights the verifications that have to be met by the design of local protection measures.

Linking the vulnerability assessment to engineering science supports the idea that the utility of cost-benefit analysis goes far beyond the pure selection of optimal management options out of an available bundle of measures; instead, if employed in earlier phases of the risk management process such an approach may serve as an additional planning tool. Analyzing the time-varying vulnerability of elements at risk – having a crucial impact on the expected consequences of flood impacts – is increasingly becoming important for a wide spectrum of management activities within the risk governance process. Intervention planning, for example, which

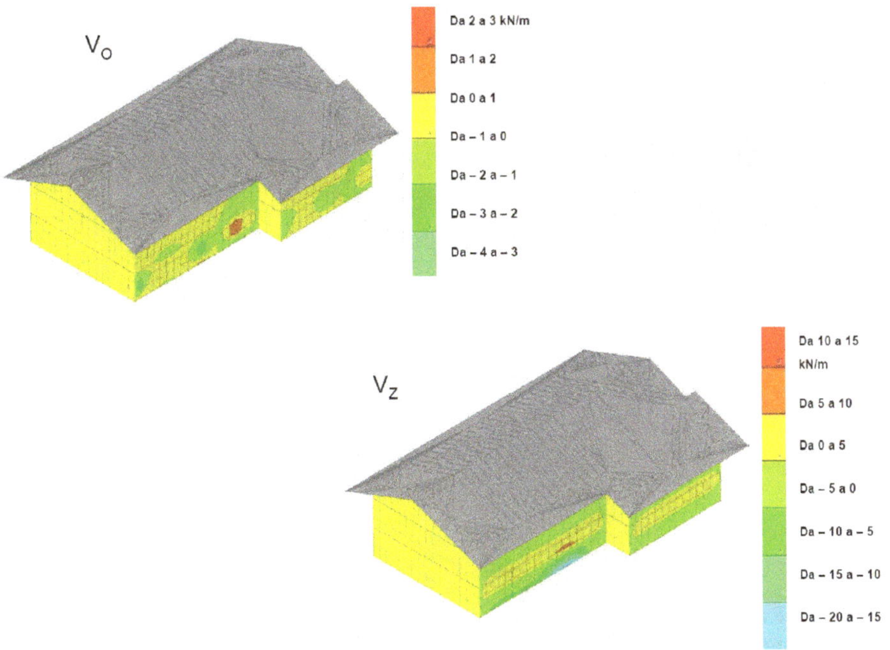

Figure 17. Shear forces (V_O and V_Z).

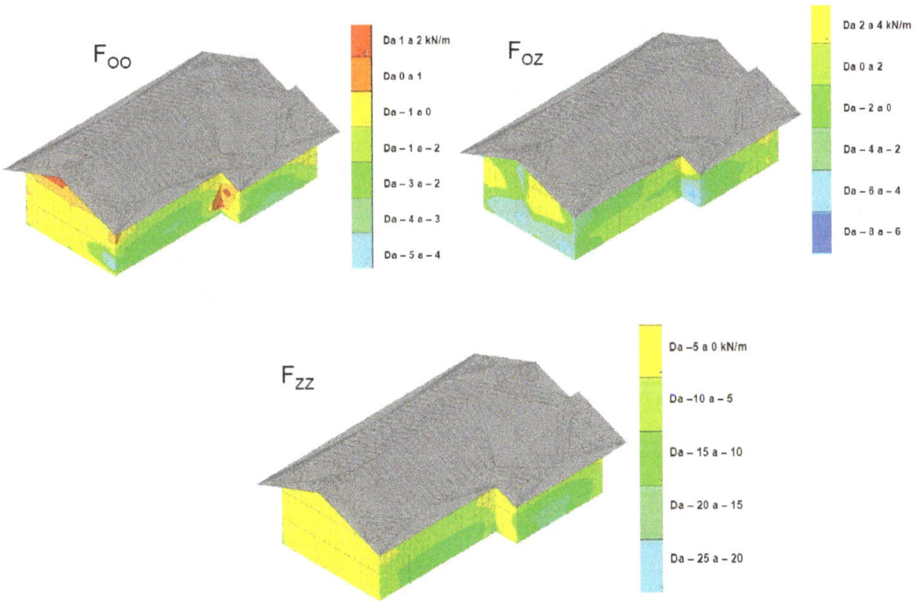

Figure 18. Tensile stresses (F_{OO} and F_{ZZ}) and shear stress component – F_{OZ}.

is recognized to be an effective tool to mitigate flood risk, is strongly based on the quality of the analysis of both the spatial and the temporal dynamics either of the flood hazard process or of the corresponding damaging impacts on elements at risk (Mazzorana et al., 2012b).

The method proposed, however, is very data demanding and is so far only applicable on the local scale of individual buildings located on torrent fans. Therefore, an area-wide application of this approach to an entire region still is challenging. Nevertheless, both the physical foundation and the traceability and reproducibility of the proposed vulnerability assessment method supports the identification of dynamics in natural hazard risk and contributes to an improved understanding of current risk levels.

To conclude, different concepts of vulnerability have different roots, different scientific objects, and therefore

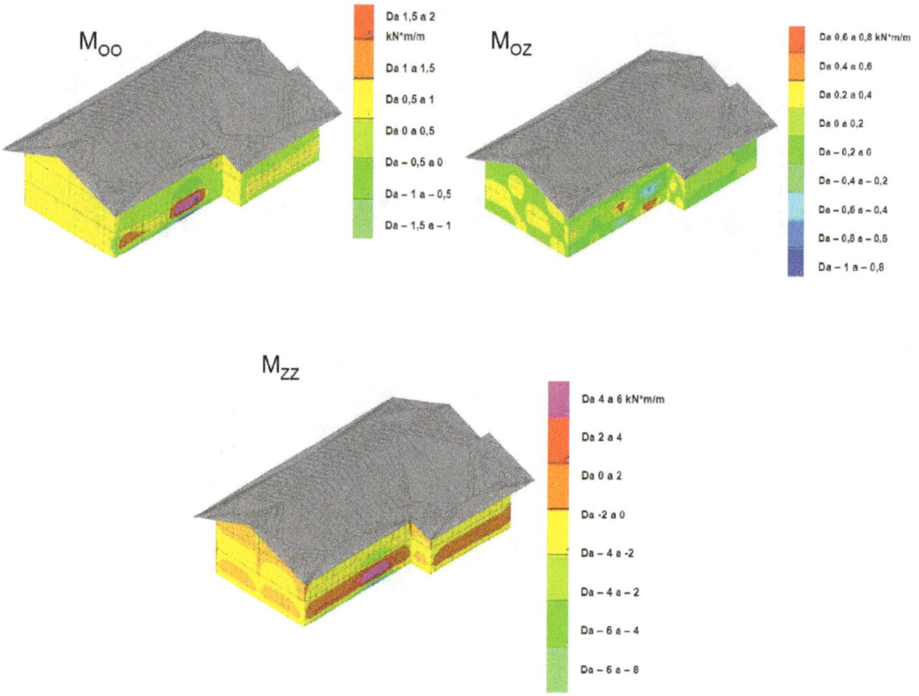

Figure 19. Bending moments (M_{OO} and M_{ZZ}) and torque – M_{OZ}.

different informative values. Combining contributions from empirical studies with in-depth studies on the damage patterns will allow us to better understand the triggers responsible for vulnerability, and will lead to a deeper understanding of mountain hazard risk. This is a first step to increase the resilience of mountain communities.

Acknowledgements. The authors wish to kindly acknowledge P. Ronco, O. Mavrouli and one anonymous referee for their constructive suggestions improving earlier versions of this manuscript. Moreover the authors would like to express their sincere thanks to the editor, M. Mikoš.

Edited by: M. Mikos

References

Armanini, A., Fraccarollo, L., and Rosatti, G.: Two-dimensional simulation of debris flows in erodible channels, Comput. Geosci., 35, 993–1006, 2009.

Armanini, A., Larcher, M., and Odorizzi, M.: Dynamic impact of a debris flow against a vertical wall, Ital. J. Eng. Geol. Environ., 11, 1041–1049, 2011.

Birkmann, J., Cardona, O. M., Carreño, M. L., Barbat, A. H., Pelling, M., Schneiderbauer, S., Kienberger, S., Keiler, M., Alexander, D., Zeil, P., and Welle, T.: Framing vulnerability, risk and societal responses: the MOVE framework, Nat. Hazards, 67, 193–211, 2013.

Cavalli, M., and Marchi, L.: Identificazione preliminare delle aree di pericolo legate a fenomeni torrentizi, Consiglio Nazionale delle Ricerche – CNR, Istituto di Ricerca per la Protezione Idrogeologica Padova – IRPI, Padova, 2006.

Comiti, F., Mao, L., Preciso, E., Picco, L., Marchi, L., and Borga, M.: Large wood and flash floods: evidences from the 2007 event in the Davča basin (Slovenia), in: Monitoring, simulation, prevention and remediation of dense and debris flow II, edited by: De Wrachien, D., Brebbia, C. A., and Lenzi, M. A., WIT Transactions on Information and Communication Technologies 39, WIT Press, Southampton, 173–182, 2008.

Concrete srl: Sismicad 12.1 manuale d'uso, http://www.concrete.it/sismicad12/, last access: 12 March 2013, 2012.

Cutter, S. and Finch, C.: Temporal and spatial changes in social vulnerability to natural hazards, P. Natl. Acad. Sci. USA, 105, 2301–2306, 2008.

de Vries, D.: Being temporal and vulnerability to natural disasters, in: Perspectives on social vulnerability, edited by: Warner, K., United Nations University, Institute for Environment and Human Security, Bonn, 36–49, 2007.

Diehl, T.: Potential drift accumulation at bridges, Washington Publication No. FHWA-RD-97-028, US Department of Transportation, Federal Highway Administration Research and Development, Turner-Fairbank Highway Research Center, Springfield, Virginia, 1997.

Feix, J. and Walkner, R.: Betonbau: Grundlagen der Bemessung nach EC2, Studia Universitätsverlag, Innsbruck, 2012.

Fell, R., Corominas, J., Bonnard, C., Cascini, L., Leroi, E., and Savage, W.: Guidelines for landslide susceptibility, hazard and risk zoning for land-use planning, Eng. Geol., 102, 85–98, 2008.

Fuchs, S.: Susceptibility versus resilience to mountain hazards in Austria – paradigms of vulnerability revisited, Nat. Hazards Earth Syst. Sci., 9, 337–352, doi:10.5194/nhess-9-337-2009, 2009.

Fuchs, S.: Cost-benefit analysis of natural hazard mitigation, in: Encyclopedia of natural hazards, edited by: Bobrowski, P., Springer, Dordrecht, 121–125, 2013.

Fuchs, S., Heiss, K., and Hübl, J.: Towards an empirical vulnerability function for use in debris flow risk assessment, Nat. Hazards Earth Syst. Sci., 7, 495–506, doi:10.5194/nhess-7-495-2007, 2007.

Fuchs, S., Birkmann, J., and Glade, T.: Vulnerability assessment in natural hazard and risk analysis: current approaches and future challenges, Nat. Hazards, 64, 1969–1975, 2012a.

Fuchs, S., Ornetsmüller, C., and Totschnig, R.: Spatial scan statistics in vulnerability assessment – an application to mountain hazards, Nat. Hazards, 64, 2129–2151, 2012b.

Fuchs, S., Keiler, M., Sokratov, S. A., and Shnyparkov, A.: Spatiotemporal dynamics: the need for an innovative approach in mountain hazard risk management, Nat. Hazards, 68, 1217–1241, 2013.

Gall, M., Borden, K., and Cutter, S.: When do losses count? Six fallacies of natural hazards loss data, B. Am. Meteorol. Soc., 90, 799–809, 2009.

Gallerani, V., Viaggi, D., and Zanni, G.: Manuale di estimo, McGraw-Hill, Milano, 2011.

Gulvanessian, H.: EN 1990 Eurocode "Basis of structural design" – the innovative head Eurocode, Steel Construct., 2, 222–227, 2009.

Gulvanessian, H., Calgaro, J.-A., Holický, M.: Designers' guide to EN 1990, Eurocode: Basis of structural design, Thomas Telford Ltd, London, 2004.

Hawkesbury-Nepean Floodplain Management Steering Committee (Ed.): Reducing vulnerability of buildings to flood damage, Hawkesbury-Nepean Floodplain Management Steering Committee, Parramatta, 2006.

Holub, M. and Fuchs, S.: Benefits of local structural protection to mitigate torrent-related hazards, in: Risk Analysis VI, edited by: Brebbia, C. and Beriatos, E., WIT Transactions on Information and Communication Technologies 39, WIT, Southampton, 401–411, 2008.

Holub, M. and Fuchs, S.: Mitigating mountain hazards in Austria – legislation, risk transfer, and awareness building, Nat. Hazards Earth Syst. Sci., 9, 523–537, doi:10.5194/nhess-9-523-2009, 2009.

Holub, M., Suda, J., and Fuchs, S.: Mountain hazards: reducing vulnerability by adapted building design, Environ. Earth Sci., 66, 1853–1870, 2012.

Hübl, J., Bunza, G., Hafner, K., and Klaus, W.: ETAlp – Erosion, Transport in Alpinen Systemen "Stummer Zeugen Katalog", Projektteam ETAlp, Wien, 2003.

Hufschmidt, G.: A comparative analysis of several vulnerability concepts, Nat. Hazards, 58, 621–643, 2011.

Ishikawa, Y.: Studies on disasters caused by debris flows carrying logs down mountains, SABO Division, Public Works Research Institute, Ministry of Construction, Tokyo, 45–75, 1990.

Iverson, R.: The physics of debris flows, Rev. Geophys., 35, 245–296, 1997.

Jakob, M.: Events on cones and fans: recurrence interval and magnitude, in: Dating torrential processes on fans and cones, edited by: Schneuwly-Bollschweiler, M., Stoffel, M., and Rudolf-Miklau, F., Springer, Dordrecht, 95–108, 2013.

Jakob, M., Stein, D., and Ulmi, M.: Vulnerability of buildings to debris flow impact, Nat. Hazards, 60, 241–261, 2012.

Kappes, M., Keiler, M., von Elverfeldt, K., and Glade, T.: Challenges of analyzing multi-hazard risk: a review, Nat. Hazards, 64, 1925–1958, 2012a.

Kappes, M., Papathoma-Köhle, M., and Keiler, M.: Assessing physical vulnerability for multi-hazards using an indicator-based methodology, Appl. Geogr., 32, 577–590, 2012b.

Kienholz, H., Krummenacher, B., Kipfer, A., and Perret, S.: Aspects of integral risk management in practice – considerations with respect to mountain hazards in Switzerland, Öster. Wasser Abfallw., 56, 43–50, 2004.

Mao, L. and Comiti, F.: The effects of large wood elements during an extreme flood in a small tropical basin of Costa Rica, in: Debris flow III, edited by: De Wrachien, D. and Brebbia, C. A., WIT Transactions on Information and Communication Technologies 39, WIT Press, Southampton, 225–236, 2010.

Mazzorana, B. and Fuchs, S.: Fuzzy Formative Scenario Analysis for woody material transport related risks in mountain torrents, Environ. Modell. Softw., 25, 1208–1224, 2010.

Mazzorana, B., Comiti, F., Volcan, C., and Scherer, C.: Determining flood hazard patterns through a combined stochastic-deterministic approach, Nat. Hazards, 59, 301–316, 2011.

Mazzorana, B., Comiti, F., Scherer, C., and Fuchs, S.: Developing consistent scenarios to assess flood hazards in mountain streams, J. Environ. Manage., 94, 112–124, 2012a.

Mazzorana, B., Levaggi, L., Formaggioni, O., and Volcan, C.: Physical vulnerability assessment based on fluid and classical mechanics to support cost-benefit analysis of flood risk mitigation strategies, Water, 4, 196–218, 2012b.

Mazzorana, B., Levaggi, L., Keiler, M., and Fuchs, S.: Towards dynamics in flood risk assessment, Nat. Hazards Earth Syst. Sci., 12, 3571–3587, doi:10.5194/nhess-12-3571-2012, 2012c.

Mazzorana, B., Comiti, F., and Fuchs, S.: A structured approach to enhance flood hazard assessment in mountain streams, Nat. Hazards, 67, 991–1009, 2013.

Papathoma-Köhle, M., Kappes, M., Keiler, M., and Glade, T.: Physical vulnerability assessment for alpine hazards: state of the art and future needs, Nat. Hazards, 58, 645–680, 2011.

Papathoma-Köhle, M., Keiler, M., Totschnig, R., and Glade, T.: Improvement of vulnerability curves using data from extreme events: debris flow event in South Tyrol, Nat. Hazards, 64, 2083–2105, 2012.

Pierson, T. C. and Costa, J. E.: A rheologic classification of subaerial sediment-water flows, Geol. Soc. Am. Rev. Eng. Geol., 7, 1–12, 1987.

Pitman, E. and Le, L.: A two-fluid model for avalanche and debris flows, Philos. T. Roy. Soc. A, 363, 1573–1601, 2005.

Plaxis: Scientific manual, http://www.plaxis.nl/files/files/2D2011-4-Scientific.pdf, last access: 12 February 2013, 2011.

Quan Luna, B., Blahut, J., van Westen, C. J., Sterlacchini, S., van Asch, T. W. J., and Akbas, S. O.: The application of numerical debris flow modelling for the generation of physical vulnerability curves, Nat. Hazards Earth Syst. Sci., 11, 2047–2060, doi:10.5194/nhess-11-2047-2011, 2011.

Rigon, R., D'Odorico, P., and Bertoldi, G.: The geomorphic structure of the runoff peak, Hydrol. Earth Syst. Sci., 15, 1853–1863, doi:10.5194/hess-15-1853-2011, 2011.

Rosatti, G. and Begnudelli, L.: Two-dimensional simulation of debris flows over mobile bed: Enhancing the TRENT2D model by using a well-balanced Generalized Roe-type solver, Comput. Fluids, 71, 179–195, 2013.

Rosatti, G. and Fraccarollo, L.: A well-balanced approach for flows over mobile-bed with high sediment transport, J. Comput. Phys., 220, 312–338, 2006.

Slaymaker, O.: The distinctive attributes of debris torrents, Hydrolog. Sci. J., 33, 567–573, 1988.

Steinke, P.: Finite-Elemente-Methode, Springer, Heidelberg, 2012.

Totschnig, R. and Fuchs, S.: Mountain torrents: quantifying vulnerability and assessing uncertainties, Eng. Geol., 155, 31–44, 2013.

Totschnig, R., Sedlacek, W., and Fuchs, S.: A quantitative vulnerability function for fluvial sediment transport, Nat. Hazards, 58, 681–703, 2011.

Wakker, P. P.: Prospect theory for risk and ambiguity, Cambridge University Press, Cambridge, 2010.

Walhorn, E., Kölke, A., Hübner, B., and Dinkler, D.: Fluid-structure coupling within a monolithic model involving free surface flows, Comput. Struct., 83, 2100–2111, 2005.

Wisner, B.: Assessment of capability and vulnerability, in: Mapping vulnerability. Disasters, development and people, edited by: Bankoff, G., Frerks, G., and Hilhorst, D., Earthscan, London, 183–193, 2004.

Zienkiewicz, O. C., Taylor, R. L., and Zhu, J. Z.: The Finite Element method: Its basis and fundamentals, Butterworth-Heinemann, Oxford, 2005.

2

Effects of variability in probable maximum precipitation patterns on flood losses

Andreas Paul Zischg[1,2], Guido Felder[1], Rolf Weingartner[1], Niall Quinn[3], Gemma Coxon[2], Jeffrey Neal[2], Jim Freer[2], and Paul Bates[2]

[1]University of Bern, Institute of Geography, Oeschger Centre for Climate Change Research, Mobiliar Lab for Natural Risks, Bern, 3012, Switzerland
[2]School of Geographical Sciences, University of Bristol, Bristol, BS8 1SS, UK
[3]Fathom Ltd., Bristol, BS1 6QF, UK

Correspondence: Andreas Paul Zischg (andreas.zischg@giub.unibe.ch)

Abstract. The assessment of the impacts of extreme floods is important for dealing with residual risk, particularly for critical infrastructure management and for insurance purposes. Thus, modelling of the probable maximum flood (PMF) from probable maximum precipitation (PMP) by coupling hydrological and hydraulic models has gained interest in recent years. Herein, we examine whether variability in precipitation patterns exceeds or is below selected uncertainty factors in flood loss estimation and if the flood losses within a river basin are related to the probable maximum discharge at the basin outlet. We developed a model experiment with an ensemble of probable maximum precipitation scenarios created by Monte Carlo simulations. For each rainfall pattern, we computed the flood losses with a model chain and benchmarked the effects of variability in rainfall distribution with other model uncertainties. The results show that flood losses vary considerably within the river basin and depend on the timing and superimposition of the flood peaks from the basin's sub-catchments. In addition to the flood hazard component, the other components of flood risk, exposure, and vulnerability contribute remarkably to the overall variability. This leads to the conclusion that the estimation of the probable maximum expectable flood losses in a river basin should not be based exclusively on the PMF. Consequently, the basin-specific sensitivities to different precipitation patterns and the spatial organization of the settlements within the river basin need to be considered in the analyses of probable maximum flood losses.

1 Introduction

Floods are one of the most damaging natural hazards, accounting for a majority of all economic losses from natural events worldwide (UNISDR, 2015). Managing flood risks requires knowledge about hazardous processes and the impacts of floods. Typically the impacts of design floods with a certain (extreme) return period (IPCC, 2012) or the impacts of worst-case floods are required for sound risk analysis and for the planning of risk reduction measures. In particular, for portfolio risk analyses of insurance companies, the estimation of the probable maximum loss is important for fulfilling financial regulations and stability criteria. Furthermore, critical infrastructure, such as power stations, has to be protected against extreme floods. Since floods are expected to increase due to climatic changes (Asadieh and Krakauer, 2015; Arnell and Gosling, 2016; Beniston et al., 2007; Bouwer, 2013; Fischer and Knutti, 2016; Millán, 2014; Pfahl et al., 2017; Rajczak et al., 2013; Scherrer et al., 2016), flood risk analyses and the management of extreme events will become even more relevant (Smolka, 2006; Yuan et al., 2017). Hence, insurance companies and governmental institutions are increasingly interested in quantifying flood risks, and especially in estimating the impacts of probable maximum floods leading to high cumulative losses (Burke et al., 2016; Morrill and Becker, 2017) or the destruction of critical infrastructure (Hasan and Foliente, 2015; Mechler et al., 2010; Michaelides, 2014).

An important aspect in flood risk analysis is the modelling of worst-case floods and their impacts (Büchele et al., 2006). One main question herein is the search for the upper physical limits of discharge in a river basin, i.e. the maximum outflow from a catchment that is possible with the given catchment characteristics and the maximum rainfall in the climate region (Felder and Weingartner, 2017). Here, the hydrological modelling undertaken to derive probable maximum flood (PMF) from probable maximum precipitation (PMP) is an important first step as a basis for inundation modelling (Felder et al., 2017). The PMP is defined as "the theoretical maximum precipitation for a given duration under modern meteorological conditions" (World Meteorological Organization, 2009). Differently, the PMF is defined as "the theoretical maximum flood that poses extremely serious threats to the flood control of a given project in a design watershed" (World Meteorological Organization, 2009). The PMF is estimated on the basis of the PMP and is commonly used in practice for the planning of hydropower dams. However, there is still a controversial discussion on the underlying concept of PMP, particularly on the assumption that the upper tail of flood distributions is bounded (Micovic et al., 2015). Comprehensive summaries of this discussion are provided by Salas et al. (2015) and by Rouhani and Leconte (2016). Nevertheless, PMP/PMF estimation methods have been continuously developed and improved. Beauchamp et al. (2013), Lagos-Zuniga and Vargas (2014), and Felder and Weingartner (2016) discuss the role of the spatio-temporal distribution of the PMP on the PMF, while Rousseau et al. (2014) and Stratz and Hossain (2014) discuss climate change and stationarity issues. Hence, Faulkner and Benn (2016), Micovic et al. (2015), Rouhani and Leconte (2016), and Salas et al. (2014) have proposed incorporating uncertainty bands into the PMP estimation.

Nevertheless, the detailed triggering mechanism and the temporal evolution of large flood events, specifically of worst-case scenarios, are not yet fully understood. An important question concerns how the peak discharge and the volume of a flood depend on the intensity and track of the triggering precipitation events, i.e. the spatio-temporal pattern of precipitation (Adams et al., 2012; Bruni et al., 2015; Cristiano et al., 2017; Emmanuel et al., 2015, 2016; Ochoa-Rodriguez et al., 2015; Paschalis et al., 2014; Rafieeinasab et al., 2015; Zhang and Han, 2017). In addition to the storm track dynamics, the peak flow depends on the watershed characteristics (Singh, 1997). In mountainous catchments with high topographical complexity, the storm track and the precipitation pattern are influenced by the mountain ranges. Furthermore, the river network is influenced by geological and tectonic structures and is thus more complex in mountainous terrain than in low-lying areas. Thus, in upland areas high variability in the spatio-temporal pattern of a probable maximum precipitation event and the resulting river flows has to be assumed. The definition of the spatio-temporal characteristics of PMP scenarios is a crucial step in the analysis of the impacts of extreme flood events. Hence, different approaches in distributing PMP in space and time over a catchment have been developed recently (Beauchamp et al., 2013; Dodov and Foufoula-Georgiou, 2005; Foufoula-Georgiou, 1989; Franchini et al., 1996; Felder and Weingartner, 2016). Regarding mountainous meso-scale catchments with an area of a few thousand km^2, insights into precipitation patterns leading to the most extreme floods are rather rare. The precipitation pattern leads to a specific pattern of the outflows from the sub-catchments. Depending on the geometry of the main river network, this timing of the outflows from the sub-catchments influences peak discharge in the individual river reaches. Hence, the relative timing of peak discharge arrivals in river confluences as a consequence of the spatio-temporal distribution of the rainfall pattern has to be addressed (Nicótina et al., 2008; Nikolopoulos et al., 2014; Pattison et al., 2014; Emmanuel et al., 2016; Zoccatelli et al., 2011). Thus, sound analysis of extreme floods in a complex river basin requires an assessment of the variability of chronological superimpositions of flood waves in tributaries and the effect of this on the probability of inundation. Neal et al. (2013) highlight the importance of spatial dependence between tributaries in terms of inundation probability and magnitude. Consequently, the amount of flood losses is also expected to vary with the timing of peak flows in the tributaries. Ochoa-Rodriguez et al. (2015) also stated that the temporal variation of rainfall inputs affects hydrodynamic modelling results remarkably. Emmanuel et al. (2015) showed that the spatio-temporal organization of rainfall plays an important role in the discharge at the outlet of the catchment and stated that a simulation approach is needed to study the effects of rainfall variability in complex river basins. The effects vary with the catchment size and its characteristics. Nevertheless, they state that there is a knowledge gap in this field. Probably the study that is most clearly focused on the role of the tributary relative timing and sequencing for extreme floods is presented by Pattison et al. (2014). They showed that tributary relative timing and synchronization is important in the determination of flood peak downstream. Thus, the distribution of extreme rainfall in space and time must play a critical role in determining the PMF and the peak discharge at the catchment outlet.

While the influence of rainfall variability on catchment response is under investigation, the further influence on flood losses is rarely investigated. To our knowledge, so far only Sampson et al. (2014) have analysed the effects of different precipitation scenarios on flood losses in depth. However, the Sampson et al. study focused on an urban area and on a (relatively) small scale. Thus far, no studies have been conducted in mountainous river basins to our knowledge.

In addition to the variability in precipitation patterns, other uncertainties have to be considered in flood loss estimation. Besides uncertainties in hydrological modelling that are not considered in this study, other factors lead to uncertainties in inundation modelling and in flood loss estimation. Uncertainties in inundation modelling and flood risk analysis are addressed by Apel et al. (2008), Di Baldassarre et al. (2010), Gai et al. (2017), Merz and Thieken (2009), and Neal et al. (2013). Savage et al. (2015) and Fewtrell et al. (2008) describe the effects of spatial scale on inundation modelling. Altarejos-García et al. (2012), Chatterjee et al. (2008), Horritt and Bates (2001, 2002), Kvočka et al. (2015), and Neal et al. (2012b) discuss the effects of the chosen inundation model, its parametrization, and the role of input data on flood modelling results. Other uncertainties in flood modelling outputs are related to uncertainties in levee heights (Sanyal, 2017) or digital elevation models (Saksena and Merwade, 2015). Beside the uncertainties in flood modelling, observational uncertainties also need to be recognized with recent studies highlighting the importance of observational errors in rainfall and discharge data (McMillan et al., 2012; Coxon et al., 2015).

Furthermore, uncertainties in the economic models used to estimate flood losses and flood damages are relevant (de Moel et al., 2015). Herein, the input data, the choice of the impact indicators, the scale, and the vulnerability models are relevant sources of uncertainty (Ward et al., 2013; Apel et al., 2008; Merz and Thieken, 2009; de Moel and Aerts, 2011). In particular, vulnerability functions are considered as one of the most relevant sources of uncertainty in flood loss estimation (Ward et al., 2013; Sampson et al., 2014). Thus, uncertainty analysis is a key aspect in flood risk assessment. Some of the limitations and uncertainties mentioned above are addressed by several recent studies. Especially with regard to coupled models, uncertainty and sensitivity analyses are important for assessing the propagation of cascading uncertainties to the final result (Ward et al., 2013; Rodríguez-Rincón et al., 2015). Uncertainty analysis focuses on quantifying the spread of uncertainty in the model input on the model outputs, i.e. the forward propagation of the uncertainties to the prediction variables. In contrast, sensitivity analysis focuses on apportioning output uncertainty to the different sources of uncertainty (input factors). A global sensitivity analysis investigates how the variation in the output of a numerical model can be attributed to variations of its input factors (Pianosi et al., 2016). However, uncertainty analyses and sensitivity analyses of coupled models or model chains are rarely investigated topics.

In summary, we identify a research gap in our understanding of the effects of spatio-temporal precipitation patterns on the amount of flood losses in a river basin. The main goals of this study are to analyse the effects of variability in probable maximum precipitation patterns on flood losses, and to compare these effects with other uncertainties in flood loss modelling in a complex mountain catchment (i.e. choice of inundation models or vulnerability functions). One important question is whether the variability in precipitation patterns is more or less influential than other uncertainties in flood loss estimation. A second question is whether the maximum discharge at the catchment outlet is a reliable proxy indicator for identifying the scenario(s) for worst case flood loss.

2 Methods

To address the above questions using a numerical experiment we constructed an inundation modelling framework composed of several coupled modules. The model chain was developed for the Aare River basin in Switzerland (3000 km^2) and consists of five main components: a precipitation module, a hydrology module, a hydrodynamic routing module, a hydrodynamic inundation module, and a damage module. The model chain computes the flood losses (model output) on the basis of a specified rainfall event (model input). In the following, the setup of the model chain is described. The uncertainties related to the precipitation pattern were subsequently compared with selected other uncertainty factors in the model chain, i.e. uncertainties related to the inundation modelling approach and to the chosen vulnerability functions. Hence, we conducted a global sensitivity analysis of the model chain with the objective to rank the uncertainty in the rainfall pattern and the uncertainties in the model setup (choice of sub-models) according to their relative contribution to the output variability after Pianosi et al. (2016). The uncertainties in the model setup are considered in the sensitivity analysis by varying the setup of the submodules for flood modelling and loss modelling.

2.1 Probable maximum precipitation and probable maximum discharge

The probable maximum precipitation PMP for the whole catchment was estimated using the guidelines of World Meteorological Organization (2009). The method for distributing the PMP in space and time is based on a Monte Carlo approach proposed by Felder and Weingartner (2016). This approach aims at identifying a PMP pattern leading to the PMF by testing a high number of randomly generated spatio-temporal patterns considering physical plausibility criteria. To consider the spatio-temporal patterns of precipitation in the river basin, the same amount of areal precipitation in the PMP scenario (300 mm for a 72 h event over 3000 km^2) was distributed in different spatio-temporal patterns across the entire river basin in a Monte Carlo simulation framework after Felder and Weingartner (2016). We focused on a precipitation event lasting 3 days, since this timespan corresponds to the typical event duration within the river basin and leads to the highest floods. The PMP scenarios are assumed to occur during the summer season with a height of the freezing level above the maximal altitudes. This means that snowfall is not considered. In the first step, a random temporal distribution of the total precipitation for the chosen duration was generated. The variation of rainfall between one time step and the following was limited to 20 % at maximum. This avoids implausible temporal distributions. In the second step, the temporal pattern of the rainfall was distributed spatially in three meteorological regions, and in the sub-catchments within each meteorological region. The sub-catchments and the meteorological regions were defined to consider the relatively independent behaviour of specific parts of the catchment, e.g. lowlands and mountainous regions, in terms of precipitation amount and intensity. The randomly created precipitation pattern was checked against the spatial dependencies to fulfil a spatial consistency within neighbouring catchments. Intensive precipitation must be concentrated in adjacent meteorological regions and affiliated sub-catchments. The concentration of intense rainfall in meteorological regions and thus in adjacent sub-catchments implicitly allows taking into account the storm movement and the effects of the mountain crests. For further details see Felder and Weingartner (2016). From a set of 10^6 Monte Carlo simulations with a simplified but computationally efficient hydrological model based on unit hydrographs, we selected 150 scenarios with the highest discharge at the basin outlet in Bern. The number of scenarios is chosen to allow for analysing the variability of PMP patterns but at the same time allowing to be computationally feasible. These precipitation scenarios are then used as inputs for the detailed rainfall–runoff model, which is set up for each tributary and delivers the input hydrographs for the hydrodynamic model. For the rainfall–runoff modelling, we used the hydrological model PREVAH (Viviroli et al., 2009b), which is a deterministic, semi-distributed model based on hydrological response units (HRU) that are directly routed to the catchment outlet. The model is set up for 15 sub-catchments that are located within the Aare River basin upstream of Bern using an hourly time steps. The calibration and validation of the hydrological model is described in Felder et al. (2017). The output of the hydrological model of each sub-catchment is used as an upper boundary condition for the hydrodynamic model, in this case the 1-D hydrodynamic model BASEMENT-ETH (Vetsch et al., 2017) that accounts for the retention effects of lakes and floodplains. The model is based on the continuity equation and solves the Saint-Venant equations for unsteady 1-D flow. Lakes and their outlet weirs are considered in the hydrodynamic model. Here, we considered only the discharge from the lakes with maximal open weirs. No lake or reservoir regulation is considered, since lake regulation can be assumed to be irrelevant in case of extreme floods. The hydrologic and the hydrodynamic models were calibrated and validated separately, and then again together in the coupled version. The hydrological model was calibrated with all available gauged observation data at the outflow of 8 out of the 15 sub-catchments. The models for the ungauged sub-catchments were regionalized by applying the parameter regionalization method proposed by Viviroli et al. (2009a). The 1-D hydrodynamic model was calibrated by empirically adjusting the friction coefficients in the river channels with particular regard to the water surface elevation in the main channel at peak discharge. However, the coupled hydrological–hydraulic model was validated against the observation at the catchment outlet. In the validation period 2011–2014, the coupled hydrological–hydraulic model has a NSE value of 0.85 (Nash–Sutcliffe efficiency; Nash and Sutcliffe, 1970), and a KGE value of 0.85 (Kling–Gupta efficiency; Gupta et al., 2009; Kling et al., 2012).

2.2 Inundation modelling

The coupled simulations of the 150 rainfall patterns provide the basis for the inundation modelling. The 1-D hydrodynamic model routes the water flow from the sub-catchments towards the catchment outlet. We defined the coupling points between the hydrological and the hydraulic model with a bottom-up approach: first, we delimited the floodplains for which the flood loss estimation will be valid (system delimitation). Second, we defined the upper boundary conditions of these floodplains. Third, we delimited the upstream catchments for the hydrological model based on the coupling points. However, the location of the gauging stations was also considered in the definition of the coupling points in order to calibrate and validate the hydrological model. The 1-D hydrodynamic model computes the level of the lakes and the outflow from the lakes. However, we used a 2-D inundation model as reference model for estimating the flow depths in the floodplains required for flood loss analysis. We nested the 2-D inundation models into the 1-D hydrodynamic model (see schematic of the approach in Fig. 1) to avoid the computationally demanding simulation of the lake retention with the 2-D model. We simulated all scenarios with the 1-D model and nested the 2-D model into the outcomes of the 1-D model at specific locations (boundary conditions). Hence, the 2-D model is always started after the simulation with the 1-D model in a cascading approach. The lake outflow hydrographs and lake level hydrographs from the 1-D hydrodynamic model and the hydrographs computed by the hydrological model that are directly flowing into the floodplains considered by the 2-D models were used as upper or lower boundary conditions for the 2-D flood inundation modelling. Minor tributaries are neglected as upper boundary condition. However, the outflows from their catchments are taken into account by aggregating all minor tributaries to sub-catchment level. The spatial setup of the model experiment, as well as the interfaces between the hydrological model and the floodplains modelled in 2-D, are shown in Fig. 2. In the 1-D model, the outflow from the sub-catchments is fed directly in the main river without considering flooding in the alluvial fans of the tributaries. In contrast, the outflows from the sub-catchments are fed into the 2-D model at the coupling points as shown in Fig. 2. Thus, the 2-D model considers flooding of the alluvial fans of the tributaries.

We used the LISFLOOD-FP model for the 2-D inundation simulation and as a basis for flood loss modelling. The model and its validation is described by Bates and de Roo (2000), Bates et al. (2010), and Neal et al. (2009, 2011, 2012a). The model was set up with a subgrid representation of the channel and a spatial resolution on the floodplain of 50 m. The digital terrain model (DTM) was upscaled from a lidar DTM with high spatial resolution (0.5 m). The basis of this terrain data is a digital terrain model (DTM) provided by the Canton of Bern. This terrain model was created from lidar measurements collected in 2014 and 2015 with a resolution of about four points per m^2. The lidar data were processed by the data provider to create a raster DTM with a cell size of 0.5 m. The buildings and the most important hydraulic structures in the main rivers (main bridges) were removed by this process. We corrected this raw raster model by (a) manually eliminating the remaining hydraulic obstacles in the river reaches, (b) correcting the height of the riverbanks in the Aare and Gürbe rivers reaches on the basis of DGPS measurements along the riverbanks, and (c) interpolating the altitudes of the raster cells of the river bed on the basis of surveyed bathymetric cross sections provided by the Federal Office for the Environment (BAFU). The result is a DTM with a spatial resolution of 0.5 m and the above mentioned corrections. This hydraulically correct DTM provides the basis for the aggregation at coarser spatial resolution for the flood inundation models.

The subgrid channel module requires the heights of the river bed and of the lateral dams, the river width, and the shape of the river bed. These data were computed at high resolution and aggregated onto the target resolution of the inundation model by conserving the cross-sectional area of the river channel from the high-resolution terrain model.

The 2-D hydrodynamic model was calibrated in terms of reproducing the stage–discharge relationships at the gauging stations and the known channel capacity along the river reaches. The model was validated on the basis of documented flooding. The fit of the inundation model (after Bates and de Roo, 2000) computed on the basis of observed discharges of the flood event in August 2005 and a comparison between modelled and observed inundation extents ranges between 0.5 and 0.9, depending on the floodplain. The lower values can be explained by dam breaks that occurred in reality but are not considered in the model, or by recent changes in the river geometry since the last flood event (implementation of new flood defence measures).

In addition to the 2-D inundation model, we elaborated inundation maps from the 1-D hydrodynamic simulations. We constructed water surface elevation (WSE) maps by interpolating the WSE values at the cross sections of the 1-D model. The projection of these WSE maps onto the digital terrain model (spatial resolution of 10 m) and the comparison with the DTM subsequently lead to a map of flow depths.

2.3 Flood loss modelling

In this study, we focused on structural damage to buildings (residential, public, and industrial buildings) without considering losses to mobile assets, building contents, and infrastructure. The flood loss module of this model chain consists of a dataset of buildings similar to that described in Röthlisberger et al. (2017) and Fuchs et al. (2015). Each building is represented by a polygon and is classified by type, functionality, construction period, volume, reconstruction costs, and number of residents. Furthermore, we delineated the height of the ground floor above sea level of each building on the basis of a lidar terrain model with sub-metre resolution.

The resulting flow depths (FDs) and WSEs from the hydrodynamic module were attributed to each building (exposure analysis) and used for deriving the object-specific degree of loss from the vulnerability functions and consequently for the estimation of object-specific losses. The flow depth was attributed to the building following two different approaches. The first approach is a direct attribution of the flow depth from the FD maps to each building. The second approach is an indirect attribution where the flow depth at each building results from the difference between the WSE raster of the flood simulation and the minimum ground floor level of the building. The idea behind this approach is to take into account local small-scale elevations of the houses. If a building footprint covers more than one cell, we used the maximum flow depth of all relevant cells of the inundation map (Bermúdez and Zischg, 2018).The flow depth was used to calculate the degree of loss on the basis of a vulnerability function. The degree of loss resulting from the flow depth and the vulnerability function was subsequently multiplied with the reconstruction value of the building. This results in the expected loss to the building structure. The object-specific losses were subsequently summed to give the cumulative losses of a simulated precipitation scenario.

Five vulnerability functions were considered in the damage calculation procedure. We used the functions of Totschnig et al. (2011; V1), Papathoma-Köhle et al. (2015; V2), Hydrotec (2001; V3) as cited in Merz and Thieken (2009), Jonkman et al. (2008; V4), and Dutta et al. (2003; V5). We used different vulnerability functions because there is no regionally adopted and validated vulnerability function available for Switzerland, and because we aimed explicitly at exploring the range of uncertainties related to the choice of the function and its relevance for the maximum uncertainties in the outcomes. A direct validation of the vulnerability functions was not possible because of a lack of loss data at the level of single objects due to privacy restrictions. The selected vulnerability functions consider flow depths as the only input variable for the estimation of the degree of loss. We did not consider flow velocity because the inundation models used in this study do not provide flow velocities and we wanted to use comparable loss models.

2.4 Benchmarking against other selected uncertainty factors

The effects of variability in probable maximum precipitation patterns on flood losses are compared with selected other

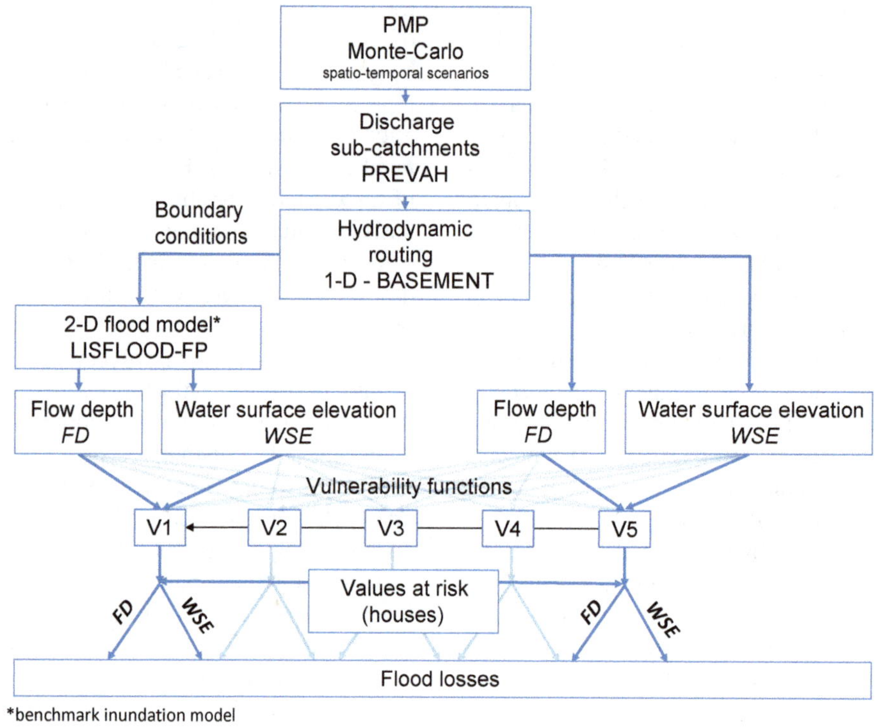

Figure 1. Schematic of the nesting approach. The 2-D flood inundation models and the loss models are nested in a 1-D routing model.

uncertainty factors. The comparison was made by following the parallel models approach first presented by Visser et al. (2000) for the example of climate simulations. Merz and Thieken (2009) adopted this approach for the identification of principal uncertainty sources in flood risk calculations. In summary, this approach computes a number of model runs with varying input parameters. In the first step, the minimum and maximum values of all simulation outcomes (flood losses in financial units in this study) were extracted. The difference between both is defined as the maximum uncertainty range (MUR). In the second step, the uncertainty range (UR_{sub}) of a specific subset of model runs was computed. The subsets from all model runs can be defined by specific criteria, e.g. a subset of all model runs with the same flood model or a subset of model runs using the same vulnerability function. The uncertainty range of this subset is given by the difference between the minimum and maximum values of all simulation outcomes of this specific subset. Third, the reduced uncertainty range (RUR) was computed according to Eq. (1). This indicator describes the relative role of an uncertainty source to the maximum uncertainty range of all model runs.

$$\mathrm{RUR} = \frac{(\mathrm{MUR} - \mathrm{UR_{sub}})}{\mathrm{MUR}} \cdot 100\,\% \qquad (1)$$

The RUR is related to the maximum uncertainty range of all models but is not relative to the RUR of other subsets. Furthermore, Eq. (1) does not isolate all the contributions of the different components to the maximum uncertainty range but they remain intertwined, except the selected uncertainty factor. However, the RUR values of the subsets are comparable. A high value of RUR means that the subset contributes significantly to the maximum uncertainty range. Alternatively, a small value of RUR ($\mathrm{RUR} \ll 100\,\%$) indicates that the subset has a reduced effect on the overall uncertainty (Visser et al., 2000). In the model experiment for this study, we analysed the relative contribution of (a) the spatio-temporal rainfall pattern, (b) the choice of the inundation model and the exposure analysis approach, and (c) the choice of the vulnerability function. Hence, we followed a hierarchical approach for the selection of the subsets. For assessing the contribution of the spatio-temporal rainfall pattern to the overall uncertainty, we analysed 150 rainfall scenarios (hierarchical level 1 – precipitation). For each of these rainfall scenarios, the losses were computed with two different flood inundation models (LISFLOOD-FP and BASEMENT-1D) in combination with two different exposure modelling approaches (FD and WSE; hierarchical level 2 – flood model) and five different vulnerability functions identified previously (hierarchical level 3 – vulnerability). For each PMP scenario, 20 loss estimations were computed (four flood models times five vulnerability functions). Overall, the whole ensemble amounts to 3000 model runs (i.e. flood loss estimations). The RUR values were computed on the basis of subsets selected by the hierarchical levels representing the uncertainty factors considered in this analysis.

3 Study area

We set up the flood inundation models for the main valley of the Aare River basin upstream of Bern, Switzerland. The catchment elevation ranges from 500 to 4200 m a.s.l., with a mean elevation of 1600 m a.s.l. The southern part of the river basin consists of relatively high alpine mountains. Several alpine peaks within this area exceed 4000 m a.s.l., and parts of it are glaciated (8 % of the total catchment area). The main valley of the Aare River basin consists of a relatively flat floodplain with two lakes, where widespread flooding can occur. The lakes are natural but artificially managed, and are oriented along an approximately east–west axis in the lowland part of the catchment. The study area covers 3000 km^2, and the following main river reaches are considered in the model chain (see Fig. 2):

1. Hasliaare river, from Meiringen to Lake Brienz (floodplain: 15 km^2; contributing area: 451 km^2);
2. Lake Brienz static inundation model (lake area: 31 km^2; contributing area: 1138 km^2);
3. Interlaken, area between Lake Brienz and Lake Thun and the fan of the Lütschine River (floodplain: 28 km^2);
4. Lake Thun static inundation model (lake area: 50 km^2; contributing area: 2450 km^2);
5. Thun (floodplain: 8 km^2);
6. Aare River reach between Thun and Bern (floodplain: 42 km^2);
7. Gürbe River reach between Burgistein and Belp (floodplain: 15 km^2; contributing area: 116 km^2).

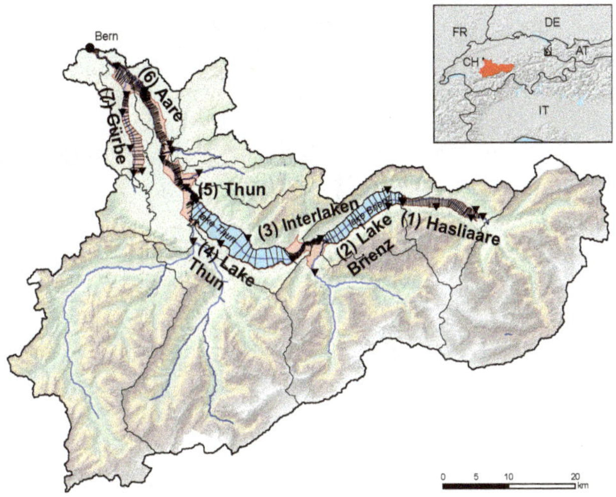

Figure 2. The Aare River catchment upstream of Bern, Switzerland. The sub-catchments of the hydrological model are divided by black lines. The black triangles indicate the coupling points between the hydrologic and the 2-D inundation model. The 1-D routing model covers all floodplains (red lines) and the lakes (blue). The floodplains that are covered by the individual 2-D inundation models nested into the 1-D routing model are marked and labelled in red.

4 Results

The main results of the coupled model simulations are the discharges at the outlet of each of the sub-catchments, the discharge at the outlet of the Aare River basin at Bern, and the flood losses for 150 PMP simulations. Figure 3 shows the hydrographs of the 150 PMP scenarios at the outlet of the river basin in Bern. The outflow from the river basin varies remarkably in peak discharge and time to peak. The peak discharges for each ensemble member were in the range 906 to 1296 $m^3 s^{-1}$. Thus, the highest peak discharge is 43 % higher than the lowest in the selected set of scenarios. Moreover, Fig. 3 shows the discharges of the tributaries downstream of Lake Thun during peak flow of the Aare River at Bern. It is shown that the highest peak discharge at Bern depends on both a high flow in the main river and high flows in the tributaries. Upstream of Thun, the synchronization of flood peaks is represented by the lake levels.

The flood inundation modelling resulted in a set of flood maps representing the 150 PMP scenarios. The overlay of these flood maps leads to an inundation extent map that estimates a spatial probability of inundation, conditional on the rainfall sum of a PMP event in the river basin. Each inundation map is treated as equally weighted in the probabilistic map. This map represents the probability that a model grid cell is flooded in one PMP scenarios. An extract of this map is shown in Fig. 4. The map shows that not all of the PMP scenarios lead to flooding of the same areas. Thus, despite the narrow framing of floodplains in mountainous areas by topography, high variability in flood extent can be observed. The discharge in the Lütschine River at Interlaken and the lake levels of both lakes, Lake Brienz and Lake Thun, have the strongest influence on the inundation probability map. In particular, the level of Lake Thun and the flooding by the Lütschine River determine a remarkable portion of the flooded area.

Depending on the chosen approach for inundation modelling and exposure analysis, the number of affected buildings varies remarkably. At minimum 2423 buildings and at maximum 5371 buildings are affected across the whole domain (not shown). The high variability between the PMP patterns is also shown by the number of exposed residents (Fig. 5). The exposure shows a bimodal distribution in the case of the 2-D model and an unimodal distribution in the case of the 1-D model. This is related to the exposure of houses at the alluvial fan of the Lütschine River. This floodplain is flooded only in some of the scenarios but when flooded, the number of affected buildings increases remarkably. This is not the case in the 1-D model because this model

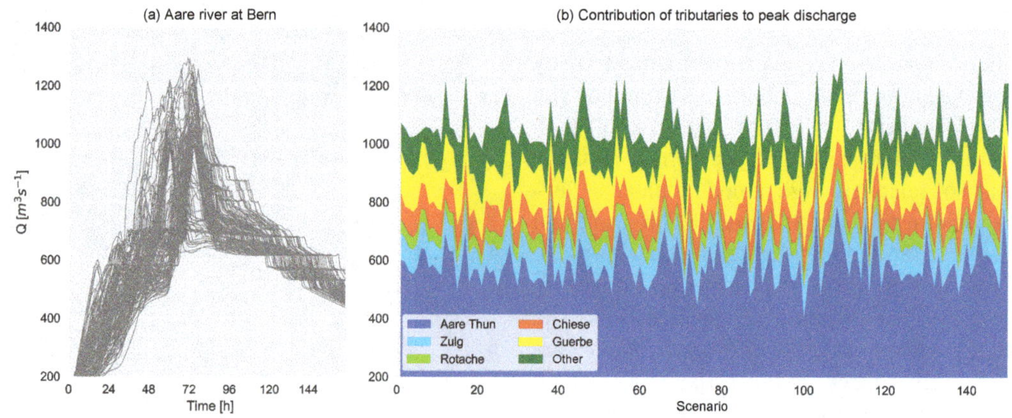

Figure 3. (a) Hydrographs at the outlet of the Aare River basin in Bern resulting from the coupled hydrologic-hydrodynamic modelling of the 150 PMP scenarios. **(b)** Superimposition of the tributaries downstream of Lake Thun during peak flow of the Aare River at Bern.

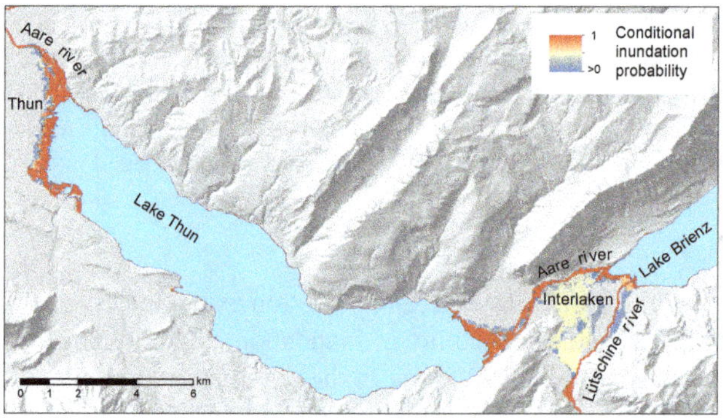

Figure 4. Detailed example of the conditional probability flood map for the floodplains of Thun and Interlaken. Predicted flood inundation extents can change significantly depending on the specific spatial properties of a few of the PMP scenarios and hence have lower mapped inundation probabilities.

only considers flooding by the main river Aare and neglects the tributaries.

The flood simulation mapped outputs (flow depth maps and water surface elevation maps) were used separately to calculate the flood losses at the individual building level. Subsequently, the flood losses at building scale were aggregated at a catchment level. Figure 6 shows the distribution of the aggregated flood losses. It is shown that – depending on the model ensemble member – the losses vary between CHF 0.06 and 2.87 billion. Thus, the losses are remarkably influenced by all the experimental uncertainty factors previously discussed in the modelling chain. However, even if the effect of the vulnerability function and the choice of the exposure analysis approach are not considered, the losses still vary markedly depending on the PMP scenario. Maximum losses are still approximately 3–5 times the minimum losses for some of the vulnerability functions. The vulnerability function V4 (Jonkman et al., 2008) results in the lowest losses. This function was calibrated for lowland floodplains and thus has generally lower degrees of loss. However, this vulnerability function might be more representative for the areas affected by lake flooding than the others. In the 2-D FD model runs, the exposure is higher compared to the 2-D WSE model runs. In contrast, the losses are higher in the 2-D WSE run. This relates to the mean flow depths at the buildings. The mean flow depth over all affected buildings is 0.54 m in the 2-D FD model runs and 0.87 m in the 2-D WSE model runs. This results in higher losses although the number of exposed buildings is lower. The flow depths in the 1-D FD and 1-D WSE model runs are 1.08 and 1.36 m respectively. This explains the generally higher losses in the 1-D model runs compared to the 2-D model runs.

The benchmark against other uncertainties such as the flood modelling in combination with the exposure analysis approach and the vulnerability functions shows that the uncertainties considered in the model experiment contribute significantly to the sensitivity of the model chain to the assumptions made. Each member of the ensemble runs represents a rainfall pattern and a resulting flood loss computed on a basis of a combination of a specific flood model with a specific loss model. The difference between the ensemble member with the absolute minimum and the member with the absolute maximum of flood losses represents the maximum uncertainty range MUR. The total number of runs was divided into subsets that represents in each case the uncertainty range of a specific combination of the variables. The difference between the member with the absolute minimum of this subset and the member with the absolute maximum of this subset represents the reduced uncertainty range UR_{sub}. Consequently, the reduced uncertainty range RUR is computed after Eq. (1). The reduced uncertainty range RUR of all subsets ranges between 14 and 92 % of the maximum uncertainty range MUR. The reduced uncertainty range of the subset of ensemble members considering only the vari-

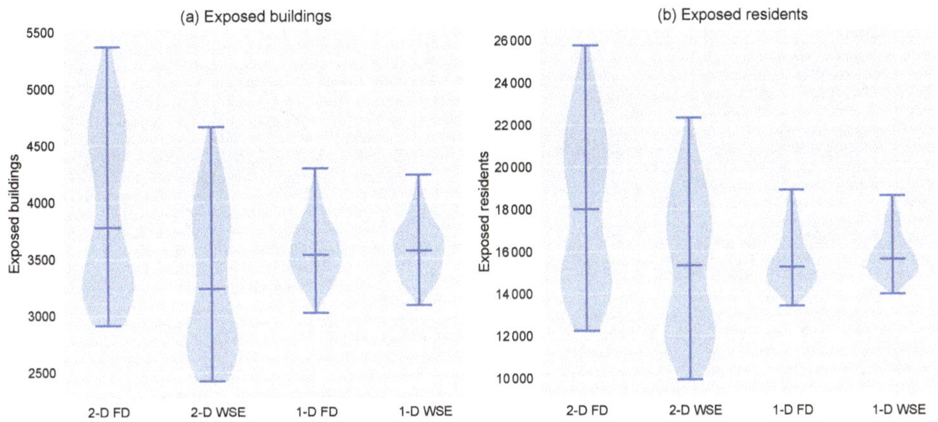

Figure 5. Exposed buildings **(a)** and residents **(b)** aggregated at river basin level. Flood losses aggregated at river basin level. The variation between the PMP scenarios is shown on the y axis, whereas the x axis shows the variability inherent to the choice of the flood model (2-D: LISFLOOD-FP; 1-D: BASEMENT-1D) in combination with the approach for attributing flow depths to the buildings (FD: flow depths are calculated on the basis of flow depths maps; WSE: flow depths are calculated on the basis of water surface elevation maps and the object-specific ground floor level).

ability in rainfall scenarios lies between 42 and 92 % with a median of 72 %. Hence, the highest RUR of all subsets is dominated by the subsets regarding the variability in probable maximum precipitation pattern. Figure 7 shows the comparison between the RUR values of the subsets in which the variability of one of the three considered uncertainty factors was analysed. This analysis makes evident that the rainfall pattern contributes most to the maximum uncertainty range.

In Fig. 8 (left column), we plotted the results of all model outcomes with focus on the 2-D inundation model in terms of exposed number of buildings and persons, and in terms of flood losses against the peak discharge of the respective precipitation pattern at the catchment outlet. The hypothesis that the flood losses increase with peak discharge at the outlet of the river basin can be verified in the sense that there is a significant correlation. This relationship is weaker for exposed buildings and residents than for the flood losses. However, the rainfall scenario leading to the highest peak discharge at the basin outlet does not correspond with the highest flood losses. Instead, the flood losses are more correlated with high lake levels in Lake Thun (see Fig. 8, right column). The correlation between flood losses and the level of Lake Thun (Spearman's rank correlation coefficient ranges from 0.54 to 0.94, depending on the flood model and the vulnerability function) is stronger than between losses and the peak discharge at the catchment outlet (Spearman's rank correlation coefficient ranging from 0.43 to 0.71). Thus, in the Aare River basin, the level of Lake Thun is a more relevant proxy indicator for the amount of flood losses in the whole river basin than the peak discharge at the outlet of the river basin (i.e. the so-called PMF of the river basin). This can be explained by the local situation of the city of Thun where the density of the building stock is very high along the shoreline of Lake Thun and along the Aare River. The major area of the Aare River basin contributes to the lakes. Only 20 % of the catchment area is located downstream of Lake Thun. Although the area of Lake Thun covers only about 2 % of its contributing area, this means that the river basin has relevant retention areas that attenuate the outflow from the river basin and thus the PMF. Vice versa, this retention effect increases flood losses because a relevant number of buildings are located in neighbourhood of the lake shorelines. Likewise, not all of the PMP scenarios lead to flooding by the Lütschine River in Interlaken. As shown in Fig. 4, the floodplain of this river is flooded only in a minority of the ensemble runs. Depending on whether this floodplain is flooded or not, up to 1500 exposed buildings and therefore up to one-third of the total number of maximally exposed buildings in the whole river basin could be affected. Thus, the highest loss of all simulated scenarios is related to a combination of a high lake level in Thun with high river discharge of the Lütschine River. This shows that the maximum loss depends on both the spatio-temporal pattern of the rainfall and the internal organization of the river basin in terms of the spatial distribution of the values at risk (i.e. exposure) within the floodplains.

5 Discussion and conclusions

In this study, we set up a coupled component model for estimating flood losses of extreme flood events in a complex mountainous river basin. On the basis of a Monte Carlo approach, we computed an ensemble of extreme flood events for different precipitation patterns of a 3-day probable maximum precipitation scenario. With this model experiment, we analysed the effects of the spatial distribution of the rainfall within a mountainous river basin on flood losses. Further-

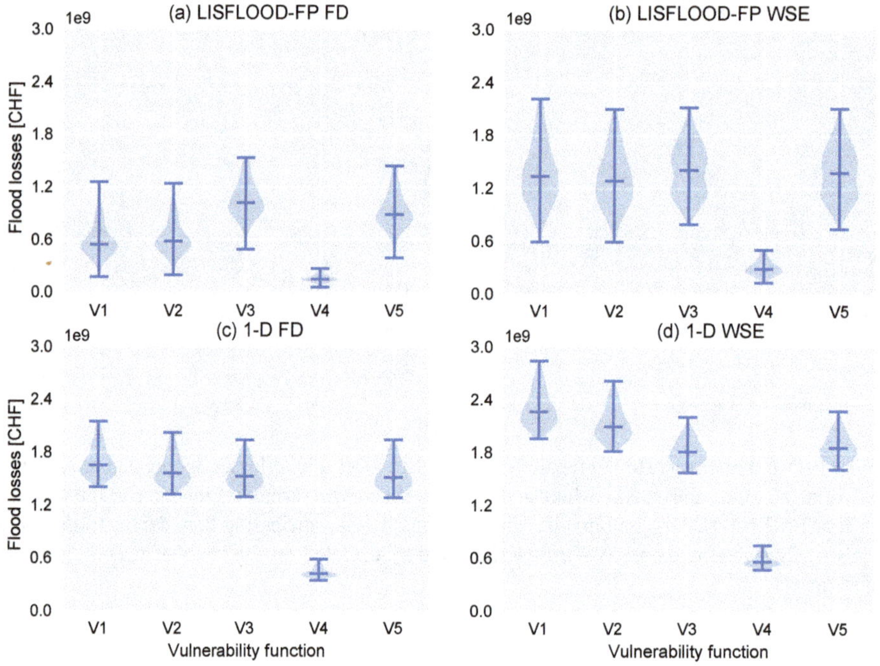

Figure 6. Flood losses aggregated at river basin level. The variation between the PMP scenarios is shown in the y axis, whereas the x axis shows the variability inherent to the vulnerability functions. The diagram in **(a)** shows flood losses that are calculated based on the flow depths as modelled by LISFLOOD-FP, the diagram in **(b)** shows the flood losses that are calculated based on the water surface elevation and the object-specific ground floor level. The flood losses estimated by the 1-D model are shown in **(c)** and **(d)**.

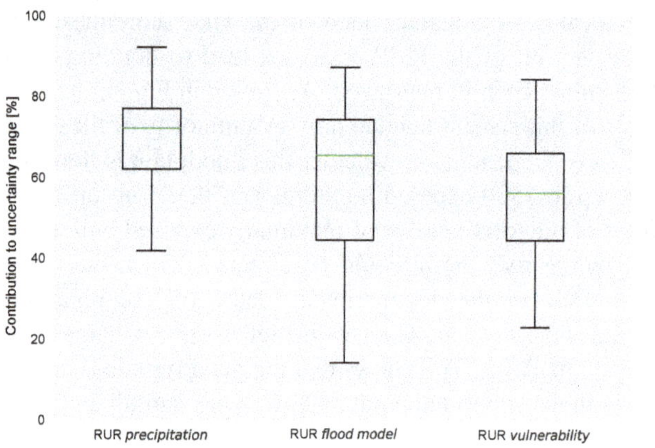

Figure 7. Reduced uncertainty ranges RUR of the subsets of model runs representing the three main uncertainty sources.

more, we benchmarked these effects with other uncertainties in flood loss modelling.

The model experiment showed that the sensitivity of flood losses to the variability of spatial distribution of rainfall within a river basin with a complex topography is larger than for the other considered uncertainty factors. The PMP pattern determines the magnitude and timing of the flood peaks coming from the sub-catchments and flowing through the floodplains along the main valleys and the lakes. Thus, the rainfall pattern could lead to a superimposition of flood waves as described by the model experiments of Neal et al. (2013) and Pattison et al. (2014). In addition to the superimposition of flood waves, it is shown that lake levels, as a proxy for the water volumes coming from different sub-catchments, are also relevant for the determination of flood losses. This complements the findings of Sampson et al. (2014) on the impacts of precipitation variability on insurance loss estimates. With the present study, we extended the Sampson et al. study, which was focussed on urban environments, with a focus on complex mountainous river basins.

Furthermore, the model experiment showed that the peak flow coming from a single sub-catchment can be responsible for a relevant share of the total sum of exposed buildings and flood losses. Thus, the physical variability of the river basin is coupled with the topological situation of the main settlements within the floodplains, i.e. the spatial pattern of exposure. The inundation probability maps and the variability in flood losses show that two floodplains are mainly responsible for a high amount of flood losses. This documents that flood losses depend on both the spatio-temporal pattern of the rainfall and the internal organization of the river basin in terms of the spatial distribution or aggregation of the values at risk within the floodplains. Moreover, the spatial setup of the values at risk within the floodplains leads to its specific sensitivity to flood magnitude and lake level. However, these specific sensitivities of the single floodplains together with

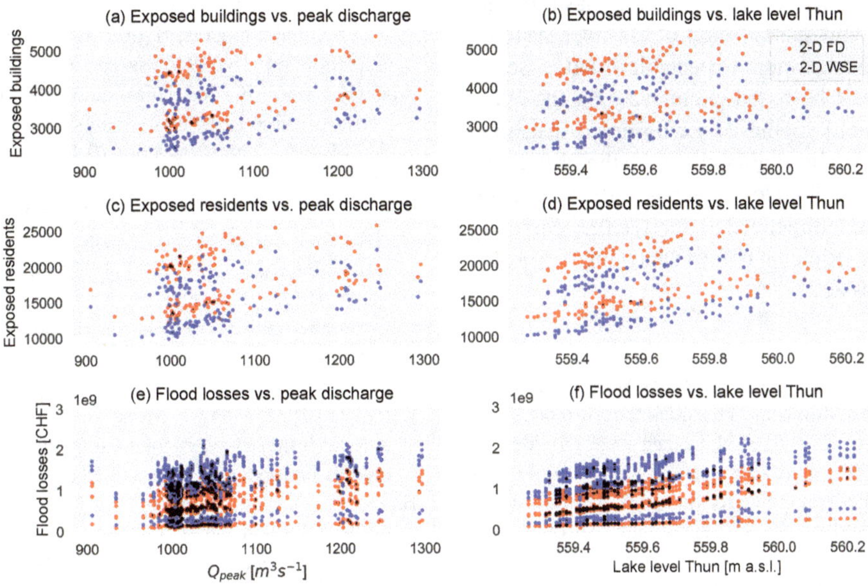

Figure 8. This figure shows the aggregated flood losses for the 150 PMP scenarios. The red dots show the exposed entities and losses that are computed based on the flow depths, the blue dots show the exposed entities and losses that are computed based on water surface elevation. The figures in the last row show the losses resulting from all vulnerability functions.

the variability in rainfall pattern lead to a specific sensitivity of the whole river basin to a certain pattern of rainfall. This behaviour has to be analysed and generalized in further studies and considered in the estimation of probable maximum flood losses.

Despite the topographical confinement of the floodplains by the mountain hillslopes, the flooded areas vary markedly with different rainfall patterns. Thus, the probabilistic map shows high spatial variability, caused by a few of the PMP scenarios significantly increasing inundation areas. Hence, the flow depths even at the individual building level, and consequently the total flood losses, vary remarkably with rainfall scenario. This case study in a mountainous environment and in an environment with remarkable retention capacities due to the presence of lakes may even lead to an attenuated illustration of this effect. These retention effects attenuate the PMF on one side but control the flood losses on the other side if settlements are located alongside the lakes. However, in mountain areas without lakes, the effects of spatio-temporal variability in precipitation patterns on flood losses may be even more accentuated. However, a modelling approach is needed to analyse these effects as stated by Emmanuel et al. (2015).

Nevertheless, the other uncertainty factors considered in this study, i.e. the role of the flood model, the exposure assessment approach and the vulnerability functions, are also contributing markedly to the maximum uncertainty range. This is in line with the findings of other studies (Jongman et al., 2012; de Moel and Aerts, 2011). Consequently, these uncertainties also have to be taken into account in portfolio analysis or in the analysis of probable maximum flood losses.

In summary, we conclude that the analysis of a broader set of extreme floods with different precipitation patterns leads to more a comprehensive view of flood losses in a river basin compared to standard deterministic PMP/PMF methods. The spatio-temporal characteristics of rainfall patterns must be considered in complex mountainous river basins. Moreover, the analysis of the probable maximum flood losses in a river basin should consider the systemic vulnerability of the floodplains or the behaviour of floodplains as human–water systems as stated by Di Baldassarre et al. (2013, 2014). This involves the identification of key locations of exposure that contribute most to the overall flood losses. Probabilistic inundation maps provide a first overview of key locations of flooded areas with high sensitivity against the rainfall pattern. Furthermore, it is shown that the presented model experiment provides a valuable instrument for the consideration of all components in the analysis of the variability of rainfall patterns to flood losses in a river basin, from hazard to exposure to vulnerability.

However, the approach for simulating rainfall patterns presented here has its limitations. Although it has been shown that it can reproduce past flood events (Felder and Weingartner, 2016) and results in more robust PMF estimations than a uniform rainfall distribution (Felder and Weingartner, 2017), it is not comparable to a regional climate model or weather forecast model. In future research, an inverse modelling approach may be followed by searching the worst case precipitation pattern leading to the worst case flood losses on the basis of the system characteristics of the river basin (sensitivities of floodplains and spatial setup of the river system). The calculation of the maximum expectable flood losses in a river basin should not be based exclusively on the PMF. In contrast to the initial hypothesis, we observed that other catchment characteristics in combination with the PMF could remarkably influence the flood losses. Consequently, in complex river basins it is recommended to analyse the sensitivity of the most relevant floodplains before analysing the probable maximum flood losses.

Code availability. Data of cross section surveys were provided the Federal Office for the Environment. The lidar terrain model was provided by the Canton of Bern. Basic GIS data were provided by the Federal Office for Topography swisstopo. The residential register was provided by the Federal Office for Statistics. The data about values at risk are restricted by privacy regulations. All other data produced in this study and the codes for the model experiment are available from the leading author on request. The inundation model LISFLOOD-FP is available at http://www.bristol.ac.uk/geography/research/hydrology/models/lisflood/ (Bates, 2018).

Author contributions. The study was designed by APZ, JF, PB, and RW. The hydrological model was set up and run by GF. Model coupling and the set up of the hydraulic model were done by APZ, NQ, GC, and JN. The loss model was developed by APZ. The analyses were performed by APZ with the support of all co-authors. The manuscript was prepared by APZ with the contribution of all co-authors.

Competing interests. The authors declare that they have no conflict of interest.

Acknowledgements. The work was partially funded by the Swiss National Foundation (grant no. IZK0Z2_170478/1), by the Swiss Mobiliar, by NERC grant SINATRA (Susceptibility of catchments to INTense RAinfall and flooding, grant no. NE/K008781/1), and by NERC grant MaRIUS (Managing the Risks, Impacts and Uncertainties of droughts and water Scarcity, grant no. NE/L010399/1). We thank the Federal Government of Switzerland and the Canton of Bern for providing the data.

Edited by: Erwin Zehe

References

Adams, R., Western, A. W., and Seed, A. W.: An analysis of the impact of spatial variability in rainfall on runoff and sediment predictions from a distributed model, Hydrol. Process., 26, 3263–3280, https://doi.org/10.1002/hyp.8435, 2012.

Altarejos-García, L., Martínez-Chenoll, M. L., Escuder-Bueno, I., and Serrano-Lombillo, A.: Assessing the impact of uncertainty on flood risk estimates with reliability analysis using 1-D and 2-D hydraulic models, Hydrol. Earth Syst. Sci., 16, 1895–1914, https://doi.org/10.5194/hess-16-1895-2012, 2012.

Apel, H., Merz, B., and Thieken, A. H.: Quantification of uncertainties in flood risk assessments, Int. J. River Basin Manage., 6, 149–162, https://doi.org/10.1080/15715124.2008.9635344, 2008.

Arnell, N. W. and Gosling, S. N.: The impacts of climate change on river flood risk at the global scale, Clim. Change, 134, 387–401, https://doi.org/10.1007/s10584-014-1084-5, 2016.

Asadieh, B. and Krakauer, N. Y.: Global trends in extreme precipitation: climate models versus observations, Hydrol. Earth Syst. Sci., 19, 877–891, https://doi.org/10.5194/hess-19-877-2015, 2015.

Bates, P.: LISFLOOD-FP. Model description and download, available at: http://www.bristol.ac.uk/geography/research/hydrology/models/lisflood/, last access: 4 May 2018.

Bates, P. D. and de Roo, A. P. J.: A simple raster-based model for flood inundation simulation, J. Hydrol., 236, 54–77, https://doi.org/10.1016/S0022-1694(00)00278-X, 2000.

Bates, P. D., Horritt, M. S., and Fewtrell, T. J.: A simple inertial formulation of the shallow water equations for efficient two-dimensional flood inundation modelling, J. Hydrol., 387, 33–45, https://doi.org/10.1016/j.jhydrol.2010.03.027, 2010.

Beauchamp, J., Leconte, R., Trudel, M., and Brissette, F.: Estimation of the summer-fall PMP and PMF of a northern watershed under a changed climate, Water Resour. Res., 49, 3852–3862, https://doi.org/10.1002/wrcr.20336, 2013.

Beniston, M., Stephenson, D. B., Christensen, O. B., Ferro, C. A. T., Frei, C., Goyette, S., Halsnaes, K., Holt, T., Jylhä, K., Koffi, B., Palutikof, J., Schöll, R., Semmler, T., and Woth, K.: Future extreme events in European climate: An exploration of regional climate model projections, Clim. Change, 81, 71–95, https://doi.org/10.1007/s10584-006-9226-z, 2007.

Bermúdez, M. and Zischg, A. P.: Sensitivity of flood loss estimates to building representation and flow depth attribution methods in micro-scale flood modelling, Nat. Hazards, 14, 253, https://doi.org/10.1007/s11069-018-3270-7, 2018.

Bouwer, L. M.: Projections of future extreme weather losses under changes in climate and exposure, Risk analysis an official publication of the Society for Risk Analysis, 33, 915–930, https://doi.org/10.1111/j.1539-6924.2012.01880.x, 2013.

Bruni, G., Reinoso, R., van de Giesen, N. C., Clemens, F. H. L. R., and ten Veldhuis, J. A. E.: On the sensitivity of urban hydrodynamic modelling to rainfall spatial and temporal resolution, Hydrol. Earth Syst. Sci., 19, 691–709, https://doi.org/10.5194/hess-19-691-2015, 2015.

Büchele, B., Kreibich, H., Kron, A., Thieken, A., Ihringer, J., Oberle, P., Merz, B., and Nestmann, F.: Flood-risk mapping: contributions towards an enhanced assessment of extreme events and associated risks, Nat. Hazards Earth Syst. Sci., 6, 485–503, https://doi.org/10.5194/nhess-6-485-2006, 2006.

Burke, N., Rau-Chaplin, A., and Varghese, B.: Computing probable maximum loss in catastrophe reinsurance portfolios on multi-core and many-core architectures, Concurrency Computat.: Pract. Exper., 28, 836–847, https://doi.org/10.1002/cpe.3695, 2016.

Chatterjee, C., Förster, S., and Bronstert, A.: Comparison of hydrodynamic models of different complexities to model floods with emergency storage areas, Hydrol. Process., 22, 4695–4709, https://doi.org/10.1002/hyp.7079, 2008.

Coxon, G., Freer, J., Westerberg, I. K., Wagener, T., Woods, R., and Smith, P. J.: A novel framework for discharge uncertainty quantification applied to 500 UK gauging stations, Water Resour. Res., 51, 5531–5546, https://doi.org/10.1002/2014WR016532, 2015.

Cristiano, E., ten Veldhuis, M.-C., and van de Giesen, N.: Spatial and temporal variability of rainfall and their effects on hydrological response in urban areas – a review, Hydrol. Earth Syst. Sci., 21, 3859–3878, https://doi.org/10.5194/hess-21-3859-2017, 2017.

de Moel, H. and Aerts, J. C. J. H.: Effect of uncertainty in land use, damage models and inundation depth on flood damage estimates, Nat. Hazards, 58, 407–425, https://doi.org/10.1007/s11069-010-9675-6, 2011.

de Moel, H., Jongman, B., Kreibich, H., Merz, B., Penning-Rowsell, E., and Ward, P. J.: Flood risk assessments at different spatial scales, Mitig. Adapt. Strateg. Glob. Change, 20, 865–890, https://doi.org/10.1007/s11027-015-9654-z, 2015.

Di Baldassarre, G., Schumann, G., Bates, P. D., Freer, J. E., and Beven, K. J.: Flood-plain mapping: A critical discussion of deterministic and probabilistic approaches, Hydrol. Sci. J., 55, 364–376, https://doi.org/10.1080/02626661003683389, 2010.

Di Baldassarre, G., Kooy, M., Kemerink, J. S., and Brandimarte, L.: Towards understanding the dynamic behaviour of floodplains as human-water systems, Hydrol. Earth Syst. Sci., 17, 3235–3244, https://doi.org/10.5194/hess-17-3235-2013, 2013.

Di Baldassarre, G., Kemerink, J. S., Kooy, M., and Brandimarte, L.: Floods and societies: the spatial distribution of water-related disaster risk and its dynamics, WIREs Water, 1, 133–139, https://doi.org/10.1002/wat2.1015, 2014.

Dodov, B. and Foufoula-Georgiou, E.: Incorporating the spatio-temporal distribution of rainfall and basin geomorphology into nonlinear analyses of streamflow dynamics, Adv. Water Resour., 28, 711–728, https://doi.org/10.1016/j.advwatres.2004.12.013, 2005.

Dutta, D., Herath, S., and Musiake, K.: A mathematical model for flood loss estimation, J. Hydrol., 277, 24–49, https://doi.org/10.1016/S0022-1694(03)00084-2, 2003.

Emmanuel, I., Andrieu, H., Leblois, E., Janey, N., and Payrastre, O.: Influence of rainfall spatial variability on rainfall–runoff modelling: Benefit of a simulation approach?, J. Hydrol., 531, 337–348, https://doi.org/10.1016/j.jhydrol.2015.04.058, 2015.

Emmanuel, I., Payrastre, O., Andrieu, H., Zuber, F., Lang, M., Klijn, F., and Samuels, P.: Influence of the spatial variability of rainfall on hydrograph modelling at catchment outlet: A case study in the Cevennes region, France, E3S Web Conf., 7, 18004, https://doi.org/10.1051/e3sconf/20160718004, 2016.

Faulkner, D. and Benn, J.: Reservoir Flood Estimation: Time for a Re-think, in: Dams – Benefits and Disbenefits; Assets or Liabilities?, edited by: Pepper, A., ICE Publishing, London, 2016.

Felder, G. and Weingartner, R.: An approach for the determination of precipitation input for worst-case flood modelling, Hydrol. Sci. J., 61, 2600–2609, https://doi.org/10.1080/02626667.2016.1151980, 2016.

Felder, G. and Weingartner, R.: Assessment of deterministic PMF modelling approaches, Hydrol. Sci. J., 62, 1591–1602, https://doi.org/10.1080/02626667.2017.1319065, 2017.

Felder, G., Zischg, A., and Weingartner, R.: The effect of coupling hydrologic and hydrodynamic models on probable maximum flood estimation, J. Hydrol., 550, 157–165, https://doi.org/10.1016/j.jhydrol.2017.04.052, 2017.

Fewtrell, T. J., Bates, P. D., Horritt, M., and Hunter, N. M.: Evaluating the effect of scale in flood inundation modelling in urban environments, Hydrol. Process., 22, 5107–5118, https://doi.org/10.1002/hyp.7148, 2008.

Fischer, E. M. and Knutti, R.: Observed heavy precipitation increase confirms theory and early models, Nat. Clim. Change, 6, 986–991, https://doi.org/10.1038/nclimate3110, 2016.

Foufoula-Georgiou, E.: A probabilistic storm transposition approach for estimating exceedance probabilities of extreme precipitation depths, Water Resour. Res., 25, 799–815, https://doi.org/10.1029/WR025i005p00799, 1989.

Franchini, M., Helmlinger, K. R., Foufoula-Georgiou, E., and Todini, E.: Stochastic storm transposition coupled with rainfall–runoff modeling for estimation of exceedance probabilities of design floods, J. Hydrol., 175, 511–532, https://doi.org/10.1016/S0022-1694(96)80022-9, 1996.

Fuchs, S., Keiler, M., and Zischg, A.: A spatiotemporal multi-hazard exposure assessment based on property data, Nat. Hazards Earth Syst. Sci., 15, 2127–2142, https://doi.org/10.5194/nhess-15-2127-2015, 2015.

Gai, L., Baartman, J. E. M., Mendoza-Carranza, M., Wang, F., Ritsema, C. J., and Geissen, V.: A framework approach for unravelling the impact of multiple factors influencing flooding, J. Flood Risk Manage, published online first, https://doi.org/10.1111/jfr3.12310, 2017.

Gupta, H. V., Kling, H., Yilmaz, K. K., and Martinez, G. F.: Decomposition of the mean squared error and NSE performance criteria: Implications for improving hydrological modelling, Hydrology Conference 2010, 377, 80–91, https://doi.org/10.1016/j.jhydrol.2009.08.003, 2009.

Hasan, S. and Foliente, G.: Modeling infrastructure system interdependencies and socioeconomic impacts of failure in extreme events: emerging R&D challenges, Nat. Hazards, 78, 2143–2168, https://doi.org/10.1007/s11069-015-1814-7, 2015.

Horritt, M. S. and Bates, P. D.: Effects of spatial resolution on a raster based model of flood flow, J. Hydrol., 253, 239–249, https://doi.org/10.1016/S0022-1694(01)00490-5, 2001.

Horritt, M. S. and Bates, P. D.: Evaluation of 1D and 2D numerical models for predicting river flood inundation, J. Hydrol., 268, 87–99, https://doi.org/10.1016/S0022-1694(02)00121-X, 2002.

Hydrotec: Hochwasser-Aktionsplan Angerbach, Teil I: Berichte und Anlagen, Studie im Auftrag des Stua Dusseldorf, Aachen, Germany, 2001.

IPCC: Managing the risks of extreme events and disasters to advance climate change adaptation: Special report of the Intergovernmental Panel on Climate Change, Cambridge University Press, New York, x, 582, 2012.

Jongman, B., Kreibich, H., Apel, H., Barredo, J. I., Bates, P. D., Feyen, L., Gericke, A., Neal, J., Aerts, J. C. J. H., and Ward, P. J.: Comparative flood damage model assessment: towards a European approach, Nat. Hazards Earth Syst. Sci., 12, 3733–3752, https://doi.org/10.5194/nhess-12-3733-2012, 2012.

Jonkman, S. N., Bočkarjova, M., Kok, M., and Bernardini, P.: Integrated hydrodynamic and economic modelling of flood damage in the Netherlands, Special Section: Integrated Hydro-Economic

Modelling for Effective and Sustainable Water Management, 66, 77–90, https://doi.org/10.1016/j.ecolecon.2007.12.022, 2008.

Kling, H., Fuchs, M., and Paulin, M.: Runoff conditions in the upper Danube basin under an ensemble of climate change scenarios, Hydrology Conference 2010, 424–425, 264–277, https://doi.org/10.1016/j.jhydrol.2012.01.011, 2012.

Kvočka, D., Falconer, R. A., and Bray, M.: Appropriate model use for predicting elevations and inundation extent for extreme flood events, Nat. Hazards, 79, 1791–1808, https://doi.org/10.1007/s11069-015-1926-0, 2015.

Lagos-Zuniga, M. A. and Vargas, M. X.: PMP and PMF estimations in sparsely-gauged Andean basins and climate change projections, Hydrol. Sci. J., 59, 2027–2042, https://doi.org/10.1080/02626667.2013.877588, 2014.

McMillan, H., Krueger, T., and Freer, J.: Benchmarking observational uncertainties for hydrology: Rainfall, river discharge and water quality, Hydrol. Process., 26, 4078–4111, https://doi.org/10.1002/hyp.9384, 2012.

Mechler, R., Hochrainer, S., Aaheim, A., Salen, H., and Wreford, A.: Modelling economic impacts and adaptation to extreme events: Insights from European case studies, Mitig. Adapt. Strateg. Glob. Change, 15, 737–762, https://doi.org/10.1007/s11027-010-9249-7, 2010.

Merz, B. and Thieken, A. H.: Flood risk curves and uncertainty bounds, Nat. Hazards, 51, 437–458, https://doi.org/10.1007/s11069-009-9452-6, 2009.

Michaelides, S.: Vulnerability of transportation to extreme weather and climate change, Nat. Hazards, 72, 1–4, https://doi.org/10.1007/s11069-013-0975-5, 2014.

Micovic, Z., Schaefer, M. G., and Taylor, G. H.: Uncertainty analysis for Probable Maximum Precipitation estimates, J. Hydrol., 521, 360–373, https://doi.org/10.1016/j.jhydrol.2014.12.033, 2015.

Millán, M. M.: Extreme hydrometeorological events and climate change predictions in Europe, J. Hydrol., 518, 206–224, https://doi.org/10.1016/j.jhydrol.2013.12.041, 2014.

Morrill, E. P. and Becker, J. F.: Defining and Analyzing the Frequency and Severity of Flood Events to Improve Risk Management from a Reinsurance Standpoint, Hydrol. Earth Syst. Sci. Discuss., https://doi.org/10.5194/hess-2017-167, in review, 2017.

Nash, J. E. and Sutcliffe, J. V.: River flow forecasting through conceptual models part I – A discussion of principles, J. Hydrol., 10, 282–290, 1970.

Neal, J., Schumann, G., Fewtrell, T., Budimir, M., Bates, P., and Mason, D.: Evaluating a new LISFLOOD-FP formulation with data from the summer 2007 floods in Tewkesbury, UK, J. Flood Risk Manage, 4, 88–95, https://doi.org/10.1111/j.1753-318X.2011.01093.x, 2011.

Neal, J., Schumann, G., and Bates, P. D.: A subgrid channel model for simulating river hydraulics and floodplain inundation over large and data sparse areas, Water Resour. Res., 48, 1–16, https://doi.org/10.1029/2012WR012514, 2012a.

Neal, J., Villanueva, I., Wright, N., Willis, T., Fewtrell, T., and Bates, P. D.: How much physical complexity is needed to model flood inundation?, Hydrol. Process., 26, 2264–2282, https://doi.org/10.1002/hyp.8339, 2012b.

Neal, J., Keef, C., Bates, P., Beven, K., and Leedal, D.: Probabilistic flood risk mapping including spatial dependence, Hydrol. Process., 27, 1349–1363, https://doi.org/10.1002/hyp.9572, 2013.

Neal, J. C., Bates, P. D., Fewtrell, T. J., Hunter, N. M., Wilson, M. D., and Horritt, M. S.: Distributed whole city water level measurements from the Carlisle 2005 urban flood event and comparison with hydraulic model simulations, J. Hydrol., 368, 42–55, https://doi.org/10.1016/j.jhydrol.2009.01.026, 2009.

Nicótina, L., Alessi Celegon, E., Rinaldo, A., and Marani, M.: On the impact of rainfall patterns on the hydrologic response, Water Resour. Res., 44, 311, https://doi.org/10.1029/2007WR006654, 2008.

Nikolopoulos, E. I., Borga, M., Zoccatelli, D., and Anagnostou, E. N.: Catchment-scale storm velocity: Quantification, scale dependence and effect on flood response, Hydrol. Sci. J., 59, 1363–1376, https://doi.org/10.1080/02626667.2014.923889, 2014.

Ochoa-Rodriguez, S., Wang, L.-P., Gires, A., Pina, R. D., Reinoso-Rondinel, R., Bruni, G., Ichiba, A., Gaitan, S., Cristiano, E., van Assel, J., Kroll, S., Murlà-Tuyls, D., Tisserand, B., Schertzer, D., Tchiguirinskaia, I., Onof, C., Willems, P., and ten Veldhuis, M.-C.: Impact of spatial and temporal resolution of rainfall inputs on urban hydrodynamic modelling outputs: A multi-catchment investigation, J. Hydrol., 531, 389–407, https://doi.org/10.1016/j.jhydrol.2015.05.035, 2015.

Papathoma-Köhle, M., Zischg, A., Fuchs, S., Glade, T., and Keiler, M.: Loss estimation for landslides in mountain areas – An integrated toolbox for vulnerability assessment and damage documentation, Environ. Modell. Softw., 63, 156–169, https://doi.org/10.1016/j.envsoft.2014.10.003, 2015.

Paschalis, A., Fatichi, S., Molnar, P., Rimkus, S., and Burlando, P.: On the effects of small scale space?: Time variability of rainfall on basin flood response, J. Hydrology, 514, 313–327, https://doi.org/10.1016/j.jhydrol.2014.04.014, 2014.

Pattison, I., Lane, S. N., Hardy, R. J., and Reaney, S. M.: The role of tributary relative timing and sequencing in controlling large floods, Water Resour. Res., 5444–5458, https://doi.org/10.1002/2013WR014067, 2014.

Pfahl, S., O'Gorman, P. A., and Fischer, E. M.: Understanding the regional pattern of projected future changes in extreme precipitation, Nat. Clim. Change, 7, 423–427, https://doi.org/10.1038/nclimate3287, 2017.

Pianosi, F., Beven, K., Freer, J., Hall, J. W., Rougier, J., Stephenson, D. B., and Wagener, T.: Sensitivity analysis of environmental models: A systematic review with practical workflow, Environ. Modell. Softw., 79, 214–232, https://doi.org/10.1016/j.envsoft.2016.02.008, 2016.

Rafieeinasab, A., Norouzi, A., Kim, S., Habibi, H., Nazari, B., Seo, D.-J., Lee, H., Cosgrove, B., and Cui, Z.: Toward high-resolution flash flood prediction in large urban areas – Analysis of sensitivity to spatiotemporal resolution of rainfall input and hydrologic modeling, J. Hydrol., 531, 370–388, https://doi.org/10.1016/j.jhydrol.2015.08.045, 2015.

Rajczak, J., Pall, P., and Schär, C.: Projections of extreme precipitation events in regional climate simulations for Europe and the Alpine Region, J. Geophys. Res.-Atmos., 118, 3610–3626, https://doi.org/10.1002/jgrd.50297, 2013.

Rodríguez-Rincón, J. P., Pedrozo-Acuña, A., and Breña-Naranjo, J. A.: Propagation of hydro-meteorological uncertainty in a model cascade framework to inundation prediction, Hydrol. Earth Syst. Sci., 19, 2981–2998, https://doi.org/10.5194/hess-19-2981-2015, 2015.

Röthlisberger, V., Zischg, A. P., and Keiler, M.: Identifying spatial clusters of flood exposure to support decision making in risk management, Sci. Total Environ., 598, 593–603, https://doi.org/10.1016/j.scitotenv.2017.03.216, 2017.

Rouhani, H. and Leconte, R.: A novel method to estimate the maximization ratio of the Probable Maximum Precipitation (PMP) using regional climate model output, Water Resour. Res., 52, 7347–7365, https://doi.org/10.1002/2016WR018603, 2016.

Rousseau, A. N., Klein, I. M., Freudiger, D., Gagnon, P., Frigon, A., and Ratté-Fortin, C.: Development of a methodology to evaluate probable maximum precipitation (PMP) under changing climate conditions: Application to southern Quebec, Canada, J. Hydrol., 519, 3094–3109, https://doi.org/10.1016/j.jhydrol.2014.10.053, 2014.

Saksena, S. and Merwade, V.: Incorporating the effect of DEM resolution and accuracy for improved flood inundation mapping, J. Hydrol., 530, 180–194, https://doi.org/10.1016/j.jhydrol.2015.09.069, 2015.

Salas, J. D., Gavilán, G., Salas, F. R., Julien, P. Y., and Abdullah, J.: Uncertainty of the PMP and PMF, in: Handbook of Engineering Hydrology, vol. 2: Modeling, Climate Change and Variability, 575–603, 2014.

Salas, J. D., Tarawneh, Z., and Biondi, F.: A hydrological record extension model for reconstructing streamflows from tree-ring chronologies, Hydrol. Process., 29, 544–556, https://doi.org/10.1002/hyp.10160, 2015.

Sampson, C. C., Fewtrell, T. J., O'Loughlin, F., Pappenberger, F., Bates, P. B., Freer, J. E., and Cloke, H. L.: The impact of uncertain precipitation data on insurance loss estimates using a flood catastrophe model, Hydrol. Earth Syst. Sci., 18, 2305–2324, https://doi.org/10.5194/hess-18-2305-2014, 2014.

Sanyal, J.: Uncertainty in levee heights and its effect on the spatial pattern of flood hazard in a floodplain, Hydrol. Sci. J., 62, 1483–1498, https://doi.org/10.1080/02626667.2017.1334887, 2017.

Savage, J. T. S., Bates, P., Freer, J., Neal, J., and Aronica, G.: When does spatial resolution become spurious in probabilistic flood inundation predictions?, Hydrol. Process., 30, 2014–2032, https://doi.org/10.1002/hyp.10749, 2015.

Scherrer, S. C., Fischer, E. M., Posselt, R., Liniger, M. A., Croci-Maspoli, M., and Knutti, R.: Emerging trends in heavy precipitation and hot temperature extremes in Switzerland, J. Geophys. Res.-Atmos., 121, 2626–2637, https://doi.org/10.1002/2015JD024634, 2016.

Singh, V. P.: Effect of spatial and temporal variability in rainfall and watershed characteristics on stream flow hydrograph, Hydrol. Process., 11, 1649–1669, https://doi.org/10.1002/(SICI)1099-1085(19971015)11:12<1649::AID-HYP495>3.0.CO;2-1, 1997.

Smolka, A.: Natural disasters and the challenge of extreme events: Risk management from an insurance perspective, Philos. T. R. Soc. A, 364, 2147–2165, https://doi.org/10.1098/rsta.2006.1818, 2006.

Stratz, S. A. and Hossain, F.: Probable Maximum Precipitation in a Changing Climate: Implications for Dam Design, J. Hydrol. Eng., 19, 6014006, https://doi.org/10.1061/(ASCE)HE.1943-5584.0001021, 2014.

Totschnig, R., Sedlacek, W., and Fuchs, S.: A quantitative vulnerability function for fluvial sediment transport, Nat. Hazards, 58, 681–703, https://doi.org/10.1007/s11069-010-9623-5, 2011.

UNISDR: Making development sustainable: The future of disaster risk management, Global assessment report on disaster risk reduction, 4.2015, United Nations, Geneva, 311 p., 2015.

Vetsch, D., Siviglia, A., Ehrbar, D., Facchini, M., Gerber, M., Kammerer, S., Peter, S., Vonwiler, L., Volz, C., Farshi, D., Mueller, R., Rousselot, P., Veprek, R., and Faeh, R.: BASEMENT – Basic Simulation Environment for Computation of Environmental Flow and Natural Hazard Simulation, Zurich, 2017.

Visser, H., Folkert, R. J. M., Hoekstra, J., and de Wolff, J. J.: Identifying Key Sources of Uncertainty in Climate Change Projections, Clim. Change, 45, 421–457, https://doi.org/10.1023/A:1005516020996, 2000.

Viviroli, D., Mittelbach, H., Gurtz, J., and Weingartner, R.: Continuous simulation for flood estimation in ungauged mesoscale catchments of Switzerland – Part II: Parameter regionalisation and flood estimation results, J. Hydrology, 377, 208–225, https://doi.org/10.1016/j.jhydrol.2009.08.022, 2009a.

Viviroli, D., Zappa, M., Gurtz, J., and Weingartner, R.: An introduction to the hydrological modelling system PREVAH and its pre- and post-processing-tools, Environ. Modell. Softw., 24, 1209–1222, https://doi.org/10.1016/j.envsoft.2009.04.001, 2009b.

Ward, P. J., Jongman, B., Weiland, F. S., Bouwman, A., van Beek, R., Bierkens, M. F. P., Ligtvoet, W., and Winsemius, H. C.: Assessing flood risk at the global scale: Model setup, results, and sensitivity, Environ. Res. Lett., 8, 44019, https://doi.org/10.1088/1748-9326/8/4/044019, 2013.

World Meteorological Organization: Manual on estimation of probable maximum precipitation (PMP), 3rd ed., WMO, no. 1045, World Meteorological Organization, Geneva, xxxii, 259, 2009.

Yuan, X.-C., Wei, Y.-M., Wang, B., and Mi, Z.: Risk management of extreme events under climate change, J. Clean. Prod., 166, 1169–1174, https://doi.org/10.1016/j.jclepro.2017.07.209, 2017.

Zhang, J. and Han, D.: Assessment of rainfall spatial variability and its influence on runoff modelling: A case study in the Brue catchment, UK, Hydrol. Process., 31, 2972–2981, https://doi.org/10.1002/hyp.11250, 2017.

Zoccatelli, D., Borga, M., Viglione, A., Chirico, G. B., and Blöschl, G.: Spatial moments of catchment rainfall: rainfall spatial organisation, basin morphology, and flood response, Hydrol. Earth Syst. Sci., 15, 3767–3783, https://doi.org/10.5194/hess-15-3767-2011, 2011.

3

Hydrodynamics of pedestrians' instability in floodwaters

Chiara Arrighi[1,*], **Hocine Oumeraci**[2], **and Fabio Castelli**[1]

[1]Department of Civil and Environmental Engineering, University of Florence, Via di S. Marta 3, 50139 Firenze, Italy

[2]Leichtweiß-Institute for Hydraulic Engineering and Water Resources, TU Braunschweig, Beethovenstrasse 51a, 38106 Braunschweig, Germany

[*] *Invited contribution by C. Arrighi, recipient of the EGU Outstanding Student Poster (OSP) Award 2015.*

Correspondence to: Chiara Arrighi (chiara.arrighi@dicea.unifi.it)

Abstract. People's safety is the first objective to be fulfilled by flood risk mitigation measures, and according to existing reports on the causes of casualties, most of the fatalities are due to inappropriate behaviour such as walking or driving in floodwaters. Currently available experimental data on people instability in floodwaters suffer from a large dispersion primarily depending on the large variability of the physical characteristics of the subjects. This paper introduces a dimensionless mobility parameter θ_P for people partly immersed in flood flows, which accounts for both flood and subject characteristics. The parameter θ_P is capable of identifying a unique threshold of instability depending on a Froude number, thus reducing the scatter of existing experimental data. Moreover, a three-dimensional (3-D) numerical model describing the detailed geometry of a human body and reproducing a selection of critical pairs of water depth and velocity is presented. The numerical results in terms of hydrodynamic forces and force coefficients are analysed and discussed. Both the mobility parameter θ_P and the numerical results hint at the crucial role of the Froude number and relative submergence as the most relevant dimensionless numbers to interpret the loss of stability. Finally, the mobility parameter θ_P is compared with an analogous dimensionless parameter for vehicles' instability in floodwaters, providing a new contribution to support flood risk management and educating people.

1 Introduction

Floods are among the main natural disasters in terms of the deadliest events and economic damage (Munich Re, 2015b). The 2011 flood in Thailand caused USD 40 billion of overall damages (Munich Re, 2012),and the 2014 flood affecting India and Pakistan caused 665 fatalities (EM-DAT, 2012; Munich Re, 2015a). Although the number of fatalities caused by floods is lower than other hazards (i.e. earthquakes), flood events are those affecting the largest number of people (EM-DAT, 2012).

Among the possible human interactions with the hydrological cycle, the loss of life in case of inundation represents a crucial phenomenon where flood and subject characteristics dynamically interact. The loss of stability of a human body in floods can be seen as the most direct, tangible and fastest interaction between water and human systems. This topic has been less studied in recent years with respect to other branches of socio-hydrology, which have well conceptualized long-term human–water interactions (Di Baldassarre et al., 2013a, b, 2015).

Research on loss of life in floods is sparse, and has been so far focused on dam break catastrophes (Aboelata and Bowles, 2008; Chakraborty et al., 2005), physical experiments (Abt et al., 1989; Karvonen et al., 2000; Jonkman and Penning-Rowsell, 2008; Xia et al., 2014) and conceptual models (Love, 1987; Lind et al., 2004; Milanesi et al., 2015). Most loss of life models are based on the location of the population at risk measured by its distance from the dam and account for the depth of flooding, population distribution and effectiveness of warning and evacuation processes

(Jonkman et al., 2002; Aboelata and Bowles 2008; US Department of Homeland Security, 2011; Penning-Rowsell et al., 2005). Other models relate the mortality to past flood events (Brown and Graham, 1988), which may no longer be representative of the current situation (Jonkman et al., 2002). In the last decade, two approaches to flood fatalities assessment, namely individual and societal risk, have been identified (Tapsell et al., 2002; Beckers et al., 2012; de Bruijn et al., 2014).

The characteristics of the flood and floodwater along with the characteristics and behaviour of the population determine the likelihood of death due to flooding (Di Mauro et al., 2012). It is widely recognized that, in developed countries, the majority of flood-related fatalities occurs as a result of inexperienced people entering floodwater either in boats, vehicles or on foot (Franklin et al., 2014). Many studies (Jonkman and Kelman, 2005; Maples and Tiefenbacher, 2009; Fitzgerald et al., 2010; Kellar, 2010) have shown that the first cause of death during a flood event is related to roads and vehicles (Arrighi et al., 2015). Jonkman and Kelman (2005) reported that in the Netherlands 33 % of deaths from drowning occur in a vehicle and 25 % as a pedestrian. Many casualties in fact occur when people try to move in floodwaters (Di Mauro et al., 2012; Chanson et al., 2014); in this case previous experiences may play a role (Siegrist and Gutscher, 2008). Thus, understanding the instability mechanisms and identifying the safest behaviour when in a vehicle or as a pedestrian unexpectedly facing a flood might be of crucial importance for management strategies (Franklin et al., 2014; Di Mauro et al., 2012) and emergency planning (Simonovic and Ahmad, 2005).

Two hydrodynamic mechanisms that can cause human instability have been distinguished in existing studies: moment instability (toppling) and friction instability (sliding). Toppling occurs when the mobilizing moment caused by the incident flow exceeds the resisting moment caused by the resultant weight of the body (Abt et al., 1989; Jonkman and Penning-Rowsell, 2008). Sliding occurs if the drag force induced by the flow is larger than the frictional resistance between the person's feet and the substrate surface (Keller and Mitsch, 1993).

Foster and Cox (1973) tested the instability perception of children with different physical characteristics (i.e. height and mass combinations) in a laboratory flume and found that also physical, emotional and dynamic factors deeply affect human stability under water flow. They observed that sliding instability prevailed, since the tests were performed with high-flow velocities and low water depths. Further tests by Abt et al. (1989) showed that toppling instability is crucial for higher water depths. More recently, several laboratory tests were performed on real adults and children (Takahashi et al., 1992; Keller and Mitsch, 1993; Karvonen et al., 2000; Yee, 2003) considering different training, wearing, environmental conditions and definitions of instability. These studies provide an extensive dataset, which has been used to define inversely proportional linear relationships between mean flow velocity and depth (Cox et al., 2010; Smith, 2015), which are often adopted as a reference for flood hazard zoning. These empirical approximating functions are, however, purely regressive and do not allow for linking hazard levels and physical effects. Jonkman and Penning-Rowsell (2008) extended the existing experimental data by testing an adult stuntman in real channel conditions of low depth and significant velocity. Moreover, they calibrated a simplified model for adults, which accounts for both slipping and toppling using the data by Abt et al. (1989) and Karvonen et al. (2000). The buoyancy force is however neglected.

Recently, Xia et al. (2014) carried out experiments on a rigid human body model with a geometric scale of 1 : 5.54. They developed a parametric scheme, introducing buoyancy force and considering both toppling and slipping failure mechanisms. They derived two formulae for the critical velocity for slipping and toppling instability mechanisms.

Conceptual models were introduced to describe the human stability as a function of flow velocity and water depth in order to provide an interpretative framework for the experimental activities. These models are based on different assumptions regarding the shape of the body, the involved forces and the failure mechanisms. Love (1987) modelled the human body as a rectangular monolith and recognized the role of the buoyancy force on toppling instability. Lind et al. (2004) tested both conceptual and empirical formulae and calibrated a relation based on the concept of the depth–speed product number (i.e. water depth multiplied by flow velocity). They modelled the human body as a rigid circular cylinder and proposed an equation for toppling instability, which yields the critical depth speed product number as a function of drag coefficient and submergence. Walder et al. (2006), studying a tsunami induced by a debris flow, developed a simplified approach to predict critical velocity for slipping to occur, disregarding toppling instability and the role of the buoyancy force and assuming a fixed drag coefficient. They also supposed that, in waters of some sufficient depth, people could not stand even if the flow velocity is negligible. Milanesi et al. (2015) recently introduced a conceptual model for people instability in a fluid flow also considering the effects of the local bottom slope and the density of the fluid.

Over the last 4 decades, a number of laboratory-based experimental studies have been undertaken to define the limits of stability under different flow regimes. Moreover, different conceptual models have been developed to derive formulae for these stability limits, usually assuming fixed values for the drag coefficient. The very wide scatter of critical pairs of water depth and velocity is the main evidence of the existing experiments on people instability. A large scatter exists within the same dataset and, to a more significant degree, when all datasets are combined (Cox et al., 2010; Russo et al., 2013). In fact, instability conditions are strongly affected by diverse "non-hydraulic" parameters (Martinez-Gomariz et al., 2016), including the physical characteristics of the subjects (i.e. weight and height), their level of training, clothing and experimental conditions. Thus, a synthetic identification of hazard regimes in dimensional terms is quite difficult.

The aim of this work is to overcome the scatter of existing experiments on people instability under water flow, introducing a dimensionless criterion capable of accounting for both flood and human characteristics and to understand its dependency on flow regimes (Sect. 2). The dimensional analysis is undertaken to clarify if a limited number of parameters (i.e. related to hydraulics and body shape) are capable of explaining most of the variability observed in the experiments or if non-hydraulic parameters are still relevant. The dimensionless criterion also allows for comparing the instability conditions of people with the incipient motion conditions of vehicles (Arrighi et al., 2015), thus providing a framework for societal risk assessment, risk management and education. Particularly for educational purposes, the use of dimensionless quantities may favour the definition of safety rules; e.g. recognizing a level of submergence (water depth reaching knees, ankles or waist) is easier than referring to absolute water depths. Since examples of numerical models can be hardly found in literature, in order to better understand the hydrodynamic interaction between the human body and mean flood flow, a simplified three-dimensional (3-D) numerical model, describing a detailed human geometry partly immersed in water, is introduced (Sect. 3) and used to reproduce a selection of the existing experimental data available in literature.

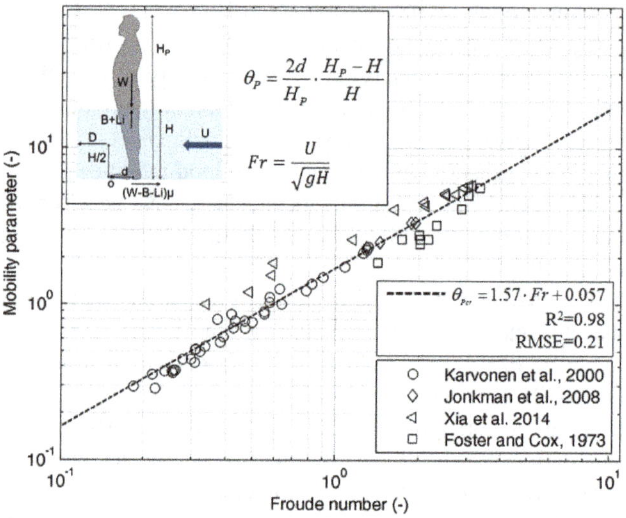

Figure 1. Instability diagram "Dimensionless mobility parameter θ_P versus Froude number" for the selected studies (Foster and Cox, 1973; Karvonen et al., 2000; Jonkman and Penning-Rowsell, 2008; Xia et al., 2014).

2 Instability conditions of a human body under water flow

2.1 Geometric representation of the human body and acting forces

The shape of the human body is extremely complex, thus leading to different conceptualization schemes of its geometry, such as prisms or cylinders (Abt et al., 1989; Lind et al., 2004; Milanesi et al., 2015). Moreover, relative motion, posture, clothing and physical parameters (i.e. body type, size and build) influence the hydrodynamic interaction between the human body and water flow. The two mechanisms by which the stability of people is lost in floodwaters are sliding and toppling (Abt et al., 1989; Lind et al., 2004; Jonkman and Penning-Rowsell, 2008). Incipient sliding on a horizontal bed occurs when drag force on the human body just exceeds the friction force of the feet on the bottom, while motion due to toppling occurs when the moment exerted by drag force just exceeds the weight-induced moment. For a stationary body in a moving flow, lift force and drag force are the force components acting normal and parallel to the mean direction of the undisturbed flow respectively (Vickery, 1966).

In order to minimize the number of parameters, the shape of the human body is mechanically schematized as in Lind et al. (2004), with reference to an approximating prism of height H_P, width l and length d (Fig. 1, panel a). In the inset of Fig. 1 (panel a), W is the weight, B is the buoyancy, Li is the lift force and D is the drag force. H is the water depth and it is assumed that the resultant drag force acts on one-half the water depth $H/2$ (Lind et al., 2004). The lever arm of the stabilizing force, which is the weight minus buoyancy and lift effect, is d, which is assumed as commutable with the full length of the foot. For a uniform prism, the lever arm of the stabilizing moment should be equal to $d/2$, but here it is preferred to use the length of the foot d in order to partly accounting for the natural adjustment of the posture of the subject observed in the experiments. In the panel (a) in Fig. 1, the rotation point O is placed on the toe for average flow velocity U coming from right to left. Otherwise, for a flow velocity oriented from left to right, the rotation point O would be placed on the heel.

2.2 Dimensionless mobility parameters

The definition of the dimensionless mobility parameter for people instability under water flow follows the procedure adopted for the introduction of the mobility parameter for vehicles' incipient motion as in Arrighi et al. (2015). It starts with defining the forces acting on the body and then proceeds with the separation of dynamic and static actions in order to identify relevant dimensionless groups of variables. The two mechanisms by which the stability of people is lost in dynamic conditions in floodwaters (i.e. sliding and toppling) are separately analysed. For hydrostatic conditions (i.e. zero flow velocity), the hydrodynamic actions are null and the static equilibrium is obtained equalling weight and buoyancy force.

Sliding equilibrium is considered first. Incipient sliding on a horizontal bed occurs when drag force D on the human body just exceeds the friction force of the feet on the bottom. Referring to Fig. 1 (panel a), the friction force is equal to the effective weight (weight W minus buoyancy B and lift force Li) multiplied by the static friction coefficient μ. The sliding instability condition is then

$$D > (W - B - Li) \cdot \mu. \tag{1}$$

The weight W is the product of constant human body density ρ_P, acceleration of gravity g and body volume $H_\mathrm{P} \cdot d \cdot l$. The width of the prism l (Fig. 1, panel b) assumed equal to the waist diameter, has been graphically found as a good proxy for the average width of the human body for a mesomorphic individual (Beashel and Taylor, 1997)

$$W = \rho_\mathrm{P} \cdot g \cdot (H_\mathrm{P} \cdot d \cdot l). \tag{2}$$

Buoyancy force B is the product of water density ρ, acceleration of gravity g and the immersed volume of the prism

$$B = \rho \cdot g \cdot (H \cdot d \cdot l). \tag{3}$$

Drag and lift forces are a function of the square of flow velocity U and are referred to in the same total frontal area of the prism, normally projected to the flow $H_\mathrm{P} \cdot l$. This reference area has been preferred to the wetted area because the determination of the actual wet area requires the study of the water profile due to the flow–body interaction; i.e. the wetting water depth does not coincide with the undisturbed water depth H (see also Sect. 3.2). In fact, as shown in Fig. 3 the difference between actual and undisturbed water depth is not negligible for super-critical flows.

$$D = \frac{1}{2} \cdot \rho \cdot U^2 \cdot C_\mathrm{D} \cdot H_\mathrm{P} \cdot l, \tag{4}$$

$$\mathrm{Li} = \frac{1}{2} \cdot \rho \cdot U^2 \cdot C_\mathrm{l} \cdot H_\mathrm{P} \cdot l, \tag{5}$$

where C_D and C_l are the drag and lift coefficient respectively. As shown by Arslan et al. (2013), Zhang et al. (2014) and by Arrighi et al. (2015), lift force can also play a significant role for partly submerged objects. The average density of the human body ($\rho_\mathrm{P} = 1062\,\mathrm{kg\,m^{-3}}$) is generally assumed equal to the density of muddy water; thus, ρ_P is substituted with ρ in Eq. (2). The assumption $\rho_\mathrm{P} = \rho$ implies that a human body immersed in water can experience a condition of static equilibrium. Substituting Eqs. (2–5), in Eq. (1) and putting equal the left and right term to define the equilibrium condition, the following equation is obtained

$$\frac{1}{2} \cdot \rho \cdot U^2 \cdot C_\mathrm{D} \cdot H_\mathrm{P} \cdot l = \left(\rho \cdot g \cdot (H_\mathrm{P} \cdot d \cdot l) - \rho \cdot g \cdot (H \cdot d \cdot l) - \frac{1}{2} \cdot \rho \cdot U^2 \cdot C_\mathrm{l} \cdot H_\mathrm{P} \cdot l\right) \cdot \mu. \tag{6}$$

The variables l and ρ multiply all the terms of Eq. (6) and thus they can be simplified. Separating the dynamic terms ($\propto U^2$) from the static terms Eq. (6) is simplified as

$$\frac{1}{2} \cdot U^2 \cdot C_\mathrm{D} \cdot H_\mathrm{P} + \left(\frac{1}{2} \cdot U^2 \cdot C_\mathrm{l} \cdot H_\mathrm{P}\right) \cdot \mu = \left[(g \cdot H_\mathrm{P} \cdot d) - (g \cdot H \cdot d)\right] \cdot \mu. \tag{7}$$

Collecting U^2 in the left term and d in the right term, then dividing both terms for $1/2 \cdot \mu \cdot H \cdot g$, the equilibrium condition yields

$$\frac{U^2}{gH} \cdot \left(C_\mathrm{l} + \frac{C_\mathrm{D}}{\mu}\right) = \frac{2d}{H_\mathrm{P}} \cdot \frac{H_\mathrm{P} - H}{H}, \tag{8}$$

where

$$\mathrm{Fr}^2 = \frac{U^2}{gH} \tag{9}$$

is the square of the Froude number of the undisturbed flow,

$$C_\mathrm{s} = \frac{C_\mathrm{D}}{\mu} + C_\mathrm{l} \tag{10}$$

and C_s includes the coefficients for drag C_D, for lift C_l and for friction μ forces.

$$\theta_\mathrm{P} = \frac{2d}{H_\mathrm{P}} \cdot \frac{H_\mathrm{P} - H}{H} \tag{11}$$

is defined as the dimensionless mobility parameter for sliding instability of people standing in floodwaters. θ_P is composed by two factors: the shape factor $2d/H_\mathrm{P}$ and the relative dry surface of the body $(H_\mathrm{P} - H)/H$. θ_P depends on Froude number and on the dimensionless force coefficients. If the assumption $\rho_\mathrm{P} = \rho$ is removed, a factor ρ_P/ρ is introduced in Eq. (11), which turns into the more general form of Eq. (12)

$$\theta_\mathrm{P} = \frac{2d}{H_\mathrm{P}} \cdot \frac{\frac{\rho_\mathrm{P}}{\rho} H_\mathrm{P} - H}{H}. \tag{12}$$

It should be noticed that with the general form of Eq. (12), the height of the subject appears virtually increased by about 6 %, which corresponds to an increased stability of the subject. Moreover, the water density ρ varies with temperature and concentration of dissolved compounds and suspended load; thus, Eq. (12) can be used to account for any fluid/body density.

Toppling instability occurs when the moment induced by drag force around a pivot point (i.e. the heel or toe) just exceeds the moment of the resultant vertical force (body weight W minus buoyancy B and lift force Li) as shown in Fig. 1 (panel a)

$$(W - B - \mathrm{Li}) \cdot d = D \cdot \frac{H}{2}. \tag{13}$$

Substituting the forces W, B, Li and D (Eqs. 2–5) in Eq. (13), the following threshold condition for incipient toppling is obtained:

$$\left[(\rho \cdot g \cdot l \cdot H_{\mathrm{P}} \cdot d) - (\rho \cdot g \cdot l \cdot H \cdot d) - \frac{1}{2}\rho \cdot U^2 C_{\mathrm{l}} \cdot H_{\mathrm{P}} \cdot l\right] \cdot d = \left(\frac{1}{2} \cdot \rho \cdot U^2 \cdot C_{\mathrm{D}} \cdot H_{\mathrm{P}} \cdot l\right) \cdot \frac{H}{2}, \quad (14)$$

where ρ and l can be dropped on both sides of Eq. (14), which after some manipulation and simplification yields

$$\frac{U^2}{gH} \cdot \left(\frac{H}{2d} \cdot C_{\mathrm{D}} + C_{\mathrm{l}}\right) = \frac{2d}{H_{\mathrm{P}}} \cdot \frac{H_{\mathrm{P}} - H}{H}. \quad (15)$$

This represents a relationship between the square of Froude number $\frac{U^2}{gH}$ together with the dimensionless parameter C_{t}

$$C_{\mathrm{t}} = \left(\frac{H}{2d} \cdot C_{\mathrm{D}} + C_{\mathrm{l}}\right) \quad (16)$$

on the left-hand side, and on the right-hand side a mobility parameter for toppling instability conditions for a person in floodwaters θ_{Pt}

$$\theta_{\mathrm{Pt}} = \frac{2d}{H_{\mathrm{P}}} \cdot \frac{H_{\mathrm{P}} - H}{H}. \quad (17)$$

The mobility parameter θ_{Pt} obtained for toppling is equal to the mobility parameter θ_{P} introduced for sliding (Eq. 11). However, the combination of coefficients C_{s} (Eq. 10) and C_{t} (Eq. 16) that define the instability limit is different. In fact, for toppling instability conditions, C_{D} is multiplied by $H/2d$ in Eq. (16), which can be interpreted as a measure of the relevance of the moment induced by the drag force for larger water depths H. Therefore, although there are two different incipient motion mechanisms, a unique parameter θ_{P} accounting for a limited number of human body parameters (H_{P} and d) and flow characteristics is able to represent both mechanisms. θ_{P} is meaningful for $0 < H < H_{\mathrm{P}}$. From the physical point of view, the limit $H = 0$ corresponds to extremely high Fr tending to infinity, and $H = H_{\mathrm{P}}$ corresponds to fully submerged condition where static equilibrium occurs given the assumption $\rho_{\mathrm{P}} = \rho$. It should be noticed that the mobility parameter for people θ_{P} could be also obtained from the mobility parameter for vehicles θ_{V}, defined by Arrighi et al. (2015), considering a human body as a "special" vehicle model with the elevation of the planform h_c equal to zero, length equal to d and density ρ_c equal to water density ρ.

For the general equation of the mobility parameter θ_{P} (Eq. 12), the sensitivity has been evaluated with respect to length of the foot d, height of the subject H_{P} and human body density ρ_{P}. The sensitivity is assessed with a local method, i.e. calculating the partial derivative of θ_{P} with respect to the selected factors X_j. The analytical formulae allow for calculating the sensitivity for each value of the water depth H, thus identifying possible critical ranges. Table 1 shows the sensitivity functions with respect to the selected parameters. The units of measurement of the sensitivity function are length^{-1} and length^3/mass for the geometric parameters and density parameter respectively. The sensitivities of θ_{P} to ρ_{P} and d decrease with increasing water depth H. The sensitivity to ρ_{P} and d are of the order of a magnitude of 10^{-3} and 10^{-1}-10^{1} respectively, for the experimental range of water depths. This means that small variations of ρ_{P} are negligible for θ_{P}; thus the assumption $\rho_{\mathrm{P}} = \rho$ is not significantly affecting the results. High sensitivity to d is found particularly for water depths lower than 0.5 m. Thus, d is a more sensitive parameter, although its variation is physically constrained because the foot to height ratio is in the range 0.149–0.169, according to allometry studies (Davis, 1990; Pawar and Dadhich, 2012; Fessler et al., 2004). The sensitivity to Hp is of the order of magnitude of 10^{-1} for the height of the subjects between 1 and 2 m (i.e. children and adults).

Therefore, since the sensitivity of the parameter θ_{P} is the product of the sensitivity function and the variation of the parameter, θ_{P} is robust enough, although obviously its regression function depends on the experimental data used (see Fig. 1).

The dimensionless mobility parameter θ_{P} indicates that the stability of a human body in floodwaters is related to relative submergence and the Froude number. The mass does not appear in the parameter definition because with the dimensional analysis the mass becomes a density ρ_{P}. All human subjects tested in the experiments had different mass/weight but had the same density, and the dimensional analysis allows for identifying dimensionless combinations of the variables of the system for a given set of independent fundamental units. Also if we do not assume $\rho_{\mathrm{P}} = \rho$ (Eq. 12), we obtain a constant factor 1.062, which virtually increases the height. The height in fact can be seen as a sort of "proxy" of the weight for a mesomorphic individual, since the mass is the product of body density and body volume (and the body volume depends on the height of the subject).

The mobility parameter θ_{P} is introduced for null bed slope and density of floodwater coinciding with the density of clear water to strictly follow the experimental set-up of the selected studies (Sect. 2.3); however, a further study could also modify Eq. (17) to account for any terrain slope and water density.

2.3 Dimensionless instability threshold from Foster and Cox (1973), Karvonen et al. (2000), Jonkman and Penning-Rowsell (2008) and Xia et al. (2014) flume experiments.

A selection of the existing flume experiments on people instability in flood flows has been made to test the applicability of the mobility parameter θ_{P}. This selection covers a wide range of Froude numbers and accounts for different subjects' characteristics and for a human-scale model. The available datasets (Foster and Cox, 1973; Karvonen et al., 2000; Jonkman and Penning-Rowsell, 2008; Xia et al., 2014) provide the experimental pairs of water depth and ve-

Table 1. Sensitivity of the general θ_P (Eq. 12) with respect to geometry and density parameters.

	Parameter for the sensitivity X_j		
	$X_j = d$ length of the foot	$X_j = H_\mathrm{P}$ height of the subject	$X_j = \rho_\mathrm{P}$ human body density
Sensitivity function $\frac{\partial \theta_\mathrm{P}}{\partial X_j}$	$\frac{2\rho_\mathrm{P}}{\rho H} - \frac{2}{H_\mathrm{P}}$	$\frac{2d}{H_\mathrm{P}^2}$	$\frac{2d}{\rho H}$

locity (H, U) in which the subjects lose their stability together with subjects' physical characteristics (i.e. weight and height). The length of the foot d is calculated as a fraction of the height, which is a standard assumption in human allometry (Davis, 1990; Pawar and Dadhich, 2012; Fessler et al., 2004). The dataset by Abt et al. (1989) and by Takahashi et al. (1992) have not been included because in the first case the experimental conditions are considered not fully representative of a 3-D flow and limited in the investigated range of flow regimes; in the latter it was not possible to retrieve the heights of the tested subjects to calculate the mobility parameter.

A diagram showing the mobility parameter θ_P against the Froude number for the selected experimental data is drawn in Fig. 1. The mobility parameter θ_P evaluated for experimental pairs (H, U) (Foster and Cox, 1973; Karvonen et al., 2000; Jonkman and Penning-Rowsell, 2008; Xia et al., 2014) defines in the diagram in Fig. 1 a unique dimensionless critical threshold of instability $\theta_{\mathrm{P_{cr}}}$ for people under water flow that can be approximated as

$$\theta_{\mathrm{P_{cr}}} = 1.57 \cdot \mathrm{Fr} + 0.057. \tag{18}$$

The determination coefficient R^2 and root mean square error (RMSE) of the regression curve are 0.98 and 0.21 respectively. Since the regressed critical threshold curve is linear, it may appear inconsistent with Eqs. (8) or (15) where θ_P depends on the square of the Froude number. The 3-D numerical model described in Sect. 3 and the numerical results of the parameter study (Sect. 4) will help clarify this apparent inconsistency demonstrating the dependency of C_s (Eq. 10) and C_t (Eq. 16) on the inverse of the Froude number.

The critical mobility parameter $\theta_{\mathrm{P_{cr}}}$ ranges from 0.3 for low Froude numbers (i.e. sub-critical conditions) up to 6 for super-critical flows and identifies a threshold, which separates stable conditions above the curve from unstable conditions below the curve, with no discontinuity between the two motion mechanisms. While the datasets by Karvonen et al. (2000) and by Jonkman and Penning-Rowsell (2008), represented with circles and diamond symbols respectively, are well aligned, the datasets by Foster and Cox (1973) and by Xia et al. (2014) appear to be more scattered. The first two datasets refer to adult subjects with different age, weight and height, the third refers to children and the latter to the human-scale model. Particularly, the selection of points calculated from the data by Xia et al. (2014) are above the threshold curve, i.e. they lie in the stable side of the diagram. This confirms that the experimental instability conditions obtained for a human-scale model are more conservative than critical condition for human subjects as argued by the authors (Xia et al., 2014). Some of the data by Foster and Cox (1973) instead are under the curve, and thus in the unstable portion of the diagram. A lower estimation of the mobility parameter may be due to the values assigned to the foot length. In fact, the growth of the feet is not proportional to the growth in height for children in the development age and common foot to height ratios are valid for adults (Davis, 1990; Pawar and Dadhich, 2012; Fessler et al., 2004).

The mobility parameter θ_P demonstrates that a reduction in the scatter of the existing instability diagrams is possible if the analysis of the instability threshold is done in dimensionless terms and accounts for both flood and subject characteristics. Moreover, a dependence of θ_P on the dimensionless force and friction coefficients has been found (Eqs. 10, 17). The analysis of the force coefficients requires a separate and dedicated analysis through a numerical model, which might help clarify the hydrodynamics of instability mechanisms (Sect. 3).

3 Numerical model

3.1 Model description

The main aim of the numerical simulations is to understand how different mean flow regimes, in which people instability is experimentally observed, affect the drag and lift forces and the motion mechanisms. Thus, the focus is to assess the physical dependencies among the involved parameters (i.e. force coefficients and Froude number) and relate them to the mean flow properties. The study is focused on the estimation of integral quantities, such as forces, rather than on the detailed description of the flow properties in terms of local distributions. Thus, the numerical simulations were performed using the "laminar" turbulence settings of the numerical code, avoiding the calibration of the turbulence model coefficients, which however could not have been possible with the existing data. Laminar settings of the code do not force a laminar flow simulation, which would not be physically consistent, but they simply refer to the absence of turbulence modelling. A turbulence model was not selected for two main reasons: first, a turbulence model needs the calibration and/or validation of some coefficients and existing experiments were not available for this purpose; second, a rigid body approximates the experimental conditions for subjects allowed to move freely. This obviously bears an error in the estimation of the forces on the subject; thus, this simplifying assumption was considered adequate for the intrinsic uncertainties of the simulated problems. As in Arrighi et al. (2015), preliminary tests have shown the substantial independence of the results on the particular choice of the closure model for the selected mesh size. Moreover, the model adequately reproduced the flow around a circular cylinder used as a benchmark test, with a correct estimation of pressures and drag coefficients for the selected range of the Reynolds number.

For the numerical simulations, the CFD toolbox OpenFOAM® (www.openfoam.com) is used since it has been proven suitable for numerical modelling of a wide number of applications in coastal and hydraulics engineering (Leclercq and Doolan, 2009; Seo et al., 2010; Arrighi et al., 2015). The code includes several tools and utilities for wave/current generation/absorption, mesh manipulation and turbulence modelling. The solver waveFoam included within the library waves2Foam (Jacobsen et al., 2012) is selected because it handles two incompressible, isothermal, immiscible fluids by capturing the fluid–fluid interface through the volume of fluid method. It solves the Reynolds-Averaged Navier Stokes (RANS) equations implemented in OpenFOAM and applies the relaxation zone technique for current generation together with absorption of its reflection. This "active sponge" layer is a practical boundary condition, which allows for reducing the number of cells of the computational domain. Mayer et al. (1998) and Jacobsen et al. (2012) provided a detailed description of the structure of the relaxation function and of the use of relaxation zones as boundary conditions.

3.2 Numerical model set-up

Among the subjects used in the flume experiments, three subjects (i.e. subjects 2, 4 and 5) tested by Karvonen et al. (2000), the subject tested by Jonkman and Penning-Rowsell (2008) and a selection of pairs (H, U) of the scale human model used by Xia et al. (2014) were chosen. This selection has been made in order to cover a wide range of flow regimes (both sub-critical and super-critical) and different subjects' physical characteristics. To generate the mesh around the human body, a free triangulated geometry of a man (STereo Lithography interface format *.stl), downloaded from www.thingiverse.com, was used. The heights of the different subjects were adjusted using the 3-D scaling functions available in the code for the triangulated geometries.

The mesh domain has a cylindrical shape so that the relaxation zone (with a similar shape and 1.5 m thick) can fully control the generation/absorption of the flood conditions (i.e. water depth and velocity) avoiding possible boundary effects.

A mesh sensitivity analysis has been performed with the laminar turbulence model for the numerical simulation of subject 2 (Karvonen et al., 2000) (water depth 0.6 m and velocity 2.0 m s^{-1}). Three different mesh sizes around the human surface have been tested: 0.015, 0.01 and 0.005 m. The differences in the estimated drag and lift average coefficients were of the order of a few percent and smaller than the standard deviation of the instantaneous values computed during the simulation. Thus, the 0.015 m mesh has been preferred for its shorter computational time. The total number of cells is around 4.5×10^5. The snappyHexMesh tool allows for refining the mesh close to the human body (cell size is set to 0.015 m), while in the whole mesh domain the maximum size is 0.25 m. The refinement close to the human body can be observed in Fig. 2, where the 3-D view of the mesh in a longitudinal cross section is shown for the whole body (panel a), the legs (panel b) and the feet (panel c). The 3-D geometry describes a naked body since clothes are difficult to be represented as soft and flexible; thus, rigid clothes could affect the estimation of the forces. The time step is set to be automatically adjusted during the simulation according to the maximum Courant number set to 0.7. The order of magnitude was around 10^{-3}–10^{-4} s to ensure stability. With a time step equal to 2×10^{-4} s and 4.5×10^5 cells, 1 s of simulation takes 30 min without running in parallel (i.e. one core).

The average water elevation H and flow velocity U are initialized in the domain according to the experimental conditions and these values are fixed at the inlet and outlet boundary to a constant value during all the simulation.

The wall function used is the standard nutWallFunction available in OpenFOAM®. The pressure and the velocity fields, needed for the drag and shear forces evaluation, are directly calculated through the continuity and momentum equations (RANS equations) implemented in the model for steady, incompressible and immiscible fluids (Morgan, 2013). The reference "undisturbed" velocity (U) and an area of reference A_{ref} are set to calculate the instantaneous drag and lift coefficients considering the force acting on the human body in the flow direction, D (Eq. 18), and in the vertical direction, Li (Eq. 18), respectively. Drag force is positive when oriented with the flow, and lift force is positive when upward directed. The reference area A_{ref} is the total frontal area of the prism approximating the body normally projected to the flow, equal to $l \cdot H_{\mathrm{P}}$

$$C_{\mathrm{D}} = \frac{D}{0.5 \cdot \rho \cdot U^2 \cdot A_{\mathrm{ref}}}, \tag{19}$$

$$C_{\mathrm{l}} = \frac{\mathrm{Li}}{0.5 \cdot \rho \cdot U^2 \cdot A_{\mathrm{ref}}}. \tag{20}$$

The total frontal area is selected instead of the wet area because the actual wet area is not simply equal to $l \cdot H$. The determination of the actual wet area would require a dedicated analysis of the flow profile for different flow regimes. Moreover, the total frontal area A_{ref} allows for better comparing the pushing efficiency for different submergence levels.

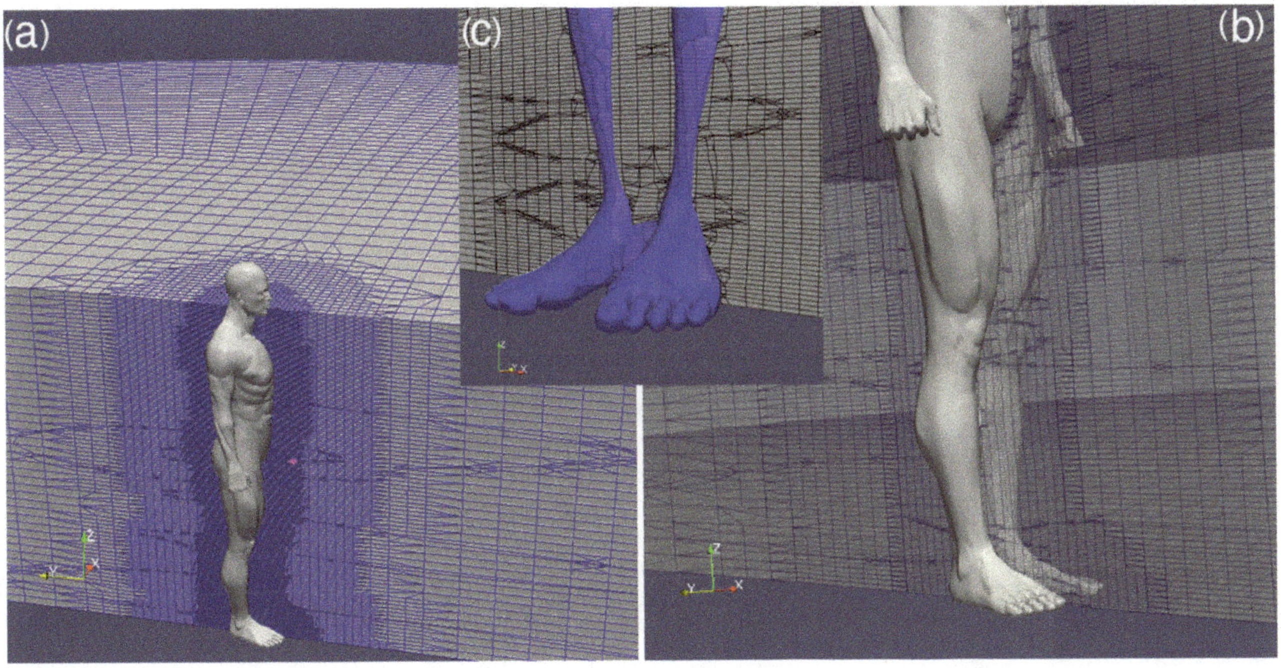

Figure 2. Computational mesh around the human body shown in a longitudinal cross section for the whole body **(a)**, the legs **(b)** and a detail of the feet **(c)**.

However, the selection of the reference area for the hydrodynamic forces is arbitrary and the use of the wetted area is optional. Drag and lift coefficients in the form of Eqs. (19, 20) are derived from dimensional analysis and the reference area is a scale factor with dimensions of (length)^2. Thus, wetted area and full frontal area are commonly used in engineering practice (Fox and McDonald, 2011; Hoerner, 1965; Bertin and Smith, 1979).

D and Li include both pressure and viscous forces acting in the flow and vertical direction respectively, although the contribution of the viscous forces is negligible with respect to pressure forces (they differ of 6–7 orders of magnitude). To obtain the force coefficients, the time average is calculated once the coefficients have reached the steady state, which is confirmed by the absence of a linear trend.

3.3 Tests programme

Three experimental datasets on the instability of people are considered (Karvonen et al., 2000; Jonkman et al., 2008; Xia et al., 2014) because they cover a wide range of flow regimes (i.e. Froude numbers) and include different physical characteristics and a human body model. All simulations account for a frontal impact of the water flow on the human body. Only one flow orientation is considered because most of the experimental studies neglects the effect of the angle of flow incidence. The investigation of a walking condition is considered outside the scope of the manuscript since it would bear different boundary conditions, mesh and working assumptions. The experimental pairs (H, U) recognized as critical in the laboratory tests and used for the numerical simulations are summarized in Table 2 for the different datasets. The experimental data for the human model (Xia et al., 2014) have been scaled to actual size through Froude similarity using the scale ratio $\lambda = 5.54$. The total number of numerical simulations is 33.

4 Results

4.1 Forces and force coefficients

The numerical results are analyzed in terms of flow characteristics and hydrodynamic forces. For super-critical flows, a significant splashing area is detected in correspondence with the impact zone (Fig. 3, panels a, c). Figure 3 depicts the simulated flow around the subject tested by Jonkman and Penning-Rowsell (2008) for the pair $H = 0.35$ m and $U = 2.40\,\mathrm{m\,s^{-1}}$. For these flow condition, the free surface elevation decreases downstream after passing the ankles where the flow accelerates, then there is a sudden energy dissipation (behind the ankles, panel b) and the free surface is restored (panel c). The rough aspect of the free surface in Fig. 3 panel a, corresponds to areas with strong mixing between air and water, which has been experimentally observed by Jonkman and Penning-Rowsell (2008).

Panel c in Fig. 3 also shows the distribution of pressures on feet and legs of the subject. Red areas correspond to high pressures located on the inner side of the feet and above the

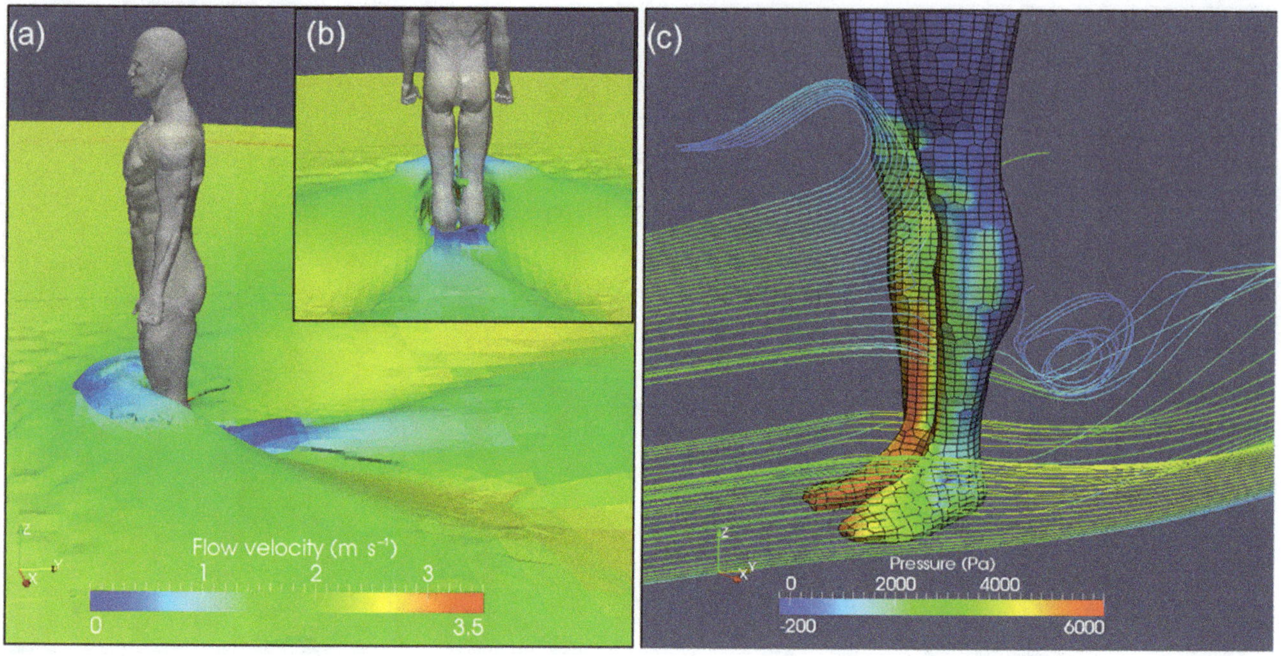

Figure 3. Splashing effect for super-critical flows shown as flow velocity **(a)**, streamlines **(c)** and inset view parallel to flow direction upstream-oriented **(b)**, for the subject tested by Jonkman and Penning-Rowsell (2008), $H = 0.35\,\text{m}$, $U = 2.40\,\text{m}\,\text{s}^{-1}$. Panel **(c)** also shows the pressure distribution on the feet and the legs of the subject.

ankles where the flow decelerates. On the other hand, in the external side of the feet depicted in light blue, the flow accelerates with a consequent decrease in pressure.

For the sub-critical flow condition, the flow is disturbed upstream of the human body, where a slight deceleration occurs. Vortices occur immediately downstream of the obstacle.

Drag and lift forces are integrated over the human geometry during the simulations and the force coefficients are calculated using the frontal reference areas A_{ref} in Table 3, which are evaluated graphically.

Figure 4 shows the drag coefficient and lift coefficients versus the Froude number on the right-hand side of the figure in the top and bottom panels respectively. Drag coefficient ranges from 0.1 for high Froude numbers, up to approximately 1 for low Froude numbers.

Drag coefficients decrease exponentially with increasing Froude number, i.e. with decreasing submergence. The drag coefficients of all the human subjects (Karvonen et al., 2000; Jonkman and Penning-Rowsell, 2008) are very similar for the same simulated flow regimes. Drag coefficients for the human-scale model (Xia et al., 2014) in the range of Froude number 0.4–1.5 appear lower than the coefficients evaluated for human subjects. In fact, the human model is "weaker" than the real human subjects in facing the water flow, as demonstrated by the comparison between dimensional thresholds of instability for the model and real humans (Xia et al., 2014). For Froude numbers above 1.5, the drag coefficient for the human model remains almost constant.

Lift coefficients (left and right bottom panels in Fig. 4) range from −0.49 up to 0.06. Except for subject 4, which is represented with a diamond symbol, the lift coefficients are negative. This means that the vertical force contributes to stability because it is directed downward. The two positive values for subject 4 (Karvonen et al., 2000) are due to the relative submergence of the subject H/H_{P}, which is higher than 0.6 (see Fig. 4, bottom left panel). For this level of submergence the water reaches the lower part of the body trunk and thus can exert its action pushing it upward. The negative lift coefficients are the result of the downward directed force acting on the upper boundary of the feet, which is shown in terms of pressures in Fig. 3 (panel c). This occurs because the subject's feet are placed directly on the bottom as a consequence of the assumption of the rigid body. In actual conditions, when a human subject is allowed to move, the pressure distribution and vertical forces would change significantly because the sole would also experience the hydrodynamic forces.

The left-hand side panels of Fig. 4 depict drag and lift coefficients versus the relative submergence H/H_{P}. Drag coefficient increases quadratically as the relative submergence increases since a larger portion of body surface is affected by the water flow, thus increasing the lever arm of the soliciting moment. Moreover, the lift coefficient linearly decreases with increasing relative submergence.

The human body has a complex shape and its hydrodynamic interaction is affected not only by the flow but also

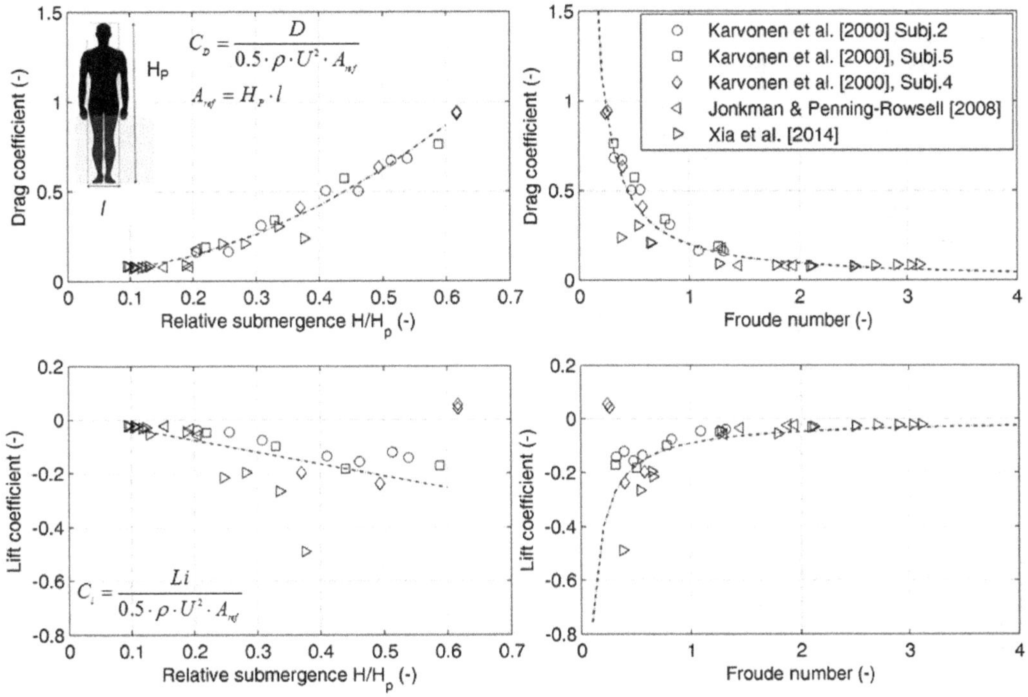

Figure 4. Estimated drag and lift coefficients versus Froude number (top left and bottom left panels respectively) and versus the relative submergence (top right and bottom right panels respectively) for the four human subjects (Karvonen et al., 2000; Jonkman and Penning-Rowsell, 2008) and the human-scale model (Xia et al., 2014). The inset in the first subplot shows the reference area used for the force coefficients calculation.

by the portions of the body involved. For the analysed range of water depths, three parts can be distinguished: feet, legs and trunk. Since the lift force is the integral of pressures on the surface, its value is affected by submergence. In fact, for low water depths, legs only contribute to drag force and feet are subject to a vertical force downward directed, given the assumption of adherence between bottom and feet. Once the pelvis is wetted, and this may occur for undisturbed water depth lower than body trunk due to backwater effects, an upward directed action is added to the downward directed feet action (conventionally negative). With the increase of submergence, the upward component increases until the global vertical force becomes fully positive and this explains the lift force behaviour (Fig. 5).

Figure 5 depicts the lift and drag forces versus the Froude number for all the simulated subjects (top and bottom panels respectively). For human subjects, which have been tested in the range of Froude numbers 0.2–2, drag force increases for $0.2 < Fr < 1$, reaching a peak for $Fr \sim 1$, then it decreases. The values of drag force for human subjects range from 100 N up to 350 N. Subject 2 tested by Karvonen et al. (2000), which is the tallest and heaviest subject in the dataset, is able to face the highest forces with respect to the other subjects. Subject 4 and 5 are weaker according to the diagram, subject 4 is a woman and subject 5 is a 60 years old man. The estimated forces for the human model (Xia et al., 2014) have been scaled according to Froude similarity, using the scale ratio 5.54^3. This allows for comparing the dimensional forces of the human model with the forces acting on the human subjects. The behaviour of the human model, whose drag force values are represented in Fig. 5 (bottom panel) with right-oriented triangles, appear different from the human subjects. In fact, drag force values increase linearly with Froude number without reaching a peak for Froude of around 1. The peak of drag force observed for human subjects is the result of a balance between drag-induced moment and immersed weight and the ability to actively react to the action of the water flow. Moreover, for $Fr = 1$, where the peak of drag force occurs, the lift force reaches its maximum absolute value (Fig. 5, top panel). Therefore, since the stabilizing effect of the vertical force increases the effective weight, the change of position of real human subjects, with a consequent change of lever arm d (Eq. 13), increases the resisting moment. Thus, a larger drag force can be faced. This is not possible for the human model, since it behaves passively in the water flow without adjusting its posture.

For Froude number between 0.5 and 1 there is a minimum of lift force (Fig. 5, top panel), which reaches about −90° N. For a low Froude number and relative submergence equal to 0.62 (see Fig. 4, bottom left panel), subject 5 (Karvonen et al., 2000) experiences a positive vertical force since a portion of the lower body trunk is immersed in water. These values

Table 2. Simulated pairs of water depth H and flow velocity U for human subjects and scale model (Karvonen et al., 2000; Jonkman and Penning-Rowsell, 2008; Xia et al., 2014).

Water depth H (m)	Flow velocity U ($\mathrm{m\,s^{-1}}$)	Froude number Fr (–)
Karvonen et al. (2000); subject 2		
0.40	2.60	1.31
0.50	2.40	1.08
0.60	2.00	0.82
0.80	1.55	0.55
0.90	1.40	0.47
1.00	1.20	0.38
1.05	1.00	0.31
Karvonen et al. (2000); subject 4		
0.6	1.4	0.58
0.8	1.1	0.39
1	0.75	0.24
1	0.8	0.26
Karvonen et al. (2000); subject 5		
0.40	2.50	1.26
0.60	1.90	0.78
0.80	1.40	0.50
1.07	1.00	0.31
Jonkman and Penning-Rowsell (2008); stuntman		
0.26	3.00	1.88
0.26	3.10	1.94
0.33	2.60	1.45
0.35	2.40	1.30
Xia et al. (2014); human model (Froude scaled H, U)		
0.64	0.85	0.34
0.57	1.15	0.49
0.48	1.27	0.59
0.42	1.21	0.60
0.32	2.05	1.16
0.22	2.40	1.63
0.21	3.03	2.11
0.20	2.93	2.09
0.18	3.35	2.51
0.18	3.30	2.50
0.18	3.60	2.71
0.17	3.70	2.91
0.16	3.80	3.03
0.16	3.90	3.11

correspond, in fact, to low values of drag force in Fig. 5 (bottom panel). With the rigid body assumption for high Froude numbers, the human model is protected by an increasing absolute value of the vertical force, which allows for resisting increasing drag forces. For both drag and lift forces there is a compensation of the opposite effects of submergence and the Froude number (i.e. velocity); in fact, when sub-

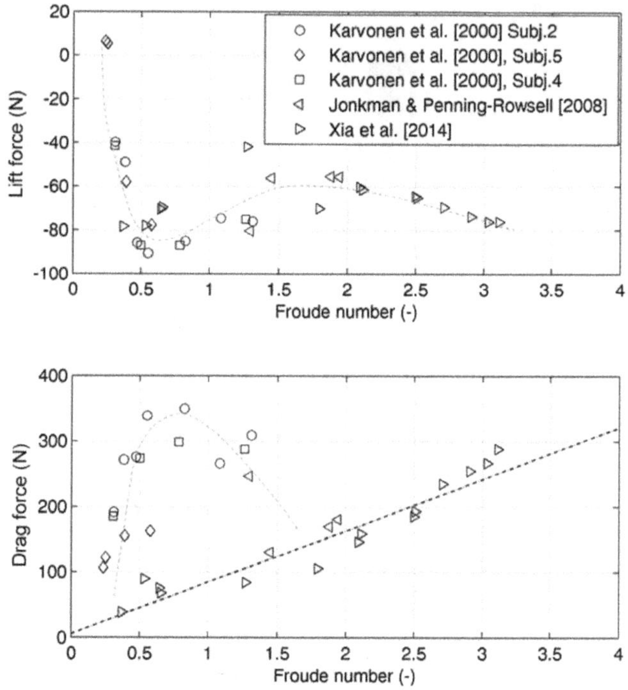

Figure 5. Estimated lift (top panel) and drag (bottom panel) forces versus the relative submergence for the four human subjects (Karvonen et al., 2000; Jonkman and Penning-Rowsell, 2008) and the human-scale model (Xia et al., 2014).

mergence increases, force coefficients and Froude number increase (in absolute value) and decrease respectively. Unfortunately, only recently human subjects have been tested for highly super-critical flows (Martinez-Gomariz et al., 2016); therefore, a direct comparison between human subjects and human model was not possible for those regimes. While for sub-critical flow regimes, it is clear that the ability of a human subject to actively resist to the flow adjusting its position is an advantage in terms of safety with respect to the human model. However, the passive behaviour of the human model can be seen as representative of the weakest class of people, such as the elderly or sick, as suggested by Xia et al. (2014).

4.2 Motion mechanisms

Since literature distinguishes two motion mechanisms, namely sliding and toppling (see Sect. 2), the identification of these mechanisms is further investigated in this section. The normalized moment is defined as the ratio of drag-induced moment and resisting moment, where the effective weight of the subject is calculated subtracting (adding) the vertical force from (to) the weight.

$$\text{Norm moment} = \frac{D \cdot H}{2(W - B - \text{Li}) \cdot d} \tag{21}$$

The normalized moment is represented against Froude number in Fig. 6. In the diagram, there are two regions identified

Table 3. Reference areas for force coefficients calculation and physical characteristics (height H_P, weight W and length of the foot d) of human subjects and human-scale model.

Subject	No. 2 Karvonen et al. (2000)	No. 4 Karvonen et al. (2000)	No. 5 Karvonen et al. (2000)	Jonkman and Penning-Rowsell (2008)	Model scale 5.54, Xia et al. (2014)
A_{ref} (m^2)	0.49	0.42	0.46	0.43	0.014
H_P (m)	1.95	1.62	1.82	1.7	0.31
W (kg)	100	57	94	68.2	0.334
d (m)	0.30	0.25	0.28	0.26	0.048

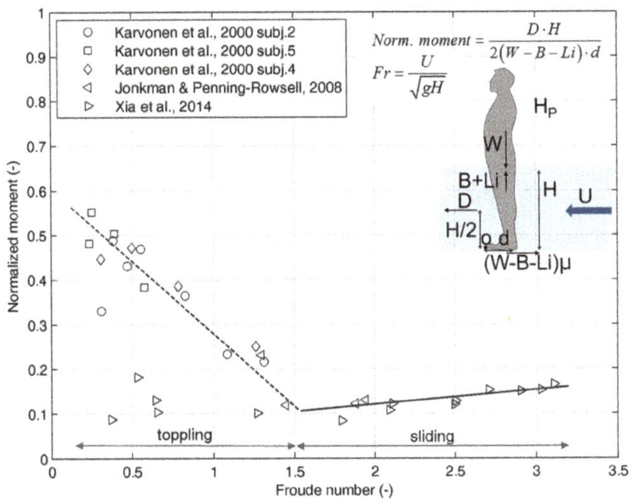

Figure 6. Normalized moment against Froude number for the four human subjects (Karvonen et al., 2000; Jonkman and Penning-Rowsell, 2008) and the human model (Xia et al., 2014).

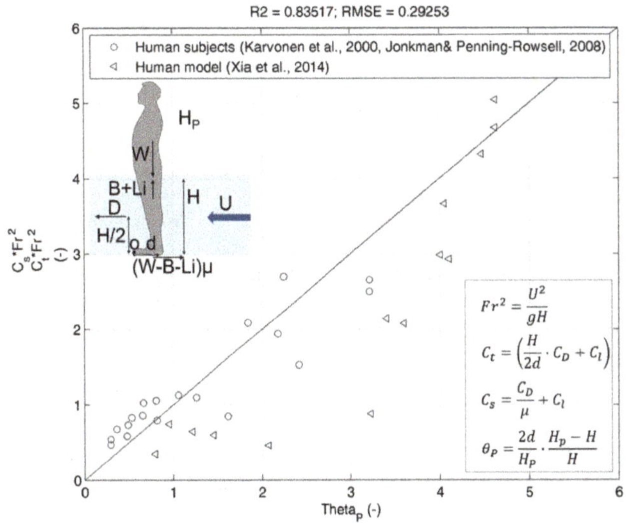

Figure 7. Comparison between experiments in terms of mobility parameter θ_P and numerical results, with a distinction between the human subjects (circles) and human model (triangles). In the top of the Figure the determination coefficient R^2 and RMSE for the data on human-scale model Xia et al. (2014) removed.

by the calculated normalized moment. As the Froude number increases, the submergence decreases in the diagram. In the left side of the diagram the normalized moment decreases with Froude number until approximately Fr = 1.5. Then for Froude number higher than 1.5, the normalized moment increases slowly. The region with Fr < 1.5 is interpreted as the toppling instability area, while for Fr >= 1.5 sliding instability occurs. The separation of the two regions, with low values of normalized moment around Fr = 1.5 hints that a mix of the two instability mechanism might occur while approaching Fr = 1.5 (Jonkman and Penning-Rowsell, 2008). In fact, for low Froude numbers (i.e. high relative submergence) full toppling instability is expected; vice versa, for high Froude numbers, full sliding instability takes place.

The identification of the two motion mechanisms helps in defining the dimensionless groups C_t and C_s defined in Sect. 2.2 (Eqs. 10, 16), which are used for the comparison between experiments and numerical results.

4.3 Comparison with experimental data

The numerical results obtained from the simulations are compared to the experimental datasets (Karvonen et al., 2000; Jonkman and Penning-Rowsell, 2008; Xia et al., 2014) using the analytical relation between the mobility parameter θ_P, Froude number and the group accounting for the force coefficients (Sect. 2.2). The groups accounting for the combination of the force coefficients are C_s or C_t for sliding or toppling instability respectively (Eqs. 10, 16). Since the two motion mechanisms have been identified in Fig. 6, C_s is calculated for the Froude number equal to or larger than 1.5 and C_t for the Froude number lower than 1.5. The friction coefficient is assumed constant and equal to 0.3, which is in the range used in literature (Milanesi et al., 2015).

The mobility parameter θ_P is calculated from the experimental water depth H and the Froude number is calculated from the experimental pairs H and U. The length of the foot assumed for the different subjects is shown in Table 3.

Figure 7 shows the scatter plot of experimental and numerical results. On the horizontal and vertical axis there are the mobility parameters θ_P and the product of the square of Fr and C_s or C_t according to the type of motion mechanism.

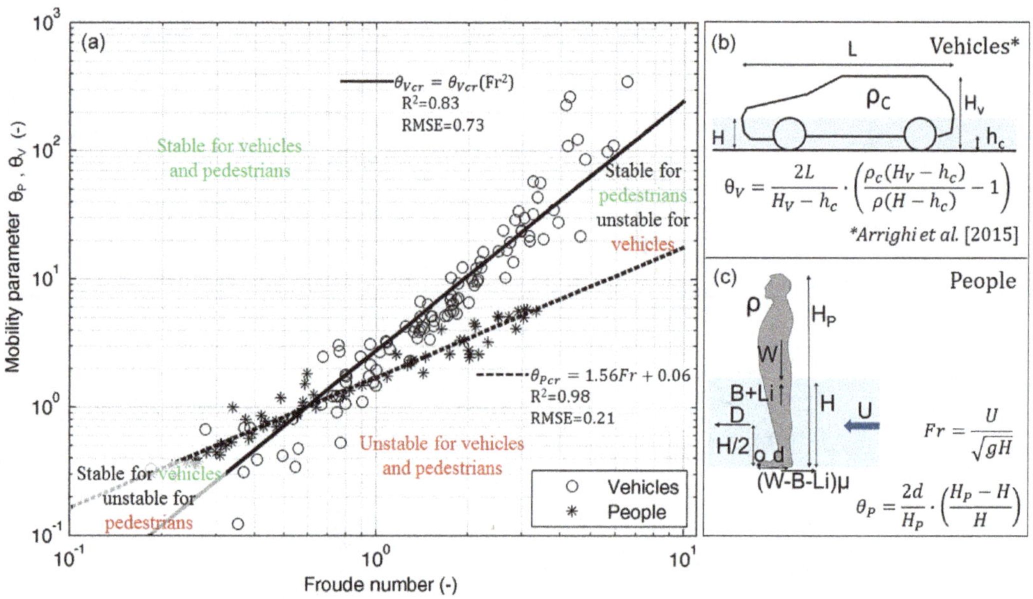

Figure 8. Comparison between dimensionless mobility parameter for people instability in flood flows θ_P and dimensionless mobility parameter for incipient motion of flooded vehicles (Arrighi et al., 2015) **(a)**, definitions of the parameters and geometric sketches for vehicles **(b)** and people **(c)**. The black continuous and dashed lines represent the critical dimensionless incipient motion curve for flooded vehicles and people respectively.

The determination coefficient is 0.76 and the RMSE is 0.63. The comparison is overall satisfactory, given the different data sources; however, there are some points that are below the $1:1$ curve. Thus, the datasets related to human subjects are separately analysed since they have shown a different behaviour in terms of hydrodynamic forces. Different symbols represents human subjects (circles) and human-scale models (triangles). As expected, the numerical results of the human model compare less well with the mobility parameter and are in general below the $1:1$ curve. This is due to the lower estimated drag coefficient/force for the human model. Moreover, since the mobility parameter accounts for the full length of the foot d, which is relevant to calculate the resisting moment, its definition may not be appropriate for a human model, which is not able to adjust its position in order to take advantage of the full length of the foot to react to the instability. If the dataset on the human model is removed, the determination coefficient R^2 is 0.82 and the RMSE is 0.28; thus, the comparison between numerical model and experiments improves.

A sensitivity analysis to d and friction coefficient μ has been carried out to understand how a change in these parameters affects the goodness of fit between numerical results and experiments. The parameters d and μ play a role in the calculation of C_t and C_s respectively (Eqs. 16 and 10). A variation of ± 10 and $\pm 30\,\%$ has been applied to both d and μ one at time and the change in the determination coefficient R^2 and RMSE of the fit has been calculated. The results are summarized in Table 4. The results of the sensitivity analysis are overall satisfactory since the determination coefficient R^2 does not decrease significantly when modifying the parameters d and μ, both considering only experiments on human subjects all the datasets. In fact, the determination coefficient R^2 does not decrease under 0.7. The RMSE tends to increase for larger variations of the parameters especially considering all datasets. A more accurate comparison between numerical results and experiments would be possible if friction and length of the foot were measured during experiments, which is strongly encouraged in future research.

5 Discussion

Flood hazard and flood risk maps, as required by the European Flood Directive 60/2007/EC (European Commission, 2007), should identify the areas that can be affected by floods for different probability scenarios and their potential adverse consequences on the environment, structures and people. Nevertheless, despite the increased capability of hydrologic–hydraulic modelling and damage assessment models, the direct consequences of flood parameters (e.g. water depth and velocity) on human health are often overlooked in hazard and risk maps. This is also due to sparse research on the subject and to the difficulties in identifying precise relationships between flood characteristics and people instability. Usually different hazard zones are classified according to the product number $H \cdot U$ (Cox et al., 2010). The curves defined as such attempt to interpret the large scatter observed in dimensional pairs of water depth H and velocity U in which instability

Table 4. Sensitivity of the goodness of fit to the parameters d and μ.

Exp.	Human subjects	All data	Human subjects	All data	Human subjects	All data	Human subjects	All data	Human subjects	All data
	Base case $d=0.15H_P$		d+10 %		d−10 %		d+30 %		d−30 %	
R^2	0.82	0.76	0.82	0.73	0.81	0.70	0.81	0.64	0.77	0.62
RMSE	0.28	0.67	0.29	0.67	0.31	0.69	0.31	0.97	0.32	1.26
	Base case	$\mu=0.3$	μ +10 %		μ −10 %		μ +30 %		μ −30 %	
R^2	0.82	0.76	0.82	0.72	0.82	0.74	0.78	0.69	0.80	0.71
RMSE	0.28	0.67	0.25	0.68	0.32	0.67	0.22	0.71	0.46	0.75

occurred in flume experiments, but are not capable of discerning stability conditions among different individuals.

For this reason, in the paper a dimensionless instability criterion for people under water flow has been proposed. The mobility parameter θ_P is a function of the physical characteristics of the human subject (i.e. height H_P and length of the foot d). It also shows a strong dependence with Froude number and accounts for the two recognized instability mechanisms, which are sliding and toppling. The evaluation of the mobility parameter for a selection of experiments available in literature (Foster and Cox, 1973; Karvonen et al., 2000; Jonkman and Penning-Rowsell, 2008; Xia et al., 2014) identifies a unique threshold for people instability $\theta_{P_{cr}}$ capable of reducing the scatter of dimensional critical combinations of water depth and velocity. Since θ_P is dimensionless, it allows for comparing the instability conditions for vehicles (Arrighi et al., 2015) and people in the same dimensionless diagram (Fig. 8).

The critical dimensionless threshold curves drawn in Fig. 8 for vehicles (black continuous line) and people (black dashed line) intersect for a Froude number approximately equal to 0.6. Thus, four different portions (i.e. hazard zones) can be observed in the diagram. Above both the curves, both pedestrians and vehicles can be classified as stable for a given flow regime (i.e. Froude number). On the other hand, below the curves both people and vehicles are in unstable and, consequently, dangerous conditions. For practical applications and risk mapping a safety factor could be applied to shift down the threshold curves and account for hydraulic model uncertainties and experimental variance. For a Froude number between 0.1 and 0.6 moving in floodwaters by car is safer than moving on foot since the $\theta_{P_{cr}}$ threshold curve lies above the $\theta_{V_{cr}}$ curve. For a Froude number above 0.6, the $\theta_{V_{cr}}$ curve lies above the $\theta_{P_{cr}}$ curve for people; thus, for these flow regimes moving on foot is better than use a car. Simply put, wading in a creek is safer on foot, wading in a shallow river is safer by car. In fact, the two curves $\theta_{V_{cr}}$ and $\theta_{P_{cr}}$ show the different dominant modality of instability for vehicles and pedestrians, which depend on the different geometric configuration and mass distribution. For a low Froude number, the dominant instability mechanism is toppling, to which pedestrians are more vulnerable than vehicles. For high Froude numbers, sliding instability prevails, which in the case of pedestrians is counterbalanced by a lower lift effect and in the case of vehicles instead contributes to a lower adherence. Since higher Froude numbers in the diagram correspond to lower water depths, this result may not be intuitive for a person facing a flood flow. In fact, a hazard in low water depths is usually underestimated. In fact, for lower water depths, which can be felt as less threatening, a person can be induced to move by car, which is perceived as a safe shelter. That is why education can play a crucial role.

A more popular version of this diagram may help support education because it clarifies the instability mechanisms of vehicles and people, which are recognized as responsible for most of the casualties. Moreover, the critical thresholds proposed here can be easily coupled with existing flood maps adding further information on hazard levels to be adopted for mitigation strategies and emergency activities.

The 3-D numerical model, although very simplified since the human body is modelled as rigid, is the first example of numerical investigation on the instability conditions of people in under water flow. It demonstrates the importance of peoples' ability of counteracting the hydrodynamic forces, through the adjustment of their posture. In fact, the forces evaluated for the instability conditions of the human-scale model (Xia et al., 2014) appear lower than those for human subjects. As suggested by Xia et al. (2014) these conservative conditions can be adopted to account for particularly weak categories of people like elderly or sick.

Moreover, the numerically evaluated forces show that subjects with larger weight and height are able to resist higher solicitations, confirming the observed experimental variability between the subjects (Cox et al., 2010; Russo et al., 2013). Further experiments on human subjects should investigate the instability conditions in super-critical flow regimes, which have been currently addressed only by Jonkman and Penning Rowsell (2008) and recently by Martinez-Gomariz et al. (2016). The evaluated force coefficients, which are a dimensionless measure of the forces, are strongly similar for the different human subjects and can be adopted in conceptual models, which usually account for standard values for cylinders.

Further studies should better investigate the role of the friction coefficient for the occurrence of instability (Martinez-Gomariz et al., 2016), which might be crucial especially for super-critical flow regimes. Moreover, the effect of different physical (i.e. body type, size and build) and psychological human characteristics on the hydrodynamic solicitations should be better understood as well as the role of relative motion, posture, and clothing. Then more detailed laboratory experiments and numerical models, with turbulence measured and accounted for, could investigate important environmental aspects such as local turbulence effects (Chanson and Brown, 2015). A more reliable estimation of the hydrodynamic forces on the human body could be achieved removing the strong assumption of the rigid body and feet–bottom adherence hypothesis. This would suggest the use of a fully coupled CFD–CSD (Computational Fluid Dynamics-Computational Structural Dynamics) model capable of accounting for the different hydrodynamic response to changes in posture.

6 Conclusions

People safety is the primary objective for flood risk managers in the definition of non-structural risk mitigation measures. Numerous studies demonstrated that most of the casualties for drowning during a flood occur because of unwise high-risk behaviours such as driving and walking in floodwaters. Current hazard zoning rely on the product number $H \cdot U$, which helps in explaining the large scatter of experimental pairs of water depth and velocity found in the last decades. However, the $H \cdot U$ criterion is empirical and neglects subject characteristics, whose variability is not physically accounted for.

This paper provides a new approach for hazard assessment of people in floodwaters. The dimensionless mobility parameter introduced here, calculated for selected existing experimental datasets, is capable of identifying a unique critical threshold of instability $\theta_{\mathrm{P_{cr}}}$ regardless of the type of motion mechanism (i.e. sliding and toppling), which is a function of relative submergence and Froude number. The scatter of dimensional experimental data is reduced because the mobility parameter θ_{P} accounts for both flood (H, U) and subject characteristics (height H_{P} and length of the foot d). The diagram of Fig. 8 allows for risk management specialists to assess pedestrians' instability through the comparison of θ_{P} and critical threshold $\theta_{\mathrm{P_{cr}}}$, thus distinguishing different individuals from their height. Thanks to its dimensionless definition, the mobility parameter for people can be compared to the existing mobility parameter for vehicles (Arrighi et al., 2015). Thus, it can support the development of behavioural rules conceived for educating people. Moreover, it can also be mapped over existing flood hazard maps showing water depth and velocity, for an average subject used as a reference or with a probabilistic distribution of human characteristics. The sensitivity analysis carried out with respect to geometric and density parameters of the human subjects hints that θ_{P} is robust since the length of the food d, which is the most sensitive parameter, may vary in a very small range according to allometry observations.

The 3-D numerical model presented in this paper, although simplified, demonstrate through the evaluation of the hydrodynamic forces and force coefficients that relative submergence and Froude number are the most relevant dimensionless parameters for people instability. The human body is modelled as rigid and is described by a detailed 3-D triangulated geometry; 33 steady flow numerical simulations have been carried out to reproduce three different experimental datasets (Karvonen et al., 2000; Jonkman and Penning-Rowsell, 2008; Xia et al., 2014) and subject characteristics, covering a wide range of flow regimes (i.e. Froude between 0.2 and 3.5). The numerical results also clarified the different behaviour of human subjects and human-scale models. A further study, both numerically and experimentally, should better investigates the role of other aspects, which affect people instability in flood waters, such as local turbulence effects, friction, relative motion, posture, clothing and water density.

7 Data availability

Full experimental datasets of Table 2 are available in the papers by Karvonen et al. (2000), Jonkman and Penning-Rowsell (2008), and Xia et al. (2014). The original dataset of this manuscript is available at https://www.researchgate.net/publication/312563449_Dataset_Hydrodynamics_of_pedestrians_instability_in_floodwaters (Arrighi et al., 2017).

Author contributions. The research work was designed and carried out by the first author during the PhD activities under the joint supervision of the two co-authors.

Competing interests. The authors declare that they have no conflict of interest.

Acknowledgements. A PhD research fellowships for the first author is provided by the University of Florence, Italy. The original data about people instability can be found in the cited papers, whose authors are acknowledged for providing an experimental substrate to this work. Authors gratefully thank the editor Hannah Cloke and the anonymous reviewers for their remarks and suggestions, which helped improving the quality of the manuscript.

Edited by: H. Cloke

References

Aboelata, M. and Bowles, D. S.: LIFESim?: A Tool for Estimating and Reducing Life-Loss Resulting from Dam and Levee Failures, Proceedings of the Association of State Dam Safety Officials "Dam Safety 2008" Conference, Indian Wells, CA, 2008.

Abt, S. R., Wittler, R. J., Taylor, A., and Love, D. J.: Human Stability in a High Flood Hazard Zone1, J. Am. Water Resour. As., 25, 881–890, doi:10.1111/j.1752-1688.1989.tb05404.x, 1989.

Arrighi, C., Alcèrreca-Huerta, J. C., Oumeraci, H., and Castelli, F.: Drag and lift contribution to the incipient motion of partly submerged flooded vehicles, J. Fluid. Struct., 57, 170–184, 2015.

Arrighi, C., Oumeraci, H., and Castelli, F.: Dataset Hydrodynamics of pedestrians instability in floodwaters, link to supplementary material: https://www.researchgate.net/publication/312563449_Dataset_Hydrodynamics_of_pedestrians_instability_in_floodwaters, 2017.

Arslan, T., Malavasi, S., Pettersen, B., and Andersson, H. I.: Turbulent flow around a semi-submerged rectangular cylinder, J. Offshore Mech. Arct., 135, 801–812, 2013.

Beashel, P. and Taylor, J.: The world of sport examined, Nelson Thornes ltd, Cheltenham, UK, 224 pp., ISBN-10: 0174387199, 1997.

Beckers, J. V. L., De Bruijn, K. M., and Riedstra, D.: Life safety criteria for flood protection standards, 5th International Conference on Flood Management, p. 2600, Tokyo, 27–29 September 2012.

Bertin, J. J. and Smith, M. L: Aerodynamics for Engineers, Prentice-Hall, Englewood Cliffs, New Jersey, 410 pp, 1979.

Brown, C. A. and Graham, W. J.: Assessing the threat to life from dam failure, Water Resour. Bull., 24, 1303–1309, 1988.

Chakraborty, J., Tobin, G. A., and Montz, B. E.: Population Evacuation: Assessing Spatial Variability in Geophysical Risk and Social Vulnerability to Natural Hazards, Natural Hazards Review, 6, 23–33, 2005.

Chanson, H. and Brown, R.: New criterion for the stability of a human body in floodwaters, J. Hydraul. Res., 53, 540–541, doi:10.1080/00221686.2015.1054321, 2015.

Chanson, H., Brown, R., and McIntosh, D.: Human body stability in floodwaters: the 2011 flood in Brisbane CBD, Hydraulic structures and society – Engineering challenges and extremes, January 2011, 1–9, available at: http://espace.library.uq.edu.au/view/UQ:329775 (last access: 20 March 2016), 2014.

Cox, R. J., Shand, T. D., and Blacka, M. J.: Australian Rainfall & Runoff, Revision Project 10: Appropriate Safety Criteria for People, Stage 1 Report, 2010.

Davis, K. T.: The foot length to stature ratio: a study of racial variance, Thesis in anthropology, Faculty of Texas Tech University, available at: https://ttu-ir.tdl.org/ttu-ir/handle/2346/8468 (last access: 7 March 2016), 1990.

de Bruijn, K. M., Diermanse, F. L. M., and Beckers, J. V. L.: An advanced method for flood risk analysis in river deltas, applied to societal flood fatality risk in the Netherlands, Nat. Hazards Earth Syst. Sci., 14, 2767–2781, doi:10.5194/nhess-14-2767-2014, 2014.

Di Baldassarre, G., Viglione, A., Carr, G., Kuil, L., Salinas, J. L., and Blöschl, G.: Socio-hydrology: conceptualising human-flood interactions, Hydrol. Earth Syst. Sci., 17, 3295–3303, doi:10.5194/hess-17-3295-2013, 2013a.

Di Baldassarre, G., Kooy, M., Kemerink, J. S., and Brandimarte, L.: Towards understanding the dynamic behaviour of floodplains as human-water systems, Hydrol. Earth Syst. Sci., 17, 3235–3244, doi:10.5194/hess-17-3235-2013, 2013b.

Di Baldassarre, G., Viglione, A., Carr, G., Kuil, L., Yan, K., Brandimarte, L., and Bloeschl, G.: Debates-Perspectives on socio-hydrology: capturing feedbacks between physical and social processes, Water Resour. Res., 51, 4770–4781, doi:10.1002/2014WR016416, 2015.

Di Mauro, M., De Bruijn, K. M., and Meloni, M.: Quantitative methods for estimating flood fatalities: towards the introduction of loss-of-life estimation in the assessment of flood risk, Nat. Hazards, 63, 1083–1113, 2012.

EM-DAT: Disasters in numbers (October 2000), International Disaster Database, Université catholique de Louvain Brussels, Belgium, available at: www.emdat.be (last access: 7 March 2016), 2012.

European Commission: Directive on the assessment and management of flood risk (2007/60/EC), available at: http://eur-lex.europa.eu/legal-content/EN/TXT/?uri=CELEX:32007L0060 (last access: 4 April 2016), 2007.

Fessler, D. M. T., Haley, K. J., and Lal, R. D.: Sexual dimorphism in foot length proportionate to stature, Ann. Hum. Biol., 32, 44–59, 2004.

Fitzgerald, G., Du, W., Jamaal, A., Clark, M., and Hou, X. Y.: Flood fatalities in contemporary Australia (1997–2008): Disaster medicine, Emerg. Med. Australas., 22, 180–186, 2010.

Foster, D. N. and Cox, R. J.: Stability of children on roads used as floodways, Technical Report No. 73/13, Water Research Laboratory of the University of New South Wales, Manly Vale, Australia, 1973.

Fox, R. V. and McDonald, A. T.: Introduction to Fluid Mechanics, 2nd ed., John Wiley & Sons, NY, 684 pp., 2011.

Franklin, R. C., King, J. C., Aitken, P. J., and Leggat, P. A.: "Washed away"-assessing community perceptions of flooding and prevention strategies: A North Queensland example, Nat. Hazards, 73, 1977–1998, 2014.

Hoerner, S. F.: Fluid dynamic drag: theoretical, experimental and statistical information, Hoerner Fluid Dynamics, 455 pp., Washington DC, ISBN-10: 9993623938, 1965.

Jacobsen, N. G., Fuhrman, D. R., and Fredsoe J.: A wave generation toolbox for the open-source CFD library: OpenFoam, Int. J. Numer. Meth. Fl., 70, 1073–1088, 2012.

Jonkman, S. N. and Kelman, I.: An analysis of the causes and circumstances of flood disaster deaths, Disasters, 29, 75–97, 2005.

Jonkman, S. N. and Penning-Rowsell, E.: Human instability in flood flows, J. Am. Water Resour. As., 44, 1208–1218, doi:10.1111/j.1752-1688.2008.00217.x, 2008.

Jonkman, S. N., Van Gelder, P. H. A. J. M., and Vrijling, J. K.: Loss of life models for sea and river floods, Flood Defence, 2002, 196–206, 2002.

Karvonen, R. A., Hepojoki, H. K., Huhta, H. K., and Louhio, A.: The use of physical models in dam-break analysis, RESCDAM Final Report, Helsinki University of Technology, Helsinki, Finland, available at: https://www.google.it/url?sa (last access: 24 January 2017), 2000.

Kellar, D. M. M.: The examination of vehicle related flood fatalities in the United States, Commonwealth of Puerto Rico and the U.S. Territories of the Virgin Island and Guam: 1995–2005, A thesis submited to Kent State University, available at: https://etd.ohiolink.edu/!etd.send_file?accession=

kent1290537007&disposition=inline (last access: 4 March 2016), 2010.

Keller, R. J. and Mitsch, B.: Safety aspects of design roadways as floodways, Research Report No. 69, Urban Water Research Association of Australia, Melbourne, Australia, 1993.

Leclercq, D. J. J. and Doolan, C. J.: The interaction of a bluff body with a vortex wake, J. Fluid. Struct., 25, 867–888, 2009.

Lind, N., Hartford, D., and Assaf, H.: Hydrodynamic models of Human Stability in a Flood, J. Am. Water Resour. As., 8, 89–96, 2004.

Love, D. J.: Analysis of a high hazard flood zone. Technical Report prepared for City of Boulder Public Works Department, Boulder, Colorado, 1987.

Maples, L. Z. and Tiefenbacher, J. P.: Landscape, development, technology and drivers: The geography of drownings associated with automobiles in Texas floods, 1950–2004, Appl. Geogr., 29, 224–234, doi:10.1016/j.apgeog.2008.09.004, 2009.

Martinez-Gomariz, E., Gomez, M., and Russo, B.: Experimental studies of the stability of pedestrians exposed to urban pluvial flooding, Nat. Hazards, 82, 1259–1278, doi:10.1007/s11069-016-2242-z, 2016.

Mayer, S., Garapon, A., and. Sørensen, L. S.: A fractional step method for unsteady free surface flow with applications to non-linear wave dynamics, Int. J. Numer. Meth. Fl., 28, 293–315, 1998.

Milanesi, L., Pilotti, M., and Ranzi, R.: A conceptual model of people's vulnerability to floods, Water Resour. Res., 7206–7230, doi:10.1002/2014WR016172, 2015.

Morgan, G. C. J.: Application of the interFoam VOF code to coastal wave/structure interaction, Thesis submitted for the degree of Doctor of Philosophy, University of Bath, UK, 2013.

Munich Re: Great natural catastrophes worldwide 1950–2011, Number of events with trend, available at: https://www.munichre.com/en/media-relations/publications/press-releases/2012 (last access: 10 February 2015), 2012.

Munich Re: Loss events worldwide 1980–2014, 10 costliest events ordered by overall losses, available at: https://www.munichre.com/en/media-relations/publications/press-releases/index.html, last access: 10 February 2015a.

Munich Re: Loss events worldwide 2014 (January), available at: https://www.munichre.com/site/wrap/get/documents_E-581009931/mram/assetpool.munichreamerica.wrap/PDF/2014/2014_globalmap.pdf, last access: 10 February 2015b.

Pawar, P. K. and Dadhich, A.: Study of correlation between human height and foot length in residents of Mumbai, International Journal of Biological and Medical Research, 3, 2232–2235, 2012.

Penning-Rowsell, E., Floyd, P., Ramsbottom, D., and Surendran, S.: Estimating injury and loss of life in floods: A deterministic framework, Nat. Hazards, 36, 43–64, doi:10.1007/s11069-004-4538-7, 2005.

Russo, B., Gómez, M., and Macchione, F.: Pedestrian hazard criteria for flooded urban areas, Nat. Hazards, 69, 251–265, 2013.

Seo, J. H., Seol, D. M., Lee, J. H., and Rhee, S. H.: Flexible CFD meshing strategy for prediction of ship resistance and propulsion performance, International Journal of Naval Architecture and Ocean Engineering, 2, 139–145, 2010.

Siegrist, M. and Gutscher, H.: Natural Hazards and Motivation for Mitigation Behavior: People Cannot Predict the Affect Evoked by a Severe Flood, Risk Analysis, 3, 771–778, doi:10.1111/j.1539-6924.2008.01049.x, 2008.

Simonovic, S. P. and Ahmad, S.: Computer-based model for flood evacuation emergency planning, Nat. Hazards, 34, 25–51, 2005.

Smith, G. P.: Expert opinion: Stability of people, vehicles and buildings in flood water, WRL Technical Report 2015/11, 2015.

Takahashi, S., Endoh, K., and Muro, Z. I.: Experimental study on people's safety against overtopping waves on breakwaters, rep. 31-04 The Port and Harbour Res. Inst., Yokosuka, Japan, 1992.

Tapsell, S. M., Penning-Rowsell, E. C., Tunstall, S. M., and Wilson, T. L.: Vulnerability to flooding: health and social dimensions, Philos. T. R. Soc. A, 360, 1511–1525, doi:10.1098/rsta.2002.1013, 2002.

US Department of Homeland Security: Estimating Loss of Life for Dam Failure Scenarios, Dams Sector, available at: http://www.damsafety.org/media/Documents/Security/DamsSectorConsequenceEstimation-LossofLife.pdf (last access: 6 January 2016), 2011.

Vickery, B. J.: Fluctuating lift and drag on a long cylinder of square cross-section in a smooth and in a turbulent stream, J. Fluid Mech., 25, 481–494, 1966.

Walder, J. S., Watts, P., and Waythomas, C. F.: Case Study?: Mapping Tsunami Hazards Associated with Debris Flow into a Reservoir, J. Hydraul. Eng.-ASCE, 132, 1–11, 2006.

Xia, J., Falconer, R. A., Wang, Y., and Xiao, X.: New criterion for the stability of a human body in floodwaters, J. Hydraul. Res., 52, 93–104, doi:10.1080/00221686.2013.875073, 2014.

Yee, M.: Human stability in floodways, Undergraduate honours Thesis, University of New South Wales, Australia, 2003.

Zhang, X., Yan, J., Zhao, J., Wang, Y., and Qinmin P.: Vertical force acting on partly submerged spindly cylinders, AIP Advances, 4, 047118, doi:10.1063/1.4871695, 2014.

4

The role of storm scale, position and movement in controlling urban flood response

Marie-claire ten Veldhuis[1,2], Zhengzheng Zhou[2,3,4], Long Yang[2], Shuguang Liu[4], and James Smith[2]

[1]Delft University of Technology, Watermanagement Department, Delft, 2628CN, the Netherlands
[2]Princeton University, Hydrometeorology Group, Princeton, NJ 08544, USA
[3]Tongji University, School of Ocean and Earth Science, Shanghai, 200092, China
[4]UNEP-Tongji Institute of Environment for Sustainable Development Shanghai, Shanghai, 20002 China

Correspondence: Marie-claire ten Veldhuis (j.a.e.tenveldhuis@tudelft.nl) and Zhengzheng Zhou (zhouzhengzhengzzz@126.com)

Abstract. The impact of spatial and temporal variability of rainfall on hydrological response remains poorly understood, in particular in urban catchments due to their strong variability in land use, a high degree of imperviousness and the presence of stormwater infrastructure. In this study, we analyze the effect of storm scale, position and movement in relation to basin scale and flow-path network structure on urban hydrological response. A catalog of 279 peak events was extracted from a high-quality observational dataset covering 15 years of flow observations and radar rainfall data for five (semi)urbanized basins ranging from 7.0 to 111.1 km^2 in size. Results showed that the largest peak flows in the event catalog were associated with storm core scales exceeding basin scale, for all except the largest basin. Spatial scale of flood-producing storm events in the smaller basins fell into two groups: storms of large spatial scales exceeding basin size or small, concentrated events, with storm core much smaller than basin size. For the majority of events, spatial rainfall variability was strongly smoothed by the flow-path network, increasingly so for larger basin size. Correlation analysis showed that position of the storm in relation to the flow-path network was significantly correlated with peak flow in the smallest and in the two more urbanized basins. Analysis of storm movement relative to the flow-path network showed that direction of storm movement, upstream or downstream relative to the flow-path network, had little influence on hydrological response. Slow-moving storms tend to be associated with higher peak flows and longer lag times. Unexpectedly, position of the storm relative to impervious cover within the basins had little effect on flow peaks. These findings show the importance of observation-based analysis in validating and improving our understanding of interactions between the spatial distribution of rainfall and catchment variability.

1 Introduction

The interactions between spatial and temporal variability of rainfall and hydrological response characteristics have been the topic of numerous empirical and modeling studies in recent decades (Anquetin et al., 2010; Lobligeois et al., 2014; Morin et al., 2006; Segond et al., 2007; Syed et al., 2003; Tetzlaff and Uhlenbrook, 2005; Volpi et al., 2012; Yakir and Morin, 2011). They have shown that interactions depend on the complex interplay between rainfall variability and catchment heterogeneity in ways that remain poorly understood. This is the case in particular for urban catchments where strong variability in land-use, high degree of imperviousness and the presence of stormwater drainage and detention infrastructure increase the complexity of hydrological response (e.g. Bruni et al., 2015; Fletcher et al., 2013; Meierdiercks et al., 2010; Smith et al., 2005, 2013a; Yang et al., 2016).

Urbanization tends to be associated with higher peak flows induced by reduced infiltration rates on impervious surfaces and with shorter response times. (e.g. Rose and Peters, 2001; Cheng and Wang, 2002; Du et al., 2012; Huang et al., 2008). However, several studies have found mixed effects of urbanization on peak flows and response times, associated with a combination of imperviousness and flood mitigation measures, especially for basins where urbanization has predominantly taken place after implementation of stormwater control legislation (e.g. Smith et al., 2013a; Hopkins et al., 2015; Miller et al., 2014). Niemczynowicz (1999) and Schilling (1991) pointed out the importance of spatially distributed rainfall information at high resolution to study response in urban basins. Thanks to the advances of weather radar, such information is becoming increasingly available (Krajewski and Smith, 2002; Berne and Krajewski, 2013), typically at 1 km spatial resolution (Smith et al., 2007), and in some cases down to less than 100 m (Otto and Russchenberg, 2011; Chen and Chandrasekar, 2015; Thorndahl et al., 2017). (Wright et al., 2014b) analyzed flow variability in three suburbanized catchments in relation to different radar rainfall products and found that storm event water balance and hydrological response times varied with the radar product used for analysis. Berne et al. (2004) derived relationships for critical rainfall resolution for urban hydrology, using high-resolution radar rainfall datasets over six basins in the Mediterranean region. They found that the temporal and spatial rainfall resolution required for urban hydrological analysis varied from about 5 min, 3 km for basins $\sim 10\,\mathrm{km}^2$, to about 3 min, 2 km for basins of $\sim 1\,\mathrm{km}^2$ scale. Radar rainfall data have been used in various studies in recent decades to drive hydrological models and sensitivity of urban hydrological response to spatial and temporal rainfall variability. Bruni et al. (2015) and Ochoa-Rodriguez et al. (2015) used rainfall data from a polarimetric rainfall radar, at $\sim$ 30–100 m and minute resolution to drive semidistributed hydrodynamic models of one and seven highly urbanized catchments, respectively, in northwestern Europe to study urban hydrological response for a range of rainfall input resolutions. They found that sensitivity of flows to rainfall variability increased for smaller basin sizes and that hydrological response was more sensitive to change in temporal than in spatial rainfall input resolution. Gires et al. (2012) quantified the impact of unmeasured small-scale rainfall variability on urban runoff for an urban catchment in London, by downscaling radar rainfall data from 1 km and 5 min resolution to a resolution 9–8 times higher in space and 4–1 times higher in time. Uncertainty in simulated peak flow associated with small-scale rainfall variability reached 25 and 40 % respectively for frontal and convective events. Rafieeinasab et al. (2015) analyzed sensitivity of hydrological response to rainfall variability for five urban catchments of different sizes, located in the City of Arlington and Grand Prairie (US), using a distributed hydrological model. They found that while flow variability was better captured using higher resolution rainfall input, errors in reproducing flow by the models remained equally large, with peak flow over- and underestimations of more than 100 %.

(Wright et al., 2014a) analyzed hydrological response for four semiurbanized basins in Charlotte watershed, North Carolina, using a Gridded Surface Subsurface Hydrologic Analysis (GSSHA) model to examine the effect of rainfall time and length scales on flood response. They found that peak flows in the larger basins ($\sim$ 50–100 km^2) were dominated by large-scale storms, while more concentrated organized thunderstorm systems dominated in the smaller basins ($\sim$ 7–30 km^2). They also identified limitations of this and similar modeling studies, where hydrologic response may be attributable to errors in radar rainfall estimates or to features that were omitted or poorly represented in the model, such as detention ponds, the spatial distribution of layered soils and, in particular, initial soil moisture.

Smith et al. (2002) used a data-driven approach to study relationships between temporal and spatial rainfall variability and hydrological response in urban basins. They introduced the concept of rainfall-weighted flow distance, representing storm position and movement relative to the flow-path network in the basin. In their study, they analyzed hydrological response in five semiurbanized basins in the US for five extreme flood-producing storms based on detailed radar rainfall and flow observation datasets. They found that fractional coverage of a basin by heavy rainfall is a key element of scale-dependent flood response: storm event scales, i.e. spatial (area, length) and temporal (duration) scales smaller than the basin scale (basins length, response time), lead to lower runoff ratios and flood peak compared to when scales of rainfall and basin are similar. Storm motion was found to be amplifying peak flow under particular conditions: storm motion from the lower basin to the upper basin on a timescale of approximately 2 h served to amplify peak discharge for the case of a large, $\sim 100\,\mathrm{km}^2$ basin, relative to other modes of storm motion. In Smith et al. (2005), spatial rainfall variability in relation to the flow-path network was analyzed for 25 flash-flood-producing storms in a $14\,\mathrm{km}^2$ urban watershed. They found that spatial rainfall variability was strongly smoothed by the flow-path network, resulting in hydrological responses for storms with widely varying spatial rainfall variability being strikingly similar.

Other authors have used similar concepts to study hydrological response in natural basins. In an extensive study of 300 events over a $148\,\mathrm{km}^2$ basin in Arizona, Syed et al. (2003) found that runoff volume and peak were strongly correlated with areal coverage by the storm core ($> 25\,\mathrm{mm\,h}^{-1}$ rainfall intensity). The importance of the storm core's position increased with basin size, with storm cores positioned in the central portion of the watershed producing more runoff and higher flood peaks. Morin et al. (2006) found that the sensitivity of flood response (in terms of flood peak magnitude and peak timing) to spatial rainfall variability increased with storm intensity, which they attributed to high flow velocities during intense storms. Similar results were found by Lobligeois et al. (2014), who analyzed the influence of spatial rainfall variability on hydrological response in 181 catchments in France based on spatial rainfall variability, storm position and catchment-scale storm velocity indices. They found that flow simulations by hydrological models benefited from spatially distributed rainfall input for large catchments and strongly spatially distributed rainfall fields. Nicotina et al. (2008) analyzed rainfall variability in a numerical study for large basins up to several thousand square kilometers and found that spatial variability of a storm was more important than variability in total rainfall volume over the basins. This was attributed to the dominant influence of hillslope flow on scales typically smaller than the rainfall variability scale, smoothing differences in travel times to the basin outlet. Channel flow only became more important in very large basins (> 8000 km^2), leading to stronger sensitivity to spatial rainfall variability. Zoccatelli et al. (2011) analyzed rainfall coverage, storm position and movement relative to the flow-path network for five storms in five different basins in southeastern Europe. Based on a model sensitivity study, they found that peak timing error introduced by neglecting spatial rainfall variability ranged between 30 and 72 % of the corresponding catchment response time. Nikolopoulos et al. (2014) analyzed the role of storm motion using radar rainfall data to drive two models of varying complexity. They found that storm motion did not play a significant role in generating hydrologic response for a large storm event, in basins sized 8–623 km^2. Emmanuel et al. (2015) investigated the impacts of spatial rainfall variability on hydrological response using a model simulation approach and found significant dispersion in results obtained for events for different simulation scenarios, showing the need for studying larger sets of events to derive robust general conclusions. Modeling studies reported in the literature have remained inconclusive with respect to the interactions between rainfall and catchment scales (Ogden et al., 2011; Morin et al., 2006; Nicotina et al., 2008; Rafieeinasab et al., 2015). This emphasizes the importance of using field observations to corroborate preliminary conclusions drawn from model simulations.

In this study, we extracted a catalog of 279 flood events from 15 years of high-quality flow observations, in five nested (semi)urbanized basins in Charlotte region, North Carolina (US). By flood events we understand the set of events associated with the top five largest peak flows per year, on average. The term "flood response" is used to refer to hydrological response associated with these high flow events, on the (sub)catchment scale. In the catchments we investigated, it is hard to distinguish between "bank-full" flow and inundating flows, since channels and natural floodplains were heavily modified as a consequence of urbanization. As a result, what used to be considered bank-full flow in a natural channel could be considered flooding (of private properties, gardens) in the urbanized context (Turner-Gillespie et al., 2003). Observational resources for the Charlotte metropolitan region are exceptionally rich (e.g. Smith et al., 2002; Wright et al., 2013). The region is covered by two National Weather Service WSR-88D (Weather Surveillance Radar-1988 Doppler) radar instruments, both of which were deployed in 1995. A dense network of rain gauges and stream gauges was installed by the US Geological Survey (USGS) in 1995. We analyze the influence of spatial scale, position and movement of storms relative to the flow-path network as well as interactions with spatial distribution of imperviousness on urban flood response. We aimed to address the following questions.

- How does rainfall scale interact with basin scale in determining urban flood response? We use fractional coverage to express the relation between rainfall scale and basin scale and to investigate the dependencies of flood peak magnitude and lag time on rainfall scale.

- Does the position of a storm in relation to the flow-path network influence flood response? We use the concept of rainfall-weighted flow distance (RWD) to identify the position of a storm relative to the flow-path network and analyze whether storms concentrated in the upstream part of the catchment are associated with significantly different responses compared to storms concentrated in the center or near the basin outlet.

- How does storm direction and velocity in relation to the flow-path network influence flood response? We use first-order differences in RWD to characterize storm movement and investigate if storms passing over the basin in the downstream direction lead to significantly different hydrological responses compared to storms moving in the upstream direction and storms moving perpendicular to the main flow direction.

- How does the position of a storm in relation to the spatial distribution of imperviousness influence flood response?

This paper is organized as follows: in Sect. 2, the case study area, datasets and methods used in this study are introduced. Results are presented and discussed in Sect. 3, followed by summary and conclusions in Sect. 4.

2 Data and methods

2.1 Study region, rainfall and flow datasets

The data used in the study were collected at five USGS stream gauging stations in Charlotte-Mecklenburg county, North Carolina. Gauging stations are located at the outlet of hydrological basins that range from 7.0 to 111.1 km^2 in size. The area is largely covered by low- to high-intensity urban development, covering 60 to 100 % of basin areas. The percentage of impervious cover varies from 25 % in the least developed to 48 % in the most urbanized basin covering the city center of Charlotte. Figure 1 shows a map with the location of the area, catchment boundaries and location of stream gauges used in the analysis. High-resolution (30 m) gridded datasets were used for terrain elevation (National Map of USGS, http://viewer.nationalmap.gov/), impervious cover,

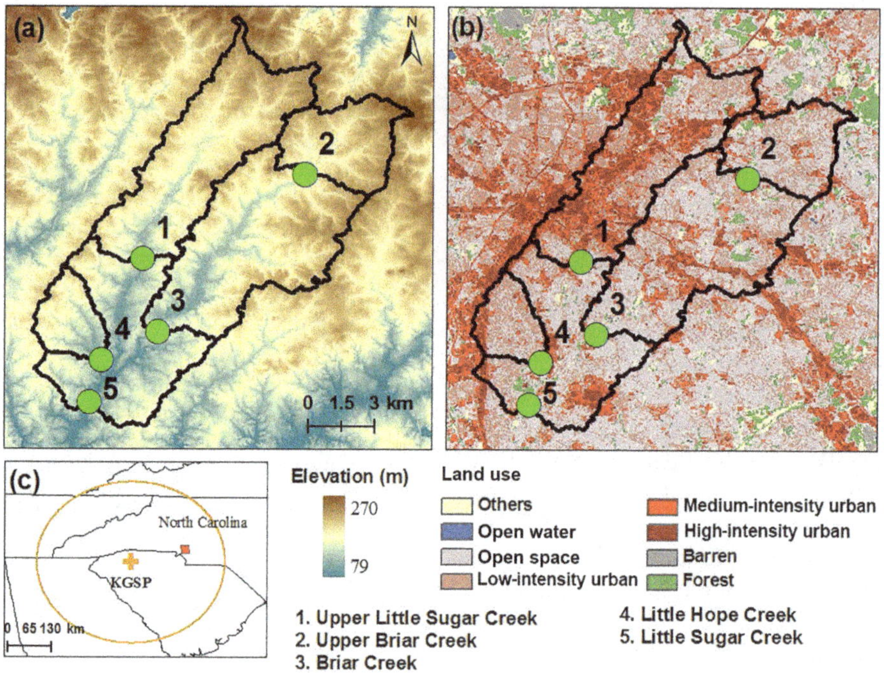

Figure 1. Location of Little Sugar Creek catchment **(c)**, topography **(a)**, land use and land cover **(b)**, and location and boundaries of subbasins, including locations of flow gauges and the location of rainfall radar.

land use and land cover (LULC, from National Land Cover Dataset NLCD, available at: http://www.mrlc.gov/).

The focus of this was Little Sugar Creek catchment, upstream of the flow gauge at Archdale, with a total drainage area of 111 km^2. Additionally, we used data from basins nested within the main basin, sized 7.0, 13.3, 31.5 and 48.5 km^2. Stream gage data were collected at 5 to 15 min intervals over the period 2001–2015. For this study, all flow data were linearly interpolated 1 min values and converted to UTC time. Gauges measure water depth using pressure transducers, using an accuracy standard set by the USGS Office of Surface Water for stage measurement at approximately 0.01 foot (ft) or 0.2 percent of the effective stage. Flows are derived from stage–discharge curves that were established based on protocols developed by USGS and include manual flow measurements during site visits performed by USGS staff. As part of this procedure, stage–discharge curves are checked and recalibrated during site visits several times per year. More information on gauge data and field measurements is available at http://waterdata.usgs.gov/nc/nwis. Flow datasets for the Charlotte region are of exceptionally high quality and consistency as data collection protocol and gauge locations have remained unchanged over decades.

A summary of basin characteristics in Little Sugar Creek catchment is provided in Table 1. (Sub)basin areas range from 7.0 to 111.1 km^2, with impervious cover from 23.9 to 48.2 % and urban land use (excluding parks and lawns) covering 47.1 to 79.1 % of the basin area. Upper Little Sugar (Upper LSugar hereafter) is the most urbanized basin, covered by the urban core of the city of Charlotte. Upper and lower Briar (hereafter Upper Briar and Lower Briar) are the least urbanized basins, with impervious cover of 23.9 and 24.7 % respectively; Little Hope (LHope) is the smallest basin in size. Maximum flow distance along the flow-path network varies from 49 km for the smallest to 213 km for the largest basin. Basin compactness, computed as the ratio of basin area over perimeter squared, is highest for Little Hope and lowest for Upper LSugar, showing that the latter is the most elongated basin. Dams have been implemented in three of the basins, all for recreational purposes, according to the National Inventory of Dams (nid.usace.army.mil/cm_apex). Storage volume varies from approximately 0.1 to 2 mm (dam storage volume divided by basin area).

Based on data from the USGS flow datasets, we established a catalog of flood events, based on "peak-over-threshold" selection such that we have, on average, five events per year over the period 2001–2015. Since radar rainfall data were only available for the summer season, April to September, events were extracted exclusively for this period. Flood events are local maxima in discharge for which there is not a larger discharge in a time window of 12 h centered on the peak time. Events with incomplete rainfall or discharge data were excluded from the dataset. This resulted in a catalog of 50 to 69 storm events per basin (see Table 1).

Rainfall amounts were computed for the time period associated with each of the flood events, based on radar rainfall data. A total of 15 years (2001–2015) of high-resolution (15 min, 1 km^2) Hydro-NEXRAD radar rainfall fields were

Table 1. Summary of hydrological basins in the Little Sugar Creek catchment: basin area (km^2), imperviousness (%), slope (–), land use coverage (high intensity, medium intensity, low intensity urban development) (%), maximum flow distance (km), number of dams regulating stormwater flows (–), number of POT flood events used for analysis (–).

Name	USGS ID	Drainage area (km^2)	Slope (–)	Max. flow distance (km) (–)	Basin compactness (%)	Imperviousness	Land use coverage (%) high int.	med. int.	low int.	No. of dams (–)	No. of events (–)
Little Hope	02146470	7.0	2.2	49	2.6	32.2	9.3	9.4	48.5	0	54
Upper Briar	0214642825	13.3	1.9	58	2.3	23.9	3.6	9.3	34.2	1	50
Upper Little Sugar	02146409	31.5	2.2	128	1.4	48.2	22.5	24	32.6	0	69
Lower Briar	0214645022	48.5	2.4	168	1.6	24.7	4.5	9.9	32.8	5	54
Lower Little Sugar	02146507	111.1	2.4	213	1.6	32.0	10.3	14.1	32.8	8	52

available for this study, based on volume scan reflectivity observations from the NWS-operated Weather Surveillance Radar 1988 Doppler (WSR-88D) radar in Greer, South Carolina (radar code KGSP, see Fig. 1c). The Hydro-NEXRAD processing system was developed to generate radar rainfall estimates for hydrologic applications by converting three-dimensional polar-coordinate volume scan reflectivity fields from NWS WSR-88D radars into two-dimensional Cartesian surface rainfall fields (Krajewski et al., 2011). The standard convective rainfall–reflectivity (Z–R) relationship ($R = aZ^b$, where $a = 0.017$, $b = 0.714$; R is rain rate in millimeters per hour, Z is radar reflectivity in millimeters to the power six per cubic meter), a 53 dBZ hail threshold, and several standard quality control algorithms are used (see Seo et al., 2011 for more details). No range correction algorithms are used in this study. The dataset has been extensively validated in Wright et al. (2014b) and used for rainfall frequency analysis in Wright et al. (2013). Mean field bias correction of the radar rainfall is done on the daily scale using 71 rain gages from the Charlotte rain gauge network (CRN) (see Wright et al., 2014b). Radar-based rainfall estimates captured rainfall variability on timescales of 5–15 min based on the sampling resolution of the radar beam, and space scales of 1 km^2. We used rainfall data at a temporal resolution of 15 min to avoid sensitivity to sampling error on the 5 min timescale. Radar rainfall data were spatially resampled at 30 m resolution using inverse-distance interpolation between radar pixel centroids, to enable computation of rainfall redistribution relative to the flow-path network and imperviousness, within the radar pixel (as will be explained in the next section). Basin-average rainfall rates were also computed, based on spatial aggregation of rainfall values over 1 km^2 pixels within the catchment boundaries of the individual basins (percent of each 1 km^2 grid in the basin was computed for pixels overlapping catchment boundaries). While 15 min estimates derived from 5 min radar sampling may smooth some of the rainfall variability, especially for fast-moving storms, they sufficiently capture the rainfall information relevant for this study, i.e. minimum, mean and maximum distance of storms relative to the outlet and movement of storms relative to the flow-path network.

2.2 Methods

2.2.1 Hydrograph and basin average rainfall characteristics

The following rainfall metrics were defined per event, based on basin-average rainfall rates derived from radar rainfall data at 15 min, 1 km^2 resolution.

- Basin-average rainfall rate ($mm\,h^{-1}$):

$$R_b(t) = \int_0^T R(t,x)\mathrm{d}x, \tag{1}$$

where $R_b(t)$ is the basin-average rainfall rate at times t ($mm\,h^{-1}$); $R(t,x)$ is the rain rate at pixel x ($1 \times 1\,km^2$) at time t (time step is 15 min), and T is the time period of the selected event, from 12 h before the time of the maximum peak flow for a storm event until 12 h after the time of peak flow.

- Rainfall duration R_d (hours), duration of rainfall above a minimum threshold of 1 $mm\,h^{-1}$ within the rainfall event:

$$R_d = \int_0^T I\,(R_b(t) > 1)\,\mathrm{d}t, \text{ where } I\,(R_b(t,x) > 0) = \begin{cases} 1 \text{ for } R_b(t,x) > 1\,mm\,h^{-1} \\ 0 \text{ otherwise.} \end{cases} \tag{2}$$

– Total rainfall depth per event (mm):

$$R_{\mathrm{b,tot}} = \int_0^T R_{\mathrm{b}}(t). \tag{3}$$

– Maximum 15 min rainfall intensity ($\mathrm{mm\,h^{-1}}$):

$$R_{\mathrm{b,max}} = \max\left\{ R_{\mathrm{b}}(t) : t \in [0, T] \right\}. \tag{4}$$

The following metrics were used to analyze relationships between rainfall and hydrologic response; flow values were normalized by basin area and expressed in cubic meters per second per square kilometer ($\mathrm{m^3\,s^{-1}\,km^{-2}}$), to allow comparison among different basins.

– Maximum normalized peak flow ($\mathrm{m^3\,s^{-1}\,km^{-2}}$):

$$Q_{\max} = \max\left\{ Q(t)A^{-1} : t \in [0, T] \right\}, \tag{5}$$

where Q is the instantaneous flow observation, at 1 min intervals ($\mathrm{m^3\,s^{-1}}$); A is the basin area ($\mathrm{km^2}$).

– Total normalized runoff volume ($\mathrm{m^3}$):

$$Q_{\mathrm{tot}} = \int_0^T Q(t)A^{-1}\mathrm{d}t. \tag{6}$$

– Flood event duration (hours): T_Q, defined as the interval between the time when the unit hydrograph continuously rises above 0.05 and falls below $0.01\,\mathrm{m^3\,s^{-1}\,km^{-2}}$. Thresholds were established based on visual inspection of the hydrographs and work well for flood events with a single peak (or events separated from other flood peaks by at least 6 h). For flood events with multiple peaks (i.e. flood peaks that are either preceded or followed by another flood peak within a short time, e.g. 1 h), these thresholds can result in anomalously long event durations that are not representative of hydrological response behavior. For these events, we manually determined the start and end time for each of the "multi-peak" events by visually inspecting the hydrographs. We further checked the duration for "single-peak" events through visual inspections, to ensure consistency in the definition of event duration.

– Lag time (hours): T_{l}, defined as the time difference between basin-average rainfall peak and maximum peak flow, computed from the time distance between the time of peak flow and time of basin-average maximum rainfall intensity during the preceding 12 h time period. In our initial analyses, we used two methods to compute lag times, based on peak-to-peak and on distance between centroids of hyetograph and hydrograph. The latter resulted in a large number of negative lag time values, associated with events with multiple rainfall and/or peak flows. After visual inspection of hyetographs and hydrograph peaks, we decided that peak-to-peak time gave a better representation of the response between rainfall and peak flows for most events, and hence we decided to stick to this lag time definition in our analyses.

– Runoff ratio (–): normalized runoff divided by total basin-average rainfall over the duration of the flood event (T_Q).

– Peak ratio (–): normalized peak flow (flow divided by basin area) divided by rainfall peak intensity.

2.2.2 Rainfall spatial characteristics: spatial variability, fractional coverage and rainfall-weighted flow distance

We used fractional coverage of the basin by rainfall above a given threshold to analyze the influence of rainfall scale in relation to basin scale on hydrological response. Additionally we used the concept of rainfall-weighted flow distance, as first introduced by Smith et al. (2002). RWD provides a representation of rainfall variability relative to a distance metric imposed by the flow-path network. The methodology has been used in multiple previous studies (Smith et al., 2002, 2005; Zoccatelli et al., 2011; Nikolopoulos et al., 2014; Emmanuel et al., 2015). It represents the position of a storm relative to the flow-path network and is used to analyze how storm position and movement influence hydrological response.

Rainfall fractional coverage (–) was computed as follows:

$$R_c(t) = \max\left\{ \frac{1}{A} \int_A I\left(R(t,x)\right) \mathrm{d}x \right\}, \tag{7}$$

where $I(R(t,x))$ is the indicator function and equals 1 when $R(t,x) \geqslant r$ or 0 otherwise; $R_c(t)$ is the maximum portion of basin area receiving rainfall equal to or exceeding $r\ \mathrm{mm\,h^{-1}}$ rainfall. We used a threshold of $r = 25\,\mathrm{mm\,h^{-1}}$, representative of high-intensity rainfall. This threshold corresponds with the 1 in threshold that is used by the flood hazard community in US, specifically the National Weather Service, as an index for potential flash flooding. It has also been used previously in the literature to investigate the influence of storm core versus overall rainfall (e.g. Syed et al., 2003).

Rainfall-weighted flow distance (RWD(t), in m) was computed as follows:

$$\mathrm{RWD}(t) = \int_A w(t,x)\mathrm{d}(x)\mathrm{d}x, \tag{8}$$

where distance function $\{\mathrm{d}(x); x \in A\}$ is the flow distance from point x within the basin to the outlet of the basin and $w(t,x)$ is the rainfall weight function:

$$w(t,x) = \frac{R(t,x)}{\int_A R(t,x)\mathrm{d}x}. \tag{9}$$

RWD is normalized by maximum flow distance in the network, as follows:

$$D(t) = \frac{1}{d_{\max}} \int_A w(t,x)\mathrm{d}(x)\mathrm{d}x, \tag{10}$$

where $D(t)$ is the rainfall-weighted flow distance, normalized by maximum flow distance (–), $d_{\max} = \{\mathrm{d}(x); x \in A\}$, maximum flow distance in the flow-path network (m).

The random variable $D(t)$ takes values from 0 to 1: low values of $D(t)$ are associated with rainfall that is spatially concentrated near the outlet, high values with rainfall concentrated near the headwaters of the basin. For uniformly distributed rainfall, all weights across the basin are equal and $D(t)$ represents the mean flow distance imposed by the flow-path network:

$$\overline{d} = \int_A \mathrm{d}(x)\mathrm{d}x. \tag{11}$$

Normalized, rainfall-weighted flow distances were computed per time step as well as for the total accumulated rainfall per storm event. The first provides information on storm movement over the basin relative to the flow-path network and combines both temporal and spatial rainfall variation (Smith et al., 2002), while the latter focuses on the spatial aspect of rainfall distribution, summarizing it for the total accumulated rainfall per storm event (Smith et al., 2005).

RWD dispersion was computed, to provide an indication of whether spatial rainfall variability as imposed by the flow-path network is unimodal or multimodal. The normalized RWD dispersion (–) was defined as follows (Smith et al., 2005).

$$S(t) = \frac{1}{\overline{s}} \left\{ \int_A w(t,x)\left[\mathrm{d}(x) - \overline{d}\right]^2 \mathrm{d}x \right\}^{\frac{1}{2}} \tag{12}$$

where $\overline{s}$ is the dispersion for uniform rainfall:

$$\overline{s} = \left\{ \int_A \left[\mathrm{d}(x) - \overline{d}\right]^2 \mathrm{d}x \right\}^{\frac{1}{2}}. \tag{13}$$

RWD dispersion takes the value 1 for uniform rainfall; values below 1 are associated with unimodal spatially distributed rainfall and values above 1 represent multimodal spatially distributed rainfall peaks in relation to the flow-path network.

To further investigate the influence of spatial distribution of urbanization on urban flood response, we computed normalized RWD strictly for pixels with impervious cover larger than 80 %, classified as high-intensity development in the NLCD dataset. Thus, imperviousness-weighted, normalized, rainfall-weighted flow distance ($D_I(t)$) was computed as follows:

$$D_I(t) = \frac{1}{d_{\max}} \int_A I(x)w(t,x)\mathrm{d}(x)\mathrm{d}x, \tag{14}$$

where $I(x)$ is an impervious indicator and takes value 1 for pixels with impervious cover $>80\,\%$ and 0 for pixels with impervious cover $<80\,\%$.

2.2.3 Summary statistics and correlation analysis

Metrics associated with normalized RWD are sensitive to the length of the time window over which they are computed (Smith et al., 2002; Nikolopoulos et al., 2014). We used a range of time windows of x h rainfall, x varying from 0.5 to 3 h, corresponding to the timescales of storm duration and lag time for the largest two basins (median storm durations 3 and 3.5 h, median lag times 1.7 and 2.0 h respectively). Results based on a 2 h window are shown in Sect. 3. The time window was centered over the time of event-maximum rainfall intensity. The following summary statistics were retained for normalized RWD: mean, minimum, maximum, coefficient of variation (CV) and gradient as well as RWD for event-total accumulated rainfall. We analyzed time-varying spatial coverage by the storm core ($>25\,\mathrm{mm\,h^{-1}}$), $\Delta R_{\mathrm{cov}}/\Delta t$, in relation to basin-average rainfall $\Delta R/\Delta t$ to see how much of change in rainfall intensity is associated with change in storm core coverage of the basin. We analyzed $\Delta R/\Delta t$ versus $\Delta \mathrm{RWD}/\Delta t$ to see how change in rainfall intensity relates to movement of the storm relative to the flow-path network. Correlation analyses were performed for all combinations of metrics associated with basin-average rainfall, flow hydrograph, spatial rainfall variability and imperviousness distribution, based on Spearman rank correlations. Correlations were tested for significance at the 5 % level (p value >0.05, based on t test).

3 Results and discussion

3.1 Rainfall and hydrograph characteristics of the selected events

In Fig. 2, box plots of rainfall and flow characteristics are shown for the catalog of selected events, for the five basins.

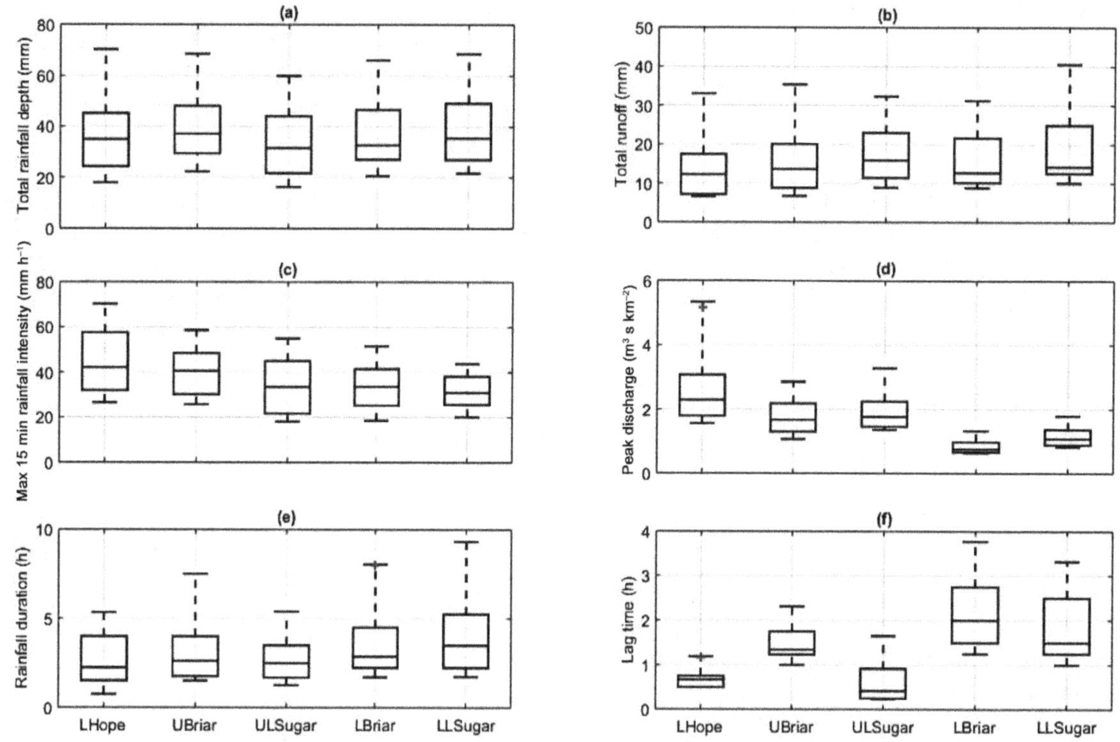

Figure 2. Box plots showing 10, 25, 50, 75 and 90 % quantiles of characteristic rainfall and flow values for all events, per basin: total basin-average rainfall depth **(a)**, total normalized runoff volume (mm) **(b)**, max 15 min rainfall intensities (mm h^{-1}) **(c)**, normalized peak flows ($\text{m}^3\,\text{s}^{-1}\,\text{km}^{-2}$) **(d)**, rainfall duration in hours **(e)**, lag time **(f)**. Box plots are based on 50 to 69 events per basin, as listed in Table 1.

The plots show that basin-average rainfall depth was of the same order of magnitude for all basins, with median values varying between 32.2 and 37.0 mm. Runoff volumes are slightly lower for the smallest two basins in terms of their median values and less skewed. Peak rainfall intensities show stronger variation with basin size: median for peak 15 min rainfall intensity decreases from 41.7 mm h^{-1} for the smallest to 31.2 mm h^{-1} for the largest basin. Peak rainfall intensity varied by factor of 10 approximately across the set of selected peak events per basin (9.5 to 87.6 mm h^{-1} for Lower LSugar; 9.3 to 83.2 mm h^{-1} for Lower Briar; 9.7 to 91.7 mm h^{-1} for Upper LSugar; 8.8 to 90.7 mm h^{-1} for Upper Briar; 10.4 to 118.5 mm h^{-1} for LHope). Figure 2d shows large differences in peak flows between the basins, as indicated by 25–75 and 10–90 % ranges per basin. Lower Briar has lowest median normalized peak flows and narrowest quantile ranges, tied to a combination of large area size and low impervious cover compared to other basins, resulting in strongly smoothed flood response. The smallest basin, LHope, has a strongly skewed peak flow distribution, with the highest median as well as the largest quantile ranges of normalized peak flow values compared to the other basins. The lowest flow variability is found for the most urbanized basin (size 31.5 km^2), which suggests a smoothing effect of imperviousness on flow variability. Upper LSugar, the most impervious basin, shows a high median peak flow value relative to its basin size and quantile ranges similar to the much smaller UBriar basin. This is confirmed by coefficient of variation values of the flow distributions per basin: 0.37 and 0. 46 for Upper and Lower LSugar; 0.65, 0.46 and 0.44 for LHope, Upper and Lower Briar. Similar results were found for a wider range of basins in this region in (Ten Veldhuis and Schleiss, 2017), who concluded that for the basins in the Charlotte catchment, flow regulation and peak flow restrictions induced by capacity constraints result in an overall effect of peak flow reduction associated with urbanization. The only quantitative information available to us about stormwater infrastructure in the Charlotte catchment is the number of dams, which is low for all 5 catchments (0, 1, 0, 5 and 8 for the smallest to largest catchment). In a recent study by (Bell et al., 2016), additional information was collected for basins in this region. They computed the percentage area of mitigated area by detention structures: 5.5, 5.8 and 3.2 % for Little Hope, Upper Briar and Upper Little Sugar, respectively. These numbers show that the impact of detention structures on hydrological response is likely to be very small.

Flow peaks for our event catalog (maximum flow peaks per basin were 3.4 and 10.4 $\text{m}^3\,\text{s}^{-1}\,\text{km}^{-2}$, respectively) were associated with 100-year return periods in 1990 and 1992, respectively, decreasing to 8 and 20 years in 2007, following (Villarini et al., 2009), who reported flood frequency distributions for Lower LSugar Creek and for LHope Creek, based on a generalized additive model fitted to annual flood peaks in these 2 basins. For rainfall, we compared return intervals of maximum 15 min rainfall intensities (over $1 \times 1\,\mathrm{km}^2$ with point rainfall frequency estimates provided by NOAA (NOAA, 2017); no frequency estimates were available on a $1 \times 1\,\mathrm{km}^2$ scale. Maximum values per event varied from 8.8. to $132\,\mathrm{mm\,h}^{-1}$, associated with return intervals of less than 1 year up to 25 years on the point scale.

Rainfall duration varied from approximately 0.5 to 14 h, representing a wide range from concentrated, single-peak events to prolonged, multi-peak events (Fig. 2e). Distributions show large quantile ranges (2.5 to 4 h, 25–75 % range) and are highly skewed. Values in the upper percentiles were mainly associated with storm events with multiple rainfall peaks. Lag times (Fig. 2f), computed as time between maximum rainfall intensity and peak flow, are strongly tied to a combination of basin area size and impervious cover. Upper LSugar, the most urbanized basin, has the shortest median lag time (26 min); the two largest basins have median lag times of 1.7 and 2 h, whereas Lower LSugar has a slightly shorter median lag time than Lower Briar, despite its larger size. This confirms findings in an earlier study by Smith et al. (2002), who found that peaks at Lower LSugar are mostly linked to discharge from the highly urbanized Upper LSugar basin. Lag time values in the upper percentiles are generally associated with multi-peak events, where multiple rainfall peaks caused one or more peak flows over a prolonged period of time. Runoff ratios vary mainly with imperviousness degree: the largest median runoff ratio was found for Upper LSugar (0.51), followed by Lower LSugar (0.44), Lower Briar (0.38) and the two smallest basins, Upper Briar (0.35) and LHope (0.34). Variability in runoff ratio, expressed in terms of coefficient of variation, is low for Upper and Lower LSugar basins compared to the other basins (figure not shown). This effect is even stronger for peak-to-peak ratios: variability in terms of CV is very low for the more impervious basins (0.5 and 0.6 respectively for Upper and Lower LSugar) compared to the other basins (CV values 5.1, 4.2 and 3.7 for LHope, Upper and Lower Briar, respectively).

3.2 Spatial rainfall variability and fractional basin coverage

Spatial rainfall variability was analyzed based on the coefficient of variation of rainfall intensities per time step. Mean CV values vary from 1.24 for the smallest to 3.51 for the largest basin, showing that rainfall tends to be more spatially uniform for smaller basins compared to larger basins. Spatial variability is high compared to temporal rainfall variability based on basin-average rainfall, where CV values vary between 0.94 and 1.03 (no clear relation with basin size). This is partially a result of the difference in aggregation scales: basin-average rainfall is aggregated over 7 to $111\,\mathrm{km}^2$ and 15 min, while spatially variable rainfall is aggregated over $1\,\mathrm{km}^2$ and several hours of rainfall duration. Additionally, spatially varied rainfall data include far more zero values, which leads to strongly skewed distributions, as is confirmed by large differences between mean and median, while these differences are small for temporal rainfall variability. Still, these results show that rainfall for the selected flood events tends to be highly spatially variable. Moreover, spatial variability changes over the duration of events, more strongly so for the larger than for the smaller basins. This is a characteristic of hydroclimatic conditions in this region northeast of the Appalachians, as confirmed for instance by Zhou et al. (2017). Similar results were found by Lobligeois et al. (2014), who analyzed spatial variability of storm events associated with the largest 20 flood events in 181 basins in France. They showed that spatial rainfall variability was strongly dependent on hydroclimatic regions, with high variability occurring in the Mediterranean area, associated with summer convective storms, and low variability over much of the northern and western regions of France.

Figure 3 shows box plots and empirical histograms of fractional rainfall coverage, i.e. the maximum percentage of basin area covered by rainfall intensities larger than $25\,\mathrm{mm\,h}^{-1}$ during storm events, representing the most intense core of the storm. The box plots show that storm cores exceed basin scale for 43 and 23 % of the storms in the two smallest basins (7 and $13.3\,\mathrm{km}^2$, respectively). For the larger basins this decreases to 10, 4 and 2 % (for basin sizes 31.5, 48.5 and $111.1\,\mathrm{km}^2$, respectively). Similar results were shown by Smith et al. (2002) and Syed et al. (2003) for the same range of (sub)basin sizes, for 5 storms using radar rainfall data and for 300 summer storms in Arizona using interpolated rain gauge data, respectively. Another interesting feature appears in the empirical histograms: for the smaller basins, fractional coverage values tends to be either small compared to basin size (coverage 0–20 %) or approaching basin size (coverage 80–100 %). Zhou et al. (2017) showed that the hydro-climatology of flood events in this region reflects a mixture of flood agents, consisting of thunderstorms and tropical cyclones. The largest fraction of events in the upper tail of flood distributions for basins in this area is associated with organized thunderstorms, which could explain the spatially concentrated nature of storm cores over LSugar Creek subbasins. Table 2 shows the degree of overlap in selected storm events between the five (sub)basins. The table shows that 54 to 69 % of events in the largest basin (Lower LSugar) is represented in the flood event catalog for the smaller basins (first row), indicating that these events are likely to have been large-scale events, affecting the entire basin. Overlap between flood-producing events in Upper Briar and Lower Briar is 59 %. The lowest overlap occurs for LHope, indicating that a substantial part of flood events in this smaller basin is associated with a different collection of storm events compared to the other basins. As we can see in Fig. 2, a higher degree of overlapping storms between basins does not result in more similar rainfall or flow patterns: rainfall and flow characteristics are as similar or dis-

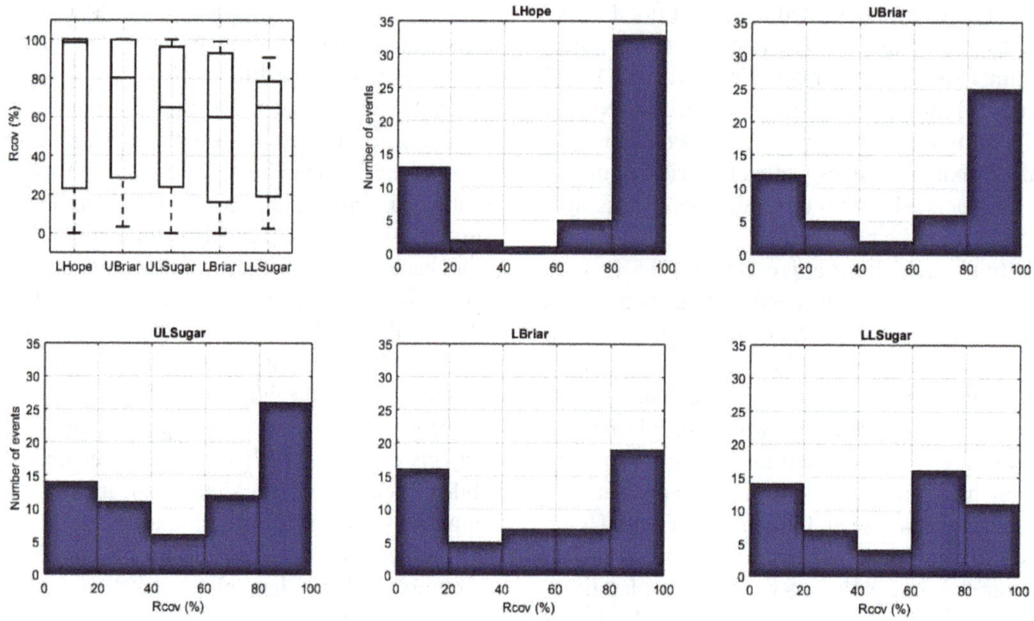

Figure 3. Box plots showing 10, 25, 50, 75 and 90 % quantiles **(a)** and empirical histograms **(b)** of fractional basin coverage by maximum rainfall intensities $> 25\,\mathrm{mm\,h^{-1}}$, representative of the storm core, for the five basins in the Little Sugar Creek catchment.

Table 2. Overlap in top flood producing storms for the five basins in Little Sugar Creek catchment, absolute numbers of events.

Basin name	LLSugar	LBriar	ULSugar	UBriar	LHope
LLSugar	52	36	36	32	28
LBriar		54	30	32	21
ULSugar			69	30	34
UBriar				50	20
LHope					54

similar for Upper compared to Lower LSugar Creek as they are for LHope and UBriar or other sets of non-overlapping basins. Even if flood events in different catchments are generated by the same rainfall events, the characteristics of the rainfall as it affects the catchments is very different.

Figure 4 shows scatter plots of fractional coverage versus peak flow. The plots show that there is a tendency for peak flows to increase with fractional coverage and that the top peak flow values are generally associated with 100 % basin coverage by the storm core. This confirms results found by Smith et al. (2002), who concluded that the relation between storm scale and basin was an important driver for flood response, and Syed et al. (2003), who found that areal coverage of the storm core was better correlated with runoff than area coverage of the entire storm. Our results show that for the urbanized basins in Little Sugar Creek, some of the highest peak flows (top 10 events in flood catalog) occur for fractional coverage well below 100 %. This could be associated with urbanization effects changing the upper tail of the peak flow distribution, as was suggested by Zhou et al. (2017), resulting in a different representation of storm events in the highest quantile peak flows.

We analyzed relationships between fractional coverage and rainfall intensity to see whether changes in basin-average rainfall are strongly tied to change in fractional coverage by the storm core, associated with the storm core moving into or out of the basin. Spearman rank correlation between first-order differences in rainfall intensity and rainfall coverage with time ($\Delta R/\Delta t$ versus $\Delta R_{\mathrm{cov}}/\Delta t$) were significant for all basins, with correlation values varying between 0.38 and 0.69. This confirms that for the selected set of largest flow events in these basins, change in fractional coverage by the storm core is an important driver for change in basin-average rainfall intensity.

3.3 Rainfall position and movement relative to flow-path network and effects on hydrological response

An important aim of this study was to investigate how position and movement of rainfall in relation to the flow-path network, influences hydrological response. Figure 5 shows time-series of basin-average rainfall, fractional coverage by storm core ($> 25\,\mathrm{mm\,h^{-1}}$) and normalized RWD and RWD dispersion for two selected events in Lower LSugar basin. The two events (Fig. 5a and b) represent events from the top 10 highest peak flows in this basin. The third row in the figure illustrates development of normalized RWD as a function of time, the dashed line shows the flow distance for uniform

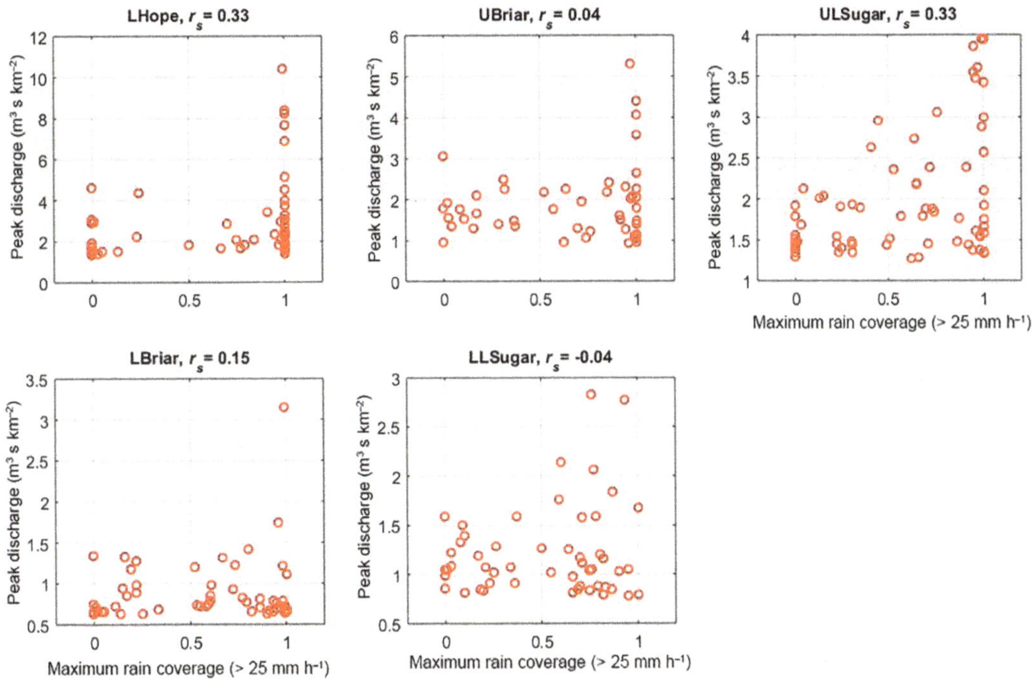

Figure 4. Scatter plots of basin fractional coverage by rainfall intensities > 25 mm h^{-1} versus peak flow, per event, for the five basins in Little Sugar Creek catchment and associated values for Spearman rank correlation coefficients.

rainfall, 0.53. The figure shows that normalized RWD values vary in a relatively small range around the mean: mean values are 0.41 and 0.40, for a 3 h time window centered on the rainfall peak. Associated coefficient of variation values are 0.30 and 0.23. This indicates that, on average, rainfall was concentrated slightly closer to the basin outlet compared to uniform rainfall. Normalized RWD dispersion shows whether rainfall is distributed uniformly, unimodally or multimodally with respect to the flow-path network (see also Eq. 12). Mean normalized RWD dispersion values are 0.83 and 0.93, for a 3 h window centered on the rainfall peak. Maximum normalized RWD dispersion is 1.04 for the first and 1.39 for the second event. This indicates that on average rainfall was mildly concentrated in space compared to uniform rainfall, the first event being more unimodal and concentrated in space during the peak of the storm and the second event breaking into a multimodal structure in between the two rainfall peaks. Storm movement relative to the flow-path network can be derived from the time series of normalized RWD, by analyzing gradients in RWD over time. As Fig. 5 shows, normalized RWD was more or less constant during the period of the most intense rainfall for the first event (cf. period with rainfall intensities > 25 mm h^{-1}), indicating that storm position relative to the flow-path network changed little during the event. For the second event, RWD decreased from 0.64 to 0.24, the main decrease happening at the same time rainfall intensities decreased. This implies that the storm moved into the basin at the upstream end of the flow-path network and moved towards the outlet at the end of the event, to about 0.24 of the maximum flow distance (storm centered over the outlet corresponds to flow distance value of zero).

3.3.1 Relationship between storm position relative to flow-path network and hydrological response

Figure 6 shows box plots of normalized RWD values for event-total accumulated rainfall depth (Fig. 6a) and for the mean and gradient of 2 h temporally varied RWD (Fig. 6b and c) for the five basins. Results show that differences in normalized RWD between events tend to be small: 25–75 % ranges smaller than 0.1 for many of the basins. Differences increase with a combination of basin size and shape: the largest 25–75 and 10–90 % ranges occur for Upper LSugar, the most elongated basin (see compactness values Table 1). This effect is emphasized for normalized RWD dispersion, where median values are lower and percentile ranges are much higher for the larger and elongated basins than for the two smallest basins (Fig. 6c). These results show that spatial rainfall variability is strongly smoothed by the flow-path network and that distribution of rainfall-weighted flow distances tends to be near uniform for the smallest basins. This suggests that the position of the storm relative to the flow-path network is likely to affect hydrological response, mainly in the larger basins. Relatively more spatially unimodal events occur in the larger and more elongated basins (Fig. 6c), yet this does not result in large differences in position along the flow-path network, as indicated by normalized RWD.

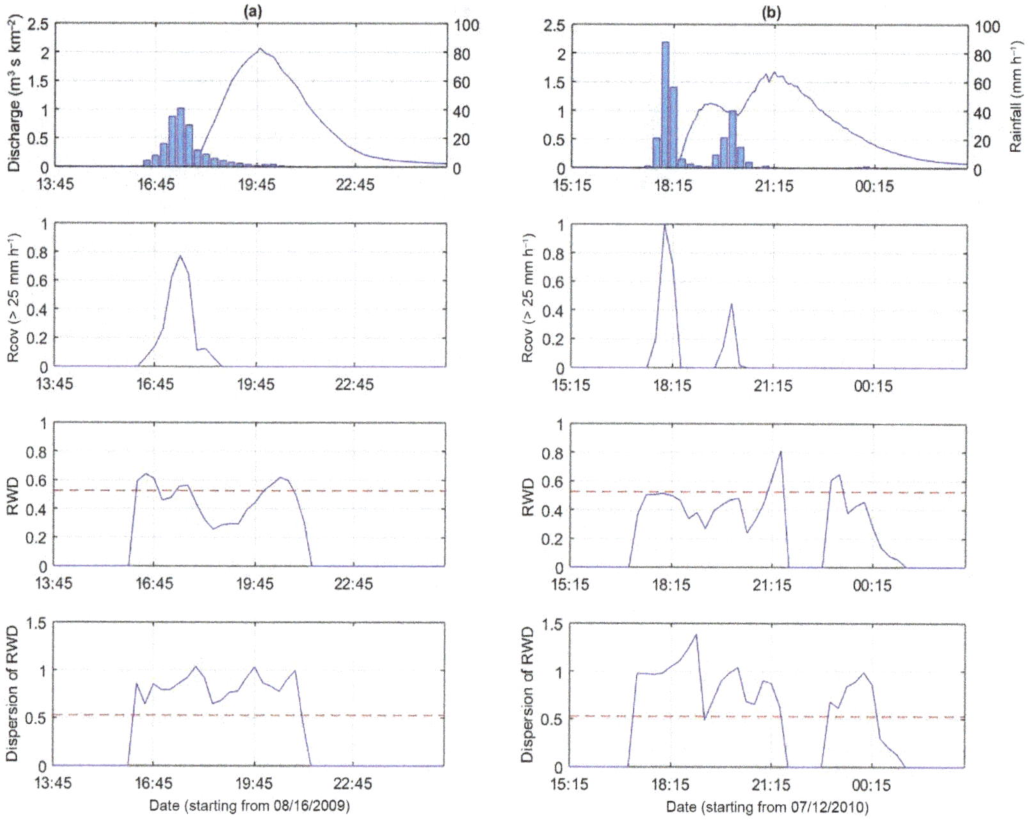

Figure 5. Time series of basin-average rainfall, flow, portion of basin covered by high-intensity rainfall (>25 mm h^{-1}), normalized rainfall-weighted flow distance (RWD) and RWD dispersion in Lower LSugar, for two events that occurred on 16 August 2009 **(a)** and 12 July 2010 **(b)**.

Figure 7a shows a scatter plot of RWD computed for total accumulated rainfall depth per storm event versus lag time. For the smaller basins, no clear signal can be observed, yet for the larger basins (Lower Briar and Lower LSugar), lag time was significantly and positively correlated with storm-total RWD. This indicates that in these basins, storm events concentrating in the upstream parts of the flow-path network are associated with longer lag times. No significant correlations with peak flow were found, as shown in Table 3, which summarizes Spearman rank correlation values between storm-total RWD (RWD_{tot}) and hydrological response characteristics, peak flow and lag time.

3.3.2 Relationship between storm movement relative to flow-path network and hydrological response

In this section we investigate how the combination of storm position and movement in time influence hydrological response. We analyzed correlations with peak flow and lag time for minimum, mean, maximum and gradient in normalized RWD over a range of time windows. Table 3 summarizes correlation values for peak flow and lag time, in relation to rainfall depth, rainfall intensity and RWD. The highest correlations were found for rainfall depth and maximum intensity; significant correlations were found for mean RWD and peak flow (LHope, ULSugar, LLSugar), for mean RWD and lag time (LBriar), and for gradient in RWD with lag time (UBriar, LLSugar). Figure 7b shows a scatter plot of maximum RWD versus peak flow; the plot shows there is no clear relationship between RWDmax and flow peak in LHope, UBriar and LBriar, either because the scale of these basins is too small compared to the scale of most storms (LHope) or because spatial rainfall variability is strongly smoothed by the basin (UBriar, LBriar). In ULSugar and LLSugar, the highest peak flows occur for storms that concentrate over the central and downstream parts of the basin, resulting in a negative correlation. A possible explanation for the negative correlation between RWD and peak flow for the Upper and Lower LSugar basins is the spatial distribution of impervious areas associated with the urban core of Charlotte. This will be analyzed in more detail in Sect. 3.4. No significant correlations between RWD and peak flow were found for Upper and Lower Briar, which suggests that spatial rainfall distribution does not influence peak flows, possibly due to a strong smoothing effect of the flow-path network in these basins. Figure 7c shows that large peak flows tend to occur for gradients near zero, i.e. slow-moving, near-stationary storms (relative to the flow-path network) or moving storms of larger

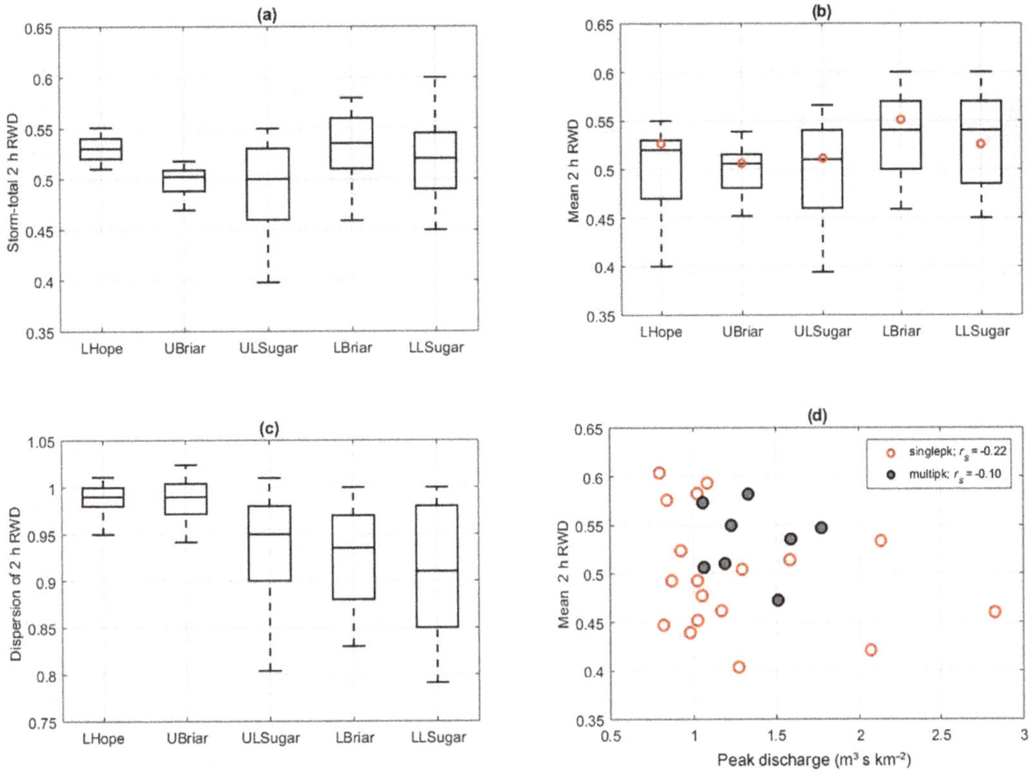

Figure 6. Box plots of RWD values for storm total rainfall **(a)**; mean RWD for a 2 h window **(b)** and RWD dispersion for a 2 h window **(c)**, for all events, for the five basins; scatter plot of mean RWD versus peak flow **(d)**, for Lower LSugar, distinguishing between events with single and with multiple flow peaks. Red circles in box plots indicate RWD associated with spatially uniform rainfall.

Table 3. Summary of correlations between both peak flow (Q_{peak}) and lag time (T_{lag}) and total basin-average rainfall (R_{tot}), peak rainfall intensity (R_{max}), normalized RWD associated with storm event total accumulated rainfall (RWD_{tot}), mean normalized RWD for a 2 h time window (RWD_m) and gradient in RWD for a 2 h time window (RWDgrad).

Basin	Peak flow					Lag time			
Name	vs. R_{tot}	vs. R_{max}	vs. RWD_{tot}	vs. RWD_m	vs. RWD_{max}	vs. R_{tot}	RWD_{tot}	vs. RWD_m	vs. RWD_{grad}
LHope	0.30*	0.40*	0.07	0.31*	0.09	0.39*	0.20	0.18	−0.08
UBriar	0.32*	0.33*	0.14	−0.03	−0.03	0.31*	0.12	−0.15	−0.37*
ULSugar	0.49*	0.43*	−0.18	−0.27*	−0.32*	0.29*	0.05	−0.08	−0.20
LBriar	0.53*	0.38*	0.08	0.06	−0.05	0.56*	0.41*	0.25*	−0.09
LLSugar	0.48*	0.32*	−0.16	−0.29*	−0.23	0.43*	0.32*	0.05	−0.49*

* Indicates significant correlations at the 5 % level.

size than the basin area (especially for smaller basins like LHope).

We separately investigated correlations between rainfall-weighted flow distance and hydrological response for a subset of clear, single-peak events, to exclude more complex correlation patterns associated with multi-peak events. Single-peak events tend to show slightly higher correlations compared to multi-peak events, between rainfall properties or rainfall-weighted flow distances and peak flow or lag time (Fig. 6d). We also investigated whether correlations were different for small-scale storms compared to large-scale storms, by splitting the storm catalog into events with maximum rainfall coverage > 25 mm h^{-1} above and below 50 %. Correlation values for the two subsets improved for some cases, but improvements were not consistent across different basins. Finally, we investigated correlations for a subset of the storm event catalog, with a strong relation between storm movement and rainfall-weighted flow distance, as indicated by a strong correlation between the two, implying that change in rainfall intensity is closely associated with rainfall moving across the basin. The number of events with significant $\Delta R_b/\Delta t$ versus $\Delta D_{Rw}/\Delta t$ correlation varied from 12 for

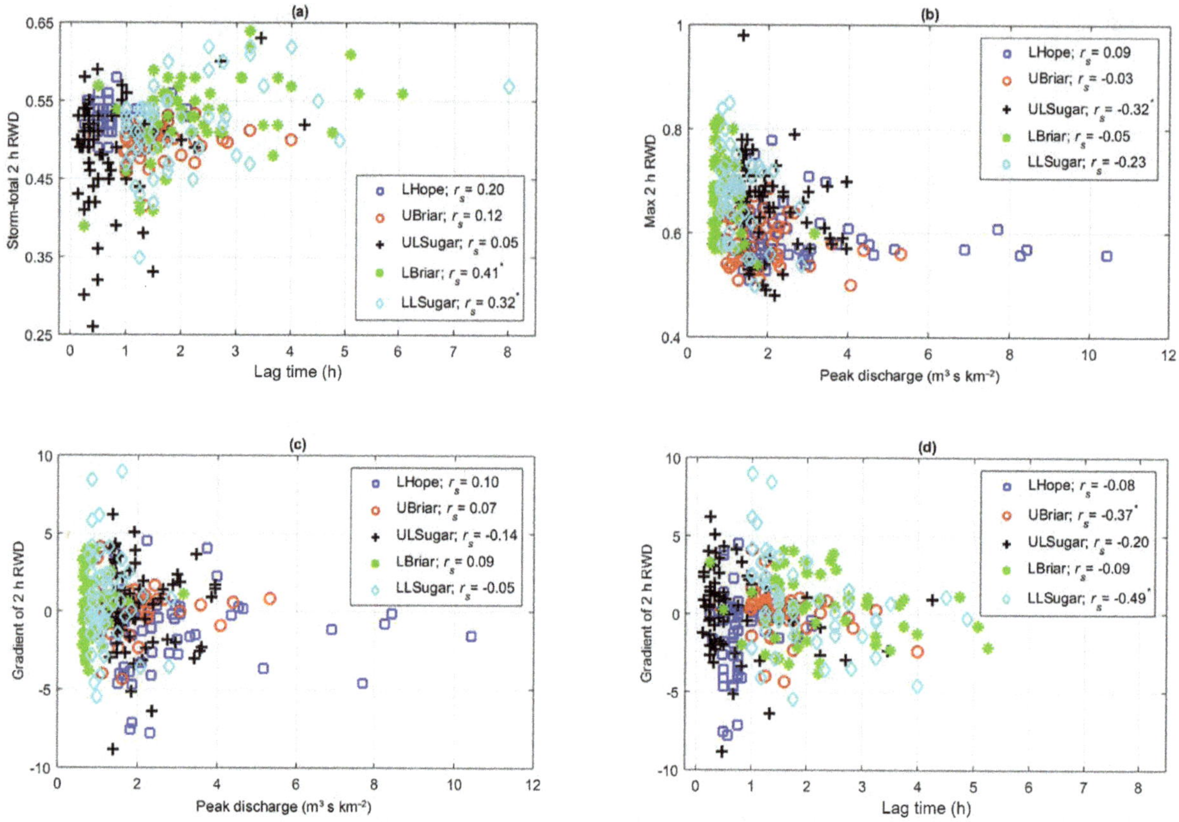

Figure 7. Scatter plots for storm-total RWD (2 h window) versus lag time **(a)**, maximum RWD (2 h window) versus peak flow **(b)**, gradient in RWD (2 h window) versus peak flow **(c)** and gradient in RWD (2 h window) versus lag time **(d)**.

Lower Briar to 22 for Upper LSugar, i.e. 22 to 34 % of the storm catalog. Generally, correlations with peak flow and lag time improved, indicating that storm movement into and out of the basin, leading to changes in basin-average rainfall intensity, significantly contributes to an explanation of the variability in hydrologic response. Investigations for event subsets served as a first exploration of potential multivariate relationships in the datasets. Results showed that explaining variability in hydrological response based on rainfall-weighted flow distance is more straightforward for single-peak events than for multi-peak events and that storm movement into and out a basin plays a significant role in explaining variability in hydrological response.

Table 3 shows that lag time was significantly negatively correlated with gradient in RWD associated with storm movement, for Upper Briar and Upper and Lower LSugar. This implies that storms moving faster towards the basin outlet were associated with slightly shorter lag times. Figure 7d shows that the relationship with RWD gradient is more subtle: small (near zero) gradients tend to be associated with longer lag times, while fast-moving storms tend to be associated with short lag times. Negative correlation with lag time is explained by negative gradients dominating over positive gradients. No significant correlations were found between dispersion of rainfall-weighted flow distance and peak flow or lag time, showing that temporal variability in uni- or multimodality of storm events does not have a significant influence on hydrological response.

In this section we analyzed the influence of the position and movement of storms relative to the flow-path network on hydrological response. Results showed that spatial rainfall variability was strongly smoothed by the flow-path network, confirming similar results found by Smith et al. (2005) for a small (14.3 km^2) basin. We found that, in small basins, rainfall concentrated in the upstream part of the basins was associated with higher peak flows, while in larger basins rainfall concentrated near the outlet was associated with significantly higher peak flows. Correlations were of the same order of magnitude or slightly weaker than those between total rainfall depth or peak rainfall intensity and peak flow. This confirms results found by Smith et al. (2002), who found that for only one of five storms they analyzed, storm position and movement amplified peak flow. While Syed et al. (2003) found that the importance of storm position increased with basin size, this effect was not clearly visible for the basins we investigated in our study. Slow-moving, near-stationary storms (relative to the flow-path network) were associated with longer lag times in some but not all basins;

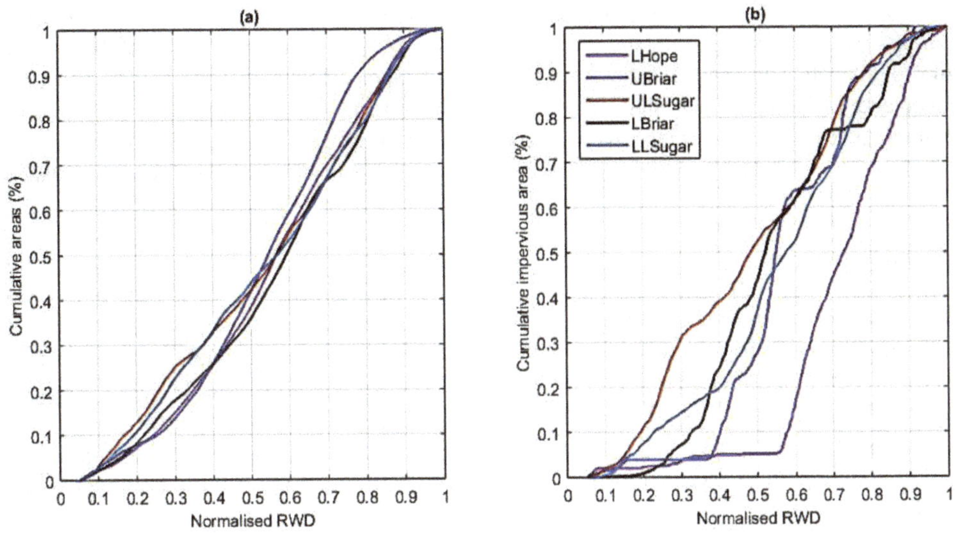

Figure 8. Cumulative distribution of catchment area **(a)** and of impervious areas **(b)** as a function of distance along the flow-path network, for the five basins in Little Sugar Creek catchment.

near-stationary storms also tend to be associated with higher peak flows. Earlier studies have surmised sensitivity of hydrological response to storm position and movement to be highest when computed over time windows equal to the basin lag time (Zoccatelli et al., 2011; Nikolopoulos et al., 2014). In our analyses, we found no relation between the time windows for computation of storm position or movement and basin response time.

3.4 Spatial distribution of impervious areas, spatial rainfall variability and hydrological response

Spatial distribution of rainfall in relation to the distribution of impervious areas in the basins is expected to have an influence on peak flow and lag time, since rainfall on impervious areas generates relatively more runoff and runs off faster compared to pervious areas. The degree of interaction between spatial rainfall variability and spatial imperviousness distribution is likely to depend on two factors: degree of impervious cover in a basin and degree of spatial variation in imperviousness. Figure 8a shows the cumulative distribution of basin area as a function of distance along the flow-path network for the five basins in Little Sugar Creek. Figure 8b shows the cumulative distribution for impervious areas. Gradients steeper than the 1–1 line indicate where impervious areas are relatively concentrated along the flow-path network.

Imperviousness is most inhomogeneously distributed for LHope, where it is almost entirely concentrated in the upstream part of the basin (above 0.55 normalised distance along the flow-path network). In Upper Briar, impervious areas are more concentrated between 0.4 and 0.6 normalized RWD. In Upper LSugar, imperviousness is nearly homogeneously distributed along the flow-path network. In Lower LSugar and Lower Briar, impervious areas are slightly more concentrated near and just downstream of the mean flow-path distance.

We analyzed the influence of spatial rainfall variability in relation to the distribution of impervious areas based on a binary weighting of normalized RWD by imperviousness, $D_I(t)$, as described in Sect. 2.2.2. We found that differences in normalized RWD between events increased by imperviousness weighting only for the smallest basin, LHope, while they remained more or less neutral for Upper Briar and Upper LSugar and slightly decrease for Lower Briar and Lower LSugar. This is illustrated in the scatter plots for RWD and imperviousness-weighted RWD versus peak flow in Fig. 9. We analyzed influence of imperviousness on hydrological response based on Spearman correlations among imperviousness-weighted RWD, peak flow and lag time. As Fig. 9 shows, relationships between imperviousness-weighted RWD and peak flow changed little or decreased slightly compared to those based on total basin area. The overall effect was that correlations based on imperviousness-weighted RWD for both peak flow and lag time were weak and no longer significant at the 5 % level. This shows that position of the storm relative to impervious cover within the basins had little effect on flow peaks. This was mainly due to imperviousness being relatively homogeneously distributed in four of the five basins; by contrast, for LHope, Fig. 9 shows that higher flow peaks were all associated with rainfall over the upper part of the basin, where imperviousness is concentrated. Future studies covering a wider range of basin scales and variability in impervious cover will be needed, to investigate to what extent this conclusion holds for other urbanized basins and what combinations of storm scales and imperviousness distribution lead to sensitivity of peak flows to impervious cover. Apart from impervious cover, the effect of spatial distribution of urban soils with relatively lower permeability than natural soils can be analyzed using the same approach. This will provide better insights into characteristic imperviousness cover and variability scales that determine sensitivity of hydrological response to spatial rainfall variability.

4 Summary and conclusions

The objective of this study was to provide insights into how spatial and temporal rainfall variability interact with catchment scale and flow-path network structure to generate hydrological response in urbanized basins, based on extensive observational datasets. The study comprised analysis of a catalog of the largest 279 flood events extracted from 15 years of rainfall and flow data over 5 nested basins of varying size and degree of urban development. We analyzed rainfall coverage over the basin and over impervious areas in the basin to analyze spatial variability effects on peak flow and lag time. We used the concept of rainfall-weighted flow distance introduced by Smith et al. (2002) to analyze how storm position and movement relative to the flow-path network influenced hydrological response. The following conclusions were drawn from the analyses.

1. Catchment scale determines the type of storm events that produce largest peak flows at the catchment outlet: storm events for the catalog of the largest peak flows in the small (7 km^2) basin show only 39–54 % overlap with those for the larger basins. The largest overlap in storm events, 69 %, is found for the two largest basins, 48.5 and 111.1 km^2 in size. This confirms results reported by Smith et al. (2013b) and Zhou et al. (2017), who also found markedly different rainfall climatologies for flood-producing storms in basins of different size.

2. Catchment scale determines the degree of variability in peak flows and peak rainfall intensities for the catalog of largest flood events. Coefficients of variation in peak flows vary from 0.46 for the largest to 0.65 for the smallest basin. The lowest flow variability is found for the most urbanized basin (size 31.5 km^2), which suggests a smoothing effect of imperviousness on flow variability. Similar results were found by other authors and were attributed to the effect of constraints in the drainage network (Smith and Smith, 2015; Ten Veldhuis and Schleiss, 2017).

3. Scale of the storm core, measured by maximum coverage of a basin by rainfall intensities above 25 $mm\,h^{-1}$, varies strongly with basin scale: for the smallest (7 km^2) basin, intense storm cores exceed basin scale for 43 % of the storms, while 30 % of the storms cover less than half of the basin. For the largest basin, storm cores exceed basin scale for only 2 % of the storms and 44 % of events cover less than half the basin area. Empirical histograms of rainfall coverage for intensities above 25 $mm\,h^{-1}$ show that for the smaller basins, up to 31.5 km^2, storm events largely fall into two groups: large-scale events, with intense storm cores exceeding basin-scale and small-scale events, with storm cores covering less than 20 % of the basin.

4. Dynamics of rainfall coverage by the storm core are an important driver for temporal variability of basin-average rainfall. Spearman rank correlation between first-order differences in rainfall intensity and rainfall coverage with time ($\Delta R/\Delta t$ versus $\Delta R_{\mathrm{cov}}/\Delta t$) were significant for all basins; correlation values varying between 0.38 and 0.69. This suggests that storm movement over the basin drives increases and decreases in basin-average rainfall intensity more strongly than development of storm cells during storm passage over the basin.

5. There is a tendency for peak flows to increase with fractional coverage and the highest peak flow values are generally associated with 100 % basin coverage by the storm core. This confirms results found by Smith et al. (2002), who concluded that the relation between storm scale and basin was an important driver for flood response, and Syed et al. (2003), who found that areal coverage of the storm core was better correlated with runoff than area coverage of the entire storm. Our results also show that for the urbanized basins in Little Sugar Creek, some of the highest peak flows (top 10 events in flood catalog) occur for fractional coverage well below 100 %. This could be associated with urbanization effects changing the upper tail of the peak flow distribution, as was suggested by Zhou et al. (2017), resulting in a different representation of storm events in the highest quantile peak flows.

6. The combination of spatial rainfall structure and flow-path network (expressed in terms of rainfall-weighted flow distance) plays a smaller role in explaining variability in hydrological response compared to rainfall volume and peak intensity. This could be explained by spatial rainfall variability having a relatively small contribution to flow variability compared to climatological rainfall variability, as shown by Peleg et al. (2017). Another explanation is that spatial rainfall variability is strongly smoothed by the flow-path network, as was also shown in earlier studies for a more limited range of observations (Smith et al., 2005).

7. The role of storm movement relative to the flow-path network is investigated based on temporal gradients in rainfall-weighted flow distance. Movement of storms upstream or downstream along the main axis of the flow-path network have no significant influence on peak

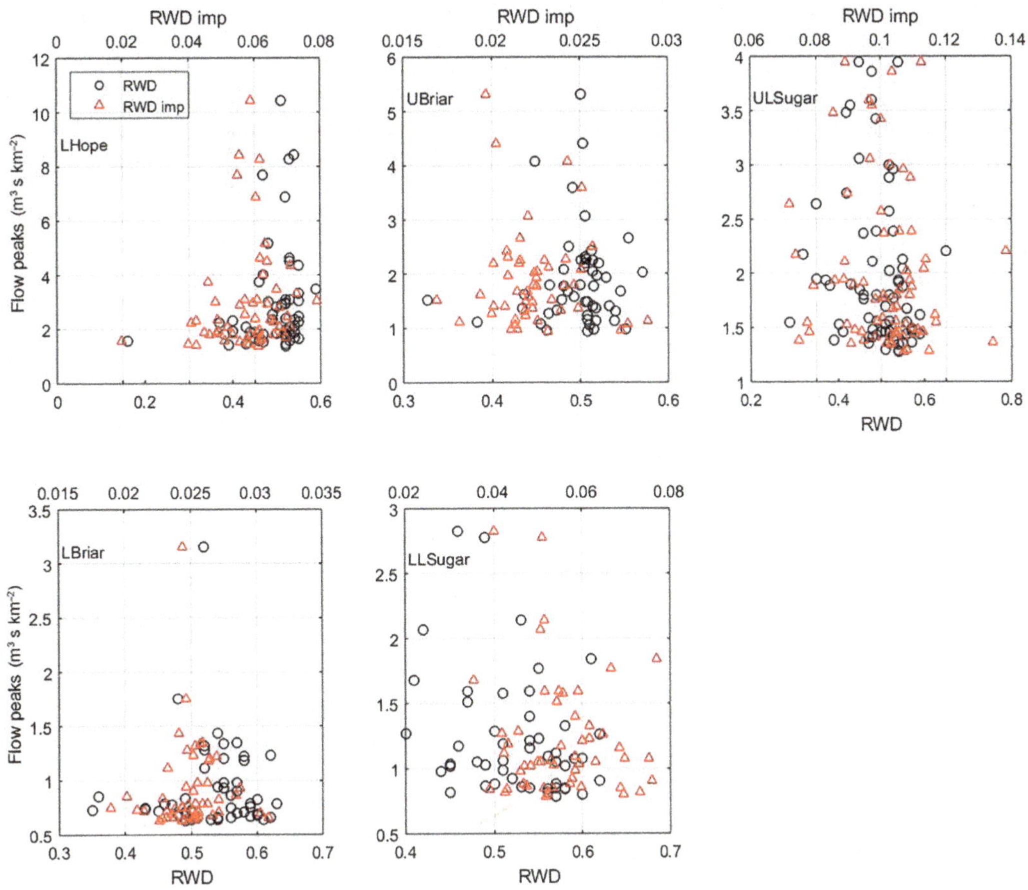

Figure 9. Scatter plots of 2 h-mean RWD versus peak flow, for RWD based on all areas (lower x axis) and for normalized RWD weighted by imperviousness (upper x axis), for the five basins in LSugar Creek catchment.

flows. Slow-moving, (near) stationary storms relative to the flow-path network tend to be associated with higher peak flows. Additionally, slow-moving storms are generally associated with longer lag times.

8. The impact of spatial variability in urban land cover on hydrological response is investigated based on rainfall-weighted flow distance over impervious areas. We find that position of the storm relative to impervious cover within the basins had little effect on flow peaks. A possible explanation is that for the largest basins, where spatial rainfall variability is higher, imperviousness is relatively homogenously distributed, and more smoothing by the flow-path network occurs. By contrast, for the smallest basin, where imperviousness is concentrated in the upper part of the basins, the highest peak flows were all associated with rainfall over this part of the basin.

Results of this study, based on 279 flood events for a range of basin sizes, clearly show that the relation between rainfall and basin scales is an important driver for generating the largest peak flows. Rainfall spatial structure and storm movement seem to play a less important role, being strongly smoothed by the flow-path network. Additional analyses for a larger number of basins are needed to further look into the role of storm position and movement in generating hydrological response. Additionally, the influence of spatial variability in impervious cover on peak flows and lag time needs further investigation to better understand the interplay between the spatial distribution of rainfall and urbanization. The role of other spatially variable catchment characteristics like topography and (urban) soil properties have not been considered in this study. In a recent study by Zhou et al. (2017) the effect of antecedent watershed wetness was investigated for the Charlotte region. They did not find a significant influence of antecedent rainfall on flood response. Direct observations of soil moisture content could help to shed more light on the effect of soil moisture in urban regions and how that affects hydrological response. The importance of variability in topography, soil moisture and urbanization in relation to spatial rainfall variability and climatological variability remain important topics for future research. Future work will focus on analyses for a larger number of basins and a larger set of storms, including smaller, more concentrated storms relative to the catchment scale, to investigate the role of spatial rainfall variability compared to climatological rainfall variability in explaining hydrological response.

Competing interests. The authors declare that they have no conflict of interest.

Acknowledgements. Flow data used in this study are available at http://waterdata.usgs.gov/nc/nwis. The radar rainfall data used in this study can be made available upon request. We are grateful to Mary Lynn Baeck for making available the NEXRAD radar rainfall datasets used in this study. We would like to thank Julia Signel for organizing the USGS flow datasets for the hydrological basins in Charlotte. The first author would like to thank NWO Aspasia and Delft University of Technology for the grant that supported this research collaboration. The authors would like to acknowledge support for this research from the National Science Foundation (CBET-1444758 and AGS-1522492).

Edited by: Thomas Kjeldsen

References

Anquetin, S., Braud, I., Vannier, O., Viallet, P., Boudevillain, B., Creutin, J.-D., and Manus, C.: Sensitivity of the hydrological response to the variability of rainfall fields and soils for the Gard 2002 flash-flood event, J. Hydrol., 394, 134–147, https://doi.org/10.1016/j.jhydrol.2010.07.002, 2010.

Bell, C., McMillan, S., Clinton, S., and Jefferson, A.: Hydrologic response to stormwater control measures in urban watersheds, J. Hydrol., 541, 1488–1500, https://doi.org/10.1016/j.jhydrol.2016.08.049, 2016.

Berne, A. and Krajewski, W.: Radar for hydrology: Unfulfilled promise or unrecognized potential?, Adv. Water Resour., 51, 357–366, https://doi.org/10.1016/j.advwatres.2012.05.005, 2013.

Berne, A., Delrieu, G., Creutin, J.-D., and Obled, C.: Temporal and spatial resolution of rainfall measurements required for urban hydrology, J. Hydrol., 299, 166–179, https://doi.org/10.1016/j.jhydrol.2004.08.002, 2004.

Bruni, G., Reinoso, R., Van De Giesen, N., Clemens, F., and Ten Veldhuis, J.: On the sensitivity of urban hydrodynamic modelling to rainfall spatial and temporal resolution, Hydrol. Earth Syst. Sci., 19, 691–709, https://doi.org/10.5194/hess-19-691-2015, 2015.

Chen, H. and Chandrasekar, V.: The quantitative precipitation estimation system for Dallas-Fort Worth (DFW) urban remote sensing network, J. Hydrol., 531, 259–271, https://doi.org/10.1016/j.jhydrol.2015.05.040, 2015.

Cheng, S.-J. and Wang, R.-Y.: An approach for evaluating the hydrological effects of urbanization and its application, Hydrol. Process., 16, 1403–1418, https://doi.org/10.1002/hyp.350, 2002.

Du, J., Qian, L., Rui, H., Zuo, T., Zheng, D., Xu, Y., and Xu, C.-Y.: Assessing the effects of urbanization on annual runoff and flood events using an integrated hydrological modeling system for Qinhuai River basin, China, J. Hydrol., 464/465, 127–139, https://doi.org/10.1016/j.jhydrol.2012.06.057, 2012.

Emmanuel, I., Andrieu, H., Leblois, E., Janey, N., and Payrastre, O.: Influence of rainfall spatial variability on rainfall-runoff modelling: Benefit of a simulation approach?, J. Hydrol., 531, 337–348, https://doi.org/10.1016/j.jhydrol.2015.04.058, 2015.

Fletcher, T., Andrieu, H., and Hamel, P.: Understanding, management and modelling of urban hydrology and its consequences for receiving waters: A state of the art, Adv. Water Resour., 51, 261–279, https://doi.org/10.1016/j.advwatres.2012.09.001, 2013.

Gires, A., Onof, C., Maksimovic, C., Schertzer, D., Tchiguirinskaia, I., and Simoes, N.: Quantifying the impact of small scale unmeasured rainfall variability on urban runoff through multifractal downscaling: A case study, J. Hydrol., 442/443, 117–128, https://doi.org/10.1016/j.jhydrol.2012.04.005, 2012.

Hopkins, K., Morse, N., Bain, D., Bettez, N., Grimm, N., Morse, J., Palta, M., Shuster, W., Bratt, A., and Suchy, A.: Assessment of regional variation in streamflow responses to urbanization and the persistence of physiography, Environ. Sci. Technol., 49, 2724–2732, https://doi.org/10.1021/es505389y, 2015.

Huang, H.-J., Cheng, S.-J., Wen, J.-C., and Lee, J.-H.: Effect of growing watershed imperviousness on hydrograph parameters and peak discharge, Hydrol. Process., 22, 2075–2085, https://doi.org/10.1002/hyp.6807, 2008.

Krajewski, W. and Smith, J.: Radar hydrology: rainfall estimation, Adv. Water Resour., 25, 1387–1394, 2002.

Krajewski, W., Kruger, A., Smith, J., Lawrence, R., Gunyon, C., Goska, R., Seo, B.-C., Domaszczynski, P., Baeck, M., Ramamurthy, M., Weber, J., Bradley, A., DelGreco, S., and Steiner, M.: Towards better utilization of NEXRAD data in hydrology: An overview of Hydro-NEXRAD, J. Hydroinform., 13, 255–266, https://doi.org/10.2166/hydro.2010.056, 2011.

Lobligeois, F., Andréassian, V., Perrin, C., Tabary, P., and Loumagne, C.: When does higher spatial resolution rainfall information improve streamflow simulation? An evaluation using 3620 flood events, Hydrol. Earth Syst. Sci., 18, 575–594, https://doi.org/10.5194/hess-18-575-2014, 2014.

Meierdiercks, K., Smith, J., Baeck, M., and Miller, A.: Heterogeneity of Hydrologic Response in Urban Watersheds, J. Am. Water Resour. As., 46, 1221–1237, https://doi.org/10.1111/j.1752-1688.2010.00487.x, 2010.

Miller, J., Kim, H., Kjeldsen, T., Packman, J., Grebby, S., and Dearden, R.: Assessing the impact of urbanization on storm runoff in a peri-urban catchment using historical change in impervious cover, J. Hydrol., 515, 59–70, https://doi.org/10.1016/j.jhydrol.2014.04.011, 2014.

Morin, E., Goodrich, D., Maddox, R., Gao, X., Gupta, H., and Sorooshian, S.: Spatial patterns in thunderstorm rainfall events and their coupling with watershed hydrological response, Adv. Water Resour., 29, 843–860, https://doi.org/10.1016/j.advwatres.2005.07.014, 2006.

Nicotina, L., Alessi Celegon, E., Rinaldo, A., and Marani, M.: On the impact of rainfall patterns on the hydrologic response, Water Resour. Res., 44, 1–14, https://doi.org/10.1029/2007WR006654, 2008.

Niemczynowicz, J.: Urban hydrology and water management – present and future challenges, Urban Water, 1, 1–14, 1999.

Nikolopoulos, E., Borga, M., Zoccatelli, D., and Anagnostou, E.: Catchment-scale storm velocity: Quantification, scale dependence and effect on flood response [Vitesse d'averse à l'échelle du bassin: Quantification, dépendance d'échelle et effets sur la crue correspondante], Hydrolog. Sci. J., 59, 1363–1376, https://doi.org/10.1080/02626667.2014.923889, 2014.

NOAA: NOAA atlas 14 point precipitation frequency estimates: NC, https://hdsc.nws.noaa.gov/hdsc/pfds/pfds_map_cont.html?bkmrk=nc (last access: 4 August 2017), 2017.

Ochoa-Rodriguez, S., Wang, L.-P., Gires, A., Pina, R., Reinoso-Rondinel, R., Bruni, G., Ichiba, A., Gaitan, S., Cristiano, E., Van Assel, J., Kroll, S., Murlà-Tuyls, D., Tisserand, B., Schertzer, D., Tchiguirinskaia, I., Onof, C., Willems, P., and Ten Veldhuis, M.-C.: Impact of spatial and temporal resolution of rainfall inputs on urban hydrodynamic modelling outputs: A multi-catchment investigation, J. Hydrol., 531, 389–407, https://doi.org/10.1016/j.jhydrol.2015.05.035, 2015.

Ogden, F., Raj Pradhan, N., Downer, C., and Zahner, J.: Relative importance of impervious area, drainage density, width function, and subsurface storm drainage on flood runoff from an urbanized catchment, Water Resour. Res., 47, W12503, https://doi.org/10.1029/2011WR010550, 2011.

Otto, T. and Russchenberg, H.: Estimation of specific differential phase and differential backscatter phase from polarimetric weather radar measurements of rain, IEEE Geosci. Remote Sens. Lett., 8, 988–992, https://doi.org/10.1109/LGRS.2011.2145354, 2011.

Peleg, N., Blumensaat, F., Molnar, P., Fatichi, S., and Burlando, P.: Partitioning the impacts of spatial and climatological rainfall variability in urban drainage modeling, Hydrol. Earth Syst. Sci., 21, 1559–1572, https://doi.org/10.5194/hess-21-1559-2017, 2017.

Rafieeinasab, A., Norouzi, A., Kim, S., Habibi, H., Nazari, B., Seo, D.-J., Lee, H., Cosgrove, B., and Cui, Z.: Toward high-resolution flash flood prediction in large urban areas – Analysis of sensitivity to spatiotemporal resolution of rainfall input and hydrologic modeling, J. Hydrol., 531, 370–388, https://doi.org/10.1016/j.jhydrol.2015.08.045, 2015.

Rose, S. and Peters, N.: Effects of urbanization on streamflow in the Atlanta area (Georgia, USA): A comparative hydrological approach, Hydrol. Process., 15, 1441–1457, https://doi.org/10.1002/hyp.218, 2001.

Schilling, W.: Rainfall data for urban hydrology: what do we need?, Atmos. Res., 27, 5–21, https://doi.org/10.1016/0169-8095(91)90003-F, 1991.

Segond, M.-L., Wheater, H., and Onof, C.: The significance of spatial rainfall representation for flood runoff estimation: A numerical evaluation based on the Lee catchment, UK, J. Hydrol., 347, 116–131, https://doi.org/10.1016/j.jhydrol.2007.09.040, 2007.

Seo, B.-C., Krajewski, W., Kruger, A., Domaszczynski, P., Smith, J., and Steiner, M.: Radar-rainfall estimation algorithms of Hydro-NEXRAD, J. Hydroinform., 13, 277–291, https://doi.org/10.2166/hydro.2010.003, 2011.

Smith, B. and Smith, J.: The flashiest watersheds in the contiguous United States, J. Hydrometeorol., 16, 2365–2381, https://doi.org/10.1175/JHM-D-14-0217.1, 2015.

Smith, B., Smith, J., Baeck, M., Villarini, G., and Wright, D.: Spectrum of storm event hydrologic response in urban watersheds, Water Resour. Res., 49, 2649–2663, https://doi.org/10.1002/wrcr.20223, 2013a.

Smith, J., Baeck, M., Morrison, J., Sturdevant-Rees, P., Turner-Gillespie, D., and Bates, P.: The regional hydrology of extreme floods in an urbanizing drainage basin, J. Hydrometeorol., 3, 267–282, https://doi.org/10.1175/1525-7541(2002)003<0267:TRHOEF>2.0.CO;2, 2002.

Smith, J., Baeck, M., Meierdiercks, K., Nelson, P., Miller, A., and Holland, E.: Field studies of the storm event hydrologic response in an urbanizing watershed, Water Resour. Res., 41, W10413, https://doi.org/10.1029/2004WR003712, 2005.

Smith, J., Baeck, M., Meierdiercks, K., Miller, A., and Krajewski, W.: Radar rainfall estimation for flash flood forecasting in small urban watersheds, Adv. Water Resour., 30, 2087–2097, https://doi.org/10.1016/j.advwatres.2006.09.007, 2007.

Smith, J., Baeck, M., Villarini, G., Wright, D., and Krajewski, W.: Extreme flood response: The june 2008 flooding in Iowa, J. Hydrometeorol., 14, 1810–1825, https://doi.org/10.1175/JHM-D-12-0191.1, 2013b.

Syed, K., Goodrich, D., Myers, D., and Sorooshian, S.: Spatial characteristics of thunderstorm rainfall fields and their relation to runoff, J. Hydrol., 271, 1–21, https://doi.org/10.1016/S0022-1694(02)00311-6, 2003.

Ten Veldhuis, M.-C. and Schleiss, M.: Statistical analysis of hydrological response in urbanising catchments based on adaptive sampling using inter-amount times, Hydrol. Earth Syst. Sci., 21, 1991–2013, https://doi.org/10.5194/hess-21-1991-2017, 2017.

Tetzlaff, D. and Uhlenbrook, S.: Significance of spatial variability in precipitation for process-oriented modelling: results from two nested catchments using radar and ground station data, Hydrol. Earth Syst. Sci., 9, 29–41, https://doi.org/10.5194/hess-9-29-2005, 2005.

Thorndahl, S., Einfalt, T., Willems, P., Ellerbæk Nielsen, J., Ten Veldhuis, M.-C., Arnbjerg-Nielsen, K., Rasmussen, M., and Molnar, P.: Weather radar rainfall data in urban hydrology, Hydrol. Earth Syst. Sci., 21, 1359–1380, https://doi.org/10.5194/hess-21-1359-2017, 2017.

Turner-Gillespie, D., Smith, J., and Bates, P.: Attenuating reaches and the regional flood response of an urbanizing drainage basin, Adv.Water Resour., 26, 673–684, https://doi.org/10.1016/S0309-1708(03)00017-4, 2003.

USGS: National Water Information System: Web Interface, USGS Water Data for North Carolina: http://waterdata.usgs.gov/nc/nwis, last access: 9 March 2017.

Villarini, G., Smith, J., Serinaldi, F., Bales, J., Bates, P., and Krajewski, W.: Flood frequency analysis for nonstationary annual peak records in an urban drainage basin, Adv. Water Resour., 32, 1255–1266, https://doi.org/10.1016/j.advwatres.2009.05.003, 2009.

Volpi, E., Di Lazzaro, M., and Fiori, A.: A simplified framework for assessing the impact of rainfall spatial variability on the hydrologic response, Adv. Water Resour., 46, 1–10, https://doi.org/10.1016/j.advwatres.2012.04.011, 2012.

Wright, D., Smith, J., Villarini, G., and Baeck, M.: Estimating the frequency of extreme rainfall using weather radar and stochastic storm transposition, J. Hydrol., 488, 150–165, https://doi.org/10.1016/j.jhydrol.2013.03.003, 2013.

Wright, D., Smith, J., and Baeck, M.: Flood frequency analysis using radar rainfall fields and stochastic storm transposition, Water Resour. Res., 50, 1592–1615, https://doi.org/10.1002/2013WR014224, 2014a.

Wright, D., Smith, J., Villarini, G., and Baeck, M.: Long-term high-resolution radar rainfall fields for urban hydrology, J. Am. Water

Resour. As., 50, 713–734, https://doi.org/10.1111/jawr.12139, 2014b.

Yakir, H. and Morin, E.: Hydrologic response of a semi-arid watershed to spatial and temporal characteristics of convective rain cells, Hydrol. Earth Syst. Sci., 15, 393–404, https://doi.org/10.5194/hess-15-393-2011, 2011.

Yang, L., Smith, J., Baeck, M., and Zhang, Y.: Flash flooding in small urban watersheds: Storm event hydrologic response, Water Resour. Res., 52, 4571–4589, https://doi.org/10.1002/2015WR018326, 2016.

Zhou, Z., Smith, J., Yang, L., Baeck, M., Chaney, M., Ten Veldhuis, M.-C., Deng, H., and Liu, S.: The complexities of urban flood response: Flood frequency analyses for the Charlotte metropolitan region, Water Resour. Res., 53, 7401–7425, https://doi.org/10.1002/2016WR019997, 2017.

Zoccatelli, D., Borga, M., Viglione, A., Chirico, G., and Blöschl, G.: Spatial moments of catchment rainfall: Rainfall spatial organisation, basin morphology, and flood response, Hydrol. Earth Syst. Sci., 15, 3767–3783, https://doi.org/10.5194/hess-15-3767-2011, 2011.

5

More frequent flooding? Changes in flood frequency in the Pearl River basin, China, since 1951 and over the past 1000 years

Qiang Zhang[1,2,3]**, Xihui Gu**[4]**, Vijay P. Singh**[5]**, Peijun Shi**[1,2,3]**, and Peng Sun**[6]

[1]Key Laboratory of Environmental Change and Natural Disaster, Ministry of Education, Beijing Normal University, Beijing 100875, China
[2]State Key Laboratory of Earth Surface Processes and Resource Ecology, Beijing Normal University, Beijing 100875, China
[3]Faculty of Geographical Science, Academy of Disaster Reduction and Emergency Management, Beijing Normal University, Beijing 100875, China
[4]Department of Atmospheric Science, School of Environmental Studies, China University of Geosciences, Wuhan 430074, China
[5]Department of Biological and Agricultural Engineering and Zachry Department of Civil Engineering, Texas A&M University, College Station, Texas, USA
[6]College of Territory Resources and Tourism, Anhui Normal University, Anhui 241000, China

Correspondence: Qiang Zhang (zhangq68@bnu.edu.cn) and Xihui Gu (guxihui421@163.com)

Abstract. Flood risks across the Pearl River basin, China, were evaluated using a peak flood flow dataset covering a period of 1951–2014 from 78 stations and historical flood records of the past 1000 years. The generalized extreme value (GEV) model and the kernel estimation method were used to evaluate frequencies and risks of hazardous flood events. Results indicated that (1) no abrupt changes or significant trends could be detected in peak flood flow series at most of the stations, and only 16 out of 78 stations exhibited significant peak flood flow changes with change points around 1990. Peak flood flow in the West River basin increased and significant increasing trends were identified during 1981–2010; decreasing peak flood flow was found in coastal regions and significant trends were observed during 1951–2014 and 1966–2014. (2) The largest three flood events were found to cluster in both space and time. Generally, basin-scale flood hazards can be expected in the West and North River basins. (3) The occurrence rate of floods increased in the middle Pearl River basin but decreased in the lower Pearl River basin. However, hazardous flood events were observed in the middle and lower Pearl River basin, and this is particularly true for the past 100 years. However, precipitation extremes were subject to moderate variations and human activities, such as building of levees, channelization of river systems, and rapid urbanization; these were the factors behind the amplification of floods in the middle and lower Pearl River basin, posing serious challenges for developing measures of mitigation of flood hazards in the lower Pearl River basin, particularly the Pearl River Delta (PRD) region.

1 Introduction

Climatic extremes are one of the crucial drivers of meteorological and hydrological hazards, such as floods and droughts (IPCC, 2007; Li et al., 2016). Meanwhile, climate change is expected to intensify the global hydrological cycle, which will potentially lead to a general increase in the intensity and frequency of extreme climatic events (Ohmura and Wild, 2002; Alan et al., 2003; Zhang et al., 2013). This will, in turn, have direct implications for hydrological extremes, such as floods and droughts (IPCC, 2013). However, the impacts of climate change on hydrological extremes are expected to vary across different regions over the globe due to the prevailing hydrometeorological regimes and the nature of climate change in specific regions (Beniston and Stephenson, 2004; Burn et al., 2015).

Due to remarkable differences in the hydrometeorological processes that generate floods, climate change can increase or decrease the magnitude, duration, frequency and even nonstationarity of extreme hydrological events, such as floods considered in this study (Gu et al., 2016; Vormoor et al., 2016; Zhang et al., 2016). A very recent study by Zhang et al. (2015a) corroborated the changes in hydrological extremes across China but also found the increasing impact of human activities on fluvial hydrological processes. Changes in hydrometeorological triggers are believed to be the first step to project likely future changes in flood-generating processes (Hall et al., 2014; Vormoor et al., 2016). This is particularly the case with flood processes in the Pearl River basin, the second largest river basin in China in terms of flow volume, in a region with a highly developed economy, a dense population, and important megacities, such as Guangdong, Macau, and Hong Kong. This constituted the motivation for this study. Hydrometeorological extremes often have disastrous impacts on society, water resources, agricultural activities, urban infrastructure, and also ecosystems (Das et al., 2013; Li et al., 2016). Floods, in particular, damage infrastructure, take away many lives, and are one of the costliest types of natural disaster in economic and human terms (Bouwer and Vellinga, 2003). This is also true for China where floods tend to have more significant impacts on agriculture than droughts (Zhang et al., 2015b).

Increasing catastrophic losses due to natural hazards have attracted widespread public awareness of extreme events in recent years (e.g., Beniston and Stephenson, 2004; Zolina et al., 2004). By 2100, the mean annual global surface temperature will increase by 1.4–5.8 °C, and future climatic and hydrological extremes will tend to increase and intensify correspondingly (Beniston et al., 2007; IPCC, 2007). Therefore, it is important to investigate flood behavior, and related studies can be of practical value in water resources management. It should be noted that precipitation extremes have a predominant effect on floods (Jena et al., 2014). Studies on precipitation extremes across the Pearl River basin have indicated that the amount of rainfall has changed little but the variability has increased over the time interval divided by change points (Zhang et al., 2009). Further, changes in the characteristics of precipitation extremes across the Pearl River basin are similar to those around the globe (Hirsch and Archfield, 2015); i.e., frequencies of precipitation extremes are increasing but magnitudes have moderate changes. However, increasing precipitation extremes are observed mainly in the lower Pearl River basin, including the Pearl River Delta (PRD) region (Zhang et al., 2012), and also partly in the middle Pearl River basin. Therefore, it can be expected that flood risk should be higher in the middle and lower Pearl River basin or coastal regions (Pino et al., 2016).

In general, extreme floods are rare and hence there is limited opportunity to collect adequate samples of such events in order to make reliable predictions. Therefore, the question is how best to extrapolate limited data to extreme events, when no or only short series of such events are available (Kjeldsen et al., 2014). High quality data and analyses of long historical records of peak extreme events are important to determine whether climate is becoming extreme or variable (Nicholls, 1995). To that end, flood records of 1000 years from Guangdong Province (which covers the lower Pearl River basin) and Guangxi Province (which covers the middle Pearl River basin) were collected to overcome the limitations of short gauge-station-based flood records for analyzing floods, and this is also the significance of this study.

The historical flood records were collected from two books compiled by Wen and Song (2006) and Wen and Yang (2007). These two books include abundant records relevant to various meteorological disasters, such as tropical cyclones, droughts, floods, and frosts. The historical flood records should be screened out from these abundant records, and this is quite a time-consuming job. Therefore, only a few reports were found concerning flooding changes over a long period such as 1000 years in this study based on historical records. In addition, historical flood records in other regions of the globe have been used to analyze the changes in flood frequency (e.g., Mudelsee et al., 2003). Mudelsee et al. (2003) collected flood records from AD 1000 to AD 2000, and pointed out no upward trends in the occurrence of extreme floods in central Europe. Mudelsee et al. (2004) indicated that historical flood records can provide reliable and unique information on heavy floods at least since AD 1500 in the Elbe and Oder rivers, which further emphasized the merits of historical records in the study of flooding frequency from a long-term perspective.

Therefore, the objectives of this study are (1) to quantify abrupt changes and trends of flood events; (2) to characterize temporal changes of 10-year flood flow and spatial distribution of flood magnitude > 10-year flood magnitude (the flood peak is expected to occur, on average, once every 10 years); and (3) to determine frequency and occurrence rate based on 1000-year flood records. Potential causes of spatiotemporal patterns of floods across the Pearl River basin and related implications are also discussed. This study provides a clear picture showing the evolution of floods in both space and time in a humid river basin and shows the response of hydrological extremes to climate change and human activities.

2 Study region and data

2.1 Study region

The Pearl River (97°39′E–117°18′E; 3°41′N–29°15′N) (Fig. 1), with a drainage area of 4.42×10^5 km^2, is the second largest river in China in terms of flow volume (PRWRC, 1991). It includes three major tributaries: West River, North River, and East River. The West River (region I) is the largest

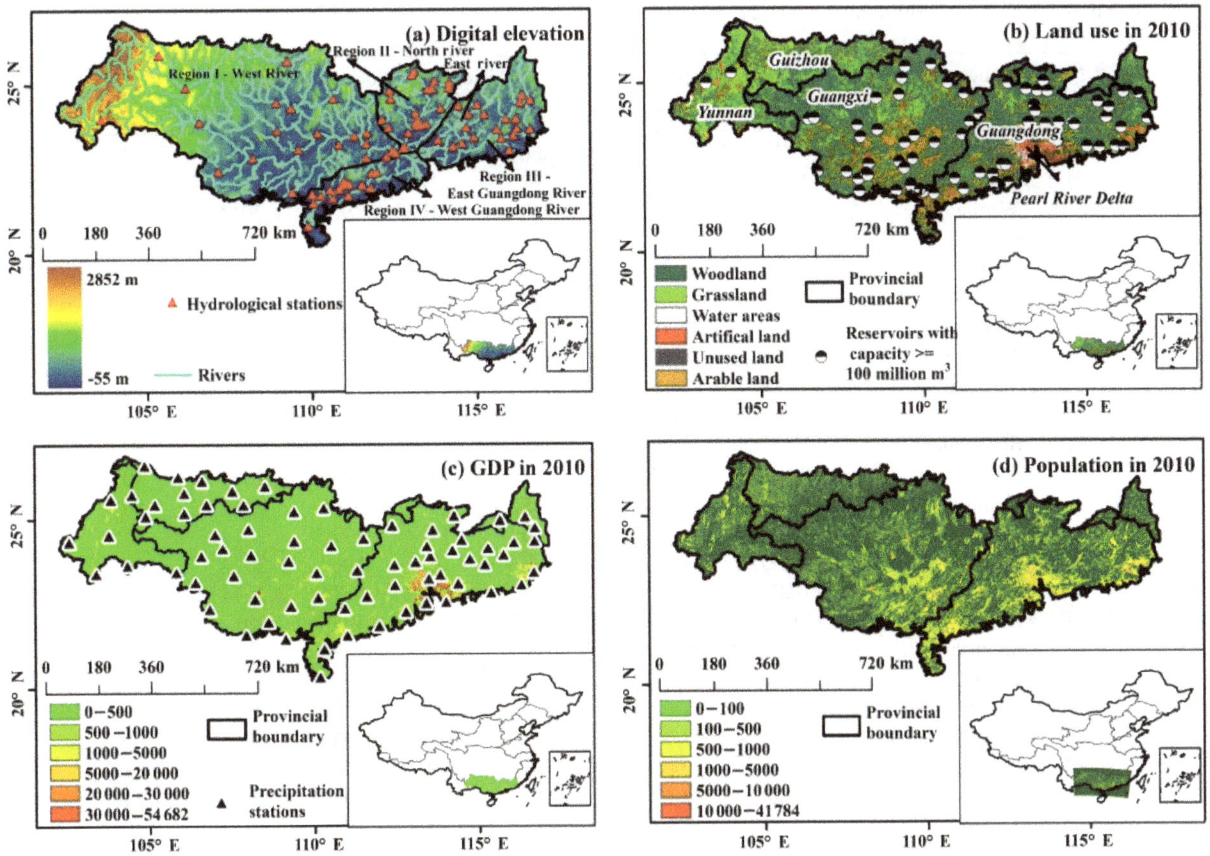

Figure 1. Locations of hydrological stations, precipitation gauging stations, and water reservoirs, and spatial patterns of land use, socio-economy, and population across the Pearl River basin.

tributary, accounting for 77.8 % of the total drainage area of the basin. The North River (region II) is the second largest one, with a drainage area of 46 710 km^2. The East River (region III) accounts for 6.6 % of the total area of the Pearl River. And region IV, which is beyond the three major tributaries, is located in the west of the Guangdong Province (Fig. 1). The annual mean temperature ranges between 14 and 22° C and the precipitation mainly occurs during April–September (Zhang et al., 2009), accounting for 72–88 % of the annual precipitation (PRWRC, 1991).

The Pearl River basin is covered mainly by two provinces, i.e., Guangdong and Guangxi (Fig. 1b). Numerous water reservoirs have been built in northern, eastern, and western Guangdong and also central and southern Guangxi (Fig. 1b). In addition, widespread urbanization can be observed in the PRD, eastern Guangdong, and coastal regions of Guangdong (Chen et al., 2009) (Fig. 1b), which has a highly developed economy (Fig. 1c) and dense population settlements (Fig. 1d). Central and southern Guangxi is dominated by croplands (Fig. 1b). The streamflow variations of the Pearl River basin have a considerable influence on the hydrological processes of the PRD, one of the most complicated deltaic drainage systems in the world (Chen et al., 2009). Flat terrain at low-lying altitude and the downstream location, together with rapid economic development and population growth over the past 3 decades, have made the PRD region more and more vulnerable to natural hazards, such as floods, salinity intrusion, and storm surges. In recent years, engineering facilities and other modifications of the Pearl River network have been designed to strengthen flood protection and to cater for huge requirements of building materials.

2.2 Data

The annual largest 1-day streamflow data (i.e., annual maxima) were collected from 78 hydrological stations across the Pearl River basin (Table 1). Locations of these hydrological stations are shown in Fig. 1a. Additionally, daily precipitation data were also collected from 74 stations across the Pearl River basin and their locations are shown in Fig. 1c. All the precipitation and hydrological data cover the period of 1951–2014. Detailed information of these hydrological (Table 1) and precipitation data can be found in Fig. 2. The hydrological data were provided by the Water Conservancy Bureau of the Pearl River Water Conservancy Commission, and the precipitation data were collected from the National Climate

Table 1. Detailed information of hydrological stations in this study.

No.	Station name	Longitude (° E)	Latitude (° N)	Basin area (km^2)	Region	Starting year	Ending year	Record length
1	Qilinzui2	113.85	23.35	2866	III	1954	2014	61
2	Pingshi2	113.05	25.28	3567	II	1964	2014	51
3	Wenjiang	113.93	24.30	2000	II	1955	2014	60
4	Chixi4	113.13	25.38	396	II	1967	2014	48
5	Lishi2	113.53	24.85	6976	II	1955	2014	60
6	Xiaogulu	114.20	25.07	1881	II	1958	2014	57
7	Renhua3	113.75	25.10	1476	II	1964	2014	51
8	Jielongwan	114.18	24.90	281	II	1958	2014	57
9	Sanshui2	112.83	23.17	46 646	II	1951	2014	64
10	Makou	112.80	23.12	353 100	II	1951	2014	64
11	Shuangqiao	112.57	22.97	938	I	1958	2014	57
12	Dulin	109.90	20.83	47	IV	1975	2014	40
13	Hedishuiku	110.30	21.72	1495	IV	1965	2014	50
14	Gangwajiao3	110.07	21.50	3086	IV	1970	2014	45
15	Ruipo	110.03	21.77	208	IV	1967	2014	48
16	Gaozhou4	110.83	21.92	2905	IV	1975	2014	40
17	Xinhe	111.12	21.72	649	IV	1958	2014	57
18	Shigushuiku1	111.04	22.07	509	IV	1965	2014	50
19	Dabai	111.15	22.05	394	IV	1967	2014	48
20	Huazhoucheng	110.65	21.65	6151	IV	1956	2014	59
21	Liangdeshuiku	110.98	22.15	494	IV	1965	2014	50
22	Gaoyao	112.47	23.05	351 535	I	1951	2014	64
23	Gulan	111.68	23.57	8273	I	1954	2007	54
24	Xiaoluo	111.67	23.25	76.2	I	1977	2014	38
25	Lingxia	114.57	23.25	20 557	III	1953	2014	62
26	Boluo2	114.30	23.17	25 325	III	1953	2014	62
27	Jianshan	115.63	23.67	1578	III	1958	2014	57
28	Shuikou2	115.90	23.98	6480	III	1953	2014	62
29	Tangjin	116.22	23.98	267	III	1959	2014	56
30	Hengshan2	116.35	24.47	12 954	III	1954	2014	61
31	Xikou	116.65	24.53	9228	III	1959	2014	56
32	Baokeng	116.42	24.68	437	III	1958	2014	57
33	Lantang2	114.93	23.43	1080	III	1958	2014	57
34	Shuntian	114.77	24.12	1357	III	1966	2014	49
35	Heyuan	114.70	23.73	15 750	III	1951	2014	64
36	Longchuan	115.25	24.12	7699	III	1952	2014	63
37	Lianping2	114.47	24.37	388	III	1971	2014	44
38	Xingfeng2	115.04	24.40	290	III	1972	2014	43
39	Jinshan	111.53	22.03	950	IV	1959	2014	56
40	Shigushuiku2	111.02	22.05	509	IV	1965	2013	49
41	Pomian_qudao	112.00	22.40	768	IV	1958	2014	57
42	Pomian3	111.83	22.38	768	IV	1954	2014	61
43	Shuangjie	111.80	21.95	4345	IV	1952	2014	63
44	Huangjingtang	112.42	24.58	595	II	1958	2014	57
45	Gaodao	113.17	24.17	7007	II	1954	2014	61
46	Shijiao	112.95	23.57	38 363	II	1954	2014	61
47	Mawu2	113.16	23.85	34.7	II	1972	2014	43
48	Damiaoxia	113.50	23.83	472	II	1960	2014	55
49	Gaolang2	113.30	23.86	216	II	1972	2014	43
50	Chaoan	116.65	23.67	29 077	III	1951	2014	64
51	Chikan	116.25	23.68	641	III	1967	2014	48
52	Fukou	115.77	23.40	355	III	1959	2014	56

Table 1. Continued.

No.	Station name	Longitude (° E)	Latitude (° N)	Basin area (km^2)	Region	Starting year	Ending year	Record length
53	Cijiao	116.02	23.05	820	III	1955	2014	60
54	Dongqiaoyuan	116.13	23.48	2016	III	1953	2014	62
55	Guanliang	111.67	22.83	3164	I	1958	2014	57
56	Yaogu	112.28	22.87	1776	I	1958	2014	57
57	Hejiang2	110.57	21.90	3000	IV	1958	2014	57
58	Daxiang2	112.15	23.97	671	II	1959	2005	47
59	Fenghuangshan	112.38	24.83	1084	II	1959	2005	47
60	Machi	113.20	23.90	300	II	1959	2005	47
61	Zhuzhou	112.35	23.73	553	II	1959	2005	47
62	Qianjiang	108.97	23.63	128 938	I	1951	2010	60
63	Dahuangjiangkou	110.20	23.57	288 544	I	1951	2010	60
64	Wuzhou	111.30	23.48	327 006	I	1951	2010	60
65	Jiangbian	103.62	24.00	25 116	I	1951	2010	60
66	Panjiangqiao	105.38	25.88	14 492	I	1951	2010	60
67	Zhexiang	106.20	24.92	82 480	I	1951	2009	59
68	Yongwei	109.28	25.70	13 045	I	1951	2010	60
69	Sancha	108.95	24.47	16 280	I	1951	2010	60
70	Liuzhou	109.40	24.32	45 413	I	1951	2010	60
71	Pingle	110.67	24.60	12 159	I	1951	2010	60
72	Baise	106.63	23.90	21 720	I	1951	2010	60
73	Xinhe	107.20	22.45	5791	I	1951	2010	60
74	Nanning	108.23	22.83	72 656	I	1951	2010	60
75	Guigang	109.62	23.08	86 333	I	1951	2010	60
76	Jinji	110.83	23.22	9103	I	1951	2010	60
77	Changba	113.68	24.87	6794	II	1951	2010	60
78	Changle	109.42	21.83	6645	I	1951	2010	60

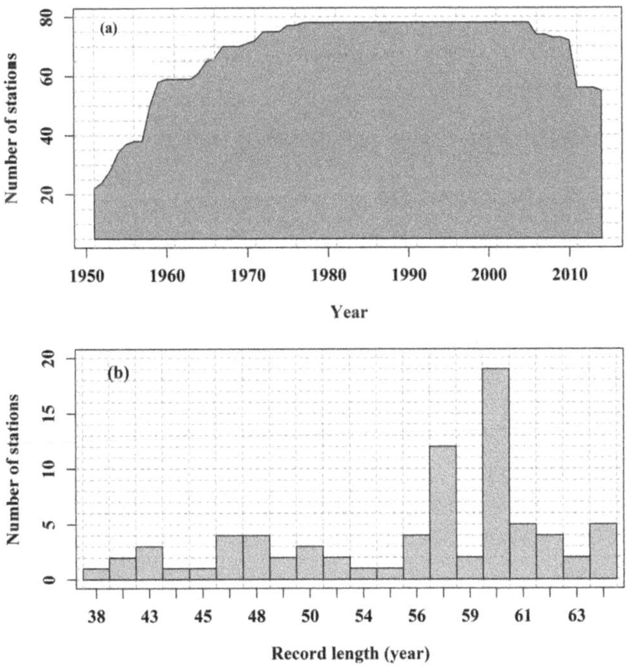

Figure 2. Information on the peak flood flow dataset.

Center, which can be obtained at http://data.cma.cn/ (last access: 23 April 2018). The quality of these data was firmly controlled before release.

There are fewer than 1 % missing values in daily precipitation data (Zhang et al., 2018). The missing precipitation data for 1–2 days were filled by the average precipitation of the neighboring days. Consecutive days with missing data were interpolated by the long-term average of the same days of other years. For the objectives of this study, the gap-fill method did not significantly affect the final results. A similar method was used by Zhang et al. (2011) to fill daily missing precipitation values. The annual largest 1-day streamflow data from 78 hydrological stations were directly collected from the Water Conservancy Bureau of the Pearl River Water Conservancy Commission. The annual largest 1-day streamflow data were compiled before release of the data. The missing values of annual largest 1-day streamflow data were filled by the average value of the neighboring years.

Mudelsee et al. (2003) classified floods into three types, based on inundation area and flood-induced losses: (1) floods that occur locally with short duration and little damage; (2) regional floods that have a relatively longer duration and cause damage to hydraulic infrastructure and also cause casualties; and (3) fluvial disastrous floods that have a longer lasting duration (usually days or weeks) and cause serious and even disastrous damage to hydraulic infrastructure and cause massive casualties. In this study, historical flood records were collected from documented flood records compiled by Wen and Song (2006) and by Wen and Yang (2007). The documented flood records for Guangdong and Guangxi provinces covered a period of 383–2000 and 107–2000, respectively. The disasters were recorded in history books, local chronicles, water conservancy archives, documents, and so on. For the sake of the study on relations between climate change and disasters, the group was developed to compile the documented nature disaster records spanning almost 2000 years for each province in China based on multisource information. The group selected the recorded flood events with mutual confirmation in different documents as far as possible. In addition, the flood event with more relevant information, such as magnitude, mortality, flood-damaged and flood-affected cropland areas, and flood-induced damaged water conservancy facilities, is more likely to be selected.

The director of the group is Wen, who served as the director of the China Meteorological Administration, and one of the group is Ding, who is an academician of the Chinese Academy of Sciences. The members of the group, who come from a senior government authority or who are famous scientists, can largely ensure the quality of the data. Based on flood types defined by Mudelsee et al. (2003), only disastrous flood events were singled out, since floods occurred almost annually. Meanwhile, flood records before AD 1000 were not complete and contained missing information; thus disastrous flood records during a period of 1000–2000 were singled out and analyzed in this study. A flood event, which caused loss of lives, submersed more than 10 000 farmland areas, or destroyed important water conservancy facilities, will be classified as a disastrous flood event.

3 Methods

3.1 Detection of change points and trends

The Pettitt method (Pettitt, 1979) is a nonparametric test and enables the detection of change in the mean (median) when the change point time is unknown. This method has been widely used in detection of change points (Villarini et al., 2009) and was also used in this study. The test is based on the Mann–Whitney statistic for testing whether the two samples $X_1,\dots, X_m$ and $X_{m+1}, \dots, X_n$ come from the same population. The p value, in statistic testing, is computed using the limiting distribution approximated by Pettitt (1979), which is valid for continuous variables (e.g., Villarini et al., 2009). The 95 % confidence level was used to evaluate the significance of change point in the study.

Trends were tested by nonparametric trend detection methods which are less sensitive to outliers than parametric statistics are. In this study, the modified version of the Mann–Kendall (MMK) trend test method was used which was proposed by Hamed and Rao (1998) based on effective or equivalent sample size to eliminate the effect of autocorrelation. MMK has been used in analyzing the effect of global warming on small aquatic ecosystems (Daufresne et al., 2009). In this study MMK was employed to explore trends in flood series, with the significance level set at 5 %. For the computation procedure one can refer to Daufresne et al. (2009). The change point and trend detection methods are only applied for the observations during 1951–2014.

3.2 Generalized extreme value (GEV) model

The GEV distribution has been widely used in the analysis of hydrometeorological extremes (e.g., Gu et al., 2016) and has three parameters, i.e., the location, μ, the scale, α ($\alpha > 0$), and the shape, κ. In this paper, the GEV is used to calculate the return period of flood events. The cumulative density function (cdf) of a random variable y drawn from a GEV distribution is given as follows (Cannon, 2010):

$$\begin{aligned} F(y;\mu,\alpha,\kappa) &= \exp\left[-\left\{1-\kappa\frac{y-\mu}{\alpha}\right\}^{1/\kappa}\right], \\ &\kappa \neq 0, 1-\kappa\frac{y-\mu}{\alpha} > 0 \\ F(y;\mu,\alpha,\kappa) &= \exp\left[-\exp\left\{1-\frac{y-\mu}{\alpha}\right\}\right], \\ &\kappa = 0. \end{aligned} \tag{1}$$

3.3 Kernel density estimation of occurrence rates of floods

The kernel density estimation method is used to estimate the occurrence rates of historical floods. The estimation of occurrence rates of time-dependent extreme events can be computed as follows(Mudelsee et al., 2003, 2004):

$$\lambda(t) = h^{-1}\sum_{i=1}^{m} K\left(\frac{t-T_i}{h}\right), \tag{2}$$

where T_i is the timing of the ith flood event with a unit of days; m is the number of floods; $K(\cdot)$ is the kernel function; and h is the width of the kernel function. The Gaussian kernel function is the widely used kernel function, which can use the Fourier space and produce a smoothed estimation of the occurrence rates of extreme events (Mudelsee et al., 2003, 2004):

$$K(y) = \frac{1}{\sqrt{2\pi}}\exp\left(-\frac{y^2}{2}\right), \tag{3}$$

where $y = (t-T_i)\,h^{-1}$. The occurrence rate of an extreme event, $\lambda(t)$, denotes the number of an extreme event exceeding threshold values given a certain time interval, t. The time

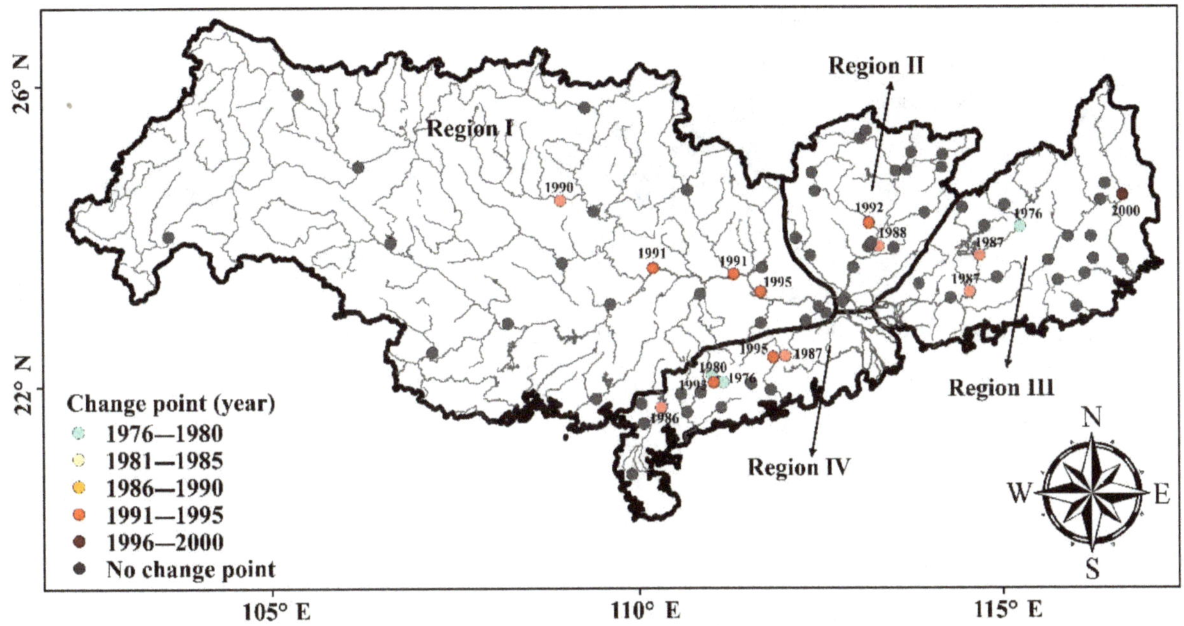

Figure 3. Spatial distribution of change points using the Pettitt test for peak flood flow changes.

interval of time series is $[t_1, t_m]$. Since no data are available outside of the time interval, i.e., $[t_1, t_m]$, $\lambda(t)$ near the boundaries of the time interval is usually underestimated. In this case, a kind of pseudodata is used to reduce the error as a result of underestimated $\lambda(t)$. A mapping technique is used to produce the pseudodata (Mudelsee et al., 2004). pT is the pseudodata outside of the time interval of $[t_1, t_m]$ for the flood series. For $t < t_1$, $pT[i] = t_1 - [T_i - t_1]$; and the same procedure was done for $t > t_m$. The extended series is 1.5 times longer than the original one. The computation of $\lambda(t)$ based on the extended data series was based on

$$\lambda(t) = h^{-1} \sum_{i=1}^{m*} K\left(\frac{t - T_i}{h}\right), \tag{4}$$

where T_i is the timing of the ith flood event based on the extended data series with a unit of day; m^* is the sample size of the extended data series. Also, the selection of window width, h, is important for the estimation of $\lambda(t)$. Too small a window width, h, selected for the computation of $\lambda(t)$ will substantially influence the randomness of $\lambda(t)$; too large a window width, h, may cause over-smoothing of the data series, and hence details in information may be excluded. The cross-validation method was used to determine the width of the window (Mudelsee et al., 2003). The kernel density estimation method is only applied for the historical floods.

3.4 Confidence interval by Bootstrap technique

The bootstrap technique and Eq. (4) can be combined to enable uncertainty analysis of the occurrence rate of floods, $\lambda(t)$, using the following procedure (Mudelsee et al., 2004).

1. Based on the extended data series, T_i^*, the simulated T^+ of the same series length can be obtained using the bootstrap technique.
2. The occurrence rates, $\lambda^+(t)$, of sample extreme events, T^+, can be computed using Eq. (5).
3. Steps 2 and 3 above will be repeated 2000 times, and $\lambda^+(t)$ of 2000 samples can be obtained.
4. The 90 % confidence interval for $\lambda^+(t)$ will be obtained using the quantile method.

4 Results

4.1 Change points and trends of peak flood flow

Analyses of change points and trends were only applied in observed flood events (i.e., annual maxima of period of 1951–2014). Figure 3 illustrates spatial patterns of stations with different change points of peak flood flow. It can be observed from the figure that only 16 out of 78 stations, accounting for 20.5 % of the total stations, were characterized by significant change points of peak flood flow changes, and most of these stations are found in the middle and lower Pearl River basin. In the coastal regions of the lower Pearl River basin, 10 out of 16 stations with significant change points were observed, accounting for 62.5 % of the total stations, characterized by significant change points of peak flood flow. Generally, flooding in the Pearl River basin is mainly attributed to precipitation extremes which were observed mainly in the middle and lower Pearl River basin

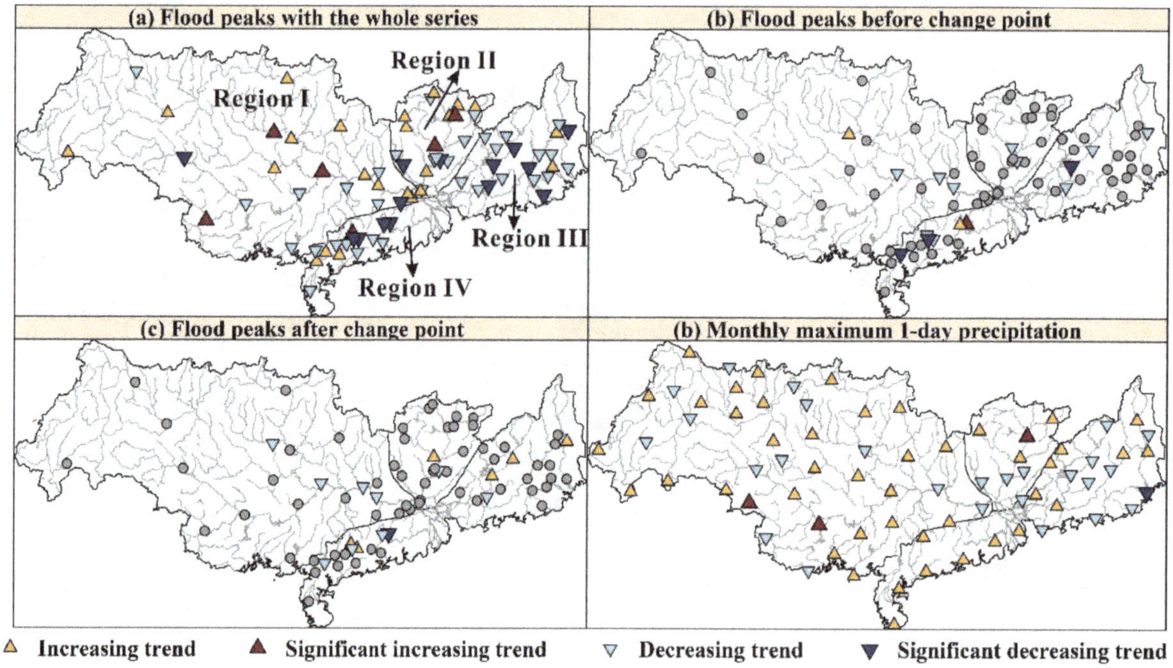

Figure 4. Trends in **(a)** flood peaks with the whole series, **(b)** flood peaks before the change point, **(c)** flood peaks after the change point, and **(d)** precipitation extremes. The gray dots in **(b)** and **(c)** indicate the stations without a change point.

and particularly in the lower Pearl River basin (Zhang et al., 2012). Results of change points of precipitation maxima by Zhang et al. (2009) indicated that precipitation maxima were dominated by significant change points during 1980–1993, and significant change points of peak flood flow series detected in this study were during 1986–1995, showing significant impacts of precipitation extremes on flooding. These results showed that significant change points of flood processes were found mainly in the middle Pearl River basin and particularly in the lower Pearl River basin. In addition, human impacts on flood processes cannot be ignored, and this is particularly the case for the East River basin (Zhang et al., 2015c), where three large water reservoirs were built that controlled 11 700 km^2 of drainage area.

Significant increasing peak flood flow was observed mainly in the northeastern West River basin, the mainstream of the Pearl River basin, the northern North River basin, the southeastern West River basin, and the southern North River. Significant decreasing peak flood flow was observed mainly in the southeastern West River, the southern North River basin, and also parts of rivers along the coastal regions of the lower Pearl River basin (Fig. 4a). Most stations show decreases in flood peaks both before and after the change point, especially in regions I and IV (Fig. 4b, c). However, the flood peaks in region III changed from a decreasing trend before the change point to an increasing trend after the change point, suggesting shifted and/or modified physical mechanisms behind flood generation processes. Significant increasing precipitation extremes were found in the northeastern West River basin and the northern North River basin, and significant decreasing precipitation extremes were detected in the East River basin. Hence, spatial patterns of peak flood flow matched those of precipitation extremes (Fig. 4a, d), implying that floods in these regions were impacted mainly by precipitation extremes. The southeastern West River basin and rivers in the west parts of region III were dominated by significant increasing precipitation extremes but significant decreasing peak flood flow (Fig. 4). Human activities exerted considerable impacts on flood processes in these regions. Cropland in the Guangxi Province was found mainly in the southeastern Jiangxi Province (Fig. 1b), and irrigated cropland showed a significant increase (Zhang et al., 2015b). The volume of water withdrawal for agricultural irrigation during 2014 only reached $2.09 \times 1^{10}\,m^3$. Meanwhile, the total water storage capacity of water reservoirs of the Guangxi Province reached $6.74 \times 10^{10}\,m^3$, and more than half of the reservoirs were built in the southeastern West River basin (Fig. 1b). The western parts of the region III were also dominated by croplands and large-scale reservoirs (Fig. 1b), agricultural water consumption reached $2.24 \times 10^{10}\,m^3$, and the total storage capacity of reservoirs reached $4.48 \times 10^{10}\,m^3$ during 2014. These human activities greatly decreased peak flood flow volume in these regions. Therefore, increasing human impacts on flood processes should attract considerable concern for the management of water resources and mitigation of flood hazards (Zhang et al., 2015a).

To determine trends of peak flood flow during specific time intervals, multi-scale trend analysis was done (Fig. 5). Trends

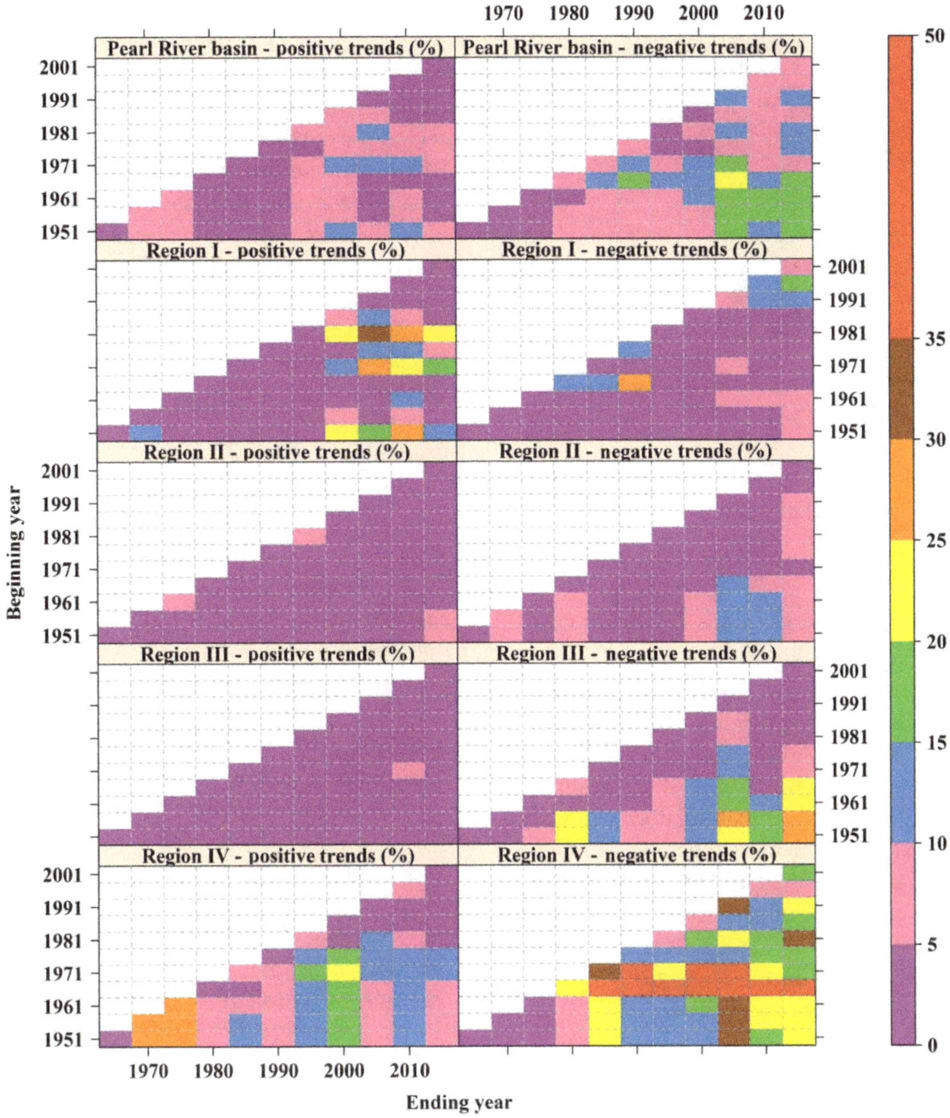

Figure 5. Percentage of stations with significant trends in peak flood flow.

were identified by changing the time interval by shifting the beginning and ending time of the interval by a time step of 5 years. The shortest time interval was 15 years to ensure the validity of statistical analysis. The percentages of stations with significant trends were also analyzed (Fig. 5). The percentage of stations with significant trends in almost all time intervals was relatively low, being about 15 % and even lower. However, stations with significant decreasing trends of peak flood flow during 1966–2005 accounted for 20–25 % of the total stations considered in the study (Fig. 5). Significant increasing peak flood flow was identified during 1981–2010 in the West River basin, and stations with significant increasing peak flood flow during 1981–2010 accounted for 25–35 % of the total stations. Stations with significant decreasing peak flood flow during 1966–1990 accounted for 25–30 % of the total stations (Fig. 5). Peak flows in the North River basin had moderate changes without statistically detectable trends (Fig. 5). Significant decreasing peak flood flow can be observed at the stations in the East River basin or eastern parts of the region III, and stations with significant decreasing peak flood flow during 1951–1980 and 1951–2014 accounted for 20–25 and 25–30 % of the total stations (Fig. 5). Stations with significant decreasing peak flood flow were fewer in number after 1981 (Fig. 5), implying amplified flood regimes after 1981 in the eastern parts of the region III. Larger changing variability of peak flood flow in the western parts of the region III was observed. Stations with significant increasing peak flood flow during 1951–1975 accounted for 30–35 %, and fewer stations were characterized by significant increasing peak flood flow after 1966. Peak flood flow after 1966 turned out to be significantly decreasing (Fig. 5); stations

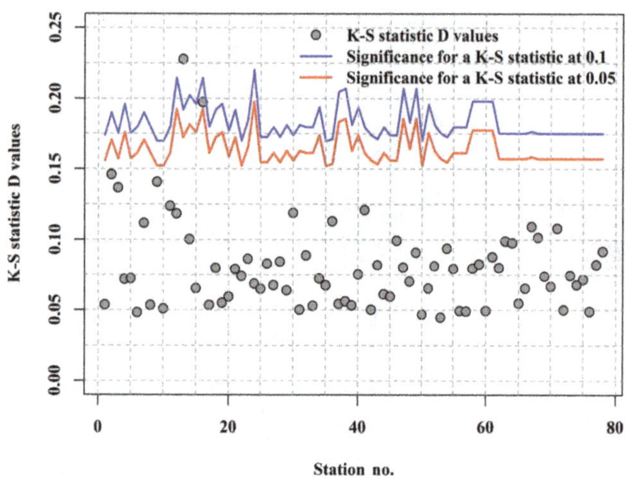

Figure 6. K–S test results of performance of GEV fitting of peak flood flow of the Pearl River basin.

with significant decreasing peak flood flow accounted for 35–50 % of the total stations.

The detailed information of flood events that occurred in the past 60 years can be used to verify the observed results in Fig. 5. For example, we observed significant increasing peak flood flow during 1981–2010 in the West River basin. The recorded flood events also showed that the floods with high magnitude intensively occurred in this period (i.e., 1981–2010). During 20 years from 1981 to 2000 only, the West River basin was hit by five floods with return periods larger than 20 years: (1) a flood during 18–23 June 1983, which caused 147 deaths; (2) a flood during 21 August–September 1988, which caused 58 deaths; (3) a flood during 12–17 June 1994, which caused 224 deaths; (4) a flood during 16–19 July 1996, which caused 252 deaths; and (5) a flood during 16–26 June 1998, which caused 81 deaths.

4.2 GEV-based flood frequency

The GEV model was used to fit peak flood flow series (i.e., annual maxima of period of 1951–2014) and the Kolmogorov–Smirnov (K–S) statistic D was used to evaluate the goodness of fit of GEV-based fitting performance (Fig. 6). Figure 6 indicated that peak flood flow series at almost all stations, except two stations, was well modeled by the GEV at 0.05 significance level. The peak flood flow series at these two stations were also modeled by the GEV at the 0.1 significance level. Therefore, the GEV was used for flood frequency analysis across the Pearl River basin. Return periods of floods at all hydrological stations were estimated and spatial patterns were also characterized across the basin. It can be observed from Fig. 7 that floods of > 10-year flood magnitude occurred with high frequency. However, large floods occurred in a clustering manner at the annual timescale. About 40 % of the total number of the three largest flood events of all stations occurred during two time intervals, i.e., 1965–1970 and 1993–2002 (i.e., 90 of total 236) (Fig. 7). This is particularly true of region I, where 38 out of 66 three largest floods occurred at 22 stations during these two time intervals (region I in Fig. 7). There was no temporal clustering observed for the three largest floods that occurred in the North River basin, but the spatial concentration was identified (region II in Fig. 7). Taking the great floods that occurred during May 1982 across the entire North River basin as an example, flood events > 10-year floods were observed at 9 out of 20 stations, and the largest three floods measured were observed at 7 stations.

The survey of floods across the West and North River basins indicated that higher probability was expected for the simultaneous occurrence of floods in both North and West River basins. For example, 1994 was a serious flooding year and floods that occurred in the West River basin at 11 stations were larger than 10-year floods and 7 out of 11 stations were dominated by the largest three floods of the recorded floods. Meanwhile, peak flood flows at 8 stations in the North River basin were larger than 10-year flood and 6 out of 8 stations were dominated by the three largest floods recorded. The occurrence of large floods in the east parts of region III was evidently uneven in time and the measured largest three floods occurred mainly during 1958–1969, and decreased occurrence rates were observed for large floods after 2005. However, floods > 10-year floods were amplified after 2005. The occurrence of large floods in the eastern parts of region III was also subject to spatial clustering, and floods > 10-year floods were usually observed at numerous stations at the same time (region III in Fig. 7). Moreover, large floods occurred in a clustering manner during 1966–1974 and occurrence rates of large floods after 1980 exhibited moderate changes (region IV in Fig. 7).

The percentage of stations with flood regimes > 10-year floods to the total stations for each region was counted and trends were evaluated by the 11-year moving average method (Fig. 8), with the aim to determine the occurrences of large floods in both space and time. It can be seen from Fig. 8a that the percentage of stations dominated by the occurrence of large floods in West River basin had moderate changes with a slight increasing tendency (Fig. 8a), and particularly after 1990. The percentage of stations dominated by the occurrence of large floods had an increasing tendency, and this increasing tendency was maintained during the entire time interval considered in this study (Fig. 8b). The percentage of stations with the occurrence of large floods followed similar changing patterns, i.e., increase and then decrease, implying enhanced risks of floods across the entire region (Fig. 8c ,d).

4.3 Flood risks based on historical flood records

Based on historical flood records, the occurrence rates of floods during the past 1000 years in the Guangdong and Guangxi provinces were analyzed, and a local polynomial regression fitting technique was used to smooth the series. It

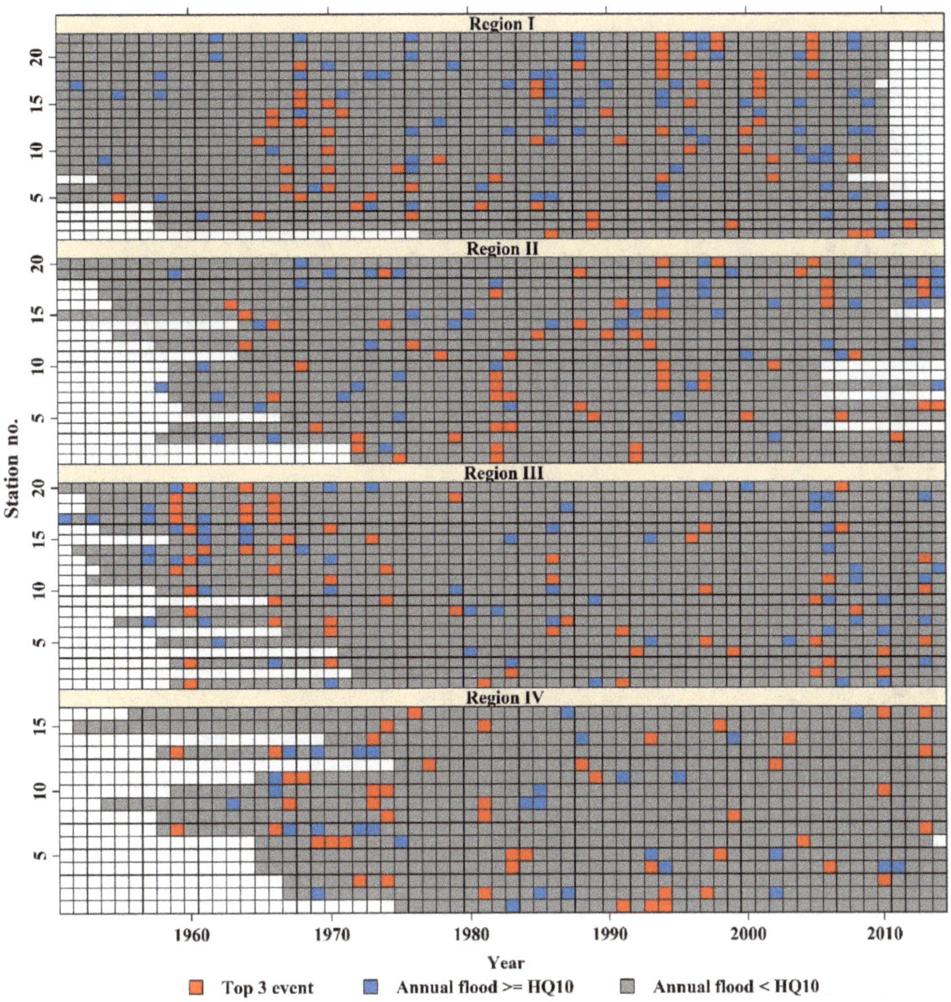

Figure 7. GEV-model-based estimated return periods of peak flood flow at hydrological stations considered in this study across the Pearl River basin.

can be observed from Fig. 9a that the occurrences of floods had increasing trends before AD 1600 and reached the peak value in about AD 1600 in Guangdong Province. The occurrences of floods had moderate variations during 1600–1900 with moderate variability. These results will be further evaluated using the kernel density estimation method in the next section. However, the occurrence of floods in Guangxi Province told another story when compared to those in Guangdong Province (Fig. 9b). A moderate increasing tendency of occurrence rates of floods was observed before 1800 AD and the time interval after AD 1800 witnessed abruptly elevating occurrence rates of floods, and this is particularly the case during the past 100 years, i.e., 1900–2000 (Fig. 9b).

Basin-scale hazardous flood events were identified based on the flood criterion defined by Mudelsee et al. (2003, 2004). Meanwhile, flood risks of the past 1000 years were evaluated using the kernel estimation method (Fig. 10). The width of the time window was 56 years and 41 years for hazardous floods in the Guangdong and Guangxi provinces based on the cross-validation method (Fig. 10b, d). Moreover, the time window of 30 years was used to have a closer look at the occurrence rates of hazardous floods (Fig. 10a, c). It can be seen from Fig. 10 that hazardous floods had an increasing tendency in general, except the time interval of 1400–1800, which was characterized by decreasing occurrence rates. The past 200 years witnessed a sharp amplification of floods in the Guangxi and Guangdong provinces. Significant amplification of floods in the middle and lower Pearl River basin, and particularly in the past 200 years, should attract considerable concern.

Because the period of the past 60 years is a segment in the past 1000 years, analyzing the historical flood records is beneficial for understanding the changes in flooding during the past 60 years. For example, we observed increasing trends in floods in region I (most parts in Guangxi Province) during the past 60 years. Actually, basin-scale hazardous flood events have shown a sharp amplification in the past 200 years in Guangxi Province. As we all know, the influences of hu-

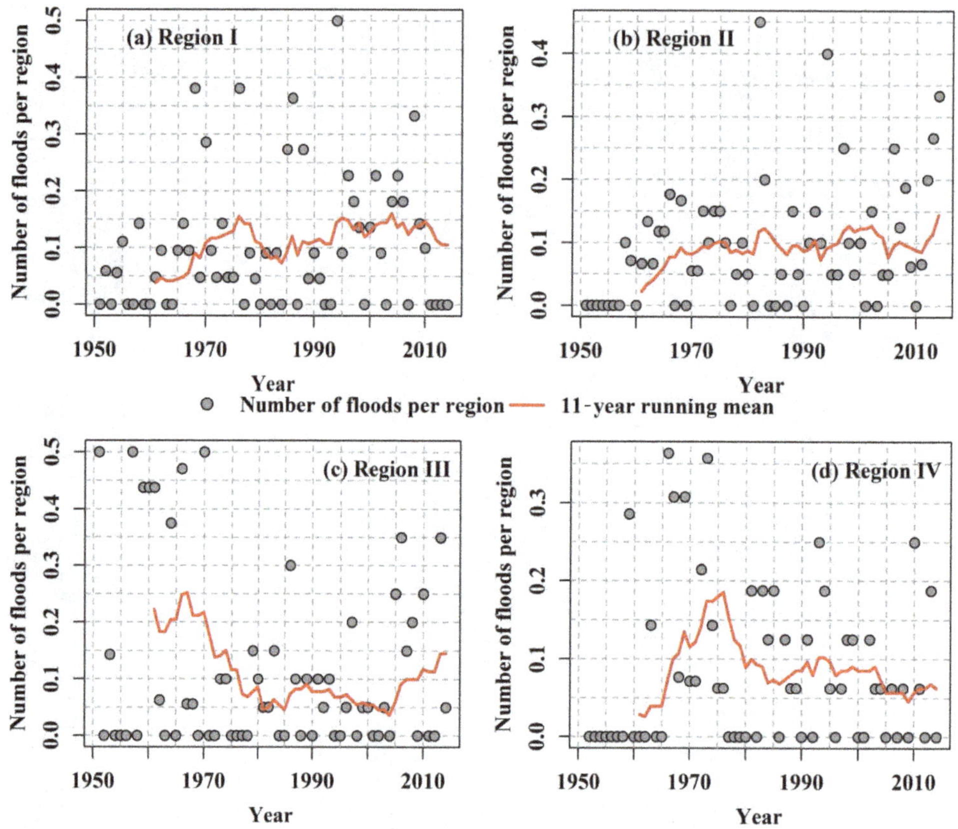

Figure 8. Temporal changes of percentage of stations with flood events of magnitude of > 10-year flood magnitude.

man activities on flood generations are considerable smaller in the past 200 years (except for the past 60 years) than in the past 60 years and are even neglected. However, human-induced climate change has enhanced continually in the past 200 years when the world experienced the industrial revolution. Therefore, the increasing flooding in the past 60 years, beginning in the past 200 years in Guangxi Province, is very likely caused by climate change.

5 Discussions

Change points and trends analyses showed that only a few stations showed a change point or significant trend in the flood peaks. In other words, the flood peaks are stationary in most of the stations considered in this study. Our previous study has also detected the trends in flood peaks before and after the change points, indicating that no significant trends have been found (e.g., Zhang et al., 2014). Taking change points in the West River as an example, change points of flood peaks in the mainstream of the West River occurred in approximately 1990 in spite of a few differences. The flood peaks of the West River basin are heavily influenced by the confluences of tributaries on the upstream of the West River, and the factors causing abrupt changes in the mean are complicated and unclear. The influence of hydraulic facilities is considerable. However, after the 1990s a few hydraulic facilities were constructed and their influence can be ignored. Analysis of precipitation extremes in the Pearl River basin indicated that the amount of rainfall changed little but its variability increased over the time interval divided by change points. Abrupt changes of precipitation maxima shifted in different seasons. However, change points of precipitation maxima in summer occurred in 1990, 1988, and 1991, which are in line with changes points of flood peaks of the West River basin. It should be noted that floods mainly occur during the summer season. Therefore, it can be tentatively stated that abrupt changes of flood peaks of the West River basin are mainly the result of abrupt behavior of precipitation maxima. However, due to spatiotemporal patterns of precipitation maxima in the Pearl River basin and the production and confluence of flood streamflow, the abrupt behavior of flood peaks usually does not match that of precipitation maxima. Moreover, human interference also introduces considerable uncertainty and causes obscure relations between abrupt changes of flood peaks and precipitation maxima. This analysis implies abrupt changes of flood peaks due to various influencing factors.

The Guangdong Province is dominated by high urbanization, a highly developed socio-economy, and a high popula-

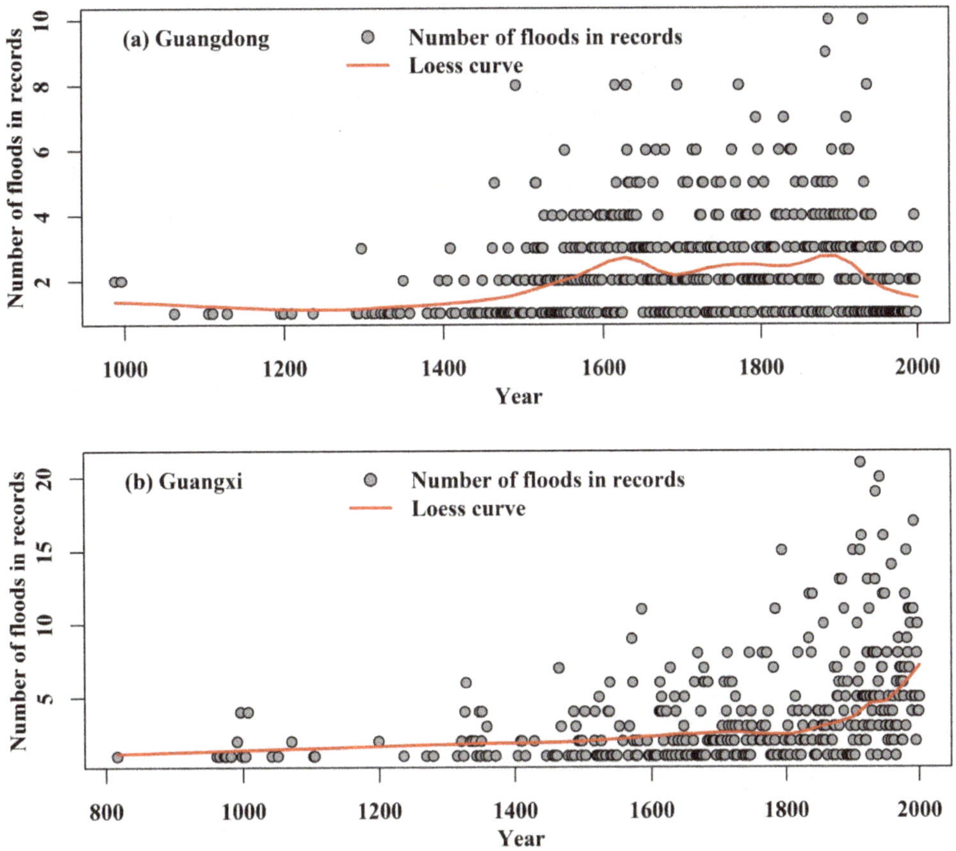

Figure 9. Temporal changes in occurrence rates of flood hazards of the past 1000 years in Guangdong **(a)** and Guangxi provinces **(b)**.

tion density, and this is particularly the case for the PRD region (Fig. 1b, c, and d). Intense human activities, such as in-channel sand dredging, building of levees, and fast urbanization, have greatly altered physical and geographical features of underlying surfaces and hence modified the flooding processes. The volume of sand dredged during the 1990s in the North and East River basins was, respectively, 3.38×10^6 and 1.50×10^6 m^3 year^{-1}, causing deepening of the river channel (e.g., Luo et al., 2007). Massive building of levees and simplification of river channel systems have caused widespread gathering of floodwaters and hence amplification of floods.

Taking the PRD as an example, during the past 60 years, more than 20 000 levees were combined with 400 levees, and the length of river channel was reduced from 10 000 to 5000 km. In addition, the construction of large-scale reservoirs greatly reduced the occurrence rates and magnitude of floods (Fig. 11a, b and c). However, fast and massive urbanization, such as the urbanization rate of the Guangdong Province reaching 67.67 %, caused fast production of floods and hence enhanced flood risk (Fig. 10a). Increasing flood magnitudes in the past 60 years (Fig. 3a) and increasing occurrence rates of floods in the past 100 years (Fig. 9b) caused increased losses of agricultural production and increased numbers of casualties (Fig. 11c, d, and f). However, when compared to Guangdong Province, Guangxi Province was dominated by lower urbanization and a lower population density (Fig. 1d); human activities did not exert significant impacts on floods. Increasing precipitation extremes and particularly increasing precipitation concentration (Zhang et al., 2012, 2013) triggered discernable amplification of floods in the Guangxi Province. Therefore, the past 200 years also witnessed the intensification of hazardous floods, which undoubtedly posed a challenge for the mitigation of flood hazards in the lower Pearl River basin, particularly the PRD region. Although the fluvial disastrous floods may be ignored in earlier time periods, the increases in the number of extreme floods are significant and sharp. The lack of reported flood events in earlier years may be one of the reasons for these sharp increases. However, we think it is not enough to explain this. Taking Guangxi Province as an example, the significant increase is continual, especially for the past 200 years (Fig. 9b). In the past 200 years, the lack of reported extreme floods did not make so much difference and the number of floods was still significantly increasing. When researchers try to use historical flood records, the lack of reported flood events is the problem that all users must face; it was not only a problem for us but also for Mudelsee et al. (2003). In addition, the time span is larger, the problem is more difficult

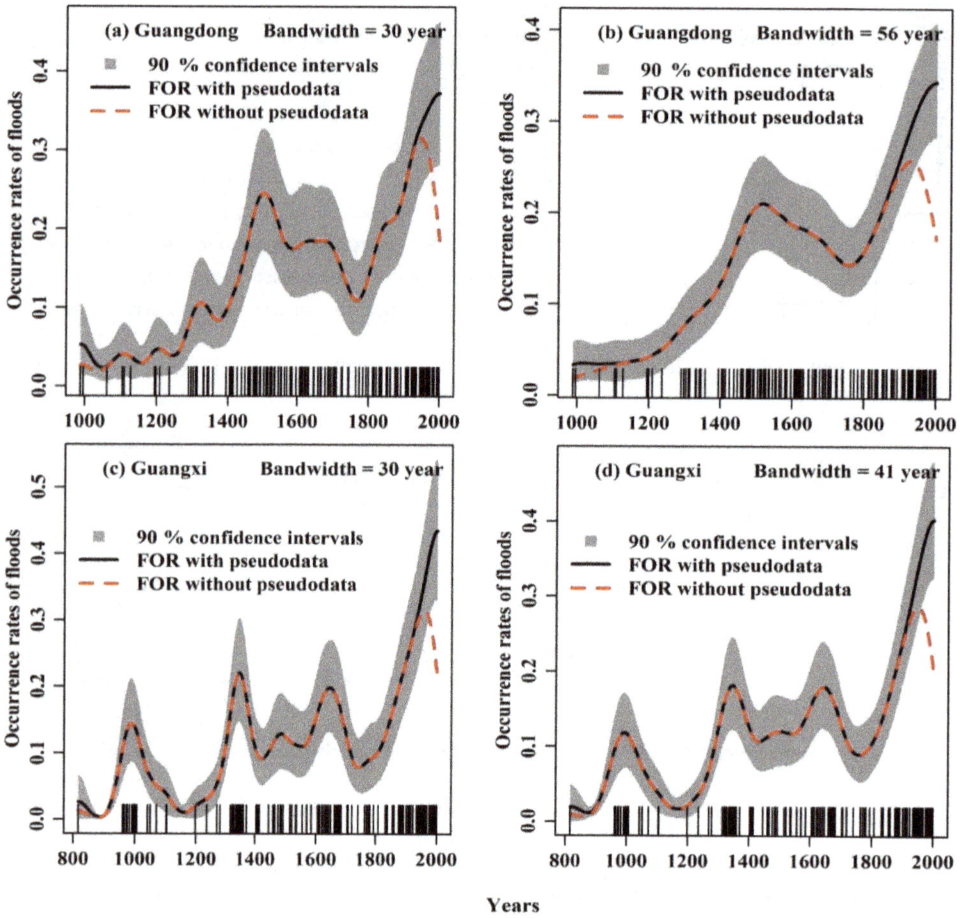

Figure 10. Temporal variations of frequency of flood hazards during the past 1000 years in Guangdong and Guangxi provinces.

to solve. Nevertheless, historical flood information can definitely provide valuable information to improve our understanding of the changes in flood frequency.

6 Conclusions

Evaluation of flood risks was done in both space and time across the Pearl River basin, China, based on peak flood flow data from 78 hydrological stations during the period of 1951–2014 and 1000-year flood hazard records. The following conclusions can be drawn from this study.

No statistically significant changes can be detected in the peak flood flow series at most of the stations, but significant changes were observed at 16 out of 78 stations. Stations with significant peak flood flow changes were found in the mainstream of the West River basin, the East River basin, and rivers in the western parts of the coastal regions, and the change points were mainly during the 1990s. Abrupt changes of peak flood flow in the West River basin were attributed to the abrupt behavior of precipitation extremes. The construction of large-scale hydraulic facilities and reservoirs was the major cause behind abrupt behavior of peak flood flow in the coastal regions.

The northern parts and mainstream of the West River basin and northern North River basin were dominated by significant increasing peak flood flow, implying amplification of floods. Peak flood flow in the East River basin however had significant decreasing trends which were attributed to the changes in precipitation extremes. It should be emphasized that precipitation extremes were increasing in the southeastern West River basin and western parts of the coastal regions, and peak flood flow in these regions was decreasing. Expanding agricultural irrigation and hydrological regulation of reservoirs were the causes of decreasing peak flood flow in these regions. A closer look at the abrupt behavior of peak flood flow indicated that significant increasing peak flood flow was identified during 1981–2010 at 25–35 % of the stations in the West River basin; significant decreasing peak flood flow was observed during 1951–2014 at 25–30 % of the stations in the East River basin; and 30–35 % of the stations in the western parts of the coastal region were dominated by significant increasing peak flood flow during 1951–1975,

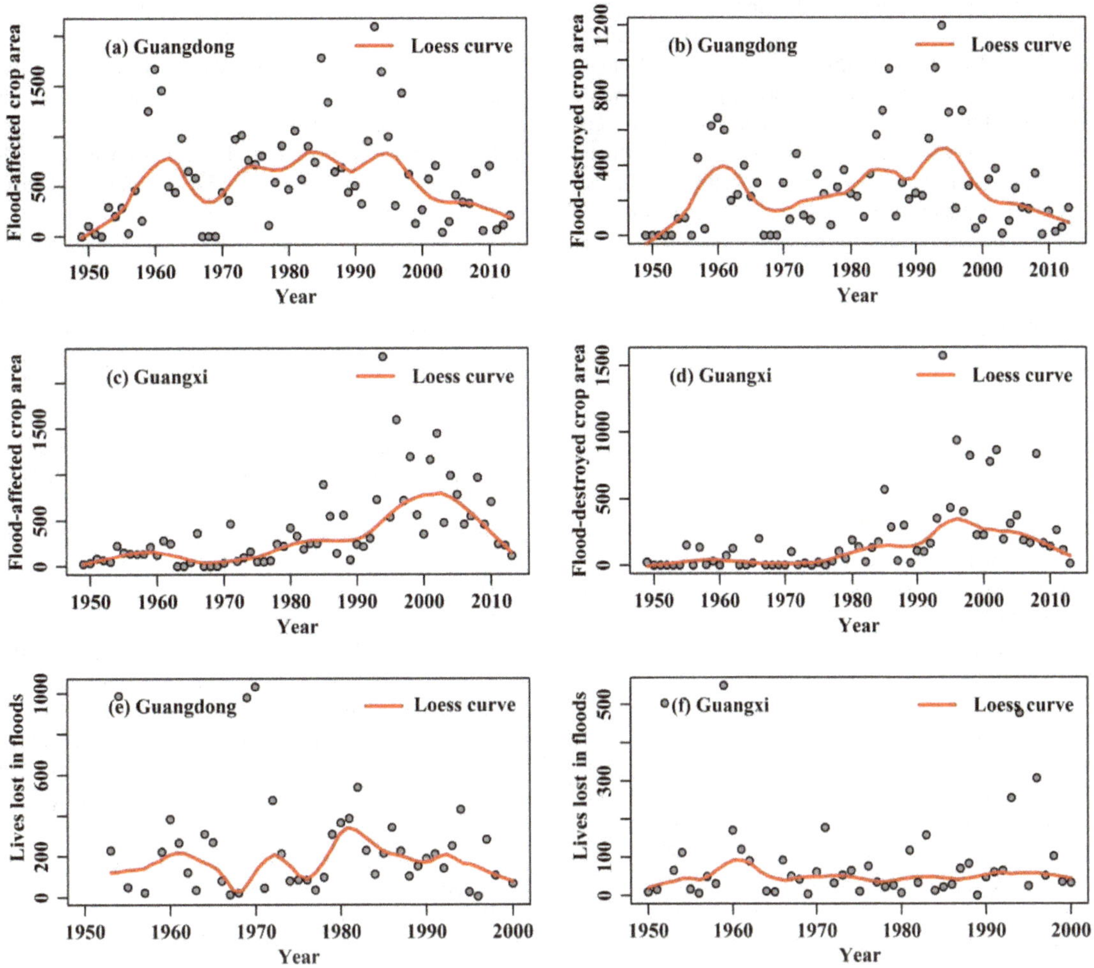

Figure 11. Temporal changes of flood-hazard-induced crop areas and mortality in Guangdong and Guangxi provinces.

and 35–50 % of the stations were dominated by significant decreasing peak flood flow.

The largest three flood events were concentrated during two time intervals, i.e., 1965–1970 and 1993–2002. The percentage of stations characterized by floods > 10-year floods increased after 1975. The East River basin was dominated by the concentrated occurrence of the three largest flood events during 1958–1969, and the percentage of stations with floods > 10-year floods increased after 2000. Results indicated temporal and spatial clustering of flood hazards. This point should attract considerable concern for the mitigation to flood hazards.

Historical flood records of the past 1000 years have told an interesting story about flood risks in basin-scale hazardous flood events from a long-term perspective. Flood risks of the middle and lower Pearl River basin were enhanced, and this is particularly the case in the past 100 years. Particularly, the flood risks in the middle and lower Pearl River basin in terms of disastrous flood regimes increased, posing serious challenges for the mitigation of flood hazards in the PRD region.

Data availability. The annual largest 1-day streamflow data (i.e., annual maxima) were collected from the Water Conservancy Bureau of the Pearl River Water Conservancy Commission. These datasets are not publicly accessible due to governmental restrictions, but can be obtained by writing to the corresponding authors. Daily precipitation data were provided by the National Climate Center, China, which can be publicly accessed at http://data.cma.cn/ (last access: 23 April 2018). The information from historical flood records was collected from two books, i.e., Collections of meteorological hazards in China: Guangdong volume and Guangxi volume (Wen and Song, 2006; Wen and Yang, 2007). Both of these books have been published in public.

Competing interests. The authors declare that they have no conflict of interest.

Acknowledgements. This work is financially supported by the Fund for the National Natural Science Foundation of China (grant no. 41771536), the National Science Foundation for Distinguished Young Scholars of China (grant no. 51425903), the Creative

Research Groups of the National Natural Science Foundation of China (41621061), and the Fundamental Research Funds for the Central Universities, China University of Geosciences (Wuhan) (grant no. CUG180614). In addition, our cordial gratitude should be extended to the editor, Fuqiang Tian, two anonymous reviewers, and Natascha Töpfer as well for their professional and pertinent comments and suggestions, which were greatly helpful for further quality improvement of this manuscript. Detailed information such as data can be obtained by writing to the corresponding author at zhangq68@mail.sysu.edu.cn.

Edited by: Fuqiang Tian

References

Alan, D. Z., Justin, S., Edwin, P. M., Bart, N., Eric, F. W., and Dennisa, P. L.: Detection of intensification in global- and continental-scale hydrological cycles: Temporal scale of evaluation, J. Climate, 16, 535–547, 2003.

Beniston, M. and Stephenson, D. B.: Extreme climatic events and their evolution under changing climatic conditions, Global Planet. Change, 44, 1–9, 2004.

Beniston, M., Stephenson, D. B., Christensen, O. B., Ferro, C. A. T., Frei, C., Goyette, S., Halsnaes, K., Holt, T., Jylhä, K., Koffi, B., Palutikof, J., Schöll, R., Semmler, T., and Woth, K.: Future extreme events in European climate: an exploration of regional climate model projections, Climatic Change, 81, 71–95, 2007.

Bouwer, L. and Vellinga, P.: Changing climate and increasing costs-implications for liability and insurance climatic change: implications for the hydrological cycle and for water management, edited by: Beniston, M., Springer, Netherlands, 429–444, 2003.

Burn, D. H. and Whitfield, P. H.: Changes in floods and flood regimes in Canada, Can. Water Resour. J., 1784, 1–12, 2015.

Cannon, A. J.: A flexible nonlinear modelling framework for nonstationary generalized extreme value analysis in hydroclimatology, Hydrol. Process., 24, 673–685, 2010.

Chen, Y. D., Zhang, Q., Xu, C.-Y., and Yang, T.: Change-point alterations of extreme water levels and underlying causes in Pearl River Delta, China, River Res. Appl., 25, 1153–1168, 2009.

Das, T., Maurer, E. P., Pierce, D. W., Dettinger, M. D., and Cayan, D. R.: Increases in flood magnitudes in California under warming climates, J. Hydrol., 501, 101–110, 2013.

Daufresne, M., Lengfellner, K., and Sommer, U.: Global warming benefits the small in aquatic ecosystems, P. Natl. Acad. Sci. USA, 106, 12788–12793, 2009.

Hamed, H. K. and Rao, R. A.: A modified Mann-Kendall trend test for autocorrelated data, J. Hydrol., 204, 182–196, 1998.

Gu, X., Zhang, Q., Singh, V. P., and Liu, L.: Nonstationarity in the occurrence rate of floods in the Tarim River basin, China, and related impacts of climate indices, Global Planet. Change, 142, 1–13, 2016.

Hall, J., Arheimer, B., Borga, M., Brázdil, R., Claps, P., Kiss, A., Kjeldsen, T. R., Kriauciuniene, J., Kundzewicz, Z. W., Lang, M., Llasat, M. C., Macdonald, N., McIntyre, N., Mediero, L., Merz, B., Merz, R., Molnar, P., Montanari, A., Neuhold, C., Parajka, J., Perdigão, R. A. P., Plavcová, L., Rogger, M., Salinas, J. L., Sauquet, E., Schär, C., Szolgay, J., Viglione, A., and Blöschl, G.: Understanding flood regime changes in Europe: a state-of-the-art assessment, Hydrol. Earth Syst. Sci., 18, 2735–2772, https://doi.org/10.5194/hess-18-2735-2014, 2014.

Hirsch, M. R. and Archfield, S. A.: Not higher but more often, Nat. Clim. Change, 5, 198–199, 2015.

IPCC: Climate change: The physical science basis, United Kingdom and New York, NY, USA, Cambridge University Press, 2007.

IPCC: Summary for policymakers, in: The Physical Science Basis, Contribution of Working Group I to the Fifth Assessment Report of the Intergovernmental Panel on Climate Change, edited by: Stocker, T. F., Qin, D., Plattner, G.-K., Tignor, M., Allen, S. K., Boschung, J., Nauels, A., Xia, Y., Bex, V., Midgley, P. M., Cambridge University Press, 2013.

Jena, P. P., Chatterjee, C., Pradhan, G., and Mishra, A.: Are recent frequent high floods in Mahanadi basin in eastern India due to increase in extreme rainfalls?, J. Hydrol., 517, 847–862, 2014.

Kjeldsen, T. R., Macdonald, N., Lang, M., Mediero, L., Albuquerque, T., Bogdanowicz, E., Brazdil, R., Castellarin, A., David, V., Fleig, A., Gul, G. O., Kriauciuniene, J., Kohnova, S., Merz, B., Nicholson, O., Roald, L. A., Salinas, J. L., Sarauskiene, D., Šraj, M., Strupczewski, W., Szolgay, J., Toumazis, A., Vanneuville, W., Veijalainen, N., and Wilson, D.: Documentary evidence of past floods in Europe and their utility in flood frequency estimation, J. Hydrol., 517, 963–973, 2014.

Li, J., Chen,Y. D., Zhang, L., Zhang, Q., and Chiew, F. H. S.: Future changes in floods and water availability across China: Linkage with changing climate and uncertainties, J. Hydrometeorol., 17, 1295–1314, 2016.

Luo, X. L., Zeng, E. Y., Ji, R. Y., and Wang, C. P.: Effects of in-channel sand excavation on the hydrology of the Pearl River Delta, China, J. Hydrol., 343, 230–239, 2007.

Mudelsee, M., Börngen, M., Tetzlaff, G., and Grünewald, U.: No upward trends in the occurrence of extreme floods in central Europe, Nature, 425, 166–169, 2003.

Mudelsee, M., Börngen, M., Tetzlaff, G., and Grünewald, U.: Extreme floods in central Europe over the past 500 years: Role of cyclone pathway "Zugstrasse Vb", J. Geophys. Res., 109, D23101, https://doi.org/10.1029/2004JD005034, 2004.

Nicholls, N.: Long-term climate monitoring and extreme events, Climatic Change, 31, 231–245, 1995.

Ohmura, A. and Wild, M.: Is the hydrological cycle accelerating?, Science, 298, 1345–1346, 2002.

Pettitt, A. N.: A non-parametric approach to the change-point problem, Appl. Stat., 28, 126–135, 1979.

Pino, D., Ruiz-Bellet, J. L., Balasch, J. C., Romero-León, L., Tuset,J., Barriendos, M., Mazon, J., and Castelltort, X.: Meteorological and hydrological analysis of major floods in NE Iberian Peninsula, J. Hydrol., 541, 63–89, 2016.

PRWRC (Pearl River Water Resources Committee): The Zhujiang Archive, vol 1, Guangdong Science and Technology Press, Guangzhou, 1991 (in Chinese).

Villarini, G., Serinaldi, F., Smith, A. J., and Krajewski, F. W.: On the stationarity of annual flood peaks in the continental United States during the 20th century, Water Resour. Res., 45, W08417, https://doi.org/10.1029/2008WR007645, 2009.

Vormoor, K., Lawrence, D., Schlichting, L., Wilson, D., and Wong, W. K.: Evidence for changes in the magnitude and frequency of observed rainfall vs. snowmelt driven floods in Norway, J. Hydrol., 538, 33–48, 2016.

Wen, K. and Song, L.: Collections of meteorological hazards in China-Guangdong version, Beijing, Meteorological Press, 2006.

Wen, K. and Yang, N.: Collections of meteorological hazards in China-Guangxi version, Beijing, Meteorological Press, 2007.

Zhang, Q., Xu, C.-Y., Becker, S., Zhang, Z. X., Chen, Y. D., and Coulibaly, M.: Trends and abrupt changes of precipitation maxima in the Pearl River basin, China, Atmos. Sci. Let., 10, 132–144, 2009.

Zhang, Q., Singh, V. P., Li, J., and Chen, X.: Analysis of the periods of maximum consecutive wet days in China, J. Geophys. Res., 116, D23106, https://doi.org/10.1029/2011JD016088, 2011.

Zhang, Q., Singh, V. P., Peng, J., Chen, Y. D., and Li, J.: Spatial-temporal changes of precipitation structure across the Pearl River basin, China, J. Hydrol., 440–441, 113–122, 2012.

Zhang, Q., Li, J., Singh, V. P., and Xiao, M.: Spatio-temporal relations between temperature and precipitation regimes: implications for temperature-induced changes in the hydrological cycle, Global Planet. Change, 111, 57–76, 2013.

Zhang Q., Gu X., Singh V. P., Xiao M., and Xu C.-Y.: Stationarity of annual flood peaks during 1951–2010 in the Pearl Riverbasin, China, J. Hydrol., 519, 3263–3274, 2014.

Zhang, Q., Gu, X., Singh, V. P., Xu, C.-Y., Kong, D., Xiao, M., and Chen, X.: Homogenization of precipitation and flow regimes across China: changing properties, causes and implications, J. Hydrol., 530, 462–475, 2015a.

Zhang, Q., Gu, X., Singh, V. P., Kong, D., and Chen, X.: Spatiotemporal behavior of floods and droughts and their impacts on agriculture in China, Global Planet. Change, 131, 63–72, 2015b.

Zhang, Q., Gu, X., Singh, V. P., Xiao, M., and Chen, X.: Evaluation of flood frequency under non-stationarity resulting from climate change and human activities in the East River basin, China, J. Hydrol., 527, 565–575, 2015c.

Zhang, Q., Liu, J., Singh, V. P., Gu, X., and Chen, X.: Evaluation of impacts of climate change and human activities on streamflow in the Poyang Lake basin, China, Hydrol. Process., 30, 2562–2576, 2016.

Zhang, Q., Gu, X., Li, J., Shi, P., and Singh, V. P.: The impact of tropical cyclones on extreme precipitation over coastal and inland areas of China and its association to the ENSO, J. Climate, 31, 1865–1880, https://doi.org/10.1175/JCLI-D-17-0474.1, 2018.

Zolina, O., Kapala, A., Simmer, C., and Gulev, K. S.: Analysis of extreme precipitation over Europe from different reanalysis: a comparative assessment, Global Planet. Change, 44, 129–161, 2004.

6

Assessing downstream flood impacts due to a potential GLOF from Imja Tsho in Nepal

M. A. Somos-Valenzuela[1], **D. C. McKinney**[1], **A. C. Byers**[2], **D. R. Rounce**[1], **C. Portocarrero**[3], **and D. Lamsal**[4]

[1]Center for Research in Water Resources, University of Texas at Austin, Austin, Texas, USA
[2]The Mountain Institute, Washington DC, USA
[3]Independent Consultant, Huaraz, Peru
[4]Graduate School of Environmental Studies, Nagoya University, Japan

Correspondence to: D. C. McKinney (daene@aol.com)

Abstract. Glacial-dominated areas pose unique challenges to downstream communities in adapting to recent and continuing global climate change, including increased threats of glacial lake outburst floods (GLOFs) that can increase risk due to flooding of downstream communities and cause substantial impacts on regional social, environmental and economic systems. The Imja glacial lake (or Imja Tsho) in Nepal, which has the potential to generate a GLOF, was studied using a two-dimensional debris-flow inundation model in order to evaluate the effectiveness of proposed measures to reduce possible flooding impacts to downstream communities by lowering the lake level. The results indicate that only minor flood impact reduction is achieved in the downstream community of Dingboche with modest (~ 3 m) lake lowering. Lowering the lake by 10 m shows a significant reduction in inundated area. However, lowering the lake by 20 m almost eliminates all flood impact at Dingboche. Further downstream at Phakding, the impact of the GLOF is significant and similar reductions in inundation are likely as a result of lake lowering.

1 Introduction

Recent worldwide retreat of glaciers (WGMS, 2013) has been very evident in the Mt. Everest region of Nepal where glacial lakes continue to form and grow, significantly increasing the risk of glacial lake outburst floods (GLOFs) (Bajracharya et al., 2007a; ICIMOD, 2011; Ives et al., 2010; Shrestha and Aryal, 2011). Many of these lakes are considered potentially dangerous (Bajracharya et al., 2007a; Bolch et al., 2008; Watanabe et al., 2009; ICIMOD, 2011); therefore, risk and vulnerability assessments of communities and assets located downstream of glacial lakes in this region have become necessary. Remedial actions have been taken to reduce the risk of GLOFs, in one case at Tsho Rolpa lake (Rana et al., 2000) and another under design at Imja Tsho (or Imja Lake) (UNDP, 2013). In the region near Imja Tsho (Fig. 1), there have been 2 GLOFs in recent decades (Nare in 1977 and Dig Tsho in 1985) resulting in significant damage to farms, villages, trails and some loss of life (Buchroithner et al., 1982; Ives, 1986; Vuichard and Zimmermann, 1986).

Imja Tsho, located in the Khumbu region (27.9° N, 86.9° E; Fig. 1), is a supraglacial lake formed on top of Imja glacier, and it is bounded on the east by the Lhotse Shar and Imja glaciers, on the north and south by lateral moraines, and to the west by a 700 m wide by 700 m long ice-cored terminal moraine complex that has an outlet that drains the lake feeding into the Imja Khola (or Imja River) (Watanabe et al., 2009; Somos-Valenzuela et al., 2013). The lake, which did not exist in 1960, has experienced rapid growth in area and volume; by 2002 it had a volume of 35.8 ± 0.7 million m^3 (Sakai et al., 2007), and by 2012 the volume had increased to 61.7 ± 3.7 million m^3 (Somos-Valenzuela et al., 2014). The western, down-valley expansion has stabilized in recent years, while the eastern expansion continues unabated (Watanabe et al., 2009), mostly through calving from the glacier terminus. Avalanche debris falling from surrounding high mountains and hanging ice is prevented from entering the lake by the high lateral moraines, which are separated

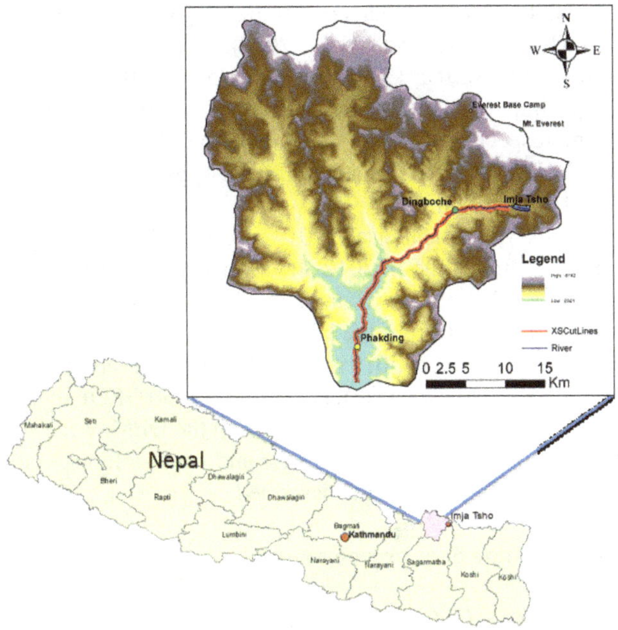

Figure 1. Location of Imja Tsho in the Khumbu region of Nepal.

Figure 2. The village of Dingboche on the Imja Khola showing the river (right) and the relative height from the river course to the arable land and houses (about 22 m).

from the surrounding mountains by several tens of meters (Hambrey et al., 2008). The bottom of the lake has continued to lower as the ice of the glacier beneath the lake melts (Watanabe et al., 1995; Fujita et al., 2009; Somos-Valenzuela et al., 2014).

The characterization of the risk of Imja Tsho is somewhat controversial, with some researchers declaring it to be relatively dangerous (Hammond, 1988; Kattelmann, 2003; Ives et al., 2010), and others concluding that it may be stable (Fujita et al., 2009; Watanabe et al., 2009; ICIMOD, 2011). ICIMOD (2011) identified Imja Tsho as one of six high-priority glacial lakes in Nepal that require detailed investigation, while other studies have stated that Imja Tsho is safe (Fujita et al., 2013) or very low risk (Hambrey et al., 2008). These conflicting classifications are confusing and can be misleading to the general public and communities downstream, who are the stakeholders these studies are meant to assist. Imja Tsho is among six glacial lakes identified in the Nepal National Adaptation Plan of Action (NAPA) as having at the most immediate risk of bursting (MoE, 2010). The United Nations Development Program (UNDP) is implementing the Community Based Flood and Glacial Lake Outburst Risk Reduction Project in an effort to reduce the possible risk to downstream communities posed by the lake. According to the UNDP project strategy (UNDP, 2013), the "GLOF risks arising from Imja Tsho will be significantly reduced by reducing the lake volume through an artificial controlled drainage system combined with a community-based early warning system." They recommend lowering the lake level by at least 3 m to achieve this risk reduction.

Dingboche is probably the most risk prone area from a potential Imja GLOF. The villages of Chukkung (~4 km) and Dingboche (~8 km) are the two nearest settlements from the lake. The former is located relatively off the Imja Khola (stream), so at less risk, whereas the latter is the largest settlement along the stream and it has extensive agricultural lands and buildings within 10–20 m elevation from the stream that will be flooded in the event of a GLOF unless flood prevention measures are taken. Two villages in the path of a potential GLOF from Imja Tsho have been the focus of the work reported here: Dingboche (27°53.563′ N, 86°50.092′ E; 4410 m) about 8 km downstream from the lake and Phakding (27°44.624′ N, 86°42.767′ E; 2569 m) about 33 km below Imja Tsho. Dingboche is a village of about 200 residents with an economy that depends on local agriculture and trekking and climbing tourism. Figure 2 shows the Imja Khola and the relative height from the river course to the arable land and houses (about 22 m above the river). About 34 km downstream of the lake outlet are low-lying portions of the village Phakding, which is a village of about 1500 residents with an economy that depends on local agriculture and trekking tourism. Most of the village is quite high above the river and is not at risk of damage from a GLOF. However, several farms and lodges are quite close to the river. Figure 3 shows the bridge crossing the Dudh Koshi and the relative height from the river course to the Star Lion lodge (about 13 m above the river). Lukla, a gateway to the Everest trekking area, can be excluded from consideration here because of its high location from the current riverbed; therefore, the discussion on the section between the lake and Phakding is appropriate.

In this paper we present a new, two-dimensional debris-flow model for predicting the potential GLOF hazard from Imja Tsho in terms of inundation depth in downstream communities and present a measure of uncertainty in the GLOF inundation predictions. We analyze four scenarios: current lake conditions, and three risk mitigation scenarios with the lake water level lowered 3, 10 or 20 m below the current level. Finally, we discuss possible methods for lowering the lake water level to reduce the GLOF hazard. To the authors' knowledge, this is the first attempt to quantify the impact

Figure 3. Bridge across the Dudh Koshi at the Star Lion Resort near the village of Phakding showing the bridge and the relative height from the river course to the arable land and houses (about 10 to 13 m).

that various flood control alternatives would have on potential GLOF damage in downstream villages.

2 Methodology

2.1 Data

To model the propagation of a GLOF from Imja Tsho to the downstream community of Dingboche, we used two digital elevation models (DEMs) for the Imja Tsho GLOF model: (1) a 5 m × 5 m grid cell DEM of the Imja–Lhotse Shar glacier and the moraine surrounding the lake generated from a 2006 Advanced Land Observing Satellite (ALOS) imagery (Lamsal et al., 2011), and (2) a DEM extending from the lake to just below Dingboche derived using the method of Lamsal et al. (2011). These DEMs provide adequate resolution and terrain data for flooding and inundation modeling; however, they cover only 11 km of the river basin downstream from the lake. Expanded 5 m × 5 m DEM coverage downstream of Dingboche could be produced, but ALOS imagery was not available for this work. Instead, we used a lower resolution DEM for the region downstream of Dingboche to just below the village of Phakding. Initially a 30 m × 30 m resolution DEM was produced from Advanced Space borne Thermal Emission and Reflection Radiometer (ASTER L1) data (Tachikawa, 2011). However, ASTER L1 data has too many unrealistic features, such as many ponds between Imja Tsho and Phakding, that do not exist according to our field observations. Therefore, we decided to use the DEM created from 40 m interval contour topographic maps produced by Bajracharya et al. (2007b). The modeled portion of the river has a length of 38.5 km from the lake outlet to a point 5 km downstream of the village of Phakding.

Roughness coefficients for eight categories of land cover in the basin were assigned using land cover maps derived from 2006 ASTER imagery for the Sagarmatha National park (Bajracharya and Uddin, 2010). These values agreed well with those that Cenderelli and Wohl (2001) calculated for the Imja Khola (0.15 and 0.30 for the riverbed and floodplain, respectively), and values that the FLO-2D manual (FLO-2D, 2012) recommends for the types of land cover found in the basin.

Somos-Valenzuela et al. (2014) conducted a bathymetric survey of Imja Tsho in 2012 and estimated the lake volume was 61.7 ± 3.7 million m^3 and that 34.1 ± 1.08 million m^3 of water could drain from the lake if the lake surface elevation decreases 35 m from 5010 m to 4975 m (the elevation of the valley floor below the lake). For the Imja Tsho GLOF model, the lake bathymetry was combined with the DEM of the surrounding moraines and the glacier and used as input to the moraine dam breach model described below.

2.2 Moraine dam breach model

In order for a GLOF to occur from Imja Tsho, a triggering event is necessary. Such triggers may include slow melting of the ice core within the damming moraine, seepage and piping through the dam and earthquakes (Kattelmann and Watanabe, 1998; Somos-Valenzuela et al., 2013). Other factors that may trigger a GLOF from Imja Tsho include excessive rain and potential blockage of the outlet that may be produced by the ice that has calved at the glacier terminus.

We observed seepage from the base of the southern portion of the damming moraine during five visits to the lake between 2011 and 2014. In September 2013 the seepage was measured using a tape measure and porTable velocity meter (Global Water Flow Probe FP111 turboprop positive displacement sensor with a range of 0.1–6.1 $m\,s^{-1}$ and an accuracy of 0.03048 $m\,s^{-1}$). At the seepage outlet, two sets of measurements were taken and an average flow of 0.005 $m^3\,s^{-1}$ was calculated. In addition, three sets of flow measurements were made at the Imja Tsho outlet (bridge over the Imja Khola) and an average flow of 2.2 $m^3\,s^{-1}$ was calculated.

To model a potential moraine breach initiating a GLOF from Imja Tsho, we use a combination of moraine breach analysis tools. First, the shape, final size and failure time of the breach are estimated from empirical equations. Failure time is the time needed for complete development of the breach from the initial breakthrough to the end of lateral enlargement (Froehlich, 2008). Second, these parameters are used in a Hydrologic Engineering Center – River Analysis System (HEC-RAS) dam breach model (USACE, 2010) to simulate the breach hydrograph, which is then used as input to a 2-D downstream inundation model.

There are a number of empirical dam breach equations in the literature (Wahl, 2010; Westoby et al., 2014). However, the equations developed by Froehlich (1995) were selected for use here because Wahl (2004) found these equations to have the lowest uncertainty among a large number of equa-

Table 1. Moraine parameter values used in the breaching equations.

Parameter	Scenario			
	Current conditions	Lake lowering		
		3 m	10 m	20 m
Moraine height (h_d, m)	35	32	25	15
Breach height (h_b, m)	35	32	25	15
Water height (h_w, m)	35	32	25	15
Water volume above breach invert (V_w, million m^3)	33.5	29.5	22.4	12.5

tions studied. Froehlich's equations (Froehlich, 1995) were used to predict breach width (B, m), failure time (t_f, h) and peak discharge (Q_p, $m^3\,s^{-1}$) are

$$B = 0.1803 k V_w^{0.32} h_b^{0.19}, \tag{1}$$

$$t_f = 0.00254 V_w^{0.53} h_b^{-0.9}, \tag{2}$$

$$Q_p = 0.607 V_w^{0.295} h_w^{1.24}, \tag{3}$$

where the moraine parameters in these equations are the breach height (h_b, m), the drainable water volume (V_w, m^3), the depth of water above the breach invert at the time of failure (h_w, m) and overtopping multiplier k ($k = 1$ for no overtopping, and $k = 1.4$ for overtopping). The values of these parameters are shown in Table 1. The value of V_w in Table 1 was taken from the 2012 bathymetric survey results of Somos-Valenzuela et al. (2014). From a large database of dam breach cases, Wahl (2004) derived equations to calculate upper (P_u) and lower (P_l) bounds for the breach parameters

$$\{P_l, P_u\} = \left\{P_p \cdot 10^{-e-2Se}, P_p \cdot 10^{-\bar{e}+2Se}\right\}, \tag{4}$$

where P_p is the predicted breach parameter value (B, t_f, or Q_p) estimated by Eqs. (1)–(3), e and 2Se are the mean prediction error and the uncertainty band, respectively (Wahl, 2004) (see Table 2).

Froehlich's equations provide estimates of the breaching parameters, but to simulate the downstream inundation, the full hydrograph of the breaching event is needed. To obtain full breach hydrographs (lower, predicted and upper), we use the HEC-RAS dam break model (USACE, 2010) with the breach width (B) and failure time (t_f) calculated from Eqs. (1)–(2). These hydrographs were adjusted to match the peak discharge (Q_p) values estimated from Eq. (3).

2.3 Inundation model

FLO-2D is used to calculate the flooding downstream of Imja Tsho due to a potential GLOF with the breaching hydrograph discussed in the previous section. The model is suitable to simulate the propagation of the debris flow (FLO-2D, 2012), since the effects of sediments and debris have been shown to be very important factors in GLOF events (Osti and Egashira, 2009). Although the geometry of the grid within FLO-2D is two dimensional, the flow is modeled in eight directions and the model solves the one-dimensional Saint Venant equation independently in each direction. The continuity and momentum equations are solved with a central, finite difference method using an explicit time-stepping scheme. The total friction slope can be expressed as (O'Brien et al., 1993; Julien, 2010; FLO-2D, 2012)

$$S_f = S_y + S_v + S_{td} = \frac{\tau_y}{\gamma_m h} + \frac{K \eta \omega}{8 \gamma_m h^2} + \frac{n^2 V^2}{h^{4/3}}, \tag{5}$$

where S_y is the yield slope, S_v is the viscous slope, S_{td} is the turbulent-dispersive slope, τ_y is the Mohr–Coulomb yield stress, γ_m is the specific weight of the sediment mixture, K is a resistance parameter, η is the Bingham dynamic viscosity, V is the depth-averaged velocity and n is the Manning roughness coefficient. Rheological properties, η and τ_γ, are formulated as exponential functions of the sediment volume concentration c_v (Julien and Leon, 2000; Julien, 2010)

$$\eta = \alpha_2 e^{\beta_2 c_v}, \tag{6}$$

$$\tau_\gamma = \alpha_1 e^{\beta_1 c_v}, \tag{7}$$

where α_i and β_i are empirical coefficients defined by laboratory experiment (FLO-2D, 2009). Since we have very limited geological information for the study area, the values recommended by the FLO-2D manual for α_i and β_i are used ($\alpha_1 = 0.0765$, $\beta_1 = 16.9$, $\alpha_2 = 0.0648$ and $\beta_2 = 6.2$). Rickenmann (1999) and Julien and Leon (2000) recommend using a concentration of 50 % as an upper limit for debris flows when no other information is available.

3 Results

The Imja GLOF model described above was used to model four scenarios of a GLOF occurring from Imja Tsho: current lake conditions with the water surface at 5010 m, and three flood mitigation scenarios with the lake water level lowered 3, 10 and 20 m. The flood mitigation scenarios represent possible lake lowering efforts starting with the current UNDP project to lower the lake at least 3 m. In case this scenario does not provide any significant flood reduction downstream at Dingboche, the other scenarios can provide some guidance as to how much more the lake might need to be lowered to achieve reduced risk. It is important to note that no other studies have analyzed the potential benefits of lowering Imja Tsho, and the selection of a preferred lake lowering alternative needs to be based on such an analysis as that presented here.

3.1 Moraine breaching model

3.1.1 Breach parameters

Table 3 shows the results of using Eqs. (1)–(3) and the moraine characteristics in Table 1 to calculate the lower

Table 2. Prediction error and uncertainty bands for the Froehlich breaching equations.

Parameter	Mean prediction error (e)	Uncertainty band ($\pm$ 2Se)
Breach width (B, m)	0.01	±0.39
Failure time (t_f, h)	−0.22	±0.64
Peak discharge (Q_p, $m^3\,s^{-1}$)	−0.04	±0.32

bound, predicted and upper bound values of the breaching parameters (B, t_f, and Q_p). The upper and lower bounds of the breaching parameters were calculated from Eqs. (4)–(5) using the prediction errors and uncertainty bands from Table 2. Lowering the lake level by 3 m does not result in a significant change in the failure time and only a 13.8 % decrease in the peak discharge. However, lowering the level by 10 m has a major impact on peak discharge, reducing it by 58.5 % and further lowering of the level to 20 m reduces the discharge by 73.8 %.

3.1.2 Breach hydrographs

Discharge hydrographs for potential moraine breaches at Imja Tsho were computed using the HEC-RAS dam break module and the lower bound, predicted and upper bound breach parameters under the current conditions scenario (see Table 4). The HEC-RAS hydrograph peak discharges were matched to the peak discharge values in Table 3 by adjusting the failure time within the range shown in the table. The predicted peak discharge is 8394 $m^3\,s^{-1}$ (see Table 4 – Imja Tsho) compared to 8274 $m^3\,s^{-1}$ computed with Froehlich's equation, a difference of 1.4 %. The range of peak discharge (upper minus lower bound) is 14728 $m^3\,s^{-1}$ compared to 14613 $m^3\,s^{-1}$ computed by Froehlich's equation, about 0.8 % difference. These results indicate good agreement between the HEC-RAS computed hydrograph values and the empirical Froehlich equation values.

3.2 Inundation model

The FLO-2D inundation model was used to compute the results of the four potential Imja Tsho GLOF scenarios. The first scenario considers the lake in its current condition with the lake level at 5010 m above mean sea level. Then alternatives with lake levels 3, 10, and 20 m lower than this were considered.

3.2.1 Current conditions scenario

The results (lower bound, expected value, upper bound) of modeling a potential GLOF from Imja Tsho under current conditions are shown in Table 4 and Figs. 4–6 at Dingboche (at the cross section indicated in Fig. 4). Table 4 also shows

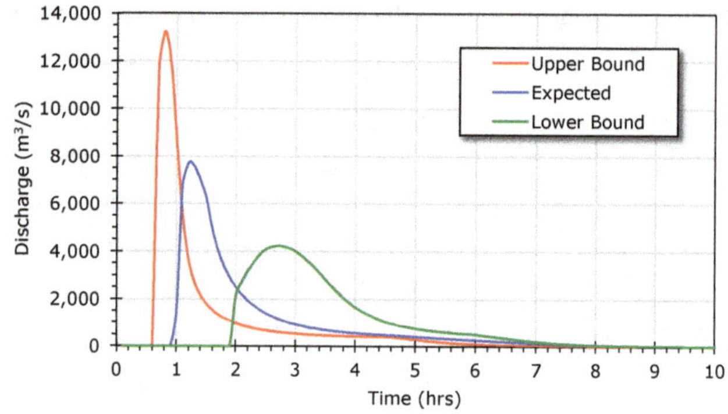

Figure 4. Upper bound, expected and lower bound GLOF hydrograph at Dingboche (cross section shown in Fig. 4) under current lake conditions.

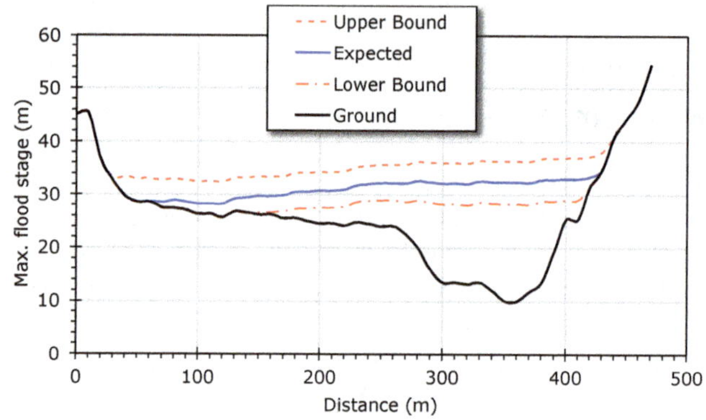

Figure 5. Upper bound, expected and lower bound GLOF flood stage at Dingboche (cross section shown in Fig. 4) under current conditions.

the flood arrival time, peak time, peak stage and flood peak discharge just downstream of Imja Tsho and at Dingboche. Fig. 4 shows the expected GLOF discharge hydrograph and bounds at Dingboche. The flood arrives at Dingboche 1 h after the breaching begins (range 0.6–1.9 h), peaks at 1.3 h (range 0.8–2.8 h) and is over after about 7 h. Figure 5 shows the flood stage at Dingboche (upper bound, expected value, lower bound). The highest expected flood stage is 22.4 m (range 18.4–26.4 m) and the peak flow is 7544 $m^3\,s^{-1}$ (range 4208–13248 $m^3\,s^{-1}$). Figure 6a shows the expected inundation at Dingboche. The lower and upper bounds are also shown in Fig. 6b and c, respectively.

The inundated area at Dingboche was mapped in Geographic Information System (GIS) and shows that, under the expected value simulation, most of the inundation is in the farming terrace areas and not the main lodges and other infrastructure along the primary trekking trail through the village (see Fig. 6a). With no lake lowering, about 9.4 ha of farmland will be inundated and 29 structures impacted (see Table 5, 0 m lowering scenario).

Further downstream at Phakding, the flooding also has an impact on potential flooding. At Phakding, the flood ar-

Table 3. Breach parameter expected values and uncertainty bands for four scenarios.

Scenario	Value type	Breach width B (m)	Failure time t_f (h)	Peak discharge Q_p ($m^3 s^{-1}$)
Current conditions	lower bound	36	0.38	4342
	predicted	91	1.01	8274
	upper bound	218	7.32	18955
Lower 3 m	lower bound	34	0.39	3742
	predicted	86	1.02	7131
	upper bound	206	7.39	16336
Lower 10 m	lower bound	30	0.42	2539
	predicted	75	1.1	4838
	upper bound	180	7.97	11083
Lower 20 m	lower bound	22	0.49	1135
	predicted	56	1.28	2163
	upper bound	134	9.27	4955

Table 4. Inundation model expected values and uncertainty bands at Imja Tsho, Dingboche and Phakding for current lake conditions.

Station	Value	Arrival time (h)	Peak time (h)	Peak discharge ($m^3 s^{-1}$)	Peak stage (m)
Below Imja Tsho	lower bound	0.8	2.3	4272	12.1
	predicted	0.3	1.0	8394	16.6
	upper bound	0.2	0.5	19 000	33.4
Dingboche	lower bound	1.9	2.8	4208	18.4
	predicted	1.0	1.3	7544	22.4
	upper bound	0.6	0.8	13 248	26.4
Phakding	lower	4.4	4.7	3171	
	predicted	3.1	3.2	3412	
	upper	2.4	2.6	3473	

rives 3.1 h (range 2.4–4.4 h) after the breaching begins and peaks at 3.2 h (range 2.6–4.7 h) with a peak discharge of 3412 $m^3 s^{-1}$ (range 3171–3473 $m^3 s^{-1}$) (see Fig. 7). The lag time between the peak flow at Imja Tsho and the peak at Phakding is 2.2 h (see Table 4).

3.2.2 Lake lowering scenarios

A proposal to reduce the risk of a GLOF from Imja Tsho that is currently (2014) under implementation is to lower the water level of the lake at least 3 m (UNDP, 2013). The Imja GLOF model was used to assess the potential flood reduction at Dingboche if such a plan were to be implemented. To this end, the model was run with lake levels 3, 10 and 20 m lower than the current conditions scenario level (5010 m). The results for these scenarios are shown in Table 5 and Figs. 8–10. Figures 8 and 9 show the hydrographs and flood stage, respectively, at Dingboche for the 0, 3, 10 and 20 m lake lowering scenarios. Figure 10 maps the inundation depth at Dingboche for the different lake lowering scenarios. Lowering the lake 3 m (Fig. 10a) results in a 2.7 % reduction in the peak flood depth at Dingboche (compared to the 0 m lowering scenario) with the peak flood height lowering 0.6 m (from 22.4 to 21.8 m). This flood height still leads to significant inundation of homes and farmlands. With the lake lowered by 3 m about 8.6 ha of farmland and 25 structures are impacted by the flooding. In contrast, lowering the lake 10 m (Fig. 10b) or 20 m (Fig. 10c) results in a 14 and 36 % flood height reduc-

Table 5. Inundation model results at Dingboche and Phakding for lake lowering scenarios under current conditions.

Lake lowering scenario (m)	Arrival time (h)	Peak time (h)	Peak discharge ($m^3 s^{-1}$)	Peak discharge reduction* (%)	Peak depth (m)	Peak depth reduction* (%)	Farm area inundated (m^2)	Buildings inundated (#)
				Dingboche				
0	1.0	1.3	7544	0	22.4	0	93 650	29
3	1.1	1.5	7053	6.5	21.8	2.7	86 262	25
10	1.3	1.6	4479	40.6	19.2	14.3	40 226	18
20	1.3	1.8	1975	73.8	14.4	35.9	10 686	0
				Phakding				
0 m	3.1	3.2	3412	0				
3 m	3.2	3.5	2937	13.9				
10 m	3.9	4.2	1730	49.3				
20 m	5.8	6.1	629	81.8				

* Relative to the peak value for 0 m lake lowering.

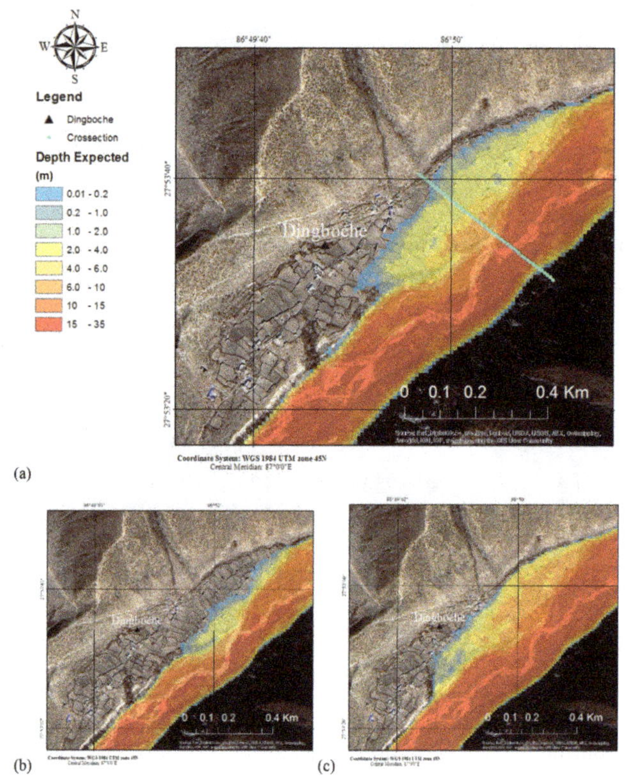

Figure 6. Inundation at Dingboche under current lake conditions: (**a**) expected inundation and the location of the cross section where the different scenarios are compared, (**b**) lower bound and (**c**) upper bound of the possible inundation.

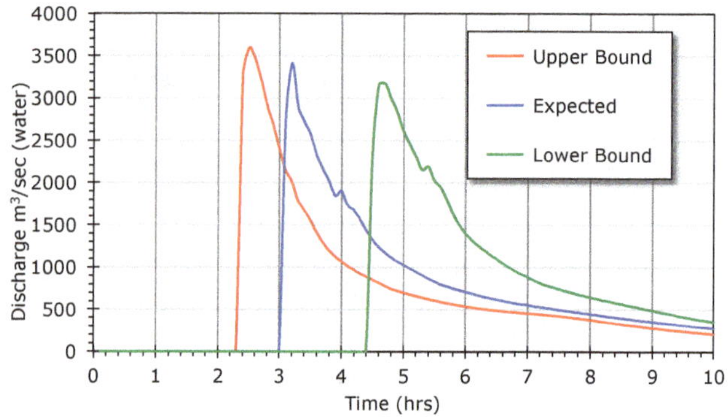

Figure 7. Upper bound, expected and lower bound GLOF hydrograph under current conditions at Phakding.

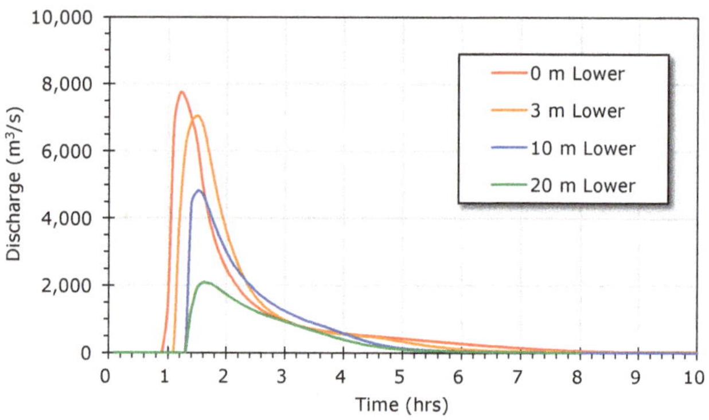

Figure 8. GLOF hydrographs at Dingboche under current lake conditions for 0, 3, 10 and 20 m lake lowering scenarios.

tion, respectively, at Dingboche, with respective peak flood heights of 19.2 and 14.4 m. These scenarios lead to considerable reduction in inundated area, especially the 20 m lowering scenario where the flood stays mostly in the historic flood plain of the river, inundates little farmland and floods no structures. When the lake is lowered 10 m about 4 ha of farmland will be inundated and 18 structures impacted and at 20 m lowering about 1 ha of farmland will be inundated and 0 structures impacted. Additionally, the peak discharge is reduced by 6.5, 40.6 and 73.8 % as a result of lowering the lake by 3, 10 or 20 m, respectively (Table 5).

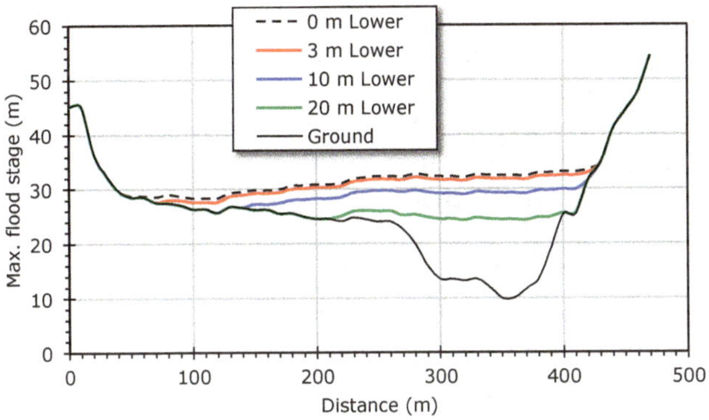

Figure 9. GLOF flood stage at Dingboche under current lake conditions for 0 m (expected), 3, 10 and 20 m lake lowering scenarios.

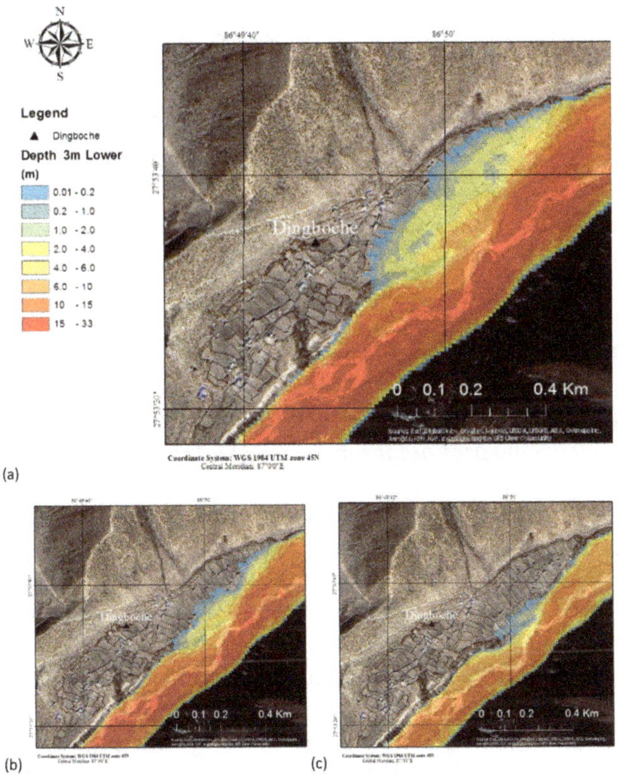

Figure 10. Inundation depth at Dingboche under current lake conditions: **(a)** 3 m lake lowering, **(b)** 10 m lake lowering and **(c)** 20 m lake lowering.

Further downstream at Phakding, the lake lowering scenarios have an impact on potential flooding as well (see Fig. 11). Lowering the lake 3 m results in a 13.9 % reduction of peak flow at Phakding. In contrast, lowering the lake 10 m results in 49.3 % reduction at Phakding, and lowering 20 m results in an 81.6 % reduction at Phakding (see Table 5).

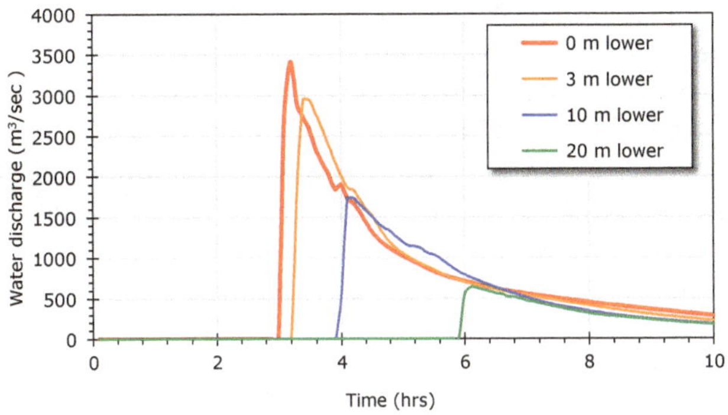

Figure 11. GLOF hydrographs at Phakding under current conditions for 0, 3, 10 and 20 m lake lowering scenarios.

4 Discussion

4.1 Comparison to previous Imja Tsho GLOF modeling

HEC-RAS has been used to simulate GLOFs in the Nepal Himalaya by several other researchers. Cenderelli and Wohl (2001) used one-dimensional, steady-flow HEC-RAS modeling to estimate peak discharges of the 1977 Nare and 1985 Dig Tsho GLOFs. Osti and Egashira (2009) modeled the 1998 GLOF at Tam Pokhari using HEC-RAS to perform one-dimensional, unsteady-flow calculations; however, the model could not be used to model the debris flow. They note that the GLOF was very strong and damaging, and the peak discharge was much higher than the results of the water-only computations. Other models have been used to model GLOFs. Dwivedi (2007) modeled the 1998 Tam Pokhari GLOF using the SOBEK flood model (Alkema and Middelkoop, 2005) and a 40 m resolution DEM. Several breaching scenarios were simulated, and eroded sediments were not considered in the model. Shrestha et al. (2013) modeled a potential debris-flow GLOF originating at Tsho Rolpa in the Rolwaling Valley of Nepal including the moraine breaching process due to an assumed seepage failure. Laboratory experiments were conducted to verify the model and good agreement with model results were obtained. Worni et al. (2012) who used the dynamic, erosion-based dam break model BASic EnvironMENT for simulation of environmental flow and natural hazard simulation (BASEMENT) (Faeh et al., 2011) to model a debris-flow GLOF in the Argentinian Patagonia. BASEMENT is a tool for the analysis of breaching processes of non-cohesive earthen dam structures and water-sediment flows (Volz et al., 2010). Schneider et al. (2014) simulated the cascade of mass movement processes of an avalanche triggered GLOF from Lake 513 in the Cordillera Blanca of Peru by coupling different physically based numerical models. Glacial lake dam overtopping hydrographs and water volumes were used as input for downstream debris-flow modeling with RAMMS (Christen et al., 2010).

Bajracharya et al. (2007b) developed a water-flow GLOF model for Imja Tsho that simulated flood flow in the Imja Khola and Dudh Kosi from the lake to about 45 km downstream of the outlet near Phakding. That one-dimensional model used a DEM derived from satellite data (30 m × 30 m grid cells) and one interpolated from 40 m contour maps (5 m × 5 m grid cells). This is the same DEM that we used for the reach from Dingboche to Phakding. The bathymetry of Imja Tsho was taken from a 2002 survey indicating the total volume of the lake was 35.8 ± 0.7 million m^3 (Sakai et al., 2007), rather than the 61.7 ± 3.7 million m^3 total volume used in this study based on the more recent 2012 survey (Somos-Valenzuela et al., 2014). The US National Weather Service (NWS) BREACH model (Fread, 1988) was used to generate moraine breach hydrographs that were passed to a NWS Flood Wave model (FLDWAV) model (Fread and Lewis, 1998) and routed downstream. Peak flows at the cross sections of the FLDWAV model were input to a steady-state US Army Corps of Engineers HEC-RAS model (USACE, 2010) to predict inundation at key cross sections. ICIMOD (2011) extended the work of Bajracharya et al. (2007b) using additional field results to more accurately define the geotechnical parameters of the moraine. The lake bathymetry was updated from 2009 fieldwork with the total volume reported to be 35.5 million m^3 (ICIMOD, 2011). The moraine-breaching trigger was not specified and might be either overtopping or piping. The simulated breach depth was 30 m, the same as we used here.

We can compare the results of ICIMOD (2011) with those reported here, since this is being asked of the consultants working on the UNDP Imja Tsho risk reduction project (UNDP, 2013). For the breaching process, ICIMOD reported a breaching time of 2.9 h with a peak discharge of 5817 $m^3 s^{-1}$, whereas we calculated 1.01 h (range 0.38 to 7.32 h) and a peak of 8394 $m^3 s^{-1}$ (range 4272 to 19000 $m^3 s^{-1}$). At Dingboche, ICIMOD reported a flood arrival of 3.1 h with a peak of 3000 $m^3 s^{-1}$ (estimated from Fig. 8.2, p. 65), whereas we show flood arrival at 1 h (range 0.6–1.9 h) and a peak of 7544 $m^3 s^{-1}$ (range 4208–13248 $m^3 s^{-1}$). At Ghat near Phakding, ICIMOD reported arrival at 4.2 h with a peak of 2300 $m^3 s^{-1}$, whereas we calculated 3.1 h (range 2.4–4.4 h) with a peak of 3412 $m^3 s^{-1}$ (range 3171–3473 $m^3 s^{-1}$). The reason for the differences here is most likely the use of the significantly smaller Imja Tsho volume in the ICIMOD calculations due to the bathymetry used. This causes faster propagation of larger flows downstream. In assessing the possibly reduced risk to downstream communities from implementing a lake lowering alternative, it is recommended that the latest estimates of the volume and bathymetry of Imja Tsho be used, e.g., 2012 or later.

4.2 Options for Imja Tsho risk reduction

To date there is no agreed upon set of hazard indicators for Imja Tsho, or other potentially dangerous glacial lakes for that matter (Somos-Valenzuela et al., 2013); however, the definition of GLOF hazard from Imja Tsho was discussed in consultations with community members in Dingboche in September 2012 and subsequently. The hazard of an Imja Tsho GLOF did not exist 30 years ago (see Somos-Valenzuela et al. (2014) and Watanabe et al. (2009) for images showing the evolution of the lake), and the community members' vulnerabilities stem from the location of their homes and farms relative to the flood plain. For them, hazard is having their farms or homes flooded or washed away, a prospect that they want reduced and preferably eliminated (Somos-Valenzuela et al., 2013).

There are many impacts that might occur from a rapid uncontrolled GLOF from Imja Tsho that will be felt downstream, in particular there are several stretches of the main trekking trail from Namche Bazar to Lukla that run quite close to the river and would be washed away, as they were in the 1985 Dig Tsho GLOF (Ives, 1986; Vuichard and Zimmermann, 1986). In addition, some parts of villages along the trail have fields and houses near the river, and they may also be impacted. The feasibility of possible remedial actions at Imja Tsho to reduce the hazard to downstream communities was evaluated. One scenario that appears to have significant risk reduction possibility is the slow, controlled lowering of the lake by 20 m. Lowering the lake by any amount will reduce the probability of GLOF occurrence for at least two reasons: the hydrostatic pressure on the west to east width of the moraine at the water level would be increased and more difficult to breach, and reducing the GLOF's occurrence probability would decrease the hazard level downstream.

Of the methods to reduce glacial lake risk, e.g., relocation of people and assets from the flood path, strengthening the lake outlet (Kattelmann and Watanabe, 1998), the one that has been employed the most is lowering the lake level. This has been used at nearly 40 dangerous glacial lakes in Peru since the 1950s (Portocarrero, 2014). Typically, the lake is lowered to a safe level by siphoning or draining and then excavating the damming moraine and installing a drainage channel at the desired elevation. Often, a reinforced earthen dam is then constructed to replace the original unconsolidated moraine dam, such that if a surge wave overtops the dam it will contain much of the excess water and not fail from erosion (Somos-Valenzuela et al., 2013). In order to lower glacial lakes, siphons are often used, e.g., at Hualcán Lake (Lake 513) in Peru (Portocarrero, 2014). Lowering glacial lakes more than about 5 m is infeasible at altitudes of 5000 m, but greater lowering can be achieved using an incremental method as discussed below (Somos-Valenzuela et al., 2013).

The UNDP Imja Tsho project suggests that lowering the lake at least 3 m will achieve significant risk reduction downstream (UNDP, 2013), but there is no requirement to estimate the remaining risk when the lake is lowered to different levels (3, 10, 20 m). This work has attempted to analyze this question. Siphons may be used at Imja Tsho to progressively lower the level in 3–5 m increments followed by excavation of the lake outlet.

Previous studies have suggested deepening and strengthening the outlet of Imja Tsho (Maskey, 2012). However, there are many difficulties in implementing this method. First, the natural flow of the outlet must be interrupted somehow in order to perform any excavation of the channel. In the siphoning method discussed above, the lake is lowered and then the outlet can be excavated to that level without needing to divert the outlet flow. One method that has been proposed is to build a coffer dam and divert water to flow over another part of the damming moraine and then excavate the existing outlet channel of the lake to increase its depth and discharge (Maskey, 2012). The difficulties of employing this method include (1) possibly encountering ice during the excavation, significantly weakening the moraine and possibly inducing a GLOF; (2) diversion of the outlet flow might cause excessive erosion that could weaken the moraine and potentially lead to a GLOF; and (3) the existence of small ponds in the outlet complex that are separated with shallow necks (with as little as 1.5 m depth) through which the lake water flows might prevent the draining of the lake unless they were also excavated (Somos-Valenzuela et al., 2013). The difficulty of encountering buried ice exists in any method employing excavation of the damming moraine and the moraine must be examined in detail with geophysical methods before this can be done safely. The example of Tsho Rolpa is being used as a model lake lowering system for Imja Tsho (UNDP, 2013). An outlet channel was constructed at Tsho Rolpa and 3 m lowering was achieved; however, the design called for lowering the lake by 20 m which was never attempted because of funding limitations (Rana et al., 2000; Mool et al., 2001). Our results show that lowering Imja Tsho 3 m would not lead to a significant inundation reduction downstream. The lake should be lowered at least 10 m and probably 20 m to achieve significant hazard reduction. Lowering Imja Tsho will require draining: (1) the normal inflow to the lake, (2) the volume of the lake expansion during the time of drainage and (3) the volume of the lake necessary to achieve 3 m lowering per drainage cycle (Somos-Valenzuela et al., 2013). Lake discharge was measured in May 2012 by a group from Kathmandu University using a tracer dilution method (Maskey, 2012) and by the authors using a timed float method (Somos-Valenzuela et al., 2013). In both cases the flow was found to be approximately 1 $m^3\ s^{-1}$.

The authors again measured the flow with a flow meter in September 2013 and found the discharge to be approximately 2 $m^3\ s^{-1}$ (see above for description of method). The lake area was $1.257 \pm 0.104\ km^2$ in September 2012, and increasing by about $0.04\ km^2\ yr^{-1}$. (Somos-Valenzuela et al., 2014). This will require $1.353\ m^3\ s^{-1}$ of drainage to lower the lake 3 m during a 5-month period in the melt season using 13 siphon pipes of 350 mm diameter.

5 Conclusions

Methods for reducing the downstream inundation hazard from a GLOF originating at Imja Tsho in Nepal were explored. A two-dimensional debris-flow model was developed to assess the downstream inundation. Inundation reducing scenarios were analyzed and an alternative under design, lowering the lake at least 3 m, was found not to have significant flood reduction benefits. The results indicate that the lake needs to be lowered about 20 m in order to completely reduce the impacts that a GLOF could have at Dingboche and further downstream. The results show that a GLOF occurring under the current lake conditions would result in inundation of much of the farming areas (about 9.4 ha and 29 structures impacted) at Dingboche but not the main lodges and other infrastructure along the primary trekking trail through the village. Lowering lake 3 m does not change this result much, but 10 m lowering reduces the impact substantially with about 4 ha of farmland and 18 structures impacted, and at 20 m lowering almost all impact at Dingboche is prevented. All cases involving lowering the lake would require a coordinated sequence of siphoning to lower the water level in 3 m increments, followed by outlet excavation to maintain the new level. The process would be repeated as needed to reach the desired lake level.

Acknowledgements. The authors acknowledge the support of the USAID Climate Change Resilient Development (CCRD) project and the Fulbright Foundation for the support of Somos-Valenzuela. The support of the software developers of FLO-2D made much of the work reported here possible. The comments of T. Watanabe, S. Bajracharya and an anonymous reviewer are greatly appreciated.

Edited by: M. Mikos

References

Alkema, D. and Middelkoop, H.: The Influence of Floodplain Compartmentalization on Flood Risk within the Rhine-Meuse Delta, Nat. Hazards, 36, 125–145, 2005.

Bajracharya, B. and Uddin, K.: Study of Land Cover Dynamics in Sagarmatha National Park and Buffer Zone, 10th Int. Symp. High Mt. Remote Sens. Cartogr. (Kathmandu, Nepal, 12–19 September 2008), 125–132, 2010.

Bajracharya, S. R., Mool, P. K., and Shrestha, B. R.: Impact of Climate Change on Himalayan Glaciers and Glacial Lakes Case Studies on GLOF and Associated Hazards in Nepal and Bhutan, International Centre for Integrated Mountain Development (ICIMOD), Kathmandu, 2007a.

Bajracharya, B., Shrestha, A. B., and Rajbhandari, L.: Glacial lake outburst floods in the Sagartmatha regions: hazard assessment using GIS and hydrological modeling, Mountain Res. Develop., 27, 336–344, 2007b.

Bolch, T., Buchroithner, M. F., Peters, J., Baessler, M., and Bajracharya, S.: Identification of glacier motion and potentially dangerous glacial lakes in the Mt. Everest region/Nepal using spaceborne imagery, Nat. Hazards Earth Syst. Sci., 8, 1329–1340, doi:10.5194/nhess-8-1329-2008, 2008.

Buchroithner, M. F., Jentsch, G., and Wanivenhaus, B.: Monitoring of recent geoligical events in the Khumbu Area (Himalaya, Nepal) by Digital Processing of Landsat MSS Data, Rock Mechan., 15, 181–197, 1982.

Cenderelli, D. A. and Wohl, E. E.: Peak discharge estimates of glacial-lake outburst floods and "normal" climatic floods in the Mount Everest region, Geomorphology, 40, 57–90, 2001.

Christen, M., Kowalski, J., and Bartelt, P.: RAMMS: numerical simulation of dense snow avalanches in three-dimensional terrain, Cold Reg. Sci. Technol., 63, 1–14, 2010.

Dwivedi, S. K.: Two Dimensional Simulation of a Glacial Lake Outburst Flood (A Case Study of Tam Pokhari Lake; Nepal Himalaya), MS Thesis, International Institute for Geo-information Science and Earth Observation, Enshede, The Netherlands, February, 2007.

Faeh, R., Mueller, R., Rousselot, P., Veprek, R., Vetsch, D., Volz, C., Vonwiller, L., and Farshi, D.: BASEMENT – Basic Simulation Environment for Computation of Environmental Flow and Natural Hazard Simulation, VAW, ETH Zurich, available at: http://www.basement.ethz.ch (last access: 13 February 2015), 2011.

Flo-2D: Flo-2D User's Manual, FLO-2D Software, Inc., Nutrioso, AZ, 2009.

Flo-2D: Flo-2D Pro Reference Manual, FLO-2D Software, Inc., Nutrioso, AZ, 2012.

Fread, D. L.: BREACH, an Erosion Model for Earthen Dam Failures, United States National Weather Service, Hydrologic Research Laboratory, Silver Spring, Maryland, 58 pp., 1988.

Fread, D. L. and Lewis, J. M.: NWS FLDWAV Model, Theoretical Development, User Document, Silver Spring, MD, 1998.

Froehlich, D. C.: Embankment dam breach parameters revisited, Proc., 1st Int. Conf. on Water Resources Engineering, American Society of Civil Engineers, 14–18 August 1995, New York, 887–891, 1995.

Froehlich, D. C.: Embankment dam breaches and their uncertainties, J. Water Resour. Plann. Manage., 121, 90–97, 2008.

Fujita K., Sakai, A., Nuimura, T., Yamaguchi, S., and Sharma, R. R.: Recent changes in Imja Glacial Lake and its damming moraine in the Nepal Himalaya revealed by in-situ surveys and multi-temporal ASTER imagery, Environ. Res. Lett. 4, 045205, doi:10.1088/1748-9326/4/4/045205, 2009.

Fujita, K., Sakai, A., Takenaka, S., Nuimura, T., Surazakov, A. B., Sawagaki, T., and Yamanokuchi, T.: Potential flood volume of Himalayan glacial lakes, Nat. Hazards Earth Syst. Sci., 13, 1827–1839, doi:10.5194/nhess-13-1827-2013, 2013.

Hambrey, M. J., Quincey, D. J., Glasser, N. F., Reynolds, J. M., Richardson, S. J., and Clemmens, S.: Sedimentological, geomorphological and dynamic context of debris-mantled glaciers, Mountain Everest (Sagarmatha) region, Nepal, Quaternary Sci. Rev., 27, 2361–2389, 2008.

Hammond, J. E.: Glacial lakes in the Khumbu region, Nepal: An assessment of the hazards, unpublished MA Thesis, University of Colorado, Boulder, CO, 1988.

ICIMOD-International Centre for Integrated Mountain Development: Glacial lakes and glacial lake outburst floods in Nepal, International Centre for Integrated Mountain Development (ICIMOD), Kathmandu, Nepal, 2011.

Ives, J.: Glacial Lake Outburst Floods and Risk Engineering in the Himalaya, International Centre for Integrated Mountain Development (ICIMOD) Occasional Paper No. 5, Kathmandu, Nepal, 1986.

Ives, J. D., Shrestha, R. B., and Mool, P. K.: Formation of glacial lakes in the Hindu Kush-Himalayas and GLOF risk assessment. International Centre for Integrated Mountain Development (ICIMOD), Kathmandu, Nepal, 2010.

Julien, P. Y.: Erosion and Sedimentation, 2nd Edn., Cambridge University Press, Cambridge, UK, 2010.

Julien, P. Y. and Leon, C. A.: Mud floods, mudlows and debris flows classification, rheology and structural design, Int. Work. Mudflows debris flows, 1–16, Caracas, Venezuela, 27 November–1 December, 2000.

Kattelmann, R.: Glacial Lake Outburst Floods in the Nepal Himalaya: A Manageable Hazard?, Nat. Hazards, 28, 145–154, 2003.

Kattelmann, R. and Watanabe, T.: Approaches to Reducing the Hazard of an Outburst Flood of Imja glacier Lake, Khumbu Himal. Proc. of International Conference on Ecohydrology of High Mountain Areas, Kathmandu, Nepal, 24–28 March 1996, 359–366, UNESCO, 1998.

Lamsal, D., Sawagaki, T., and Watanabe, T.: Digital Terrain Modelling Using Corona and ALOS PRISM Data to Investigate the Distal Part of Imja glacier, Khumbu Himal, Nepal. J. Mt. Sci., 8, 390–402, 2011.

Maskey, R. K.: Topographic Survey and Engineering Design of the Outlet Channel and Pre-feasibility Study for a Mini-Hydropower Generation Facility from Imja Lake. USAID ADAPT Asia-Pacific Support to UNDP/Nepal: Community Based GLOF and Flood Risk Reduction Project, United States Agency for International Development, Bangkok, 2012.

MoE-Ministry of the Environment: National Adaptation Programme of Action to Climate Change, Kathmandu, Nepal, 2010.

Mool, P. K., Bajracharya, S. R., and Joshi, S. P.: Risk Assessment of Lake Rolpa Glacial Lake along the Rolwaling and Tama Kosi Valleys Dolakha District, Nepal, International Centre for Integrated Mountain Development (ICIMOD), Kathmandu, Nepal, 2001.

O'Brien, J. S, Julien, P. Y., and Fullerton, W. T.: Two-Dimensional water Flood and mudlow simulation, J. Hydraul. Eng., 119, 244–261, 1993.

Osti, R. and Egashira, S.: Hydrodynamic characteristics of the Tam Pokhari Glacial Lake outburst flood in the Mt . Everest region, Nepal, Hydrol. Process., 23, 2943–2955, doi:10.1002/hyp.7405, 2009.

Portocarrero, C.: The Glacial Lake Handbook: Reducing Risk from Dangerous Glacial Lakes in the Cordillera Blanca, Peru, United States Agency for International Development, Washington, DC, 2014.

Rana, B., Shrestha, A. B., Reynolds, J. M., Aryal, R., Pokhrel, A. P., and Budhathoki, K. P.: Hazard Assessment of the Lake Rolpa Glacier Lake and Ongoing Remediation Measures, J. Nepal Geol. Soc., 22, 563–570, 2000.

Rickenmann, D.: Empirical Relationships for Debris Flows, Nat. Hazards, 19, 47–77, 1999.

Sakai, A., Saito, M., Nishimura, K., Yamada, T., Iizuka, Y., Harada, K., Kobayashi, S., Fujita, K., and Gurung, C. B.: Topographical survey of end-moraine and dead ice area at the Imja Glacial Lake in 2001 and 2002, B. Glaciol. Res., 24, 29–36, 2007.

Schneider, D., Huggel, C., Cochachin, A., Guillén, S., and García, J.: Mapping hazards from glacier lake outburst floods based on modelling of process cascades at Lake 513, Carhuaz, Peru, Adv. Geosci., 35, 145–155, doi:10.5194/adgeo-35-145-2014, 2014.

Shrestha, A. B. and Aryal, R.: Climate change in Nepal and its impact on Himalayan glaciers, Reg. Environ. Change, 11 (Suppl 1), S65–S77, 2011.

Shrestha, B. B, Nakagawa, H., Kawaike, K., Baba, Y., and Zhang, H.: Glacial hazards in the Rolwaling valley of Nepal and numerical approach to predict potential outburst flood from glacial lake, Landslides, 10, 299–313, doi:10.1007/s10346-012-0327-7, 2013.

Somos-Valenzuela, M., McKinney, D. C., Byers, A. C., Rounce, D. R., and Portocarrero, C.: Modeling Mitigation Strategies for Risk Reduction at Imja Lake, Nepal, High Mountain Glacial Watershed Program, CRWR Online Report 13-06, Center for Research in Water Resources, University of Texas at Austin, 2013

Somos-Valenzuela, M. A., McKinney, D. C., Rounce, D. R., and Byers, A. C.: Changes in Imja Tsho in the Mount Everest region of Nepal, The Cryosphere, 8, 1661–1671, doi:10.5194/tc-8-1661-2014, 2014.

Tachikawa, T., Hato, M., Kaku, M., and Iwasaki, A.: Characteristics of ASTER GDEM Version 2, Geoscience and Remote Sensing Symposium (IGARSS), Institute of Electrical and Electronics Engineers (IEEE), 3657–3660, 24–29 July, Vancouver, British Columbia, Canada, doi:10.1109/IGARSS.2011.6050017, 2011

UNDP-United Nations Development Programme: Community Based Glacier Lake Outburst and Flood Risk Reduction in Nepal. Project Document, UNDP Environmental Finance Services, Kathmandu, Nepal, 2013.

USACE-U.S.: Army Corps of Engineers: HEC-RAS River Analysis System Hydraulic Users Manual (Version 4.1), Hydrological Engineering Center, Davis, CA, 2010.

Volz, C., Rousselot, P., Vetsch, D., Mueller, R., Faeh, R., and Boes, R.: Numerical modeling of dam breaching processes due to overtopping flow. In: Proc. 8th ICOLD European Club Symposium 2010, 22–23 September, Innsbruck, Austria, 691–696. 2010.

Vuichard, D. and Zimmermann, M.: The Langmoche Flash-Flood, Khumbu Himal, Nepal, Mount. Res. Develop., 6, 90–94, 1986.

Wahl, T. L.: Uncertainty of Predictions for Embankment Dam breach Parameters, J. Hydraul. Eng., 130, 389–397, 2004.

Wahl, T. L.: Dam Breach Modeling–An Overview Of Analysis Methods, Joint Federal Interagency Conference on Sedimentation and Hydrologic Modeling, 27 June–1 July, Las Vegas, NV, 2010.

Watanabe, T., Kameyama, S., and Sato, T.: Imja glacier dead-ice melt rates and changes in a supra-glacial lake, 1989–1994, Khumbu Himal, Nepal: Danger of lake drainage, Mountain Res. Develop., 15, 293–300, 1995.

Watanabe T., Lamsal, D., and Ives, J. D.: Evaluating the growth characteristics of a glacial lake and its degree of danger of outburst flooding: Imja glacier, Khumbu Himal, Nepal, Norsk Geografisk Tidsskrift, 63, 255–267, 2009.

Westoby, M. J., Glasser, N. F., Brasington, J., Hambrey, M. J., Quincey, D. J., and Reynolds, J. M.: Modelling outburst floods from moraine-dammed glacial lakes, Earth Sci. Rev., 134, 137–159, doi:10.1016/j.earscirev.2014.03.009, 2014.

WGMS-World Glacier Monitoring Service: Preliminary Glacier Mass Balance Data 2010/2011, available at: http://www.wgms.ch/mbb/sum11.html, last access: 17 January 2013.

Worni, R., Stoffel, M., Huggel C., Volz, C., Casteller, A., and Luckman, B.: Analysis and dynamic modeling of a moraine failure and glacier lake outburst flood at Ventisquero Negro, Patagonian Andes (Argentina), J. Hydrol., 444–445, 134–145, 2012.

7

Basin-scale impacts of hydropower development on the Mompós Depression wetlands, Colombia

Héctor Angarita[1,2], Albertus J. Wickel[3], Jack Sieber[4], John Chavarro[5], Javier A. Maldonado-Ocampo[6], Guido A. Herrera-R.[6,7], Juliana Delgado[1], and David Purkey[3]

[1]The Nature Conservancy, Bogotá, Colombia

[2]Grupo de ecología y territorio, Facultad de estudios ambientales y rurales, Pontificia Universidad Javeriana, Bogotá, Colombia

[3]Stockholm Environment Institute US Center, Davis, California, USA

[4]Stockholm Environment Institute US Center, Somerville, Massachusetts, USA

[5]Centro de Investigación en Ciencias y Recursos GeoAgroAmbientales CENIGAA, Neiva, Colombia

[6]Laboratorio de Ictiología, Unidad de Ecología y Sistemática (UNESIS), Departamento de Biología, Facultad de Ciencias, Pontificia Universidad Javeriana, Bogotá, Colombia

[7]Laboratoire Evolution et Diversité Biologiques (EDB), Paul Sabatier University, Toulouse III, France

Correspondence: Héctor Angarita (hangarita@javeriana.edu.co)

Abstract. A number of large hydropower dams are currently under development or in an advanced stage of planning in the Magdalena River basin, Colombia, spelling uncertainty for the Mompós Depression wetlands, one of the largest wetland systems in South America at 3400 km^2. Annual large-scale inundation of floodplains and their associated wetlands regulates water, nutrient, and sediment cycles, which in turn sustain a wealth of ecological processes and ecosystem services, including critical food supplies. In this study, we implemented an integrated approach focused on key attributes of ecologically functional floodplains: (1) hydrologic connectivity between the river and the floodplain, and between upstream and downstream sections; (2) hydrologic variability patterns and their links to local and regional processes; and (3) the spatial scale required to sustain floodplain-associated processes and benefits, like migratory fish biodiversity. The implemented framework provides an explicit quantification of the nonlinear or direct response relationship of those considerations with hydropower development. The proposed framework was used to develop a comparative analysis of the potential effects of the hydropower expansion necessary to meet projected 2050 electricity requirements. As part of this study, we developed an enhancement of the Water Evaluation and Planning system (WEAP) that allows resolution of the floodplains water balance at a medium scale ($\sim$ 1000 to 10 000 km^2) and evaluation of the potential impacts of upstream water management practices. In the case of the Mompós Depression wetlands, our results indicate that the potential additional impacts of new hydropower infrastructure with respect to baseline conditions can range up to one order of magnitude between scenarios that are comparable in terms of energy capacity. Fragmentation of connectivity corridors between lowland floodplains and upstream spawning habitats and reduction of sediment loads show the greatest impacts, with potential reductions of up to 97.6 and 80 %, respectively, from pre-dam conditions. In some development scenarios, the amount of water regulated and withheld by upstream infrastructure is of similar magnitude to existing fluxes involved in the episodic inundation of the floodplain during dry years and, thus, can also induce substantial changes in floodplain seasonal dynamics of average-to-dry years in some areas of the Mompós Depression.

1 Introduction

Hydropower is a fundamental component of many countries' energy supply due to comparative advantages such as long-term economic efficiency, flexibility to adapt to high-frequency demand fluctuations, and greater regulation of hydrologic variability for other water users. Recently, climate change considerations have reawakened interest in hydropower development for its potential contributions to low-carbon economies and reduced dependency on fossil fuels.

Dam and reservoir construction and operations are one of the main drivers of global change in freshwater systems (Dynesius and Nilsson, 1994; Grill et al., 2015; Zarfl et al., 2014). There are numerous examples worldwide of how changes in flow, sediment, and temperature regimes; loss of river connectivity; and other impacts associated with reservoirs and dams cumulatively affect the physical and ecological processes that determine the integrity of major river systems, and in particular, of riverine lowland floodplains and wetlands (Arias et al., 2014; Dang et al., 2016; Grill et al., 2015; Opperman et al., 2010; Tockner and Stanford, 2002).

Riverine floodplains and wetlands are ecosystems of high biodiversity and productivity (Tockner and Stanford, 2002), providing numerous benefits, including stable water supply, support for fisheries, flood risk mitigation, carbon regulation, and improved water quality (Zedler and Kercher, 2005). Floodplain systems – despite their comparatively small spatial footprint – generally exceed the productivity of purely terrestrial or purely aquatic ecosystems (Bayley, 1995; Tockner and Stanford, 2002). Due to their central role in processes operating at the basin scale, and to the economic value of the numerous services they provide, hydrologically and ecologically functional riverine floodplains should be factored into sustainable water management infrastructure development. Such consideration should go beyond project-scale environmental impact assessments to consider the cumulative effect of all interventions located upstream (Dang et al., 2016; Fitzhugh and Vogel, 2011; Yang and Lu, 2014).

Basin-scale analysis aims to explicitly take into account the benefits of water management infrastructure along with potential repercussions to long-range processes and services that freshwater systems naturally provide; such analysis is especially relevant because the hierarchical and nested character of river networks and their associated ecosystems lead to nonlinearity of impacts (Fullerton et al., 2010; Grill et al., 2015). Habitat fragmentation, for example, is highly dependent on the geographic configuration of artificial barriers (Fausch et al., 2002). Unique disturbances at specific locations can consequently have system-wide impacts, and multiple dams, while individually disconnecting relatively small parts of the river network, can together disconnect large portions of non-substitutable habitat. This in turn, can constrain key ecological or physical processes, like fish migration from floodplains to upstream spawning habitats, or sediment and nutrient transport (López-Casas et al., 2016; Yang and Lu, 2014).

Floodplains and associated wetlands rely on longitudinal, lateral, and vertical connectivity which all affect the extent, depth, duration, and frequency of inundation. Cumulative flow alteration associated with upstream reservoir operation disrupts these hydrologic processes, which, in turn, affect multiple physical and ecosystem characteristics and processes, like floodplain topography; deposition of nutrients and organic matter in the floodplain; recharge of the water table; recruitment, dispersion, and colonization of plants; fish migration triggers; and access to soil moisture, among many others (Arias et al., 2014; Poff and Zimmerman, 2010).

Like habitat fragmentation, changes in the magnitude, frequency, duration, and timing of river flows also exhibit nonlinear cumulative behavior (Dang et al., 2016; Poff et al., 1997; Richter et al., 1998). While the artificial regulation effect of individual dams on hydrologic alteration depends both on reservoir storage capacity in comparison to the natural river discharge and on the operational rules (Williams and Wolman, 1984), at the basin level, dam placement determines both the spatial extent and the degree of alteration. Certain relative dam locations can therefore enable (or preclude) attenuation of streamflow from tributary rivers, and multiple dams located in the same river branch or sub-basin can amplify artificial regulation – resulting in hydrologic alteration greater than the sum of the individual effects of single reservoirs and propagating impacts hundreds or thousands of kilometers downstream (Angarita et al., 2013; Fitzhugh and Vogel, 2011; Piman et al., 2016; Richter et al., 1998).

The decrease in sediment loading due to reservoir trapping is another important driver of change in freshwater systems (Vörösmarty et al., 2003). Deficits in sediment loads are responsible for a number of impacts, like erosion and subsidence of river deltas (Syvitski et al., 2009), progressive incision or incremental changes in channel sinuosity and bank erosion (Grant et al., 2003), and transformation of wetlands and floodplains into permanent water bodies; and indirectly, as consequences of these impacts, destabilization of infrastructure like bridges, bank protections, levees, etc.

Medium and large hydropower plants in the Magdalena River basin (MRB) with a total capacity of 6.89 GW currently supply 49 % of the electricity consumed in Colombia. Faced with growing demand – by 2050, electricity use in Colombia is expected to increase by between 105 and 147 % with respect to 2010 (UPME, 2015) – there is great interest in further developing the remaining MRB hydroelectric potential, estimated at ~ 35 GW (Departamento Nacional de Planeación, 1979). Due to its proximity to existing transmission infrastructure and to urban areas that represent 75 % of the energy demand of the country, the Magdalena River and its tributaries make an attractive target for further hydropower expansion. Recently, basin-level impacts of MRB hydropower have been discussed in terms of (a) cumulative hydrologic alteration (Angarita et al., 2013); (b) loss of longi-

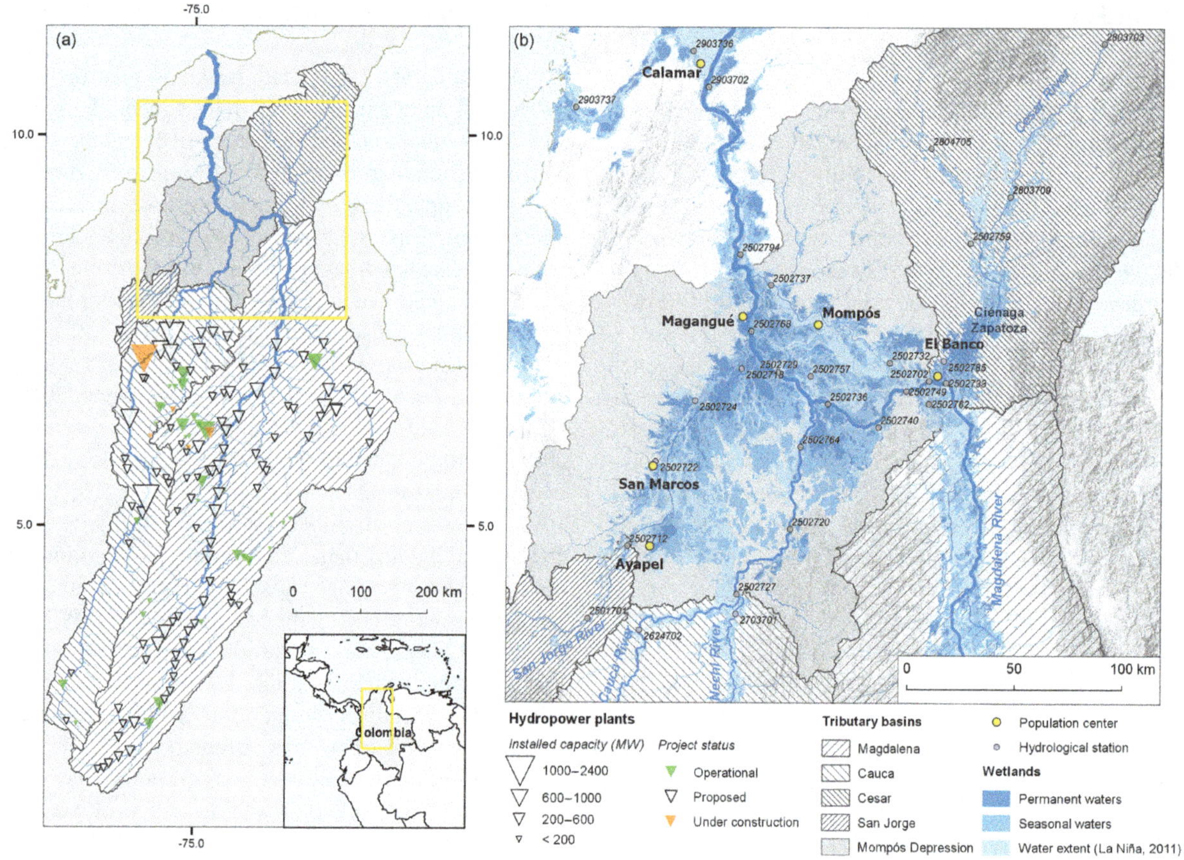

Figure 1. Map of the Magdalena River basin showing existing and proposed hydropower dams **(a)**, and the Mompós Depression low floodplains system and hydrological stations (numbered) referenced in the text **(b)**.

tudinal connectivity (Opperman et al., 2015); (c) contribution to changes in fish productivity, extinction risk, species distribution, community composition, and extent of spawning habitat (Carvajal-Quintero et al., 2017; Jiménez-Segura et al., 2014; Pareja-Carmona and Ospina-Pabón, 2014); and d) reproductive biology of fish of economic importance (López-Casas et al., 2014, 2016; Villa-Navarro et al., 2014).

However, none of the above mentioned studies included an integrated basin-level analysis of cumulative impacts on lowland riverine floodplains in the MRB. In this paper, we present an assessment of the current and potential basin-scale impacts of hydropower expansion on these floodplains – the Mompós Depression wetlands. We propose an integrated framework that takes basin-level and local factors into consideration to assess system alteration. From a basin-level perspective, we first developed an integrated analysis of three main factors associated with cumulative impacts of hydropower infrastructure: (1) flow regime alteration; (2) sediment trapping; and (3) connectivity losses with upper tributaries, with an emphasis on migratory fish species. Second, to estimate long-range hydrologic dynamics of floodplains, we developed an enhancement of the Water Evaluation and Planning system, or WEAP (SEI, 2017), capable of reproducing floodplain fluxes and storage, to resolve the Mompós Depression floodplains' water balance at a medium scale ($\sim$ 1000 to 10 000 km^2) and evaluate its relationship to upstream and local water management.

2 System description

The Magdalena River is located in the northern Andes Mountains and drains a biodiverse mosaic of ecosystems along its journey northward to the Caribbean Sea. The basin covers nearly one quarter of Colombia's national territory, providing sustenance, and acting as an economic and cultural life force, especially for the more than 35 million Colombians – 70 % of the country's population – who live within its bounds (Fig. 1).

With a length of 1540 km, the main stem of the Magdalena is the principal riverine trade artery of the country and the main connection to the Atlantic Ocean (ARCADIS Nederland BV and JESYCA S.A.S., 2015). Following the Strahler system of stream order classification (Strahler, 1957) the MRB network ranges from small mountain tributaries (order 1), to the Magdalena at its mouth in the Caribbean Sea (order 8). The combined network comprises a total length of approximately 101 109 km, of which 11 997 are medium to large rivers (Strahler order ≥ 4). Average flows range from $46 \pm 30\,m^3\,s^{-1}$ (order 4 rivers) to $7359 \pm 203\,m^3\,s^{-1}$ (order 8).

The Magdalena River flows between the Eastern and Central Cordillera of the northern Andes. Tanner (1974) argued that the Magdalena River valley is an "incomplete flood plain", a term he defined in a submission by the same name. Floodplain incompleteness, according to Tanner, can result either from rapid changes in sea level or from continued tectonic deformation, the latter being a likely explanation in this intermontane basin within the active Andes orogenous zone. Incomplete floodplains are characterized by lakes, marshes, wetlands, and swamps – depressions inundated by a high water table – and lack signs of prior meandering or channel migration. Near the town of El Banco (23.5 m a.s.l.), situated just upstream of what is considered the lower Magdalena, the Magdalena River is joined by the Cesar River. Downstream of El Banco, it splits into numerous channels, and is joined by two more tributaries: the Cauca and the smaller San Jorge (Fig. 1). The tectonically active foreland basin of the lower Magdalena "consists of vertically accreting, levee-confined channels and adjacent extensive [Mompós] wetlands, which are interpreted as an anastomosing river sedimentary system" (Smith, 1986, p. 177). A notable feature of this basin is extensive and waterlogged negative-relief elements (Lewin and Ashworth, 2014). The wetlands, dissected by numerous tie channels, together with the permanent and temporary lentic waterbodies called "ciénagas" encompass approximately 3400 km^2, comprising one of the largest wetland systems in South America. About 200 km from the Caribbean Sea, downstream of the city of Mangangué (10 m a.s.l.), the numerous braids of the Magdalena converge and meander as a single channel until the Magdalena splits again at Calamar, with part of the flow diverted westward to Cartagena through an altered channel system that serves as a navigation canal and part flowing into a 100 km long delta, while the main river continues to its mouth in Barranquilla.

The Magdalena is among the rivers with the highest sediment yields in South America: $560\,t\,km^{-2}\,yr^{-1}$ – a rate approximately three times that in the Amazon, La Plata, and Orinoco rivers (Restrepo et al., 2006). The most recent estimate of annual sediment flux (suspended sediments) of the Magdalena is $142.6 \times 10^9\,kg\,yr^{-1}$ (Restrepo et al., 2015). High rates of sediment transport have shaped the basin-scale morphologic and hydrologic dynamics that determine the complex storage and exchange patterns of water in the river and adjacent plains (Posada and Rhenals, 2006).

The discharge pattern of the Magdalena to the Mompós Depression is largely determined by the Inter Tropical Convergence Zone (ITCZ), which annually oscillates from the Equator to the northern Andes and back, resulting in two rainy seasons: April–May and September–November (Poveda et al., 2011). This weather pattern typically results in predictable bimodal discharge peaks in April–May and October–November (Poveda et al., 2001; Smith, 1986). The roles of topography, soil–atmosphere interactions, the Atlantic Ocean, and the Amazon also influence temporal and spatial rainfall patterns, resulting in the bimodal character not being equally strong across the basin (Poveda et al., 2011). The lower basin near the Caribbean coast – including the Mompós Depression – is often suggested to be unimodal in character, and the southeastern portion of the basin (approximately below 2° N) is characterized by a distinct unimodal pattern, with a June–August wet season (IDEAM, 2014).

During intense El Niño–Southern Oscillation (ENSO) events, the ITCZ can extend anomalously far south, bringing drought conditions to the MRB. In contrast, during La Niña events the MRB experiences heavier than normal rains and colder conditions that often extend – sometimes even bridging ITCZ events, leading to rainy periods that can last a year or longer (Poveda et al., 2001; Poveda and Mesa, 1997). The strong relation between anomalously high or low stream flow conditions at four stations in the MRB and the Oceanic Niño Index, a measure of ENSO, is illustrated in Fig. 2. Observed climate variability in the MRB also exhibits oscillations at decadal or interdecadal timescales, represented by multiple macroclimatic oscillations including Pacific Decadal Oscillation and Atlantic Multidecadal Oscillation (IDEAM, 2014).

The hydrologic variation of the lower Magdalena River and its resulting hydroperiod in the Mompós wetland system are crucial to the system's high ecological complexity and species diversity. The wetland ecosystems depend on seasonal inundation and the nutrients and sediment delivered by floodwaters. The system contains more than 226 native fish species with 129 (57 %) endemic (Maldonado-Ocampo et al., 2008), and at least 16 that undertake reproductive migration from the low floodplain to the foothills of the Andes (López-Casas et al., 2016). This richness and high species endemism, in addition to the proximity to main human settlements, has made the river the country's main and most productive fishery, which is based on at least 40 species (FAO, 2015). Fish are the main source of dietary protein for many MRB communities (Galvis and Mojica, 2007; Lasso et al., 2011). Additionally, the wetlands and lagoons of the lower Magdalena are critical stopovers for migrating and wintering birds along the Pacific Americas Flyway, where episodic inundation is critical to fish and bird reproduction, while low-flow conditions are important for reptile reproduction, propagation of riparian flora, and nutrient and organic matter storage (Jaramillo et al., 2015).

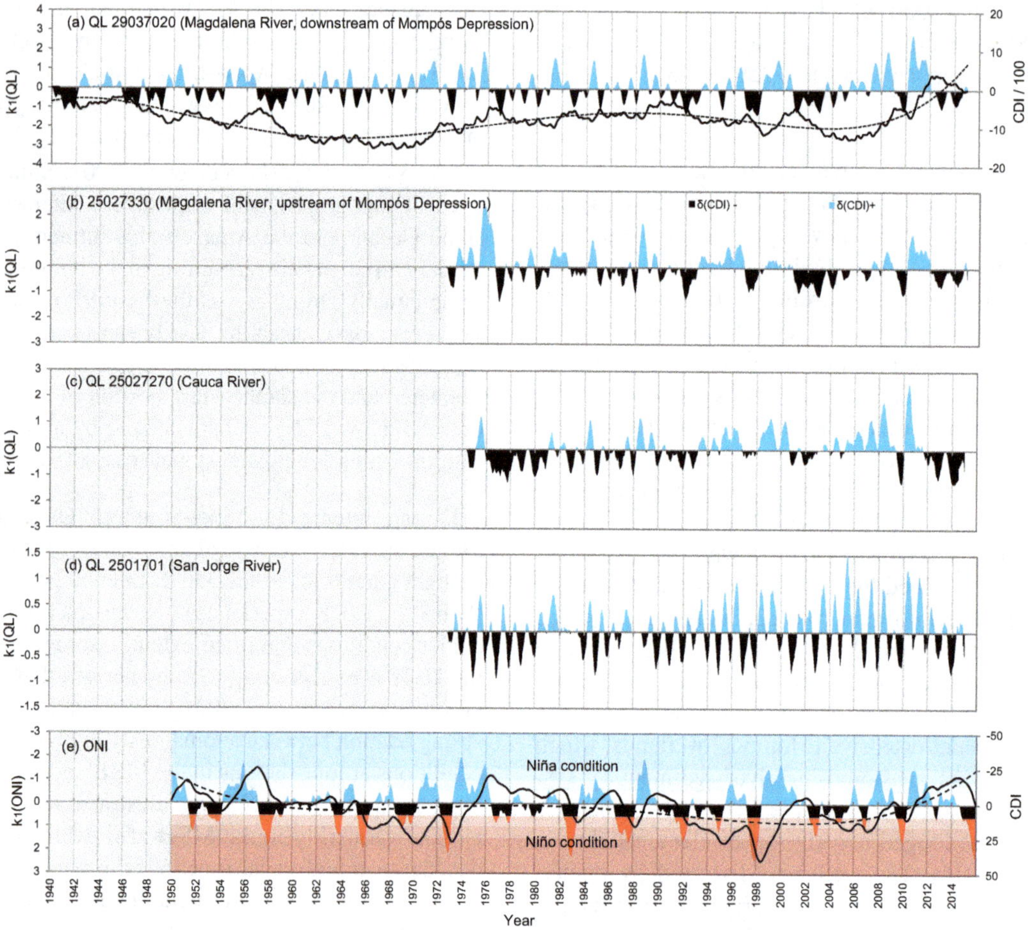

Figure 2. Streamflow inter-annual variability, expressed as the 6-month moving average of the k_1 anomaly (blue and red areas) and the corresponding cumulative anomaly (continuous black line) observed at streamflow (QL) gauges **(a–d)** in comparison to the Oceanic Niño Index (ONI; **e**). Data gaps are shaded grey.

3 Data and methods

3.1 Basin-level considerations

3.1.1 Defining dam sets for current and potential development

This study focused on existing and proposed medium and large hydropower projects, including reservoirs and run-of-river plants. Such projects can reduce river network connectivity or produce downstream alterations. Currently the MRB upstream of the Mompós Depression provides 70 % of Colombia's hydropower, equivalent to 49 % of the country's electricity supply (XM, 2014). Ninety-five percent of the capacity is distributed over 35 plants (32 in operation and 3 expected to be completed in 2018), with an aggregate installed capacity of 6.89 GW (and expected expansion to 9.35 GW in 2018) and 17.2 billion m^3 of storage (equivalent to 8.4 % of the basin's average annual runoff). The remaining 5 % corresponds to small hydro plants (< 20 MW).

In Colombia there is no centralized or coordinated planning for hydropower site identification; expansion occurs on an individual project basis in response to rolling auctions issued by the government based on 5- to 15-year projected needs of additional generation capacity (Cramton and Stoft, 2007; UPME, 2012).

To account for this uncertainty, our analysis first identified and compared a set of 1000 possible future scenarios – starting from a baseline condition that includes existing and under-construction dams – using a catalog of 97 potential project sites identified in Colombia's 1979 hydropower inventory (Departamento Nacional de Planeación, 1979) (Table 1), considered to be reliable by government and developers (see locations in Fig. 1). We evaluated each scenario with respect to the cumulative basin-level impacts of (a) loss of river network longitudinal connectivity between wetlands and upstream tributaries, (b) boundary conditions of flow regime alteration, and (c) loss of sediment input due to reservoir entrapment. Based on results from the first 1000 scenarios, four additional sets of 100 scenarios were generated by applying some restrictions to the potential sites, to avoid one or more criteria: projects located on Mompós Depression tributaries (order 4+) not yet affected by artificial barriers, mainstem projects upstream of existing projects, projects that would inundate areas with > 300 inhabitants, and projects that would inundate productive lands > 300 ha. In the context of Colombia's regulatory framework for energy expansion, this second set of scenarios demonstrates some examples of the sensitivity of developable hydropower potential to basin-level policy for site identification guidelines.

From the subset of scenarios that meet projected hydropower expansion by year 2050 – an equivalent hydropower capacity of 15.25 ± 0.5 GW, or +125 % with respect to 2010 (UPME, 2015) – we selected five scenarios representative of the range of impacts and trade-offs in the basin on which to perform a more detailed analysis of the potential changes in streamflow regime and hydrologic dynamics of the Mompós Depression wetlands. This analysis consists of a 33 year simulation of reservoir operations (using 1981 to 2013 as reference the period). The simulation results allowed us to estimate the potential changes in streamflow regime and hydrologic dynamics of the associated Mompós Depression wetlands.

3.1.2 Flow regime alteration

As part of this study, we developed a new indicator, named the weighted degree of regulation (DOR_w), to perform a comparative analysis of potential cumulative impacts of the natural flow regime of multiple reservoirs at the level of an entire river basin. The indicator is based on the original DOR, applied in several regional and global assessments as a first-level approximation of flow alteration (Grill et al., 2015; Lehner et al., 2011). DOR is the fraction of a river's annual flow volume that can be withheld by reservoirs upstream of a river reach, and is calculated as the relationship between the cumulative reservoir storage upstream and the total annual river flow in a river section. Higher values indicate a greater potential alteration of the natural flow regime – particularly of seasonal patterns – due to the effect of the operations of reservoirs; however, the DOR indicator does not consider the attenuation of artificial regulation from the fraction of basin runoff not affected by reservoir operations, and as a result DOR cannot differentiate the effect of proximity of the reservoir to the interest point. In order to overcome the above limitation of the DOR, we included a weighting based on the percentage of yearly upstream runoff effectively controlled by artificial storage, or

$$DOR_{wr} = \frac{Q_{cr}}{Q_r} \frac{\sum_{\text{upstream}_r} V}{Q_r} \cdot 100\,\%, \tag{1}$$

where Q_c is the upstream annual runoff affected by artificial storage ($m^3\,yr^{-1}$), V the reservoir volume (m^3), and Q the total annual river runoff ($m^3\,yr^{-1}$), with the "r" sub-index referring to specific reaches. In comparison with the previous DOR index, the weighting factor explicitly considers the attenuation of artificial regulation from the fraction of basin runoff not affected by reservoir operations. As DOR_w provides a basin-scale index of basin-level flow alteration it is thought to be particularly useful as a metric for basin-scale impacts on downstream wetland systems as found in the Mompós wetlands.

For the five selected scenarios of hydropower expansion thought to be representative of the potential range of alteration, we performed a 33 year simulation of the system to estimate boundary conditions (monthly streamflow) at the three main tributaries upstream of the Mompós Depression – the Magdalena, Cauca, and Nechí rivers – using Matlab's *ReservoirSimulator* model (Angarita et al., 2013; Ritter, 2016). This model performs a water balance of the inflows from tributary sub-basins of the reservoirs, coupled to a reservoir operations routine for hydropower production, along with other requirements such as water diversions and environmental flow obligations, when applicable (see SI-1 in the Supplement).

For a given reservoir, the model takes physical and technical constraints into account, such as volume–elevation curve, tail-water elevation, operational levels (inactive, buffer, technical, and safety), turbine type, capacity, and efficiency. Physical characteristics for existing dams were obtained from project official documentation archives, and for projected dams from the 1979 inventory (Departamento Nacional de Planeación, 1979). MRB river topology, sub-basins, and volume–area–elevation curves were derived using the HydroSHEDS dataset (Lehner et al., 2008; Lehner and Grill, 2013). Unimpaired flows for each sub-basin were lumped at dam sites based on observed runoff records from 1981 to 2013.

Water allocation for hydropower is based on basin-level target generation for a given time step. Target generation for a multi-reservoir system is an extremely complex problem, subject to many interlinked factors operating at multiple timescales, including water inflows, operational rules and technical constraints, firm energy obligations, fuel prices, and energy market competition (Cramton and Stoft, 2007; Ritter, 2016). In order to provide a plausible estimate of the monthly variability of generation targets of hydro plants in the MRB, we evaluated the historical monthly average plant-factor (PF; Fig. 3) – the average percentage use of installed capacity – of existing medium and large hydro plants in the MRB from 2000 to 2015, based on market data (XM, 2014). Monthly average PFs for the MRB range from 41 to 85 %; with most of the variation associated with hydro-climatic oscillations, like the 2008–2011 sequence of Niña–Niño–Niña events (Fig. 2). On the other hand, intra-annual monthly variation of PF in non-extreme years shows relatively stable values within a year, with a variation of 10 to 16 % from dry to wet months. This is consistent with the prominent role hydropower plays in Colombian energy supply and base-load

Table 1. Existing and proposed hydropower projects and other related infrastructure in the MRB, used to identify dam sets.

Project name	ID	Generation capacity (MW)	Gross volume estimate (million m^3)	Dam height (m)	Median discharge ($m^3\ s^{-1}$)
Existing					
Amoyá*	42	80	*	5	21.2
Ayurá (Transfer)	134	19	*		0.6
Betania	5	540	1488.0	58	388.4
Cadena1_Casalaco*	36	261	*		
Cadena2_Pagua*	212	580	*		
Calderas	17	26	0.0	25	7.6
Canoas*	74	50	*	0	117.5
Carlos Lleras*	56	78.2	*	5	68.3
Cucuana*	36	55	*	5	5.9
El Colegio*	77	300	*		119.4
Florida 2*	121	24	*		44.3
Ituango	21	2400	1850.0	197	1133.5
Jaguas–San Lorenzo	9	170	185.0	63	55.3
Laguneta*	76	80	*	0	117.7
Miel	3	396	591.0	188	118.9
Miraflores	14	0	99.0	0	4.7
Muña	1	270	0.8	13	1.2
Neusa	60	0	101.0	0	1.6
Palmas	147	12	NA	10	
Penol-Guatapé	6	560	1071.0	36	112.2
Piedras Blancas	135	11	2.9	0	0.8
Playas	13	201	76.8	46	128.2
Porce_2	29	426	142.7	118	172.5
Porce_3	4	660	170.0	151	201.9
Prado	12	55	1034.0	92	113.8
Quimbo	26	400	3205.0	151	228.8
Río Grande 1	7	19.9	0.5	0	99.5
Río Grande 2	8	0	153.0	65	0.1
Rio Negro	78	10	13.4	14	139.3
Salto I–II *	75	120	*		117.5
Salvajina	2	285	865.0	148	201.8
San Carlos–Punchiná	10	1020	72.0	70	145.1
San Francisco	11	135	2.3	8	0.0
San Miguel	41	44	0.3	5	102.5
San Rafael (supply storage)	61	0	71.0	59.6	1.0
Sisga	62	0	101.2	0	2.8
Sogamoso	20	820	4800.0	190	504.0
Tafetanes *	16	0	*	0	2.3
Tasajera *	213	306	*	0	39.8
Tominé (multipurpose storage)	63	0	690.0	30	6.9
TR Guarinó (transfer)*	39	0	*	5	63.4
TR Manso (transfer)*	40	0	*	5	12.0
Troneras	15	42	31.0	48	40.2
Proposed					
Aguadas	128	124	6.9	27	67.0
Alto Saldaña	141	124	423.2	155	97.0
Ambalema	158	208	154.4	19	1340.0
Apaví	132	1920	2639.3	120	1229.1
Aranzazu	66	102	252.6	120	119.4
Atá	142	109	197.1	135	46.0

Table 1. Continued.

Project name	ID	Generation capacity (MW)	Gross volume estimate (million m^3)	Dam height (m)	Median discharge ($m^3\ s^{-1}$)
Proposed					
Basilio	139	253	12680.7	112	204.2
Basillas	155	126	251.0	27	575.0
Bateas	154	145	67.4	31	520.0
Bellavista	140	197	156.6	57	109.3
Boquerón	73	104	0.6	22	30.0
Buenos Aires	69	106	1402.1	140	110.9
Butantán	79	268	1999.6	170	131.7
Cabrera	31	605	1510.1	177	327.4
Cambao	53	189	46.0	10	1260.6
Cañafisto	22	965	6487.8	139	1039.2
Cañaveral	34	80	1.0	32	19.1
Carare	117	582	1408.8	22	2287.4
Carbonero	115	269	217.4	14	2085.2
Carolina	116	349	213.1	16	2123.3
Carrasposo	156	150	151.0	27	675.0
Cepitá	103	172	19.7	25	192.0
Chacipay	86	164	310.2	85	167.1
Chagualo	137	100	188.1	97	116.5
Chillurco	149	161	359.1	105	126.0
Chimurro	120	146	NA	0	27.3
Cocorná	97	33	7.0	42	22.3
Coyaima	145	110	360.8	34	246.0
Cuerquia	130	75	8.8	57	5.1
El Indio	90	107	245.6	70	125.9
El Juncal	107	115	202.1	27	421.3
El Manso	152	118	163.8	29	425.0
El Neme	143	480	5670.0	185	182.0
El Palmar	131	91	0.2	20	7.7
El Tablón	102	171	6.2	25	144.2
Encimadas	33	94	2.7	35	10.5
Escuela_Minas	38	55	0.1	5	66.2
Espíritu Santo	18	885	185.3	81	1167.5
Farallones	127	2120	11916.9	220	802.2
Filo Cristal	105	262	125.1	36	527.0
Fonce	100	343	77.7	65	113.0
Furatena	85	125	2989.9	115	122.6
Guaira	93	115	357.8	66	43.8
Guane	104	426	1063.5	160	337.5
Guarapo	148	104	533.4	100	106.0
Guarquina	94	69	60.5	71	68.8
Hispania	129	145	3.6	27	43.3
Honda	159	374	663.3	31	1370.0
Horta	88	114	1463.2	150	101.3
Icononzo	72	117	0.2	20	25.6
Isnos	64	103	33.3	105	16.3
Julumito	122	53	165.1	80	55.0
La Cascada	70	70	0.3	18	12.5
La Chamba	110	169	231.3	19	981.4
La Dorada	112	323	229.6	21	1385.3
La Miel II	35	120	0.5	5	41.1
La Plata	68	159	225.6	120	60.2

Table 1. Continued.

Project name	ID	Generation capacity (MW)	Gross volume estimate (million m^3)	Dam height (m)	Median discharge ($m^3\,s^{-1}$)
Proposed					
La Playa	71	84	2.9	25	22.0
La Suecia	82	66	38.0	100	14.7
La Vieja	124	80	1246.2	90	151.5
Lagunilla	83	60	0.3	15	30.9
Lame	157	334	236.6	28	1270.0
Lebrija	106	187	3269.4	145	108.4
Mamaruco	98	167	678.4	135	185.2
Marañal	113	461	612.1	26	1555.7
Mayaba	32	242	230.2	50	455.3
Nariño	50	356	118.0	20	1161.8
Natagaima	108	154	231.1	26	606.2
Nus	91	189	12.7	95	99.5
Ombale	146	105	98.0	34	238.0
Oporapa	150	180	699.7	130	130.0
Páez	67	143	81.8	90	54.2
Paicol	65	311	1570.6	170	184.2
Palmalarga	144	496	7737.3	160	296.0
Palmera	95	312	838.8	106	135.1
Patagón	114	170	102.2	12	1729.4
Pericongo	151	240	1245.6	120	136.0
Piedra del Sol	30	420	257.1	125	127.4
Piedras Negras	55	299	13.7	15	1343.1
Porce 4	19	404	2198.1	195	223.4
Porvenir 1	24	364	1384.9	167	166.6
Porvenir 2	23	352	463.0	145	186.2
Puente Linda	80	52	88.9	90	55.1
Riachón	136	100	1.4	50	10.9
Ricaurte	111	141	90.8	16	1043.0
Risaralda	125	93	25.8	60	23.0
Samal	84	107	623.0	140	53.4
Samaná Medio	25	175	1668.8	177	130.3
San Diego	81	54	109.9	87	8.9
San Juan	37	114.3	0.2	5	64.6
Santo Domingo	96	48	3.1	23	35.5
Simacota	99	162	140.3	90	245.0
Socotá	101	124	1.6	22	109.2
Tamar	92	132	642.6	60	111.1
Timba	123	60	782.4	46	254.2
Toloso	133	334	167.7	26	1309.1
Troya	89	151	2341.2	150	123.8
Valdivia	138	700	728.9	128	140.6
Veraguas	153	110	202.3	26	490.0
Vigía	109	132	80.4	20	618.4
Wilches	119	308	34.8	11	3269.1
Xarrapa	126	330	351.0	66	776.7
Yátaro	87	150	1589.9	90	144.4
Yondó	118	308	129.3	12	2684.4

Note: main projects are labeled with ID in Fig. 1. * Run of river projects. NA = not available.

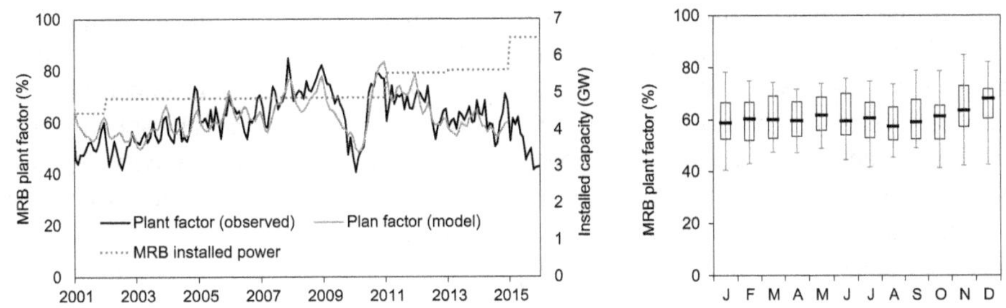

Figure 3. Aggregated observed and modeled plant factor of Magdalena River basin (MRB) hydropower plants (2001–2015), and seasonal variation of the plant factor over the observed period.

generation; cumulative storage and water allocation is able to compensate – on a monthly basis – for seasonal hydrologic variability. Based on observed PFs, we developed the following regression model to estimate average monthly PFs for the full simulation period 1981–2013 (Adj $R^2 = 0.62$, SE $= 5.8\,\%$):

$$\begin{aligned}\mathrm{PF} = &-0.031 \cdot \mathrm{ONI} + 1.205 \times 10^{-5} \cdot \mathrm{QL_{Calamar}} \\ &+ 0.233 \cdot \log\left(\mathrm{MA_6}\left(\mathrm{QL_{calamar}}\right)\right) - 0.371, \end{aligned} \tag{2}$$

where ONI is the Oceanic Niño Index, $\mathrm{QL_{Calamar}}$ the monthly average streamflow at Calamar (station 2903702, shown in Fig. 2), and $\mathrm{MA_6}$ a moving average operator applied over a six month period.

3.1.3 Sediment trapping

We estimated basin-level entrapment or S_e, defined as the percentage of total sediment throughput retained by upstream reservoirs, considering two main factors: individual reservoirs' retention efficiency, and the relative locations of multiple upstream reservoirs.

To estimate trapping efficiency for each reservoir, we used Dendy's formula (Dendy, 1974). Dendy's method is a revised Brune curve, which uses an empirical expression to estimate the long-term average reservoir sediment retention efficiency based on the ratio between capacity (C) and average annual inflow (I). A higher ratio indicates higher sediment retention efficiency, TE, as described by the following equation:

$$\mathrm{TE} = 100 \cdot \left(0.97^{0.1^{\log\left(\frac{C}{I}\right)}}\right). \tag{3}$$

Similar to the case of flow regime alteration, relative locations of reservoirs play an important role in sediment entrapment because upstream reservoirs can significantly reduce sediment input to downstream reservoirs, and sediment yields vary across the basin (see Restrepo et al., 2006, for a detailed analysis of the MRB). To consider the effects of relative dam locations and of sediment yield heterogeneity, we developed a routing model for reach-level sediment balance, as described by the following recursive equation:

$$\mathrm{SST_r} = \left(\sum_{u \in \mathrm{Inflow_r}} \mathrm{SST_u} + E_\mathrm{r} \cdot A_\mathrm{r}\right) \cdot (1 - \mathrm{TE}), \tag{4}$$

where $\mathrm{SST_r}$ is the sediment load downstream of reach r, $\mathrm{Inflow_r}$ the set of river reaches directly upstream of reach r, A_r the drainage area, and E_r the contribution of sediments generated by laminar erosion and storage on the slopes, based on the Revised Universal Soil Loss Equation (RUSLE) methodology:

$$E_\mathrm{r} = R \cdot K \cdot L_\mathrm{s} \cdot C \cdot P, \tag{5}$$

where E is laminar erosion ($\mathrm{t\,m^{-2}\,yr^{-1}}$), R rain erosivity ($\mathrm{MJ\,mm\,m^{-2}\,h^{-1}}$), K soil erodibility ($\mathrm{t\,ha\,h\,ha^{-1}\,MJ^{-1}\,mm^{-1}}$), L_s topographic factor (dimensionless), C soil cover (dimensionless), and P management practices (dimensionless). Values for each of the corresponding variables were adopted from Jimenez (2016) for the MRB. Our simplified approach focuses on the primary inputs and outputs in a section of a stream according to Wilkinson et al. (2009), where the primary production process corresponds to the contribution of slope and channel erosion in the upper parts of the basin (Strahler order 1). Our main purpose was to provide a basis for comparative analyses of sediment retention in the tributary rivers of the Mompós Depression for the different hydropower expansion scenarios; therefore, we do not provide a comprehensive description of the other components of the channel sediment balance, such as sediment production by lateral migration of the channel, or bank overflow events and sediment deposition.

3.2 Floodplains hydrologic dynamics

We developed a conceptual hydrological model with a surface storage component that includes episodic interactions between river and wetland systems as an enhancement to the WEAP platform's existing Soil Moisture Model (SMM) (Yates et al., 2005b). The model dynamically simulates evapotranspiration, surface runoff, subsurface runoff or interflow, and deep percolation at the sub-basin level, as well as bidirectional water transfer between river and wetland systems. The water balance is defined using a semi-distributed approach that reflects the topological relationships between basin areas or catchments, stream networks, and wetlands. The model allows for the evaluation of hydrologic dynamics associated with several factors, including alteration in the upstream flow regime, climate variability and change, and impacts of local and upstream water resource management practices, such as flood control structures and changes in connectivity between river and wetland systems.

WEAP SMM enhancements included two main modifications: the inclusion of surface storage for water balance representation at the catchment level; and the topological representation of interactions between surface storage, subsurface storage, and the river network. WEAP's original SMM represents the water mass balance through two soil layers – the root zone and the deep zone – in lumped portions of the watershed called catchment objects, each divided into N fractional areas, j, representing different land cover types, with a water balance computed for each fractional area. The model "uses empirical functions that describe evapotranspiration, surface runoff, subsurface runoff or interflow, and deep percolation" (Yates et al., 2005a, p. 491). The modified version introduces a third storage volume (or "bucket"), corresponding to a fractional area of the catchment that accounts for surface storage. The water balance in the third bucket is determined by (a) bidirectional exchanges of water (flood and return flow) with one or more sections of river and (b) local inputs/outputs such as precipitation, evaporation, or percolation (Fig. 4).

Water balance in the soil root zone and soil deep zone are calculated, respectively, by land cover type:

$$\mathrm{Sw}_j \frac{\mathrm{d}z_{1,j}}{\mathrm{d}t} = P + \mathrm{Ir} - \mathrm{PET} \cdot k_{\mathrm{c},j}(t)\left(\frac{5z_{1,j} - 2z_{1,j}^2}{3}\right) - (P_\mathrm{e} + I_\mathrm{r})\, z_{1,j}^{\mathrm{RRF}_j} - \left(1 - f_j\right) k_\mathrm{s} z_{1,j}^2 \tag{6}$$

$$\mathrm{Dw}_j \frac{\mathrm{d}z_{2,j}}{\mathrm{d}t} = \left(1 - f_j\right) k_\mathrm{s} z_{1,j}^2 - k_\mathrm{d} z_{2,j}^2. \tag{7}$$

The total runoff Ro (volume) and baseflow Bf (volume) of a given catchment are then calculated as sums of the contributions of the land cover types:

$$\mathrm{Ro}(t) = \sum_{j=1}^{N} A_j \left[(P + \mathrm{Ir})\, z_{1,j}^{\mathrm{RRF}_j} + f_j k_\mathrm{s} z_{1,j}^2 \right] \tag{8}$$

$$\mathrm{Bf}(t) = \sum_{j=1}^{N} A_j \left[k_\mathrm{d} z_{2,j}^2 \right], \tag{9}$$

where Sw_j is soil root zone water storage capacity (length), Dw_j, deep zone water storage capacity (length), z_1, water stored in the root zone, relative to its total storage capacity (%), z_2, water stored in the deep zone, relative to its total storage capacity (%), P, precipitation and snowmelt in the catchment (length), Ir, irrigation (length), PET, Penman–Monteith reference crop potential evapotranspiration ($\mathrm{L\,T^{-1}}$), $k_{\mathrm{c},j}$, crop coefficient (dimensionless), f_j, flow direction (dimensionless), k_s, conductivity of the root zone ($\mathrm{L\,T^{-1}}$), k_d, conductivity of the deep zone ($\mathrm{L\,T^{-1}}$), RRF_j, runoff resistance factor (dimensionless), and A_j, area of land cover of type j.

Likewise, the mass balance at the floodplain and the connected river reaches (V_river), is represented by

$$\frac{\mathrm{d}V_{3,j}}{\mathrm{d}t} = Q_\mathrm{l} - R_\mathrm{l} - A_3 \cdot \left[P_\mathrm{e} \cdot z_{1,j}^{\mathrm{RRF}_j} - \mathrm{PET}(t)\left(1 - k_{\mathrm{c},j}\right) \left(\frac{5z_{1,j} - 2z_{1,j}^2}{3}\right)\right] \tag{10}$$

$$\frac{\mathrm{d}V_{\mathrm{river}_i}}{\mathrm{d}t} = Q_\mathrm{h} - Q_\mathrm{l} - \mathrm{Ir} + R_\mathrm{l} + \mathrm{Ro} + \mathrm{Bf}, \tag{11}$$

where $V_{3,j}$ is storage volume in the floodplain (volume), $V_{\mathrm{river},i}$, water stored in the connected river reach (volume), A_3, extent (area) of flooded area, given the volume of floodwater in catchment, Q_h, river reach input streamflow, Q_l, lateral flow between river and floodplain (vol. $\mathrm{T^{-1}}$), defined as percentage T_f of the river reach streamflow, above a certain flow threshold:

$$Q_\mathrm{l} = \begin{cases} T_\mathrm{f} \cdot (Q_\mathrm{h} - Q_\mathrm{threshold}) & \text{if } Q_\mathrm{h} > Q_\mathrm{threshold} \\ 0, & \text{if } Q_\mathrm{h} < Q_\mathrm{threshold} \end{cases} \tag{12}$$

and R_l, return flow from floodplain to river reach (vol. $\mathrm{T^{-1}}$), defined as the percentage T_r of water above a floodplain storage threshold, that flows out of the floodplain in one time step:

$$R_\mathrm{l} = \begin{cases} T_\mathrm{r} \cdot \left(V_3 - V_{3,\mathrm{threshold}}\right), & \text{if } Q_\mathrm{h} < Q_\mathrm{threshold} \\ 0, & \text{if } Q_\mathrm{h} < Q_\mathrm{threshold} \end{cases}. \tag{13}$$

While there is a wide range of modeling approaches to study floodplain systems dynamics, including MIKE21 (DHI, 2016), ANUGA HMP (Roberts, 2017), and HEC-RAS (USACE and RMA, 2016), conceptual approaches have several advantages, as previously discussed by Dutta et al. (2013). Our lumped-topological model has fewer information requirements and a much shorter execution time than a hydrodynamic model. Therefore, the approach is suitable for the simulation of long periods of time, and for comparative analysis of multiple scenarios for planning and management. Also, this type of model allows for long-term evaluation of floodplain dynamics and broader potential management implications.

The WEAP enhancements were developed for the Mompós Depression and adjacent lowland basin, with a total area of 32 198 km^2, or 11.8 % of the total area of the entire MRB. The area receives flows from the Magdalena, Cauca, San Jorge, and Cesar rivers (Figs. 1 and 5). Catchments were determined by selecting basin-scale natural "breaks" in river system topology to allow the identification of basins, inter

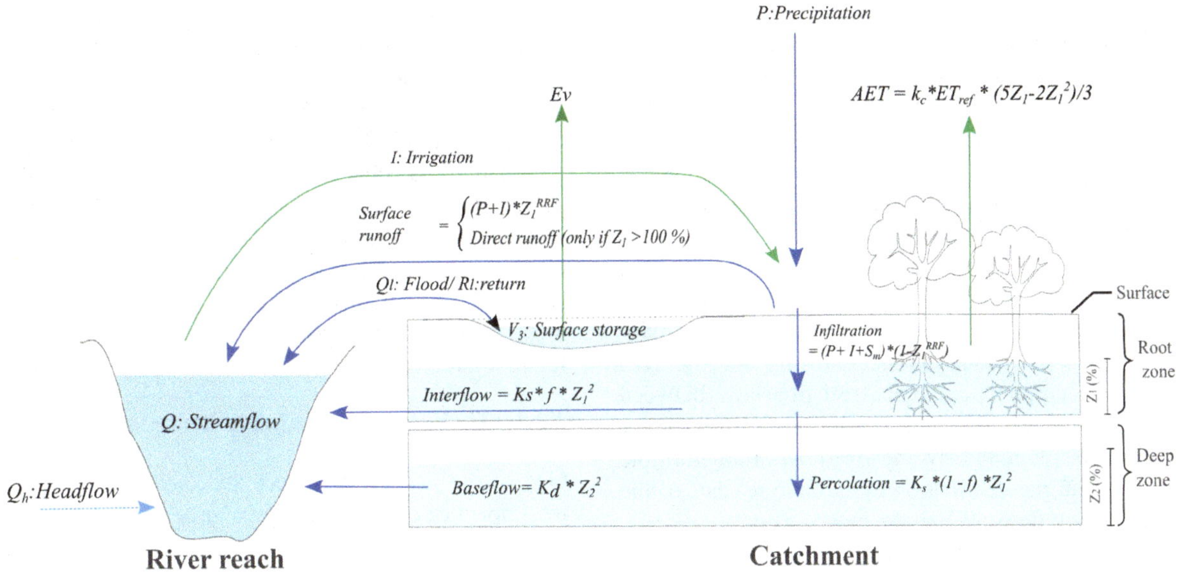

Figure 4. Schematic of the enhanced two-layer soil moisture model including a surface storage component.

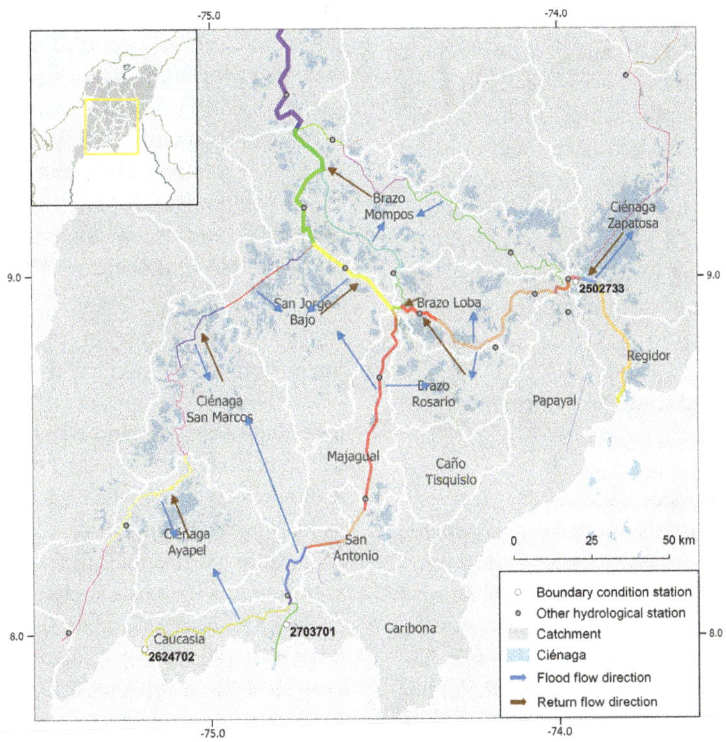

Figure 5. WEAP model hydrological units (catchments), river reaches (shown in different colors to illustrate the discretization of the fluvial network), and topological relationships between river reaches and wetland/floodplain areas (flood flows and returns). Stations corresponding to streamflow boundary conditions are labeled: 2502733 (Magdalena at Peñoncito), 2624702 (Cauca at La Coquera), and 2703701 (Nechí at La Esperanza).

basins, and internal basins based on the Pfafstetter hierarchical basin coding approach (Verdin and Verdin, 1999), implemented in the recently released HydroBASINS product (Lehner and Grill, 2013). Comparison of the hydrographic units with the basin morphogenic classification (IDEAM, 2010), revealed a strong coincidence between these units. This is consistent with morphogenic classification being conditioned by factors such as geologic structure, bioclimatic conditions, topography, and slope. Land cover classification is based on seven differentiated categories in terms of their physiognomy: forests, shrubs, grasslands, agricultural zones, water bodies, hydrophytes and others, which were derived from Colombia's ecosystem map (IDEAM et al., 2007).

3.2.1 Topological representation of the floodplain system

Using WEAP's semi-distributed modeling approach, Eqs. (6)–(11) can be set independently for multiple river reach and floodplain connections, allowing for the representation of complex topological relationships between catchments, river reaches, and floodplains (Fig. 5). For example, a floodplain fed by the overflow from multiple river reaches, and the distribution to multiple reaches of the floodplain's return flow can both be represented.

In practice, most of the model catchment sub-units are described only by Eqs. (6) and (7), representing areas of the basin not subject to flooding. For the subset of catchments that represent floodplains (as shown in Fig. 5), the model is set up to include Eqs. (10) and (11). To reduce the number of model calibration parameters, topological connections between the river and floodplains were pre-identified using multiple sources of contextual information. In the case of the Mompós Depression, clues for permanent and episodic connectivity were derived from a review of remote sensing data (Landsat 5, 7, and 8) over time and of topological data derived from a high-resolution DEM recently developed by Colombia's (Climate) Adaptation Fund in the area between the Cauca and San Jorge rivers, as documented by Sanchez-Lozano et al. (2015).

3.2.2 Model calibration, validation, and uncertainty estimation

The WEAP model was calibrated (1981–1998) and validated (1999–2013) for monthly streamflow at 13 discharge gauges and for water level at four stations with long-term records in the Mompós Depression (Fig. 1). Historical monthly precipitation, temperature, discharge data ($m^3\,s^{-1}$), and water levels (m) were obtained from Colombia's National Meteorology, Hydrology, and Environmental Studies Institute (IDEAM). The longest available records date back to 1940 for station QL (2903702, Calamar), located at the outlet of the Mompós Depression (Fig. 1). Other stations provide relatively high serial-complete streamflow records starting in 1972.

We adopted Nash–Sutcliffe efficiency (NSE) and relative bias (P-BIAS) for streamflow data, and R^2 between wetland water levels and storage as orthogonal performance metrics; in the case of wetlands, a correlation between water levels and storage was adopted due to a lack of topo-bathymetrical data, which prevented the conversion of the model state variable (storage volume) to effective water levels in wetland units. Despite this limitation, the R^2 metric reflects the model's ability to capture the dynamic character of water levels in wetland areas.

In both cases, acceptance ranges were chosen based on Moriasi et al. (2007). Model parameters (54 in total) were then calibrated using a three-stage random hypercube sampling. The first stage was derived from 10 000 simulations and the subsequent two were derived from 1000 simulations each. Sets of model parameters above acceptance criteria ranges of 30 simultaneous metrics (13 NSE, 13 P-BIAS, and 4 R^2) were used to assess model uncertainty by analyzing the range of predicted average and maximum floodplain storage.

3.2.3 Hydrologic alteration of floodplains

One of the most widely accepted methodologies to assess the impact of changes of flow regime on aquatic ecology is the concept of Indicators of Hydrologic Alteration (IHA), as proposed by Richter et al. (1996). IHA is a set of 32 statistics related to magnitude, timing, duration, frequency, and rate of change, which allows a detailed comparative analysis of diverse flow components. Many of the statistics are intercorrelated, rendering part of this vast amount of information redundant for high-level assessments (Gao et al., 2009; Vogel et al., 2007). In order to simplify IHA, Gao et al. (2009) demonstrated that "Ecodeficits" and "Ecosurpluses" (EDS), defined as relative changes of flow duration curves, can provide a comprehensive simplified representation of hydrologic alteration impacts, as compared with the use of the more complex IHA approach.

In this study we employed seasonal EDS to assess the impact of variations in the hydrologic regime of wetlands storage. We divided the year into four seasons: Subienda (December–February), Bajanza I (March–May), Mitaca (June–August), and Bajanza II (September–November). These periods were selected based on their biologic and hydrologic relevance in the basin, in particular to fish migration, as in Jiménez-Segura et al. (2014). We differentiated ranges of duration corresponding to storage magnitude for extreme high (months with percentage of time exceeded $< 10\,\%$: max to P_{10}), seasonal (P_{10} to P_{75}), low (P_{75} to P_{90}), and extreme low flows (P_{90} to Min), also relevant to diverse ecological processes (DePhilip and Moberg, 2013).

3.2.4 Habitat fragmentation in the upstream tributaries

We estimated fluvial length loss over the gradient 0 to 3000 m a.s.l., with a focus on reaches used by species of migratory fish present in the Mompós Wetlands. Loss of river length is a proxy for fractionation of populations and communities, and for reduction or isolation of available habitat necessary for the different life stages of species and/or groups with specific distribution ranges (Carvajal-Quintero et al., 2017; Fullerton et al., 2010).

We used biological data derived from species distribution models (SDMs) fitted with MaxEnt v3.3.4 for 13 of the 16 species in the MRB known to migrate upstream from the floodplains: *Brycon henni, Brycon moorei, Curimata mivartii, Cyphocharax magdalenae, Leporinus muyscorum, Pimelodus blochii, Pimelodus grosskopfii, Plagioscion magdalenae, Prochilodus magdalenae, Pseudoplatystoma magdaleniatum, Saccodon dariensis, Salminus affinis*, and *Sorubim cuspicaudus*. Fish records consist of information available in principal ichthyological collections and surveys of migratory fish since 1940, which provide information on the historical distribution of fish in the MRB prior to hydroelectric development. A total of 31 environmental variables describing climate, soil, and geomorphology were considered. Principal component analysis (PCA) between those variables were used in SDMs to avoid multicollinearity. An "All Target Group" approach was used in SDMs to reduce error associated with sampling bias (Phillips et al., 2009). To evaluate model performance, we used the mean value of the area under the curve from the receptor of operator characteristic resulting from 10 random cross-validation sets (70 % of data for calibration and 30 % for testing). The threshold that maximized the sum of specificity and sensitivity resulted from cross-validation and was used to obtain fish distributions in presence–absence format (Liu et al., 2013).

To perform connectivity analysis using the topological river network, we assigned SDMs as an attribute (presence–absence) to each river reach; as a result, a total of 11 434 km of medium and large rivers (Strahler order 4 or higher) were found to be historically associated with one or more migratory species. Migratory fish habitats are predominantly located below 1000 m a.s.l. (9371 km; 85.1 % of the total river network). To account for the different elevation ranges associated with different life stages of migratory fish – *Pseudoplatystoma magdaleniatum* and *Sorubim cuspicaudus* do not exceed 500 m; *Pimelodus grosskopfii* can reach 900 m; *Prochilodus magdalenae, Salminus affinis*, and *Brycon moorei* are reported to perform reproductive migrations up to elevations of 1500 m; and *Brycon henni* can reach 2000 m (Jiménez-Segura et al., 2014) – we evaluated the total loss of connectivity in three elevation ranges: 0 to 400 m a.s.l. (juvenile fish growth), 400 to 1000 m a.s.l., and 1000 to 1500 m a.s.l. (migration and spawning).

4 Results

4.1 Upstream impacts

4.1.1 Baseline conditions

The baseline length of the river network associated with migratory fish (Strahler order ≥ 4) and connected to the floodplains is 6789 km in the elevation range of 0 to 400 m a.s.l., 1104 km between 400 and 1000 m a.s.l., and 123 km between 1000 and 1500 m a.s.l. Compared to a total pre-dam length of 11 434 km (6963, 2402, and 941 km, respectively, in the specified elevation ranges), this represents a loss of 28.8 % of connected river length, with the greatest connectivity loss at high elevations; only 2.5 % of the total river length is affected by fragmentation at 0 to 400 m a.s.l., while between 400 and 1000 m a.s.l. the figure is 54.0 %, and between 1000 and 1500 m a.s.l., 86.9 % (Fig. 6). Figure 6 illustrates the distinct differences in topographic profiles of the mainstem and its tributaries, and could be used to identify potential natural breaks in connectivity and local hotspots for endemism due to steep variations in gradient. Altitudinal distribution of fish species and habitat loss with increasing elevation is shown in Fig. 6d and e.

The baseline cumulative hydrologic alteration – expressed as DOR_W – is 3.2 %. Peñoncito station on the Magdalena River (2502733), La Coquera station on the Cauca (2624702), and La Esperanza station on the Nechí (2703701) show relatively low levels of DOR_W at 5.2, 3.0, and 3.2 %, respectively, but with high levels of controlled runoff: 48, 80, and 25 %, respectively (Fig. 7a). Current low levels of regulation are explained by the comparatively low storage capacity of existing reservoirs in comparison with basin flows. However, sediment loads are estimated to have been reduced due to reservoir trapping of 40.9, 61.3, and 39.9 % at the three locations, respectively (Fig. 7b).

4.1.2 Future scenarios

Figure 8 presents the expected cumulative impacts of 1400 generated future scenarios (1000 randomly generated – shown as grey dots, and 400 following four sets of potential basin-level restrictions – shown as colored dots), highlighting those in the range of projected expansion by 2050 (15 250 ± 500 MW). Scenarios of comparable energy capacity show wide ranges of increased cumulative impacts due to nonlinearity. Regarding river fragmentation (Fig. 8a), 6763 to 4391 km of connected river length between 0 and 400 m a.s.l. remain in the different scenarios (a loss of 2.9 to 36.9 % from pre-dam conditions). The range of potential loss of connectivity in elevations between 400 and 1000 m a.s.l. is particularly dramatic, with outcomes between 1104 and 68.5 km of remaining connected network, a 15-fold impact range. The worst-case scenario (equivalent to a loss of 97.1 % with respect to pre-dam conditions) would eliminate virtually all connections between lowland floodplains and upstream spawning areas, while the best-case scenario presents no additional impacts. Figure 8b and c present downstream impacts of hydrologic alteration and sediment trapping, respectively. The expected range of basin-level cumulative DOR_W is 4.1 to 18.1 %, equivalent to 1.3 to 5.7 times the baseline condition. Ranges of additional DOR_W impacts also vary substantially between the Magdalena and the Cauca, being much higher in the latter. While this is mostly a result of the relative size of Magdalena in terms of flow (the Magdalena is

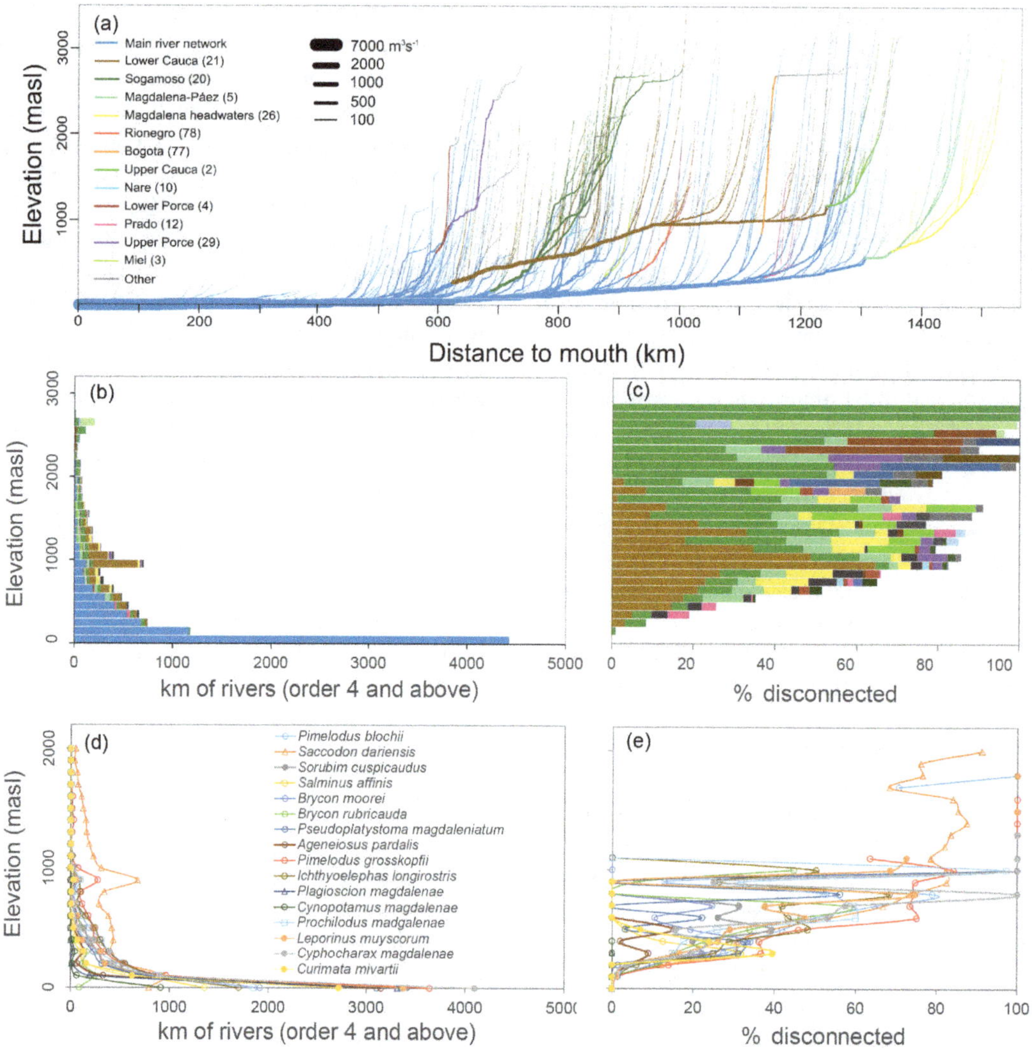

Figure 6. Baseline conditions of remaining river network connectivity by elevation (rivers of order 4 and above). Network fragments associated with specific barriers shown in different colors (**a–c**; Project IDs from Table 1). Habitat availability and loss by elevation ranges of migratory fish species (**d, e**).

approximately twice the size), it is worth noting that most of the largest reservoirs projected in the basin are located in the Cauca River, which is characterized by a much narrower and steeper river valley. Cumulative sediment trapping lies in the range of 41.0 to 68.9 %, representing an additional change of between 1.1 and 29 % over the baseline (39.9 %).

There is a wide range of expected impacts associated with scenarios of comparable hydropower capacity (Fig. 9). Some trade-offs in the set can be clearly identified, such as regulation between the Cauca and Magdalena (we did not attempt to establish the Pareto-optimal set, since the purpose of our study was not to perform an optimization). Through our analysis we found no statistically significant correlation between DOR_w and connectivity or between DOR_w and sediment trapping. This finding indicates the complementarity of the proposed metrics. In contrast, we found a high inverse correlation ($R^2 > 0.84$) between migratory connectivity and sediment trapping, indicating that future work could use sediment trapping as a proxy for connectivity loss, or vice versa (Fig. 9). However, this relationship may be unique to the Magdalena system as some of the remaining basin's migratory routes are associated with large free-flowing tributaries that contribute significant sediment loads. It is worth noting that in all the scenarios considered, additional regulation in the Cauca has little to no additional effect on sediment transport reduction; this is due to the high sediment trapping of the baseline condition, and specifically due to the high sediment retention efficiency of Projects 2 and 21. (Those two projects' high sediment input will affect their longevity.)

Figures 8 and 9 also allow comparison of the range of basin-level impacts resulting from scenarios derived from the proposed sampling strategies following basin-level guide-

Table 2. Indices of basin-level cumulative alteration of selected scenarios at Mompós Depression boundary conditions. Percentage loss of the connected main river network in parentheses. See Fig. 5 for station locations.

Scenario	Installed capacity	Weighted degree of regulation (%)			Connected main river network (km) and loss (%)		Cumulative sediment trapping (%)		
	(MW)	Magdalena	Cauca	Nechí	0–400 m a.s.l.	400–1000 m a.s.l.	Magdalena	Cauca	Nechí
Baseline	9781	5.2	4.8	0.6	6789 (2.5)	1104 (54)	40.9	79.2	24.6
A	14 856	8.5	4.9	2.9	6763 (2.9)	1021 (57.5)	47.2	79.3	27.1
B	15 603	6.2	39.1	4.3	6637 (4.7)	975 (59.4)	40.3	66.7	66.7
C	15 081	15.3	19.0	2.1	6433 (7.6)	485 (79.8)	60.7	67.9	52.6
D	15 635	23.5	19.3	24.5	4791 (31.2)	143 (94.1)	80	78.7	66.2
E	14 771	13.2	5.7	2.9	6703 (3.7)	937 (61)	58	66.6	50.7

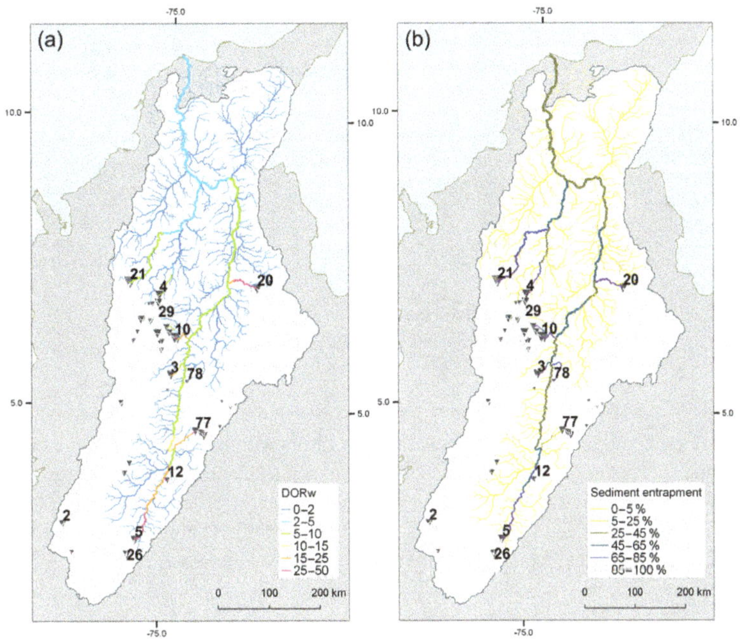

Figure 7. Baseline cumulative impacts of existing and under-construction dams in the basin (symbolized by triangles): **(a)** DOR_W weighted degree of regulation and **(b)** percentage of sediment entrapment due to upstream reservoirs. Fragmented sections of river network are greyed out. Selected projects labeled with IDs used in Table 1.

lines to restrict certain projects sites. In this case, we did not attempt to comprehensively explore how different restrictions can enable better outcomes. Rather, we illustrated how the potential application of a bottom-up approach of providing key information to decision makers in the basin could enable local and individual decisions (i.e., site selection, project size, etc.) that "scale-up" to better basin-level outcomes. As shown, in some cases simple restrictions result in expansion pathways consistently better in most of the analyzed impact and benefits metrics. In particular, as shown in Fig. 9, scenarios that avoid projects located on tributaries not yet affected by artificial barriers and mainstem projects upstream of existing reservoirs, are characterized by lower basin level impacts on all four dimensions considered. Additionally, this type of analysis can illustrate that certain restrictions – while they may help circumvent local impacts like projects affecting populated areas – are not sufficient to avoid basin-level impacts.

The five selected scenarios (highlighted in Fig. 9 and summarized in Table 2) are representative of the wide range of potential boundary conditions of the Mompós Depression: A and B are equivalent in terms of low sediment trapping and fragmentation of spawning habitats, but with contrasting geographical distribution of DOR_W. Scenario A adds artificial regulation in the Magdalena sub-basin, B to the Cauca sub-basin. C and E correspond to "mediocre" cases, while D was in the group of worst-case scenarios in terms of impact on artificial regulation, sediment load loss, and upstream connectivity. It should be noted that all five scenarios are plausible under Colombia's current regulatory framework.

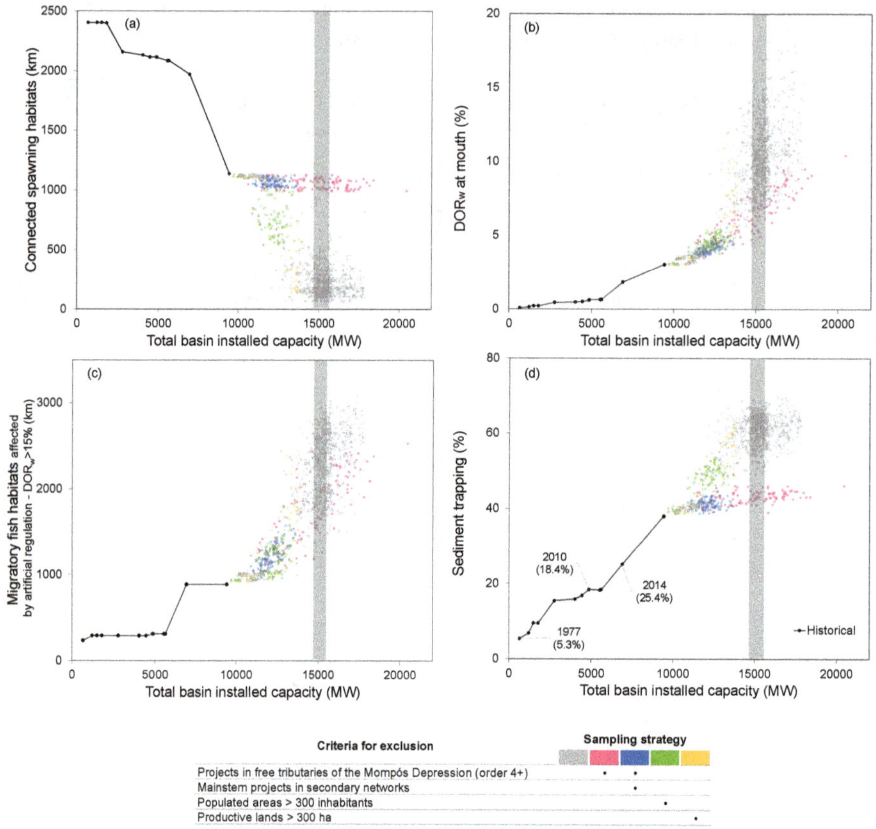

Figure 8. Indicators of basin-level cumulative alteration of historical hydropower development and randomly generated expansion scenarios (dots) using different sampling strategies (differentiated by color). Shaded area shows the range of expected capacity by 2050 (15 250 ± 500 MW). **(a)** Longitudinally connected migratory fish spawning habitat (river length) at 400–1000 m a.s.l. **(b)** Cumulative streamflow regulation measured as weighted degree of regulation (DOR_W). **(c)** Migratory fish habitat (river length) affected by artificial regulation (DOR > 15 %). **(d)** Total sediment trapping in reservoirs upstream of the Mompós Depression.

Simulated average streamflow of the baseline and selected scenarios across stations 2502733 (Magdalena), 2624702 (Cauca), and 2703701 (Nechí) shows the two annual storage–release cycles (Storage: March–May and September–November, and Release: December–February and June–August), with consequent cumulative attenuation of the seasonal streamflow signal and the overall regulation effect of dry, average, and wet years (Fig. 10). DOR_W levels as low as 10 to 15 % (corresponding to scenarios A and C for the Magdalena and C for the Cauca), effectively reduce the amplitude of seasonal oscillations, especially in years with extreme dry macroclimatic conditions like 1992 and 1998 Niño events. Scenarios with higher DOR_W (> 23 %) (D for the Magdalena and Cauca, and B for the Cauca), can eliminate the seasonal signal altogether in average to dry years. None of the evaluated artificial regulation scenarios affect seasonal patterns or magnitudes during wet or extremely wet periods.

It must be noted that flow alteration impacts are highly influenced by operational rules, and even reservoir configurations with a high DOR_W can be operated to mimic the natural flow regime. While this study did not explore the implications of alternative operational rules in detail (our analysis only attempted to reproduce historical seasonal generation targets for the basin), the multiple simulations performed are representative of a wide range of DOR_W (from 3 to 29 %) and can serve as a reasonable approximation of the envelope of expected operational behavior of multiple reservoirs with similar build-out storage capacities.

4.2 Floodplains analysis

4.2.1 WEAP model implementation

Figure 11 summarizes the model calibration and validation metrics for the sub-set (15 out of 12 000, 0.12 %) of randomly generated model parameters with highest performance, above or closest to the acceptance ranges (NSE > 0.65 and P-Bias < 10 %) – or "good-fit" model set. As shown, performance is consistent across the 13 streamflow gauges and calibration and validation periods, with the exception of streamflow gauges 2502749 and 2502757 (cal-

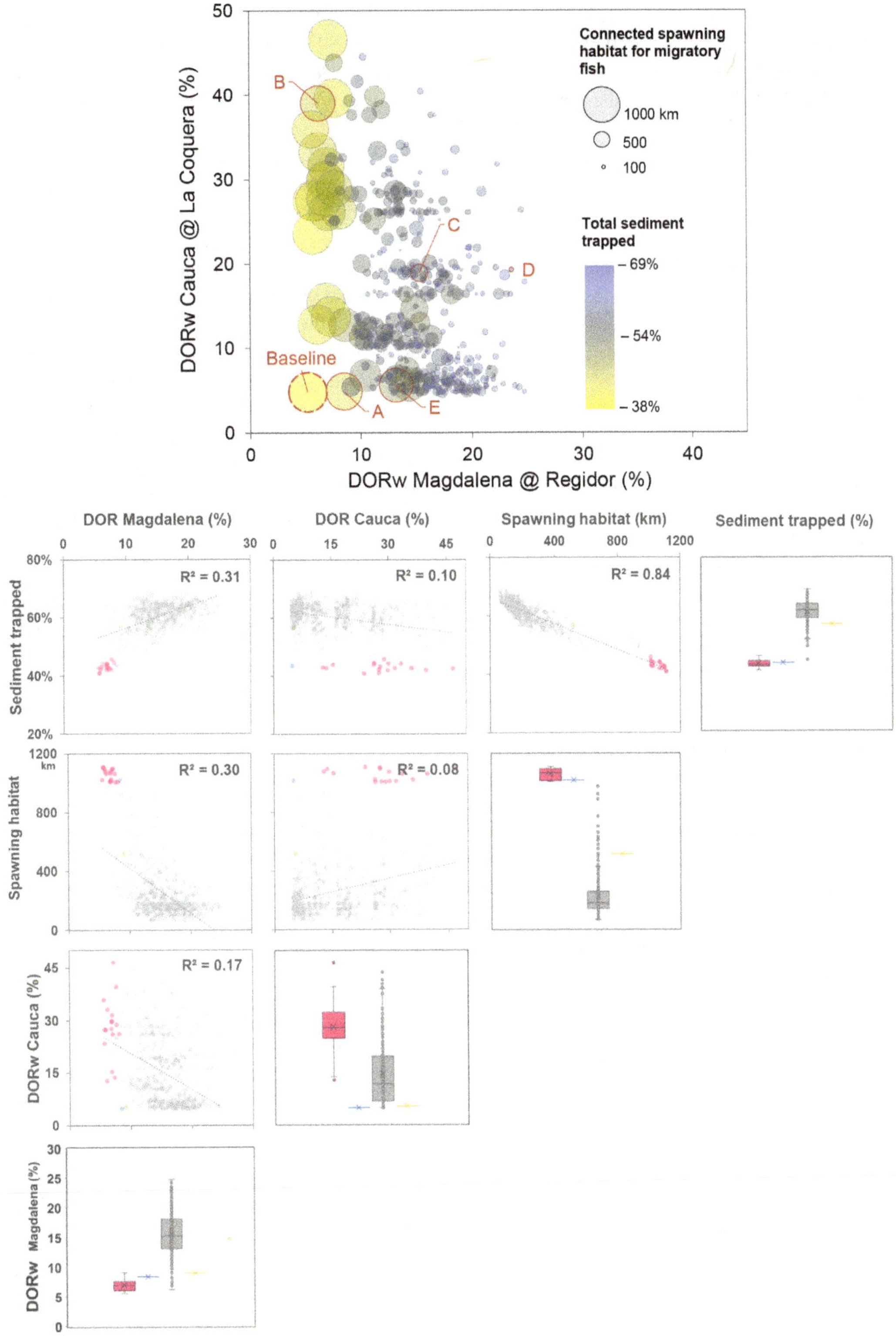

Figure 9. Trade-off plot for scenarios in the range of expected hydropower expansion (15 250 ± 500 MW). Top panel: x and y axes are expected DOR_W upstream of the Mompós Depression on the Magdalena and the Cauca, respectively; bubble size represents length of connected network in the range of 400–1000 m a.s.l. (spawning habitat), and color indicates the expected loss of sediment load due to reservoir trapping. Selected scenarios for detailed analyses are labeled as A–E. Bottom panels: 2-D plots and box-plots of individual metrics of basin-level impacts. Colors identify different sampling strategies following legend shown in Fig. 8.

ibration). However, at the same locations, performance increases during the validation period (1999–2013), which may indicate errors in the observed record at those sites during the period 1981–1998. Sharp performance decreases in gauges 2502720 and 2502764 are due to the Cauca levee breach that occurred during a 2010–2011 La Niña event.

Model sensitivity analysis of average and maximum volume storage in the main floodplain sub-units, shows results vary in the range of ±25 % of the mean value of the set estimate in most of the sub-units, with the exception of C24 (Ciénaga de Ayapel), where observed variation of estimates was up to ±35 % of the mean value of the subset of "good-fit" models.

Model limitations

The model developed runs on a monthly time step and represents large units. As a result, we were unable to evaluate high-frequency floodplain dynamics such as backwater effects on tributaries, and rates of increase in the depth and extent of flows. The extent of the flooded area was not directly reproduced by the model.

4.2.2 Hydrologic alteration of floodplain dynamics

Lastly, the new model allowed us to evaluate the potential changes in wetland hydrological dynamics for each of the considered configurations of hydropower in the MRB. Figure 12 shows the simulated changes for the baseline condition and for all hydropower expansion configurations aiming for hydropower production (A to E), and alternative operation schemes aiming to reduce peak flows during extreme high events (B' and D').

Results show a heterogeneous response of the different floodplain units to upstream hydrologic alterations; units with the highest sensitivity to increased DOR_w alteration are the Zapatosa, Rosario, Brazo de Loba, and Brazo Mompós, all of which are directly influenced by the Magdalena River. The Bajo San Jorge unit, which is influenced by the San Jorge, Cauca, and Magdalena, showed a comparatively lower sensitivity to upstream hydrologic alteration. The Ayapel and San Marcos units showed the lowest sensitivity to upstream alteration, consistent with the fact that the connection between the Cauca River and Ayapel and San Marcos floodplains became limited in the 1970s by the construction of a lateral levee west of the Cauca River (Dique Marginal del Cauca); currently those wetlands units are only influenced by the San Jorge River. Episodic levee failures, like the ones observed during the La Niña event of 2010–2011, have reestablished connection between the Cauca River and the San Marcos and Ayapel systems; however, such events during extreme wet periods are not affected by dam operations, as shown in the previous section.

Low and extremely low storage events showed the highest impacts from increased regulation of upstream tributaries. Under the baseline condition and all expansion scenarios, extremely low storage events (P_{90} to min) are expected to have much higher magnitude and be much less variable, especially in floodplains with a permanent connection between the river and wetlands systems, like the Zapatosa, Rosario, Brazo Mompós, and Bajo San Jorge. Alteration is higher during the first half of the year, which typically oscillates with higher amplitude between dry and wet periods. Scenarios with the highest cumulative DOR_w at station 2502733 on the Magdalena River (Scenario D), also induced significant changes in the magnitude of low storage events (P_{75} to P_{90}), modifying the amplitude of seasonal variation of floodplain and wetlands storage. Low and extremely low storage events support biodiversity by enabling several different ecological processes such as reptile reproduction, propagation of riparian vegetation communities, and nutrient and organic matter storage. Low storage also keeps invasive and introduced species in check by eliminating those that are not adapted to variable conditions.

Seasonal storage events corresponding to ranges of duration between P_{10} and P_{75} were found to change in floodplain units characterized by long periods of disconnection between floodplain and river systems, such as the Brazo Loba unit; with a higher sensitivity to seasonal ecodeficits in the range of P_{10} to P_{75} during the second half of the year. Reduced seasonal storage in this area could consequently have severe impacts on local ecosystem functioning, as episodic yearly inundation is critical for water, nutrient, and sediment delivery to the floodplain system. Connectivity times and storage volume also determine habitat availability for migratory and resident fish.

In scenarios with the highest cumulative DOR_wat station 2502733 (D), floodplain units with permanent connections like the Zapatosa, Brazo Mompós, and Rosario, also experienced small changes in storage in the range of P_{10} to P_{75}, and a reduction of small seasonal flood events, potentially affecting the extent of wetlands oscillation. Seasonal oscillation also supports multiple ecosystem processes, including the prevention of the invasion of riparian vegetation into the channel, and a general contribution to habitat heterogeneity.

Regarding extreme high storage events, development of hydropower dams has very low impact on high flows/flood magnitude, as extreme high flows continue to occur even under alternative operation rules focused on increased buffer capacities for regulating extreme wet events (represented by scenarios B' and D'). None of the proposed scenarios would substantially reduce the magnitudes or duration of extreme floods associated with periodic high flow events (occurring every 10 years or more), such as those that occurred around La Niña in 2010–2011. Operation regimes aimed at maximizing energy production (maintaining higher storage to increase working head) as well as those aimed at reducing the

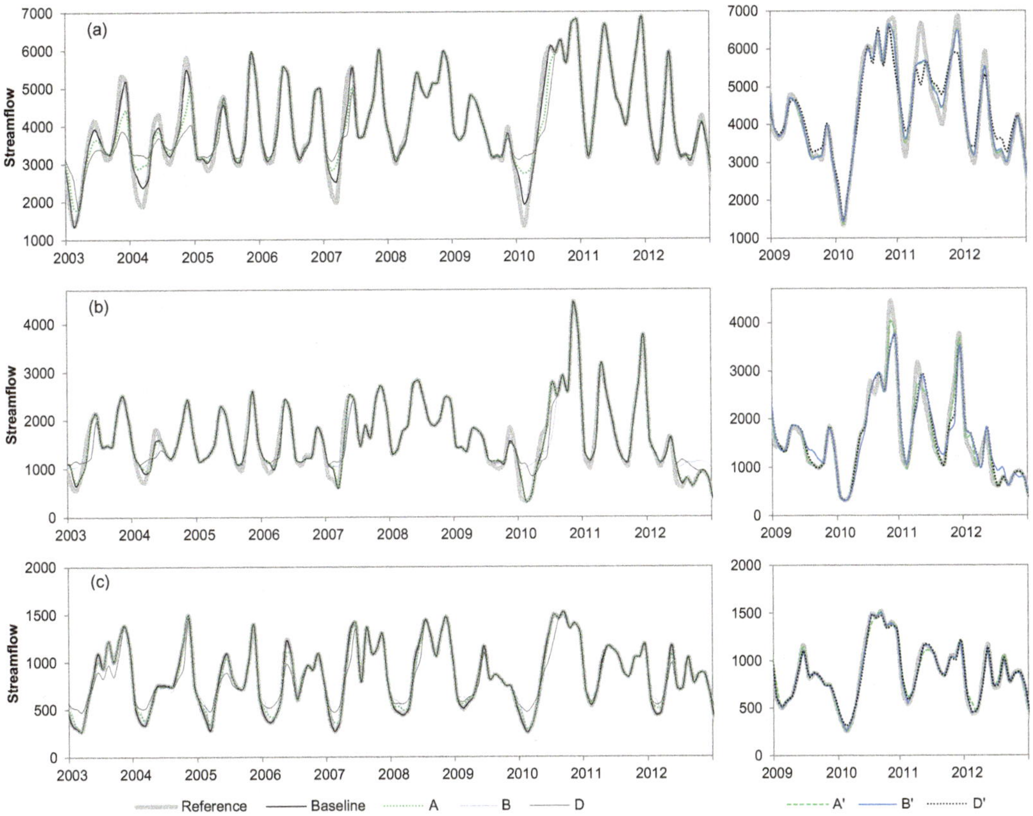

Figure 10. Comparison of 10-year sample (2003–2012) of simulated boundary conditions (monthly average streamflow) resulting from selected hydropower configurations A, B and D. Streamflow values are shown for stations on the **(a)** Magdalena (2502733), **(b)** Cauca (2624702), and **(c)** Nechí (2703701) rivers, upstream of the Mompós Depression. Full period of boundary conditions is 1981–2013. Left plots show resulting simulation from scenarios from a hydropower priority operation. Right plots show examples of operation aiming to reduce flood peak magnitudes during the Niño–Niña 2009–2011 event by maintaining low storage in reservoirs to regulate peak flows.

magnitude of peak flows (maintaining lower storage to increase buffer capacity to store peak flows) show little-to-no effect on the magnitude of extreme high events. This is consistent with the fact that even at the highest DOR_W levels (up to 39.1 % in the Cauca, or 24.7 % in the Magdalena), usable reservoir buffering capacity during extreme wet events can be surpassed in less than two months at peak flow volume, rendering reservoirs unable to substantially affect the magnitudes of extensive wet seasons – like those experienced during 2010 and 2011 – and forcing operators to spill water for dam safety. Nevertheless, extreme flooding events deposit nutrients and organic matter in the floodplain, recharge the water table, and determine geomorphologic dynamics of the system. As discussed in Sect. 4.1.2, proposed scenarios can also reduce sediment loads up to 69 %. Through reduced sediment loads during peak flood events, wetlands and floodplains could experience reduced productivity and a progressive transformation into permanent water bodies.

5 Discussion

5.1 Contributions of this research

From a general perspective, we believe this research can contribute to the adoption of effective frameworks for strategic decision-making in the configuration of hydropower expansion. Our research shows that integrated and basin-level considerations focused on avoiding cumulative impacts on long-range, key environmental processes and components can be effectively adopted as criteria for the multiple stages of hydropower planning and development, from site selection to identification of long-term expansion potential

In this specific case, we focused our attention on key attributes of ecologically functional floodplains (Opperman et al., 2010), based on (1) hydrologic connectivity between the river and the floodplain, and between upstream and downstream sections; (2) hydrologic variability patterns and their links to local and regional processes; and (3) the spatial scale required to sustain floodplain-associated processes and benefits, like migratory fish biodiversity. Our proposed framework

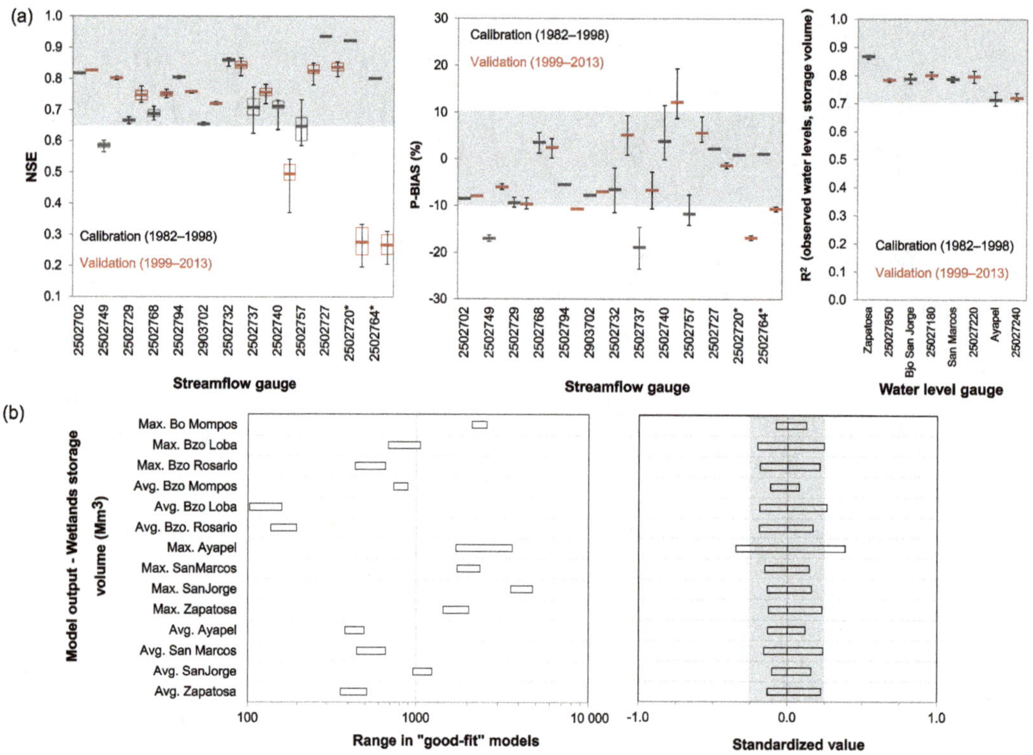

Figure 11. Comparison of the subset of models with highest performance obtained from Monte Carlo calibration: **(a)** NSE and percentile bias of streamflow, and correlation coefficient of water levels and storage volumes. Acceptance ranges highlighted in grey. **(b)** Model sensitivity of "good-fit models", in terms of average and maximum volume storage in the main floodplain sub-units of the Mompós Depression.

provides an explicit quantification of the nonlinear or direct response relationship of those considerations to hydropower expansion. Changes in connectivity, hydrologic variability patterns, and the spatial scale of processes result from a wide range of scenarios that produce equivalent levels of energy generation capacity. This finding underscores the advantage of system-level integrated approaches to hydropower planning and development as well as the potential to minimize impacts without sacrificing generating capacity (Hartmann et al., 2013; Nardini and Franco-Idarraga, 2016; Opperman et al., 2015), and demonstrates how consideration of the trade-offs between impacts and benefits can serve as a basis for a preventive approach. Another important finding of this research is related to how to design and evaluate transparent guiding principles that can be adopted by both policy makers and project developers; our case study illustrates some examples that take advantage of the nonlinearity of impacts on freshwater systems, and explores how to inform decision makers through simple rules that can enable conditions that avoid or reduce impacts on basin-level key processes.

Another relevant contribution is the enhancements to the WEAP modeling platform to resolve water balance dynamics of floodplains and wetlands. Our study shows that the hydrologic dynamics of water storage in floodplains on a monthly to decadal scale can be represented with these enhancements. In the case of the MRB, this enables WEAP to successfully resolve the lowland floodplains water balance at medium scales (~ 1000 to $10\,000\,\mathrm{km}^2$), while linking the simulation of these dynamics to upstream water management practices. By providing an improved understanding of the linkages between climate variability, system operation, and floodplain dynamics, this modeling approach can contribute in the consideration of floodplains dynamics into water management infrastructure development and operation decisions as well as in ecosystem conservation or restoration projects.

Colombia's regulatory framework – as other countries' – currently omits any consideration of basin-level impacts of hydropower expansion; the current study provides a method to include such considerations. The wide range of scenarios, from those producing outcomes with relatively small additional environmental impacts, to those that virtually eliminate basin-level processes, provides huge potential to avoid undesirable outcomes through a comprehensive integration of system-level performance metrics into hydropower planning. The challenge is integrating these considerations into policy design, which is currently highly reactionary and market driven.

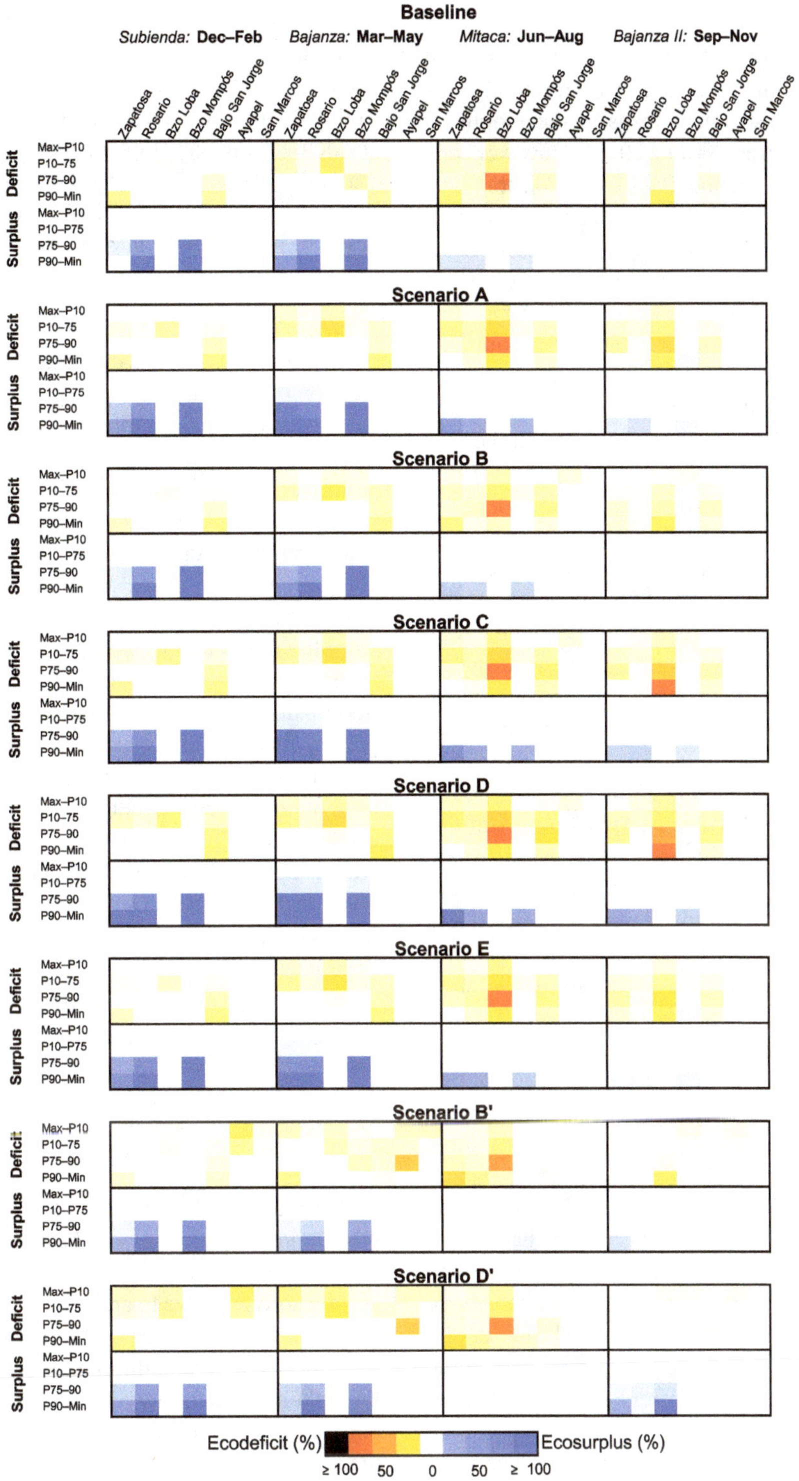

Figure 12. Impacts of upstream regulation scenarios in wetland dynamics for the different floodplain sub-units (see locations in Fig. 5), expressed as ecodeficits or ecosurpluses in the hydroperiod. Seasons correspond to periods of biologic and hydrologic relevance, particularly to fish migration: Subienda (December–February), Bajanza I (March–May), Mitaca (June–August), and Bajanza II (September–November). Ranges of durations representing extreme high (Max–P_{10}), seasonal (P_{10}–P_{75}), low (P_{75}–P_{90}), and extreme low events (P_{90}–Min) are representative of events associated with different ecological or physical processes. Scenarios B' and D' consider an alternative operational regime of configurations B and D, to reduce flood peak magnitudes by maintaining low storage in reservoirs to allow regulation of peak flows.

5.2 Implications of the case study

The most recent analysis of sediment yield changes, performed using records from 1972 to 2010, shows no significant trend in observed sediment loads at the mouth of the Magdalena River (Restrepo et al., 2015). However, our study estimated sediment reduction due to reservoir trapping in 1977 and 2010 at 5.3 and 18.4 %, respectively, equivalent to an average decrease of 0.40 % yr^{-1}. In addition to reservoir effects, sediment trapping must be discussed in relation to other controls on sediment yield and transport, in particular to the clearing of natural vegetation for land cultivation, which is likely to result in increased river sediment yields (Walling and Fang, 2003). Over the same period of the study of Restrepo et al. (2015), average rates of natural cover loss in the MRB were estimated at 1.4 to 1.9 % yr^{-1} (Etter et al., 2006; Restrepo et al., 2006). While the sediment retention/release dynamics of the Mompós floodplains are not well understood, the apparent equilibrium in basin-level sediment transport at the river mouth might be the result of the wetlands acting to buffer the sediment balance – with sediment added from land cover change being balanced by increased retention in the wetlands and/or additional sediment trapped by reservoirs being balanced by increased sediment released from the wetlands.

Despite the uncertain contribution of the Mompós floodplains to the MRB sediment balance, we must note that the baseline condition – which includes projects with an expected completion in 2018 – represents a significant increase in sediment trapping (from 18.4 to 39.9 %) over the reference period (1972–2010) reported by Restrepo et al. (2015). Further observation of the sediment balance of the Mompós floodplain can provide more definitive evidence of project impacts. Such analysis is urgent and relevant because under certain conditions, sediment deficits could induce basin-scale system transformations, such as net subsidence of wetland and floodplain areas and a progressive transformation into permanent water bodies. The wide range of increased sediment retention in future scenarios must also be a consideration in the assessment of hydropower contributions to carbon budgets, as studies have indicated a relationship between reservoirs' retention of organic sediments and greenhouse gas emissions (Deemer et al., 2016; Maeck et al., 2013); sediment retention is also important to the operation and longevity of hydropower dams, from a system-level perspective.

Loss of longitudinal connectivity by dams has been reported as one of the major threats to fish in the MRB, especially for migratory species and commonly fished species (Carvajal-Quintero et al., 2017; López-Casas et al., 2016). Those findings are supported by the results presented here, with the highest values of habitat fragmentation (up to 97.3 %) incurred by dams situated between 400 and 1500 m a.s.l. (Fig. 6). Loss of longitudinal connectivity through river fragmentation could be affecting more than the migratory species evaluated here; it is important to note that this elevation range (400 to 2000 m a.s.l.) contains the highest fish species richness in the MRB, including several endemic species distributed along the tributaries having the densest dam development (Carvajal-Quintero et al., 2015; Jaramillo-Villa et al., 2010). This study prioritized evaluation of the impacts of longitudinal loss, but dams and associated reservoirs also affect lateral (local) connectivity as well as vertical connectivity (connection to groundwater).

Additionally, and as illustrated, upstream hydrologic alteration can produce heterogeneous effects in the floodplain lowlands, but the most immediate consequences seem related to changes in the amplitude, magnitude, extension, and seasonal variation of floodplain inundation and wetland water storage in low- and extreme-low flow conditions (Fig. 12). These, along with changes in sediment inputs due to discharge regulation in the Mompós Depression, can alter important environmental signals and stimuli for fish migration, from the floodplain to the upstream tributaries. Loss of sediment inputs – and consequently of nutrient inputs – to the floodplains, which form a nursery and feeding area for migratory fish, can affect available energy reserves for the migration and reproductive maturation essential for reproduction in the upstream tributaries, as discussed by López-Casas et al. (2016). There are other important biological effects which should be evaluated in relation to changes in the composition and functional structure of the floodplain fish assemblages in the Mompós Depression. These changes have been documented in other basins, such as the Amazon (Röpke et al., 2017). Hydrologic alteration in combination with overfishing and habitat conversion in the lowland floodplain in the Mompós Depression could profoundly affect the food security of the people that live in the lower MRB and depend on fisheries for their food supply and income.

Our findings also reveal a distinct response of the Mompós Depression floodplains based on the relative locations of dams in the basin. Under current conditions, this system seems more sensitive to artificial regulation in the Magdalena River than in the Cauca. Hydropower in the Cauca River seems to have little additional effect in terms of alteration of floodplain inundation dynamics, as significant loss of lateral connectivity four decades ago continues to affect marshes on the west bank (the Ayapel and San Marcos). Additionally, the reservoirs of the Cauca have little influence over regulation of extreme events. This result, however, should be viewed in light of some proposals to replace the current levee on the west bank of the Cauca with infrastructure that could restore the hydraulic connection between these systems. The WEAP model developed in this study can contribute to the evaluation of such measures.

6 Conclusion

This paper presents a framework to quantify impacts and trade-offs to inform hydropower expansion decisions, thus enabling an integrated approach of basin-level physical, environmental, and ecosystem processes. Following Opperman et al. (2010), we focused on functional lowland floodplain systems as key basin-level environmental features, considering the impacts of hydropower expansion on (1) hydrologic connectivity between the river and the floodplain, and between upstream and downstream sections; (2) hydrologic variability patterns and their links to local and regional processes; and (3) the spatial scale required to sustain floodplain-associated processes and benefits, like migratory fish biodiversity. Our analysis illustrates the nonlinear behavior of cumulative impacts, characterized by a wide range of potential outcomes for equivalent energy expansion configurations, and demonstrates a practical approach to inform decision makers on how to design effective guidelines to protect – or avoid additional impacts on – key basin-scale processes and ecosystems.

As part of this study we developed a set of enhancements to WEAP that allow for simulation of the water balance dynamics of floodplains and wetlands. By providing an improved understanding of the linkages between climate variability, system operation, and floodplain dynamics, these new routines can guide the implementation of water management infrastructure development as well as ecosystem conservation or restoration projects. Both components are critical to the sustainable development of Colombia and many other countries.

From a planning perspective, we compared possible scenarios of hydropower development (as combinations of projects) that meet expected national expansion goals for 2050. In the case of the MRB, our analysis shows that baseline hydropower conditions have already significantly altered multiple basin-level processes vital to the health of the Mompós wetlands floodplains – in particular, loss of longitudinal connectivity of spawning habitats of migratory fish (−54.8 %) and decreased sediment transport (−39 %) – while flow regime and wetland hydrological variability maintain near natural conditions. Development scenarios, however, show a potential range of up to one order of magnitude of additional impacts across comparable hydropower capacity. Some future development scenarios can result in significant physical or hydrologic alteration, i.e., a loss of longitudinal connectivity to virtually all remaining spawning habitat for migratory fish and significant reductions of sediment loads, while substantially altering floodplain (lateral) seasonal inundation dynamics in extensive areas of the Mompós Depression. Our analysis of possible scenarios, however, indicates that other scenarios would result in much lower differential changes. This emphasizes the need for comprehensive basin-level approaches to water infrastructure planning that integrate broader environmental and cumulative impacts

Glacier Lake and Ongoing Remediation Measures, J. Nepal Geol. Soc., 22, 563–570, 2000.

to achieve balanced outcomes across a wide range of objectives.

We recognize that the metrics used in this analysis, while selected to provide an objective insight into multiple basin-scale key processes, are still proxies with no direct representation of the specific ecological processes of the MRB. Nevertheless, the proposed framework can serve as a basis to guide detailed studies at the reach scale to establish direct relationships.

Data availability. The following datasets were used in this research: HydroSHEDS 3-second grids (https://hydrosheds.cr.usgs.gov/dataavail.php, Lehner et al., 2006) and HydroBASINS (http://www.hydrosheds.org, Lehner and Grill, 2013); Colombian energy market data – daily inflows, storage, and spills (http://informacioninteligente10.xm.com.co/hidrologia/Paginas/HistoricoHidrologia.aspx, XM, 2005); Colombian Water Resources Information System (sistema de información del recurso hídrico) (http://sirh.ideam.gov.co:8230/Sirh/faces/observatorio.jspx, IDEAM, 2015).

Competing interests. The authors declare that they have no conflict of interest.

Acknowledgements. This work was supported by USAID Cooperative Agreement Award No. AID-S14-A-13-00004 and AID-514-A-12-00002, the Rio Magdalena Watershed Management Program, and "Generación del Bicentenario" scholarship program funded by Colombia's Departamento administrativo de ciencia, tecnología e innovación – Colciencias. The authors would like to thank Anne G. Hereford for her contributions in writing assistance, technical editing, language editing, and proofreading.

Edited by: Pieter van der Zaag

References

Angarita, H., Delgado, J., Escobar-Arias, M. I., and Walschburger, T.: Escenarios de alteración regional del regimen hidrológico en la cuenca Magdalena-Cauca por intensificación de la demanda para hidroenergía, in: Memorias del Congreso Internacional AGUA, Universidad del Valle, Cali, Colombia, 2013.

ARCADIS Nederland BV and JESYCA S.A.S.: Plan Maestro Fluvial de Colombia 2015, prepared for Ministerio de Transporte and Departamento Nacional de Planeación, Bogotá, Colombia, 2015.

Arias, M. E., Piman, T., Lauri, H., Cochrane, T. A., and Kummu, M.: Dams on Mekong tributaries as significant contributors of hydrological alterations to the Tonle Sap Floodplain in Cambodia, Hydrol. Earth Syst. Sci., 18, 5303–5315, https://doi.org/10.5194/hess-18-5303-2014, 2014.

Bayley, P. B.: Understanding Large River–Floodplain Ecosystems, Bioscience, 45, 153–158, https://doi.org/10.2307/1312554, 1995.

Carvajal-Quintero, J. D., Escobar, F., Alvarado, F., Villa-Navarro, F. A., Jaramillo-Villa, Ú., and Maldonado-Ocampo, J. A.: Variation in freshwater fish assemblages along a regional elevation gradient in the northern Andes, Colombia, Ecol. Evol., 5, 2608–2620, https://doi.org/10.1002/ece3.1539, 2015.

Carvajal-Quintero, J. D., Januchowski-Hartley, S. R., Maldonado-Ocampo, J. A., Jézéquel, C., Delgado, J., and Tedesco, P. A.: Damming Fragments Species Ranges and Heightens Extinction Risk, Conserv. Lett., 10, 708–716, https://doi.org/10.1111/conl.12336, 2017.

Cramton, P. and Stoft, S.: Colombia Firm Energy Market, in: Proceedings of the 40th Annual Hawaii International Conference on System Sciences, HICSS, Waikoloa, Hawaii, USA, 2007.

Dang, T. D., Cochrane, T. A., Arias, M. E., Van, P. D. T., and de Vries, T.: Hydrological alterations from water infrastructure development in the Mekong floodplains, Hydrol. Process., 30, 3824–3838, https://doi.org/10.1002/hyp.10894, 2016.

Deemer, B. R., Harrison, J. A., Li, S., Beaulieu, J. J., Delsontro, T., Barros, N., Bezerra-Neto, J. F., Powers, S. M., Dos Santos, M. A., and Vonk, J. A.: Greenhouse gas emissions from reservoir water surfaces: A new global synthesis, Bioscience, 66, 949–964, https://doi.org/10.1093/biosci/biw117, 2016.

Dendy, F. E.: Sediment trap efficiency of small reservoirs, T. ASAE, 17, 898–908, https://doi.org/10.13031/2013.36994, 1974.

Departamento Nacional de Planeación: Estudio del Sector de Energía Eléctrica – Inventario de recursos hidroenergéticos, Bogotá, Colombia, 1979.

DePhilip, M. and Moberg, T.: Ecosystem flow recommendations for the Upper Ohio River Basin in Western Pennsylvania, The Nature Conservancy, Harrisburg, PA, 2013.

DHI: MIKE21, DHI Water & Environment Pty Ltd., https://www.mikepoweredbydhi.com/products/mike-21, 2016.

Dutta, D., Teng, J., Vaze, J., Lerat, J., Hughes, J., and Marvanek, S.: Storage-based approaches to build floodplain inundation modelling capability in river system models for water resources planning and accounting, J. Hydrol., 504, 12–28, https://doi.org/10.1016/j.jhydrol.2013.09.033, 2013.

Dynesius, M. and Nilsson, C.: Fragmentation and Flow Regulation of River Systems in the Northern Third of the World, Science, 266, 753–762, https://doi.org/10.1126/science.266.5186.753, 1994.

Etter, A., McAlpine, C., Wilson, K., Phinn, S., and Possingham, H.: Regional patterns of agricultural land use and deforestation in Colombia, Agr. Ecosyst. Environ., 114, 369–386, https://doi.org/10.1016/j.agee.2005.11.013, 2006.

FAO: Colombia: Pesca en Cifras/2014, Food and Agriculture Organization of the United Nations, Bogotá, Colombia, http://aunap.gov.co/wp-content/uploads/2016/05/Pesca_en_cifras.pdf (last access: 22 April 2018), 2015.

Fausch, K. D., Torgersen, C. E., Baxter, C. V., and Li, H. W.: Landscapes to Riverscapes: Bridging the Gap between Research and Conservation of Stream Fishes, Bioscience, 52, 483–498, 2002.

Fitzhugh, T. W. and Vogel, R. M.: The impact of dams on flood flows in the United States, River Res. Appl., 27, 1192–1215, https://doi.org/10.1002/rra.1417, 2011.

Fullerton, A. H., Burnett, K. M., Steel, E. A., Flitcroft, R. L., Pess, G. R., Feist, B. E., Torgersen, C. E., Miller, D. J., and Sanderson, B. L.: Hydrological connectivity for riverine fish: Measurement challenges and research opportunities, Freshwater Biol., 55, 2215–2237, https://doi.org/10.1111/j.1365-2427.2010.02448.x, 2010.

Galvis, G. and Mojica, J. I.: The Magdalena River fresh water fishes and fisheries, Aquat. Ecosyst. Health Manage., 10, 127–139, https://doi.org/10.1080/14634980701357640, 2007.

Gao, Y., Vogel, R. M., Kroll, C. N., Poff, N. L., and Olden, J. D.: Development of representative indicators of hydrologic alteration, J. Hydrol., 374, 136–147, https://doi.org/10.1016/j.jhydrol.2009.06.009, 2009.

Grant, G. E., Schmidt, J. C., and Lewis, S. L.: A Geological Framework for Interpreting Downstream Effects of Dams on Rivers, in: A Peculiar River, edited by: O'Connor, J. E. and Grant, G. E., American Geophysical Union, Washington, D.C., 209–225, 2003.

Grill, G., Lehner, B., Lumsdon, A. E., MacDonald, G. K., Zarfl, C., and Reidy Liermann, C.: An index-based framework for assessing patterns and trends in river fragmentation and flow regulation by global dams at multiple scales, Environ. Res. Lett., 10, 15001, https://doi.org/10.1088/1748-9326/10/1/015001, 2015.

Hartmann, J., Harrison, D., Opperman, J. J., and Gill, R.: The Next Frontier of Hydropower Sustainability: Planning at the System Scale, Inter-American Development Bank, Washington, D.C., 2013.

IDEAM: Sistemas morfogénicos del territorio colombiano, Instituto de Hidrología, Meteorología y Estudios Ambientales, Bogotá, Colombia, http://documentacion.ideam.gov.co/openbiblio/bvirtual/021769/Sistemas_morf_Territ_Col_Ideam_Contenido.pdf (last access: 22 April 2018), 2010.

IDEAM: Estudio Nacional del Agua, Instituto de Hidrología, Meteorología y Estudios Ambientales, Bogotá, Colombia, http://documentacion.ideam.gov.co/openbiblio/bvirtual/023080/ENA_2014.pdf (last access: 22 April 2018), 2014.

IDEAM: Observatorio del sistema de información del recurso hídrico, Sistema de Información Ambiental de Colombia, available at: http://sirh.ideam.gov.co:8230/Sirh/faces/observatorio.jspx (last access: 4 May 2018), Bogotá, Colombia, 2015.

IDEAM, IGAC, IAvH, Invemar, ISinchi, and IIAP: Ecosistemas continentales, costeros y marinos de Colombia, Instituto de Hidrología, Meteorología y Estudios Ambientales, Bogotá, Colombia, 2007.

Jaramillo-Villa, Ú., Maldonado-Ocampo, J. A., and Escobar, F.: Altitudinal variation in fish assemblage diversity in streams of the central Andes of Colombia, J. Fish Biol., 76, 2401–2417, https://doi.org/10.1111/j.1095-8649.2010.02629.x, 2010.

Jaramillo, Ú., Cortés-Duque, J., and Flórez, C. (Eds.): Colombia Anfibia. Un país de humedales, in: Vol. 1, Instituto de Investigación de Recursos Biológicos Alexander von Humboldt, Bogotá, Colombia, 2015.

Jimenez, M.: Cuentas de sedimentos a escala de cuencas usando conceptualizaciones de modelos conocidos y confiables, y aplicación de información secundaria, Medellín, Colombia, 2016.

Jiménez-Segura, L. F., Restrepo-Santamaría, D., López-Casas, S., Delgado, J., Valderrama, M., Álvarez, J., and Gómez, D.: Ictiofauna y desarrollo del sector hidroeléctrico en la cuenca del río Magdalena-Cauca, Colombia, Biota Colomb., http://revistas.humboldt.org.co/index.php/biota/article/view/317 (last access: 22 April 2018), 2014.

Lasso, C. A., Gutiérrez, F. de P., Morales-Betancourt, M. A., Agudelo, E., Ramírez-Gil, H. R., and Ajiaco-Martínez, R. E. (Eds.): Pesquerías continentales de Colombia: cuencas del Magdalena-Cauca, Sinú, Canalete, Atrato, Orinoco, Amazonas y vertiente del Pacífico, in: Serie Editorial Recursos Hidrobiológicos y Pesqueros Continentales de Colombia, Instituto de Investigación de los Recursos Biológicos Alexander von Humboldt, Bogotá, Colombia, 2011.

Lehner, B. and Grill, G.: Global river hydrography and network routing: baseline data and new approaches to study the world's large river systems, Hydrol. Process., 27, 2171–2186, 2013 (data available at: http://www.hydrosheds.org, last access: 4 May 2018).

Lehner, B., Verdin, K., and Jarvis, A.: HydroSHEDS, available at: https://hydrosheds.cr.usgs.gov/dataavail.php (last access: 4 May 2018), United States Geological Survey, Reston, VA, 2006.

Lehner, B., Verdin, K., and Jarvis, A.: New global hydrography derived from spaceborne elevation data, Eos Trans. AGU, 89, 93–94, 2008.

Lehner, B., Liermann, C. R., Revenga, C., Vörömsmarty, C., Fekete, B., Crouzet, P., Döll, P., Endejan, M., Frenken, K., Magome, J., Nilsson, C., Robertson, J. C., Rödel, R., Sindorf, N., and Wisser, D.: High-resolution mapping of the world's reservoirs and dams for sustainable river-flow management, Front. Ecol. Environ., 9, 494–502, https://doi.org/10.1890/100125, 2011.

Lewin, J. and Ashworth, P. J.: Defining large river channel patterns: Alluvial exchange and plurality, Geomorphology, 215, 83–98, https://doi.org/10.1016/j.geomorph.2013.02.024, 2014.

Liu, C., White, M., and Newell, G.: Selecting thresholds for the prediction of species occurrence with presence-only data, J. Biogeogr., 40, 778–789, https://doi.org/10.1111/jbi.12058, 2013.

López-Casas, S., Jiménez-Segura, L. F., and Pérez-Gallego, C. M.: Peces migratorios al interior de una central hidroeléctrica: caso Miel I, cuenca del río Magdalena (Caldas-Antioquia), Colombia, Biota Colomb., 15, 26–39, 2014.

López-Casas, S., Jiménez-Segura, L. F., Agostinho, A. A., and Pérez, C. M.: Potamodromous migrations in the Magdalena River basin: bimodal reproductive patterns in neotropical rivers, J. Fish Biol., 89, 157–171, https://doi.org/10.1111/jfb.12941, 2016.

Maeck, A., DelSontro, T., McGinnis, D. F., Fischer, H., Flury, S., Schmidt, M., Fietzek, P. and Lorke, A.: Sediment Trapping by Dams Creates Methane Emission Hot Spots, Environ. Sci. Technol., 47, 8130–8137, https://doi.org/10.1021/es4003907, 2013.

Maldonado-Ocampo, J. A., Vari, R., and Usma, J.: Checklist of the freshwater fishes of Colombia, Biota Colomb., 9, 143–237, 2008.

Moriasi, D. N., Arnold, J. G., Van Liew, M. W., Bingner, R. L., Harmel, R. D., and Veith, T. L.: Model evaluation guidelines for systematic quantification of accuracy in watershed simulations, Trans. Am. Soc. Agr. Biol. Eng., 50, 885–900, 2007.

Nardini, A. and Franco-Idarraga, F.: A Qualitative Hydro-Geomorphic Prediction of the Destiny of the Mojana Region (Magdalena-Cauca Basin, Colombia), to Inform Large Scale Decision Making, Resources, 5, 22, https://doi.org/10.3390/resources5030022, 2016.

Opperman, J. J., Luster, R., McKenney, B. A., Roberts, M., and Meadows, A. W.: Ecologically Functional Floodplains: Connectivity, Flow Regime, and Scale, J. Am. Water Resour. Assoc., 46, 211–226, https://doi.org/10.1111/j.1752-1688.2010.00426.x, 2010.

Opperman, J. J., Grill, G., and Hartmann, J.: The Power of Rivers: Finding balance between energy and conservation in hydropower development, Washington, D.C., http://www.nature.org/media/freshwater/power-of-rivers-report.pdf (last access: 22 April 2018), 2015.

Pareja-Carmona, M. I. and Ospina-Pabón, J. G.: Listado taxonómico de especies ícticas de importancia pesquera en tres embalses del Oriente antioqueño, cuenca del río Magdalena, Colombia, Biota Colomb., 15, 54–60, 2014.

Phillips, S. J., Dudík, M., Elith, J., Graham, C. H., Lehmann, A., Leathwick, J., and Ferrier, S.: Sample selection bias and presence-only distribution models: Implications for background and pseudo-absence data, Ecol. Appl., 19, 181–197, https://doi.org/10.1890/07-2153.1, 2009.

Piman, T., Cochrane, T. A., and Arias, M. E.: Effect of proposed large dams on water flows and hydropower production in the Sekong, Sesan and Srepok rivers of the Mekong Basin, River Res. Appl., 22, 1085–1095, https://doi.org/10.1002/rra.3045, 2016.

Poff, N. L. and Zimmerman, J. K. H.: Ecological responses to altered flow regimes: a literature review to inform the science and management of environmental flows, Freshwater Biol., 55, 194–205, https://doi.org/10.1111/j.1365-2427.2009.02272.x, 2010.

Poff, N. L., Allan, J. D., Bain, M. B., Karr, J. R., Prestegaard, K. L., Richter, B. D., Sparks, R. E., and Stromberg, J. C.: The natural flow regime, Bioscience, 47, 769–784, https://doi.org/10.2307/1313099, 1997.

Posada G., L. and Rhenals, R. L.: Controles Fluviales del Río Cauca en la Región de La Mojana, in: XVII Seminario Nacional de Hidráulica e Hidrología, Popayán, Colombia, 655–662, 2006.

Poveda, G. and Mesa, O. J.: Feedbacks between hydrological processes in tropical South America and large-scale ocean–atmospheric phenomena, J. Climate, 10, 2690–2702, https://doi.org/10.1175/1520-0442(1997)010<2690:FBHPIT>2.0.CO;2, 1997.

Poveda, G., Jaramillo, A., Gil, M. M., Quiceno, N., and Mantilla, R. I.: Seasonality in ENSO-related precipitation, river discharges, soil moisture, and vegetation index in Colombia, Water Resour. Res., 37, 2169–2178, https://doi.org/10.1029/2000WR900395, 2001.

Poveda, G., Álvarez, D. M., and Rueda, Ó. A.: Hydro-climatic variability over the Andes of Colombia associated with ENSO: a review of climatic processes and their impact on one of the Earth's most important biodiversity hotspots, Clim. Dynam., 36, 2233–2249, https://doi.org/10.1007/s00382-010-0931-y, 2011.

Restrepo, J. C., Ortíz, J. C., Otero, L., and Ospino, S. R.: Transporte de sedimentos en suspensión en los principales ríos del Caribe colombiano: magnitud, tendencias y variabilidad, Rev. la Acad. Colomb. Ciencias Exactas, Físicas y Nat., 39, 527–546, https://doi.org/10.18257/raccefyn.209, 2015.

Restrepo, J. D., Kjerfve, B., Hermelin, M., and Restrepo, J. C.: Factors controlling sediment yield in a major South American drainage basin: the Magdalena River, Colombia, J. Hydrol., 316, 213–232, https://doi.org/10.1016/j.jhydrol.2005.05.002, 2006.

Richter, B. D., Baumgartner, J. V., Powell, J., and Braun, D. P.: A Method for Assessing Hydrologic Alteration within Ecosystems, Conserv. Biol., 10, 1163–1174, https://doi.org/10.1046/j.1523-1739.1996.10041163.x, 1996.

Richter, B. D., Baumgartner, J. V., Braun, D. P., and Powell, J.: A spatial assessment of hydrologic alteration within a river network, Regul. Rivers Res. Manage., 14, 329–340, 1998.

Ritter, J.: Optimisation of hydropower dam cascade operations with respect to energy generation, flood hazard and flow regime alteration, using operational modelling: a case study in the Nechí catchment, Colombia, UNESCO-IHE, Delft, the Netherlands, 2016.

Roberts, S.: ANUGA Open Source Hydrodynamic/Hydraulic Modelling Project, http://anuga.anu.edu.au/ (last access: 22 April 2018), 2017.

Röpke, C. P., Amadio, S., Zuanon, J., Ferreira, E. J. G., de Deus, C. P., Pires, T. H. S., and Winemiller, K. O.: Simultaneous abrupt shifts in hydrology and fish assemblage structure in a floodplain lake in the central Amazon, Sci. Rep., 7, 1–10, https://doi.org/10.1038/srep40170, 2017.

Sanchez-Lozano, J., Ardila, F., Oliveros, J. J., Ramirez, W. D., Cardona, C. A., Garay, C. I., Verschelling, E., Becker, A., and Zagonjoll, M.: Hydraulic Modeling of Magdalena River Using SOBEK, in: E-proceedings of the 36th IAHR world congress, The Hague, the Netherlands, 1–13, 2015.

SEI: Water Evaluation and Planning – WEAP, [Software], Stockholm Environment Institute, Stockholm, Sweden, 2017.

Smith, D. G.: Anastomosing river deposits, sedimentation rates and basin subsidence, Magdalena River, northwestern Colombia, South America, Sediment. Geol., 46, 177–196, 1986.

Strahler, A. N.: Quantitative analysis of watershed geomorphology, Trans. Am. Geophys. Un., 38, 913–920, https://doi.org/10.1029/TR038i006p00913, 1957.

Syvitski, J. P. M., Kettner, A. J., Overeem, I., Hutton, E. W. H., Hannon, M. T., Brakenridge, G. R., Day, J., Vörösmarty, C., Saito, Y., Giosan, L., and Nicholls, R. J.: Sinking deltas due to human activities, Nat. Geosci., 2, 681–686, 2009.

Tanner, W. F.: The incomplete flood plain: Reply, Geology, 2, 281–282, https://doi.org/10.1130/0091-7613(1974)2<281a:TIFPR>2.0.CO;2, 1974.

Tockner, K. and Stanford, J. A.: Riverine flood plains: present state and future trends, Environ. Conserv., 29, 308–330, https://doi.org/10.1017/S037689290200022X, 2002.

UPME: Plan de Expansión de Referencia Generación – Transmisión 2012–2025, Unidad de Planeación Minero Energética, Bogotá, Colombia, http://www.upme.gov.co/docs/plan_expansion/2012/plan_completo_2012-2025.pdf (last access: 22 April 2018), 2012.

UPME: Plan Energético Nacional, Unidad de Planeación Minero Energética, Bogotá, Colombia, http://www.upme.gov.co/docs/pen/pen_idearioenergetico2050.pdf (last access: 22 April 2018), 2015.

USACE and RMA: HEC-RAS, [Software], US Army Corps of Engineers and Resource Management Associates, http://www.hec.usace.army.mil/software/hec-ras/ (last access: 22 April 2018), 2016.

Verdin, K. L. and Verdin, J. P.: A topological system for delineation and codification of the Earth's river basins, J. Hydrol., 218, 1–12, 1999.

Villa-Navarro, F. A., García-Melo, L. J., Zúñiga-Upegui, P., García-Melo, J. E., Quiñones-Montiel, J. M., Albornoz, J. G., Conde-Saldaña, C. C., Reinoso-Flórez, G., Gualtero-Leal, D. M., and Ángel-Rojas, V. J.: Historia de vida del bagre Imparfinis usmai (Heptapteridae: Siluriformes) en el área de influencia del proyecto hidroeléctrico El Quimbo, alto río Magdalena, Colombia, Biota Colomb., 15, 111–126, 2014.

Vogel, R. M., Sieber, J., Archfield, S. A., Smith, M. P., Apse, C. D., and Huber-Lee, A.: Relations among storage, yield, and instream flow, Water Resour. Res., 43, 1–12, https://doi.org/10.1029/2006WR005226, 2007.

Vörösmarty, C. J., Meybeck, M., Fekete, B., Sharma, K., Green, P., and Syvitski, J. P. M.: Anthropogenic sediment retention: Major global impact from registered river impoundments, Global Planet. Change, 39, 169–190, https://doi.org/10.1016/S0921-8181(03)00023-7, 2003.

Walling, D. E. and Fang, D.: Recent trends in the suspended sediment loads of the world's rivers, Global Planet. Change, 39, 111–126, https://doi.org/10.1016/S0921-8181(03)00020-1, 2003.

Wilkinson, S. N., Prosser, I. P., Rustomji, P., and Read, A. M.: Modelling and testing spatially distributed sediment budgets to relate erosion processes to sediment yields, Environ. Model. Softw., 24, 489–501, 2009.

Williams, G. P. and Wolman, M. G.: Downstream effects of dams on alluvial rivers, http://pubs.er.usgs.gov/publication/pp1286 (last access: 22 April 2018), 1984.

XM: Información inteligente. Histórico hidrología, Compañía Expertos en Mercados S.A. E.S.P, available at: http://informacioninteligente10.xm.com.co/hidrologia/Paginas/HistoricoHidrologia.aspx (last access: 4 May 2018), Medellín, Colombia, 2005.

XM: Informe de Operación del SIN y Administración del Mercado – Generación del SIN, Medellín, Colombia, http://informesanuales.xm.com.co/2014/SitePages/operacion/InformedeOperaciC3B3ndelSIN_2014.pdf (last access: 22 April 2018), 2014.

Yang, X. and Lu, X. X.: Estimate of cumulative sediment trapping by multiple reservoirs in large river basins: An example of the Yangtze River basin, Geomorphology, 227, 49–59, https://doi.org/10.1016/j.geomorph.2014.01.014, 2014.

Yates, D., Sieber, J., Purkey, D., and Huber-Lee, A.: WEAP21 – A Demand-, Priority-, and Preference-Driven Water Planning Model: Part 1: Model Characteristics, Int. Water Resour. Assoc., 30, 487–500, 2005a.

Yates, D., Sieber, J., Purkey, D., and Huber-Lee, A.: WEAP 21 – A Demand-, Priority-, and Preference-Driven Water Planning Model: Part 2: Aiding Freshwater Ecosystem Service Evaluation, Int. Water Resour. Assoc., 30, 501–512, 2005b.

Zarfl, C., Lumsdon, A. E., Berlekamp, J., Tydecks, L., and Tockner, K.: A global boom in hydropower dam construction, Aquat. Sci., 77, 161–170, https://doi.org/10.1007/s00027-014-0377-0, 2014.

Zedler, J. B. and Kercher, S.: Wetland Resources: Status, Trends, Ecosystem Services, and Restorability, Annu. Rev. Environ. Resour., 30, 39–74, https://doi.org/10.1146/annurev.energy.30.050504.144248, 2005.

8

Examining controls on peak annual streamflow and floods in the Fraser River Basin of British Columbia

Charles L. Curry[1,2] **and Francis W. Zwiers**[1]

[1]Pacific Climate Impacts Consortium, University of Victoria, Victoria, V8N 5L3, Canada
[2]School of Earth and Ocean Sciences, University of Victoria, Victoria, V8N 5L3, Canada

Correspondence: Charles L. Curry (cc@uvic.ca)

Abstract. The Fraser River Basin (FRB) of British Columbia is one of the largest and most important watersheds in western North America, and home to a rich diversity of biological species and economic assets that depend implicitly upon its extensive riverine habitats. The hydrology of the FRB is dominated by snow accumulation and melt processes, leading to a prominent annual peak streamflow invariably occurring in May–July. Nevertheless, while annual peak daily streamflow (APF) during the spring freshet in the FRB is historically well correlated with basin-averaged, 1 April snow water equivalent (SWE), there are numerous occurrences of anomalously large APF in below- or near-normal SWE years, some of which have resulted in damaging floods in the region. An imperfect understanding of which other climatic factors contribute to these anomalously large APFs hinders robust projections of their magnitude and frequency.

We employ the Variable Infiltration Capacity (VIC) process-based hydrological model driven by gridded observations to investigate the key controlling factors of anomalous APF events in the FRB and four of its subbasins that contribute nearly 70 % of the annual flow at Fraser-Hope. The relative influence of a set of predictors characterizing the interannual variability of rainfall, snowfall, snowpack (characterized by the annual maximum value, SWE_{max}), soil moisture and temperature on simulated APF at Hope (the main outlet of the FRB) and at the subbasin outlets is examined within a regression framework. The influence of large-scale climate modes of variability (the Pacific Decadal Oscillation (PDO) and the El Niño–Southern Oscillation – ENSO) on APF magnitude is also assessed, and placed in context with these more localized controls. The results indicate that next to SWE_{max} (univariate Spearman correlation with APF of $\hat{\rho} = 0.64$; 0.70 (observations; VIC simulation)), the snowmelt rate ($\hat{\rho} = 0.43$ in VIC), the ENSO and PDO indices ($\hat{\rho} = -0.40$; -0.41) and ($\hat{\rho} = -0.35$; -0.38), respectively, and rate of warming subsequent to the date of SWE_{max} ($\hat{\rho} = 0.26$; 0.38), are the most influential predictors of APF magnitude in the FRB and its subbasins. The identification of these controls on annual peak flows in the region may be of use in understanding seasonal predictions or future projected streamflow changes.

1 Introduction

1.1 Study domain and motivation

The response of nival watersheds across the Northern Hemisphere to ongoing warming of the climate system is a topic of intense interest to those interested in the water–climate nexus. Since the early reviews of Barnett et al. (2005) and Milly et al. (2005), which offered a global perspective, more recent studies have investigated the response on continental and regional scales. In mountainous regions that supply fresh water to downstream populated areas, reduced snowpack in recent decades has led to concerns about water availability for human consumption, agriculture and fisheries (Stewart, 2009; Jiménez Cisneros et al., 2014), while changes in the timing of the freshet and a widespread decrease in the snow-to-rain ratio (Danco et al., 2016) have implications for flood magnitude and frequency (Matti et al., 2016). An understanding of the mechanisms behind these changes has been greatly aided by the use of process-based hydrologic models (Park and Markus, 2014; Duan et al., 2017), which permit the analysis of a host of variables that respond to historical climate forcings via physically consistent relationships. We apply such a model to the Fraser River Basin (FRB) of British Columbia (BC), Canada, a large, representative nival watershed, to study the dominant climatic controls on both observed and modelled hydrologic change.

The FRB is one of the largest watersheds draining the western slopes of the North American Cordillera, and home to both densely populated urban centres and a diversity of ecosystems closely linked to the economic prosperity of the region (Fraser Basin Council, 2010). The basin is also a focal point for salmon migration and spawning, constituting a key component of the highly valued commercial and subsistence fisheries of the region. The FRB lies between the Coast Mountains and the Continental Divide, with the headwaters of the Fraser in the northeast (~53° N, 118° W) and its outlet at the Pacific Ocean in the southwest (Fig. 1). Its vast 240 000 km^2 area encompasses a range of climatic zones, from the snowy mountains of the eastern Rockies to dry interior plateaus and wet fertile valleys nearest the Pacific west coast. The hydrological diversity of the basin is well described in Eaton and Moore (2010), who reviewed seasonal streamflow regimes at the catchment scale across BC, and also in Moore (1991), who focused specifically on the FRB. For the most part, streamflows are unregulated in the FRB, with the exception of Kenney Dam on the Nechako River in the northwestern sector of the FRB (operational since the early 1950s) and several dams associated with the Bridge River power project in the Interior Plateau (completed in 1960). Regulated subbasins represent less than 10 % of the total area of the FRB (Bawden et al., 2015).

Streamflow in the interior catchments of the FRB is dominated by the snowmelt-fed spring freshet in April–July, leading to the usual characterization of the FRB as a nival basin. Hydrographs of major rivers in the FRB do not vary their form significantly from year to year due to the large amount of storage in the multi-year, high-elevation snowpack. Indeed, the longest record of gauged flow at the southwestern outlet of the basin, at Fraser-Hope, has never recorded an annual peak daily flow (APF) outside of the April–July period. Nevertheless, several catchments in the lower FRB, and to the west of the basin in the Coast Mountains and Western Cascades, exhibit annual streamflow peaks coinciding with the maximum of Pacific frontal rainstorm occurrence in October–December (Eaton and Moore, 2010; Padilla et al., 2015).

1.2 Previous studies of climate and streamflow change in the FRB

The focus of this work is upon the main drivers of the interannual (and to some extent, interdecadal) variability in annual peak daily flow (hereafter APF), and not upon secular trends in APF in the FRB and its subbasins. Nevertheless, as there is a growing body of work on such trends,

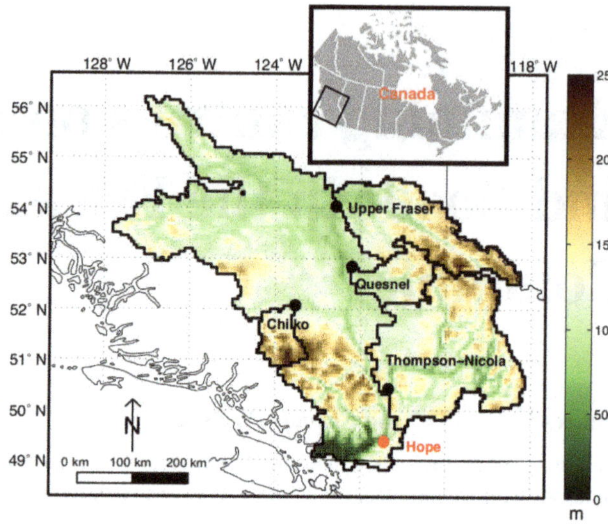

Figure 1. The Fraser River Basin of British Columbia, Canada, and four of its subbasins examined in this study. Colours correspond to elevations as used by the VIC model, at 1/16° horizontal resolution. Locations of streamflow gauge stations at the outlet to each subbasin are shown with black dots, while the major outlet for the FRB at Hope is shown with a red dot. Details of each subbasin are provided in Table 1.

which have implications for non-stationarity of the climate, we briefly review this research here, limiting the discussion to observations concerning APF magnitude. Significant long-term trends in temperature and precipitation have been detected over a network of meteorological stations in the FRB and its surroundings; a summary of these trends is available in a recent report from the BC Ministry of the Environment (BC MOE, 2016) (in what follows, we average results for three regions used in the report which cover most of the FRB area: Sub-Boreal Interior, Central Interior, and Southern Interior). Annual (summer; winter) mean temperatures have increased at the rate of +0.9 °C century^{-1} (+0.7; +1.4 °C century^{-1}) over the 1900–2013 period, while minimum winter temperature has increased at the more rapid rate of 2.2 °C century^{-1}. The latter coincides with reduced winter snow depth (−10 % decade^{-1}) and snow water equivalent (−6 % decade^{-1}; both over 1950–2014), mirroring a much larger-scale phenomenon occurring over Canada and the US (Gan et al., 2013; Knowles, 2015) and much of the Northern Hemisphere (Rupp et al., 2013; Jeong et al., 2017). On the other hand, precipitation amounts have increased in the FRB over 1900–2013, by about +2 % decade^{-1} in spring, summer, and fall, with no significant change in winter precipitation (BC MOE, 2016). However, sparse station coverage in the early decades of the twentieth century casts doubt on the robustness of this result. Restricting attention to the period 1950–2014, we used the regional data to compute precipitation trends of +3.3 % decade^{-1} in spring, +2.3 % decade^{-1} in fall and −4.1 % decade^{-1} in winter, with no significant trend detected in summer. Over the last century (1912–2012), an earlier onset of the half-annual streamflow volume date was detected in one subbasin of the FRB (Stellako, 9-day advance) as well as at the major outlet to the basin at Hope (6-day advance). The latter conclusion was reinforced by Kang et al. (2016), who noted a statistically significant advance, by ~ 10 days, of the APF at Fraser-Hope over the 1949–2006 period.

Recent decadal trends in the magnitude of annual and/or seasonal mean streamflow at gauge stations in BC and western Canada have been investigated by several authors (Pike et al., 2010; Bawden et al., 2015; DeBeer et al., 2016; BC MOE, 2016), with no significant trends detected at stations in the FRB. Hernández-Henríquez et al. (2017) conducted analyses on the FRB specifically, using a network of long-term measurements at 139 streamflow gauge stations available from the online Hydrometric Database (HYDAT; Water Survey of Canada, 2016). At Fraser-Hope specifically, Déry et al. (2012) found an increasing trend in interannual streamflow variability between 1960 and 2005, in both annual and seasonal means, suggesting an increase in the frequency and/or intensity of low- and/or high-flow conditions, but with no detectable trend in annual mean streamflow at Hope.

With respect to trends in the APF specifically, Cunderlik and Ouarda (2009) found no significant trend at most Reference Hydrometric Basin Network (RHBN) stations in the FRB over the 1974–2003 period, but noted a weak trend ($\sim$ 1–5 %) toward decreasing magnitude and earlier APF occurrence at two stations. A Canada-wide nonstationary analysis by Tan and Gan (2015), suggested that APF increased over recent decades at two stations in the FRB: the Stellako R. at Glenannan and Chilliwack R. at Chilliwack Lake. More aligned with our interests here, Burn and Hag Elnur (2002) found a weak negative correlation between APF and annual mean temperature at Quesnel in the FRB over the 1950–1997 period. We look for similar relationships between a range of climatic variables and APF at the scale of both the FRB and its major subbasins in Sect. 3 below.

Finally, it is important to recognize the influence of large-scale climate teleconnections on streamflow in the FRB. Previous researchers have investigated the influence of modes of large-scale climate variability on various river basins in western North America. Specifically, relationships between total and/or peak annual river discharge and the Pacific Decadal Oscillation (PDO), El Niño–Southern Oscillation (ENSO), and the Pacific North America index have been examined (Shabbar et al., 1997; Rood et al., 2005; Gobena and Gan, 2006; Bonsal and Shabbar, 2008; Whitfield et al., 2010; Gurrapu et al., 2016), while impacts of large-scale teleconnections on snowpacks in BC were examined by Moore and McKendry (1996) and Hsieh and Tang (2001). El Niño and La Niña typically occur every 3 to 5 years, often separated by 1 to 2 years of neutral conditions. The lower frequency PDO is a superposition of several interacting climate processes, including ENSO, mid-latitude ocean currents and atmospheric influences on mid-latitude sea surface temperatures (Alexander, 2010). El Niño events are more likely to occur during the positive phase of the PDO, while La Niña events are more common during the negative phase.

During the negative (cold) phase of the PDO, and La Niña periods, winters in western Canada are typically cooler and wetter than average, with a larger snowpack at high elevations leading to higher annual discharge than average. Roughly opposite behaviour occurs during the positive (warm) PDO phase and occurrences of El Niño. Extending earlier work by Woo and Thorne (2003) and Thorne and Woo (2011), Gurrapu et al. (2016) determined that the PDO index is significantly anti-correlated ($p < 0.05$) with APF at eight hydrometeorological stations in the FRB, while APF is correlated with the Southern Oscillation Index (SOI), which tracks ENSO phase, at 11 stations (note that SOI is anti-correlated with the NINO3.4 index, and so also the PDO index). Specifically, both Thorne and Woo (2011) and Gurrapu et al. (2016) found that the observed APF was generally higher during the negative PDO phase and during La Niña years. For this reason, decadal trends in climatic variables, including streamflow, are sensitive to the phase of the PDO, which argues for a cautious interpretation of the results cited above.

The paper is structured as follows. Data sources, the VIC model and methods of analysis are described in Section 2. The main results of the study are gathered in Sect. 3, which begins with the regression analysis of observations before presenting insights from the VIC simulation results. Section 4 presents a few case studies that illuminate the precursors of high streamflow in particular years, and also reinforce the regression-based results. We conclude in Sect. 5 with a short discussion of outstanding issues and conclusions.

2 Data and methods

2.1 Study domain and observational data

The location of the FRB within western Canada and BC is shown in Fig. 1. The observational data set used for analysis and for driving the hydrological model (see Sect. 2.2 below) is taken from the gridded data set of surface temperature and precipitation at daily temporal and $1/16^\circ$ spatial resolution described by Schnorbus et al. (2011), hereafter referred to as PCIC-OBS. The original station data, which span the period from January 1950 to December 2006, are interpolated to the grid and corrected for elevation using the Climate Data for Western North America (Climate WNA) package (https://sites.ualberta.ca/~ahamann/data/climatewna.html; Hamann et al., 2013), based on very high resolution climatologies for the region that are developed with the Parameter-elevation Regressions on Independent Slopes Model (PRISM; Daly et al., 2008). Precipitation is not partitioned into rain and snow separately in PCIC-OBS. Since we are interested in investi-

Table 1. Water Survey of Canada (WSC) hydrometric stations and corresponding basin and subbasin characteristics.

Station name (WSC ID)	Basin/subbasin name	Period of record	Subbasin area (km^2)	Mean elevation (m)
Fraser R. at Hope (08MF005)	Fraser (FRB)	1912–2014	217 000	1330
Fraser R. at Shelley (08KB001)	Upper Fraser	1951–2014	32 400	1308
Quesnel R. near Quesnel (08KH006)	Quesnel	1939–2013	11 500	1173
Thompson R. near Spences Bridge (08LF051)	Thompson–Nicola	1952–2013	54 900	1747
Chilko R. near Redstone (08MA001)	Chilko	1927–2013	6940	1756

gating the relationship between rainfall and APF specifically, we need to estimate the rainfall-only portion, R. We do this using the empirical fit of Dai (2008), which relates the fractional rain frequency to surface temperature via a hyperbolic tangent function having four fitted parameters. We chose the parameter values corresponding to land-only, annual mean precipitation (seasonal fitted coefficients were also given by Dai (2008), but do not differ much from the annual values).

Daily streamflow data were obtained from the Water Survey of Canada (WSC) Hydrometric Database (HYDAT; Water Survey of Canada, 2016) for five hydrometric stations located within the FRB, as summarized in Table 1. The main outlet at Hope, which integrates the flows from all upstream locations, receives the most attention in the paper, but four subbasin outlets are also considered. Three of these were selected on the basis of their leading contributions to the observed mean annual discharge at Fraser-Hope: Upper Fraser (29 %), Thompson–Nicola (28 %), and Quesnel (9 %) (Kang et al., 2016). These subbasins are located in the eastern FRB, cover 45% of the total area, and represent nival environments. The smaller Chilko basin, by contrast, lies on the southwestern edge of the FRB and intercepts a significant amount of rain falling on the east-facing side of the Coast Mountains, making it a hybrid (nival–pluvial) catchment. Hence, this subbasin was included in an attempt to probe the sensitivity of streamflow to rainfall. Manual snow survey (MSS) SWE measurements taken at the beginning of each non-summer month (eight times per year) were obtained from the BC Snow Survey Network Program, distributed by the BC River Forecast Centre (http://bcrfc.env.gov.bc.ca/data/). The data do not permit the exact determination of the annual maximum SWE, so we extracted the 1 April SWE from each year for analysis. Data from 19 locations that are at least 81 % complete spanning the period 1956–2014 were averaged to obtain an annual 1 April SWE time series for the entire FRB. The MSS stations are mainly located at high-elevation sites in the Coast and Rocky Mountain ranges; exact locations are shown in Fig. 1 of Najafi et al. (2017). Another source of snow cover data, from automated snow pillows at high-elevation sites, was also examined. However, as only a few of these sites have records longer than 20 years (within the 1956–2006 period of PCIC-OBS), we decided to exclude them from the analysis.

We use the PDO and NINO3.4 indices to characterize the relevant large-scale climate modes affecting the region. The PDO index is derived as the leading principal component of monthly sea surface temperature (SST) anomalies in the North Pacific Ocean northward of 20° N (http://research.jisao.washington.edu/pdo/PDO.latest.txt). For the corresponding predictor variable, we use the mean PDO index from the preceding November to March, following Gurrapu et al. (2016). The NINO3.4 index is calculated from the Hadley Centre SST and sea ice gridded data set, HadISST1, as the area average of SST from 5° S–5° N and 170–120° W, available from http://www.esrl.noaa.gov/psd/gcos_wgsp/Timeseries/Nino34/. We use the mean value from June to November of the preceding year as a predictor. Note that this differs slightly from Gurrapu et al. (2016), who instead made use of the SOI over the same months (NINO3.4 and the SOI are strongly negatively correlated). A list of all variables analyzed may be found in Table 2.

2.2 Hydrological model and boundary forcing

The gridded temperature and precipitation data described above were used to drive the Variable Infiltration Capacity (VIC) hydrological model (Liang et al., 1994) over a large portion of BC, including the FRB, from 1950 to 2006. The VIC model is applied at a horizontal resolution of 1/16° ($\sim$ 5–6 km, depending on latitude), and solves the one-dimensional water and energy balance equations within each grid cell at a daily time step (with the exception of the snow sub-model, which runs at hourly resolution). The VIC implementation used in this study incorporates five elevation bands corresponding to 200 m vertical resolution, with the number of elevation bands in any one 1/16° grid cell depending on the topography within that cell. Each VIC grid cell can be assigned up to eight major vegetation classes, with a fractional cell area assigned to each, and these land cover fractions are identical for each elevation band within a VIC grid cell. Three of the input PCIC-OBS fields, maximum and minimum temperature and precipitation, are vertically interpolated to provide values for each elevation band (the other input field, surface wind speed, is not interpolated). In

Table 2. Predictor variables and descriptions including their origin. Acronyms are as defined in the text, with the exception of ESRL/GCOS, Earth System Resource Laboratory/Global Climate Observing System (National Oceanic and Atmospheric Administration, NOAA), and JISAO, Joint Institute for the Study of the Atmosphere and Ocean (University of Washington/NOAA).

Predictor	Units	Description	Source
Maximum annual snow, SWE_{max}; 1 April SWE, SWE_{Apr1}	mm	Annual maximum snow water equivalent (VIC); 1 April snow water equivalent (OBS)	VIC; MSS
October mean total column soil moisture	mm	Previous October mean value	VIC
Cold season rainfall	mm	Sum of rainfall between 1 October and 31 March	PCIC-OBS
Spring rainfall	mm	Sum of rainfall between days of SWE_{max} (VIC) or SWE_{Apr1} (OBS) and annual maximum streamflow (APF)	PCIC-OBS
APF rainfall	mm	Sum of rainfall from 15 days prior to 5 days after APF	PCIC-OBS
Freezing degree days	°C	Absolute value of sum of negative daily mean $T < 0\,°C$ from 1 October to 31 March	PCIC-OBS
Spring warming rate	$°C\,day^{-1}$	Slope of daily mean T between days of SWE_{max} and T_{max}	PCIC-OBS
Snowmelt rate	$mm\,day^{-1}$	Slope of daily SWE between dates of SWE_{max} and APF	VIC
Date of SWE_{max}, $t_{SWE_{max}}$	day	Calendar day of maximum SWE	VIC
Melt season length, SWE_{len}	days	Date of 0.25 SWE_{max} minus date of SWE_{max}	VIC
NINO3.4 index	°C	HadISST1 anomaly over 5° N–5° S and 170–120° W	ESRL/GCOS
PDO index	°C	Leading principal component of monthly SST anomalies in the North Pacific Ocean, poleward of 20° N	JISAO

VIC, precipitation type (rain or snow) at the grid scale is determined by fixed temperature thresholds, with snow falling when $T < 0\,°C$, rain when $T > 6\,°C$, and a linearly interpolated mix of the two at intermediate temperatures. While this differs somewhat from the partitioning applied to the PCIC-OBS precipitation (Sect. 2.1) used in the regression analysis of Sect. 3 for both observations and models, the treatments are sufficiently similar that we do not expect a significant bias to arise. Snowpack is represented by a two-layer scheme – a thin surface overlying a thick deeper layer – subject to mass and energy balance, similar to other cold land process models. The snow albedo parameterization in VIC is based entirely on snow age, with a different albedo decay rate used during accumulation and snowmelt seasons. Interested readers are directed to Andreadis et al. (2009) for further details.

Glaciers are not explicitly parameterized in VIC; however, the version of VIC used here produces a perennial, accumulating snowpack at several high-elevation grid cells, many of which coincide with the locations of glaciers in the real system (also noted by Islam and Déry, 2017, who used a version of VIC with lower horizontal resolution but finer vertical resolution). These anomalous "glacier" cells cause the annual maximum of the basin average SWE, SWE_{max}, to increase approximately linearly with time t: i.e., $SWE_{max} = at + SWE_0$, where SWE_0 is the value of SWE at an affected cell at the start of the simulation ($t = 0$) and a is a fitted trend. The linear increase in SWE_{max} is clearly unrealistic and is not seen, e.g., in the corresponding observed 1 April SWE time series averaged over the FRB, which has a trend indistinguishable from zero. In order to reproduce this basin-averaged trend of approximately zero in the VIC model, we masked out the affected cells according to the criterion $a > 60\,mm\,yr^{-1}$, with the slope a determined from a linear least-squares fit over the 1950–2006 period of the calibrated VIC simulation (see below). In addition, we confirmed a posteriori that the removal of these anomalous cells had little effect on the correlation structure of the basin average SWE_{max} with any of the variables examined in Sect. 3 below.

Soil parameters in VIC are defined for each grid cell. Soil classification and parameterization are based primarily on physical data from the Soils Program in the Global Soil Data Products CD-ROM (GSD, 2000), which originate from a global pedon database produced by the International Soil Reference and Information Center (ISRIC) (Batjes, 1995) and the FAO-UNESCO Digital Soil Map of the World (DSMW) (FAO, 1995). Although VIC contains a parameterization for seasonally frozen soils (Cherkauer and Lettenmaier, 1999), it increases the computation time significantly and so was not activated (the simulation we analyzed was originally produced for a different purpose). Surface and subsurface runoff are generated for each grid cell, and subsequently directed into a surface routing network (Lohmann et al., 1996, 1998; Schnorbus et al., 2011). Simulated streamflow can be extracted at grid cells representing outlets of the

FRB or any one of its subbasins, which can be evaluated against stream gauge measurements.

VIC has been calibrated and evaluated in the FRB and its subbasins (Schnorbus et al., 2010; Shrestha et al., 2012, 2014) and also in other nearby hydrological basins (Schnorbus et al., 2011). Recently, Islam and Déry (2017) used a lower horizontal resolution version of VIC ($1/4°$) to study its sensitivity to several different gridded input data sets, including PCIC-OBS. They found that while driving VIC with PCIC-OBS tended to overestimate SWE, the resultant hydrographs for the FRB and its basins were in better agreement with observations than when competing data products were used as driving data sets. VIC model output variables, including SWE, total column soil moisture (both over the period 1950–2006), and routed streamflow at the location of WSC stations (1955–2004), were obtained from the Pacific Climate Impacts Consortium Data Portal (Pacific Climate Impacts Consortium, 2014).

2.3 Selection of predictors and analysis methods

We use regression models to study the relationship between APF at Fraser-Hope and climate variables, termed "predictors", that may influence APF. Predictors were selected based on physical intuition, inspection of the relevant literature and initial exploratory data analysis. Prior studies that were particularly helpful in this regard were Gurrapu et al. (2016), who examined the influence of the PDO on streamflow in western Canada, Jenicek et al. (2016), who examined the influence of snow accumulation and other variables on summer low flows, Coles et al. (2017), who studied snowmelt-runoff generation on Canadian prairie hillslopes, and Wever et al. (2017), who conducted model simulations of the joint effect of snowmelt and soil moisture on streamflow in a Swiss Alpine catchment. The predictor variables chosen are listed in Table 2.

Both univariate and multivariate linear regression models were constructed to explore predictor–predictand relationships. The APF was determined as the maximum annual value of the running 3-day mean discharge at Fraser-Hope. Most of the predictors are represented as basin averages, but two, the ENSO and PDO indices, describe large-scale, multiyear climate modes of variability. The influence of large-scale climate can be manifested as nonstationary behaviour (e.g., trends) in the predictand and/or predictors. Since regression models are sensitive to both trends and autocorrelation in the underlying time series, all univariate regressions were checked for the presence of both (e.g., see Shumway and Stoffer, 2017, and specifically their online supplement.)

Specifically, for the predictand (APF) $\boldsymbol{Y}_t$ and each predictor $\boldsymbol{X}_t$, we first fit the models (by linear least-squares regression):

$$\boldsymbol{Y}_t = \alpha_0 + \alpha_1 t + \boldsymbol{y}_t, \quad \boldsymbol{X}_t = \beta_0 + \beta_1 t + \boldsymbol{x}_t, \tag{1}$$

where $\boldsymbol{y}_t$ and $\boldsymbol{x}_t$ are the corresponding detrended annual time series. If, as determined from the fit, there was no statistically significant temporal trend (with p-value < 0.05) in either $\boldsymbol{Y}_t$ or $\boldsymbol{X}_t$, then the latter were used in the subsequent analysis in place of $\boldsymbol{y}_t$ and $\boldsymbol{x}_t$. Trends were detected in certain time series, as reviewed in Sect. 3.1 below. Regression models including variables with significant trends were generally found to have inflated correlation coefficients (e.g., Pearson's R^2 or Spearman's $\hat{\rho}$) compared to those using the same variables after detrending. The analysis proceeds using the fitted linear regression model to the detrended series $\boldsymbol{y}_t$ and $\boldsymbol{x}_t$, i.e., $\widetilde{\boldsymbol{y}}_t = \gamma_0 + \gamma_1 \boldsymbol{x}_t$. If a statistically significant relationship was found (again with p-value < 0.05), then the associated correlation coefficient was taken to be a conservative measure of the relationship between the predictand and predictor. We say "conservative" because it is possible that the residuals $\boldsymbol{\varepsilon}_t = \boldsymbol{y}_t - \widetilde{\boldsymbol{y}}_t$ may yet possess an autoregressive structure, i.e., $\boldsymbol{\varepsilon}_t = \varphi_1\, \varepsilon_{t-1} + \varphi_2\, \varepsilon_{t-2} + \ldots\, \varphi_i\, \varepsilon_{t-i} + \boldsymbol{w}_t$, where $\varphi_1, \varphi_1, \ldots, \varphi_i$ are constants ($\varphi_i \neq 0$) and $\boldsymbol{w}_t$ represents white noise (Shumway and Stoffer, 2017). If $\boldsymbol{\varepsilon}_t > 2/\sqrt{N_{\mathrm{yr}}}$ at any lag $i > 1$, where N_{yr} is the length of the time series, then further analysis would be required to fully specify the regression model. However, including autoregressive terms as predictors in the model will only increase the explained variance (e.g., Pearson's R^2), so we can be confident that the correlation coefficient after detrending, but without including autoregressive terms, underestimates the correlation coefficient. In practice, however, autocorrelation was detected only in a few cases (using the function acf2 in the R library astsa from the R Statistical Computing package; R Core Team, 2017), and principally amongst predictors themselves, not in the regressions of APF on predictors.

Ultimately, the nonparametric Spearman rank correlation, with sample estimator $\hat{\rho}$, was used to characterize the interannual regression results as it makes no assumptions regarding the distribution of the climatic and hydrologic data. A correlation matrix of $\hat{\rho}$ was constructed by repeated univariate regression over all variables (including detrending where necessary), and the results summarized in the correlograms presented in Sect. 3. Another nonparametric measure, the Theil–Sen slope, is used to calculate temporal trends of the predictand and predictors in Sect. 3.1. The Theil–Sen slope is a median of slopes calculated for each pair of data points and is less sensitive to outliers than the standard least-squares regression line (Sen, 1968). Multiple linear regression (MLR) analyses were also conducted by including all possible combinations of the predictors listed in Table 2. We retained the MLR model that featured 1) the most variables (N) with partial p-values less than 0.05 (N_{sig}), and (2) a Pearson-adjusted coefficient of determination R^2_{adj} larger than any MLR with $N < N_{\mathrm{sig}}$ predictors. We also tried adding predictors in a stepwise manner, obtaining similar results.

In order to discern differences between data samples drawn from potentially distinct distributions, we apply a permutation or resampling test at several points in the analysis.

Table 3. Trends in observed and VIC-simulated variables over the period of each record. Results are only shown for those variables that contain a statistically significant trend at the $p < 0.05$ level. The trend was calculated using the Theil–Sen median slope estimator (Sect. 2.3). Slightly different results are obtained for observed inputs to the VIC model due to the difference in start and end years of the time series. The residuals of each fit were checked for autocorrelation, with none detected. NA indicates this info is not available in the observations we used.

Observations (1956–2006)			VIC model (1955–2004)	
Variable (units of trend)	Trend (Sen)	Pearson R^2	Trend (Sen)	Pearson R^2
APF ($m^{-3}\,s^{-1}\,yr^{-1}$)	−36.5	0.10	–	–
Freezing degree days (°C day yr^{-1})	−6.29	0.14	−6.29	0.11
April–June mean T (°C day yr^{-1})	0.026	0.10	–	–
Spring rain (mm yr^{-1})	–	–	0.927	0.13
PDO (yr^{-1})	0.035	0.16	0.038	0.17
Snowmelt rate (mm $day^{-1}\,yr^{-1}$)	NA	NA	−0.0137	0.10
Melt season length (day yr^{-1})	NA	NA	0.225	0.12

For two input data sets, $\boldsymbol{X}$ and $\boldsymbol{Y}$ of length n_X and n_Y, respectively, the test statistic $S \equiv \text{mean}(\boldsymbol{X})/\text{mean}(\boldsymbol{Y})$ is calculated. The two sets are then combined, i.e., $\boldsymbol{Z} \equiv \boldsymbol{X} \cup \boldsymbol{Y}$, and a large number (we chose $N = 10^4$) of paired, random samples of lengths n_X, n_Y are drawn from $\boldsymbol{Z}$. For each sample (x_i, y_i), the same statistic S_i is recalculated, and the number of exceedances, $N_{\text{exc}}(S_i > S)$, summed over all $i = 1, \ldots,$ N samples. If the ratio $p = N_{\text{exc}}/N$ is sufficiently near either 0 or 1, then the original test statistic S is taken to indicate a significant difference between the samples at the p or $1 - p$ level. We adopt the commonly used threshold value of $\min(p, 1 - p) = 0.05$.

Finally, while most predictors are well characterized by their annual maximum or seasonally averaged values, daily rainfall needs special attention due to its high temporal variance even when averaged over the entire FRB. To better identify significant, multi-day rainfall episodes, we computed the current rainfall index (CRI), following Fedora and Beschta (1989) and Smakhtin and Masse (2000):

$$\text{CRI}_t = K < \times\text{CRI}_{t-1} + R_t = R_t + K R_{t-1} + K^2 R_{t-2} + \ldots, K < 1. \quad (2)$$

The CRI incorporates both the most recent daily rainfall amount (R_t) and an exponential decay in the weight given to previous rainfall events. K is the daily recession coefficient and reflects the storage capacity of the basin which depends somewhat on its physical properties (e.g., topography and area). We set $K = 0.9$ following a previous application in Pacific Northwest basins (Fedora and Beschta, 1989). The CRI proves useful for investigating intra-annual correlations between R and daily streamflow, which is covered in Sect. 3.3.

3 Results

3.1 Trends in observed time series

We begin by searching for temporal trends in the input time series. These are of intrinsic interest, but also for interpreting the results of the univariate and multivariate regression models later in this section. In addition to APF, we computed linear trends using the Theil–Sen slope estimator for the eight observed variables listed in Table 2 over the common period of record 1956–2006, with the results summarized in Table 3. Of the nine variables, four display statistically significant trends at the $p < 0.05$ level: APF, freezing degree days (absolute value of the sum of negative daily mean $T < 0\,°C$ from 1 October to 31 March, hereafter FDD), April–June mean temperature (T_{amj}), and the PDO index. The correlation coefficient R^2 is small for all the fits ($R^2 = 0.10$–0.16), indicating that the trends are modest compared to the scatter in the annual data. The decreasing trend in FDD and increasing trend in April–June mean temperature (0.26 °C decade^{-1}) are qualitatively consistent with the regional temperature trends summarized in Sect. 1.1. The trend in APF of $-37\,m^3\,s^{-1}\,yr^{-1}$, or $-4.3\,\%\,\text{decade}^{-1}$, is of the same sign but lower magnitude than that estimated for annual mean flow at Hope by BC MOE (2016) ($-5.7\,\%\,\text{decade}^{-1}$ between 1958 and 2012). However, it is worth noting that over the entire 1912–2014 period of the gauge record at Fraser-Hope, there is no significant trend detected in APF, even at the less conservative p-level of 0.1. The same is true of the PDO index over its much longer period of record (1900–2015). Nevertheless, we detrended the 1956–2006 observed time series of APF before computing the correlograms shown later in this section.

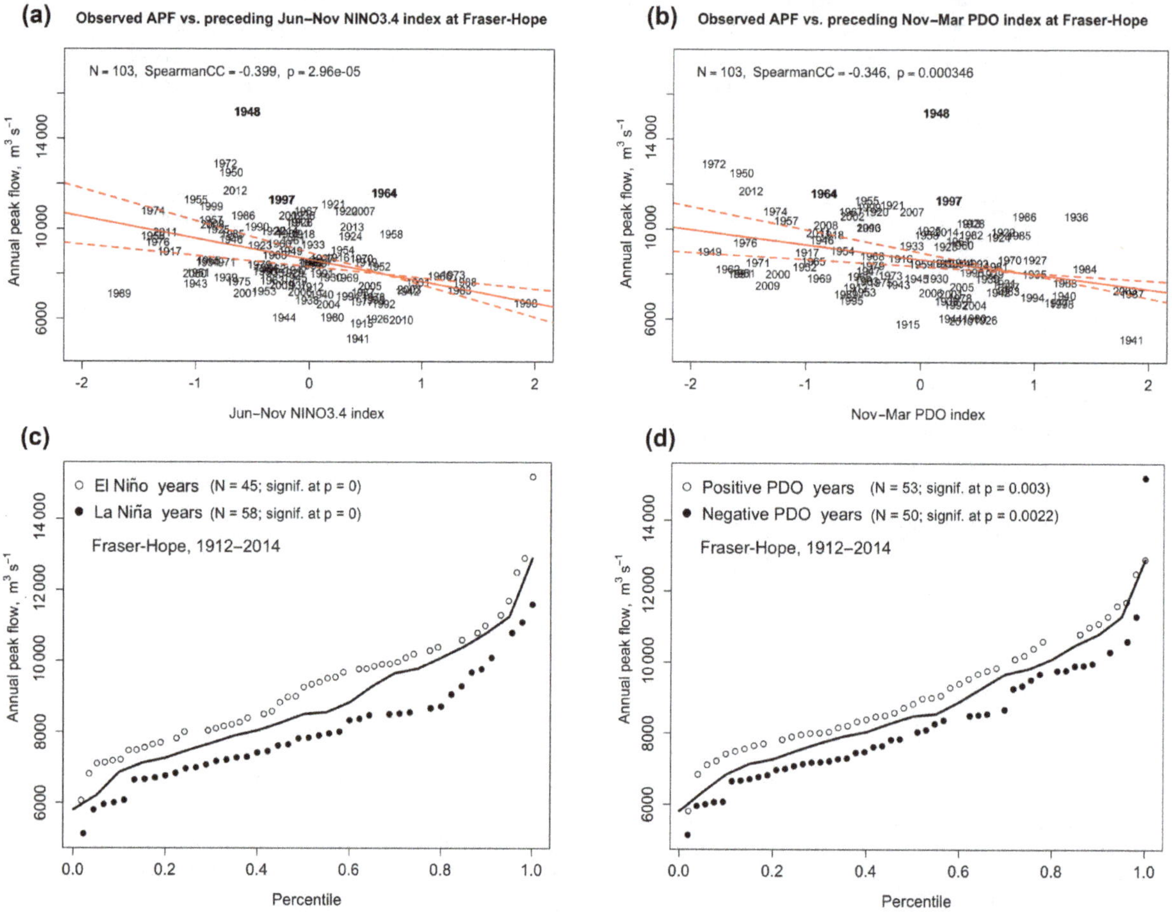

Figure 2. **(a)** Regression of observed annual peak daily streamflow (APF) magnitude at Fraser-Hope hydrometric station (vertical axis) against the NINO3.4 index over the period 1912–2014. Year labels are plotted as individual points. **(b)** Same as in **(a)** but for the PDO index. Years in boldface font are discussed in the text of Sect. 3.2. **(c)** Percentiles of APF in years when the NINO3.4 index is in the negative (La Niña) phase (filled circles) versus the positive (El Niño) phase (open circles). The solid curve shows the median result of resampling the combined data set of both ENSO phases 10^4 times. The significance of differences between APFs in either phase and corresponding samples of the combined data set is assessed using a permutation test (Sect. 2.3), resulting in the indicated p-values. **(d)** Same as in **(c)** but for the PDO index.

3.2 Influence of large-scale climate modes on observed streamflow at Fraser-Hope

Before investigating relationships between climate and APF at the basin scale, we examine the influence of the PDO and ENSO on the observed APF at the Fraser-Hope stream gauge station. This station was not included in the Gurrapu et al. (2016) study, but we derive results similar to theirs at other stations, as shown in Fig. 2. The figure shows that higher APF is associated with negative (cold) phases of the NINO3.4 (Fig. 2a) and PDO (Fig. 2b) indices over the 103-year record (1912–2014) at Fraser-Hope. While the statistical relationships between the large-scale climate modes and the APF are robust (Spearman correlation of $\hat{\rho} = -0.40$ for NINO3.4, $\hat{\rho} = -0.35$ for PDO, both with $p < 10^{-3}$), Fig. 2a and b show that the largest APF in the record (1948; shown in boldface font on the plot) occurred during a neutral PDO phase and weak La Niña conditions, as did the fifth- and sixth-largest (1964 and 1997, also in bold). The second- to fourth-largest APFs (1972, 1950, 2012) occurred during strong negative PDO phases but weak La Niña conditions. This suggests that while APFs occurring during a negative PDO or La Niña phase may be larger than average, the very largest APFs may be influenced by more local drivers, of either climatic or non-climatic nature (e.g., elevation and aspect). Indeed, our results indicate that the PDO and NINO3.4 indices explain only $\sim \hat{\rho}^2 \sim 0.12$–$0.16$ or 12–16 % of the variance (with considerable interdependence between the two modes). Correlations of similar magnitude and sign were found at many more stations within the FRB by Thorne and Woo (2011).

Another way of visualizing streamflow sensitivity to ENSO and PDO phase is exhibited in the percentile plots

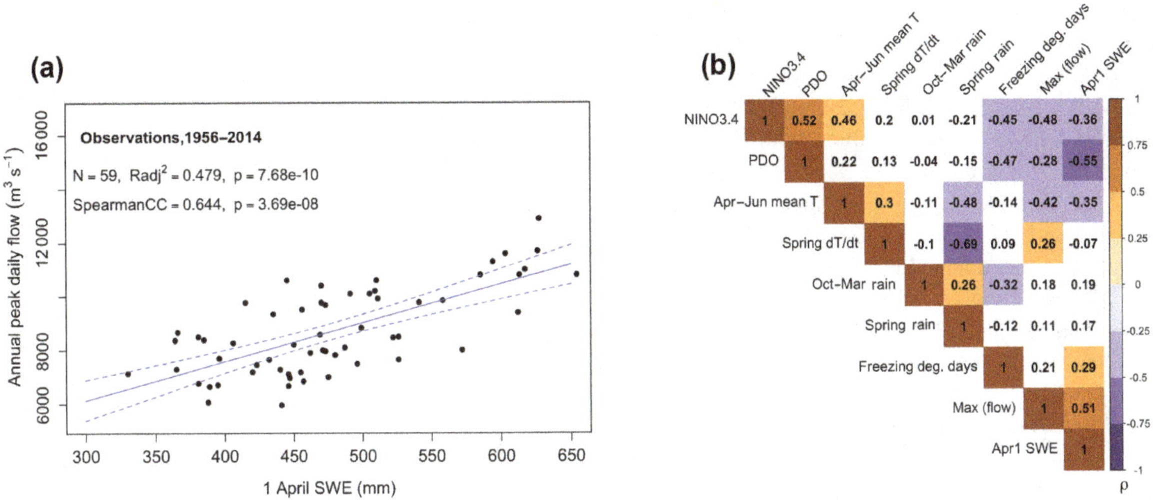

Figure 3. (a) Regression of observed APF against basin-averaged 1 April SWE over the Fraser Basin, within the period of overlapping records, 1956–2014. The solid blue line is the least-squares linear regression fit, while the dashed curves show the 95 % confidence interval. Adjusted Pearson and Spearman rank correlation coefficients, along with their associated p-values, are indicated at upper left. **(b)** Correlogram of all observed variables, averaged over the Fraser Basin over the common period of records for all variables, 1956–2006. Numerical values are Spearman rank correlation coefficients, and coloured squares indicate significant correlations at the $p < 0.1$ level.

of Fig. 2c and d. These plots can reveal differences in sample distributions more clearly than a histogram or density plot. For example, for the PDO the time series of APF was first divided into years with positive (PDO_{pos}) and negative (PDO_{neg}) PDO index. Then a resampling (permutation) test was applied to check whether the test statistic $S = [\text{mean(APF)}]_{\text{PDO,neg}}/[\text{mean(APF)}]_{\text{PDO,pos}}$ differed from that calculated from 10^4 random samples of the combined (both positive and negative PDO phase) data set (Sect. 2.3). Figure 2d shows that the APF in years with negative (cold) PDO phase is significantly larger than in years with positive (warm) PDO phase, consistent with the relationship seen in the scatter plot (Fig. 2b). Similar results were found for ENSO, as seen in Fig. 2c.

3.3 Basin-scale relationships amongst observed variables

To initiate our investigation of basin-scale drivers for APFs, we revisited the observed data. Specifically, we regressed the observed APF at Fraser-Hope against FRB-wide averages of the observed predictors in Table 2. Figure 3b shows a correlogram of the univariate regression results for all observed variables over the common period of 1956–2006. Variables with detected trends over this period (Sect. 3.1) were detrended before constructing the correlogram, as described in Sect. 2.3. We summarize the results for individual predictors below, before looking at their joint influence on APF at the end of the subsection.

3.3.1 Snow water equivalent (SWE)

As expected given the mainly nival character of the FRB, we find that interannual variations in 1 April SWE and APF are strongly correlated, with a Spearman correlation of $\hat{\rho} = 0.64$ over the common period of 1956–2014 of the MSS and WSC time series (Fig. 3a). This figure shows the raw data, while Fig. 3b shows the correlogram of all variables over the shorter common period of 1956–2006, including detrending where necessary. These differences lead to a somewhat smaller $\hat{\rho} = 0.51$ between 1 April SWE and APF. Nevertheless, the conclusion that years with higher than average SWE tend to produce higher peak streamflow at Fraser-Hope remains robust.

3.3.2 Temperature

Several diagnostics of the effect of surface air temperature T on APF were examined. First, we computed FDD from the PCIC-OBS data averaged over the entire FRB. This helps determine whether exceptionally cold winters correspond to an unusually large snowpack, potentially producing an enhanced snowmelt contribution to the spring freshet. Second, we calculated the April–June mean temperature T_{amj}, which roughly coincides with the interval between the time of 1 April SWE and APF. Finally, we computed the warming rate over the freshet period, $\mathrm{d}T/\mathrm{d}t$, by computing the linear least-squares slope of T between 1 April and the date of APF, or annual peak date (APD). Over the 1956–2006 period at Fraser-Hope, the APD ranges from 16 May to 23 July, with a median of 13 June. The corresponding warming rates in different years range from 0.093 to 0.26 °C day^{-1} (median = 0.16 °C day^{-1}), implying a typical warming over the median freshet (under the linear approximation) of $\sim$ 11 °C.

The correlations of these variables with APF are displayed in the correlogram of Fig. 3b. Here it is seen that amongst these variables, April–June mean temperature is anti-correlated with APF ($\hat{\rho} = -0.42$), while FDD and $\mathrm{d}T/\mathrm{d}^t$ are positively correlated with APF [$\hat{\rho} = 0.21$ (not significant) and $\hat{\rho} = 0.26$, respectively]. All else being equal, an unusually cold winter (high FDD) would be expected to result in a larger snowpack and a larger snowmelt contribution to streamflow consistent with the positive correlation found between FDD and APF. By the same reasoning, an unusually cold spring (low T_{amj}) resulting in a delayed, but more rapid snowmelt during the freshet, would again be expected to increase that year's APF. In years with normal summer T, this situation would produce a larger than normal warming rate, consistent with the positive correlation found between $\mathrm{d}T/\mathrm{d}^t$ and APF. Finally, we note from Fig. 3b that a positive correlation is seen between T_{amj} and $\mathrm{d}T/\mathrm{d}t$ ($\hat{\rho} = 0.30$), implying that high spring temperatures are associated with rapid warming.

3.3.3 Rainfall

As mentioned in Sect. 2.3, daily rainfall R shows a high temporal variance even when averaged over the entire FRB, which could introduce spurious noise into the regressions. For this reason, we looked at three integrated forms of R: (1) the summed rainfall over the winter months, $R_{\mathrm{Oct-Mar}}$; (2) the sum of rainfall between 1 April and the day of APF, R_{Spring}; and (3) the sum of R over the 15 days prior to the APD, R_{APF}. These metrics offer differing probes of the influence of rainfall on the APF at different lags and temporal resolution. However, none of the rainfall measures displayed a significant relationship with observed APF (Fig. 3b), reinforcing the designation of the FRB as a primarily nival basin. Indeed, R_{APF} was completely unrelated to APF ($\hat{\rho} = 0.02$, not shown in Fig. 3b). Although severe flooding in several small catchments in the US Pacific Northwest has been attributed to rain-on-snow events (McCabe et al., 2007; Surfleet and Tollos, 2013), we see no evidence of this in the much larger FRB.

Unlike SWE, the basin-averaged, annual maximum CRI, $\mathrm{CRI}_{\mathrm{max}}$, generally occurs during summer and fall (calendar days 160 to 301), although multiple peaks in a given year are often observed (see ff., Fig. 9). This contrasts with the narrower distribution of APF dates occurring in spring–summer (days 136–204), suggesting a weak relationship may exist between the two on the seasonal timescale.

Focusing exclusively on annual maxima or summed values of rainfall and APF might cause us to miss important relationships between rain and discharge on shorter timescales. To investigate these types of linkages, we interrogated the respective daily time series. Specifically, we computed the

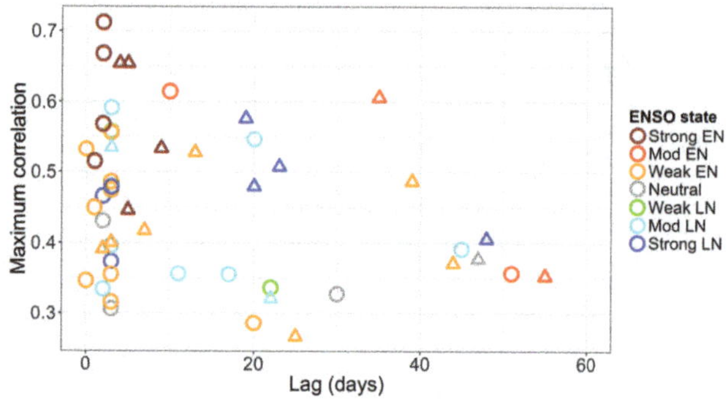

Figure 4. Results of lagged regression of FRB-averaged daily rainfall, characterized by the current rainfall index (CRI), on streamflow at Fraser-Hope. Only the subset of years wherein there exists a significant relationship between CRI and discharge are shown. The ENSO state, as specified in the legend according to colour (EN: El Niño, LN: La Niña), corresponds to the year preceding the rainfall and discharge, and was obtained from http://ggweather.com/enso/oni.htm, based on the same definition used in the analysis of Sect. 3 (i.e., NINO3.4). The maximum correlation, $\max(\hat{\rho}_{XY})$, is shown on the vertical axis, with the corresponding lag, τ, between rainfall and discharge on the horizontal axis. A positive lag means that streamflow lags CRI. Circles: observed precipitation versus observed discharge over the 1950–2006 period. Triangles: observed precipitation versus VIC-simulated discharge. All correlations are significant at the $p < 0.05$ level. Two outlier points with lags > 60 days (with none exceeding $\max(\hat{\rho}_{XY}) = 0.42$) are omitted from the plot.

annual cross-correlation function between deseasonalized streamflow (X) and CRI (Y) anomalies for each year i:

$$\hat{\rho}_{XY,i}(\tau) = \frac{\mathrm{mean}\left[X_i'(t)Y_i'(t+\tau)\right]}{\hat{\sigma}_{X,i}\hat{\sigma}_{Y,i}}, \qquad (3)$$

where $X_i'(t)$ is the anomaly time series of X (i.e., difference between X and its multi-year mean annual cycle) in year i, $\hat{\sigma}_{X,i}$ is the standard deviation of X_i' (and similarly for Y), and τ is the applied lag (days) between X_i' and Y_i', ranging over ± 183 days. If $\max(\hat{\rho}_{XY,i}) > \delta$ at $\tau > 0$, where $\delta = 2/\sqrt{N} = 2/\sqrt{365}$, then CRI both leads and positively correlates with streamflow in that year, suggesting a causal relationship. The results are displayed in Fig. 4. Each point in the scatterplot represents $\max(\hat{\rho}_{XY,i})$ calculated over $(365 - \tau)$ pairs taken from the two daily time series for the ith calendar year. Figure 4 shows that about half (26 of 50) of the years exhibit a significant relationship at some time during the year, with $\max(\hat{\rho}_{XY,i})$ ranging from 0.24 to 0.72 with lags of $\tau = 0$–51 days (Fig. 4, open circles). Two clear outliers, at $\tau = 93$ and 114 days, were disregarded (not shown). For each point plotted in Fig. 4, the corresponding ENSO state for that year, taken from historical data, is indicated; 3 of the 5 (and 4 of the 10) largest correlations were associated with strong El Niño years, each with a lag of 2 days or less between rainfall and streamflow (Fig. 4). Rainfall events in the upper reaches of the FRB can have a delayed effect on streamflow at Hope of up to ~1 week (BC River Forecast Centre, 2012), while in years with $\tau = 1$ to 8 weeks, soil moisture that is near field capacity might be responsible for successive overland flow following rainfall events. However, Fig. 4 shows that these situations tend to occur during weak or moderate La Niña conditions.

Finally, we note the possibility that significant multi-day rainfall events coinciding with frozen or saturated soils might lead to occasional flooding at local scales within the FRB. While suitable soil moisture observations are not readily available at this time (see Sect. 5), we employ the VIC model to examine the role of soil moisture in both the FRB and its sub-basins using the regression framework in Sect. 3.4.

3.3.4 Relationships amongst observed predictors

Finally, we investigated relationships amongst observational variables unrelated to streamflow revealed in the correlogram of Fig. 3b. April–June mean temperature is positively correlated with spring warming rate and negatively correlated with 1 April SWE, both intuitively reasonable results, as is the positive correlation of FDD with SWE. Strong inverse relationships also exist between spring rainfall and (i) T_{amj} ($\hat{\rho} = -0.48$), and (ii) warming rate ($\hat{\rho} = -0.69$). Both of these relations are reasonable given that the rainfall fraction diminishes approximately linearly with decreasing temperature toward 0 °C, according to the Dai (2008) parameterization used here. Finally, cold season (October–March) rainfall is anti-correlated with FDD ($\hat{\rho} = -0.32$) (Fig. 3b).

3.3.5 Multivariate regression

The above results were derived using univariate linear regression and correlations computed using the Spearman rank method. However, we also would like to attribute interannual variance in the APF to the combined variances of the predictors. As described in Sect. 2.3, we constructed a number of MLR relations including all possible combinations of the above variables that showed a significant Spearman $\hat{\rho}$ when regressed individually against APF.

The MLR procedure yields the following multilinear regression fits:

$$\widehat{\mathrm{APF}}_{\mathrm{obs}}\left(\mathrm{m^3\,s^{-1}}\right) = 4535 + 11.40\mathrm{SWE_{Apr1}} + 17\,068(\mathrm{d}T/\mathrm{d}t) - 603.2T_{\mathrm{amj}} \quad \left(R^2_{\mathrm{adj}} = 0.63,\ p < 10^{-9}\right), \tag{4}$$

$$\widehat{\mathrm{APF}}_{\mathrm{obs}}\left(\mathrm{m^3\,s^{-1}}\right) = 4106 + 10.48\mathrm{SWE_{Apr1}} + 17\,815(\mathrm{d}T/\mathrm{d}t) - 494.3T_{\mathrm{amj}} - 402.3\mathrm{NINO3.4} \quad \left(R^2_{\mathrm{adj}} = 0.65,\ p < 10^{-9}\right), \tag{5}$$

where the units of the predictors on the right-hand sides of Eqs. (4) and (5) are provided in Table 2. Equation (4) includes only local, basin-averaged predictors, while Eq. (5) includes the non-local influences of ENSO and PDO. Interestingly, only NINO3.4, not the PDO index, is a significant predictor of APF in the MLR, despite the comparable importance of both indices in the univariate regressions (Sect. 3.2). The residuals from both fits are indistinguishable from a Gaussian distribution at the 5 % significance level, according to the Kolmogorov–Smirnov statistic. Additional parameters of the fits are summarized in Table 4. The predictors on the right-hand side of Eqs. (4) and (5) are ordered from left to right by decreasing partial F value: e.g., $\mathrm{SWE_{Apr1}}$ contributes the majority of the interannual variance in APF, followed by $\mathrm{d}T/\mathrm{d}t$, T_{amj} and NINO3.4 (Table 4). Together, these variables explain 65 % of the variance, 2 % more than if the influence of ENSO is ignored. As mentioned above, rainfall variables do not contribute significantly to the interannual variability of the observed APF at Fraser-Hope.

3.4 Observed versus VIC-simulated streamflow and SWE

Before exploring relationships between APF and the wider array of variables available in the VIC hydrological model, as an evaluation exercise we compare several features of the VIC simulations with available observations in the FRB. In Fig. 5a, we compare the 10 largest APFs in observations and VIC at Fraser-Hope station over the simulation period of 1955–2004. The APFs have been ranked by their observed magnitude, with the highest flow years on the left-hand side of the bar graph. In most years, the VIC-simulated APFs are close to the observed values. Figure 5b compares the daily climatology and interannual variability of VIC and observations over the same period. VIC tends to overestimate the magnitude of the APF by ~8 % (multi-year mean) to 16 % (multi-year maximum), and also simulates an APD ~5 days later than in the observations. VIC underestimates interannual streamflow variability over most of the year, except over the period of peak flow from June to mid-August, when it displays higher variability. However, given that the interannual coefficient of variation in observed APF ($\mathrm{CV} = \sigma/\mathrm{mean[APF]}$) is 18 %, that the VIC-simulated CV = 20 %, and their degree of overlap, we conclude that the hydrographs are not significantly different.

Figure 5c shows quantile plots of APF and APD for VIC compared to observations over the 1955–2004 period. Here, the permutation test was applied using the test statistic $S = [\mathrm{mean(APF)}]_{\mathrm{VIC}}/[\mathrm{mean(APF)}]_{\mathrm{OBS}}$ (Sect. 2.3). Figure 5c shows that for APF, the VIC-simulated APF is indistinguishable from the stream gauge observations at the 5 % significance level (i.e., $p = 0.07 > 0.05$; $p = 0.24$ if the two outliers with VIC-simulated $\mathrm{APF} > 13\,000\,\mathrm{m^3\,s^{-1}}$ are removed), while the late bias in VIC-simulated APD is significant at the ~1 % level. As our main concern in this work

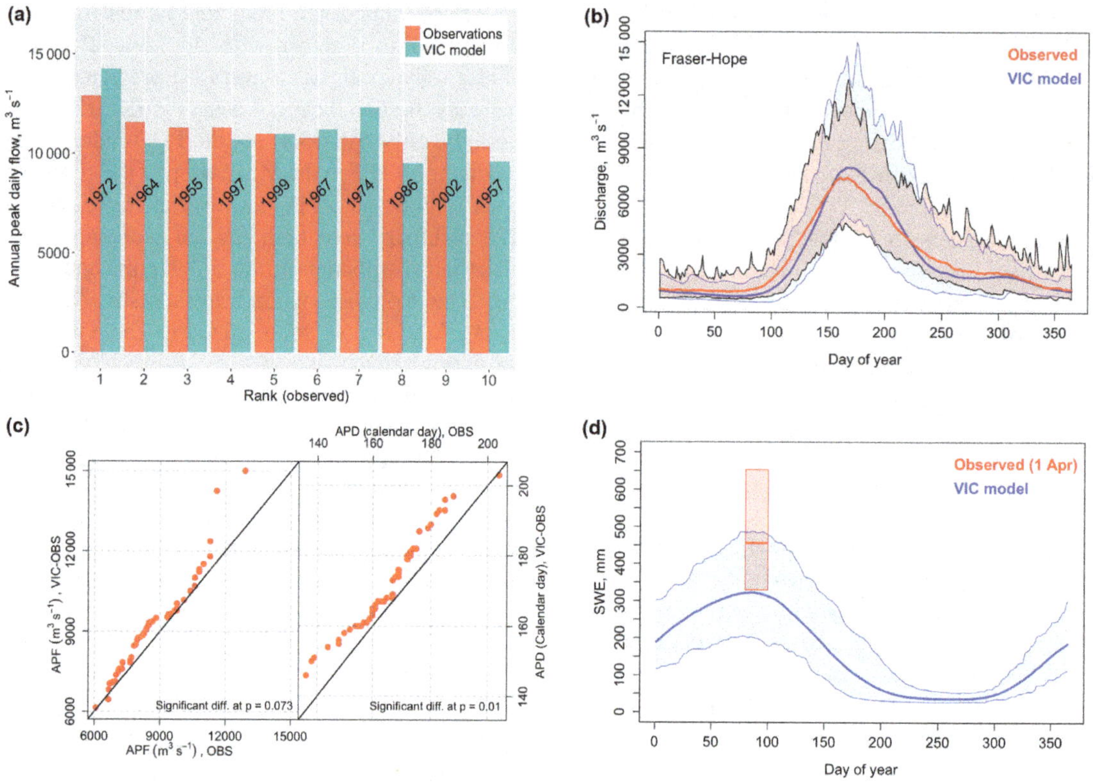

Figure 5. (a) Annual peak daily streamflow (APF) magnitude in observations (red) and in the VIC simulation (blue) at Fraser-Hope, ranked by observed values over 1955–2004. **(b)** Annual cycle of daily streamflow in observations (red) and VIC simulation (blue) over 1955–2004 at Fraser-Hope. **(c)** Quantile plots of VIC-simulated versus observed APF and APD at Fraser-Hope. Differences between the respective distributions are assessed using a permutation test with 10^4 resamples; the resulting p-values are indicated in each sub-panel. **(d)** 1 April observed SWE (red) compared with annual cycle of SWE from VIC, both averaged over the FRB for 1956–2006. Heavy curves in **(b)** and **(d)** show the multi-year mean, while shaded areas show the interannual range.

is with identifying key predictors of the APF, with less emphasis on APD, we conclude that VIC simulates APF reasonably well compared to observations.

Due to the dominant influence of annual snowpack on APF, it is also desirable to compare the VIC-simulated SWE with observed 1 April SWE measurements. In the analysis of the VIC simulation, we use SWE_{max} as a predictor instead of SWE_{Apr1} since it is expected to be more closely linked to APF on physical grounds. In Fig. 5d, the annual cycle of the corrected, VIC-simulated SWE (Sect. 2.2) is compared with the observed 1 April SWE, with both quantities represented by their basin averages. While there is significant overlap in the interannual ranges of simulated and observed SWE, VIC appears to systematically underestimate the snowpack amount. However, it is important to recognize the sampling bias inherent in the observed, basin-average SWE: since the MSS stations tend to be located at high elevation (range: 750–2200 m), the observed estimates are likely biased high compared to a true basin average, as represented in VIC. In addition, we note that the apparent VIC biases in peak streamflow and SWE over the FRB are qualitatively consistent with VIC simulations over other nival basins in the Pacific Northwest (Salathé Jr. et al., 2014).

3.5 Relationships amongst VIC-simulated variables

In this section we apply the methodology of Sect. 3.3 to probe relationships amongst the wider array of variables available in the VIC hydrological model over the FRB. We begin with an analysis of the routed model streamflow at Fraser-Hope, as a representative outlet of the entire FRB, before examining VIC-modelled discharge at the outlets of four subbasins within the FRB in Sect. 3.6.

In addition to the PCIC-OBS variables used in the regression analysis of Sect. 3.3 – which were used as daily forcings for the VIC simulation – we include a number of variables available in the model but not in observations, namely annual maximum of SWE averaged over the FRB, SWE_{max}; calendar date of SWE_{max}; snowmelt rate, $d(SWE)/dt$; melt season length, SWE_{len}; and antecedent total column soil moisture (detailed definitions are given in Table 2). The regression results are again summarized as a correlogram (Fig. 6) and in Table 4. The annual snowmelt rate, $d(SWE)/dt$, was

Table 4. Fitted parameters from multilinear regression of the form: $Y = a_0 + a_1X_1 + a_2X_2 + a_3X_3 + \ldots$ For each basin or subbasin, the first row in columns 2 to 6 indicates the relevant predictors, while the second and third rows list the fit coefficients and partial F-values, respectively (all partial p-values are less than 0.05). The total F-value and adjusted Pearson correlation for each fit is provided in columns 7 and 8, respectively. For the subbasins, only VIC results are given, due to the small number of 1 April observed SWE values available. Results given for OBS include basin-averaged predictors over the FRB, while those for OBS_{ext} include indices of large-scale climate variability.

Basin/subbasin	Int.	X_1	X_2	X_3	X_4	F	R^2_{adj}
	a_0	a_1	a_2	a_3	a_4		
		F_1	F_2	F_3	F_4		
FRB							
– OBS		SWE_{Apr1}	dT/dt	T_{amj}			
	4535	11.40	17 068	−603.2			
		60.9	14.0	13.0		29.3	0.63
– OBS_{ext}		SWE_{Apr1}	dT/dt	T_{amj}	NINO3.4		
	4106	10.48	17 815	−494.3	−402.3		
		65.4	15.0	13.9	4.46	24.7	0.65
– VIC		SWE_{max}	dT/dt	SWE_{len}	d(SWE)/dt		
	3239	37.14	26 842	−57.69	1769.6		
		101	38.8	8.67	3.70	38.1	0.75
Upper Fraser		SWE_{max}	SWE_{len}	R_{Spring}			
	2414	5.257	−28.43	3.453			
		39.0	16.9	2.64		19.5	0.53
Quesnel		SWE_{max}	dT/dt	SM_{Sep}			
	−542.0	1.834	988.3	2291.2			
		55.1	19.0	5.77		26.6	0.61
Thompson-Nicola		SWE_{max}	dT/dt	$R_{Oct\text{-}Mar}$			
	−805.8	5.181	7199.8	4.341			
		97.4	39.1	7.75		48.1	0.75
Chilko		SWE_{max}	dT/dt				
	−142.6	1.152	786.2				
		56.5	8.45			32.5	0.56

calculated as the best-fit, least-squares linear slope of SWE between the dates of SWE_{max} and APF. Formally speaking, d(SWE)/dt is the snow ablation rate, which in VIC includes snowmelt as the dominant contribution along with evaporation and rain-on-snow (other snow removal processes occurring in nature such as blowing snow or avalanches are not simulated). For convenience, however, we refer to d(SWE)/dt as simply the snowmelt rate with the understanding that these other processes may make minor contributions to snowpack disintegration.

3.5.1 Influence of large-scale climate modes on streamflow at Fraser-Hope

Through the influence of the forcing variables, the PDO and ENSO may affect the VIC-simulated APF at Fraser-Hope. Indeed, we find a slightly more robust, but qualitatively similar, relationship between the large-scale climate indices and modelled APF than for observed APF: as seen in Fig. 6, the correlations are Spearman $\hat{\rho} = -0.41$ for NINO3.4 and $\hat{\rho} = -0.38$ for PDO (both at $p < 10^{-2}$).

3.5.2 Snow water equivalent and snowmelt

As noted for the observed 1 April SWE, we find that SWE_{max} exercises a strong control on APF ($\hat{\rho} = 0.70$, $p < 0.001$; Fig. 6). The latter lags SWE_{max} by an average of 84 days (range 52–127 days) over the simulation period; examples for specific years are displayed in Fig. 9. Further, Table 5 shows that of the top 10 APF years in this period, 7 were in the top 10 of SWE_{max}. Yet, the highest APF corresponds to the 6th-largest SWE_{max} (1982), while the 4th-highest APF occurred in an average year for snow accumulation (1958). It is therefore of interest to investigate what conditions, independent of snow accumulation, led to the comparatively large APF in those years.

Snowmelt displays significant positive correlations with APF ($\hat{\rho} = 0.43$) and several other predictors, namely SWE_{max} ($\hat{\rho} = 0.63$), FDD ($\hat{\rho} = 0.38$), date of SWE_{max} ($\hat{\rho} = 0.32$), dT/dt ($\hat{\rho} = 0.25$), and maximum annual soil moisture ($\hat{\rho} = 0.64$). In years with high SWE_{max}, snowmelt in spring recharges soil moisture (over unfrozen ground; see Sect. 3.5.3), sometimes to field capacity, which leads to in-

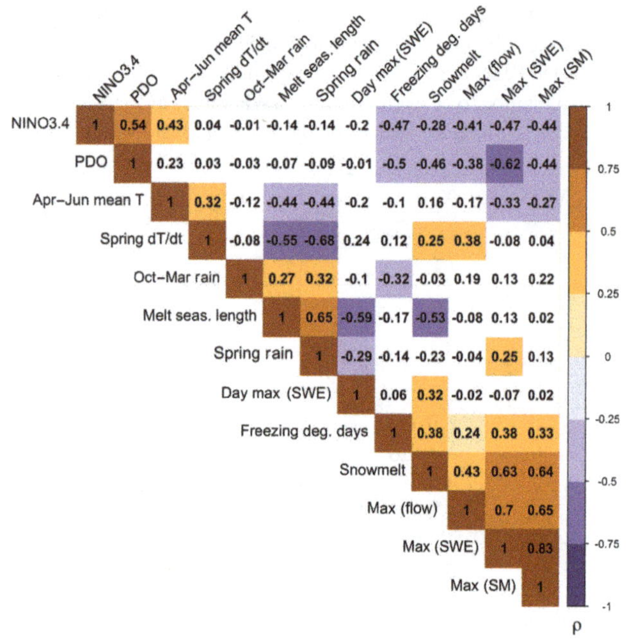

Figure 6. Correlogram of all observed and VIC-simulated variables, averaged over the Fraser Basin within the common period of records, 1955–2004. All values are Spearman rank correlation coefficients, and coloured squares indicate significant correlations at the $p < 0.1$ level. A hierarchical clustering algorithm has been applied to group like-with-like correlations.

Table 5. Top 10 APF years at Fraser-Hope in the VIC simulation over the period 1955–2004, along with corresponding ranks of other basin-averaged predictors. Years in boldface font are highlighted in Fig. 9.

Rank APF	Year APF	Rank SWE_{max}	Rank SM	Rank FDD	Rank dT/dt	Rank spring rain
1	1982	6	6	14	1	47
2	**1972**	**2**	**1**	**4**	**21**	**26**
3	1974	1	4	17	39	22
4	**1958**	**25**	**13**	**46**	**5**	**49**
5	1956	10	7	1	11	50
6	2002	15	19	26	8	23
7	1967	7	9	28	7	39
8	**1999**	**4**	**8**	**44**	**45**	**1**
9	1997	5	2	9	22	13
10	1964	18	16	33	26	15

creased runoff and the strong positive correlations between snowmelt, soil moisture and APF. Significant negative correlations are also found with melt season length ($\hat{\rho} = -0.53$) and the NINO3.4 and PDO indices ($\hat{\rho} = -0.28$ and -0.46, respectively). The inverse relationship with the large-scale indices should be considered in light of their similar relationship with SWE_{max} ($\hat{\rho} = -0.47$ and -0.62, for NINO3.4 and PDO respectively): higher snowpack accumulates during La Niña and negative PDO phases, with reduced snowmelt due to cooler temperatures.

3.5.3 Soil moisture

In our VIC simulation, the basin-averaged annual peak soil moisture, SM_{max}, occurs during the snowmelt period from mid-March to mid-June, most often near the end of May, well after the day of SWE_{max} and approximately 3 weeks in advance of the APF (for an illustration depicting individual years, see Fig. 9). The direct influence of both SWE_{max} ($\hat{\rho} = 0.83$) and snowmelt ($\hat{\rho} = 0.64$) on SM_{max} is detected at high confidence ($p < 10^{-3}$), while SM_{max} is, in turn, strongly correlated with APF ($\hat{\rho} = 0.65$, $p < 10^{-3}$) in the annual time series (Fig. 6). A cross-correlation analysis of the respective daily time series over the entire common period reveals that, on average, SWE leads SM by 68 days (maximum cross-correlation, $R = 0.65$), SM leads streamflow by 22 days ($R = 0.85$), and SWE leads streamflow by 105 days ($R = 0.74$). The higher cross-correlation between SM and streamflow indicates that the annual cycle of SM is a better predictor of the daily streamflow hydrograph than SWE, despite the above-mentioned superiority of SWE_{max} as an annual predictor of APF. This is a reasonable result, since during the freshet, daily SM integrates contributions from both snowmelt and precipitation. On the other hand, SM_{max} could be considered inferior to SWE_{max} as a predictor of APF with respect to its much shorter lead time. SM_{max} also exhibits significant relationships with FDD ($\hat{\rho} = 0.33$), T_{amj} ($\hat{\rho} = -0.27$) and the NINO3.4 and PDO indices ($\hat{\rho} = -0.44$ for both). The negative phases of ENSO and the PDO bring more rain and snow, which consequently enhances soil moisture.

Also of interest is a possible relationship between APF and SM preceding the snowmelt period, for example, in fall before snow accumulation begins. Numerous studies point to the influence of antecedent soil moisture on seasonal streamflow in nival catchments (Maurer and Lettenmaier, 2003; Berg and Mulroy, 2006; Williams et al., 2009; Harpold and Molotch, 2015). Using a suite of land surface models including VIC, Koster et al. (2010) and Mahanama et al. (2012) demonstrated improvement of March–July streamflow forecast skill over the western United States using antecedent (1 January) soil moisture in addition to snow amount as a predictor. The basic mechanism is that antecedent reduced storage capacity of wet or frozen soils leads to more of the snowmelt being routed to discharge during the spring freshet, and vice-versa for dry soils. To investigate the interannual sensitivity of APF to antecedent SM, we used monthly mean SM from the preceding August through November in turn as predictors of APF, but found no significant correlations. This insensitivity may be due to the lack of a frozen soil parameterization in the version of VIC used here. In this implementation, soil drainage over the cold season tends to be overestimated (Cherkauer and Lettenmaier, 2003), which could cause a decoupling between autumn SM and spring freshet flows.

3.5.4 Temperature and rainfall

As in the observations, FDD and spring warming rate $\mathrm{d}T/\mathrm{d}t$ are positively correlated with APF ($\hat{\rho}=0.24$ and $\hat{\rho}=0.38$, respectively; Fig. 6). The connection between $\mathrm{d}T/\mathrm{d}t$ and APF is stronger than in the observations but, interestingly, there is no significant correlation between T_{amj} and APF as exists in the observational data (Eqs. 4 and 5). Further, the results in Table 5 suggest that large APFs in average SWE years are characterized by large $\mathrm{d}T/\mathrm{d}t$ (e.g., 1982, 1958, 2002).

Again as in the observations (Sect. 3.3.3), no significant correlations are found between any of the rainfall measures and VIC-simulated APF. However, as also found in the observations, there are indications of a rainfall–streamflow connection at other times of the year. Repeating the cross-correlation analysis between streamflow and CRI as in Sect. 3.3.3 reveals that 20 of 50 years exhibit a significant relationship at some time during the year, with $\max(\hat{\rho}_{XY,i})$ ranging from 0.27 to 0.66 with lags of $\tau=2$–55 days. Two clear outliers, at $\tau=91$ and 142 days, were disregarded. Figure 4 (triangles) shows that most (nine) of the rainfall-influenced years occur during the El Niño phase, while four occur during La Niña and seven during neutral years. Twelve of the 20 rainfall-influenced years occur during the cool phase of the PDO. More often than not, however, CRI lags daily streamflow, suggesting little to no relationship. With regard to other relationships, we find that cold season rainfall is correlated with spring rainfall ($\hat{\rho}=0.32$) and anti-correlated with FDD ($\hat{\rho}=-0.32$) (Fig. 6). As mentioned in Sect. 3.3.4, spring rainfall is negatively correlated with T_{amj}, $\mathrm{d}T/\mathrm{d}t$, and snowmelt, but with slightly different $\hat{\rho}$ values due to the different lengths of averaging period in the calculations compared to the observed case (as per the definitions in Table 2).

3.5.5 Multivariate regression

As in the case of the observed variables, we constructed MLR relations including all combinations of the variables in Fig. 6 that showed a significant Spearman $\hat{\rho}$ and selected the optimal MLR based on the criteria specified in Sect. 3.3.5. One predictor that was excluded from the MLR was $\mathrm{SM_{max}}$: its high correlation with $\mathrm{SWE_{max}}$ indicates that its independent explanatory power is limited (Sect. 3.5.3). The resulting relationship is

$$\widehat{\mathrm{APF}}_{\mathrm{VIC}}\left(\mathrm{m^3\,s^{-1}}\right)=3239+37.14\mathrm{SWE_{max}}+26842(\mathrm{d}T/\mathrm{d}t) \\ -57.69\mathrm{SWE_{len}}+1770\mathrm{d(SWE)}/\mathrm{d}t \\ \left(R^2_{\mathrm{adj}}=0.75,\ p<10^{-9}\right). \quad (6)$$

In contrast to the MLR constructed for observed streamflow, Eq. (5), neither of the large-scale climate indices has a significant influence, nor is T_{amj} an important predictor. Nevertheless, the four variables on the right-hand side of Eq. (6) account for 75 % of the interannual variance in APF. Three of the four were identified in the univariate regressions as important, with the exception being the length of the melt season, $\mathrm{SWE_{len}}$. The latter displays a strong anti-correlation with snowmelt ($\hat{\rho}=-0.55$, Fig. 6), suggesting that the two variables are not independent. However, since removing each of $\mathrm{SWE_{len}}$ and $\mathrm{d(SWE)}/\mathrm{d}t$ from the MLR in turn yields a significantly poorer fit ($R^2_{\mathrm{adj}}=0.71$ for $\mathrm{d(SWE)}/\mathrm{d}t$ only and $R^2_{\mathrm{adj}}=0.69$ for $\mathrm{SWE_{len}}$ only), it seems that both predictors have some explanatory value. The absence of both the PDO and NINO3.4 indices from the MLR could be a reflection of the limitations of the driving data, inasmuch as the processing of gridded station data to the regular grid may weaken the influence of the large-scale climate drivers (Sect. 2.1).

3.6 Relationships amongst VIC-simulated variables at the subbasin scale

The same analysis as conducted for the entire FRB was repeated for each of the four subbasins comprising nearly 70 % of the annual flow at Fraser-Hope (Table 1; Kang et al., 2016). The results of the univariate regressions are presented as a correlogram in Fig. 7, while those for the MLR are provided in Table 4.

Overall, the relationships in the subbasins mirror those seen in the FRB as a whole. The univariate analysis shows that in all four subbasins, $\mathrm{SWE_{max}}$ and $\mathrm{SM_{max}}$ are good predictors of APF, while snowmelt and FDD exhibit positive correlations with APF in three of the four subbasins, Chilko being the exception (Fig. 7). While $\mathrm{SWE_{max}}$ has a slightly stronger influence on APF than $\mathrm{SM_{max}}$ in the FRB, $\mathrm{SM_{max}}$ is more influential at the subbasin scale, explaining over 75 % of the variance in APF in Quesnel (compared to 40 % for $\mathrm{SWE_{max}}$). The correlation between spring $\mathrm{d}T/\mathrm{d}t$ and APF is strong in Thompson–Nicola ($\hat{\rho}=0.50$, $p<0.05$) but weaker in Quesnel ($\hat{\rho}=0.25$, $p<0.1$) and not significant in the other two catchments. Three of the four subbasins exhibit a strong inverse relationship between APF and the NINO3.4 and PDO indices, again with the exception of Chilko. The weak dependence of streamflow on the PDO, SOI and Pacific-North American indices in this and other catchments in the western FRB was also noted by Thorne and Woo (2011), who attributed this insensitivity to the low magnitude of discharge in these tributaries. These authors speculated that the main trunk of the Fraser, by contrast, integrates the influence of regional climate forcings on upstream catchments, bolstering the teleconnections. The insensitivity of APF to the local, basin-averaged predictors might be related to the smaller size of the Chilko compared to the other three subbasins, which lowers the signal-to-noise ratio of the basin averages. This, along with the comparatively lower APFs at the basin out-

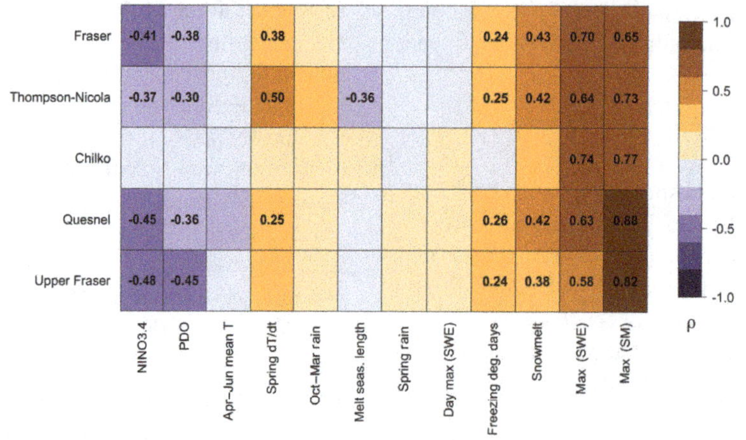

Figure 7. Correlogram of observed and VIC-simulated variables, averaged over each of the indicated subbasins within the 1955–2004 period, against APF at the subbasin outlet (Table 1). The cell values and colour scale indicate Spearman rank correlations, significant at the $p < 0.1$ level. The ordering of variable columns is the same as in Fig. 6, for ease of comparison.

let, makes the detection of significant correlations more challenging in Chilko compared with the other subbasins.

Moving now to the MLR analysis, the results in Table 4 demonstrate that in all four subbasins, SWE_{max} is the most skillful predictor of APF, again in agreement with the results for the FRB as a whole. Likewise, in three of the four catchments, dT/dt emerges as the next most significant variable. The exception is the Upper Fraser basin, where SWE_{len} is the second most skillful predictor. In this subbasin, APF is inversely correlated with SWE_{len} in the MLR, while the latter is in turn anti-correlated with both dT/dt ($\hat{\rho} = -0.81$, $p < 0.05$) and T_{amj} ($\hat{\rho} = -0.25$, $p < 0.1$) in the univariate regressions (Fig. 6). These results suggest that anomalously warm springtime temperatures (compared to the preceding winter) are at the heart of the APF–SWE_{len} relationship in the Upper Fraser, not unlike what is seen in the other subbasins.

In contrast to the FRB as a whole, rainfall does appear to have a weak influence on APF in two of the subbasins. However, in each subbasin, APF is sensitive to a different measure of rainfall. In Thompson–Nicola, the basin with the largest area and second-highest mean elevation, $R_{Oct–Mar}$ is positively correlated with APF, while in the Upper Fraser, R_{Spring} displays a somewhat weaker positive relationship with APF. In the Quesnel, a smaller basin of lower mean elevation, the preceding September mean soil moisture is an effective predictor of APF. Interestingly, neither the NINO3.4 nor the PDO index is an effective predictor of APF in the MLR of any of the subbasins, despite the fact that strong inverse relationships are still seen in the univariate correlogram (Fig. 6).

3.7 Co-dependence of streamflow predictors

The above results make it clear that, of the predictors considered in the FRB and its subbasins, APF is primarily influenced by SWE_{max} and the rate of warming in spring, dT/dt. To explore the co-dependence between predictors, we show in Fig. 8 a scatterplot of the relative anomaly of each of these two predictors, $\Delta X/\overline{X} = (X_i - \overline{X})/\overline{X}$, where X_i is the value of predictor X at year i and $\overline{X}$ is the long-term mean (1955–2004), with the corresponding streamflow relative anomaly $\Delta Q/\overline{Q}$ indicated by the point colour. This type of plot has been used previously to explore the elasticity (i.e., non-linearity) of streamflow as a function of covariates (e.g., Andréassian et al., 2016). However, here we employ it primarily as an additional illustration of the co-dependencies identified by the MLR analysis.

In the FRB, the roughly uniform pattern of scatter in the vertical and horizontal directions indicates a weak co-dependence between ΔSWE_{max} and $\Delta(dT/dt)$, consistent with expectation – dT/dt is computed only after the day of SWE_{max} each year – and with the results of Figs. 5 and 6. The corresponding $\Delta Q/\overline{Q}$ values display an overall gradient from bottom left to top right, i.e., from lower than average SWE_{max} and dT/dt to higher than average SWE_{max} and dT/dt, again consistent with the univariate and multivariate regression results. Qualitatively similar results are found in the Chilko, Thompson–Nicola and Quesnel subbasins.

In the Upper Fraser subbasin, the primary predictor remains SWE_{max}, but the secondary predictor is SWE_{len}. As a result, the scatterplot displays a weak co-dependence between relative changes in the two variables, with some clustering toward the diagonal. Furthermore, the overall gradient in $\Delta Q/\overline{Q}$ is from top left to bottom right, i.e., from lower than average SWE_{max} and higher than average SWE_{len} to higher than average SWE_{max} and lower than average SWE_{len}. That is, in years when an anomalously large snowpack ($\Delta SWE_{max} > 0$) melts fairly quickly ($\Delta SWE_{len} < 0$), streamflow tends to be larger than usual ($\Delta Q > 0$).

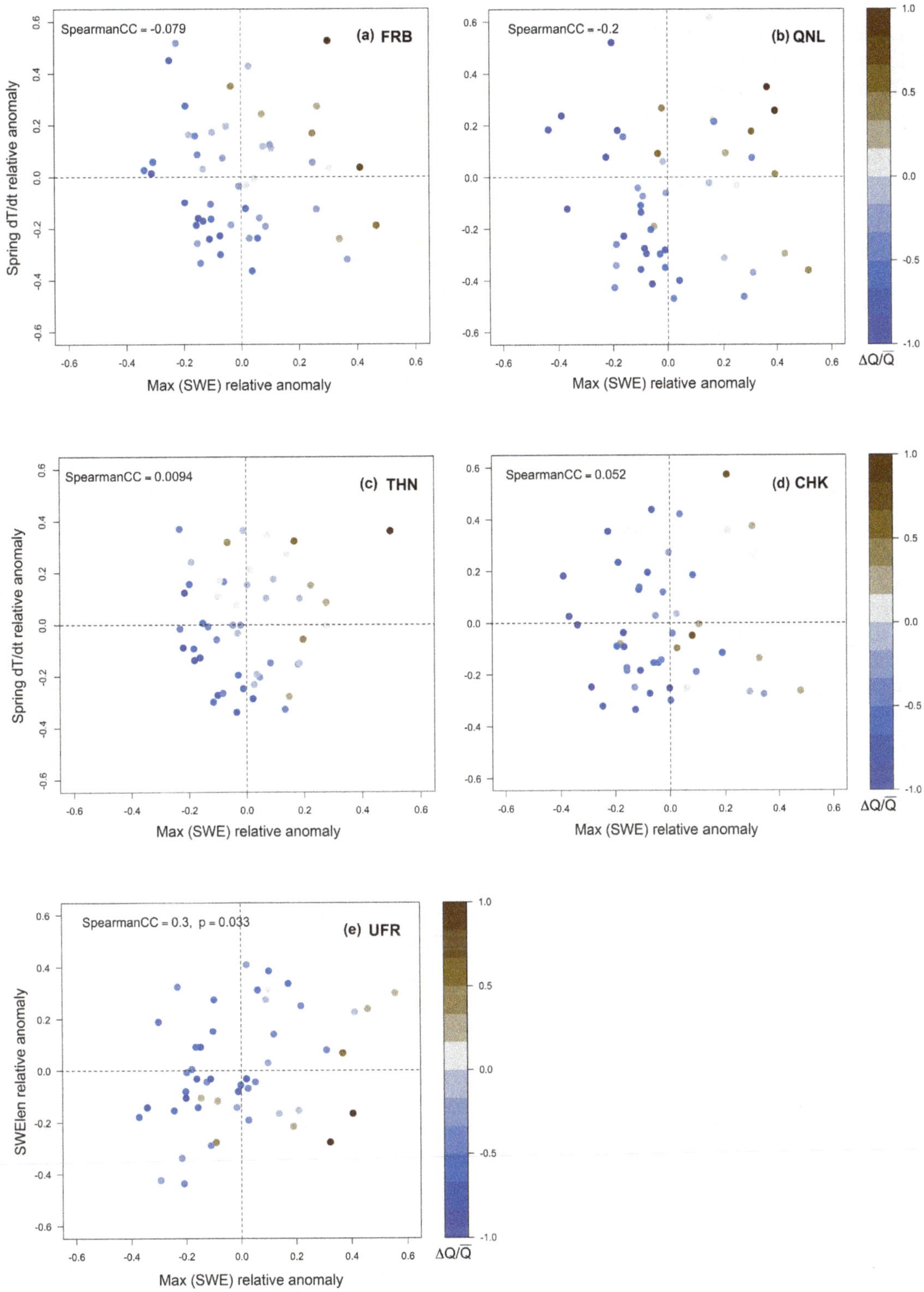

Figure 8. Scatterplots showing the co-dependence of relative APF, $\Delta Q/\overline{Q}$ (colour scale) on the two principal predictors from the MLR analysis (x- and y-axes), expressed as relative anomalies, in each basin. Counterclockwise from top left: entire Fraser (FRB), Thompson–Nicola (THN), Upper Fraser (UFR), Chilko (CHK) and Quesnel (QNL). The primary predictor in all subbasins is SWE_{max}, while the secondary predictor is dT/dt in all subbasins except UFR, where it is SWE_{len}. The Spearman rank correlation between the two predictors is shown at upper left in each panel; other than in UFR, none are significant at the 10 % ($p < 0.1$) level.

4 Case studies: high-flow years in the FRB

While the MLR approach captures the relationship between various predictors and APF in the FRB and its subbasins in a statistical manner, it can miss unusual weather factors that are important in specific years. Both historical data and anecdotal accounts of large historical floods in the region place a large emphasis on the precise seasonal development of warming temperatures and rainfall during the snowmelt period from early April to late June as being a critical factor in the development of damaging floods (BC River Forecast Centre, 2012; Septer, 2007). For this reason, we present in this section an "anatomy" of streamflow and the associated key hydrological variables in years of particularly high VIC-simulated discharge at the Fraser-Hope station. We focus on VIC-simulated variables since full time series of all variables of interest are available to construct both a climatology and annual cycles for specific years.

Table 5 shows the top 10 APFs occurring in the VIC simulation from 1955 to 2004, with corresponding rankings of other key predictors entering the regression analysis of Sect. 3. Seven of the top 10 SWE_{max} years are in this group. This highlights the dominant effect of spring snowpack on APF magnitude in the FRB. A similar result holds for observed basin-averaged 1 April SWE and APF at Fraser-Hope: 8 of the top 10 1 April SWE years are also amongst the top 10 observed APFs. Looking at results for the other predictors, 7 of the top 10 SM_{max} years (not surprising given the linkage between SWE_{max} and SM_{max} noted in Sect. 3.4.3), 4 of the top 10 spring warming rates and 3 of the top 10 FDDs are in the group of top 10 APFs. Only 1 of the top 10 spring rainfalls is in the group, which happens to be the highest simulated rainfall in 1999 (8th largest APF). These results are therefore consistent with the key predictors identified for APF in the regression analysis of Sect. 3.

Figure 9 shows the annual cycle of discharge at Fraser-Hope along with other variables of interest over the calendar year for 3 of the top 10 APF years: 1958, 1972 and 1999. The daily evolution of discharge Q at Fraser-Hope and basin-averaged SWE, T, CRI and SM are plotted, along with their 1955–2004 climatologies, as an aid to evaluating how anomalous a given year is. A 15-day smoothing filter was applied to T to better highlight sub-seasonal trends. Also shown in the bottom two subpanels of each panel are the difference between the slope of T calculated over a 61-day moving window in the year of interest and its climatology (the warming rate anomaly), and the difference of the snowmelt rate from its climatology calculated over a 15-day moving window. Both anomalies were set to zero if $T < 0$, since we are interested in behaviour during the melt season only. We consider each year in turn, as each exhibits a unique phenomenology that illuminates the development of the APF in that year. Also, in this section we provide descriptions of the two largest flooding events ever recorded in the FRB – the freshets of 1894 and 1948 – both of which precede the simulated period. It is instructive that there are similarities between the meteorological precursors and covariates in those years and the explicitly simulated years highlighted below.

4.1 Warm spring in an average SWE year: 1958

APF in the year 1958 ranked 4th over the 1955–2004 period of the simulation (Table 5) and 13th in observed APF. Yet, as simulated by VIC, 1958 was a normal SWE year, with SWE_{max} achieved near the end of March. Rainfall and soil moisture were also near normal up to this point, while winter temperatures were above normal but still below freezing (Fig. 9a). At the beginning of the melt season in April, dT/dt began to exceed its climatological value, prompting rapid snowmelt toward the end of that month. The anomalous snowmelt persisted until the end of May, about the time of the APF (APD), while the period of elevated warming rate continued into early June. The snowmelt pulse produced a coincident soil moisture anomaly, which is remarkable in that these quantities are averaged over the entire FRB, yet their behaviour is consistent with small-scale processes. Subsequent to the APD, the soil moisture anomaly became negative, apparently in response to the prolonged warming, which would lead to enhanced evaporation, and lower than normal rainfall over the summer. Figure 9a demonstrates that neither rainfall nor high soil moisture prior to freeze-up were pivotal factors in producing the anomalously large APF in this year. Indeed, rainfall amounts were well below normal between snowmelt initiation and the APD (49th out of 50 years; Table 5).

4.2 A high-SWE year: 1972

The second-highest simulated APF over the 1955–2004 period occurred in 1972, which also featured the second-highest SWE_{max} (Table 5). This year also exhibited the largest observed APF over the same period (Fig. 5a). While the preceding winter was colder than normal – evidently a factor in generating an anomalously large snowpack – the spring warming rate was above normal, resulting in a strong snowmelt anomaly lasting from May until just after the APD in early June (Fig. 9b). As in 1958, this snowmelt pulse generated a large soil moisture anomaly, which likely produced more overland flow during the freshet. This evidence suggests that the extreme APF in 1972 was primarily caused by a combination of elevated warming in spring and a heavy snowpack, which provided a large water surplus during the freshet. However, there is also an indication that a series of heavy rainfall episodes starting in early June, just days before the APD, affected the APF and particularly the duration of the high-flow period. An extended period of anomalously large rainfall is seen in the CRI between early June and late July, with a clear response in SM and in the persistence of the high-discharge anomaly until the end of August – both

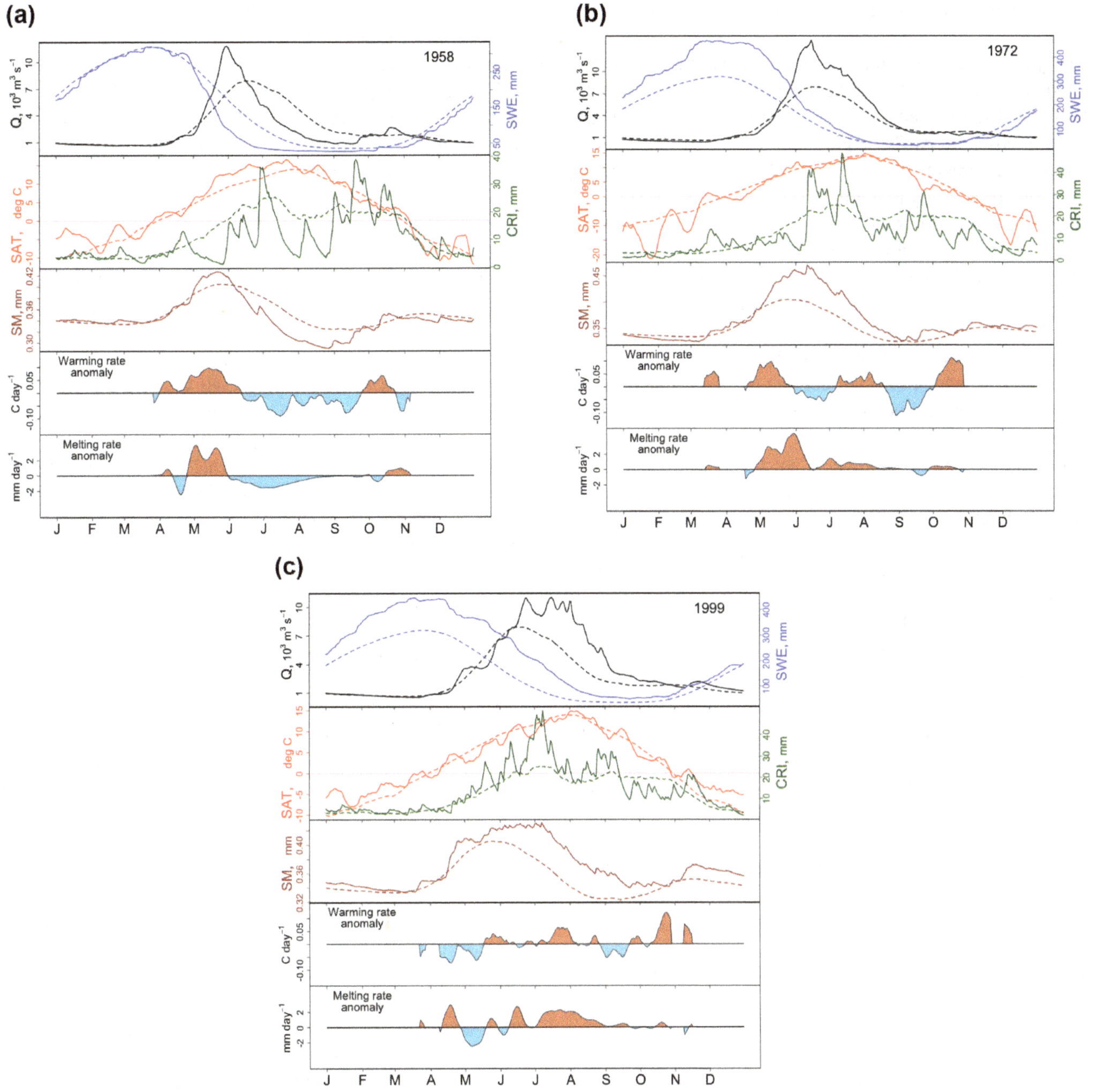

Figure 9. Annual cycles of key variables from the VIC simulation, constructed from daily output. Results for three high-APF years are shown: **(a)** 1958; **(b)** 1972; and **(c)** 1999. In each panel, sub-panels show, from top to bottom: streamflow (black, left-hand axis); SWE (blue, right-hand axis); surface air temperature (red, left-hand axis); current rainfall index, CRI (green, right-hand axis); soil moisture (brown); warming rate anomaly; and melting rate anomaly. In the upper three sub-panels, solid curves show time series for the year indicated at top right, while dashed curves show the multi-year (1955–2004) mean climatology. The calculations underlying the lower two sub-panels are described in Sect. 4.

are clearly distinguishable from their counterparts in 1958 (Fig. 9a).

Finally, it is worth noting that 1982, the year with the highest simulated APF (not shown in Fig. 9), was characterized by a very similar evolution of predictors as in 1972, including an extended, coincident period of anomalously large rainfall. However, in that case, there were two additional elements: (1) the spring warming rate was the highest of any year in the record (Table 5), and (2) a strong warm anomaly $\sim +5\,°C$ occurred in mid-June just prior to the APD, which evidently generated enough additional snowmelt runoff to position that APF as the highest over the simulated period.

4.3 Influence of rainfall in a high-SWE year: 1999

The year 1999 holds the distinction of having the highest simulated spring rainfall in the record. It also had the fourth-largest VIC-simulated SWE_{max}, while ranking eighth in APF (fifth in observed APF; see Fig. 5a and Table 5). The temperature development was unremarkable, albeit a little colder than the climatology in the freshet months of April and June (Fig. 9c). The hydrograph reflects this increased role of rainfall by its evident synoptic timescale variability, in contrast to its smoother counterpart in the snowmelt-dominated years examined above (Fig. 9a and b). Indeed, the character of the hydrograph over the freshet period is such that isolating the single largest APF misses key features of the flow development, which involves not one but four peak flows of roughly equal magnitude spanning the period from mid-June to mid-August. Consequently, the use of annual predictors with a single APF as predictand, as adopted in our univariate and multivariate regressions, is likely to underweight a strong influence of rainfall in a particular year. Table 3 shows that the maximum cross-correlation of deseasonalized daily streamflow and CRI anomalies during 1999 is 0.61 at a lag of 35 days (CRI leading streamflow), while in 1958 the maximum is just 0.38 at a lag of 47 days. This implies that rainfall should be treated differently than SWE and other predictors to correctly capture its influence on APF. The evolution of SM is also different than in the prior cases considered, insofar as it displays step-like jumps in mid-March, early April, and mid-May followed by a plateau at a high level until early July (Fig. 9c). This SM anomaly persisted for the remainder of the year, except for a brief 2-week period in November. While in snowmelt-dominated years SWE approaches its climatological value in late summer (except in 1958, when it fell below that value), in 1999 a positive SWE anomaly persisted throughout the year.

4.4 The two highest flow years in the FRB: 1894 and 1948

A description of meteorological precursors to the 1894 and 1948 floods is available from the BC MOE (BC MOE, 2008) and also the historical review, based on newspaper accounts, of Septer (2007). According to limited archival data available at two interior locations in the FRB, snowfall amounts during the winter of 1893 and 1894 were near normal over the FRB as a whole, although the snowpack remaining from the previous summer was reportedly larger than usual. While the spring of 1894 was cold and wet in the FRB, temperatures rose rapidly in late May, becoming unseasonably warm near the end of that month. By the end of May, the Fraser overtopped its banks at many locations and existing dikes were breached, leading to the "Great Chilliwack Flood" in the densely populated Lower Fraser valley. The Fraser River at Mission (near Hope) peaked on 5 June, but floodwaters did not subside in many areas until early July. A hydraulic modelling exercise conducted in 2008 estimated a peak discharge at Hope in the range of 16 000 to 18 000 $m^3 s^{-1}$, with a best guess of 17 000 $m^3 s^{-1}$ (BC MOE, 2008).

The meteorological record for the FRB in 1948 is considerably more complete than for 1894. It shows that precipitation was well above normal for a long period in advance of the 1948 freshet, with excess rainfall in autumn 1947 and heavy snowfall in the subsequent winter and early spring. As a result, soils in many areas were likely near saturation at the time of freeze-up, an important factor for the partitioning of runoff from spring snowmelt. Also, the accumulated reservoir of snow was larger than normal. The early spring of 1948 was cooler than average to 20 May, followed by a rapid increase to unseasonable warmth in late May–June. Thus, sensible heat inputs to the existing high snowpack in the FRB were large, leading to a rapid and voluminous release of meltwater to lower elevations. The peak flow at Hope on 31 May was measured at 15 200 $m^3 s^{-1}$, which remains the highest value in the instrumental record (Septer, 2007; BC MOE, 2008). Apparently, neither the 1894 nor the 1948 event was characterized by excessive rainfall coincident with the meltwater peaks.

5 Discussion and conclusions

In Sect. 3.4, we showed that the VIC model driven by gridded observations provides an adequate simulation of streamflow and maximum annual SWE in the FRB. The mutual resemblance of the correlograms (Figs. 3b and 6), which summarize the univariate linear regression fits to observed and VIC data, along with the similar forms of the respective MLR models (Eqs. 1–3), give one further confidence in the ability of the VIC model to simulate interactions between the key controls of streamflow acting in the real system. Furthermore, differences in these controls in the observed and modelled cases suggest fruitful avenues of further research. For example, the use of more complete snow survey or satellite products might permit the estimation of SWE_{len} or snowmelt rate, and confirmation of the influence of these terms appearing in the VIC-derived MLR, Eq. (6). Or conversely, improved driving data for the VIC model might reveal the influence of the PDO and/or ENSO explicitly in the MLR, or the inverse correlation with spring temperature and/or freezing degree days. The relationships derived between the basin-averaged predictors examined and streamflow at the major basin and subbasin outlets in the FRB should be relevant to other large, nival watersheds elsewhere on the globe, since the physical drivers (e.g., temperature seasonality and precipitation phase change) are generic and scale-independent. However, it is important to recognize that the influence of large-scale drivers (e.g., ENSO, PDO) will differ depending on the specific geographic setting.

Interestingly, in the historical climate record we find little prospect of using basin-averaged, rainfall-related indices as predictors of APF at Fraser-Hope. It is possible, however, that at subbasin scales, and/or in combination with an appropriate soil moisture indicator, some measure of rainfall might prove useful for predicting localized flooding. This has been a valuable strategy for APF/APD hindcasting in nival–pluvial and pluvial catchments (Neiman et al., 2011; Surfleet and Tullos, 2013). Moreover, given that the rain-to-snow ratio will increase in the FRB in response to further warming (see below), future studies of projected streamflow could uncover an explicit rainfall–streamflow connection at the basin scale.

We emphasize that the identification of the principal controls on APF at the interannual timescale within the MLR framework has its limitations. The relationships derived from historical inputs can only be considered broadly indicative of expected behaviour, and then only in a basin-averaged sense. Although based on only 50 years of simulated basin hydrology driven by observed data, the VIC results imply that a high SWE_{max}, say in the top quartile of historical values (i.e., 7 of the top 10 in Table 5), increases the chance of an upper quartile APF. The long interval between SWE_{max} and APF, of order 2–4 months, makes the former a valuable early warning indicator of possible flooding in the lower FRB (BC River Forecast Centre, 2012). However, it is also true that 3 of the top 10 SWE_{max} years (1976, ranked 3rd; 1991, 8th; and 1971, 9th) did not exhibit remarkable floods: in those years, the corresponding APFs ranked 20th, 30th and 23rd. And while SM_{max} has about the same success rate as a predictor of APF – 7 of the top 10 APF years are top 10 SM_{max} years – these are the same as for SWE_{max}, meaning that soil moisture during the freshet is of little additional predictive value. As mentioned in Sect. 3.5.3, the lack of a connection between fall SM and APF in the historical VIC simulation suggests that future model studies should include the effect of soil freezing to more realistically simulate the spring thaw. Further, the estimation of groundwater storage and its evolution using NASA's Gravity Recovery and Climate Experiment (GRACE), which has proved promising for flood forecasting in large, snowmelt-dominated basins (Reager et al., 2014; Wang and Russell, 2016), could find useful application in the FRB.

In Sect. 3, we demonstrated that the springtime warming rate, $\mathrm{d}T/\mathrm{d}t$, was the next most skillful predictor of APF in the FRB. Moreover, $\mathrm{d}T/\mathrm{d}t$ appears to provide additional predictive value over that of SWE_{max} and SM_{max}, insofar as 2 of the top 10 $\mathrm{d}T/\mathrm{d}t$ years are not top 10 SWE_{max} and SM_{max} (1958 and 2002; Table 5). Thus, the combination of an upper quartile SWE_{max} with a high $\mathrm{d}T/\mathrm{d}t$ over the snowmelt period may presage flooding at Fraser-Hope station (9 out of the top 10 APFs were characterized by one or the other; 4 featured both). The definition of $\mathrm{d}T/\mathrm{d}t$ used here is dependent upon the APD, which is of course unknown at the time of SWE_{max}; however, in a predictive context, one could simply use the most recent daily T observation to compute the warming rate within a window of increasing duration. Better still, if hydrological forecasting on the daily to seasonal timescale is of paramount interest, employing a forecast methodology based on an ensemble of hydrological simulations and multiple initializations would constitute a superior approach (Bazile et al., 2017).

In the event that future simulations of the FRB were to furnish annual time series of the basin-averaged predictors appearing in Eq. (6) and/or Table 4 – for example from a coupled global climate model – could the MLR relationships derived in this paper be used for predictions of future APF? We could answer in the affirmative if both of the following conditions were to hold: (1) the dominant predictors of APF in the late twentieth century (defining a multi-decadal reference period) remain unchanged in the future period of interest, and (2) the APF predictions comprise multi-year or decadal-scale anomalies from the reference period: e.g., APF in 2080–2100 compared to 1980–2000. Assumption (1) is placed in some doubt due to the significant warming projected for the FRB in future (Shrestha et al., 2012), which will increase the rain-to-snow ratio over large areas of the basin already characterized by an annual mean temperature near 0 °C. This suggests that rainfall may become a key predictor for high streamflow in the region, with perhaps a less pivotal role played by SWE_{max}. Regarding condition (2), the suppression of interannual variability in the MLR fits underestimates interannual variations in APF, meaning that only decadal-scale averages of the predicted APF would be meaningful.

Of what use, then, are the predictor sets derived from the MLR analysis? The application of nonstationary extreme value theory to APFs suggests at least one promising avenue of progress (Towler et al., 2010; Shrestha et al., 2017). In such models, the parameters of fitted distributions (e.g., location, scale and shape parameters of the generalized extreme value (GEV) distribution) are taken to be functions of climate covariates. Temperature and precipitation are often chosen for this purpose, due to their availability in observations and climate models and the presumption that they should influence streamflow at least under some circumstances. But as we have shown, in a large nival basin such as the FRB, rainfall has a weak influence on APF (although it would be expected to influence smaller magnitude flows), while the warming rate is more influential than temperature itself in determining APF magnitude. Hence, it may be worth introducing snowfall or SWE_{max} and/or spring $\mathrm{d}T/\mathrm{d}t$ as covariates of the GEV parameters in the fitting of nonstationary probability distributions of APFs. We leave this as an interesting topic for future investigation.

Data availability. Source data for this study are freely available from the Water Survey of Canada (daily stream gauge measurements, https://wateroffice.ec.gc.ca/search/historical_e.html), the BC River Forecast Centre (Manual Snow Survey data, https://www2.gov.bc.ca/gov/content/environment/air-land-water/water/drought-flooding-dikes-dams/river-forecast-centre), and the Pacific Climate Impacts Consortium Data Portal (VIC model gridded output and routed streamflow, https://www.pacificclimate.org/data). Driving temperature and precipitation data for the VIC model (PCIC-OBS) are available from the authors upon request.

Competing interests. The authors declare that they have no conflict of interest.

Special issue statement. This article is part of the special issue "Understanding and predicting Earth system and hydrological change in cold regions". It is not associated with a conference.

Acknowledgements. We thank Markus Schnorbus and Arelia (Werner) Schoeneberg for helpful discussions regarding the VIC model, Reza Najafi for providing observed SWE data for the Fraser basin, Faron Anslow for providing the regional temperature and precipitation time series data over BC, and Juraj Cunderlik for sharing station locations from Cunderlik and Ouarda (2009). The comments of Siraj Ul Islam and referees Stephen Déry, Michal Jenicek and an anonymous reviewer also led to substantial improvements to the final paper. Charles L. Curry is supported by the NSERC-funded Canadian Sea Ice and Snow Evolution (CanSISE) Network.

Edited by: Chris DeBeer

References

Alexander, M. A.: Extratropical Air-Sea Interaction, SST Variability and the Pacific Decadal Oscillation (PDO), in: Climate Dynamics: Why Does Climate Vary?, edited by: Sun, D. and Bryan, F., AGU Monograph #189, Washington, D.C., 123–148, 2010.

Andreadis, K. M., Storck, P., and Lettenmaier, D. P.: Modeling snow accumulation and ablation processes in forested environments, Water Resour. Res., 45, W05429, https://doi.org/10.1029/2008WR007042, 2009.

Andréassian, V., Coron, L., Lerat, J., and Le Moine, N.: Climate elasticity of streamflow revisited – an elasticity index based on long-term hydrometeorological records, Hydrol. Earth Syst. Sci., 20, 4503–4524, https://doi.org/10.5194/hess-20-4503-2016, 2016.

Barnett, T. P., Adam, J. C., and Lettenmaier, D. P.: Potential impacts of a warming climate on water availability in snow-dominated regions, Nature, 438, 303–309, 2005.

Batjes, N. H. (Ed.): A homogenized soil data file for global environmental research: A subset of FAO, ISRIC and NRCS profiles (Version 1.0), Working Paper and Preprint 95/10b, International Soil Reference and Information Centre, Wageningen, 1995.

Bawden, A. J., Burn, D. H., and Prowse, T. D.: Recent changes in patterns of western Canadian river flow and association with climatic drivers, Hydrol. Res., 46, 551–565, 2015.

Bazile, R., Boucher, M. A., Perreault, L., and Leconte, R.: Verification of ECMWF System 4 for seasonal hydrological forecasting in a northern climate, Hydrol. Earth Syst. Sci., 21, 5747–5762, https://doi.org/10.5194/hess-21-5747-2017, 2017.

BC MOE – British Columbia Ministry of the Environment: Comprehensive Review of Fraser River at Hope Flood Hydrology and Flows – Scoping Study and Final Report, Northwest Hydraulic Consultants, available at: http://www.env.gov.bc.ca/wsd/public_safety/flood/pdfs_word/review_fraser_flood_flows_hope.pdf (last access: 6 June 2017), 2008.

BC MOE – British Columbia Ministry of the Environment: Indicators of Climate Change for British Columbia: 2016 Update, available at: http://www2.gov.bc.ca/assets/gov/environment/research-monitoring-and-reporting/reporting/envreportbc/archived-reports/climate-change/climatechangeindicators-13sept2016_final.pdf (last access: 19 June 2017), 2016.

BC River Forecast Centre: https://www2.gov.bc.ca/gov/content/environment/air-land-water/water/drought-flooding-dikes-dams/river-forecast-centre, last access: 12 April 2018.

Berg, A. A. and Mulroy, K. A.: Streamflow predictability in the Saskatchewan/Nelson River basin given macroscale estimates of the initial soil moisture status, Hydrolog. Sci. J., 51, 642–654, 2006.

Bonsal, B. and Shabbar, A.: Impacts of Large-Scale Circulation Variability on Low Streamflows Over Canada: A Review, Can. Water Res. J., 33, 137–154, https://doi.org/10.4296/cwrj3302137, 2008.

British Columbia River Forecast Centre: Flow Forecasting for the Lower Fraser River (from Hope to the Ocean), internal report, available at: http://bcrfc.env.gov.bc.ca/freshet/lower_fraser/FlowForecastingforthe20LowerFraserRiver.pdf (last access: 24 April 2017), 2012.

Burn, D. H. and Hag Elnur, M. A.: Detection of hydrologic trends and variability, J. Hydrol., 255, 107–122, 2002.

Cherkauer, K. A. and Lettenmaier, D. P.: Hydrologic effects of frozen soils in the upper Mississippi River basin, J. Geophys. Res.-Atmos., 104, 19599–19610, 1999.

Cherkauer, K. A. and Lettenmaier, D. P.: Simulation of spatial variability in snow and frozen soil, J. Geophys. Res.-Atmos., 108, 8858, https://doi.org/10.1029/2003JD003575, 2003.

Coles, A. E., Appels, W. M., McConkey, B. G., and McDonnell, J. J.: The hierarchy of controls on snowmelt–runoff generation over seasonally-frozen hillslopes, Hydrol. Earth Syst. Sci. Discuss., https://doi.org/10.5194/hess-2016-564, in review, 2016.

Cunderlik, J. M. and Ouarda, T. B.: Trends in the timing and magnitude of floods in Canada, J. Hydrol., 375, 471–480, 2009.

Dai, A.: Temperature and pressure dependence of the rain-snow phase transition over land and ocean, Geophys. Res. Lett., 35, L12802, https://doi.org/10.1029/2008GL033295, 2008.

Daly, C., Halbleib, M., Smith, J. I., Gibson, W. P., Doggett, M. K., Taylor, G. H., Curtis, J., and Pasteris, P. P.: Physiographically sensitive mapping of climatological temperature and precipitation across the coterminous United States, Int. J. Climatol., 28, 2031–2064, https://doi.org/10.1002/joc.1688, 2008.

Danco, J. F., DeAngelis, A. M., Raney, B. K., and Broccoli, A. J.: Effects of a Warming Climate on Daily Snowfall Events in the Northern Hemisphere, J. Climate, 29, 6295–6318, 2016.

DeBeer, C. M., Wheater, H. S., Carey, S. K., and Chun, K. P.: Recent climatic, cryospheric, and hydrological changes over the interior of western Canada: a review and synthesis, Hydrol. Earth Syst. Sci., 20, 1573–1598, https://doi.org/10.5194/hess-20-1573-2016, 2016.

Déry, S. J., Hernández-Henríquez, M. A., Owens, P. N., Parkes, M. W., and Petticrew, E. L.: A century of hydrological variability and trends in the Fraser River Basin, Environ. Res. Lett., 7, 024019, https://doi.org/10.1088/1748-9326/7/2/024019, 2012.

Duan, K., Sun, G., McNulty, S. G., Caldwell, P. V., Cohen, E. C., Sun, S., Aldridge, H. D., Zhou, D., Zhang, L., and Zhang, Y.: Future shift of the relative roles of precipitation and temperature in controlling annual runoff in the conterminous United States, Hydrol. Earth Syst. Sci., 21, 5517–5529, https://doi.org/10.5194/hess-21-5517-2017, 2017.

Eaton, B. and Moore, R. D.: Regional hydrology, in: Compendium of Forest Hydrology and Geomorphology in British Columbia, Land Manag. Handb. 66, edited by: Pike, R. G., Redding, T. E., Moore, R. D., Winker, R. D., and Bladon, K. D., B.C. Min. For. Range, For. Sci. Prog., Victoria, BC and FORREX Forum for Research and Extension in Natural Resources, Kamloops, BC, http://www.for.gov.bc.ca/hfd/pubs/Docs/Lmh/Lmh66.htm (last access: 17 August 2016), 2010.

FAO – Food and Agriculture Organization: The digital soil map of the world, version 3.5, FAO, Rome, http://www.fao.org/geonetwork/srv/en/metadata.show?id=14116 (last access: 10 April 2018), 1995.

Fedora, M. A. and Beschta, R. L.: Storm runoff simulation using an antecedent precipitation index (API) model, J. Hydrol., 112, 121–133, 1989.

Fraser Basin Council: The Fraser: A Canadian Heritage River, 10-Year Monitoring Report, available at: http://www.fraserbasin.bc.ca/resources_publications.html (last access: 10 April 2018), 2010.

Gan, T. Y., Barry, R. G., Gizaw, M., Gobena, A., and Balaji, R.: Changes in North American snowpacks for 1979–2007 detected from the snow water equivalent data of SMMR and SSM/I passive microwave and related climatic factors, J. Geophys. Res.-Atmos., 118, 7682–7697, 2013.

GSD – Global Soil Data Task: Global Soil Data Products CD-ROM (IGBP-DIS), CD-ROM, International Geosphere-Biosphere Programme, Data and Information System, Potsdam, Germany, available at Oak Ridge National Laboratory Distributed Active Center, Oak Ridge, Tennessee, USA, 2000.

Gobena, A. K. and Gan, T. Y.: Low-Frequency Variability in Southwestern Canadian Streamflow: Links with Large-Scale Climate, Int. J. Climatol., 26, 1843–1869, https://doi.org/10.1002/joc.1336, 2006.

Gurrapu, S., St-Jacques, J.-M., Sauchyn, D. J., and Hodder, K. R.: The Influence of the Pacific Decadal Oscillation on Annual Floods in the Rivers of Western Canada, J. Am. Water Resour. Assoc., 52, 1031–1045, https://doi.org/10.1111/1752-1688.12433, 2016.

Hamann, A., Wang, T., Spittlehouse, D. L., and Murdock, T. Q.: A comprehensive, high-resolution database of historical and projected climate surfaces for western North America, B. Am. Meteorol. Soc., 94, 1307–1309, 2013.

Harpold, A. A. and Molotch, N. P.: Sensitivity of soil water availability to changing snowmelt timing in the western U.S., Geophys. Res. Lett., 42, 8011–8020, https://doi.org/10.1002/2015GL065855, 2015.

Hernández-Henríquez, M. A., Sharma, A. R., and Déry, S. J.: Variability and trends in runoff in the rivers of British Columbia's Coast and Insular Mountains, Hydrol. Process., 31, 3269–3282, 2017.

Hsieh, W. W. and Tang, B.: Interannual variability of accumulated snow in the Columbia basin, British Columbia, Water Resour. Res., 37, 1753–1759, 2001.

Islam, S. U. and Déry, S. J.: Evaluating uncertainties in modelling the snow hydrology of the Fraser River Basin, British Columbia, Canada, Hydrol. Earth Syst. Sci., 21, 1827–1847, https://doi.org/10.5194/hess-21-1827-2017, 2017.

Jenicek, M., Seibert, J., Zappa, M., Staudinger, M., and Jonas, T.: Importance of maximum snow accumulation for summer low flows in humid catchments, Hydrol. Earth Syst. Sci., 20, 859–874, https://doi.org/10.5194/hess-20-859-2016, 2016.

Jeong, D. I., Sushama, L., and Khaliq, M. N.: Attribution of spring snow water equivalent (SWE) changes over the northern hemisphere to anthropogenic effects, Clim. Dynam., 48, 3645–3658, 2017.

Jiménez Cisneros, B. E., Oki, T., Arnell, N. W., Benito, G., Cogley, J. G., Döll, P., Jiang, T., and Mwakalila, S. S.: Freshwater resources, in: Climate Change 2014: Impacts, Adaptation, and Vulnerability. Part A: Global and Sectoral Aspects, Contribution of Working Group II to the Fifth Assessment Report of the Intergovernmental Panel on Climate Change, edited by: Field, C. B., Barros, V. R., Dokken, D. J., Mach, K. J., Mastrandrea, M. D., Bilir, T. E., Chatterjee, M., Ebi, K. L., Estrada, Y. O., Genova, R. C., Girma, B., Kissel, E. S., Levy, A. N., MacCracken, S., Mastrandrea, P. R., and White, L. L., Cambridge University Press, Cambridge, UK and New York, NY, USA, 229–269, 2014.

Kang, D. H., Gao, H., Shi, X., ul Islam, S., and Déry, S. J.: Impacts of a rapidly declining mountain snowpack on streamflow timing in Canada's Fraser River basin, Scient. Rep., 6, 19299, https://doi.org/10.1038/srep19299, 2016.

Knowles, N.: Trends in Snow Cover and Related Quantities at Weather Stations in the Conterminous United States, J. Clim., 28, 7518 7528, 2015.

Koster, R. D., Mahanama, S. P., Livneh, B., Lettenmaier, D. P., and Reichle, R. H.: Skill in streamflow forecasts derived from large-scale estimates of soil moisture and snow, Nat. Geosci., 3, 613–616, 2010.

Liang, X., Lettenmaier, D. P., Wood, E. F., and Burges, S. J.: A simple hydrologically based model of land surface water and energy fluxes for general circulation models, J. Geophys. Res., 99, 14415–14428, https://doi.org/10.1029/94JD00483, 1994.

Lohmann, D., Nolte-Holube, R., and Raschke, E.: A large-scale horizontal routing model to be coupled to land surface parametrization schemes, Tellus A, 48, 708–721, 1996.

Lohmann, D., Raschke, E., Nijssen, B., and Lettenmaier, D. P.: Regional scale hydrology: I. Formulation of the VIC-2L model coupled to a routing model, Hydrolog. Sci. J., 43, 131–141, 1998.

Mahanama, S., Livneh, B., Koster, R., Lettenmaier, D., and Reichle, R.: Soil moisture, snow, and seasonal streamflow forecasts in the United States, J. Hydrometeorol., 13, 189–203, 2012.

Matti, B., Dahlke, H. E., and Lyon, S. W.: On the variability of cold region flooding, J. Hydrol., 534, 669–679, 2016.

Maurer, E. P. and Lettenmaier, D. P.: Predictability of seasonal runoff in the Mississippi River basin, J. Geophys. Res.-Atmos., 108, 8607, https://doi.org/10.1029/2002JD002555, 2003.

McCabe, G. J., Clarke, M. P., and Hay, L. E.: Rain-on-snow events in the Western United States, B. Am. Meteorol. Soc., 88, 319–328, https://doi.org/10.1175/BAMS-88-3-319, 2007.

Milly, P. C. D., Dunne, K. A., and Vecchia, A. V.: Global pattern of trends in streamflow and water availability in a changing climate, Nature, 438, 347–350, 2005.

Moore, R. D.: Hydrology and water supply in the Fraser River basi, in: Water in Sustainable Development: Exploring Our Common Future in the Fraser River Basin, edited by: Dorcey, A. H. J. and Griggs, J. R., Westwater Research Centre, The University of British Columbia, Vancouver, British Columbia, Canada, 21–40, 1991.

Moore, R. D. and McKendry, I. G.: Spring snowpack anomaly patterns and winter climatic variability, British Columbia, Canada, Water Resour. Res., 32, 623–632, 1996.

Najafi, M. R., Zwiers, F., and Gillett, N.: Attribution of the Observed Spring Snowpack Decline in British Columbia to Anthropogenic Climate Change, J. Climate, 30, 4113–4130, 2017.

Neiman, P. J., Schick, L. J., Ralph, F. M., Hughes, M., and Wick, G. A.: Flooding in western Washington: The connection to atmospheric rivers, J. Hydrometeorol., 12, 1337–1358, 2011.

Pacific Climate Impacts Consortium: Station Hydrologic Model Output, University of Victoria, available at: https://www.pacificclimate.org/data/station-hydrologic-model-output/ (last access: 10 May 2016), 2014.

Pacific Climate Impacts Consortium Data Portal: https://www.pacificclimate.org/data, last access: 12 April 2018.

Padilla, A., Rasouli, M., and Déry, S. J: Impacts of variability and trends in runoff and water temperature on salmon migration in the Fraser River Basin, Canada, Hydrolog. Sci. J., 60, 523–533, 2015.

Park, D. and Markus, M.: Analysis of a changing hydrologic flood regime using the Variable Infiltration Capacity model, J. Hydrol., 515, 267–280, 2014.

Pike, R. G., Bennett, K. E., Redding, T. E., Werner, A. T., Spittlehouse, D. L., Moore, R. D., Murdock, T. Q., Beckers, J., Smerdon, B. D., Bladon, K. D., Foord, V. N., Campbell, D. A., and Tschaplinski, P. J.: Climate change effects on watershed processes in British Columbia, in: Compendium of Forest Hydrology and Geomorphology in British Columbia, Land Manag. Handb. 66, edited by: Pike, R. G., Redding, T. E., Moore, R. D., Winker, R. D., and Bladon, K. D., B.C. Min. For. Range, For. Sci. Prog., Victoria, BC and FORREX Forum for Research and Extension in Natural Resources, Kamloops, BC, http://www.for.gov.bc.ca/hfd/pubs/Docs/Lmh/Lmh66.htm (last access: 17 August 2016), 2010.

R Core Team: R: A Language and Environment for Statistical Computing, R Foundation for Statistical Computing, Vienna, Austria, available at: https://www.R-project.org/, last access: 18 October 2015.

Reager, J. T., Thomas, B. F., and Famiglietti, J. S.: River basin flood potential inferred using GRACE gravity observations at several months lead time, Nat. Geosci., 7, 588–592, 2014.

Rood, S. B., Samuelson, G. M., Weber, J. K., and Wywrot, K. A.: Twentieth-century decline in streamflows from the hydrographic apex of North America, J. Hydrol., 306, 215–233, https://doi.org/10.1016/j.jhydrol.2004.09.010, 2005.

Rupp, D. E., Mote, P. W., Bindoff, N. L., Stott, P. A., and Robinson, D. A.: Detection and attribution of observed changes in Northern Hemisphere spring snow cover, J. Climate, 26, 6904–6914, 2013.

Salathé Jr., E. P., Hamlet, A. F., Mass, C. F., Lee, S. Y., Stumbaugh, M., and Steed, R.: Estimates of twenty-first-century flood risk in the Pacific Northwest based on regional climate model simulations, J. Hydrometeorol., 15, 1881–1899, 2014.

Schnorbus, M. A., Bennett, K. E., and Werner, A. T.: Quantifying the water resources impacts of the mountain pine beetle and associated salvage harvest operations across a range of watershed scales: Hydrologic modelling of the Fraser River Basin, MBPI Project 7.29, Natural Resources Canada, Canadian Forest Service, Pacific Forestry Centre, Information Report BC-X-423, 64 pp., available at: https://www.pacificclimate.org/resources/publications (last access: 18 July 2017), 2010.

Schnorbus, M. A., Bennett, K. E., Werner, A. T., and Berland, A. J.: Hydrologic Impacts of Climate Change in the Peace, Campbell and Columbia Watersheds, British Columbia, Canada, PCIC Internal Report, available at: https://www.pacificclimate.org/resources/publications (last access: 28 November 2012), 2011.

Sen, P. K.: Estimates of the regression coefficient based on Kendall's tau, J. Am. Stat. Assoc., 63, 1379–1389, 1968.

Septer, D.: Flooding and Landslide Events Southern British Columbia 1808–2006, BC Ministry of Environment, Victoria, available as three separate files at: https://www.for.gov.bc.ca/hfd/library/documents/bib106111south1.pdf, https://www.for.gov.bc.ca/hfd/library/documents/bib106111south2.pdf, and https://www.for.gov.bc.ca/hfd/library/documents/bib106111south3.pdf (last access: 6 June 2016), 2007.

Shabbar, A., Bonsal, B., and Khandekar, M.: Canadian Precipitation Patterns Associated with the Southern Oscillation, J. Climate, 10, 3016–3027, https://doi.org/10.1175/1520-0442(1997)010<3016:CPPAWT>2.0.CO;2, 1997.

Shrestha, R. R., Schnorbus, M. A., Werner, A. T., and Berland, A. J.: Modelling spatial and temporal variability of hydrologic impacts of climate change in the Fraser River basin, British Columbia, Canada, Hydrol. Process., 26, 1840–1860, https://doi.org/10.1002/hyp.9283, 2012.

Shrestha, R. R., Peters, D. L., and Schnorbus, M. A.: Evaluating the ability of a hydrologic model to replicate hydro-ecologically relevant indicators, Hydrol. Process., 28, 4294–4310, https://doi.org/10.1002/hyp.9997, 2014.

Shrestha, R. R., Cannon, A. J., Schnorbus, M. A., and Zwiers, F. W.: Projecting future nonstationary extreme streamflow for the Fraser River, Canada, Climatic Change, 145, 289–303, 2017.

Shumway, R. H. and Stoffer, D. S.: Time series analysis and applications, using the R statistical package, EZ Edn. 4, Sect. 3.2, available at: http://www.stat.pitt.edu/stoffer/tsa4/ (last access: 2 January 2018), 2017.

Smakhtin, V. Y. and Masse, B.: Continuous daily hydrograph simulation using duration curves of a precipitation index, Hydrol. Process., 14, 1083–1100, 2000.

Stewart, I. T.: Changes in snowpack and snowmelt runoff for key mountain regions, Hydrol. Process., 23, 78–94, 2009.

Surfleet, C. G. and Tullos, D.: Variability in effect of climate change on rain-on-snow peak flow events in a temperate climate, J. Hydrol., 479, 24–34, 2013.

Tan, X. and Gan, T. Y.: Nonstationary analysis of annual maximum streamflow of Canada, J. Climate, 28, 1788–1805, 2015.

Thorne, R. and Woo, M. K.: Streamflow response to climatic variability in a complex mountainous environment: Fraser River Basin, British Columbia, Canada, Hydrol. Process., 25, 3076–3085, 2011.

Towler, E., Rajagopalan, B., Gilleland, E., Summers, R. S., Yates, D., and Katz, R. W.: Modeling hydrologic and water quality extremes in a changing climate: A statistical approach based on extreme value theory, Water Resour. Res., 46, W11504, https://doi.org/10.1029/2009WR008876, 2010.

Wang, S. and Russell, H. A.: Forecasting snowmelt-induced flooding using GRACE satellite data: A case study for the Red River watershed, Can. J. Remote Sens., 42, 203–213, 2016.

Water Survey of Canada: HYDAT Database, Natl. Water Data Arch., https://wateroffice.ec.gc.ca/search/historical_e.html, last access: 12 April 2018.

Wever, N., Comola, F., Bavay, M., and Lehning, M.: Simulating the influence of snow surface processes on soil moisture dynamics and streamflow generation in an alpine catchment, Hydrol. Earth Syst. Sci., 21, 4053–4071, https://doi.org/10.5194/hess-21-4053-2017, 2017.

Whitfield, P. H., Moore, R. D., Fleming, S. W., and Zawadzski, A.: Pacific Decadal Oscillation and the hydroclimatology of western Canada – Review and Prospects, Can. Water Resour. J., 35, 1–27, 2010.

Williams, C. J., McNamara, J. P., and Chandler, D. G.: Controls on the temporal and spatial variability of soil moisture in a mountainous landscape: The signature of snow and complex terrain, Hydrol. Earth Syst. Sci., 13, 1325–1336, https://doi.org/10.5194/hess-13-1325-2009, 2009.

Woo, M. and Thorne, R.: Comment on "Detection of Hydrologic Trends and Variability," by Burn, D. H. and Hag Elnur, M. A., 2002, Journal of Hydrology 255, 107–122, J. Hydrol., 277, 150–160, https://doi.org/10.1016/S0022-1694(03)00079-9, 2003.

9

Daily GRACE gravity field solutions track major flood events in the Ganges–Brahmaputra Delta

Ben T. Gouweleeuw[1], **Andreas Kvas**[3], **Christian Gruber**[1], **Animesh K. Gain**[2], **Thorsten Mayer-Gürr**[3], **Frank Flechtner**[1], **and Andreas Güntner**[1]

[1]GFZ German Research Centre for Geosciences, Section 5.4 Hydrology, 14473 Potsdam, Germany
[2]Christian Albrecht University Kiel, Institute of Geography, Ludewig-Meyn-Str. 14, 24098 Kiel, Germany
[3]Graz University of Technology, Institute of Geodesy, 8010 Graz, Austria

Correspondence: Ben T. Gouweleeuw (ben.gouweleeuw@gfz-potsdam.de)

Abstract. Two daily gravity field solutions based on observations from the Gravity Recovery and Climate Experiment (GRACE) satellite mission are evaluated against daily river runoff data for major flood events in the Ganges–Brahmaputra Delta (GBD) in 2004 and 2007. The trends over periods of a few days of the daily GRACE data reflect temporal variations in daily river runoff during major flood events. This is especially true for the larger flood in 2007, which featured two distinct periods of critical flood level exceedance in the Brahmaputra River. This first hydrological evaluation of daily GRACE gravity field solutions based on a Kalman filter approach confirms their potential for gravity-based large-scale flood monitoring. This particularly applies to short-lived, high-volume floods, as they occur in the GBD with a 4–5-year return period. The release of daily GRACE gravity field solutions in near-real time may enable flood monitoring for large events.

1 Introduction

Floods are dynamic events, which may only take hours to days to develop and drain. For monitoring purposes, Earth observation products need to be available sufficiently frequently to capture the progressing stages of a flood event. Flood early-warning and forecasting systems additionally require information in near-real time (NRT) to estimate probabilistic flood risk with typical lead times of a few days for larger river basins. Total water storage anomalies (TWSAs) derived from temporal variations of the Earth's gravity field as observed by the Gravity Recovery and Climate Experiment (GRACE) twin-satellite mission (Tapley et al., 2004) have been shown to be a unique descriptor of large-scale flood events (Chen et al., 2010; Steckler et al., 2010). However, partly due to its coarse temporal (weekly to monthly) and spatial (>150 000 km^2) resolution, the evaluation of the integrated information from GRACE on total water storage variations (i.e., variations of all surface and subsurface water stores) for flood monitoring or forecasting has been limited.

Reager and Famiglietti (2009) proposed a regional monthly flood potential index using a GRACE-based saturation deficit approach, which was quantitatively evaluated by Molodtsova et al. (2016) for the continental United States. While the index agreed well with observed floods on regional and even local scales, an increased forecasting skill was found for large-scale, long-duration floods during summer. Reager et al. (2014) established a relationship between gauged river flow and GRACE-derived basin-wide water storage for the March–June 2011 Missouri river flood, potentially increasing forecasting lead time to several months. The same 500-year flood event was evaluated by Reager et al. (2015), who assimilated monthly GRACE-derived TWSAs into a land surface model, which enables state disaggregation of the vertically integrated TWSAs, a downscaling of GRACE's coarse spatial resolution and NRT analysis beyond the latest GRACE data release.

Currently, the latency in data product processing and release consists of a nominal time delay of the GRACE Level-1 instrument data (11 days) and of the derived monthly global Level-2 gravity field products (60 days). Temporal sampling

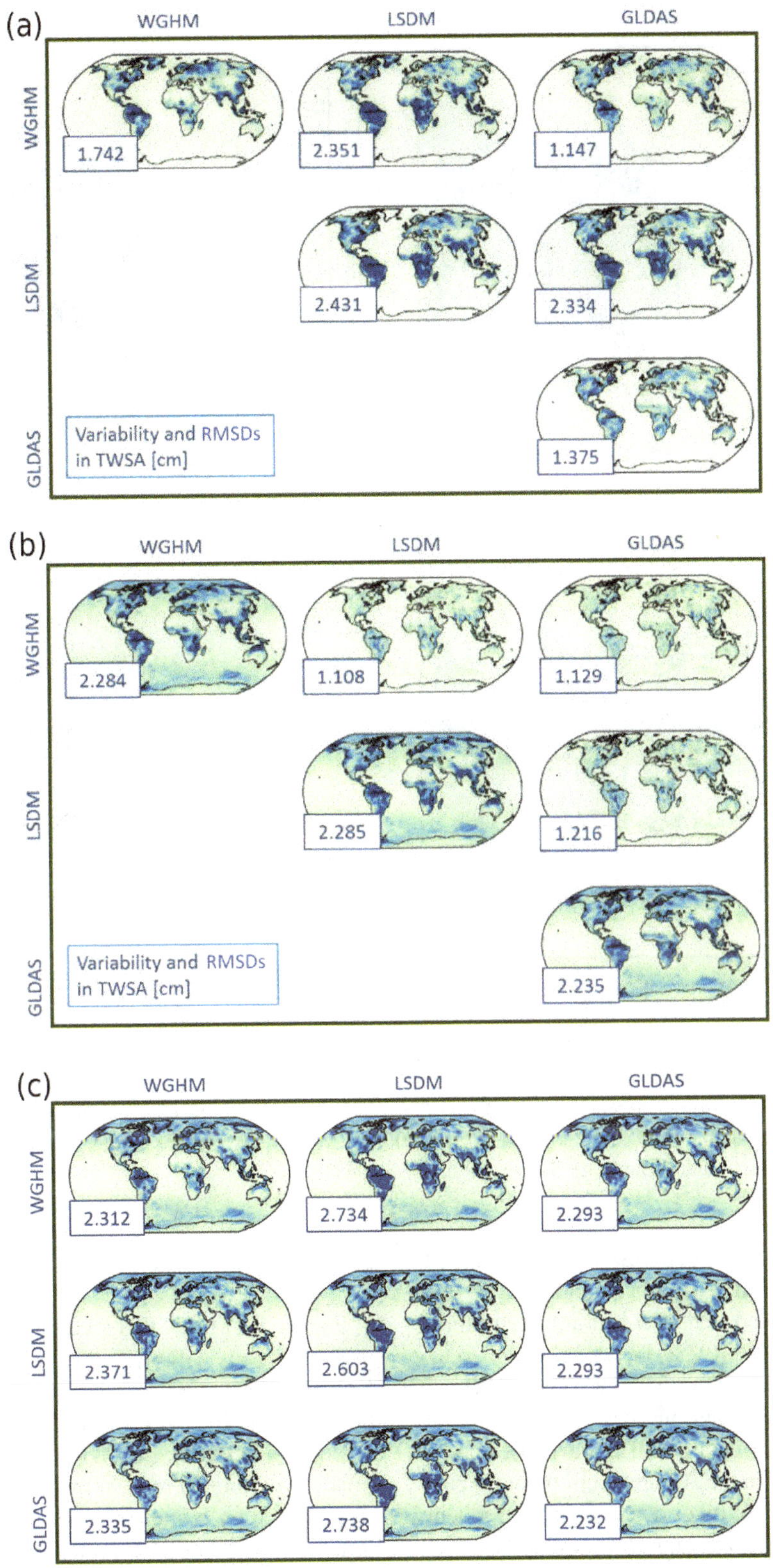

Figure 1. (a) Global average daily water mass variability (main diagonal) and root mean square differences (RMSDs) (off-diagonal) between the hydrological models used, expressed as TWSAs (2003–2014, secular and annual variations removed). **(b)** Global average daily variability (main diagonal) and RMSDs (off-diagonal) of the derived daily ITSG-Grace2014 solutions, expressed as TWSAs (2003–2014, secular and annual variations removed). **(c)** Global RMSDs in cm between the daily ITSG-Grace2014 solutions (rows) and the hydrological models used (columns), expressed as TWSAs (2003–2014, secular and annual variations removed).

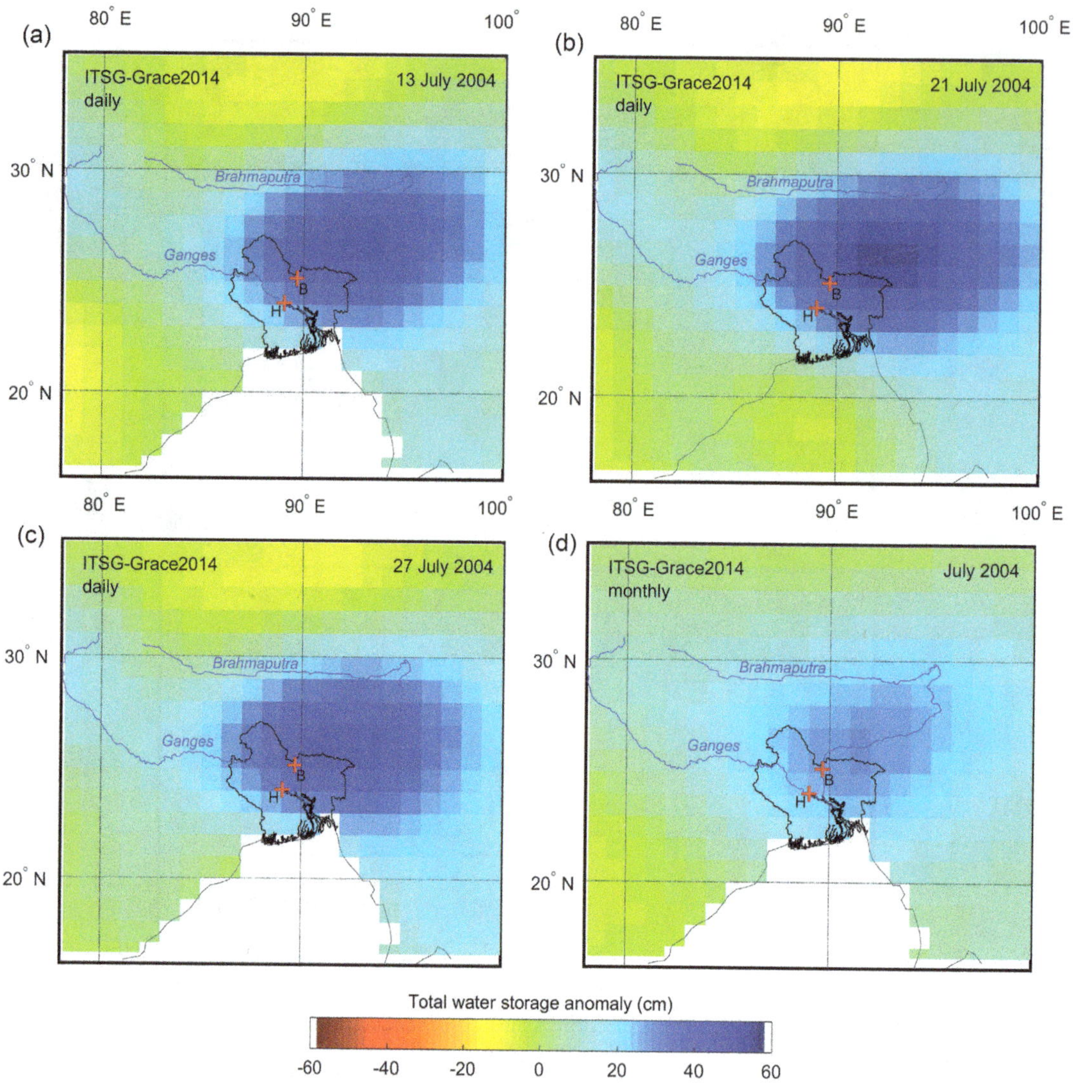

Figure 2. Daily and monthly water storage anomalies of the ITSG-Grace2014 solution for the Ganges–Brahmaputra Delta (outline indicated) on **(a)** 13 July 2004, **(b)** 21 July 2004, **(c)** 27 July 2004 and **(d)** July 2004. Increased TWSAs are related to flooding. River runoff stations are Bahadurabad (B) in the Brahmaputra and Hardinge Bridge (H) in the Ganges.

is at best 7–10 days, but most reliably 1 month, caused by a need to accumulate GRACE observations over this time period. Both latency and temporal averaging currently limit the potential use of the GRACE Level-3 products (i.e., TWSAs) for flood monitoring and early-warning systems. Daily GRACE gravity field solutions based on a Kalman filter approach (Kurtenbach et al., 2012) have been validated against ocean signals in the Antarctic circumpolar current, which showed the possibility of detecting high-frequent ocean mass variations (Bergman and Dobslaw, 2012). Recently, Sakumura et al. (2016) proposed a method for improved high-frequency signal capture via a regularized sliding window mascon (RSWM) product, which approximates a daily GRACE solution using a moving weighting scheme of 21 adjacent days of observational data, with about 10 days' delay.

For the first time, this study presents a hydrological evaluation of daily GRACE gravity field solutions based on a Kalman filter approach, which are scheduled for an operational run in 2017 with a time delay of just 5 days, in part enabled by quick-look Level-1 data with a time delay of 1 day (made available on request by NASA Jet Propulsion Laboratory (JPL)), by comparing the time series to observed river runoff in the Ganges–Brahmaputra Delta (GBD) under flood conditions. The world's largest river delta, situated at the confluence of two river systems with a combined discharge surpassed only by the Amazon and the Congo, is subject to short-lived flooding throughout summer and early autumn each year. In a typical year, 20–30 % of Bangladesh, which

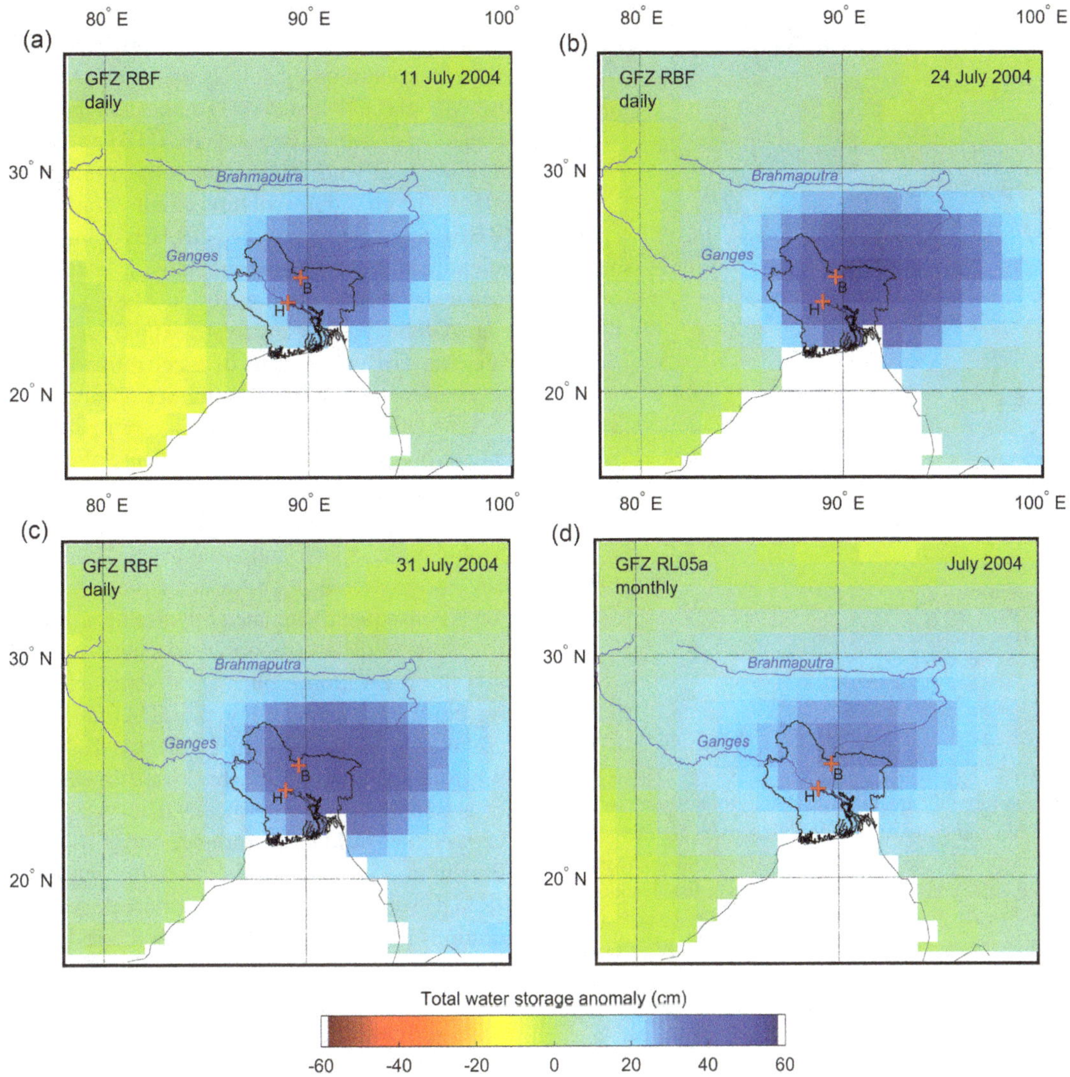

Figure 3. Daily and monthly water storage anomalies of the GFZ RBF solution for the Ganges–Brahmaputra Delta on **(a)** 11 July 2004, **(b)** 24 July 2004, **(c)** 31 July 2004 and **(d)** July 2004. Key is as in Fig. 2.

occupies most of the GBD, can be inundated for days during the monsoon, mostly in low-lying fields (Steckler et al., 2010). Major flooding events occur with a return period of 4–5 years (Hopson and Webster, 2010), causing widespread devastation in this densely populated part of the world. Two of these major flood events coincide with the GRACE mission's lifetime (March 2002–present). In July 2004, the Brahmaputra exceeded critical flood levels twice in a fortnight, inundating 38 % of the country (Best et al., 2007). In July and September 2007, two separate major flood peaks in the Brahmaputra caused inundation lasting weeks, affecting 42 % of the country (Islam et al., 2010).

2 GRACE data processing

2.1 Computation of daily GRACE Solutions

Compared to monthly solutions, the limited spatial coverage within 1 day does not allow for the GRACE satellite constellation to observe the full gravity field signal alone. Limited spatial sampling in an east–west direction means that GRACE data contribute little to no information to potential coefficients with orders higher than approximately 15. It is therefore necessary to introduce additional information to obtain reliable estimates of the full global gravity field signal. Applied to the determination of daily gravity field variations, this means that information on how the variable gravity field evolves with time is required. Since geophysical processes are not random, one can assume that the Earth's time-variable gravity field does not change arbitrarily from one day to the

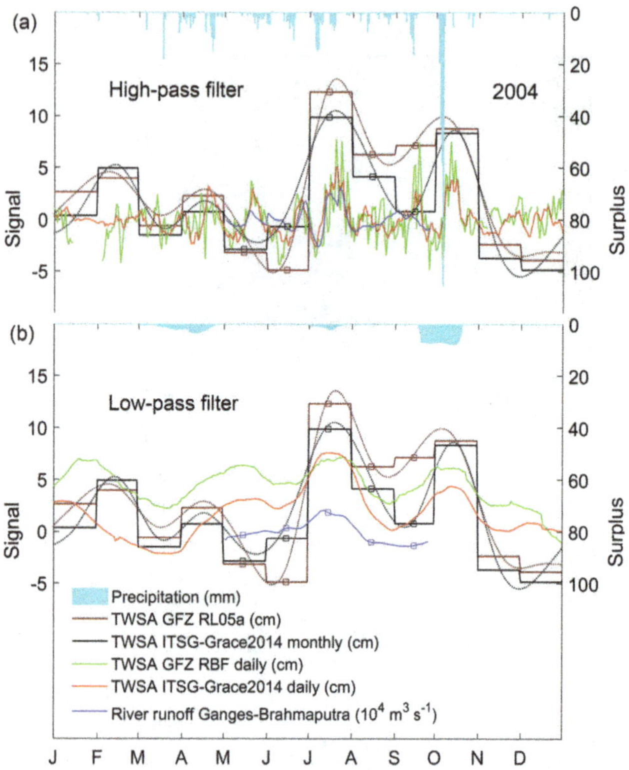

Figure 4. Daily and monthly area mean GRACE total water storage anomalies (TWSAs) and daily river runoff (left axis) together with the precipitation surplus (right axis) for the GBD in 2004. The daily data are separated into a high-frequency **(a)** and a low-frequency signal **(b)** by means of a 31-day high-pass filter. A series of cubic spline interpolations (dotted line) is fitted to the monthly solutions (step line). The squares represent (the number of) monthly values. The low-frequency signals and the monthly solutions have the mean seasonal cycle removed.

next. Kurtenbach et al. (2012) proposed to model this temporal evolution as a first-order Markov process, which can be fully described by its auto- and cross-covariance. Applied to daily GRACE solutions, the process to be modeled is the residual gravity field signal that is present in the observations after other effects, such as long-term, secular and nontidal ocean and atmosphere variations, have been reduced. The main geophysical constituents left in the GRACE data are therefore continental hydrology, cryosphere, solid earth and errors in the background models (Kurtenbach et al., 2012). For the daily solutions of the ITSG-Grace2014 release (Mayer-Gürr et al., 2014) used in this analysis, the model output of the updated ESA Earth System Model (Dobslaw et al., 2015) is used to approximate the unknown covariance structure of this residual gravity field signal. The 6-hourly model output is resampled to 1 day using daily averaging. These daily averages are subsequently reduced by their sample mean, trend and annual signal. Finally, the empirical auto- and cross-covariance is computed from the resulting state vectors.

For the daily GRACE solutions from GFZ, empirical functions for the auto- and cross-covariance matrices are derived from harmonic analysis of WaterGAP Global Hydrology Model (Döll et al., 2003) output and the Atmosphere and Ocean De-aliasing Level-1B (AOD1B) products (Dobslaw et al., 2013), as well as GFZ monthly solutions (Dahle et al., 2012). The GFZ daily solution employs radial basis functions (RBFs) to map the measured GRACE twin-satellite range accelerations into the mass anomaly (or water equivalent) surface layer. Precise dynamic orbits of the satellite trajectories using Global Positioning System (GPS) data complement the microwave measurements of acceleration in the line of sight between the GRACE twin satellites (Gruber et al., 2014).

A widely used tool to combine prior information of the underlying process and measurements of this process is the Kalman filter (Kalman, 1960). Given the previously derived process model, one can predict the Earth's gravity field for the following epoch and compute the corresponding accuracy information using covariance propagation. This prediction is consequently updated by forming a weighted mean between the predicted and observed state, whereby the weights of both observation groups are determined by their respective covariance matrix. For the ITSG-Grace2014 daily solutions (Kurtenbach et al., 2012), the Kalman filter is run in a forward as well as a backward direction. This allows for a smoothed estimate of the state vectors by computing the weighted minimum-variance mean of both time series (Rauch et al., 1965). Since the future purpose of the daily GRACE solutions is an NRT service mode, the GFZ RBF solutions in this study have been processed with the Kalman filter in forward mode only (Gruber and Gouweleeuw, 2018).

2.2 Derivation of gridded water storage anomalies from daily and monthly GRACE solutions

To derive gridded TWSAs from daily and monthly gravity field potential coefficients, the general processing scheme used for the GRACE land water mass grids provided by GRACE Tellus is followed (Swenson, 2012; Landerer and Swenson, 2012). This post-processing scheme can be split into three steps: (1) replace the C20 coefficient (Earth's oblateness), (2) transform the potential coefficients into the center of the Earth by adding degree 1 coefficients and (3) apply a spatial filter to the coefficients.

For the ITSG-Grace2014 daily solution, the C20 coefficient is replaced by linear interpolation of the monthly satellite laser ranging time series provided by Cheng et al. (2011). Similarly, daily degree 1 coefficients are obtained by linear interpolation of the monthly time series provided through Tellus, based on the methodology described in Swenson et al. (2008). The maximum degree used to calculate TWSAs equals 40. Glacial isostatic adjustment (GIA) correction has been applied using the model from A et al. (2013). Since the daily GRACE solutions are constrained within the least squares adjustment, no additional spatial filtering is nec-

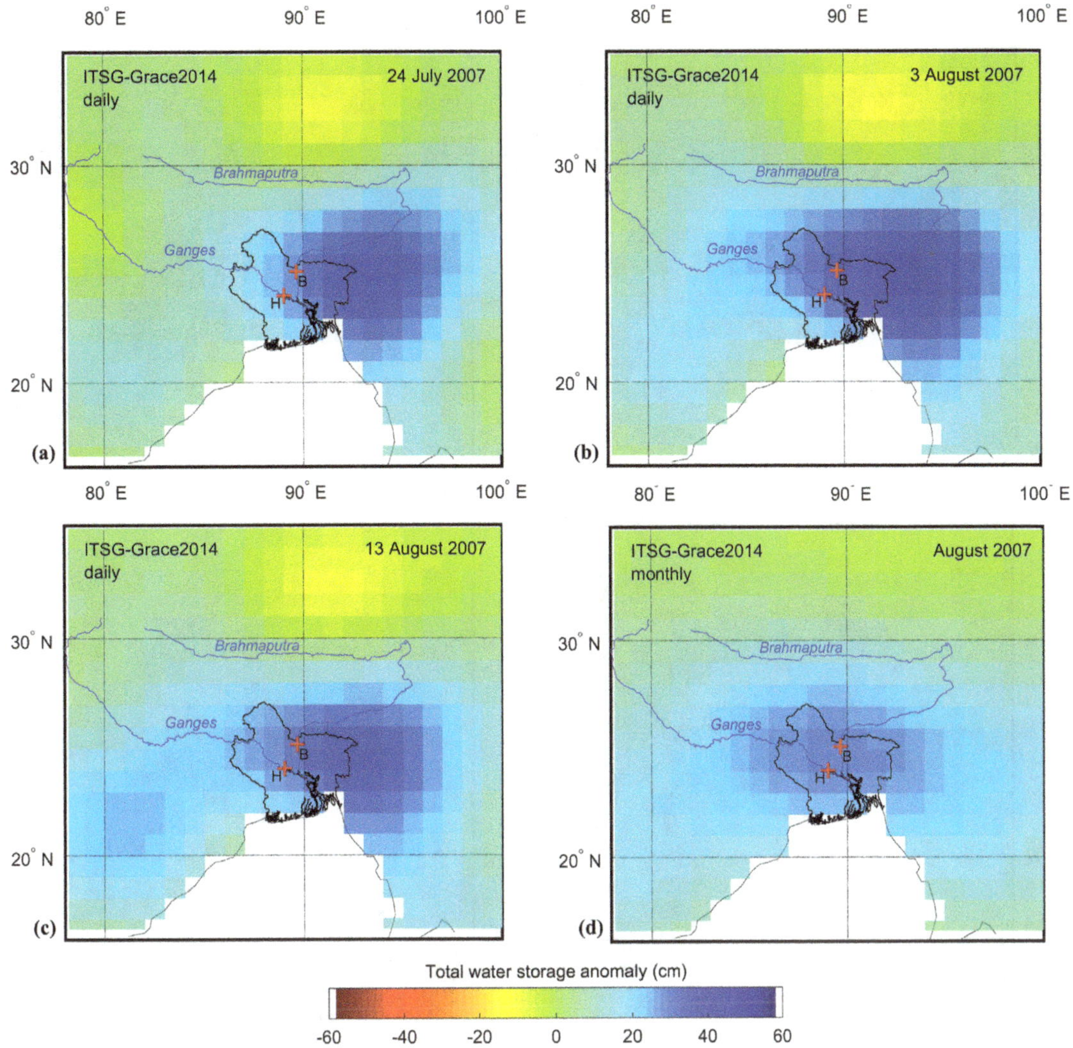

Figure 5. Daily and monthly water storage anomalies of the ITSG-Grace2014 solution for the Ganges–Brahmaputra Delta on **(a)** 24 July 2007, **(b)** 3 August 2007, **(c)** 13 August 2007 and **(d)** August 2007. Key is as in Fig. 2.

essary. For comparison, the monthly solutions of ITSG-Grace2014 (Mayer Gürr et al., 2014), calculated to a maximum spherical harmonic degree of 90, are also considered. Here, the same models as for the daily solutions are applied. However, since the monthly solutions are unconstrained, the coefficients were smoothed by a DDK2 anisotropic filter (Kusche et al., 2009).

The GFZ daily solutions make use of the same models as are used in the post-processing of ITSG-Grace2014, except for degree 1, which is also taken from a satellite laser ranging (SLR) estimate (Cheng et al., 2010). As with the daily ITSG solution, no additional spatial filtering was performed. Due to the parameterization in the spatial domain, no exact maximum degree is given, but the signal content is comparable to the ITSG-2014 daily solution. The monthly solutions from GFZ (RL05a, Dahle et al., 2012), calculated to a maximum spherical harmonic degree of 90, are corrected using the same models, and a DDK2 filter is applied. Both daily and monthly solutions are then propagated to TWSAs on a $1° \times 1°$ grid (~ 100 km at 25° latitude). The actual spatial resolution of the gridded TWSAs, however, is lower, with approximately 330 and 500 km for monthly and daily solutions, respectively.

3 Results

3.1 Process dynamics

To illustrate the possible impact of the process dynamics that may originate from the hydrological models on the daily Kalman GRACE solutions, three different daily gravity time series are computed using stochastic information from three different models, i.e., the WaterGAP Global Hydrological Model (WGHM), the Land Surface Discharge Model

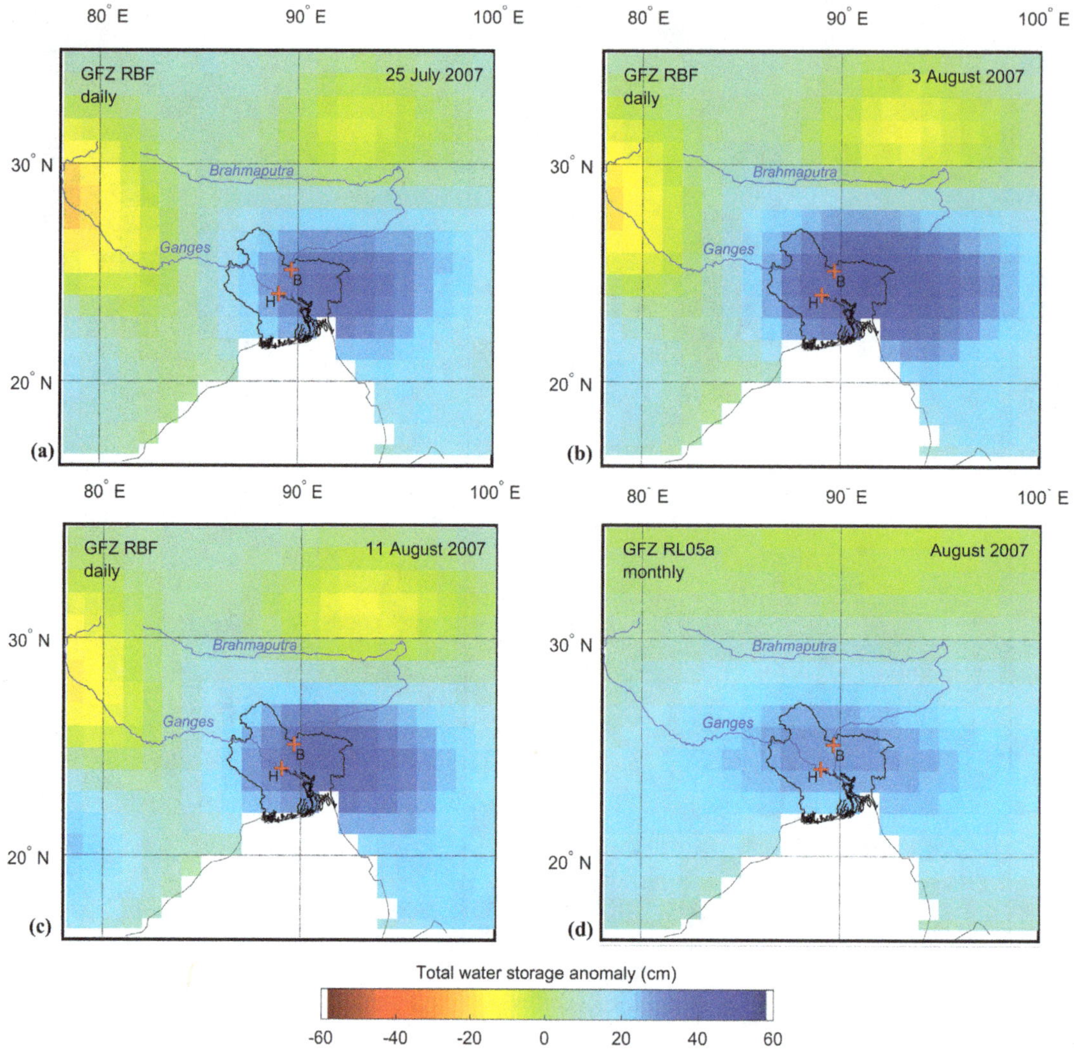

Figure 6. Daily and monthly water storage anomalies of the GFZ RBF solution for the Ganges–Brahmaputra Delta on **(a)** 25 July 2007, **(b)** 3 August 2007, **(c)** 11 August 2007 and **(d)** August 2007. Key is as in Fig. 2.

(LSDM) and the Global Land Data Assimilation System (GLDAS), respectively. The GRACE observational data input is identical for each time series. It can therefore be assumed that differences in the gravity field time series are caused by the different predictors only. Figure 1a–c show the water storage variability and the differences between the three hydrological/land surface models and the three daily GRACE solutions computed using the stochastic information of these models as well as the differences between the GRACE solutions and the hydrological models. For each time series, secular and annual variations are removed. The results show that, first, the differences between the three hydrological models may vary as much as the variability of the daily signal simulated by each hydrological model alone (Fig. 1a). Secondly, the difference between the daily GRACE solutions (Fig. 1b) is consistent and relatively low, while the variability of each daily GRACE solution alone is consistent and relatively high. Finally, the difference between a daily GRACE solution and a particular hydrological model varies for each hydrological model, but is consistent for any of the three daily GRACE solutions (Fig. 1c). It is therefore concluded that there is hardly any model-specific information left in the daily GRACE solutions and that the information from the actual GRACE observations clearly dominates.

3.2 The 2004 flood

Figures 2 and 3 show a succession of daily GRACE TWSAs for ITSG-Grace2014 on (a) 13 July, (b) 21 July and (c) 27 July 2004 and for GFZ RBF on (a) 11 July, (b) 24 July and (c) 31 July 2004, respectively, together with (d) the monthly ITSG-Grace2014 and GFZ RL05a gravity field solution for July 2004, respectively. The sampling dates are chosen such that they represent the (local) peaks in the

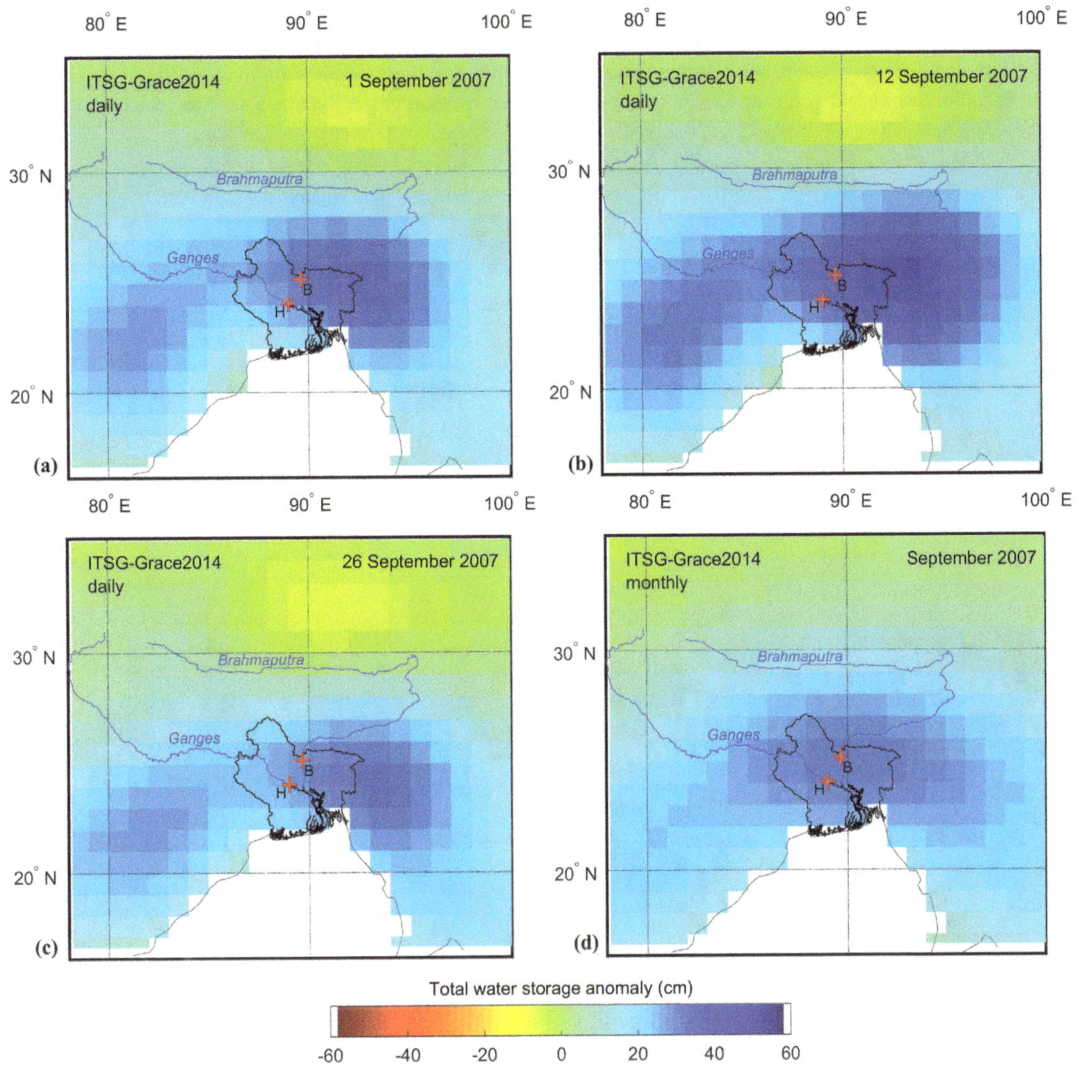

Figure 7. Daily and monthly water storage anomalies of the ITSG-Grace2014 solution for the Ganges–Brahmaputra Delta on **(a)** 1 September 2007, **(b)** 12 September 2007, **(c)** 26 September 2007 and **(d)** September 2007. Key is as in Fig. 2.

respective (high-pass filter, HPF) daily gravity time series corresponding with discharge peaks. Elevated daily TWSA values for the larger GBD ($\sim 210\,000\,\mathrm{km}^2$ area, including Bangladesh and parts of northeast India) on these dates show a progression of widespread flooding in the delta within half a month (a) just before, (b) during and (c) after peak flooding, which cannot be resolved temporally in (d) the monthly solutions. Partly due to temporal averaging and the different filtering techniques (see above), the signal amplitude of the daily and monthly gravity field solutions also cannot be compared directly. For example, lower TWSAs in the monthly solutions may be partly due to post-processing (filtering) of the GRACE observations, resulting in signal attenuation (Kusche et al., 2009). Different process dynamics, which are also partly reflected in different noise levels, cause the daily solutions to peak on different days. Spatially, the GFZ RBF solution shows more variation between the three daily snapshots, while high TWSA values are slightly more focussed. All solutions, however, show comparable spatial patterns of increased TWSAs along the Brahmaputra northeast of the GBD. Flood stages were reached between 10 and 26 July 2004 in the Brahmaputra at Bahadurabad (B) river runoff station, while the Ganges at Hardinge Bridge (H) did not reach critical flood levels (Hopson and Webster, 2010).

Figure 4 shows time series of area mean values of daily and monthly GRACE TWSAs and observed daily river runoff anomalies, together with the daily precipitation surplus. The added value of the daily GRACE solutions is demonstrated by means of a HPF with a near-monthly (31-day) window (upper panel). The HPF is applied to daily anomalies (mean reduced) of total water storage, river runoff and precipitation for the period between 2003 (start of the record of daily GRACE solutions) and 2009 (end of daily river runoff record). The remaining part of the daily time

Table 1. Correlation of daily and monthly TWSAs and daily precipitation with river runoff anomalies in(to) the GBD for the years of major flooding in 2004 and 2007. A high-pass filter (HPF) with a 31-day window separates daily data. The low-pass filter (LPF) component of the filter, the monthly data and a series of cubic spline interpolations (CSIs) fitted to the monthly data have the mean seasonal cycle removed. Pearson's linear correlation coefficient (r), sample size (n) and a (p) value for testing the hypothesis of no correlation are indicated. Time lag, if applicable, is indicated in days in brackets (a positive time lag denotes a delayed river runoff response).

	31-day high pass filter			31-day low pass filter*		
2004						
	r	n	p	r	n	p
Precipitation	0.41 (+8d)	148	< 0.01	0.64 (+7d)	148	<0.01
ITSG-Grace2014 daily	0.69 (+1d)	148	<0.01	0.95 (−1d)	148	<0.01
GFZ RBF daily	0.42 (−2d)	148	<0.01	0.79	148	<0.01
ITSG-Grace2014 monthly*				0.59	5	0.29
GFZ RL05a*				0.22	5	0.73
ITSG-Grace2014 CSI*				0.70 (−6d)	148	<0.01
GFZ RL05a CSI*				0.33 (−7d)	148	<0.01
2007						
	r	n	p	r	n	p
Precipitation	0.43 (+9d)	114	<0.01	0.77 (+12d)	114	<0.01
ITSG-Grace2014 daily	0.87 (+1d)	114	<0.01	0.95 (−1d)	114	<0.01
GFZ RBF daily	0.70 (+1d)	114	<0.01	0.85	114	<0.01
ITSG-Grace2014 monthly*				0.79	4	0.21
GFZ RL05a*				0.85	4	0.15
ITSG-Grace2014 CSI*				0.72 (−1d)	114	<0.01
GFZ RL05a CSI*				0.74 (−2d)	114	<0.01

*The mean seasonal cycle has been removed.

series, the low-pass component of the filter (LPF), is also shown (lower panel), together with a series of cubic spline interpolations (both panels, dotted line) fitted to the monthly GRACE gravity field solutions (both panels, step line). The LPF and monthly time series have the mean seasonal cycle (2003–2009) removed in order to focus on the sub-seasonal anomalies. To facilitate comparison with area mean TWSAs, the observed daily river runoff at the two stations is combined. Daily precipitation is taken from the WFDEI (WATCH Forcing Data methodology applied to ERA-Interim data) dataset (Weedon et al., 2014), using Global Precipitation Climatology Centre (GPCC) precipitation totals. The precipitation surplus, computed as an area mean for the GBD, represents the positive HPF signal (upper panel). The HPF river runoff signal peaks on 23 July, coinciding with the reported flood stage of the Brahmaputra at Bahadurabad station between 10 and 26 July (Hopson and Webster, 2010). The HPF water storage signals of ITSG-Grace2014 and GFZ RBF peak 2 days earlier and 1 day later, on 21 and 24 July, respectively. Correlation, expressed as Pearson's linear correlation coefficient (r), between the HPF signals of precipitation (surplus) and river runoff anomalies (Table 1) is strongest during a period in which the seasonally corrected LPF signals of the daily GRACE solutions increase and peak, from mid-June to the end of July ($r = 0.62$ ($p<0.01$) at a 9-day time lag). This also applies to the HPF signals of river runoff and water storage anomalies ($r = 0.89$ ($p<0.01$) at a 2-day time lag and $r = 0.60$ ($p<0.01$) at a 1-day time lag for ITSG-Grace2014 and GFZ RBF, respectively). The short time lag in the maximum correlation of the HPF signals indicates that part of the river runoff does not enter longer term floodplain or subsurface stores during this time, but is transported through the GBD and discharged into the ocean. The strong correlation of the HPF signals of precipitation, runoff and storage during this period suggests river runoff and precipitation contribute to flooding not only when regional water storage peaks, but also shortly prior to that, when the available stores are still filling up. A successive drop in the level of regional water storage, manifested by a decrease of the LPF signal of the daily GRACE solutions, is reflected in a weaker correlation of the HPF signals of precipitation, runoff and storage. River runoff data are missing to evaluate the correlation for another period of increased regional water storage, which coincides with a period of extreme precipitation surplus, with a peak of 106 mm on 6 October.

3.3 The 2007 flood

The Brahmaputra exceeded critical flood levels at Bahadurabad during two distinct periods in 2007, i.e., 26 July–

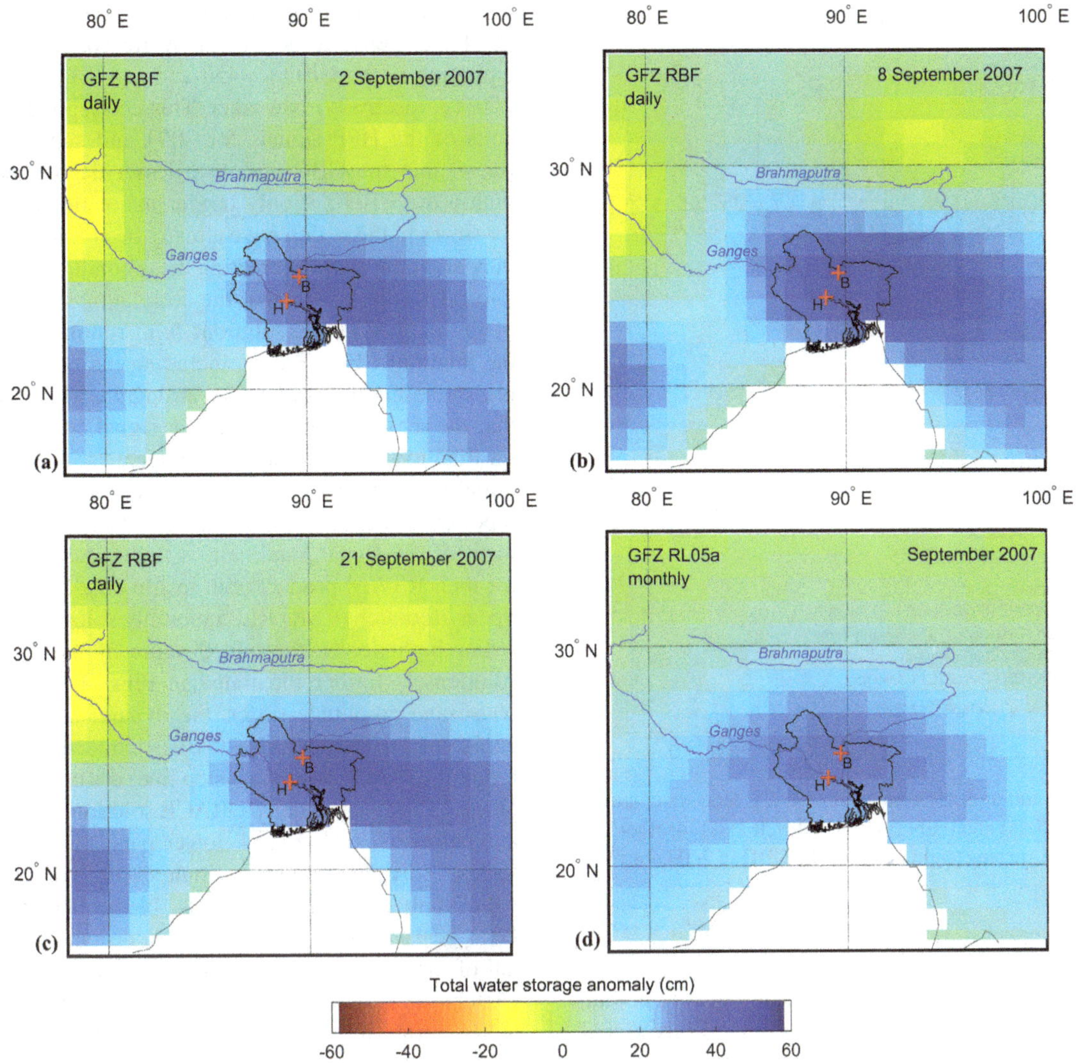

Figure 8. Daily and monthly water storage anomalies of the GFZ RBF solution for the Ganges–Brahmaputra Delta on **(a)** 2 September 2007, **(b)** 8 September 2007, **(c)** 21 September 2007 and **(d)** September 2007. Key is as in Fig. 2.

6 August and 8–17 September (Hopson and Webster, 2010). As in 2004, the Ganges at Hardinge Bridge did not reach critical flood levels. Figures 5 and 6 show a sequence of daily GRACE TWSAs for ITSG-Grace2014 for the first flood peak on (a) 24 July, (b) 3 August and (c) 13 August 2007 and for GFZ RBF on (a) 25 July, (b) 3 August and (c) 11 August 2007, respectively, together with (d) the monthly ITSG-Grace2014 and GFZ RL05a gravity field solutions for August 2007, respectively. Figures 7 and 8 show a sequence of daily GRACE TWSAs for ITSG-Grace2014 for the second flood peak on (a) 1 September, (b) 12 September and (c) 26 September 2007 and for GFZ RBF on (a) 2 September, (b) 8 September and (c) 21 September 2007, respectively, together with (d) the monthly ITSG-Grace2014 and GFZ RL05a gravity field solutions for September 2007, respectively. Again, the series of daily snapshots reflect the progression of flooding in the delta (a) just before, (b) during and (c) after peak flooding, which is beyond the temporal resolution of (d) the monthly solution. As in 2004, the two daily solutions do not necessarily peak on the same day (second flood peak), while spatial patterns of peak TWSAs show slightly different areas of concentration.

Figure 9 shows time series of the area mean values of daily and monthly GRACE TWSAs and observed daily river runoff anomalies, together with the daily precipitation surplus. The high-pass filtered daily gravity field solutions clearly reflect the two peaks of the HPF daily river runoff anomalies on 31 July and 13 September, and a smaller peak in between on 21 August.

As in 2004, correlation between the HPF signals of precipitation (surplus) and river runoff anomalies (Fig. 9, upper panel) is strongest during a period in which the LPF signals of the daily GRACE solutions peak ($r = 0.61$ at an 8-day time lag). In 2007, however, the period of strong cor-

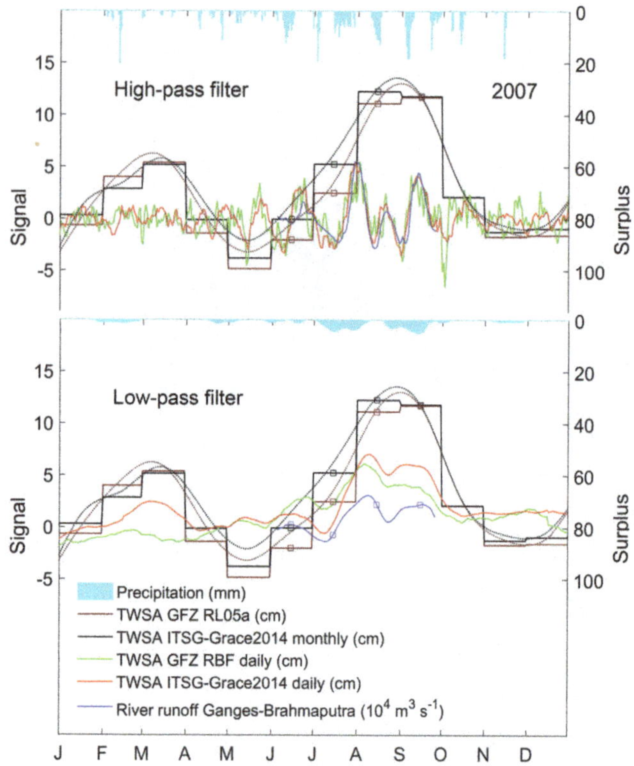

Figure 9. Daily and monthly area mean GRACE total water storage anomalies (TWSAs) and daily river runoff (left axis) together with the precipitation surplus (right axis) for the GBD in 2007. Key is as in Fig. 4.

relation is defined by a flattened peak, during which water storage plateaus and which lasts from the end of July to mid-October, with only a small drop around 23 August. Similarly, the correlation between the HPF signals of river runoff and water storage anomalies peaks during this period ($r = 0.95$ and $r = 0.77$ at a 1-day time lag for ITSG-Grace2014 and GFZ RBF, respectively). This indicates that the available water storage in the area is close to capacity during an extended period of time (~ 2 months) and additional inputs of runoff and precipitation can only be stored in the river during this time. The stronger correlation of anomalies of water storage with river runoff into the GBD than with precipitation within the GBD suggests that river runoff is a stronger driver for major flooding than precipitation in the GBD, particularly for the 2007 flood (Steckler et al., 2010; Islam et al., 2010). Both in 2004 and 2007, water storage increases slightly before river runoff, possibly due to the large GRACE satellite footprint, which detects increasing water storage in the upstream reaches of the Brahmaputra and Ganges rivers earlier than recorded as runoff at the gauges (see e.g., Fig. 2).

The strong correlation of the seasonally corrected low-frequency signals (Fig. 9, lower panel and Table 1) indicates that river runoff (volume of ~ 700 and $\sim 770\,\mathrm{km}^3$ for 2004 and 2007, respectively) also contributes predominantly to sub-seasonal storage variations (~ 100 and $\sim 110\,\mathrm{km}^3$ for 2004 and 2007, respectively), while correlation with precipitation in the GBD (~ 450 and $\sim 475\,\mathrm{km}^3$ for 2004 and 2007, respectively) is weaker. This corresponds with the results of the HPF signals for 2004 and suggests that river runoff into the GBD and, to a lesser degree, precipitation within the GBD not only trigger major flooding when water stores in the region have already been filled and peak, but they also contribute to creating these conditions for flooding. Table 1 further shows that the correlation of the LPF signal of the daily GRACE solutions with runoff exceeds that of the monthly GRACE data, including the fitted series of cubic spline interpolations. The stronger correlation indicates that the seasonally corrected LPF signal contains additional information at this frequency compared to the DDK filtered monthly GRACE data. A similar result for the 2004 flood is reported by Sakumura et al. (2016), who found good agreement of the signal amplitude at (sub-)seasonal frequencies for their RSWM product with in situ data and the Center of Space Research (CSR) RL05 monthly solutions.

For both floods, the added value of the daily GRACE solutions is further illustrated in Figs. 4 and 9. Although phase and amplitude differ, the dynamics of the series of cubic spline interpolations (CSIs, dotted line) fitted to the monthly GRACE solutions (step line) are comparable to that of the LPF signal of daily GRACE solutions and river runoff anomalies in 2004 (Fig. 4, lower panel). In 2007, the CSI series resolve the flood as a single event, while the LPF signal of daily GRACE solutions is able to distinguish the two flood peaks (Fig. 9, lower panel). Additionally, the HPF signal of the daily GRACE solutions (upper panels) is able to capture the HPF signal of the river runoff anomalies, particularly during the period in which regional water storage is filling up and peaks (2004) or plateaus (2007).

This is further illustrated in Fig. 10, which shows the frequency-separated anomalies of river runoff vs. total water storage in the GBD for the flood years of 2004 and 2007 (Riegger and Tourian, 2014; Reager et al., 2015; Sproles et al., 2015). Generally, the hypothesis that storage can drive river runoff tends to indicate a slower process evolution through subsurface water storage and baseflow generation, expressed by a strong correlation at longer (monthly) timescales. Daily HPF runoff is expected to be less correlated with and more variable than daily HPF storage, caused by precipitation that runs off quickly and does not enter storage for a significant amount of time. The fact that there is still a strong correlation between daily HPF storage and HPF river runoff, particularly for the 2007 flood (Table 1), points towards a scenario of increased storage in the river itself, in which the variation of daily total water storage reflects the inflow of river water into the delta. This water inflow can only be stored in the river during the time of flooding, when the available water storage in the area is at (near) capacity. However, while trends of the HPF signal of daily water storage and river runoff anomalies show agreement over periods of a

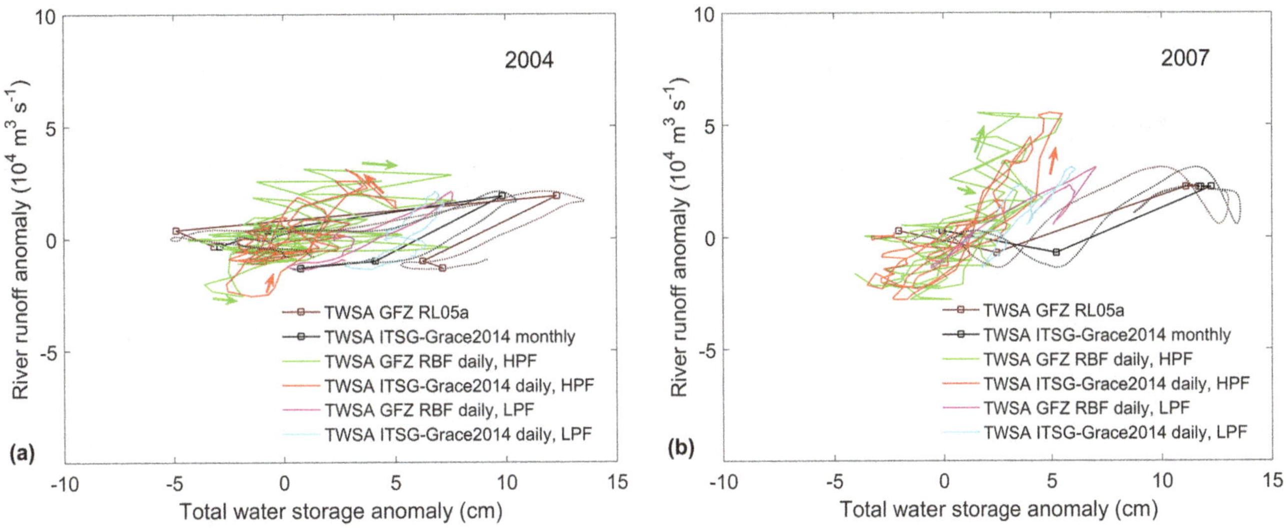

Figure 10. Anomalies of river runoff vs. total water storage for **(a)** 2004 and **(b)** 2007. A high-pass filter (HPF) with a 31-day window separates daily data into a HPF and an LPF component. A cubic spline interpolation (dotted line) is fitted to the monthly data. The LPF signals and monthly data have the mean seasonal cycle removed. Arrows indicate (local) directions in the HPF signal hysteresis loop.

few days, the higher frequency content of the daily solutions is not reflected in the daily river runoff. This high-frequency variation is attributed to process noise of the Kalman filter approach and a repeat period of 4 days for the GRACE satellites to pass over the GBD. Propagation of the full formal error matrix to the area mean value for each time step estimates the resulting noise level in the ITSG-Grace2014 and GFZ RBF daily solutions at approximately 1 and 1.45 cm TWSAs, respectively. These numbers are confirmed by an empirical estimate using the methodology of Bonin et al. (2012). The dif ference in apparent noise in the two daily time series can primarily be attributed to the process models employed, which result in different temporal constraints and degrees of spatial filtering.

4 Conclusions

Daily GRACE gravity field solutions have been evaluated against daily river runoff data for major flood events in the Ganges–Brahmaputra Delta (GBD) in 2004 and 2007. Compared to the monthly gravity field solutions, the trends over periods of a few days in the daily gravity field solutions are able to reflect temporal variations in river runoff during major flood events. This is especially true for the larger flood in 2007, for which three consecutive peaks in daily river runoff, of which two exceeded critical flood levels, are replicated. The daily temporal resolution is sufficiently high to reflect these area mean variations of water storage anomalies, but the spatial resolution is too low to accurately locate the flood-affected area. While the daily ITSG-Grace2016 solution shows relatively higher correlation with river flow and higher temporal consistency, the daily GFZ RBF solution exhibits a better spatial focus of the flooded area, possibly indicating a higher content of the hydrological signal.

GRACE total water storage anomaly data are integrated observations of multiple water storage compartments (e.g., river storage, lakes and floodplains, soil moisture and groundwater). The strong correlation of high-pass filtered daily river runoff anomalies and TWSAs suggests that river water constitutes a large part of the daily total water storage variation during flooding, when other water stores are at (near) capacity and cannot absorb additional inputs of runoff or precipitation. Strong correlation further indicates that the remaining part of the daily GRACE data, the low-pass component of the filter, also contains additional information at this frequency compared to the monthly GRACE data. The analysis further suggests that river runoff into the GBD, mainly generated by precipitation in the upstream reaches of the Ganges–Brahmaputra basin, is a stronger driver for major flooding than precipitation in the GBD, particularly for the larger flood of 2007.

This first hydrological evaluation of the daily GRACE gravity field solutions based on a Kalman filter approach confirms their potential for gravity-based large-scale flood monitoring. This particularly applies to short-lived, high-volume floods, as they occur in the GBD with a 4–5-year return period. These results imply that with the release of the daily gravity field solutions in near-real time, flood monitoring may be supported for large events.

Competing interests. The authors declare that they have no conflict of interest.

Acknowledgements. This research is funded by the European Union's Horizon 2020 project European Gravity Service for Improved Emergency Management (EGSIEM) under grant agreement no. 637010. We thank John T. Reager for his comments and suggestions, which greatly helped to improve the manuscript. Further, we thank Natthachet Tangdamrongsub and an anonymous reviewer for their input and constructive comments.

Edited by: Wouter Buytaert

References

A, G., Wahr, J., and Zhong, S.: Computations of the viscoelastic response of a 3-D compressible Earth to surface loading: an application to Glacial Isostatic Adjustment in Antarctica and Canada, Geophys. J. Int., 192, 557–572, https://doi.org/10.1093/gji/ggs030, 2013.

Bergmann, I. and Dobslaw, H.: Short-term transport variability of the Antarctic circumpolar current from satellite gravity observations, J. Geophys. Res., 117, C05044, https://doi.org/10.1029/2012JC007872, 2012.

Best, J. L., Ashworth, P., Sarker, M. H., and Roden, J.: The Brahmaputra-Jamuna River, Bangladesh, in: Large Rivers: Geomorphology and Management, 395–430, John Wiley, Chichester, UK, 2007.

Bonin, J. A., Bettadpur, S., and Tapley, B. D.: High-frequency signal and noise estimates of CSR GRACE RL04, J. Geod., 86, 1165, https://doi.org/10.1007/s00190-012-0572-5, 2012.

Chen, J. L., Wilson, C. R., and Tapley, B. D.: The 2009 exceptional Amazon flood and interannual terrestrial water storage change observed by GRACE, Water Resour. Res., 46, W12526, https://doi.org/10.1029/2010WR009383, 2010.

Cheng, M., Ries, J. C., and Tapley, B. D.: Variations of the Earth's figure axis from satellite laser ranging and GRACE, J. Geophys. Res., 116, B01409, https://doi.org/10.1029/2010JB000850, 2011.

Dahle, C., Flechtner, F., Gruber, C., König, D., König, R., Michalak, G., and Neumayer, K. H.: GFZ GRACE Level-2 Processing Standards Document for Level-2 Product Release 0005, Scientific Technical Report STR 12/02–Data, Revised Edition, January 2013, Potsdam, 21 pp., https://doi.org/10.2312/GFZ.b103-1202-25, 2012.

Dobslaw, H., Flechtner, F., Bergmann-Wolf, I. , Dahle, C., Dill, R., Esselborn, S. Sasgen, I., and Thomas, M.: Simulating high-frequency atmosphere-ocean mass variability for de-aliasing of satellite gravity observations: AOD1B RL05, J. Geophys. Res., 118, 3704–3711, doi.org/10.1002/jgrc.20271, 2013.

Dobslaw, H., Bergmann-Wolf, I., Dill, R., Forootan, E., Klemann, V., Kusche, J., and Sasgen, I.: The updated ESA Earth System Model for future gravity mission simulation studies, J. Geodesy, 89, 505–513, https://doi.org/10.1007/s00190-014-0787-8, 2015.

Döll, P., Kaspar, F., and Lehner, B.: A global hydrological model for deriving water availability indicators: model tuning and validation, J. Hydrol., 207, 105–134, https://doi.org/10.1016/S0022-1694(02)00283-4, 2003.

Grace Tellus: Geocenter estimates, C20 SLR time series, GIA model, available at: http://grace.jpl.nasa.gov, last access: 17 November 2015.

Gruber, C. and Gouweleeuw, B. T.: Short latency monitoring of continental, ocean- and atmospheric mass variations using GRACE inter-satellite accelerations, Geophysical Journal International, in review, 2018.

Gruber, C., Moon, Y., Flechtner, F., Dahle, C., Novàk, P., Koenig, R., and Neumayer, H.: Submonthly GRACE Solutions from Localizing Integral Equations and Kalman Filtering. Earth on the Edge: Science for a Sustainable Planet, Proceedings of the IAG General Assembly, Melbourne, Australia, 28 June–2 July 2011, Series: International Association of Geodesy Symposia, edited by: Rizos, C. and Willis, P., 139, 383–389, 2014.

Gruber, C., Moon, Y., Flechtner, F., Dahle, C., Novàk, P., Koenig, R., and Neumayer, H.: Submonthly GRACE Solutions from Localizing Integral Equations and Kalman Filtering, available at ftp://gfzop.gfz-potsdam.de/EGSIEM/, last access: 05 April 2016.

Hopson, M., and Webster, P. J.: A 1–10-Day Ensemble Forecasting Scheme for the Major River Basins of Bangladesh: Forecasting Severe Floods of 2003–07, J. Hydrometeor., 11, 618–641, https://doi.org/10.1175/2009JHM1006.1, 2010.

Islam, A. S., Haque, A., and Bala, S. K.: Hydrologic characteristics of floods in Ganges-Brahmaputra–Meghna (GBM) delta, Natural Hazards, 54, 797–811, https://doi.org/10.1007/s11069-010-9504-y, 2010.

Kalman, R. E.: A New Approach to Linear Filtering and Prediction Problems, J. Basic Eng.-T. Asme., 82, 35–45, https://doi.org/10.1115/1.3662552, 1960.

Kurtenbach, E., Eicker, A., Mayer-Gürr, T., Hohlschneider, M., Hayn, M., Fuhrmann, M., and Kusche, J.: Improved daily GRACE gravity field solutions using a Kalman smoother, J. Geodyn., 59–60, 39–48, https://doi.org/10.1016/j.jog.2012.02.006, 2012.

Kusche, J., Schmidt, R., Petrovic, S., and Rietbroek, R.: Decorrelated GRACE time-variable gravity solutions by GFZ, and their validation using a hydrological model, J. Geodesy, 83, 903–913, https://doi.org/10.1007/s00190-009-0308-3, 2009.

Landerer, F. W. and Swenson, F. C.: Accuracy of scaled GRACE terrestrial water storage estimates, Water Resour. Res., 48, W04531, https://doi.org/10.1029/2011WR011453, 2012.

Mayer-Gürr, T., Zehentner, N., Klinger, B., and Kvas, A.: ITSG-Grace2014: a new GRACE gravity field release computed in Graz, available at: http://www.itsg.tugraz.at/research/ITSG-Grace2014 (last access: 20 May 2015), 2014.

Mayer-Gürr, T., Zehentner, N., Klinger, B., and Kvas, A.: ITSG-Grace2014: a new GRACE gravity field release computed in Graz, available at: ftp://ftp.tugraz.at, last access: 20 May 2015.

Molodtsova, T., Molodtsov, S., Kirilenko, A., Zhang, X., and VanLooy, J.: Evaluating flood potential with GRACE in the United States, Nat. Hazards Earth Syst. Sci., 16, 1011–1018, https://doi.org/10.5194/nhess-16-1011-2016, 2016.

Rauch, H. E., Tung, F., and Striebel, C. T.: Maximum likelihood estimates of linear dynamic systems. AIAA, 3, 1445–1450, https://doi.org/10.2514/3.3166, 1965.

Reager, J. T. and Famiglietti, J.: Global terrestrial water storage capacity and flood potential using GRACE, Geophys. Res. Lett., 36, L23402, https://doi.org/10.1029/2009GL040826, 2009.

Reager, J. T., Thomas, B. F., and Famiglietti, J.: River basin flood potential inferred using GRACE gravity observations at several months lead time, Nat. Geosci., 7, 588592, https://doi.org/10.1038/ngeo2203, 2014.

Reager, J. T., Thomas, A. C., Sproles, E. A., Rodell, M., Beaudoing, H. K., Li, B., and Famiglietti, J. S.: Assimilation of GRACE Terrestrial Water Storage Observations into a Land Surface Model for the Assessment of Regional Flood Potential, Remote Sens., 7, 14663–14679, https://doi.org/10.3390/rs71114663, 2015.

Riegger, J. and Tourian, M. J.: Characterization of runoff-storage relationships by satellite gravimetry and remote sensing, Water Resour. Res., 50, 3444–3466, https://doi.org/10.1002/2013WR013847, 2014.

Sakumura, C., Bettapur, S., Save, H., and McCullough, C.: High-frequency terrestrial water storage signal capture via a regularized sliding window mascon product from GRACE, J. Geophys. Res.-Sol. Ea., 121, 4014–4030, https://doi.org/10.1002/2016JB012843, 2016.

Sproles, E. A., Leibowitz, S. G., Reager, J. T., Wigington Jr., P. J., Famiglietti, J. S., and Patil, S. D.: GRACE storage-runoff hystereses reveal the dynamics of regional watersheds, Hydrol. Earth Syst. Sci., 19, 3253–3272, https://doi.org/10.5194/hess-19-3253-2015, 2015.

Steckler, M. S., Nooner, S. L., Akhter, S. H., Chowdhury, S. K., Bettadpur, S., Seeber, L., and Kogan, M. G.: Modeling Earth deformation from monsoonal flooding in Bangladesh using hydrographic, GPS, and Gravity Recovery and Climate Experiment (GRACE) data, J. Geophys. Res., 115, B08407, https://doi.org/10.1029/2009JB007018, 2010.

Swenson, S., Chambers, D., and Wahr, J.: Estimating geocenter variations from a combination of GRACE and ocean model output, J. Geophys. Res., 113, B08410, https://doi.org/10.1029/2007JB005338, 2008.

Swenson, S. C.: GRACE monthly land water mass grids NETCDF RELEASE 5.0. Ver. 5.0. (PO.DAAC, CA, USA), available at: https://doi.org/10.5067/TELND-NC005 (last access: 20 May 2015), 2012.

Swenson, S. C. and Wahr, J. M.: Estimating signal loss in regularized GRACE gravity field solutions, Geophys. J. Int., 185, 693–702, https://doi.org/10.1111/j.1365-246X.2011.04977.x, 2011.

Tapley, B. D., Bettadpur, S., Ries, J. C., Thompson, P. F., and Watkins, M. M.: GRACE measurements of mass variability in the Earth system, Science, 305, 503–505, https://doi.org/10.1126/science.1099192, 2004.

Weedon, G. P., Balsamo, G., Bellouin, N., Gomes, S., Best, M. J., and Viterbo, P.: The WFDEI meteorological forcing data set: WATCH Forcing Data methodology applied to ERA-Interim reanalysis data, Water Resour. Res., 50, 7505–7514, https://doi.org/10.1002/2014WR015638, 2014.

10

Dealing with uncertainty in the probability of overtopping of a flood mitigation dam

Eleni Maria Michailidi and Baldassare Bacchi

DICATAM, Università degli Studi di Brescia, Via Branze 42, 25123 Brescia, Italy

Correspondence to: Eleni Maria Michailidi (e.michailidi@unibs.it)

Abstract. In recent years, copula multivariate functions were used to model, probabilistically, the most important variables of flood events: discharge peak, flood volume and duration. However, in most of the cases, the sampling uncertainty, from which small-sized samples suffer, is neglected. In this paper, considering a real reservoir controlled by a dam as a case study, we apply a structure-based approach to estimate the probability of reaching specific reservoir levels, taking into account the key components of an event (flood peak, volume, hydrograph shape) and of the reservoir (rating curve, volume–water depth relation). Additionally, we improve information about the peaks from historical data and reports through a Bayesian framework, allowing the incorporation of supplementary knowledge from different sources and its associated error. As it is seen here, the extra information can result in a very different inferred parameter set and consequently this is reflected as a strong variability of the reservoir level, associated with a given return period. Most importantly, the sampling uncertainty is accounted for in both cases (single-site and multi-site with historical information scenarios), and Monte Carlo confidence intervals for the maximum water level are calculated. It is shown that water levels of specific return periods in a lot of cases overlap, thus making risk assessment, without providing confidence intervals, deceiving.

1 Introduction

In the relatively recent literature, there is a wide application of the copula functions to model the natural variability of hydrometeorological variables, ranging from rainfall (De Michele and Salvadori, 2003; Zhang and Singh, 2007; Balistrocchi and Bacchi, 2011; Singh and Zhang, 2007; Ariff et al., 2012) to floods (Aronica et al., 2012; Balistrocchi et al., 2014; Candela et al., 2014; Domeneghetti et al., 2013; Gräler et al., 2013; Ganguli and Reddy, 2013).

An important application of this multivariate analysis is the determination of the risk of failure of a hydraulic structure. De Michele et al. (2005) were the first to check the adequacy of a dam's spillway under a bivariate hydrological load, followed by Requena et al. (2013), while Volpi and Fiori (2014) formalised the idea that the return period of a failure of a structure depends on the structure of interest, and therefore the interaction between the hydrological loads and the structure should be taken into consideration by fixing a "structure-based" return period.

In the same conceptual framework, Serinaldi (2016) suggested that the choice between a univariate and multivariate risk assessment should not be based on whether one or the other overestimate/underestimate the risk but rather on the operational criteria of the problem, or simply on what is the mechanism of failure.

Copulas are functions that combine marginal distributions with the joint cumulative distribution; therefore, the latter is only indirectly affected by the choice of the marginals. So, the practical problem of identification and estimation of the joint distribution is handled from two non-interwinding aspects: the dependence structure of the set of variables and the marginal distributions.

In the majority of the studies, the communication of the sampling uncertainty – an integral component in a univariate framework – is overlooked in a multivariate case. Serinaldi (2013) studied the effect of sample size on the confidence bands of the probability of exceedance curves of a joint peak-volume event and showed that in small and medium sample sizes these curves largely overlap. Similarly, Zhang et al. (2015) implemented a Bayesian inference approach to account for the uncertainty of parameter estimation and for the occurrence of a drought, coming to the conclusion that the 95 % confidence interval of a 20-year event can include the expected values of 10 to 50-year events.

In order to account for the sampling uncertainty of multivariate cases, where a variable of interest can be expressed as a function of one or more variables, Serinaldi (2016) proposed a Monte Carlo procedure. He also underlined the importance of including confidence intervals when providing point estimates of the variable of interest, which is even more necessary in the multivariate frequency analysis, where the unknown dependence structure contributes to the uncertainty.

The sampling uncertainty in a joint peak-volume event was quantified by Dung et al. (2015) who used two bootstrapping methods – one developed by the authors and the second by Serinaldi (2013) – and concluded, as the previous, that the model selection and parameter estimation methods are of minor significance in uncertainty estimation with respect to sampling uncertainty, even in relatively large sample sizes. They suggested that efforts should be focused on the expansion of the data set in order to achieve a reduction of uncertainty.

The data expansion can be temporal, spatial and causal (Merz and Blöschl, 2008), thus enriching the available evidence with information from neighbouring basins, previous periods and by comprehension of the flood-generating mechanisms. In the past, many researchers (Parent and Bernier, 2003; Reis Jr. and Stedinger, 2005; Gaume et al., 2010; Halbert et al., 2016; Parkes and Demeritt, 2016; Viglione et al., 2013) have dealt with the extension of the available data using information on paleo-floods, historical flood reports, marks of the river stage during important flood events, expert judgement, etc. with the aim of reducing the range of uncertainty bands or simply to reach a more realistic design value. Bayesian inference allows the integration of information from different sources and their associated uncertainty and errors and provides a means of conveying hydrological reasoning in a mathematical context.

In this research, we validate a methodology of flood risk assessment in a real case study, where risk is expressed in terms of probability of exceeding a given reservoir level in an online flood mitigation dam. We consider this level as a function of flood peak, volume and hydrograph shape and, consequently, multivariate modelling is implemented with the use of copulas. The characteristics of the reservoir – also a function of the level – are synthesised in the rating curve and the volume-level curve. The main scope is to integrate the associated sampling uncertainty and to build confidence intervals for each water level through Monte Carlo simulations. Furthermore, we incorporate additional information on the peaks in a Bayesian framework and we examine its effect on the distributions, their confidence intervals, as well as the ones of the reservoir-level frequency curve.

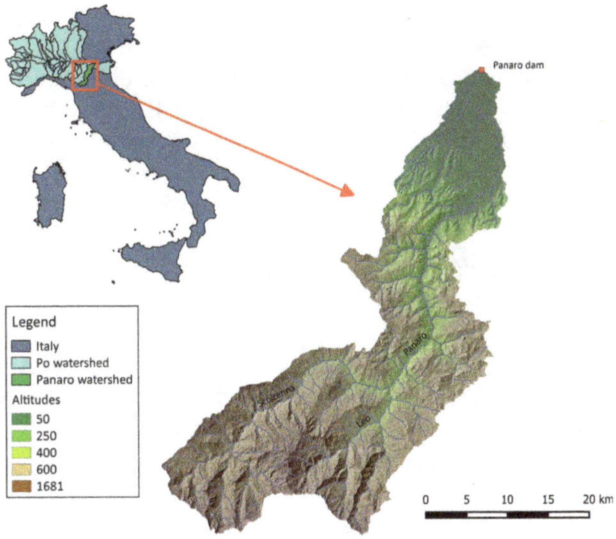

Figure 1. Panaro study watershed.

2 Case study and data

We have focused our interest on the Panaro catchment – an important influent of the Po river in northern Italy. In particular, the watershed under investigation is composed of the Panaro river itself, the Scoltenna and the Leo tributaries with an outlet upstream of the Panaro dam (Fig. 1) and occupies an area of 876 km^2. The Panaro has its source at Monte Cimone (2165 m a.s.l.) and flows into the Po at Bondeno; it takes its name from the valley of Montespecchio after converging with the Leo and Scoltenna streams that constitute the upper part of the river network. The hydrographic network of the watershed shows a low degree of hierarchy, indicating an evolving state which is also evident by the existence of torrential dynamic phenomena (Autorità di bacino del fiume Po, 2006).

The influence of snowfall is negligible due to the modest land elevation and the majority of rainfall events occurring seasonally (September–April). The average precipitation height ranges between 700 and 2000 mm yr^{-1} (Autorità di bacino del fiume Po, 2006).

The basin's permeability is low, and therefore the runoff is influenced little by water infiltration. In fact, the study basin consists mostly of sandstones and silicatic alternating sequences (44 % of total area) and marls and clay (34 %).

The Panaro dam is a concrete gravity dam (150 m in length), located near the city of Modena and constructed for flood mitigation purposes. The hydraulic system consists of two reservoirs, a principal on the river course and a secondary at the right river bank, and a series of levees that enclose them. The crest of the principal levees is at 44.85 m a.s.l. The reservoirs can hold in total 23.66 hm^3 up to the spillway's crest at 41.1 m a.s.l. There are also nine discharge outlets at the bottom of the dam that ensure constant flow to the downstream valley.

The available flood data included a 52-year discharge series (1936–1943, 1945 and 1946 were missing) with an hourly time interval from the Bomporto station located downstream near the current location of the dam. The hydrological characteristics of the study basin are briefly presented in Table 1.

Additional data included the annual peaks of the missing years from the same station (Servizio Idrografico Italiano, 1939, 1953) and recent annual peaks from upstream stations, after consulting the annual hydrological reports of ARPA – Emilia Romagna published in its website (http://www.arpae.it), in particular, for 2003 from Pievepelago, for 2004, 2005 and 2015 from Ponte Samone, and for 2006 to 2014 from Spilamberto.

In a report about natural disaster risks in the city of Modena (Nora and Ghinoi, 2009), it is also stated that the most disastrous flood events of the 20th century happened during the last 40 years (1966, 1969, 1972 and 1973). In November 1966, the flooded area from the Panaro covered 9400 ha; in September 1972, it covered 2540 ha; and in September 1973, it covered 6000 ha (Nora and Ghinoi, 2009).

3 Methodology

3.1 Data regionalisation

In order to rescale the flood information from subcatchments and from the downstream station, depending on the area, the following scale function was used:

$$Q(A_1) = Q(A_2)(A_1/A_2)^m \tag{1}$$

where $Q(A_1)$ is the rescaled discharge, $Q(A_2)$ a known discharge and m a regional-scale exponent.

De Michele and Rosso (2002) clustered basins with similar flood generation mechanisms and checked the homogeneity of the grouped regions. The study area was located in northwestern Italy and included the Panaro watershed. The proposed scale exponent m for this region is 0.772 with a standard deviation of 0.072. In our case, the rescaling regarded different locations of the same basin, although in theory neighbouring basins could have been used (e.g. the Secchia basin), but they did not add additional information here.

3.2 Incorporating additional data

Thomas Bayes' theorem expresses how an individual's degree of belief can change after the presence of new evidence. Bayes' theorem can be formulated as

$$p(\theta|D) = \frac{l(D|\theta)\pi(\theta)}{\int l(D|\theta)\pi(\theta)d\theta} \propto l(D|\theta)\pi(\theta), \tag{2}$$

where $\pi(\theta)$ is the prior density distribution of the parameters θ, $p(\theta|D)$ is the posterior distribution after the introduction of the observed information D and $l(D|\theta)$ is the likelihood of the data. The denominator serves only as a normalisation constant to ensure unity of the area under $p(\theta|D)$, so the equality sign can be substituted with the proportionality sign. This integral cannot be solved analytically, so for its computation Monte Carlo Markov chain algorithms are employed. In each Markov chain, the aim is the maximisation of the logarithm of the unnormalised joint posterior distribution starting from an initial value and proceeding iteratively, in order to arrive at each target distribution (Statisticat, LLC, 2016).

Table 1. Main hydrological characteristics of the Panaro watershed (area A, main stream length L, minimum elevation H_{min}, elevation drop ΔH, time of concentration t_{c}).

A (km^2)	876
L (km)	124.4
H_{min} (m)	32
ΔH (m)	1449.9
t_{c} (h)	10.0

In a Bayesian framework, the model's parameters are handled as stochastic variables in order to incorporate the uncertainty of their values (Ouarda and El-Adlouni, 2011). In the present case, the model's parameters were the parameter of the peak marginal distribution and the scale exponent. We used noninformative prior distribution for the marginal and a normal prior distribution for the exponent $m \backsim N$ (0.772, 0.072). We integrated a perception threshold X_{P} – a value which only in k number of years in a historic period of h years was exceeded; here, it is set as at about 1000 m^3 s^{-1}, a value thought to be exceeded only once in a historic period of 117 years since flood reports indicate that during the early years of the 1900s, when systematic records were nonexistent, the flood events were of less significance in comparison with the events occurring in the 1970s. Additionally, we have introduced the uncertainty of the scale exponent m. Therefore, the likelihood function of the data is set as

$$l(D|\theta) = \begin{bmatrix} h \\ k \end{bmatrix} F_X(X_{\mathrm{P}})^{(h-k)} \prod_{i=1}^{s} \left[\prod_{j=1}^{n_i} f_x\left(y_{ij}(A/A_i)^m\right) \right], \tag{3}$$

where $\begin{bmatrix} h \\ k \end{bmatrix} = \frac{h!}{k!(h-k)!}$ is the binomial coefficient, s is the number of different sites of the recorded flood peaks, n_i is the number of recorded peaks for each site and y_{ij} are the annual peaks from the different sites.

The Bayesian inference was conducted in R with the package LaplacesDemon (Statisticat, LLC, 2016) and the MCMC algorithm utilised was the Componentwise Hit-And-Run Metropolis. The logarithm of the posterior distribution to be maximised is the sum of the logarithm of the likelihood and the logarithm of the priors:

$$\log(p(\mu,\sigma,m|D) = \log(l(D|\mu,\sigma,m) + \log(\pi(m)), \quad (4)$$

where μ and σ are the mean and shape parameters of the peak distribution.

3.3 Copula and marginal inference

Copulas are functions that describe the dependence structure between variables independently of the choice of marginal distributions. The joint distribution functions and the marginals are linked by Sklar's theorem (Sklar, 1959):

$$F(x_1,\ldots,x_d) = C(F_1(x_1),\ldots,F_d(x_d)), \quad (5)$$

for all $\boldsymbol{x} \in R^d$, where the F_i, $i = 1, \ldots, d$ are the marginals of F and C is the copula function.

Copulas provide a powerful tool for the statistical modelling of multivariate data: for a theoretical introduction, see Nelsen (2006), Joe (2014) and Durante and Sempi (2015); for a practical engineering approach, see Genest and Favre (2007), Salvadori et al. (2007) and Salvadori and De Michele (2007).

The application of copula functions has facilitated overcoming some inadequacies of traditional multivariate distributions such as that the marginals must derive from the same distribution family and their parameters may define the dependence structure between the variables (Salvadori et al., 2007).

The degree of relation between pairs of variables was examined by measures of association. These include Kendall's τ, Spearman's ρ_S (which expresses the existence or absence of concordance) and Pearson's ρ_P (which expresses linear dependence). For the observed discharge/volume pairs, these were equal to 0.58, 0.77 and 0.81, respectively, and indicate strong dependence.

In the absence of a long sample, the copulas that fit the data can be numerous and goodness-of-fit tests cannot distinguish between them (Serinaldi, 2013). Since inferring the "correct" copula model is not the aim of this research and since this endeavour at this point can be futile, given the available data set, the final choice was based partly on the preference of previous published research of the Gumbel distribution, including conference proceedings by Balistrocchi et al. (2014) who fitted the Gumbel on peaks obtained from a peak-over-threshold method on the same discharge time series. In the present case, both the Gaussian and the Gumbel–Hougaard one-parameter copulas passed the goodness-of-fit tests (Cramér–von Mises and Kolmogorov–Smirnov) and demonstrated the smallest Akaike weights – or else the probability that the chosen model is the most apt among the tested ones (Burnham and Anderson, 2004). However, we thought that if tail dependence exists, Gumbel would be more appropriate (belonging to the extreme value copula family), as the Gaussian has no tail dependence. We recall the Gumbel–Hougaard copula as

$$C(u,v) = \exp\left[-\left((-\log(u))^{\theta} + (-\log(v))^{\theta}\right)^{1/\theta}\right], \quad (6)$$

where u, v are the pseudo-observations and θ the copula parameter.

The existence of tail dependence between peak and volume was also implied by some historical evidence. Many significant events in Italy occur when a frontal perturbation, generated by the cold high masses coming from the North Atlantic Ocean or the Arctic Ocean, meets Mediterranean southward warm fronts. Depending on the persistence of the south and north currents, the generated front begins to develop, covering a large area (e.g. $10^4\,\mathrm{km}^2$). Inside this warm front, the energy content is very high. This causes local convective phenomena enhanced by orographic effects. So, thunderstorms can appear locally producing rainfall whose values can surpass one-third of the mean annual in 24–30 h. In the vicinity of the local thunderstorms, the rainfall is moderately high, producing large soil saturation and increasing, significantly, the contribution to the groundwater. This kind of rainfall event produces not only maximum observed peaks of flood in many rivers of small ($< 100\,\mathrm{km}^2$) and medium ($< 2000\,\mathrm{km}^2$) sizes but also the largest observed volumes associated with the persistence of the global event. This is the case, for example, for the flood in Florence and Triveneto on 4 November 1966, in Valtellina on 18–25 July 1987, along the Tanaro on 5–6 November 1994, along the Po in Piedmont on 17–21 October 2000, etc.

Unfortunately, tail dependence estimators such as the ones of Frahm et al. (2005) and Schmidt and Stadtmüller (2006) can be biased and susceptible to high uncertainty even in large sample sizes (Serinaldi et al., 2015); thus, their use in this case is discouraged.

Regarding the choice of the marginal distributions, we preferred distributions that were more parsimonious, thus reducing the additional statistical uncertainty introduced by an extra parameter, following the logic of Occam's razor, and this provided a nice visual fit. The differences between the corrected Akaike information criterion (AIC), Bayesian information criterion (BIC) and Akaike-weighted values were not sufficient to make a safe distinction between the models. The peaks were modelled with the inverse Gaussian distribution (two parameters instead of three of the generalised extreme value (GEV) distribution) and their corresponding volumes with the one-parameter Rayleigh. It is, however, imperative to note that there was no clear indication of overall performance superiority of the chosen distributions.

The parameters of the inferred distributions (copula and marginals) are presented in Table 2.

3.4 Hydrograph selection

The shape of the "design hydrograph" is often considered an important factor in the design procedure and is related to the spatial and temporal rain distribution as well as the

Table 2. Estimated parameters of the inferred distributions and their confidence interval (95 %).

	Parameter name	Estimated parameter	Confidence interval (95%)	Standard deviation
Gumbel–Hougaard	θ	2.27	[1.79, 3.01]	0.38
Inverse Gaussian for peak (single site)	μ	364.12	[23.64, 416.40]	23.67
	λ	1957.16	[1288.05, 2820.61]	380.17
Inverse Gaussian for peak (multi-site	μ	398.61	[358.42, 442.54]	21.89
and historical information)	λ	1533.41	[1108.84, 2058.99]	256.37
Rayleigh for volume	σ	386.58×10^5	$[343.18, 430.53] \times 10^5$	26.54×10^5

basin's shape and behaviour (Singh, 1997). Therefore, typical hydrographs were determined from the annual maxima flood events extracted from the available time series. In particular, the events' hydrographs were clustered according to their characteristics and utilising the methodology proposed by Dyck and Peschke (1995), which suggests the normalisation of the hydrograph (after the removal of the baseflow) by

$$Q_{\text{norm}} = (Q - q_{\text{base}}) / (Q_{\max} - q_{\text{base}}) \quad (7)$$

$$t_{\text{norm}} = t / t_{Q_{\max}}, \quad (8)$$

where $Q_{\max}$ is the hydrograph's peak, q_{base} the base flow and $t_{\max}$ the time to peak, starting from the rising limb of the flood event.

Consequently, the normalised peak equals 1 at time 1. All normalised hydrographs were extended to a common duration (for comparison purposes) and cluster analysis with the Ward method and Euclidean distances was implemented (Aronica et al., 2012).

3.5 Structure-based risk analysis

Volpi and Fiori (2014) associated the return period with the structure of interest by relating the structure design parameter to the hydrological load through the function $Z = g(\mathbf{X})$. Consequently the structure-oriented return period of a value z takes the form

$$T_{\text{STR}} = \frac{\mu_T}{1 - F_Z(z)}, \quad (9)$$

where μ_T is the mean interarrival time between two consecutive occurrences of z (in our case, $\mu_T = 1$ year), F_Z is the probability distribution function of the derived variable Z, which in this case is the reservoir level and $\mathbf{X} \equiv (Q, V, \text{shape}, \text{etc.})$. Here, the structure function is very complex, since the reservoir level is a function of the spillway's rating curve and the flood's natural variables, and therefore the whole analysis must be based on Monte Carlo simulations. This adds to the computational burden, specifically when dealing with the quantification of the uncertainty.

3.6 Uncertainty estimation

In order to account for sampling uncertainty and to estimate the confidence intervals, the following Monte Carlo procedure was implemented, originally proposed by Serinaldi (2016).

1. Estimate the parameter $\hat{\theta}$ of the copula for the observed sample as well as the parameter of the flood volume distribution.
2. Simulate B bivariate samples of size n (equal to the number of years of the observed sample) using the estimated copula parameter and then transform into volume using the estimated parameter of the marginal.
3. Calculate the copula parameter $\hat{\theta}$ and the volume marginal parameter for each sample with the same estimation method used for the observed sample.
4. Simulate B bivariate samples of size M with the copula parameter $\hat{\theta}$ estimated in the previous step.
5. Transform the samples from the unit interval to discharge and volume using the estimated marginal parameters. Generate $B \times M$ hydrographs with an assigned peak, volume and shape and route them to calculate the reservoir level and the frequency curves of all B samples.
6. Build the confidence intervals of the reservoir level frequency curves.

In the present research, B was set equal to 10 000 and M equal to 1000.

The confidence intervals of the peaks' marginal distribution parameters have been estimated in a Bayesian framework, as stated previously, in order to incorporate the additional knowledge and to account for the scaling uncertainty.

The parameter uncertainty of additional distributions that fit the data could be introduced in the procedure, leading to larger confidence intervals. However, in this case, only the parameter uncertainty of the inferred models was of interest.

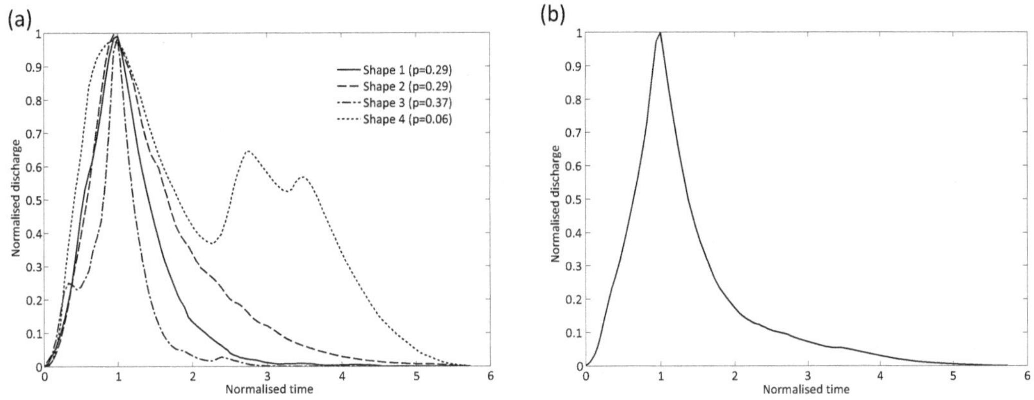

Figure 2. Characteristic normalised hydrograph shapes **(a)** with a certain probability of occurrence and **(b)** "mean" normalised hydrograph shape.

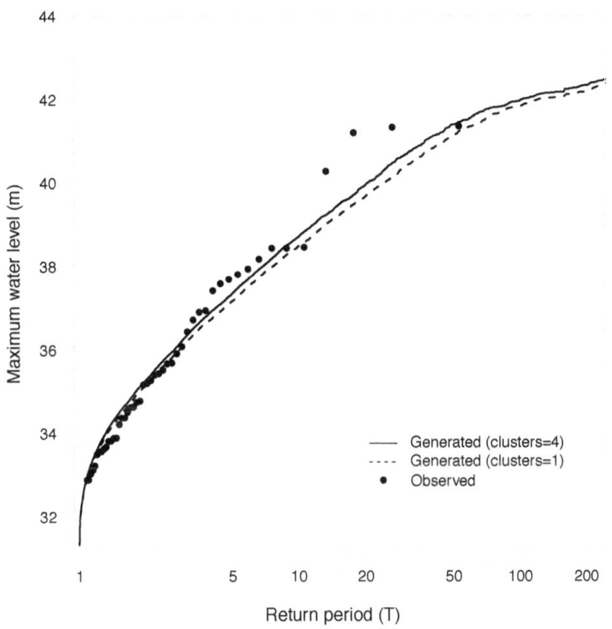

Figure 3. Frequency curves of maximum water level of synthetic hydrographs for four clusters and one cluster and corresponding levels of observed hydrographs.

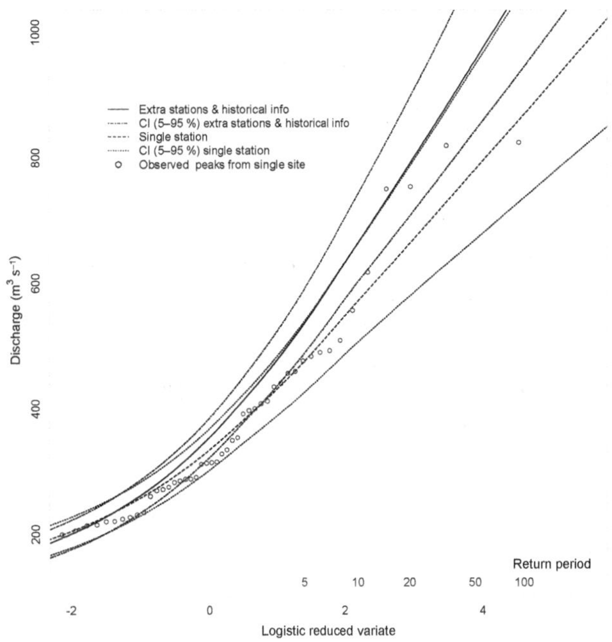

Figure 4. Flood frequency curves with 95 % confidence limits for the single-site data and the multi-site data with the extra information case. Observed peaks are also plotted with the Gringorten plotting position.

4 Results and discussion

Initially, we have clustered the hydrograph shapes into four characteristic groups. After simulating 10 000 peak-volume pairs from the inferred distributions, we assigned to each one a specific hydrograph shape (respecting their frequency of occurrence). Then, we denormalised and routed the hydrographs; we repeated the same procedure but after clustering into only one group, thus considering a global mean hydrograph. The characteristic shapes are depicted in Fig. 2a, along with the mean shape (Fig. 2b). The level frequency curve showed small differences between the two cases (Fig. 3) and, as we shall see later, this difference is negligible in comparison with the estimated uncertainty. So, we have proceeded with the uncertainty assessment considering one mean hydrograph.

We have implemented the Bayesian framework on the peaks extracted from the systematic discharge series recorded at the Bomporto station, adding also the uncertainty of the scaling exponent of the regionalisation relation. In the second scenario, we also included recently recorded annual peaks from other hydrometric stations of the same basin, mentioned previously, as well as information from flood re-

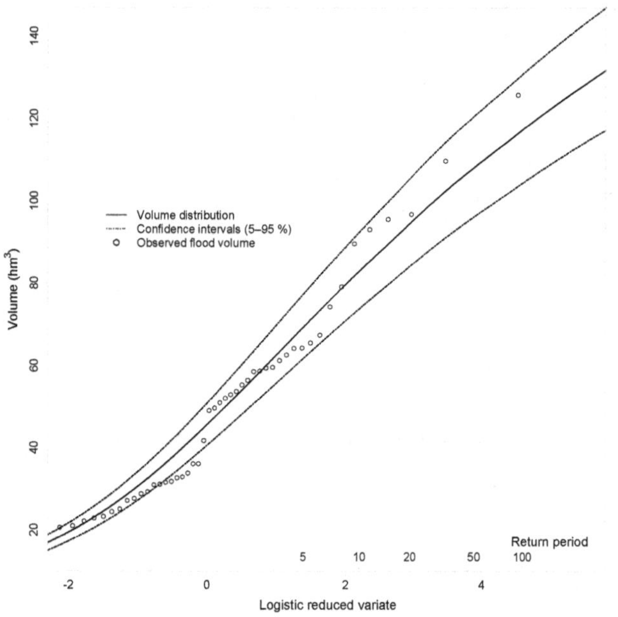

Figure 5. Flood volume curve with 95 % confidence limits. Observed flood volumes are also plotted with the Gringorten plotting position.

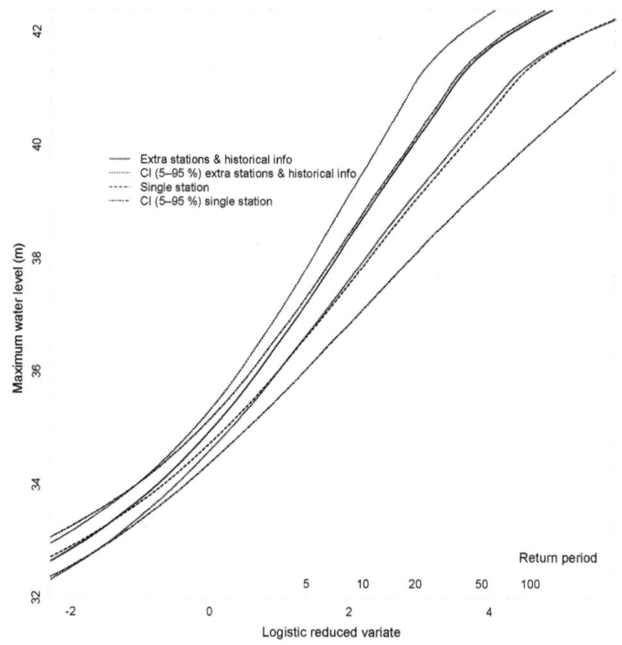

Figure 6. MWL frequency curves with 95 % confidence limits for the single-site data and the multi-site data with the extra information case.

ports, while integrating the uncertainty of the scaling exponent. As it can be seen in Fig. 4, when ignoring the additional information, the estimate of discharge peak is lower for a given return period. We focus our attention on relatively small return periods since any extrapolation beyond the available time period is subject to great uncertainty. Indicatively, a peak with a univariate return period of 50 years can increase by 18 %, exceeding the confidence intervals of the fitted distribution. This occurs because during the last 10 years crucial flood events appeared in the area. In Table 2, we note that in the second case the distribution's mean is bigger and the shape parameter is smaller with a significantly lower standard deviation.

The 95 % confidence interval of both of the peak distributions can be wide (Fig. 4); e.g. for a univariate return period of 50 years, it can span from 665 to 941 $m^3 s^{-1}$ (29 % difference) and from 837 to 1092 $m^3 s^{-1}$ (23 % difference) for the first and second cases.

Similarly, in the case of the flood volume, the 95 % confidence interval for a univariate return period of 50 years can span from 95.5 to 120 hm^3 (20 % difference) (Fig. 5).

The confidence intervals of the parameters of the inferred distributions are presented in Table 2.

The results of the increased peaks are reflected also on the frequency curve of the maximum water level (MWL). The return period here corresponds to a water level, so it is considered structure based, since the level is a function of the structural and operational characteristics of the dam, among others. As it can be seen (Fig. 6), the MWL is significantly lower in the case of no extra information, especially for greater return periods. For a return period of 50 years, the average MWL can differ by 1.2 m – a considerable magnitude in terms of volume and when considering that the safety margin above the spillway's crest is in some cases 1 m.

In Fig. 7, the highest density regions depict a sort of confidence interval of the MWL for specific return periods for each case (single-site information and multi-site with historical information cases). These regions can be defined as the smallest areas in the sample space with a certain probability coverage and they have the advantage of displaying multimodal distributions; thus, they may consist of disjoint subsets (Hyndman, 1996). They are particularly suitable in multivariate cases or for asymmetrical distributions. In the high-density region (HDR) box plots, the mode (horizontal line) substitutes the median and the darker region corresponds to a probability coverage of 50 %, the lighter to a coverage of 95 % and the points outside to the data beyond the 95 % probability.

The span of the highest density regions slightly decreases as more information is introduced. However, this decrease in uncertainty seems small and we cannot come to a conclusion, whereas the extra information has contributed to a systematic uncertainty reduction. An increase in the simulation size could lead to a slightly different picture; however, the added computational burden is prohibitive and anyhow, as Salvadori et al. (2015) stated, a clear rule of thumb regarding the simulation size does not exist. In any case, the size is considered large enough for some safe conclusions, especially for the smaller return periods.

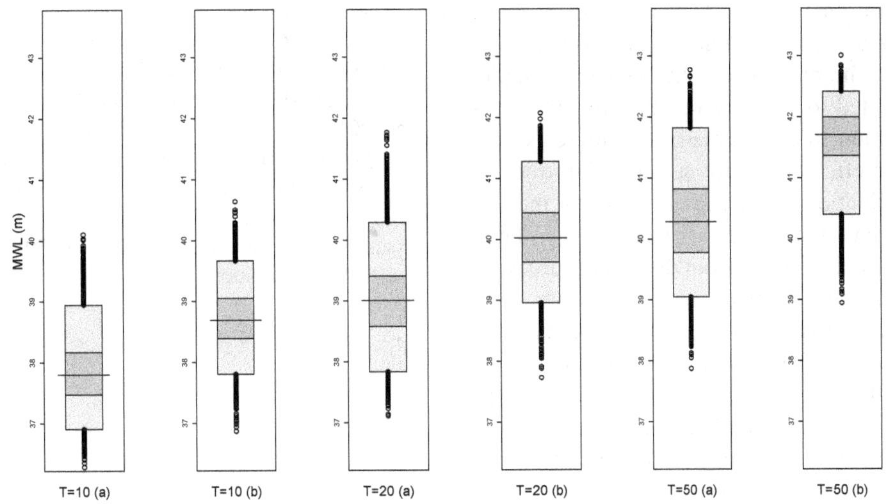

Figure 7. High-density region box plots of MWL for return periods of 10, 20 and 50 years for **(a)** single-site data and **(b)** multi-site data with historical information.

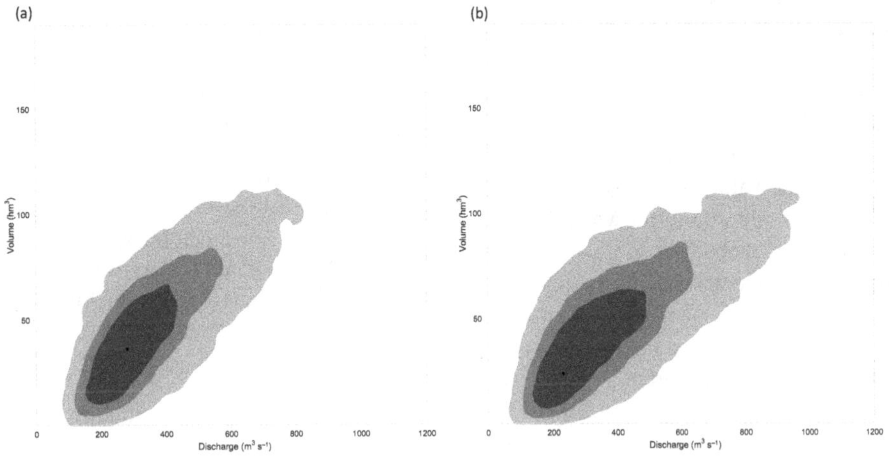

Figure 8. The 50th, 75th and 95th percentiles of the kernel density areas of MWLs with a return period of 50 years on the discharge–volume plane for single-site data **(a)** and multi-site data with historical information **(b)**.

Within a certain return period, the parameter uncertainty can lead to substantial MWL variations, e.g. for 20 years (in the case of extra information), the span of the MWL with a density of 50 and 95 % is of 0.8 and 2.3 m, respectively, which correspond to huge volume differences. These can have devastating effects not only in the case of overtopping but also because the remaining water can cause bank failure due to piping. These spans could increase for larger return periods, where the uncertainty is bound to get vaster.

As the results of previous studies suggested (Serinaldi, 2013; Dung et al., 2015; Zhang et al., 2015; Serinaldi, 2016), the regions of the return periods can overlap; in this case, the 95 % confidence interval of an event of 20 years can include, marginally, the expected values of events of 10 to 50 years (e.g. single-site scenario). For the multi-site with the extra information scenario, the overlapping region is smaller.

In Fig. 8, the highest density regions (50, 75 and 95 %) are depicted in a two-dimensional plane (discharge–volume) that correspond to a return period of 50 years. For events that result in a MWL with a specific return period, the variation of discharge and volume can be huge even when looking in the smaller density regions (e.g. 50 %). For example, in the 95 % region, the discharge can assume values with a univariate return period from 1 to 50 years (for the multi-site scenario), which is a strong indicator of the nonlinearity of the problem. The same applies for the flood volume.

5 Conclusions

This analysis focuses on the uncertainty introduced when calculating the probability of exceeding specific water levels in a flood control reservoir, which is a result of the parameter uncertainty of the marginals of the hydrological variables, as well as the copula multivariate function, due to the small size that characterises, in most cases, a hydrological sample. Therefore, we attempted to quantify this uncertainty, without aiming our attention to copula/marginals inference. Instead, we studied the effect of additional flood information not only on the distribution parameters but also on the uncertainty range in a Bayesian framework that, among others, permits the consideration of errors from different sources.

The extra flood data that included additional peaks from different hydrometric stations led to a peak distribution with bigger mean and smaller shape parameters and thus to elevated peaks, since the data include flood events of recent years that exceed the events of the historical data series in magnitude. Consequently, including the additional information translates into a general bigger estimate of the peaks, which is also reflected on the MWLs, as the peak is a driving factor of the routing process.

The uncertainty range of discharge and volume is considerable and affects, along with the copula parameter, the MWL. The variations in the MWL for the same structure-based return period correspond to significant variation in the stored water volume. Most importantly, the return period of a specific water level cannot be determined with certainty because the return periods of the events overlap. Naturally, the range of discharge and volume values for a given structure-based return period is very ample due to the wide range of the parameters of the inferred distributions.

A clear observation of whether uncertainty is systematically reduced with the introduction of additional information cannot be made here. Nonetheless, a Bayesian framework allows a certain degree of transparency (Parkes and Demeritt, 2016). Incorporating knowledge about water levels during historic events, e.g. at the locality of Navicello for the 1783 and 1842 floods, could result in a more significant change in the uncertainty range, as past research has shown. However, one must consider also the great amount of error involved in these data in the Bayesian framework.

As a general remark, one can deduce that the process of risk estimation is inherently crippled by uncertainty that can be quantified or at least approximated. Any attempt to obscure this uncertainty could create a false notion about its existence in a multivariate problem with eventual implications in dam safety.

Competing interests. The authors declare that they have no conflict of interest.

Acknowledgements. We would like to thank F. Serinaldi and an anonymous referee for their instructive comments and A. Bárdossy for his handling of the manuscript. We would also like to thank Stefano Orlandini for providing us with all the information regarding the Panaro dam. For the routing of the hydrographs, we used the model developed by Gambarelli et al. (2009).

The analysis was implemented in R Statistical Computing Software (R Core Team, 2015) with the use of the following contributed packages: CDVine (Brechmann and Schepsmeier, 2013), Cairo (Urbanek and Horner, 2015), copula (Kojadinovic and Yan, 2010; Yan, 2007), fitdistrplus (Delignette-Muller and Dutang, 2015), goftest (Faraway et al., 2015), hdrcde (Rob J Hyndman with contributions from Jochen Einbeck and Matt Wand, 2013), ks (Duong, 2016), LaplacesDemon (Statisticat, LLC, 2016), lmomco (Asquith, 2015), statmod (Smyth et al., 2015), VGAM (Yee, 2010) and wordcloud (Fellows, 2014).

Edited by: A. Bárdossy

References

Ariff, N. M., Jemain, A. A., Ibrahim, K., and Wan Zin, W. Z.: IDF relationships using bivariate copula for storm events in Peninsular Malaysia, J. Hydrol., 470–471, 158–171, doi:10.1016/j.jhydrol.2012.08.045, 2012.

Aronica, G. T., Candela, A., Fabio, P., and Santoro, M.: Estimation of flood inundation probabilities using global hazard indexes based on hydrodynamic variables, Phys. Chem. Earth A/B/C, 42–44, 119–129, doi:10.1016/j.pce.2011.04.001, 2012.

Asquith, W.: lmomco – L-moments, censored L-moments, trimmed L-moments, L-comoments, and many distributions, r package version 2.1.4, http://www.cran.r-project.org/package=lmomco (last access: 10 May 2017), 2015.

Autorità di bacino del fiume Po: Caratteristiche del bacino del fiume Po e primo esame dell'impatto ambientale delle attività umane sulle risorse idriche, Report, Parma, Italy, 2006.

Balistrocchi, M. and Bacchi, B.: Modelling the statistical dependence of rainfall event variables through copula functions, Hydrol. Earth Syst. Sci., 15, 1959–1977, doi:10.5194/hess-15-1959-2011, 2011.

Balistrocchi, M., Ranzi, R., and Bacchi, B.: Multivariate Statistical Analysis of Flood Variables by Copulas: Two Italian Case Studies, in: 3rd IAHR Europe Congress, 14–16 April 2014, Porto, Portugal, 2014.

Brechmann, E. C. and Schepsmeier, U.: Modeling Dependence with C- and D-Vine Copulas: The R Package CDVine, J. Stat. Softw., 52, 1–27, doi:10.18637/jss.v052.i03, 2013.

Burnham, K. P. and Anderson, D. R.: Multimodel inference understanding AIC and BIC in model selection, Sociolog. Meth. Res., 33.2, 261–304, 2004.

Candela, A., Brigandì, G., and Aronica, G. T.: Estimation of synthetic flood design hydrographs using a distributed rainfall–runoff model coupled with a copula-based single storm rainfall generator, Nat. Hazards Earth Syst. Sci., 14, 1819–1833, doi:10.5194/nhess-14-1819-2014, 2014.

Delignette-Muller, M. L. and Dutang, C.: fitdistrplus: An R Package for Fitting Distributions, J. Stat. Softw., 64, 1–34, doi:10.18637/jss.v064.i04, 2015.

De Michele, C. and Rosso, R.: A multi-level approach to flood frequency regionalisation, Hydrol. Earth Syst. Sci., 6, 185–194, doi:10.5194/hess-6-185-2002, 2002.

De Michele, C. and Salvadori, G.: A Generalized Pareto intensity-duration model of storm rainfall exploiting 2-Copulas, J. Geophys. Res.-Atmos., 108, 4067, doi:10.1029/2002JD002534, 2003.

De Michele, C., Salvadori, G., Canossi, M., Petaccia, A., and Rosso, R.: Bivariate Statistical Approach to Check Adequacy of Dam Spillway, J. Hydrol. Eng., 10, 50–57, doi:10.1061/(ASCE)1084-0699(2005)10:1(50), 2005.

Domeneghetti, A., Vorogushyn, S., Castellarin, A., Merz, B., and Brath, A.: Probabilistic flood hazard mapping: effects of uncertain boundary conditions, Hydrol. Earth Syst. Sci., 17, 3127–3140, doi:10.5194/hess-17-3127-2013, 2013.

Dung, N. V., Merz, B., Bárdossy, A., and Apel, H.: Handling uncertainty in bivariate quantile estimation – An application to flood hazard analysis in the Mekong Delta, J. Hydrol., 527, 704–717, doi:10.1016/j.jhydrol.2015.05.033, 2015.

Duong, T.: ks: Kernel Smoothing, r package version 1.10.4, http://CRAN.R-project.org/package=ks (last access: 10 May 2017), 2016.

Durante, F. and Sempi, C.: Principles of copula theory, CRC Press, Boca Raton, Florida, 2015.

Dyck, S. and Peschke, G.: Grundlagen der Hydrologie, Verlag für Bauwesen, Berlin, 1995.

Faraway, J., Marsaglia, G., Marsaglia, J., and Baddeley, A.: goftest: Classical Goodness-of-Fit Tests for Univariate Distributions, r package version 1.0-3, http://CRAN.R-project.org/package=goftest (last access: 10 May 2017), 2015.

Fellows, I.: wordcloud: Word Clouds, r package version 2.5, http://CRAN.R-project.org/package=wordcloud (last access: 10 May 2017), 2014.

Frahm, G., Junker, M., and Schmidt, R.: Estimating the tail-dependence coefficient: Properties and pitfalls, Insur. Math. Econ., 37, 80–100, doi:10.1016/j.insmatheco.2005.05.008, 2005.

Gambarelli, P., Moretti, G., and Orlandini, S.: Sviluppo di un Modello Matematico del Funzionamento Idraulico della Cassa di Espansione sul Fiume Panaro, Thesis, Università degli Studi di Modena e Reggio Emilia, Modena, Italy, 2009.

Ganguli, P. and Reddy, M. J.: Probabilistic assessment of flood risks using trivariate copulas, Theor. Appl. Climatol., 111, 341–360, doi:10.1007/s00704-012-0664-4, 2013.

Gaume, E., Gaál, L., Viglione, A., Szolgay, J., Kohnová, S., and Blöschl, G.: Bayesian MCMC approach to regional flood frequency analyses involving extraordinary flood events at ungauged sites, J. Hydrol., 394, 101–117, doi:10.1016/j.jhydrol.2010.01.008, 2010.

Genest, C. and Favre, A.: Everything You Always Wanted to Know about Copula Modeling but Were Afraid to Ask, J. Hydrol. Eng., 12, 347–368, doi:10.1061/(ASCE)1084-0699(2007)12:4(347), 2007.

Gräler, B., van den Berg, M. J., Vandenberghe, S., Petroselli, A., Grimaldi, S., De Baets, B., and Verhoest, N. E. C.: Multivariate return periods in hydrology: a critical and practical review focusing on synthetic design hydrograph estimation, Hydrol. Earth Syst. Sci., 17, 1281–1296, doi:10.5194/hess-17-1281-2013, 2013.

Halbert, K., Nguyen, C. C., Payrastre, O., and Gaume, E.: Reducing uncertainty in flood frequency analyses: A comparison of local and regional approaches involving information on extreme historical floods, J. Hydrol., 541, 90–98, doi:10.1016/j.jhydrol.2016.01.017, 2016.

Hyndman, R. J.: Computing and Graphing Highest Density Regions, Am. Statist., 50, 120–126, doi:10.2307/2684423, 1996.

Joe, H.: Dependence modeling with copulas, Chapman and Hall/CRC Press, London, 2014.

Kojadinovic, I. and Yan, J.: Modeling Multivariate Distributions with Continuous Margins Using the copula R Package, J. Stat. Softw., 34, 1–20, doi:10.18637/jss.v034.i09, 2010.

Merz, R. and Blöschl, G.: Flood frequency hydrology: 1. Temporal, spatial, and causal expansion of information, Water Resour. Res., 44, W08432, doi:10.1029/2007WR006744, 2008.

Nelsen, R. B.: An introduction to copulas, in: vol. 139, Springer Science & Business Media, New York, 2006.

Nora, E. and Ghinoi, A.: Alluvioni e terremoti: Principali rischi naturali di Modena nel Novecento, http://www.comune.modena.it/lecittasostenibili/documenti-cittasostenibili/annale-900-citt-ambiente/alluvioni-e-terremoti (last access: 10 May 2017), 2009.

Ouarda, T. B. M. J. and El-Adlouni, S.: Bayesian Nonstationary Frequency Analysis of Hydrological Variables, J. Am. Water Resour. Assoc., 47, 496–505, doi:10.1111/j.1752-1688.2011.00544.x, 2011.

Parent, E. and Bernier, J.: Encoding prior experts judgments to improve risk analysis of extreme hydrological events via POT modeling, J. Hydrol., 283, 1–18, doi:10.1016/S0022-1694(03)00080-5, 2003.

Parkes, B. and Demeritt, D.: Defining the hundred year flood: A Bayesian approach for using historic data to reduce uncertainty in flood frequency estimates, J. Hydrol., 540, 1189–1208, doi:10.1016/j.jhydrol.2016.07.025, 2016.

R Core Team: R: A Language and Environment for Statistical Computing, R Foundation for Statistical Computing, Vienna, Austria, http://www.R-project.org/ (last access: 10 May 2017), 2015.

Reis Jr., D. S. and Stedinger, J. R.: Bayesian MCMC flood frequency analysis with historical information, J. Hydrol., 313, 97–116, doi:10.1016/j.jhydrol.2005.02.028, 2005.

Requena, A. I., Mediero, L., and Garrote, L.: A bivariate return period based on copulas for hydrologic dam design: accounting for reservoir routing in risk estimation, Hydrol. Earth Syst. Sci., 17, 3023–3038, doi:10.5194/hess-17-3023-2013, 2013.

Rob J Hyndman with contributions from Jochen Einbeck and Matt Wand: hdrcde: Highest density regions and conditional density estimation, r package version 3.1, http://CRAN.R-project.org/package=hdrcde (last access: 10 May 2017), 2013.

Salvadori, G. and De Michele, C.: On the Use of Copulas in Hydrology: Theory and Practice, J. Hydrol. Eng., 12, doi:10.1061/(ASCE)1084-0699(2007)12:4(369), 2007.

Salvadori, G., De Michele, C., Kottegoda, N., and Rosso, R.: Extremes in Nature: An Approach Using Copulas, Water Science and Technology Library, 1st Edn., Springer Netherlands, doi:10.1007/1-4020-4415-1, 2007.

Salvadori, G., Durante, F., Tomasicchio, G. R., and D'Alessandro, F.: Practical guidelines for the multivariate assessment of the structural risk in coastal and off-shore engineering, Coast. Eng., 95, 77–83, doi:10.1016/j.coastaleng.2014.09.007, 2015.

Schmidt, R. and Stadtmüller, U.: Non-parametric Estimation of Tail Dependence, Scand. J. Stat. 33, 307–335, doi:10.1111/j.1467-9469.2005.00483.x, 2006.

Serinaldi, F.: An uncertain journey around the tails of multivariate hydrological distributions, Water Resour. Res., 49, 6527–6547, doi:10.1002/wrcr.20531, 2013.

Serinaldi, F.: Can we tell more than we can know? The limits of bivariate drought analyses in the United States, Stoch. Environ. Res. Risk A., 30, 1691–1704, doi:10.1007/s00477-015-1124-3, 2016.

Serinaldi, F., Bárdossy, A., and Kilsby, C. G.: Upper tail dependence in rainfall extremes: would we know it if we saw it?, Stoch. Environ. Res. Risk A., 29, 1211–1233, doi:10.1007/s00477-014-0946-8, 2015.

Servizio Idrografico Italiano: Dati Caratteristici dei Corsi d'Aqcua Italiani, Ministero dei Lavori Pubblici, Istituto Poligrafico dello Stato, Roma, 1939, 1953.

Singh, V. P.: Effect of spatial and temporal variability in rainfall and watershed characteristics on stream flow hydrograph, Hydrol. Process., 11, 1649–1669, doi:10.1002/(SICI)1099-1085(19971015)11:12<1649::AID-HYP495>3.0.CO;2-1, 1997.

Singh, V. P. and Zhang, L.: IDF Curves Using the Frank Archimedean Copula, J. Hydrol. Eng., 12, 651–662, doi:10.1061/(ASCE)1084-0699(2007)12:6(651), 2007.

Sklar, M.: Fonctions de répartition à n dimensions et leurs marges, Université Paris 8, Paris, 1959.

Smyth, G., Hu, Y., Dunn, P., Phipson, B., and Chen, Y.: statmod: Statistical Modeling, r package version 1.4.21, http://CRAN.R-project.org/package=statmod (last access: 10 May 2017), 2015.

Statisticat, LLC: LaplacesDemon: Complete Environment for Bayesian Inference, r package version 16.0.1, https://cran.r-project.org/web/packages/LaplacesDemon/ (last access: 10 May 2017), 2016.

Urbanek, S. and Horner, J.: Cairo: R graphics device using cairo graphics library for creating high-quality bitmap (PNG, JPEG, TIFF), vector (PDF, SVG, PostScript) and display (X11 and Win32) output, r package version 1.5-9, http://CRAN.R-project.org/package=Cairo (last access: 10 May 2017), 2015.

Viglione, A., Merz, R., Salinas, J. L., and Blöschl, G.: Flood frequency hydrology: 3. A Bayesian analysis, Water Resour. Res., 49, 675–692, doi:10.1029/2011WR010782, 2013.

Volpi, E. and Fiori, A.: Hydraulic structures subject to bivariate hydrological loads: Return period, design, and risk assessment, Water Resour. Res., 50, 885–897, doi:10.1002/2013WR014214, 2014.

Yan, J.: Enjoy the Joy of Copulas: With a Package copula, J. Stat. Softw., 21, 1–21, doi:10.18637/jss.v021.i04, 2007.

Yee, T. W.: The VGAM Package for Categorical Data Analysis, J. Stat. Softw., 32, 1–34, doi:10.18637/jss.v032.i10, 2010.

Zhang, L. and Singh, V. P.: Bivariate rainfall frequency distributions using Archimedean copulas, J. Hydrol., 332, 93–109, doi:10.1016/j.jhydrol.2006.06.033, 2007.

Zhang, Q., Xiao, M., and Singh, V. P.: Uncertainty evaluation of copula analysis of hydrological droughts in the East River basin, China, Global Planet. Change, 129, 1–9, doi:10.1016/j.gloplacha.2015.03.001, 2015.

11

Estimation of peak discharges of historical floods

J. Herget, T. Roggenkamp, and M. Krell

Department of Geography, University of Bonn, Bonn, Germany

Correspondence to: J. Herget (herget@giub.uni-bonn.de)

Abstract. There is no doubt that the hazard assessment of future floods, especially under consideration of recent environmental change, can be significantly improved by the consideration of historic flood events. While flood frequency inventories on local, regional and even European scale have already been developed and published, the estimation of their magnitudes indicated by discharges is still challenging. Such data are required due to significant human impacts on river channels and floodplains, though historic flood levels cannot be related to recent ones or recent discharges. Based on experiences from single local key studies, we present the general outline of an approach to estimate the discharge of the previous flood based on handed-down flood level and topographic data. The model for one-dimensional steady flow is based on the empirical Manning equation for the mean flow velocity. Background and potential sources of information, acceptable simplifications and data transformation for each element of the model equation are explained and discussed. Preliminary experiences regarding the accuracy of $\pm 10\,\%$ are documented, and potential approaches for the validation of individual estimations are given. A brief discussion of benefits and limitations, including a generalized statement on alternative approaches, concludes the review of the approach.

1 Introduction

Water level data from previous floods provide important information on potential magnitudes of contemporary floods. Furthermore, information on historic floods enables a comparison with recent floods to help in their classification. Recently, the European Union approved a flood risk estimation guideline that regulates by law the quantitative consideration of previous floods (EU, 2007). Previous floods can be divided into historic and palaeofloods. The distinction of historic and palaeofloods is based on the duration of historic times with handed-down historic documents or descriptions while palaeoflood events took place in prehistoric times. Note that in several previous publications (e.g. Benito et al., 2010; Brázdil et al., 2006; House et al., 2002; Thorndycraft et al., 2005) the term "palaeoflood" is used even for recent flood events quantified by means of indirect methods due to missing gauging stations. According to the established used of the prefix "palaeo", based on the old-Greek origin *palaios*, meaning "old" (e.g. in palaeoclimatology or palaeohydrology), a stricter, only temporal differentiation seems more logical. Historic times with detailed flood descriptions last for about one or two centuries, e.g. in many parts of North America, up to several millennia in the old cultures of ancient Egypt or China (e.g. Bell, 1970; Pang, 1987; Herget, 2012). Consequently, the time of the transfer of historic times flood events to palaeofloods differs regionally. Typically, most historic floods can be dated exactly with high temporal, and partly also spatial, resolution, reaching levels of hydrograph reconstructions with a temporal resolution up to minutes based on historic photographs (Roggenkamp and Herget, 2014). Temporally, palaeoflood evidence based on sedimentary or geomorphological remnants (e.g. Baker et al., 1988; Herget, 2012; House et al., 2002) can only be estimated using relative chronologies or physically based dating techniques like radiocarbon or optical stimulated luminescence and give less exact dates, but might even reach annual resolution for the entire Holocene times if dendrochronological data are available from trees rings in flood plains or varves in lakes (e.g. St. George and Nielsen, 2002; Stoffel et al., 2010; Corella et al., 2014). Palaeofloods can be analysed back throughout Earth's geological history but decrease by number and resolution in pre-Pleistocene times based on the less significant sedimentary evidence (e.g. Herget, 2012; House et al., 2002), while also quantitatively reconstructed

Figure 1. Flood marks of the River Main on the historic city fortification of Eibelstädt near Würzburg.

extraterrestrial flood and drainage events date back in astronomical timescales of billion of years (e.g. Burr et al., 2009). Here, we focus on historic floods in Europe, as their evidence and their relation to recent and near-future flood conditions are more obvious than for palaeofloods from geological times.

Historic flood levels can be found as markings on historic buildings (Fig. 1), identifying the maximum flood level, or in documentary sources (Deutsch et al., 2010). Usually, written descriptions compiled in source text compilations (e.g. Alexandre, 1987; Weikinn, 1958; www.tambora.org; Buisman and Van Engelen, 1995) are qualitative, such as "as a consequence of the flood, great damage was effected along the river at ...", but also semi-quantitative descriptions like "the water reached the doors of the church" are preserved. After careful interpretation and analysis, many of these descriptions can be used as flood level indicators for historic times, as is the case for rivers in Europe (e.g. Brázdil et al., 2012; Glaser et al., 2010; Herget, 2012), depending on the quality and quantity of the data. The approach of flood frequency analysis based on gauged flood events is well established, although the serious problem of statistical unsteadiness of data sets has to be dealt with (e.g. Benito and Thorndycraft, 2005; Kidson and Richards, 2005; Savenije, 1995). By adding a significantly increased number of large flood events before the period of instrumental gauging, these data sets can be enhanced considerably (e.g. Witte et al., 1995; Benito and Thorndycraft, 2005). Direct utilization of these stage records in order to predict actual flood discharges is impossible due to frequent, mainly anthropogenic, modification of channels and nearby floodplains since historic times (e.g. Herget et al., 2005). For comparable discharges, modern water levels would reach a different elevation, in most cases probably higher, due to the decreased cross-section areas related to dykes, constructions and settlements on the floodplain. Therefore, the historic flood levels must first be transformed into historic peak discharges. These discharge values can then be used to estimate comparable modern-day flood levels by deriving peak discharges from historic events. In view of methodological problems, flood discharge estimations based on historic flood levels in urban areas are quite rare (e.g. Benito et al., 2003; Brázdil et al., 1999, 2005, 2006; Glaser et al., 2010; Thorndycraft et al., 2003), and some exceptions prove this rule (e.g. Elleder, 2010; Elleder et al., 2013; Herget and Meurs, 2010; Macdonald et al., 2006; Roggenkamp and Herget, 2014; Wetter et al., 2011).

Below, a review of a simple, suitable and more-or-less easily applicable approach is presented for estimating the discharge of previous floods based on preserved water level data. The method of the calculation itself with a focus on the determination respectively estimation of the parameters is given in detail below and commented based on experiences from previous applications of the approach in several local key studies. A discussion of limits and advantages in comparison with other approaches concludes this review.

2 The method and parameter determination

With the insertion of the empirical Manning equation for mean flow velocity v (Chow, 1959) into the continuity equation describing discharge Q as a product of cross-section area A and flow velocity v, discharges for specified stages of historical flood events can be calculated as

$$Q_i = A_i R_i^{2/3} S_i^{1/2} n_i^{-1}, \tag{1}$$

with Q_i the discharge [$\mathrm{m^3\,s^{-1}}$], A_i the cross-section area [$\mathrm{m^2}$] of the floodplain area for the specific flood level, R_i the hydraulic radius [m] for the flood level determined as a quotient of the cross-section area A_i [$\mathrm{m^2}$] and the wetted perimeter P_i [m], S_i the energy line slope [$\mathrm{m\,m^{-1}}$], and n_i the hydraulic roughness coefficient [-] according to Manning.

For different stages of a flood event, most of the factors of the equation vary (see the following subchapters) and therefore have to be related to a specific stage, e.g. the maximum one of the peak discharge as handed down by most flood marks. Due to the empirical character of the Manning equation, Eq. (1) is not true by units (cf. Chow 1959

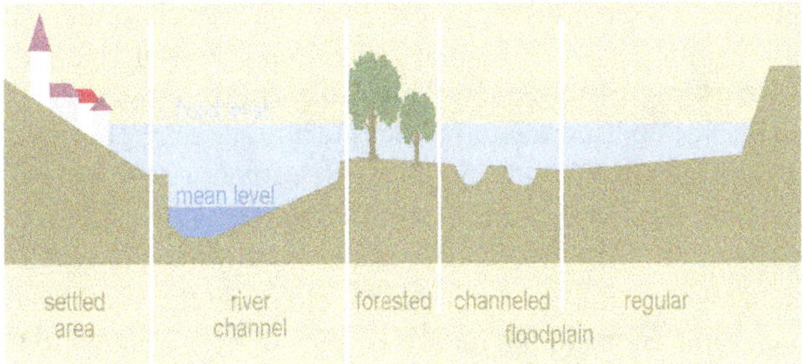

Figure 2. Scheme of homogenous units of floodplains with different hydraulic roughness characteristics (modified from Herget, 2012).

for details and discussion). As Eq. (1) determines the discharge related to a specific stage of a flood, a uniform one-dimensional steady flow is modelled. Ice-jam-related floods (Beltaos, 2008, 2014) cannot be quantified by the approach due to the temporal blockage of the channel as a reason for the flood level instead of an increased discharge.

If one looks more closely, floodplains of river valleys consist of several units with significantly different hydraulic roughness caused by obstructions like buildings or vegetation, surface roughness as a result of minor landforms like floodplain channels, or hills and depressions in addition to different land use (Fig. 2). Generally speaking, the units of settled areas, the river channel, and the floodplain obviously provide different hydraulic roughness. Additionally, they developed and changed differently in historic times, and therefore they have to be considered individually. The floodplain can be further subdivided into open ground of agricultural use, flood plain channels eroded and incised by previous flood events, and floodplain forests with dense vegetation cover dominated by trees and bushes. Consequently, the discharge is calculated separately for individual homogenous units of the inundated cross-section area A and subsequently simplified to a single value for the flood event. Each of the units has to be reconstructed for its appearance and hydraulic roughness at the point of time the historic flood event occurred. Uniform flow within each unit is assumed.

Within each of the units, the parameters of Eq. (1) are quantified according to the scheme illustrated in Fig. 3 and individually explained in detail below. In case significant uncertainties arise for the flood event itself – e.g. different water levels from different reliable and verified sources or missing information if the debris of a destroyed stone bridge filled and blocked the river channel during the flood event or not (cf. Herget et al., 2014, for details of these problems related to the July 1342 flood event) – different scenarios based on varying assumptions should be considered. Arguments for or against the plausibility of the individual scenarios can be based on the derived discharge calculations and their relation to discharge calculations at additional locations up- or downstream along the river for the same event.

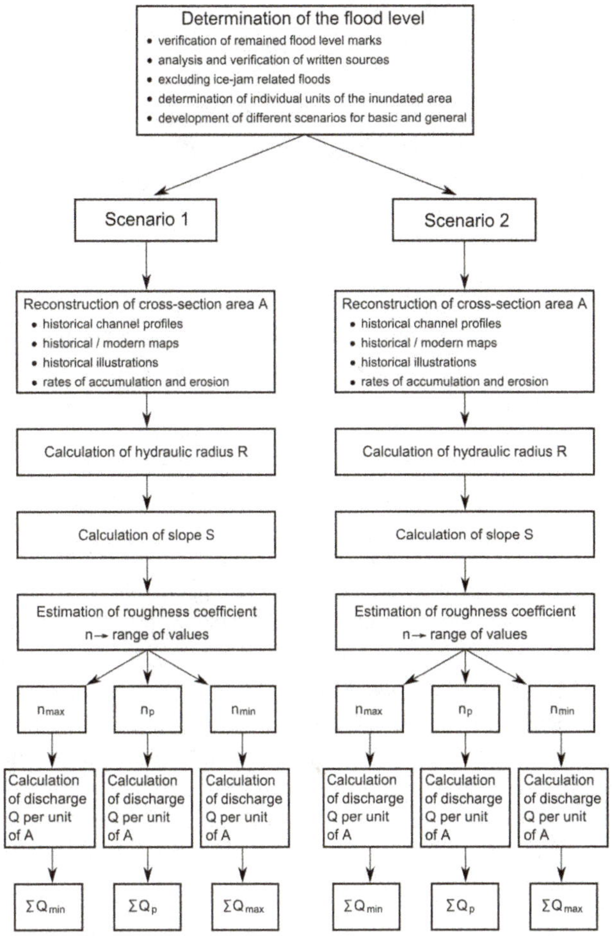

Figure 3. Scheme of discharge calculation and main aspects of parameter quantification.

2.1 Cross-section area A

As illustrated in Fig. 2, the level of the specific flood of interest dominates the magnitude of the cross-section area A. The reconstruction of the topography of the inundated floodplain area is based on data from historic maps, etchings and drawings. Typically, locations of historic importance with verified flood marks will have already experienced rather detailed investigation of their urban archaeology. Based on these illustrations and archaeological studies, any significant topographic change – including land use change on the floodplain and expansion of the settlement – can be backtracked qualitatively and partly even quantitatively by the thickness of time-specific sedimentary layers through time. For reference, modern large-scale topographic maps with detailed elevation data can be used and differences as a result of erosion or accumulation through time quantified along the profile of the cross-section area. Based on experiences it is recommended that all data be converted into metric units and related to metres above sea level, as local reference points (such as gauge datum), measurement units, and calibrations (such as map datum) were changed through historic times. The use of relative values like height above gauge datum might be a source of confusion.

According to elevation changes, the separated units of the inundated floodplain (Fig. 2) show different characteristics and require detailed investigations. For the areas of the settlement itself, a tendency towards accumulation can be observed. The background is the typical repeated rebuilding of historic settlements after destruction by fire, war or systematic modernization on top of the remnants and debris of the previous buildings. In particular, measures for the stabilization of shorelines at harbour areas in order to protect against minor floods result in significant accumulation. In Cologne, the anthropogenic embankment of the nearshore areas towards the River Rhine measures up to 10 m locally for the last 2000 years (Herget and Meurs, 2010) Due to anthropogenic measures, changes within the settled areas took place at certain points of time, while more-or-less continuous rates of aggradation or erosion can be observed in the neighbouring river channel and on the floodplain. Destructive single events, like the July 1342 flood, resulting from intensive erosive rainfall with local immense accumulations of colluvial deposits (Bork, 2014; Kiss, 2009; Zbinden, 2011) illustrate the complexity of the phenomenon. Nonetheless, for urban areas where the long-lasting handed-down flood level history is localized, the simplification of the trends mentioned above provides a framework for potential results of detailed local investigations.

As most large river channels are excavated to improve navigation and narrowed to provide space for additional settlements, the natural conditions are rarely preserved. Due to missing systematic investigations and measurements, data on natural river channel geometry from historic times are rare. Only occasionally have systematic bathymetric measurements been carried out and documented in detail and thus considered in detail for channel reconstructions (e.g. Elleder et al., 2013; Herget and Meurs, 2010). Frequently, reports and plans regarding how to improve river channel conditions in the historic near-future provide data about maximum values of natural channel depths, as the excavated channels will be deeper than the natural ones. If no historic maps or paintings exist that are more or less true to scale, the construction and lengths of bridges might support first estimations of historic channel widths (BGU, 2011). Based on the oldest data on channel geometry, previous conditions can be estimated by means of the extrapolation of handed-down geometry considering natural incision or aggradation rates. Theoretically, numerous aspects like change in trends as a result of tectonic movement, climatic change, or land use change resulting in variability of the hydrology and sediment budget might be expected to cause serious problems for such extrapolation. On the other hand, the time period back to the earliest historic flood events with sufficient data for a quantitative reconstruction in Europe dates back to late medieval times. Annual natural rates of incision of rivers of, for example, $1\ \text{mm}\,\text{a}^{-1}$ – which is a rather unrealistically high value considering differences in altitude of river terraces (Bridgland and Westaway, 2008; Schirmer, 1995) – would result in a difference of a few decimetres. As we are dealing with high-magnitude deep-water floods inundating flood plains with widths of several kilometres, depth variations of such dimensions in the relatively narrow river channel itself do not influence the dimension of entire cross-section area significantly (compare, for example, Elleder et al., 2013, or Herget and Meurs, 2010, with different observations on natural river channel trends in historic times). Note that this preliminary assessment should not be transferred arbitrarily to any river channel, as, globally speaking, more extreme trends such as more-or-less natural aggradations of > 10 m in just one century are also observable (Qingchao, 1989).

The width of the neighbouring floodplains in historic times might be considerably underestimated, as dykes allowed for the expansion of settlements and the installation of infrastructure (Schenk, 2001). For example, the width of the natural floodplain of the River Rhine at Cologne is about 9000 m, while the recent distance between the dykes or rather higher terrace levels is down to 350 m (Herget and Meurs, 2010). The floodplains have the tendency to rise as a result of the deposition of suspension load during floods. The accumulation of the sediments might have reached significant thickness, but must be differentiated by age. Geological and soil maps or archaeological excavations provide suitable information about the age of the floodplain deposits. Like for the river channel incision, a closer look at elevation changes derived from extrapolated aggradation rates reveals a minor influence for broad floodplains in Europe. Local exceptions related to extreme events – such as the 1342 flood mentioned above, or the rise of the valley bottom of 3.9 m since about 1210 in the village of Grünsfeldhausen, located in a small valley 10 km southwest of Würzburg, indicated by the level of the entrance of the church below the surface (Hahn, 1992) – are again exceptions to the rule. On the other hand, these examples again illustrate the necessity of careful investigation for local studies.

2.2 Hydraulic radius *R*

The hydraulic radius is calculated as $R = A/P$, where A is the cross-section area and P is the wetted perimeter; it considers the shape of the cross-section area, as along the shores and the channel bottom, roughness elements decrease the mean flow velocity. Like the cross-section area, the wetted perimeter can be determined from modern topographic maps with consideration of the same properties of the features along the profile as discussed for the cross-section area.

2.3 Slope S

Strictly speaking, the slope, S, is the slope of the energy line along the flow direction (Chow, 1959). It can be seen from closer inspection along river section of sufficient length that the slope of the water surface and the energy line are parallels, which significantly eases the quantification. Within the region of the cross-section profile, no significant backwater effects from narrow culverts at bridges or other obstructions like mills or weirs, including cliffs at the channel bottom, should influence the water level at the flood stage. If no significant obstacle has been introduced since the occurrence of the historic floods of interest, the recent slope of the water surface can be transferred, as incisions or aggradations occurred over a longer section, resulting in a parallel rise or lowering of the energy line. For a known slope S and assurance that the water level was not influenced along the way, heights of flood level marks from other locations within the area of the study can be transferred to the cross-section profile. Note that their absolute height must be modified considering the value of the slope.

2.4 Hydraulic roughness n

The hydraulic roughness reducing the mean flow velocity is quantified by empirical values based on experiences and is available from tables and manuals (e.g. Arcement and Schneider, 1989; Barnes, 1967; Chow, 1959). Chow (1959, 101 pp.) analysed the elements affecting the hydraulic roughness and found the principal algebraic form of

$$n = (n_1 + n_2 + n_3 + n_4 + n_5 + n_6 + n_7 + n_8 + n_9)m, \qquad (2)$$

where n_1 represents surface roughness, n_2 vegetation, n_3 channel irregularity, n_4 channel alignment, n_5 obstructions, n_6 silting and scouring, n_7 stage and discharge, n_8 sediment load (density of water), n_9 seasonal changes, and m a correction factor for channel meandering.

Assuming that the sediment load did not reach concentrations of hydraulic influence like hyper-concentrated flow during the historic flood event of interest, and considering the steady flow conditions modelled, the summands $n_6 - n_9$ do not require further consideration. Consequently, Eq. (2) is simplified to

$$n = (n_1 + n_2 + n_3 + n_4 + n_5)m. \qquad (3)$$

These roughness elements are components reducing the mean one-dimensional flow velocity as result of turbulences. Surface roughness n_1 is caused by larger or smaller grain size of the sediments at the channel bottom up to minor submerged obstacles. The influence of vegetation n_2 obviously changes throughout the year and hence differs for the same floodplain by season. Channel irregularities n_3 are typically submerged bedforms such as local scour holes, sedimentary bars, or riffles and pool structures influencing the vertical component of the current above. The channel alignment n_4 is the similar horizontal effect generated by any deviation in the lateral shores from a straight line. Obstructions n_5 are large obstacles within the channel or floodplain, like trees or houses, that might reach from the bottom up to the surface of the flood level. Any deviation in the river channel or floodplain orientation from a straight line, such as a meander, generates secondary currents which reduce the main one-dimensional flow velocity. Hence, the degree of the deviation from straight is proportional to a value of $m > 1$, which increases the roughness and decreases the mean flow velocity.

From the references mentioned above, values for each component of Eq. (3) can be taken. The degree of the strength of the roughness characteristic varies and requires experiences with the estimation of the representative value. Therefore, in the source tables, data ranges with minimum, typical and maximum values for classified degrees of the development of each element are given. As it is already challenging to estimate a suitable roughness value for recent channels, the limited detailed information on historic channel conditions increases the uncertainty significantly. Consequently, the range of n values is taken over into the final discharge calculation, resulting in minimum (for upper range roughness), maximum (for lower range roughness) and a plausibly balanced representative value for each roughness component (Fig. 3). The value of n_p that has been balanced according to all available information is not necessarily the mean value between n_{min} and n_{max} but is frequently chosen so arbitrarily due to missing detailed information. For each unit of the cross-section profile, three roughness values of a range of $n_{min} < n_p < n_{max}$ are estimated to take into account the individual aspects of hydraulic roughness, consequently resulting in three discharge values that are finally summarized separately to the flood discharge of the entire cross-section.

Based on experiences from previous key studies, the different units of a cross section have specific roughness characteristics, which are briefly summarized below.

Flood water in inundated modern cities with relatively broad, straight roads is, compared with medieval towns, frequently standing and does not flow through town (e.g. Elleder et al., 2013; Herget and Meurs, 2010; Roggenkamp and Herget, 2014). Obviously the roughness exceeds a threshold and prevents the water from flowing as fast as on the open floodplain or within the river channel. Considering that most historic towns were fortified with a surrounding city wall and typically featured narrow winding alleys instead of the recent four-lane straight roads, this effect might have been even stronger. This phenomenon, indicated by a mirror effect visible on photographs of inundated areas, has significant consequences for discharge estimation, as the dense settled areas of the floodplain might be left out since the water there is standing and not moving. Note that this important observation requires further confirmation but so far provides significant simplification, as high-resolution topographic data from within medieval cities would be hard to determine.

Table 1. Comparison chart for estimated and measured peak discharges of selected flood events (partly from Meurs, 2006, and Roggenkamp, 2012).

Flood event	River/city	Estimated peak discharge [$m^3\ s^{-1}$]			Gauge data [$m^3\ s^{-1}$]	Difference Q_p to Q_{gauge}
		Q_{min}	Q_p	Q_{max}	Q_{gauge}	
November 1882	Rhine/Andernach	8970	9785	10 762	10 700	−9 %
November 1882	Rhine/Düsseldorf	7391	8648	10 549	10 400	−17 %
November 1882	Rhine/Rees	6047	7326	9422	10 200	−28 %
January 1883	Rhine/Mainz	4455	5060	5860	6940	−27 %
January 1883	Rhine/Andernach	8317	9073	9980	< 9530	−5 %
January 1883	Rhine/Düsseldorf	6965	8142	9915	9710	−16 %
January 1883	Rhine/Rees	6200	7518	9676	10 500	−28 %
April 1983	Rhine/Cologne	7800	9100	10 200	9486	−4 %
May 1983	Rhine/Cologne	7950	9300	10 400	9724	−4 %
March 1988	Rhine/Cologne	7950	9300	10 400	9708	−4 %
December 1993	Rhine/Cologne	8750	10 250	11 450	10 836	−5 %
January 1995	Rhine/Cologne	8900	10 450	11 650	10 939	−4 %
January 2003	Rhine/Cologne	7650	8950	10 000	9329	−4 %
May 1984	Ahr/Altenahr	148	182	232	192	−5 %
March 1988	Ahr/Altenahr	143	176	225	190	−7 %

As the reconstruction of the geometry of historic river channels is already a challenge, an even more detailed determination of their roughness elements and the degree of their development appears rather unlikely. The uncertainty regarding the existence and dimensions of mobile bedforms such as gravel dunes or water plants illustrates the problem. On the other hand, the reconstruction of historic floods typically has to do with large-scale, high-magnitude events of considerable water depth. In particular, the significantly increased depth of flow in relation to mean flow conditions and its characteristic expansion of the entire floodplain obviously reduce the significance of the uncertainty regarding these relatively minor roughness elements.

Open floodplains near historic locations like cities or monasteries with localized flood level information have typically been used for agriculture. Even though knowledge on plants, techniques and methods used in historic agriculture is well developed, a high-resolution picture cannot be determined. The reason is that it is impossible to estimate, with regard to location, which kind of plant, of which size, and of which seasonal leaf development exactly was growing at the point of time of the flood occurrence. Based on the season the flood occurred, a more general picture of dense or, conversely, missing agricultural vegetation cover with characteristic roughness value ranges can be plausibly quantified. Parts of the floodplain might have remained forested, but there are uncertainties about species and densities, like for the areas of agricultural use as mentioned before. Barnes (1967) documented photographic evidence of the appearance of floodplain forests with measured roughness values that might ease estimations for historic environmental conditions, at least for a plausible magnitude of n values. Even though the floodplain channels might still be delimitable in recent urban topography (e.g. http://www.hw-karten.de/koeln/ for the example of Cologne), their historic appearance is not documented. Within the agriculturally used floodplain, the incised and rather wet channels due to close groundwater contact were only disturbing agricultural activities and not worth further mention. From the recent topography, minimum values of these channels' dimensions are indicated by their steep lateral slopes grown over with bushes, and relatively dense vegetation cover (cf. Herget and Meurs, 2010). Consideration of expanded floodplains of such uncertain characteristics like those characterized above with spread roughness value ranges explains why the approach presented here will always result in flood discharge ranges and not distinct values, regardless of what future improvements to the approach will look like.

2.5 Validation and plausibility check

Validation of the estimated discharge data is possible by the application of the method on recent flood events and comparison of the estimation with gauge data. Table 1 presents mainly unpublished data based on flood reconstruction along the rivers Rhine and Ahr, a minor tributary upstream from Bonn. Note that no improvements to the flood discharge estimations were carried out by adaptation of n values to narrow the differences with measured discharges.

Even though the comparisons documented in Table 1 are not representative, a tendency towards underestimation of flood discharge for Q_p values is obvious. Typically, Q_p estimations are up to 10 % less than the related gauge data, while floods modelled in the low-level gentle slope regions of the Lower Rhine at Düsseldorf and Rees differ even more. Due to limited possibilities for gauge calibrations, even discharge measurements of recent floods with water levels very far beyond bankfull inundating a broad differently structured floodplain are less certain (e.g. Morgenschweis, 2011).

An additional approach for plausibility testing is the repeated reconstruction of flood discharges along rivers at different locations and checking of consistency, e.g. increasing discharge downstream of confluences with major tributaries or relation to reliable locations for the same event (e.g. Elleder et al., 2013).

3 Conclusions

Based on sufficient historic background data such as water level and previous topography, the approach is suitable for estimating the discharge of historic flood events with an accuracy of approximately ±10 %. Application of the approach to recent floods and comparison with gauge data indicate a tendency towards underestimation of the discharge based on data available so far. Questionable data like contradictory handed-down flood level data/information and uncertainties about the influence of destroyed bridges probably filling the river channel (e.g. Herget et al., 2014) can be dealt with by modelling different scenarios and use of subsequent plausibility checks of the estimated discharge data with additional locations up- and downstream from the river. Additional sources of error are less significant than one might expect, as high water levels over broadly inundated floodplains compensate for less distinct values of the river channel morphology, the historic accumulation level of floodplain sediments or extrapolated incision and accumulation rates. Rather time-consuming is the research regarding historic data on river channel conditions, high-resolution historic topography, and data of annual incision or accumulation rates of the river channel and floodplain in historic times.

The model itself is rather basic, considering simplified current patterns of one-dimensional steady flow that are far below the real flow pattern of a passing-through flood wave. Two- or three-dimensional models for unsteady flow would obviously be more realistic, but usually cannot be fed with sufficient high-resolution input data based on evidence from historic times. Some exceptions (e.g. Bürger et al., 2006; Calanda et al., 2003) prove this rule and might be considered for scientific and methodological interest rather than applied flood hazard assessment. Note that an increase in model complexity does not automatically lead to an improved result, neither by spatial resolution nor accuracy, but is much more complicated to deal with (Carling et al., 2003).

Further improvement and development of the approach might occur as a result of dealing with flood flow currents passing through settled areas. High-resolution data on the detailed structure at the point of time of a specific flood event is as challenging as the flow itself. A possible perspective could be either high-resolution modelling or the estimation of hydraulic roughness n values for settled areas.

Author contributions. T. Roggenkamp and M. Krell carried out local studies along the Rivers Ahr and Rhine (T. Roggenkamp) and Rhine and Main (M. Krell). J. Herget prepared the manuscript based on their material and previous own and other publications, and the manuscript that was ultimately submitted was checked by all co-authors.

Acknowledgements. The authors thank numerous colleagues for their support through provision of data and access to material for the key studies providing the background for this review paper. The investigations were kindly support by the German Research Foundation (DFG) (HE 3006/9-1).

Edited by: G. Blöschl

References

Alexandre, P.: Le climat en Europe au Moyen Age, École des hautes études en sciences socials, Paris, 1987.

Arcement, G. J. and Schneider, V. R.: Guide for selecting Manning's roughness coefficients for natural channels and flood plains. USGS Water Supply Paper 2339, United States Geological Survey, Denver, 1989.

Baker, V. R., Kochel, R. C., and Patton, P. C. (Eds.): Flood geomorphology, Wiley, New York, 1988.

Barnes, H. H.: Roughness characteristics of natural channels. USGS Water Supply Papers 1849, United States Geological Survey, Denver, 1967.

Bell, B.: The oldest records of the Nile floods, Geograph. J., 136, 569–573, 1970.

Beltaos, S.: Progress in study and management of river ice jams, Cold Reg. Sci. Tech., 51, 51, 2–19, 2008.

Beltaos, S.: Hydrodynamic properties of ice-jam release waves in the Mackenzie Delta, Canada, Cold Reg. Sci. Technol., 103, 91–106, doi:10.1016/j.coldregions.2014.03.011, 2014

Benito, G. and Thorndycraft, V. R. (Eds.): Systematic, palaeoflood and historical data for the improvement of flood risk estimation – methodological guidelines, Centro de Ciencias Medioambientales, Madrid, 2005.

Benito, G., Díez-Herrero, A., and de Villalta, M.: Magnitude and frequency of flooding in the Tagus river (Central Spain) over the last millennium, Clim. Change, 58, 171–192, 2003.

Benito, G., Rico, M., Sánchez-Moya, Y., Sopeña, A., Thorndycraft, V. R., and Barriendos, M.: The impact of late Holocene climatic variability and land use change on the flood hydrology of the Guadalentín River, southeast Spain, Global Planet. Change, 70, 53–63, 2010.

BGU: Bayerische Gesellschaft für Unterwasserarchäologie (Ed.): Archäologie der Brücken, Pustet, Regensburg, 2011

Bork, H.-R.: Spuren in der Landschaft – extreme Witterungsereignisse während des Spätmittelalters und ihre Folgen, Deutsche Wasserhistorische Gesellschaft Schriften 22, 107–126, Siegburg, 2014.

Brázdil, R., Dobrovolný, P., Elleder, L., Kakos, V., Kotyza, O., Květoň, V., Macková, J., Müller, M., Štekl, J., Tolasz, R., and Valášek, H.: Historical and recent floods in the Czech Republic. Masaryk University/Czech Hydrometeorological Institut, Brno/Prague, 2005.

Brázdil, R., Glaser, R., Pfister, Ch., Dobrovolný, P., Antoine, J.-M., Barriendos, M., Camuffo, D., Deutsch, M., Enzi, S., Guidoboni, E., Kotyza, O., and Sanchez Rodrigo, F.: Flood events of selected European rivers in the sixteenth century, Clim. Change, 43, 239–285, 1999.

Brázdil, R., Kundzewicz, Z. W., and Benito, G.: Historical hydrology for studying flood risk in Europe, Hydrolog. Sci. J., 51, 739–764, 2006.

Brázdil, R., Kundzewicz, Z. W., Benito, G., Demarée, G., Macdonald, N., and Roald, L. A.: Historical floods in Europe in the past millennium, in: Changes in flood risk in Europe, edited by: Kundzewicz, Z. W., IAHS Special Publication 10, 121–166, Wallingford, 2012.

Bridgland, D. and Westway, R.: Preservaton patterns of Late Cenozoic fluvial deposits and their implications – results from IGCP 449, Quaternary Int., 189, 5–38, 2008.

Buisman, J. and van Engelen, A.: Duizend jaar weer wind en water in de Lage Landen, Van Wijnen, Franeker, 1995–2006 (five volumes).

Bürger, K., Dostal, P., Seidel, J., Imbery, F., Barriendos, M., Mayer, H., and Glaser, R.: Hydrometeorological reconstruction of the 1824 flood event in the Neckar River basin (southwest Germany), Hydrol. Sc. J., 51, 864–877, 2006.

Burr, D. M., Carling, P. A., and Baker, V. R. (Eds.): Megaflooding on Earth and Mars. Cambridge University Press, Cambridge, 2009.

Calanda, G., Calvani, L., and Mancini, P.: Simulation of the great flood of December 1870 in Rome, Water Maritim. Eng., 156, 305–312, 2003.

Carling, P., Kidson, R., Cao, Z., and Herget, J.: Palaeohydraulics of extreme flood events – reality and myth, in:Palaeohydrology – understanding global change, edited by: Gregory, K. J. and Benito, G., Wiley, Chichester, 325–336, 2003.

Chow, V. T.: Open channel hydraulics, McGraw-Hill, New York, 1959.

Corella, J. P., Benito, G., Rodriguez-Lloveras, X., Brauer, A., and Valero-Garcés, B. L.: Annually-resolved lake record of extreme hydro-meteorological events since AD 1347 in NE Iberian Peninsula, Quaternary Sc. Rev., 93, 77–90, 2014.

Deutsch, M., Glaser, R., Pörtge, K.-H., Börngen, M., Drescher, A., Martin, B., Riemann, D., and Schönbein, J.: Historische Hochwasserereignisse in Mitteleuropa – Quellenkunde, Interpretation und Auswertung, Geographische Rundschau 3, 18–24, 2010.

Elleder, L., Herget, J., Roggenkamp, T., and Nießen, A.: Historic floods in the city of Prague – reconstruction of peak discharges, Hydrol. Res., 44, 202–214, 2013.

Elleder, L.: Reconstruction of the 1784 flood hydrograph fort he Vlatava River in Prague, Czech Republic, Global Planet. Change, 70, 117–124, 2010.

EU: Richtlinie 2007/60/EG des Europäischen Parlamentes und des Rates vom 23. Oktober 2007 über die Bewertung und das Management von Hochwasserrisiken, Amtsblatt der Europäischen Union, L 288, 27–34, Brussels, 2007.

Glaser, R., Riemann, D. Schönbein, J., Barriendos, M., Brázdil, R., Bertolin, C., Camuffo, D. Deutsch, M., Dobrovolný, P., van Engelen, A., Enzi, S., Halíčková, M., Koenig, S. J., Kotyza, O., Limanówka, D., Macková, J., Sghedoni, M., Martin, B., and Himmelsbach, I.: The variability of European floods since AD 1500, Clim. Change, 101, 235–256, 2010.

Hahn, H.-U.: Die morphogenetische Wirksamkeit historischer Niederschläge, Würzburger Geographische Arbeiten, 82, 1–196, Würzburg, 1992.

Herget, J.: Am Anfang war die Sintflut – Hochwasserkatastrophen in der Geschichte, Primus, Darmstadt, 2012.

Herget, J. and Meurs, H.: Reconstructing peak discharges for historic flood levels in the city of Cologne - Germany, Global Planet. Change, 70, 108–116, 2010.

Herget, J., Bremer, E., Coch, T., Dix, A., Eggenstein, G., and Ewald, K.: Engineering impact on river channels in the River Rhine catchment, Erdkunde, 59-3/4, 294–319, 2005.

Herget, J., Kapala, A., Krell, M., Rustemeier, E., Simmer, C., and Wyss, A.: Neues zur Magdalenenflut vom Juli 1342, Deutsche Wasserhistorische Gesellschaft Schriften, 22, 77–106, Siegburg, 2014.

House, P. K., Webb, R. H., Baker, V. R., and Levish, D. R. (Eds.): Ancient floods, modern hazards – principles and applications of paleoflood hydrology, American Geophysical Union, Washington, 2002.

Kidson, R. and Richards, K. S.: Flood frequency analysis – assumptions and alternatives, Prog. Phys. Geog., 29, 392–410, 2005.

Kiss, A.: Floods and weather in 1342 and 1343 in the Carpathian Basin, J. Environmental Geog., II, 37–47, 2009.

Macdonald, N., Werritty, A., Black, A. R., and McEwen, L. J.: Historical and pooled flood frequency analysis for the River Tay at Perth – Scotland, Area, 38, 34–46, 2006.

Meurs, H.: Bestimmung der Spitzenabflüsse historischer Hochwasser in Köln. Diploma thesis, Department of Geography, University of Bonn, 2006.

Morgenschweis, G.: Hydrometrie, Springer, Berlin, 2011.

Pang, K. D.: Extraordinary floods in early Chinese history and their absolute dates, J. Hydrol., 96, 139–155, 1987.

Qingchao, Y.: Fluvial processes of the lower Yellow River and estimation of flood conditions, in: Taming the Yellow River – silt and floods, edited by: Brush, L. M., Wolman, M. G., and Bing-Wei, H., Kluwer, Dordrecht, 261–274, 1989.

Roggenkamp, T. and Herget, J: Reconstructing peak discharges of historic floods of the River Ahr – Germany, Erdkunde, 68, 49–59, 2014.

Roggenkamp, T.: Rekonstruktion historischer Hochwasser der Ahr. Diploma thesis, Department of Geography, University of Bonn, 2012.

Savenije, H. G. G.: Recent extreme floods in Europe and the USA – challenges for the future, Phys. Chem. Earth, 20, 433–437, 1995.

Schenk, W.: Auen als Siedlungs- und Wirtschaftsräume vor den ingenieurtechnischen Veränderungen des 19. Jhs. – das Mittelmaingebiet als Beispiel, Z. Geomorph. N.F. Suppl.-Bd., 124, 55–67, 2001.

Schirmer, W.: Valley bottoms in the late Quaternary, Z.f. Geomorph. N.F. Suppl., 100, 27–51, 1995.

St. George, S. and Nielsen, E.: Flood ring evidence and its application to paleoflood hydrology of the Red River and Assiniboine River in Manitoba, Géogr Phys. Quatern., 56, 181–190, 2002.

Stoffel, M., Bollschweiler, M., Butler, D. R., and Luckman, B. H. (Eds.): Tree rings and natural hazards – a state of the art, Springer, Dortrecht, 2010.

Thorndycraft, V. R., Benito, G., Barriendos, M., and Llasat, M. C. (Eds.): Palaeofloods, historical data & climatic variability – applications in flood risk assessment, Centro de Ciencias Medioambientales, Madrid, 2003.

Thorndycraft, V. R., Benito, G., Rico, M., Sopeña, A., Sánchez, Y., and Casas, M.: A long-term flood discharge record derived from slackwater flood deposits of the Llobregat River, NE Spain, J. Hydrol., 313, 16–31, 2005.

Weikinn, C.: Quellentexte zur Witterungsgeschichte Europas von der Zeitenwende bis zum Jahre 1850 – Band 1 – Zeitenwende bis 1500, Akademie, Berlin, 1958.

Wetter, O., Pfister, Ch., Weingartner, R., Luterbacher, J., Reist, T., and Trösch, J.: The largest floods in the High Rhine basin since 1268 assessed from documentary and instrumental evidence, Hydrol. Sci. J., 56, 733–758, 2011.

Witte, W., Krahe, P., and Liebscher, H.-J.: Rekonstruktion der Witterungsverhältnisse im Mittelrheingebiet von 1000 n.Chr. bis heute anhand historischer hydrologischer Ereignisse, Internationale Kommission für die Hydrologie des Rheingebietes KHR, Bericht II-9, Lelystad, 1995.

Zbinden, E.: Das Magdalenenhochwasser von 1342 – der hydrologische Gau in Mitteleuropa, Wasser Energie Luft, 103, 193–203, 2011.

12

Improvement of the SWAT model for event-based flood simulation on a sub-daily timescale

Dan Yu[1], **Ping Xie**[1,2], **Xiaohua Dong**[3,4], **Xiaonong Hu**[5], **Ji Liu**[3,4], **Yinghai Li**[3,4], **Tao Peng**[3,4], **Haibo Ma**[3,4], **Kai Wang**[6], **and Shijin Xu**[6]

[1]State Key Laboratory of Water Resources and Hydropower Engineering Science, Wuhan University, Wuhan, 430072, China

[2]Collaborative Innovation Center for Territorial Sovereignty and Maritime Rights, Wuhan, 430072, China

[3]College of Hydraulic & Environmental Engineering, China Three Gorges University, Yichang, 443002, China

[4]Hubei Provincial Collaborative Innovation Center for Water Security, Wuhan, 430070, China

[5]Institute of Groundwater and Earth Sciences, Jinan University, Guangzhou, 510632, China

[6]Hydrologic Bureau of Huaihe River Commission, Bengbu, 233001, China

Correspondence: Xiaohua Dong (xhdong@ctgu.edu.cn)

Abstract. Flooding represents one of the most severe natural disasters threatening the development of human society. A model that is capable of predicting the hydrological responses in watershed with management practices during flood period would be a crucial tool for pre-assessment of flood reduction measures. The Soil and Water Assessment Tool (SWAT) is a semi-distributed hydrological model that is well capable of runoff and water quality modeling under changed scenarios. The original SWAT model is a long-term yield model. However, a daily simulation time step and a continuous time marching limit the application of the SWAT model for detailed, event-based flood simulation. In addition, SWAT uses a basin level parameter that is fixed for the whole catchment to parameterize the unit hydrograph (UH), thereby ignoring the spatial heterogeneity among the subbasins when adjusting the shape of the UHs. This paper developed a method to perform event-based flood simulation on a sub-daily timescale based on SWAT2005 and simultaneously improved the UH method used in the original SWAT model. First, model programs for surface runoff and water routing were modified to a sub-daily timescale. Subsequently, the entire loop structure was broken into discrete flood events in order to obtain a SWAT-EVENT model in which antecedent soil moisture and antecedent reach storage could be obtained from daily simulations of the original SWAT model. Finally, the original lumped UH parameter was refined into a set of distributed ones to reflect the spatial variability of the studied area. The modified SWAT-EVENT model was used in the Wangjiaba catchment located in the upper reaches of the Huaihe River in China. Daily calibration and validation procedures were first performed for the SWAT model with long-term flow data from 1990 to 2010, after which sub-daily ($\Delta t = 2\,\mathrm{h}$) calibration and validation in the SWAT-EVENT model were conducted with 24 flood events originating primarily during the flood seasons within the same time span. Daily simulation results demonstrated that the SWAT model could yield very good performances in reproducing streamflow for both whole year and flood period. Event-based flood simulation results simulated by the sub-daily SWAT-EVENT model indicated reliable performances, with E_{NS} values varying from 0.67 to 0.95. The SWAT-EVENT model, compared to the SWAT model, particularly improved the simulation accuracies of the flood peaks. Furthermore, the SWAT-EVENT model results of the two UH parameterization methods indicated that the use of the distributed parameters resulted in a more reasonable UH characterization and better model fit compared to the lumped UH parameter.

1 Introduction

A flood represents one of the most severe natural disasters in the world. It has been reported that nearly 40 % of losses originating from natural catastrophes are caused by floods (Adams III and Pagano, 2016). Floods have caused enormous losses to economies, societies, and ecological environments around the world (Doocy et al., 2013; Werritty et al., 2007; Guan et al., 2015). China is a flood-prone country, which suffers from severe flooding almost every year (Zhang et al., 2002). In this situation, protection against flooding has always been the government's primary task that brooks no delay. A series of structural and non-structural flood mitigation measures have been conducted to control and manage the floods (Guo et al., 2018). However, accurate flood simulations would be particularly important for such design- or management-related issues.

Numerous hydrological models have been developed since their first appearance. According to the spatial discretization method, these existing hydrological models can be divided into two categories: lumped models and distributed (semi-distributed) models (Maidment, 1994). Although lumped models are generally accepted for flood forecast and simulation due to the structural simplicity, computational efficiency and lower data requirements, they are not applicable to complex catchments since they do not account for the heterogeneity of the catchments (Yao et al., 1998; Hapuarachchi et al., 2011). Meanwhile, distributed (semi-distributed) models subdivide the entire catchment into a number of smaller heterogeneous sub-units with dissimilar attributes. It is the advantage for distributed (semi-distributed) models to incorporate the spatial characteristics of catchment such as land cover, soil properties, topography and meteorology (Yang et al., 2001, 2004). A large number of distributed or semi-distributed hydrological models have been applied in flood simulation. Beven et al. (1984) firstly tested the applicability of the TOPMODEL in flood simulation for three UK catchments and suggested that the model could be a useful approach for ungauged catchments. The Variable Infiltration Capacity (VIC) model is also playing an increasing role in flood simulation (Wu et al., 2014; Yigzaw and Hossain, 2012). The applications of the HBV model for flood simulation could be found in many studies (Haggstrom et al., 1990; Grillakis et al., 2010; Kobold and Brilly, 2006). The HEC-HMS model was able to provide reasonable flood simulation results in the San Antonio River basin (Ramly and Tahir, 2016). Among many distributed (semi-distributed) models, the one that is capable of predicting the hydrological responses in watersheds with management practices would provide scientific reference for preventing flood and mitigating its adverse effects.

The Soil and Water Assessment Tool (SWAT) model (Arnold et al., 1998) is a typical semi-distributed hydrological model that delineates a catchment into a number of sub-basins, which were subsequently divided into hydrologic response units (HRUs) representing the unique combination of land cover, soil type, and slope class within a sub-basin. The SWAT model integrates well with the Geographic Information System (GIS), having great potential in dealing with spatial flood control measures. In addition, the SWAT model is widely applied for runoff and water quality modeling under changed scenarios (Glavan et al., 2015; Yu et al., 2018; Qiu et al., 2017; Baker and Miller, 2013; Yan et al., 2013).

SWAT is a continuous (i.e., long-term) model with a limited applicability toward simulating instantaneous hydrologic responses. Therefore, Jeong et al. (2010) extended the capability of SWAT to simulate operational sub-daily or even sub-hourly hydrological processes, the modifications of which primarily focused on the model algorithms to enable the SWAT model to operate at a finer timescale with a continuous modeling loop. Constrained by data availability in China (MWR, 2008), rainfall and discharge observations at a sub-daily timescale are usually collected during flood periods, while daily data are measured otherwise. In this respect, hydrological models are usually applied at different timescales (i.e., a daily timescale for continuous simulations and a sub-daily timescale for event-based flood simulation) according to the availability of observed rainfall and discharge data (Yao et al., 2014a). Hence, a major constraint for the application of the SWAT model as modified by Jeong et al. (2010) is the conflict between a continuous simulation loop and the discontinuous observed sub-daily data in China.

To capture the sophisticated characteristics of flood events at a sub-daily timescale, a refinement of the spatial representation within the SWAT model is necessary. A dimensionless unit hydrograph (UH), which was distributed as a triangular shape and embedded within an sub-daily overland flow routing process in the SWAT model, was applied to relate hydrologic responses to specific catchment characteristics, such as the dimensions of the main stream and basin area, through applications of GIS or remote sensing (RS) software (Jena and Tiwari, 2006). Due to the spatial discretization in the SWAT model, the model parameters are grouped into three levels: (1) basin level parameters are fixed for the whole catchment; (2) sub-basin level parameters are varied with sub-basins; (3) HRU level parameters are distributed in different HRUs. By default, the UH-specific parameter in the SWAT model is programmed on the basin level, which means that spatial variation within a catchment is disregarded when adjusting the shape of the UH in each sub-basin. Given the spatial heterogeneity of the catchment, the application of this basin level adjustment parameter seems to be rather unconvincing. Moreover, because a great deal of research has primarily focused on daily, monthly or yearly simulations using the SWAT model, little effort has actually been provided toward demonstrating the usage of the UH method in the SWAT model.

This study developed a method to perform event-based flood simulation on a sub-daily timescale based on the SWAT model and simultaneously improved the UH method used in

Table 1. SWAT model input data and sources for the Wangjiaba (WJB) catchment.

Data type	Resolution	Source	Description
DEM	90 m × 90 m	http://srtm.csi.cgiar.org/ last access: 5 January 2017	Digital elevation model
Land use	1 km × 1 km	http://www.landcover.org/ last access: 7 January 2017	Land use classification
Soil	30 arcsec	http://www.fao.org/soils-portal/ last access: 15 January 2017	Soil type classification and characterization of soil parameters
Global weather data	30 stations	https://globalweather.tamu.edu/ last access: 15 January 2017	Relative humidity, wind speed, solar radiation and the minimum and maximum air temperatures
Observed rainfall	138 gauges	Hydrologic Bureau of Huaihe River Commission	Daily data: 1991–2010; sub-daily data: flood period during 1991–2010
Observed streamflow	1 gauges	Hydrologic Bureau of Huaihe River Commission	Wangjiaba station, daily data for 1991–2010, sub-daily data for flood period during 1991–2010

the original SWAT model in the upper reaches of the Huaihe River in China. SWAT is an open-source code model, which makes it possible to produce such a modification. The source code of SWAT2005 has an internal auto-calibration module and such integrated design of model simulation and auto-calibration is easily manageable and modified since there is no need to couple external optimization algorithms. The accessible SWAT2009 (rev. 528) and SWAT2012 (rev. 664) have removed auto-calibration routines, however, an independent program SWAT-CUP (Abbaspour et al., 2007) is provided instead. Admittedly, many improvements have been made from the SWAT2005 to the latest SWAT2012. According to the SWAT model updates in Seo et al. (2014), the major enhancements focused on the water quality modeling components, whereas the runoff modeling components in new SWAT versions were not so far different from those in SWAT2005. This study was specific to the model modifications in runoff simulation; thus, SWAT2005 was considered to be appropriate. There are some other model modification studies (Dechmi et al., 2012; Jeong et al., 2010) based on the SWAT2005 version.

2 Study area and data

2.1 Study area

The Huaihe River basin (30°55′–36°36′ N, 111°55′–121°25′ E) is situated in the eastern part of China. The Wangjiaba (WJB) catchment is situated within the upper reaches of the Huaihe River basin and was chosen as the study area for this paper (see Fig. 1). The WJB catchment has a drainage area of 30 630 km^2, wherein the long channel reaches from the source region to the WJB outlet. The southwestern upstream catchment is characterized as a mountain range with a maximum elevation of 1110 m above sea level. The central and eastern downstream regions are dominated by plains. The study catchment is a subtropical zone with an annual average temperature of 15 °C. The long-term average annual rainfall varies from 800 mm in the north to 1200 mm in the south. Since the catchment is dominated by a monsoon climate, approximately 60 % of the annual rainfall is received during the flood season ranging from mid-May to mid-October. Severe rainfall events within the study area typically transpire during the summer, frequently resulting in severe floods (Zhao et al., 2011).

2.2 Model dataset

To construct and execute the SWAT model, a digital elevation model (DEM), together with land use and soil type data, is required. Climate data, including that of rainfall, temperature, wind speed, etc., are also used. Table 1 lists the model data used in this study.

The DEM data in this study were downloaded from the website of the US Geological Survey (USGS) with a spatial resolution of 90 m. The study catchment was divided into 136 sub-basins according to the catchment delineation, as shown in Fig. 1.

A land use map was produced from the Global Land Cover 2000 (GLC2000) data product with a grid size of 1 km (Bartholomé and Belward, 2005). Six categories of land use were identified for this catchment: agricultural land (80.51 %), forest-deciduous (6.76 %), forest-evergreen (2.26 %), range-brush (1.09 %), range-grasses (8.09 %), and water (1.29 %).

Soil data were obtained from the Harmonized World Soil Database (HWSD) with a spatial resolution of 30 arcseconds. The HWSD also provides an attributed database that contains the physico-chemical characteristics of soil data worldwide (FAO et al., 2012). Since the built-in soil database within the SWAT model does not cover the study area, additional soil parameters were calculated using the method proposed by Jiang et al. (2014). Soil reclassification in the study area was in accordance with the FAO-90 soil system. Consequently, Eutric Planosols and Cumulic Anthrosols are the

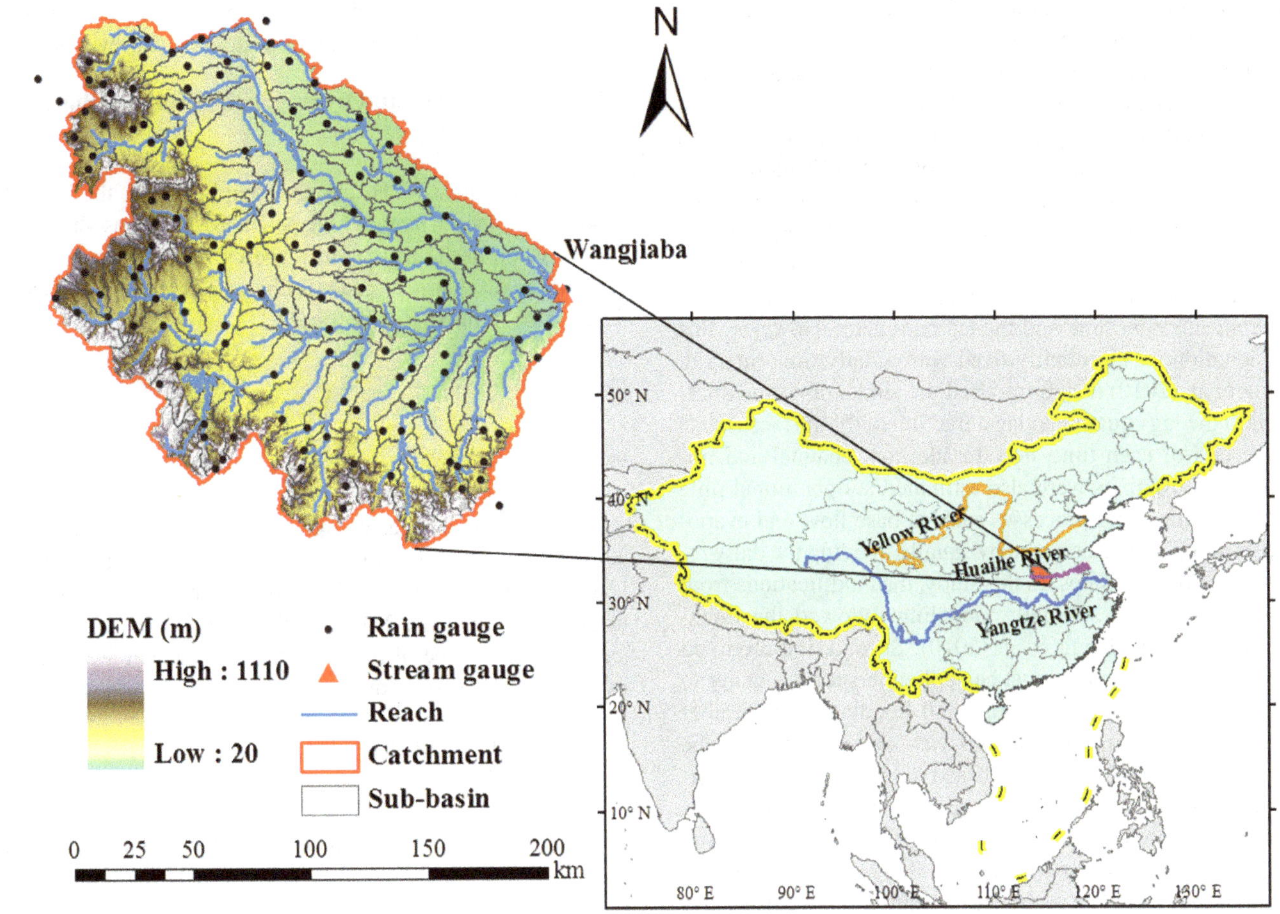

Figure 1. The Wangjiaba (WJB) catchment.

two main soil types, with area percentages of 24.71 % and 19.95 %, respectively.

The SWAT model has developed a weather generator (WXGEN) to fill the missing climate data by the use of monthly statistics. Relative humidity, wind speed, solar radiation and the minimum and maximum air temperatures were obtained from the Climate Forecast System Reanalysis (CFSR), which was designed based on the forecast system of the National Centers for Atmospheric Prediction (NCEP) to provide estimation for a set of climate variability from 1979 to the present day. There were 30 weather stations included in the study catchment.

A dense rain gauge network consisting of 138 gauges is distributed throughout the study area as illustrated in Fig. 1. By default, SWAT structure allows only one rainfall input for each delineated sub-basin. Thus, sub-basins without available rainfall gauge would be automatically assigned the nearest one. For sub-basins with multiple rainfall gauges, Thiessen polygon method (Thiessen, 1911) was utilized to derive the rainfall input. Rainfall is the main driving force for hydrological models, and therefore accurate representation of spatially distributed rainfall is essential in hydrological modeling. Cho et al. (2009) compared three different methods to incorporate spatially variable rainfall into the SWAT model and recommended the Thiessen polygon approach in catchments with high spatial variability of rainfall due to its robustness to catchment delineation. Daily observed rainfall data were retrieved from 1991 to 2010 with coverage during the entire year, while sub-daily ($\Delta t = 2$ h) rainfall data are only available for several flood events from May to September within the same time span.

3 Methodologies

3.1 Development of a sub-daily event-based SWAT model

The original SWAT model was designed for continuous simulations using a daily time step. The SWAT model operates most effectively during the prediction of long-term hydrological responses to land cover changes or soil management practices with daily time step (Jeong et al., 2011). When faced with flood simulation issues, a finer timescale is required to realistically capture the instantaneous changes representative of flood processes.

Therefore, the original daily simulation-based SWAT model first needs to be modified in order to perform sub-daily simulations. In a previous study, the sub-daily and even the sub-hourly modeling capacities of the SWAT model have been developed to allow flow simulations with any time step less than a day (Jeong et al., 2010). In the original SWAT model, the surface runoff lag was estimated by a first-order lag equation, which was represented by a function of the concentration time and the lag parameter. However, this lag equation was implicitly fixed with a daily time interval. Jeong et al. (2010) then introduced the simulation time interval into the lag equation to lag a fraction of the surface runoff at the end of each time step. In addition, channel and impoundment routings were also estimated at operational time interval while other processes such as base flow and evapotranspiration were calculated by equally dividing the daily results over the time steps. In this study, the modifications from daily modeling to sub-daily modeling followed the methods proposed by Jeong et al. (2010). Second, the modified sub-daily SWAT model must be applied in such a manner to achieve the simulation of individual flooding events rather than to simulate in a continuous way, as performed in the original SWAT model. Event-based sub-daily flood modeling is necessary for these reasons: (1) to enable the modelers to acknowledge the detailed information of upcoming floods and (2) to potentially conduct flood simulation within a watershed without possessing continuously recorded hydrologic data at a short time step. To enable the SWAT model to simulate individual flood events, the original source codes were modified and compiled into a new version known as SWAT-EVENT. In the source code of SWAT2005, the "simulate" subroutine contains the loops governing the hydrological processes following the temporal marching during the entire simulation period. Here, the continuous yearly loop was set into several flood events, meanwhile, the continuous daily loop was broken into flood events according to the specific starting and ending dates.

However, the event-based modeling requires a separate method to derive the antecedent conditions of model states. The combination of daily continuous modeling and sub-daily event-based modeling was used in this study (Fig. 2). A continuous daily rainfall sequence was imported into the original SWAT model to independently perform long-term daily simulations. In the SWAT model, there are another two subroutines "varinit" and "rchinit" initializing the daily simulation variables for the land phase of the hydrologic cycle and the channel routing, respectively. In the SWAT-EVENT model, condition judgments were added into those two initialization subroutines. That is, when the simulation process is at the beginning of a given flood event, antecedent soil moisture and antecedent reach storage are set equal to the respective values extracted from the long-term daily simulations of the original SWAT model; otherwise, they should be updated by the SWAT-EVENT model simulation states of the previous day.

3.2 Application of unit hydrographs with distributed parameters

The dimensionless UH method employed in the SWAT model exhibits a triangular shape (SCS, 1972), as shown in Fig. 3, wherein the time t (h) represents the x axis, and the ratio of the discharge to peak discharge represents the y axis. This UH is defined as follows:

$$q_{\mathrm{uh}} = \frac{t}{t_{\mathrm{p}}} \ \text{if}\ t \leq t_{\mathrm{p}},$$
$$q_{\mathrm{uh}} = \frac{t_{\mathrm{b}} - t}{t_{\mathrm{b}} - t_{\mathrm{p}}} \ \text{if}\ t > t_{\mathrm{p}}, \tag{1}$$

where q_{uh} is the unit discharge at time t, t_{p} is the time to the peak (h), and t_{b} is the time base (h). Then, the dimensionless UH is expressed by dividing by the area enclosed by the triangle (Jeong et al., 2010). There are two time factors determining the shape of the triangular UH, which are defined by the following equations:

$$t_{\mathrm{b}} = 0.5 + 0.6 \cdot t_{\mathrm{c}} + t_{\mathrm{adj}}, \tag{2}$$
$$t_{\mathrm{p}} = 0.375 \cdot t_{\mathrm{b}}, \tag{3}$$

where t_{c} is the concentration time for the sub-basin (h), and t_{adj} is a shape adjustment factor for the UH (h) (Neitsch et al., 2011).

The time of concentration t_{c} can be calculated based upon the geographic characteristics of the sub-basin considered, for which t_{c} is denoted by the accumulation of the overland flow time t_{ov} (h) and the channel flow time t_{ch} (h):

$$t_{\mathrm{c}} = t_{\mathrm{ov}} + t_{\mathrm{ch}}, \tag{4}$$
$$t_{\mathrm{ov}} = \frac{L_{\mathrm{slp}}^{0.6} \cdot n^{0.6}}{18 \cdot S_{\mathrm{sub}}^{0.3}}, \tag{5}$$
$$t_{\mathrm{ch}} = \frac{0.62 \cdot L \cdot n^{0.75}}{A^{0.125} \cdot S_{\mathrm{ch}}^{0.375}}, \tag{6}$$

where L_{slp} is the average slope length for the sub-basin under consideration (m); n is the Manning coefficient for the sub-basin; S_{sub} is the average slope steepness of the sub-basin ($\mathrm{m\,m^{-1}}$); L is the longest tributary length in the sub-basin (km); A denotes the area of the sub-basin ($\mathrm{km^2}$); and S_{ch} is the average slope of the tributary channels within the sub-basin ($\mathrm{m\,m^{-1}}$).

According to catchment discretization, Table 2 appears obvious spatial differences of the geographical attributes among sub-basins. For instance, the values of sub-basin area A vary from 0.09 to 879.16 $\mathrm{km^2}$, with a coefficient of variation (CV) of 0.74. The average slope of the sub-basin S_{sub} and the average slope of the tributary channels S_{ch} are topographic-related parameters, showing much higher values in source

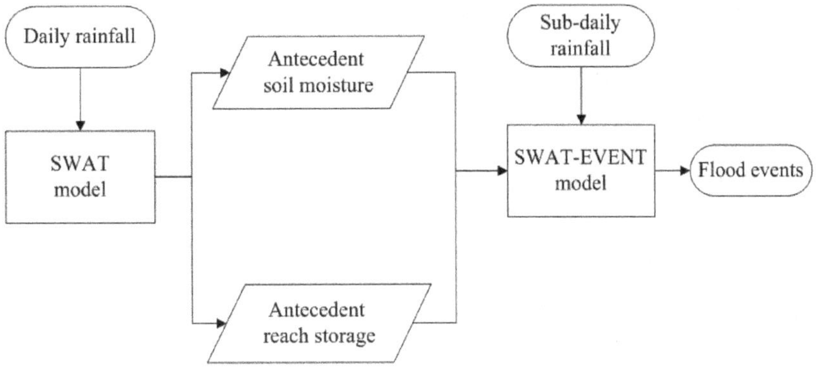

Figure 2. SWAT-EVENT model for the simulation of event-based flood data based on the initial conditions extracted from daily simulation results produced by the original SWAT model.

Table 2. Geographic features of sub-basins for the Wangjiaba (WJB) catchment.

	L_{slp} (m)	S_{sub} (m m^{-1})	L (km)	A (km^2)	S_{ch} (m m^{-1})	t_{ov} (h)	t_{ch} (h)	t_c (h)
Minimum	28.46	0.01	0.71	0.09	0.000	0.14	0.13	1.37
Maximum	121.95	0.22	96.83	879.16	0.024	2.42	33.06	34.18
Average	100.42	0.04	37.44	221.88	0.005	0.91	6.03	6.94
CV	0.29	1.28	0.52	0.74	1.18	0.37	0.91	0.81

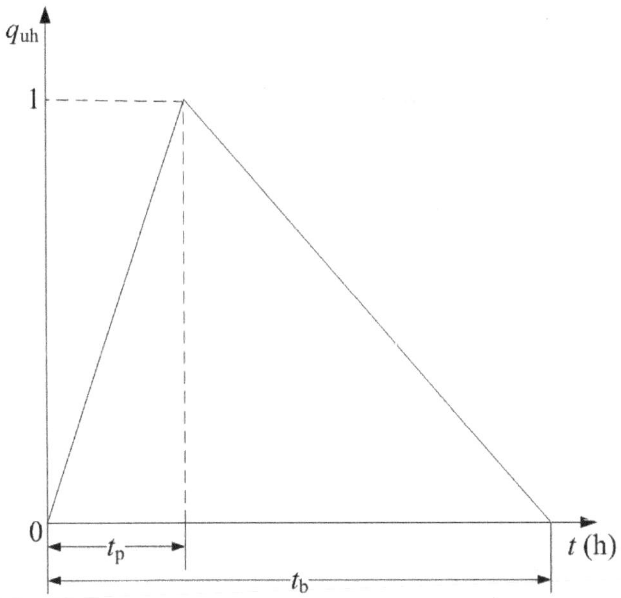

Figure 3. Shape of the dimensionless triangular UH.

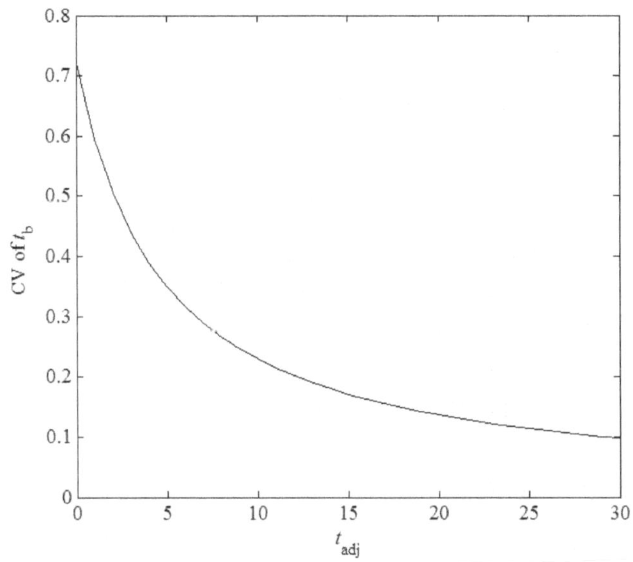

Figure 4. Effect of a basin level UH parameter t_{adj} on the CV of UH time base t_b.

sub-basins than those in downstream sub-basins. Spatially, the CV values of S_{sub} and S_{ch} in Table 2 are 1.28 and 1.18. As a result, the overland flow time t_{ov} and the channel flow time t_{ch} affected by all those geographical attributes are non-homogeneous in the spatial distribution, especially for the t_{ch} with the CV value of 0.91. Since the channel flow time t_{ch} dominates the concentration time t_c, the CV of t_c is 0.81 in Table 2. According to Eq. (2), the time base of the UH (t_b is determined by both concentration time for the sub-basin (t_c and shape adjustment factor (t_{adj} concurrently. However, the UH parameter t_{adj} in Eq. (2) is a basin level parameter possessing a lumped value for all sub-basins, meaning that the spatial heterogeneity of t_b may be homogenized. Hypothetically, the CV value of the t_b would decrease from 0.72 to 0.09

Table 3. Parameters and parameter ranges used in sensitivity analysis and the final ranks of sensitivity analysis results.

Parameter	Definition	Lower bound	Upper bound	Daily simulation with SWAT model		Event-based sub-daily simulation with SWAT-EVENT model
				Long-term period	Flood period	
ALPHA_BF	Baseflow alpha factor (days)	0	1	4	3	4
BLAI	Maximum potential leaf area index	0	1	10	8	15
CANMX	Maximum canopy storage (mm)	0	10	11	11	12
CH_K2	Effective hydraulic conductivity in main channel alluvium ($mm\,h^{-1}$)	0	150	5	5	11
CH_N2	Manning's "n" value for the main channel	0.01	0.3	1	1	1
CN2[a]	Initial SCS runoff curve number for moisture condition II	−25	25	3	4	2
EPCO	Plant uptake compensation factor	0	1	12	12	16
ESCO	Soil evaporation compensation factor	0	1	6	6	17
GW_DELAY	Groundwater delay time (days)	0	20	15	13	10
GW_REVAP[b]	Groundwater "revap" coefficient	−0.036	0.036	14	14	14
GWQMN	Threshold depth of water in the shallow aquifer required for return flow to occur (mm)	0.01	100	8	9	7
REVAPMN[b]	Threshold depth of water in the shallow aquifer for "revap" or percolation to the deep aquifer to occur (mm)	−100	100	16	16	13
SOL_AWC[a]	Available water capacity of the soil layer ($mm\,mm^{-1}$)	−30	30	7	7	5
SOL_K[a]	Saturated hydraulic conductivity ($mm\,h^{-1}$)	−50	50	13	15	8
SOL_Z[a]	Depth from soil surface to bottom of layer (mm)	−30	30	9	10	6
SURLAG	Surface runoff lag coefficient	0	20	2	2	9
t_{subadj}^{a}	Sub-basin level UH parameter (h)	−50	50			3

[a] These parameters are varied by multiplying a ratio (%) within the range.
[b] These parameters are varied by adding or subtracting a value within the range.

along with the increase of UH parameter t_{adj} from 0 to 30 h in Fig. 4. Generally, the time base of triangular UH (t_b should be reduced to produce increased peak flow for steep and small sub-basins, or should be increased to produce decreased peak flow for flat and large sub-basins. Thus, the shape adjustment parameter t_{adj} was modified from the basin level to the sub-basin level, and renamed t_{subadj} which allowed the UHs to be adjusted independently by distributed values.

3.3 Model calibration and validation

3.3.1 Sensitivity analysis

Sensitivity analysis is a process employed to identify parameters that significantly influence model performance (Holvoet et al., 2005). Generally, sensitivity analysis takes priority over the calibration process to reduce the complexity of the latter (Sudheer et al., 2011). Here, a combined Latin hypercube and one-factor-at-a-time (LH-OAT) sampling method embedded within the SWAT model (Griensven et al., 2006) was used to conduct a sensitivity analysis. LH-OAT method firstly subdivides each parameter into N stratums with a probability of $1/N$. Sampling points are randomly generated so that one parameter is sampled only once at each strata. Then, the local sensitivity of a parameter at one sampling point is calculated as

$$S_{ij} = 200 \cdot \left| \frac{\left[y(\theta_1,\ldots,\theta_i+\Delta_i,\ldots,\theta_P) - y(\theta_1,\ldots,\theta_P)\right]}{\left[y(\theta_1,\ldots,\theta_i+\Delta_i,\ldots,\theta_P) + y(\theta_1,\ldots,\theta_P)\right]\cdot\Delta_i} \right|, \quad (7)$$

where S_{ij} is the partial effect of parameter θ_i at the LH sampling point j; y is the model output (or objective function); Δ_i is the perturbation of parameter θ_i and P is the number of parameters. The final sensitivity index S_i for the parameter θ_i is derived by averaging these partial effects of each loop for all LH points (i.e., N loops). The greater the S_i, the more sensitive the model response is to that particular parameter.

It is highly recommended to identify the model parameters that can represent the hydrological characteristics of specific catchment before blindly applying sensitivity analysis. Based on the reviews of the SWAT model applications (Griensven et al., 2006; Cibin et al., 2010; Roth and Lemann, 2016) and the analysis of the SWAT model parameters, a total of 16 parameters related to the streamflow simulation in study area were involved in sensitivity analysis (see Table 3) for daily simulation with the SWAT model. When it came to the event-based sub-daily flood simulation with SWAT-EVENT model, additional distributed UH parameter t_{subadj} (i.e., a total of 17 model parameters) was also considered. For both models, the objective function y in Eq. (7) represented the residual sum

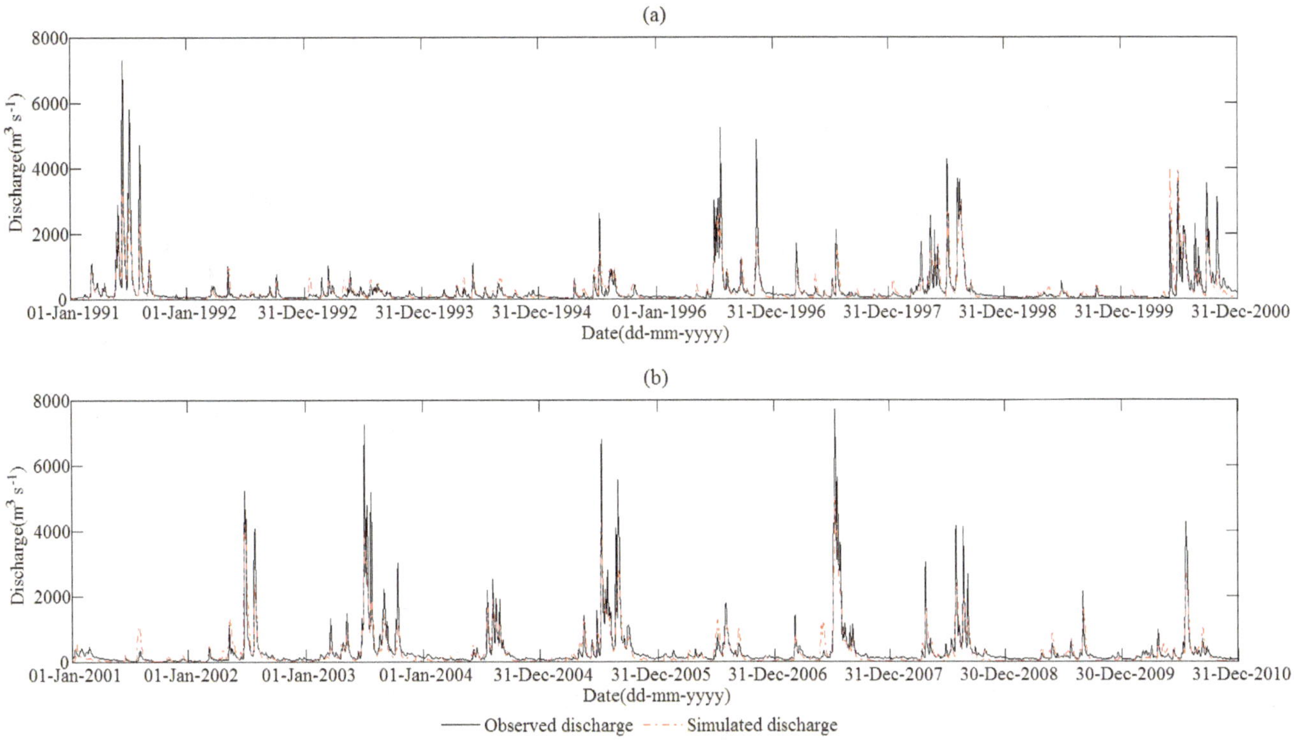

Figure 5. Comparisons between the observed and simulated daily discharges for calibration **(a)** and validation **(b)** periods at WJB.

of squares of stream flow between the simulated set and the measured set. Specifically, sensitivity analysis of the SWAT model was conducted not only for long-term period, but also for the same flood period as the SWAT-EVENT simulation. According to the sensitivity ranks of S_i , the upper-middle ranking parameters would be used for the calibration procedure, while the values of the other parameters were set to their default values.

3.3.2 Daily calibration and validation with the SWAT model

Before effectively applying a hydrological model, a calibration process aims to estimate the model parameters that minimize the errors between the observed and simulated results is usually necessary. The Shuffled Complex Evolution (SCE-UA) algorithm (Duan et al., 1992) is a global optimization technique that is incorporated as a module into the SWAT model. The SCE-UA algorithm has been applied to multiple physically based hydrological models (Sorooshian et al., 1993; Luce and Cundy, 1994; Gan and Biftu, 1996) and has exhibited good performance similar to other global search procedures (Cooper et al., 1997; Thyer et al., 1999; Kuczera, 1997; Jeon et al., 2014).

Daily simulations were performed within the time span, from 1990 to 2010, using daily observed data at the outlet of WJB. During this phase, the SWAT model was also conducted in two ways, calibrating for long-term period and calibrating for flood period. For long-term period case, one year (1990) was selected as the model warm-up period, the period from 1991 to 2000 was used for the model calibration, and the remaining data from 2001 to 2010 were employed for validation. For flood period calibrating, what was different was that the objective function only covered several flood events, which were consistent with the SWAT-EVENT application.

Multiple statistical values, including the Nash–Sutcliffe efficiency coefficient (E_{NS}) (Nash and Sutcliffe, 1970), ratio of the root mean square error to the standard deviation of measured data (R_{SR}) (Singh et al., 2005), and the percent bias (P_{BIAS}) (Gupta et al., 1999), were selected in this study to evaluate the daily model performances, as shown in Eqs. (8), (9), and (10). The E_{NS} provides a normalized statistic indicating how closely the observed and simulated data match with each other, wherein a value equal to 1 implies an optimal model performance insomuch that the simulated flow perfectly matches the observed flow. The R_{SR} index standardizes the root mean square error using the observations standard deviation, varying from 0 to a positive value. The optimal value of R_{SR} is 0, which indicates the perfect model simulation. The P_{BIAS} detects the degree that the simulated data deviates from the observed data.

$$E_{\mathrm{NS}} = 1 - \left[\frac{\sum\limits_{i=1}^{n} \left(Q_{\mathrm{obs}}(i) - Q_{\mathrm{sim}}(i)\right)^2}{\sum\limits_{i=1}^{n} \left(Q_{\mathrm{obs}}(i) - \overline{Q_{\mathrm{obs}}}\right)^2} \right], \tag{8}$$

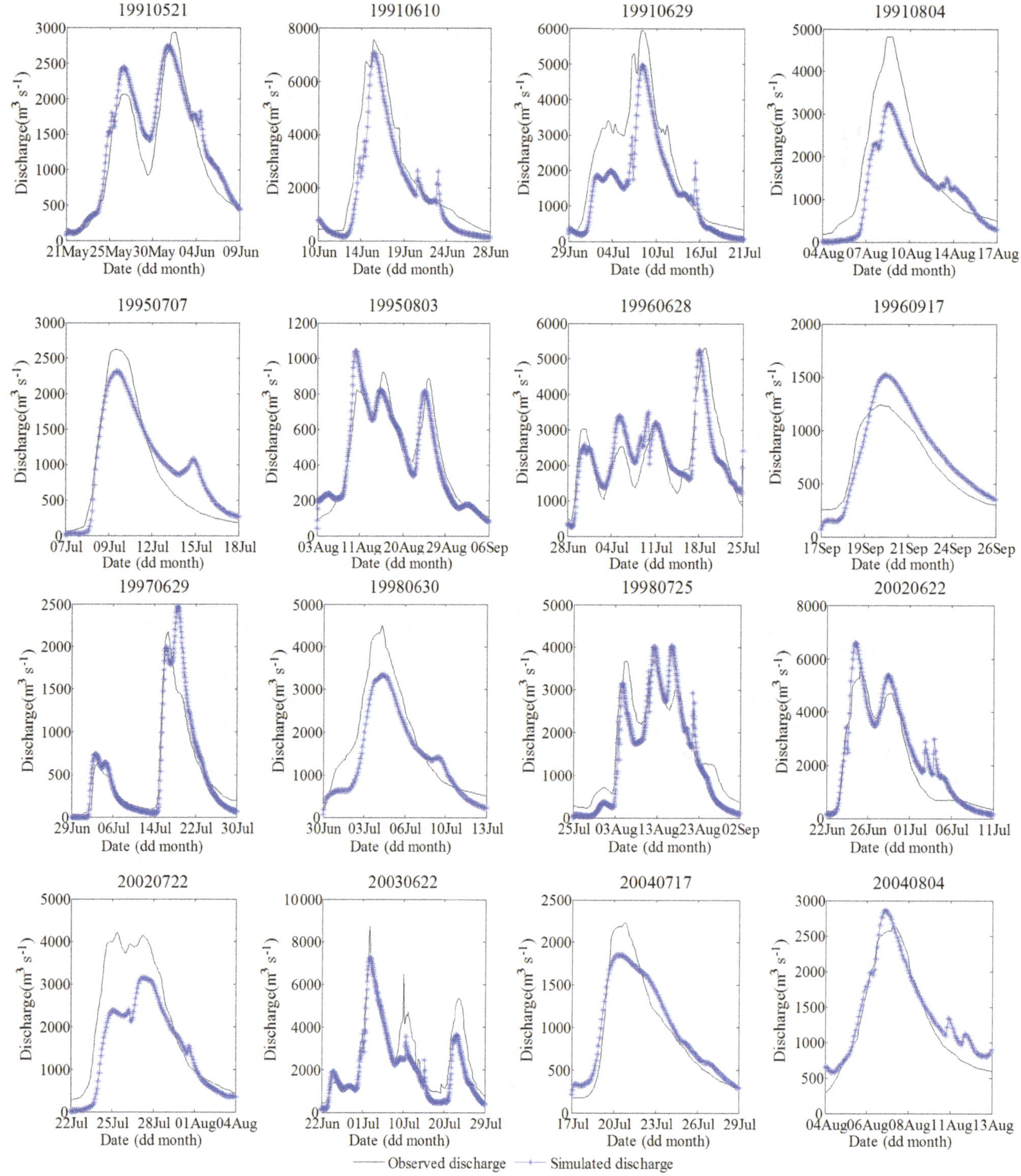

Figure 6. Comparisons between the observed and simulated sub-daily flood events for the calibration period at WJB.

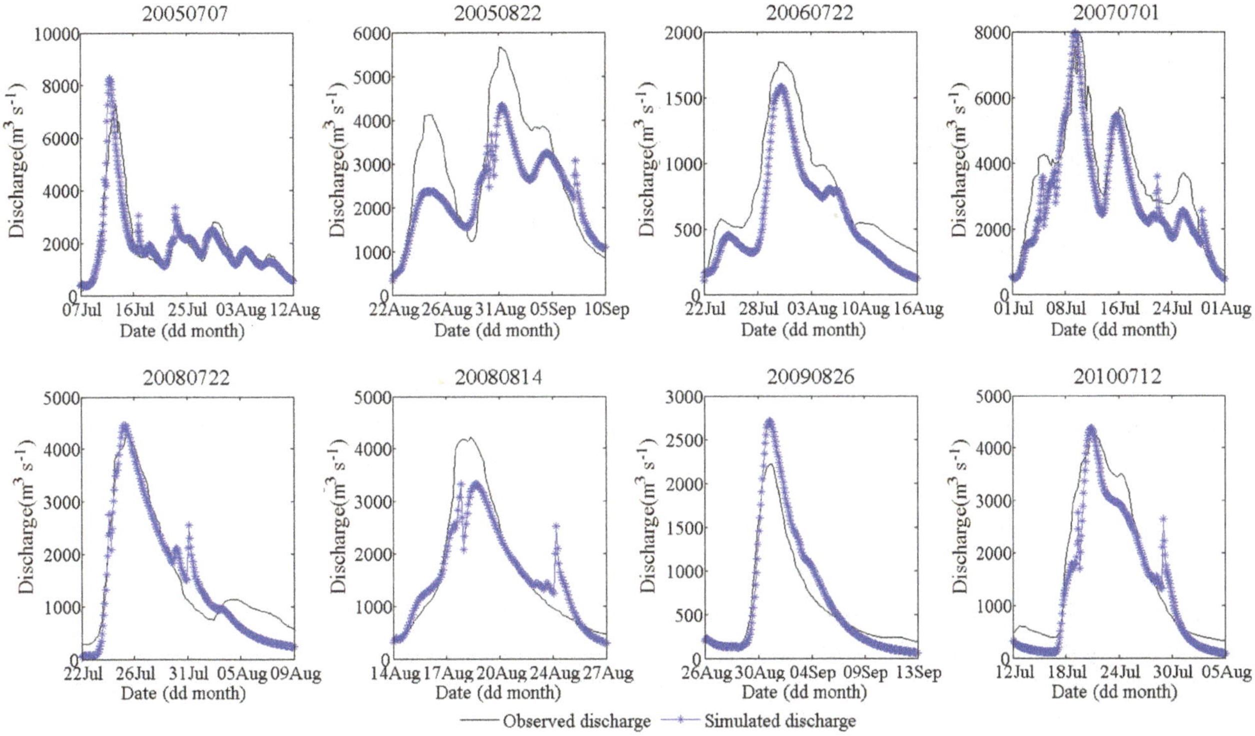

Figure 7. Comparisons between the observed and simulated sub-daily flood events for the validation period at WJB.

Table 4. Calibrated parameter values for the SWAT model and the SWAT-EVENT model.

Daily simulation with the SWAT model			Event-based simulation with the SWAT-EVENT model	
Parameter	Value for long-term period calibrating	Value for flood period calibrating	Parameter	Value
CH_N2	0.10	0.19	CH_N2	0.03
SURLAG	1.84	2.40	CN2*	24.60
CN2*	15.98	20.68	t^*_{subadj}	−10.40
ALPHA_BF	0.84	0.75	SOL_Z[a]	−7.91
CH_K2	109.90	54.00	GWQMN	0.28
ESCO	0.94	1.00	SOL_AWC[a]	−29.71
SOL_AWC*	−18.01	−9.26	ALPHA_BF	0.88
			SOL_K*	−48.84

* The final values of these parameters are derived by multiplying the percentage change (%) based on their default values. Parameter CN2 with the calibrated value of 15.98, for example, means that the default values are multiplied by (1 + 15.98 %) to obtain the optimal results.

$$R_{\text{SR}} = \frac{\sqrt{\sum_{i=1}^{n} \left(Q_{\text{obs}}(i) - Q_{\text{sim}}(i)\right)^2}}{\sqrt{\sum_{i=1}^{n} \left(Q_{\text{obs}}(i) - \overline{Q_{\text{obs}}}\right)^2}}, \tag{9}$$

$$P_{\text{BIAS}} = \left[\frac{\sum_{i=1}^{n} \left(Q_{\text{obs}}(i) - Q_{\text{sim}}(i)\right) \cdot 100}{\sum_{i=1}^{n} Q_{\text{obs}}(i)}\right], \tag{10}$$

where $Q_{\text{obs}}(i)$ is the ith observed streamflow ($\text{m}^3\,\text{s}^{-1}$); $Q_{\text{sim}}(i)$ is the ith simulated streamflow ($\text{m}^3\,\text{s}^{-1}$); n is the length of the time series.

3.3.3 Event-based sub-daily calibration and validation with the SWAT-EVENT model

In this study, the SWAT-EVENT model employed the same built-in automatic calibration subroutine as the SWAT model did. Sub-daily simulations with the SWAT-EVENT model

Table 5. SWAT model performance statistics for long-term period calibrating and flood period calibrating.

	Long-term period calibrating		Flood period calibrating	
Statistical indicator	Calibration	Validation	Calibration	Validation
E_{NS}	0.76	0.80	0.78	0.81
R_{SR}	0.49	0.44	0.48	0.44
P_{BIAS} (%)	5.72	−8.38	5.27	−6.10

were conducted within the same time span as the daily simulation, with a primary focus on the flood season with a series consisting of 24 flood events, two-thirds of which were utilized for the calibration while the rest were used for validation. Preferential implementation was applied to daily calibration from which the antecedent conditions were extracted.

E_{NS}, relative peak discharge error (E_{RP}), relative peak time error (E_{RPT}), and relative runoff volume error (E_{RR}) were selected as the performance evaluation statistics for the flood event simulations to comply with the Accuracy Standard for Hydrological Forecasting in China (MWR, 2008). E_{RP}, E_{RPT}, and E_{RR} are specific indicators used to indicate whether the accuracies of the simulations reach the national standard (MWR, 2008). They are considered to be sufficiently qualified when the absolute values are less than 20 %, 20 %, and 30 %, respectively.

4 Results

4.1 Sensitivity analysis results

Sensitivity results for daily simulation with the SWAT model are listed in Table 3. The sensitivity rank for a single parameter shows tiny differences between the two types of analysis period for SWAT simulation, with the changes in all parameter ranks less than.three According to a previous study (Cibin et al., 2010), the sensitivity of SWAT parameters was proved to vary in low, medium and high streamflow regimes. The long-term period analysis in Table 3 consists of different flow regimes, but presents almost the same sensitivity ranks as the flood period case, indicating that the high streamflow would dominate the sensitivity results in the long-term period analysis. Unexpectedly, compared to the long-term analysis, the initial SCS runoff curve number (CN2) shows less effect on streamflow output during flood period, whereas the groundwater parameter ALPHA_BF becomes more sensitive to high streamflow regime. As declared by Bondelid et al. (2010), the effects of CN2 variation on surface runoff yield decreased as the rainfall increased, especially for the larger storm events. Bondelid et al. (2010) further explained that the proportion of the rainfall that went into initial abstraction and infiltration decreased along with the increasing of rainfall, so the proportional change in surface runoff associated with a unit change in CN2 would decrease. Furthermore, from a previous sensitivity study with the SWAT model (Cibin et al., 2010), the parameter CN2 in wet year simulation was found to be less important than that in entire simulation, and the greatest sensitivity index of CN2 was found in low flow. Thus, there is reason to believe, the sensitivity ranking of CN2 would be reduced when it comes to flood period analysis in Table 3. Instead, in this process, the model output changes resulting from the perturbation of parameter ALPHA_BF would be more prominent, as there is more water recharging the shallow aquifer, and meanwhile the parameter ALPHA_BF strongly influences groundwater response to changes in recharge (Sangrey, 1984). Considering that the shallow aquifer in the Huaihe River basin has good drainage condition (Zuo et al., 2006), a relatively high value of ALPHA_BF would be expected in this study. Generally, the identified seven sensitive parameters of the daily SWAT model cover multiple main hydrological processes, i.e., channel routing (CH_N2 and CH_K2), runoff (SURLAG and CN2), groundwater (ALPHA_BF), evaporation (ESCO), and soil water (SOL_AWC), not only for the long-term period, but also for the flood period. According to Table 3, it is clear that both the year-round streamflow and the high streamflow are most sensitive to CH_N2 due to its top sensitivity rank.

Table 3 also presents the sensitivity results for event-based flood simulation with the SWAT-EVENT model at a sub-daily timescale. Sensitivity of some parameters differs widely from its performance in flood period analysis with the SWAT model at a daily timescale. The sensitivity ranks of BLAI, CH_K2, ESCO, SOL_K, and SURLAG have changed more than five, which could be caused by the differences in hydrological simulation between the SWAT model and the SWAT-EVENT model. It is noteworthy that the UH parameter t_{subadj}, peculiar to the SWAT-EVENT model, can significantly influence the event-based flood simulation at sub-daily timescales with a corresponding sensitivity ranking of three in Table 3. Though there exist differences among the daily SWAT model and the sub-daily SWAT-EVENT model, the same point is that the parameter CH_N2 is recognized as the most important parameters for both two models. In general, the top eight sensitive parameters (ALPHA_BF, CH_N2, CN2, GWQMN, SOL_AWC, SOL_K, SOL_Z and t_{subadj} are considered to influence the event-based sub-daily flood simulation significantly.

Table 6. Performance evaluations for the daily SWAT model calibrating only for flood periods, and the sub-daily SWAT-EVENT model performances with sub-basin level UH parameters and basin level UH parameters.

					Daily SWAT model simulation		Sub-daily SWAT-EVENT model simulation with sub-basin level UH parameter					Sub-daily SWAT-EVENT model simulation with basin level UH parameter				
	Flood event	Start date	End date	Observed peak flow ($m^3\,s^{-1}$)	Simulated peak flow ($m^3\,s^{-1}$)	E_{ns}	Simulated peak flow ($m^3\,s^{-1}$)	E_{RP} (%)	E_{RPT} (%)	E_{RR} (%)	E_{ns}	Simulated peak flow ($m^3\,s^{-1}$)	E_{RP} (%)	E_{RPT} (%)	E_{RR} (%)	E_{ns}
Calibration	19910521	21 May	10 Jun	2935	2160	0.68	2740	−6.64	−6.04	13.38	0.93	2880	−1.87	−10.74	13.51	0.83
	19910610	10 Jun	29 Jun	7577	4500	0.80	7050	−6.96	0.00	−23.08	0.91	6860	−9.46	−9.46	−22.98	0.90
	19910629	29 Jun	21 Jul	5931	3720	0.83	4960	−16.37	0.88	−31.25	0.85	4760	−19.74	−7.89	−31.21	0.85
	19910804	4 Aug	17 Aug	4824	2830	0.70	3250	−32.63	1.59	−28.10	0.81	3030	−37.19	−1.59	−28.05	0.80
	19950707	7 Jul	18 Jul	2613	1990	0.67	2310	−11.60	2.44	7.77	0.89	2200	−15.81	−7.32	7.83	0.84
	19950803	3 Aug	6 Sep	922.1	1000	0.70	819	−11.18	−4.88	−0.79	0.88	1220	32.31	−5.49	−0.78	0.78
	19960628	28 Jun	25 Jul	5298	3170	0.36	5200	−1.85	−4.20	0.54	0.67	5750	8.53	−5.34	0.74	0.53
	19960917	17 Sep	26 Sep	1239	1550	0.86	1520	22.68	7.32	11.04	0.82	1340	8.15	−43.90	12.45	0.79
	19970629	29 Jun	30 Jul	2171	1560	0.84	2470	13.77	9.82	7.26	0.83	2610	20.22	5.80	7.39	0.79
	19980630	30 Jun	13 Jul	4504	3050	0.78	3340	−25.84	0.00	−20.31	0.87	3010	−33.17	1.64	−20.24	0.87
	19980725	25 Jul	2 Sep	3698	3310	0.77	4030	8.98	−1.28	−13.54	0.83	3960	7.08	−1.74	−13.49	0.83
	20020622	22 Jun	11 Jul	5715	4560	0.81	6600	15.49	−14.29	14.76	0.90	6390	11.81	−22.45	14.78	0.86
	20020722	22 Jul	4 Aug	4290	2950	0.73	3150	−26.57	46.94	−30.09	0.83	3190	−25.64	42.86	−30.06	0.81
	20030622	22 Jun	29 Jul	8740	5030	0.66	7260	−16.93	0.75	−19.43	0.84	7140	−18.31	−2.99	−19.44	0.80
	20040717	17 Jul	29 Jul	2229	2020	0.44	1850	−17.00	−14.29	5.71	0.93	1810	−18.80	−18.37	5.88	0.87
	20040804	4 Aug	13 Aug	2641	1900	0.64	2870	8.67	−12.24	9.79	0.95	2800	6.02	−16.33	11.45	0.91
Validation	20050707	7 Jul	12 Aug	7331	4070	0.65	8280	12.95	−17.11	−2.87	0.82	8350	13.90	−25.00	−3.08	0.63
	20050822	22 Aug	10 Sep	5650	3200	0.50	4320	−23.54	1.65	−18.78	0.71	4380	−22.48	−7.44	−18.48	0.68
	20060722	22 Jul	16 Aug	1770	1160	0.81	1580	−10.73	1.82	−26.86	0.92	1460	−17.51	−8.18	−26.87	0.93
	20070701	1 Jul	1 Aug	7926	5580	0.77	7980	0.68	−6.50	−16.70	0.83	7910	−0.20	−9.76	−16.69	0.77
	20080722	22 Jul	9 Aug	4264	3020	0.72	4460	4.60	−4.08	−7.25	0.89	4120	−3.38	−6.12	−7.25	0.86
	20080814	14 Aug	27 Aug	4219	2580	0.69	3440	−18.46	−12.90	−5.11	0.82	3670	−13.01	−20.97	−5.04	0.78
	20090826	26 Aug	13 Sep	2221	1710	0.75	2710	22.02	−4.17	7.64	0.89	2310	24.01	−15.28	7.61	0.88
	20100712	12 Jul	5 Aug	4314	3180	0.91	4370	1.30	−2.63	−14.68	0.92	4610	6.86	−6.14	−14.65	0.92
Qualified (%)								75	95.8	91.6			70.8	79.1	91.6	

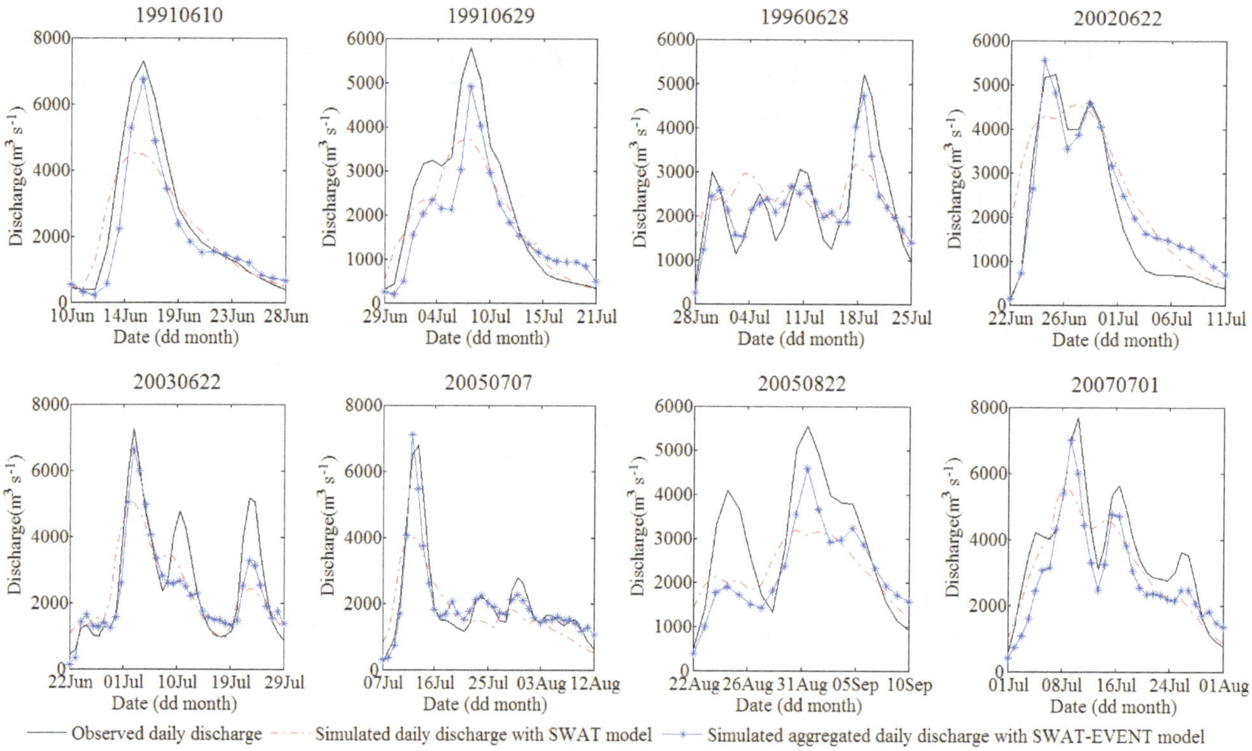

Figure 8. Comparisons of the daily simulations conducted using the SWAT model and the aggregated sub-daily simulations conducted using the SWAT-EVENT model.

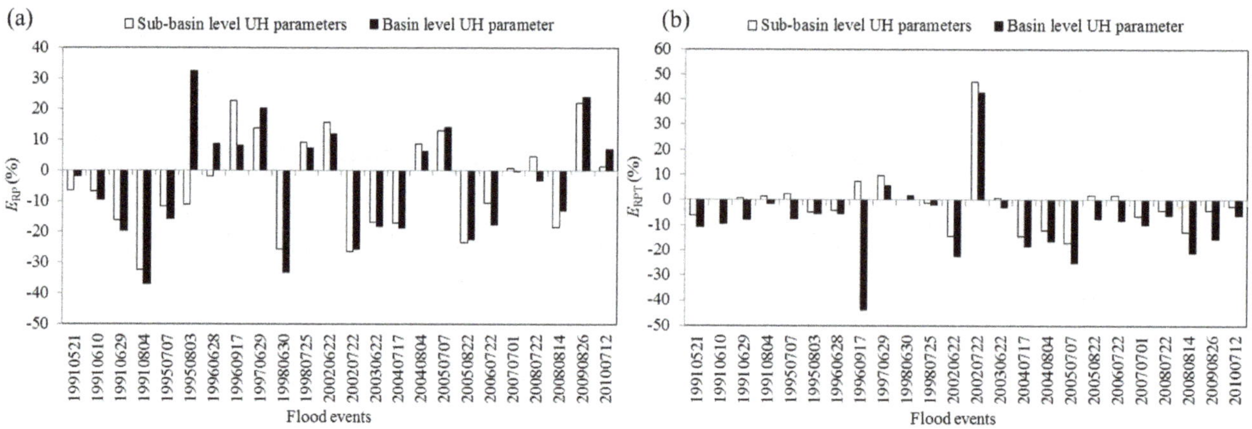

Figure 9. Comparisons between sub-basin level and basin level UH parameter cases for relative peak discharge error **(a)** and relative peak time error **(b)**.

4.2 Daily simulation results

The final calibrated parameters for daily simulation with the SWAT model are presented in Table 4. The model performances for daily streamflow simulations at outlet WJB are summarized in Table 5. For long-term calibration, the E_{NS} value is 0.76 for the calibration period and 0.80 for the validation period. These two values of the daily E_{NS} both exceed 0.75, which is considered to be "very good" according to performance ratings for evaluation statistics recommended by Moriasi et al. (2007). The daily R_{SR} values are 0.49 and 0.44 for the calibration and validation, respectively, indicating that the root mean square error values are less than half the standard deviation of measured data, i.e., the "very good" model performances suggested by Moriasi et al. (2007). The SWAT model overestimates the streamflow by 5.72 % for calibration while underestimating the streamflow by 8.38 % for validation. The calculated results of P_{BIAS} in Table 5 also attain the "very good" rating. Visual comparisons between the observed and simulated streamflows for both of the calibration and validation periods are shown in Fig. 5, from which it can be observed that the SWAT model could simulate well the temporal variation of long-term streamflow at a daily timescale. In general, the daily simulation results obtained from the SWAT model at WJB demonstrate decent applicability and can consequently represent a preliminary basis for further flood event simulation.

When focusing on event period calibration and validation, all statistical criteria in Table 5 indicate high accuracy of the daily SWAT model for flood period simulation.

4.3 Event-based simulation results

Table 4 shows the optimum values of parameters used in the SWAT-EVENT model simulation. The sub-daily simulation results for 24 flood events, as shown in Table 6, exhibit reliable performances of the SWAT-EVENT model, with E_{NS} values varying from 0.67 to 0.95. The qualified ratios of E_{RP}, E_{RPT} and E_{RR} are 75 %, 95.8 % and 91.6 %, respectively. Meanwhile, observed and simulated sub-daily flood hydrographs are displayed in Figs. 6 and 7. It is clearly that the SWAT-EVENT model has the ability to accurately simulate the sub-daily flood events, except for the event 20020722. Moreover, for specific floods (i.e., 19960628, 19980725, 20050707, and 20070701), it is remarkable to see that the SWAT-EVENT model owns the outstanding performances in simulating flood events with multiple peaks.

Table 6 also displays the model performances of the daily simulation results using the SWAT model specific for flood period. All daily E_{NS} values are lower than the sub-daily ones, indicating that the flood hydrographs simulated by the sub-daily SWAT-EVENT model are much more reliable than those simulated by the daily SWAT model. In addition, the peak flows simulated by the SWAT-EVENT model on a sub-daily timescale are much closer to the observed flows relative to the predictions obtained from the SWAT model on a daily timescale, especially for flood events with high peak flows in Table 6. There are eight flood events (19910610, 19910629, 19960628, 20020622, 20030622, 20050707, 20050822, and 20070701) that exhibit peak flows greater than 5000 m^3 s^{-1}. The sub-daily simulation results of these eight floods were aggregated into daily averages and then compared with those of the daily simulations, the results of which are illustrated in Fig. 8. It can be concluded that the daily simulations are likely to miss the high flood peaks. The more effective performances of the SWAT-EVENT model could be due to rainfall data with a higher temporal resolution and the model calculation with more detailed time steps, which can capture the instantaneous changes representative of flood processes.

All statistical indicators suggest that the SWAT-EVENT model can accurately reproduce the dynamics of observed flood events based upon antecedent conditions extracted from SWAT daily simulations.

4.4 Effects of the UH parameter level on SWAT-EVENT model performances

To analyze the effects of the level of UH parameters on SWAT-EVENT model simulations, the default lumped UH parameter t_{adj} was calibrated while the other parameters remained unchanged exactly as the sub-basin level case was calibrated in Table 4. The optimized basin level UH parameter (t_{adj}) displays a uniform value of 15.75 h for all sub-basins, while the sub-basin level UH parameters (t_{subadj}) are distributed in sub-basins, ranging from 4.81 to 120.33 h. As a consequence, the optimized t_{subadj} value enables the base time (t_b) and the peak time (t_p) of the UHs within the ranges of 6.13–141.34 and 2.30–53.00 h, respectively. While for the basin level UH parameter case, the values of t_b and t_p distribute in a relatively narrow range, i.e., 17.07–36.76 h for t_b and 6.40–13.78 h for t_p. More of a concern, according to Fig. 4, is the CV value of t_b or t_p would be reduced to less than 0.2, meaning that the spatial heterogeneity of UH time factors is homogenized due to the constrains between sub-basins when adjusting the basin level UH parameter. As expected, the application of sub-basin level UH parameters would keep the CV value of t_b or t_p at 0.79, which corresponds quite closely to the CV value of t_c in Table 2. Thus, the spatial inhomogeneity of geographical features can be better represented by the use of sub-basin level UH parameters.

The SWAT-EVENT simulation results using the basin level UH parameter are also presented in Table 4. Compared with the sub-basin level case, the basin level case induces significant decrease in the qualified ratio of E_{RPT} from 95.8 % to 79.1 %. Intuitive comparisons for relative peak discharge error (E_{RP} and relative peak time error (E_{RPT} under both UH parameter levels could be found in Fig. 9. When simulating from the sub-basin level UH case to the basin level UH case, more than half of the total 24 flood events and nearly all of the flood events show, respectively, increased peak discharge error and peak time error. Thus, it can be concluded that changing the spatial level of the UH parameter would affect the flood peak simulations significantly, especially for the peak time error. In this procedure, however, model parameters except for the UH parameter remain fixed, so it is not surprising that there is little change in the specific values of the relative runoff volume error (E_{RR}) between the two cases in Table 4. All these findings indicate that the application of sub-basin level UH parameters in the SWAT-EVENT model can improve the simulation accuracies of flood peaks.

The overall distributions of E_{NS} statistics for flood events for the two UH methods (i.e., the basin level UH parameter vs. the sub-basin level UH parameters) are plotted in Fig. 10. The box plots therein exhibit rectangle heights equal to the interquartile range (IQR), the upper and lower ends of which are separately marked with the upper and lower quartile values, respectively. The median is represented by a line transecting either of the two rectangles. The extended whiskers

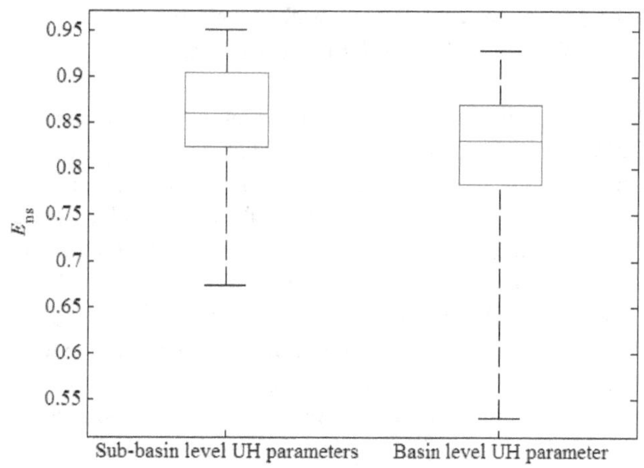

Figure 10. Box plots of ENS values for the SWAT-EVENT model results for sub-basin level UH parameters and basin level UH parameters.

denote the range of the batch data (Massart et al., 2005; Cox, 2009). According to Table 4 and Fig. 10, the SWAT-EVENT model using sub-basin level UH parameters demonstrates improvements for event-based flood simulation. For the sub-basin level case in Fig. 10, half of the E_{NS} values range from 0.83 (lower quartile) to 0.91 (upper quartile), with a median of 0.87, which can potentially represent the second flood forecasting accuracy standard (i.e., B) according to MWR (MWR, 2008). However, the basin level case performs comparatively poorly with regard to reproducing the flood hydrograph, wherein the majority of E_{NS} values vary between 0.78 and 0.88. In comparison, the application of spatially distributed UH parameters allows the SWAT-EVENT model to simulate the flood events more accurately.

5 Discussion

5.1 Sub-daily simulation vs. daily simulation

Floods are always triggered by intense rainfall events with short duration. In order to adequately capture and analyze the rapid response of flood events, simulation time step at sub-daily resolution is preferred. Normally, an appropriate simulation time step is chosen depend on the catchment response time to a rainfall event. According to the catchment delineation and geographical features of sub-basins in Table 2, the general average concentration time of sub-basins is found to be less than 24 h. Moreover, considering the time interval of observed data acquisition (i.e., 2 to 6 h), the 2 h simulation step chosen in this study was more than sufficient for flood simulation. The remarkable performances of the sub-daily SWAT-EVENT model for peak flow simulations (as shown in Table 6 and Fig. 8) adequately confirmed the superiority of using sub-daily time step in simulating flood hydrographs. In this study, daily surface runoff was calculated using the SCS curve number method in the SWAT model, whereas sub-daily surface runoff was calculated using the Green & Ampt infiltration method in the SWAT-EVENT model. In terms of the comparison of these two methods, (King et al., 1999) argued that the advantage of Green & Ampt method was the considerations of sub-daily rainfall intensity and duration, meanwhile, a rainstorm might not be fully represented by total daily rainfall used in SCS method due to its high variation in temporal distribution. Beyond that, as stated by Jeong et al. (2010), the physically based hydrological processes simulating at a short timescale would contribute to the reinforcement of model simulation accuracy.

5.2 Event-based simulation vs. continuous simulation

Pathiraja et al. (2012) may argue that the continuous simulation for design flood estimation was becoming increasingly important. Nevertheless, in operational flood simulation and prediction perspectives, many endusers and practitioners are still in favor of the event-based models (Coustau et al., 2012; Berthet et al., 2009). The emphasis on event-based modeling in this study was due to the unavailability of the long continuous hydrological data at a sub-daily timescale. Such a data scarcity issue has also promoted the applications of the event-based models in some developing countries (Hughes, 2011; Tramblay et al., 2012). More broadly, the preferred event-based approach is highlighted when the hydrological model is used for investigating the effect of heavy rainfall on environmental problems such as soil erosion and contaminant transport (Maneta et al., 2007).

Several studies have declared that the catchment's antecedent moisture conditions prior to a flood event can have a strong influence on flood responses, including the flood volume, flood peak flow and its duration (Rodrã-Guez-Blanco et al., 2012; Tramblay et al., 2012; Coustau et al., 2012). However, the major drawback of event-based models lies in its initialization: external information is needed to set the antecedent conditions of a catchment (Berthet et al., 2009; Tramblay et al., 2012). To address the initialization issue, some efforts have been made to set up the initial conditions of event-based models, such as in situ soil moisture measurements, retrieved soil moisture from the remote sensing products, and continuous soil moisture modeling. Among these methods, continuous soil moisture modeling using the daily data series to estimate sub-daily initial conditions would be a traditional solution, as suggested by Nalbantis (1995) (Tramblay et al., 2012) also tested different estimations of the antecedent moisture conditions of the catchment for an event-based hydrological model and concluded that the continuous daily soil moisture accounting method performed the best. However, there might be some deficiencies in the continuous simulation of the SWAT model in this study. On the one hand, the continuous soil moisture modeling required long data series and took a long time to implement. On the other hand, the continuous SWAT model was calibrated using the sum of squares of the residuals as the objective function, which was more sensitive to high flows than low flows. As a consequence, the SWAT model ensured the simulation accuracy at the expense of the low flow performances, which would certainly bring errors to the estimations of antecedent moisture conditions. As Coustau et al. (2012) declared, event-based models were very convenient for operational purposes, if the initial wetness state of the catchment would be known with good accuracy. Although the continuous modeling approach used in this study was not the perfect solution for the determination of the catchment antecedent conditions, it was still an effective method as the preliminary preparation for the simulation of the SWAT-EVENT model due to the good goodness-of-fit in Figs. 6 and 7. Since the goal of this research was to ascertain the applicability of the newly developed SWAT-EVENT model on event-based flood simulation, it was accepted to have a lower performance in calculating the antecedent conditions. Active microwave remote sensing has proved the feasibility and rationality of obtaining temporal and spatial soil moisture data. It means that there is a potential interest of using the remote sensing data to estimate the initial conditions (Tramblay et al., 2012).

5.3 Distributed UH parameters vs. lumped UH parameters

The UH method is used to spread the net rainfall over time and space, representing the most widely practiced technique for determining flood hydrographs. The main difference between the two applications of the UH parameter is, in essence, the method for surface runoff routing within the sub-basins. The application of the sub-basin level UH parameters allowed distributed parameter value for each sub-basin, while the basin level UH parameter application consistently applied a lumped value for all sub-basins. All but the derived UH shape of the distributed UH case were identical to these of the lumped UH case. Therefore, the difference in the simulations of the two UH parameter cases resulted from the surface runoff routing method.

As seen from the aforementioned model performance assessment in Table 6 and Fig. 9, the capability of the SWAT-EVENT model with basin level UH parameter for event-based flood simulation was downgraded relative to the sub-basin level case. It is known that Sherman (1932) first proposed the UH concept in 1932. However, because the UH proposed by Sherman is based on observed rainfall–runoff data at gauging sites for hydrograph derivations, it is only applicable for gauged basins (Jena and Tiwari, 2006). A prominent lack of observed data promoted the appearance of the Synthetic Unit Hydrograph (SUH), which extended the application of the UH technique to ungauged catchments. The triangular dimensionless UH used in this study denotes the traditional derivation of SUHs, which relates hydrologic responses to the catchment geographic characteristics according to Eqs. (2)–(6). Therefore, it can be inferred that the shape feature of the UH should be region-dependent. A lumped UH parameter used for the whole catchment would lead to either sharpening the peak flows in large sub-basins, or flattening the peak flows in small sub-basins. On the whole, hydrological behaviors among sub-basins would tend to be homogenized. As indicated in Table 6 and Figs. 9 and 10, there was a positive effect from the application of the distributed UH parameters on flood simulation.

In addition to the triangular dimensionless UH used in this study, there are many other available methods for derivation of the SUH (Bhunya et al., 2007) compared four probability distribution functions (pdfs) in developing SUH and concluded that such statistical distributions method performed better than the traditional synthetic methods. Furthermore, the instantaneous unit hydrograph (IUH) is more capable of mathematically expressing the effective rainfall hyetograph and direct runoff hydrograph relationship in a catchment (Jeng and Coon, 2003). And Yao et al. (2014b) improved the flood prediction performance of the Xinanjiang model by the coupling of the geomorphologic instantaneous unit hydrograph (GIUH) (Khaleghi et al., 2011) compared the accuracy and reliability of different UH methods and confirmed the high efficiency of the GIUH for flood simulation. There might be room for further improving the current UH method used in the SWAT-EVENT model.

6 Conclusions

The original SWAT model was not competent for flood simulation due to its initial design of long-term simulations with daily time steps. This paper mainly focused on the modification of the structure of the original SWAT model to perform event-based flood simulation, which was applicable for the area without continuous long-term observations. The newly developed SWAT-EVENT model was applied in the upper reaches of the Huaihe River. Model calibration and validation were made by the using of historical flood events, showing good simulation accuracy. To improve the spatial representation of the SWAT-EVENT, the lumped UH parameters were then adjusted to the distributed ones. Calibration and validation results revealed the improvement of event-based simulation performances, especially for the flood peak simulation. This study expands the application of the original SWAT model in event-based flood simulation. Event-based runoff quantity and quality modeling has become a challenge task since the impact of hydrological extremes on the water quality is particularly important. The improvement of the SWAT model for event-based flood simulation in this study will lay the foundation for dealing with the event-based water quality issues.

The optimal parameters of the SWAT-EVENT model were obtained by the automatic parameter calibration module that integrated the SCE-UA algorithm in this study. However, several factors such as interactions among model parameters, complexities of spatio-temporal scales, and statistical features of model residuals may lead to the parameter non-uniqueness, which is the source of the uncertainty in the estimated parameters. Uncertainty of model parameters will be finally passed to the model results, hence leading to certain risks in flood simulation. In the future, emphasis will be placed on the quantification of the parameter uncertainty to provide better support for flood operations.

Code and data availability. The DEM data were downloaded from the website http://srtm.csi.cgiar.org/ (Consortium for Spatial Information, 2017). The land use data (GLC2000) were downloaded from the website http://www.landcover.org/ (University of Maryland, 2017). The soil data (HWSD) were downloaded from the website http://webarchive.iiasa.ac.at/Research/LUC/External-World-soil-database/HTML/ (FAO, 2017). The global weather data were downloaded from the website https://globalweather.tamu.edu/ (National Centers for Environmental Prediction, 2017). The rainfall observations at 138 stations and the discharge observations at the outlet (WJB) were provided by Hydrologic Bureau of Huaihe River Commission. The source codes of the SWAT model are available at the website http://swat.tamu.edu/ (USDA Agricultural Research Service and Texas A&M AgriLife Research, 2016).

Author contributions. XD and PX contributed to the conception of this study. XD and DY contributed significantly to analysis and manuscript preparation. DY performed the data analyses and wrote the manuscript. XH, JL, YL, TP, and HM helped perform the analysis with constructive discussions. All authors read and approved the manuscript. KW and SX assisted in data acquisition and collation.

Competing interests. The authors declare that they have no conflict of interest.

Acknowledgements. This research has been supported by the Non-profit Industry Financial Program of Ministry of Water Resources of China (no. 201301066), the National key research and development program (2016YFC0402700), the National Natural Science Foundation of China (nos. 91547205, 51579181, 51409152, 41101511, and 40701024), and the Hubei Provincial Collaborative Innovation Center for Water Security.

Edited by: Markus Weiler

References

Abbaspour, K. C., Vejdani, M., and Haghighat, S.: SWAT-CUP calibration and uncertainty programs for SWAT, in: Modsim 2007 International Congress on Modelling and Simulation Land Water and Environmental Management Integrated Systems for Sustainability, Christchurch, New Zealand, 10–13 December 2007, 1603–1609, 2007.

Adams III, T. E. and Pagano, T. C.: Flood Forecasting: A Global Perspective, in: Flood Forecasting, Academic Press, Boston, USA, xxiii–xlix, 2016.

Arnold, J. G., Srinivasan, R., Muttiah, R. S., and Williams, J. R.: Large area hydrologic modeling and assessment part I: model development, JAWRA, 34, 91–101, 1998.

Baker, T. J. and Miller, S. N.: Using the Soil and Water Assessment Tool (SWAT) to assess land use impact on water resources in an East African watershed, J. Hydrol., 486, 100–111, 2013.

Bartholomé, E. and Belward, A. S.: GLC2000: a new approach to global land cover mapping from Earth observation data, Int. J. Remote Sens., 26, 1959–1977, 2005.

Berthet, L., Andréassian, V., Perrin, C., and Javelle, P.: How crucial is it to account for the antecedent moisture conditions in flood forecasting? Comparison of event-based and continuous approaches on 178 catchments, Hydrol. Earth Syst. Sci., 13, 819–831, https://doi.org/10.5194/hess-13-819-2009, 2009.

Beven, K. J., Kirkby, M. J., Schofield, N., and Tagg, A. F.: Testing a physically-based flood forecasting model (TOPMODEL) for three U.K. catchments, J. Hydrol., 69, 119–143, 1984.

Bhunya, P. K., Berndtsson, R., Ojha, C. S. P., and Mishra, S. K.: Suitability of Gamma, Chi-square, Weibull, and Beta distributions as synthetic unit hydrographs, J. Hydrol., 334, 28–38, 2007.

Bondelid, T. R., Mccuen, R. H., and Jackson, T. J.: Sensitivity of SCS Models to Curve Number Variation, JAWRA, 18, 111–116, 2010.

Cho, J., Bosch, D., Lowrance, R., Strickland, T., and Vellidis, G.: Effect of spatial distribution of rainfall on temporal and spatial uncertainty of SWAT output, T. ASABE, 52, 277–281, 2009.

Cibin, R., Sudheer, K., and Chaubey, I.: Sensitivity and identifiability of stream flow generation parameters of the SWAT model, Hydrol. Process., 24, 1133–1148, 2010.

Consortium for Spatial Information: DEM data, available at: http://srtm.csi.cgiar.org/, last access: 5 January 2017.

Cooper, V. A., Nguyen, V. T. V., and Nicell, J. A.: Evaluation of global optimization methods for conceptual rainfall-runoff model calibration, Water Sci. Technol., 36, 53–60, 1997.

Coustau, M., Bouvier, C., Borrell-Estupina, V., and Jourde, H.: Flood modelling with a distributed event-based parsimonious rainfall-runoff model: case of the karstic Lez river catchment, Nat. Hazards Earth Syst. Sci., 12, 1119–1133, https://doi.org/10.5194/nhess-12-1119-2012, 2012.

Cox, N. J.: Speaking Stata: Creating and varying box plots, Stata J., 9, 478–496, 2009.

Dechmi, F., Burguete, J., and Skhiri, A.: SWAT application in intensive irrigation systems: Model modification, calibration and validation, J. Hydrol., 470–471, 227–238, 2012.

Doocy, S., Daniels, A., Murray, S., and Kirsch, T. D.: The Human Impact of Floods: a Historical Review of Events 1980–2009 and Systematic Literature Review, Plos Curr., 5, 1808–1815, 2013.

Duan, Q., Soroosh, S., and Vijai, G.: Effective and efficient global optimization for conceptual rainfall-runoff models, Water Resour. Res., 28, 1015–1031, 1992.

FAO, IIASA, ISRIC, and ISSCAS: Harmonized World Soil Database Version 1.2, Food & Agriculture Organization of the UN, Rome, Italy, and International Institute for Applied Systems Analysis, Laxenburg, Austria, 2012.

Food and Agriculture Organization (FAO): HWSD soil data, available at: http://www.fao.org/soils-portal/soil-survey/soil-maps-and-databases/harmonized-world-soil-database-v12/en/, last access: 15 January 2017.

Gan, T. Y. and Biftu, G. F.: Automatic Calibration of Conceptual Rainfall-Runoff Models: Optimization Algorithms, Catchment Conditions, and Model Structure, Water Resour. Res., 32, 3513–3524, 1996.

Glavan, M., Ceglar, A., and Pintar, M.: Assessing the impacts of climate change on water quantity and quality modelling in small Slovenian Mediterranean catchment – lesson for policy and decision makers, Hydrol. Process., 29, 3124–3144, 2015.

Griensven, A. V., Meixner, T., Grunwald, S., Bishop, T., Diluzio, M., and Srinivasan, R.: A global sensitivity analysis tool for the parameters of multi-variable catchment models, J. Hydrol., 324, 10–23, 2006.

Grillakis, M. G., Tsanis, I. K., and Koutroulis, A. G.: Application of the HBV hydrological model in a flash flood case in Slovenia, Nat. Hazards Earth Syst. Sci., 10, 2713–2725, https://doi.org/10.5194/nhess-10-2713-2010, 2010.

Guan, M., Wright, N. G., and Andrew Sleigh, P.: Multiple effects of sediment transport and geomorphic processes within flood events: Modelling and understanding, Int. J. Sediment Res., 30, 371–381, https://doi.org/10.1016/j.ijsrc.2014.12.001, 2015.

Guo, L., He, B., Ma, M., Chang, Q., Li, Q., Zhang, K., and Hong, Y.: A comprehensive flash flood defense system in China: overview, achievements, and outlook, Nat. Hazards, 1–14, 2018.

Gupta, H. V., Sorooshian, S., and Yapo, P. O.: Status of Automatic Calibration for Hydrologic Models: Comparison With Multilevel Expert Calibration, J. Hydrol. Eng., 4, 135–143, 1999.

Haggstrom, M., Lindstrom, G., Cobos, C., Martínez, J. R., Merlos, L., Dimas Alonso, R., Castillo, G., Sirias, C., Miranda, D., and Granados, J.: Application of the HBV model for flood forescasting in six Central American Rivers, Smhi Hydrol., 27, 1–13, 1990.

Hapuarachchi, H. A. P., Wang, Q. J., and Pagano, T. C.: A review of advances in flash flood forecasting, Hydrol. Process., 25, 2771–2784, 2011.

Holvoet, K., Griensven, A. V., Seuntjens, P., and Vanrolleghem, P. A.: Sensitivity analysis for hydrology and pesticide supply towards the river in SWAT, Phys. Chem. Earth, 30, 518–526, 2005.

Hughes, D. A.: Regionalization of models for operational purposes in developing countries: an introduction, Hydrol. Res., 42, 331–337, 2011.

Jena, S. K. and Tiwari, K. N.: Modeling synthetic unit hydrograph parameters with geomorphologic parameters of watersheds, J. Hydrol., 319, 1–14, 2006.

Jeng, R. I. and Coon, G. C.: True Form of Instantaneous Unit Hydrograph of Linear Reservoirs, J. Irrig. Drain. Eng., 129, 11–17, 2003.

Jeong, J., Kannan, N., Arnold, J., Glick, R., Gosselink, L., and Srinivasan, R.: Development and Integration of Sub-hourly Rainfall-Runoff Modeling Capability Within a Watershed Model, Water Resour. Manage., 24, 4505–4527, 2010.

Jeong, J., Kannan, N., Arnold, J. G., Glick, R., Gosselink, L., Srinivasan, R., and Harmel, R. D.: Development of sub-daily erosion and sediment transport algorithms for SWAT, T. ASABE, 54, 1685–1691, 2011.

Jeon, J. H., Park, C. G., and Engel, B. A.: Comparison of Performance between Genetic Algorithm and SCE-UA for Calibration of SCS-CN Surface Runoff Simulation, Water, 6, 3433–3456, 2014.

Jiang, X. F., Wang, L., Fang, M. A., Hai-Qiang, L. I., Zhang, S. J., and Liang, X. W.: Localization Method for SWAT Model Soil Database Based on HWSD, China Water & Wastewater, 30, 135–138, 2014.

Khaleghi, M. R., Gholami, V., Ghodusi, J., and Hosseini, H.: Efficiency of the geomorphologic instantaneous unit hydrograph method in flood hydrograph simulation, Catena, 87, 163–171, 2011.

King, K., Arnold, J., and Bingner, R.: Comparisonof Green-Ampt and curve number methods on Goodwin creek watershed using SWAT, T. ASAE, 42, 919–926, 1999.

Kobold, M. and Brilly, M.: The use of HBV model for flash flood forecasting, Nat. Hazards Earth Syst. Sci., 6, 407–417, https://doi.org/10.5194/nhess-6-407-2006, 2006.

Kuczera, G.: Efficient subspace probabilistic parameter optimization for catchment models, Water Resour. Res., 33, 177–185, 1997.

Luce, C. H. and Cundy, T. W.: Parameter Identification for a Runoff Model for Forest Roads, Water Resour. Res., 30, 1057–1070, 1994.

Maidment, D. R.: Handbook of hydrology, Earth-Sci. Rev., 24, 227–229, 1994.

Maneta, M. P., Pasternack, G. B., Wallender, W. W., Jetten, V., and Schnabel, S.: Temporal instability of parameters in an event-based distributed hydrologic model applied to a small semiarid catchment, J. Hydrol., 341, 207–221, 2007.

Massart, D. L., Smeyers-Verbeke, J., Capron, X., and Schlesier, K.: Visual presentation of data by means of box plots, Lc Gc Europe, 18, 215–218, 2005.

Moriasi, D. N., Arnold, J. G., Van Liew, M. W., Bingner, R. L., Harmel, R. D., and Veith, T. L.: Model evaluation guidelines for systematic quantification of accuracy in watershed simulations, T. ASABE, 50, 885–900, 2007.

MWR: Standard for Hydrological Information and Hydrological Forecasting (GB/T 22482-2008), Ministry of Water Resources of the People's Republic of China, Standards Press of China, Beijing, 2008 (in Chinese).

Nalbantis, I.: Use of multiple-time-step information in rainfall-runoff modelling, J. Hydrol., 165, 135–159, https://doi.org/10.1016/0022-1694(94)02567-U, 1995.

Nash, J. E. and Sutcliffe, J. V.: River flow forecasting through conceptual models part I – A discussion of principles, J. Hydrol., 10, 282–290, 1970.

National Centers for Environmental Prediction: Global weather data, available at: https://globalweather.tamu.edu/, last access: 15 January 2017.

Neitsch, S. L., Arnold, J. G., Kiniry, J. R., Srinivasan, R., and Williams, J. R.: Soil and Water Assessment Tool Input/output File Documentation: Version 2009, Texas Water Resources Institute Technical Report 365, Texas Water Resources Institute, Texas, USA, 2011.

Pathiraja, S., Westra, S., and Sharma, A.: Why continuous simulation? The role of antecedent moisture in design flood estimation, Water Resour. Res., 48, 6534, https://doi.org/10.1029/2011WR010997, 2012.

Qiu, L., Wu, Y., Wang, L., Lei, X., Liao, W., Hui, Y., and Meng, X.: Spatiotemporal response of the water cycle to land use conversions in a typical hilly–gully basin on the Loess Plateau, China, Hydrol. Earth Syst. Sci., 21, 6485–6499, https://doi.org/10.5194/hess-21-6485-2017, 2017.

Ramly, S. and Tahir, W.: Application of HEC-GeoHMS and HEC-HMS as Rainfall–Runoff Model for Flood Simulation, ISFRAM 2015, Singapore, 181–192, 2016.

Rodrã-Guez-Blanco, M. L., Taboada-Castro, M. M., and Taboada-Castro, M. T.: Rainfall–runoff response and event-based runoff coefficients in a humid area (northwest Spain), Int. Assoc. Sci. Hydrol. Bull., 57, 445–459, 2012.

Roth, V. and Lemann, T.: Comparing CFSR and conventional weather data for discharge and soil loss modelling with SWAT in small catchments in the Ethiopian Highlands, Hydrol. Earth Syst. Sci., 20, 921–934, https://doi.org/10.5194/hess-20-921-2016, 2016.

Sangrey, D. A.: Predicting ground-water response to precipitation, J. Geotech. Eng., 110, 957–975, 1984.

SCS: National engineering handbook, section 4, hydrology, US Department of Agriculture, SCS, Washington, DC, USA, 640 pp., 1972.

Seo, M., Yen, H., Kim, M. K., and Jeong, J.: Transferability of SWAT Models between SWAT2009 and SWAT2012, J. Environ. Qual., 43, 869–880, 2014.

Sherman, L.: Stream Flow from Rainfall by the Unit-Graph Method, Eng. News-Rec., 108, 501–505, 1932.

Singh, J., Knapp, H. V., Arnold, J. G., and Demissie, M.: Hydrological modeling of the Iroquois River watershed using HSPF and SWAT, JAWRA, 41, 343–360, 2005.

Sorooshian, S., Duan, Q., and Gupta, V. K.: Calibration of rainfall-runoff models: Application of global optimization to the Sacramento Soil Moisture Accounting Model, Water Resour. Res., 29, 1185–1194, 1993.

Sudheer, K. P., Lakshmi, G., and Chaubey, I.: Application of a pseudo simulator to evaluate the sensitivity of parameters in complex watershed models, Environ. Model. Softw., 26, 135–143, https://doi.org/10.1016/j.envsoft.2010.07.007, 2011.

Thiessen, A. H.: Precipitation averages for large areas, Mon. Weather Rev., 39, 1082–1084, 1911.

Thyer, M., Kuczera, G., and Bates, B. C.: Probabilistic optimization for conceptual rainfall-runoff models: A comparison of the shuffled complex evolution and simulated annealing algorithms, Water Resour. Res., 35, 767–773, 1999.

Tramblay, Y., Bouaicha, R., Brocca, L., Dorigo, W., Bouvier, C., Camici, S., and Servat, E.: Estimation of antecedent wetness conditions for flood modelling in northern Morocco, Hydrol. Earth Syst. Sci., 16, 4375–4386, https://doi.org/10.5194/hess-16-4375-2012, 2012.

University of Maryland: Land use data (GLC2000), available at: http://www.landcover.org/, last access: 7 January 2017.

USDA Agricultural Research Service and Texas A&M AgriLife Research: SWAT code, available at: http://swat.tamu.edu/, last access: 16 March 2016.

Werritty, A., Houston, D., Ball, T., Tavendale, A., and Black, A.: Exploring the Social Impacts of Flood Risk and Flooding in Scotland, Report to the Scottish Executive, School of Social Sciences-Geography, University of Dundee, Dundee, UK, 2007.

Wu, H., Adler, R. F., Tian, Y., Huffman, G. J., Li, H., and Wang, J. J.: Real-time global flood estimation using satellite-based precipitation and a coupled land surface and routing model, Water Resour. Res., 50, 2693–2717, 2014.

Yan, B., Fang, N. F., Zhang, P. C., and Shi, Z. H.: Impacts of land use change on watershed streamflow and sediment yield: An assessment using hydrologic modelling and partial least squares regression, J. Hydrol., 484, 26–37, https://doi.org/10.1016/j.jhydrol.2013.01.008, 2013.

Yang, D., Herath, S., and Musiake, K.: Spatial resolution sensitivity of catchment geomorphologic properties and the effect on hydrological simulation, Hydrol. Process., 15, 2085–2099, 2001.

Yang, D., Koike, T., and Tanizawa, H.: Application of a distributed hydrological model and weather radar observations for flood management in the upper Tone River of Japan, Hydrol. Process., 18, 3119–3132, 2004.

Yao, C., Zhang, K., Yu, Z., Li, Z., and Li, Q.: Improving the flood prediction capability of the Xinanjiang model in ungauged nested catchments by coupling it with the geomorphologic instantaneous unit hydrograph, J. Hydrol., 517, 1035–1048, https://doi.org/10.1016/j.jhydrol.2014.06.037, 2014a.

Yao, C., Zhang, K., Yu, Z., Li, Z., and Li, Q.: Improving the flood prediction capability of the Xinanjiang model in ungauged nested catchments by coupling it with the geomorphologic instantaneous unit hydrograph, J. Hydrol., 517, 1035–1048, 2014b.

Yao, H., Hashino, M., Terakawa, A., and Suzuki, T.: Comparison of distributed and lumped hydrological models, Doboku Gakkai Ronbunshuu B, 42, 163–168, 1998.

Yigzaw, W. Y. and Hossain, F.: Impact of Artificial Reservoir Size and Land Use Land Cover on Probable Maximum Flood: The case of Folsom Dam on American River, J. Hydrol. Eng., 18, 1180–1190, 2012.

Yu, D., Xie, P., Dong, X., Su, B., Hu, X., Wang, K., and Xu, S.: The development of land use planning scenarios based on land suitability and its influences on eco-hydrological responses in the upstream of the Huaihe River basin, Ecol. Model., 373, 53–67, 2018.

Zhang, J., Zhou, C., Xu, K., and Watanabe, M.: Flood disaster monitoring and evaluation in China, Global Environ. Chang., 4, 33–43, 2002.

Zhao, L. N., Tian, F. Y., Wu, H., Qi, D., Di, J. Y., and Wang, Z.: Verification and comparison of probabilistic precipitation forecasts using the TIGGE data in the upriver of Huaihe Basin, Adv. Geosci., 29, 95–102, 2011.

Zuo, Z., Wang, X., Luo, W., Wang, F., and Guo, S.: Characteristics on Aquifer of the Quaternary system in Huai River Basin (Henan Section), Ground Water, 28, 25–27, 2006.

13

Reproducing an extreme flood with uncertain post-event information

Diana Fuentes-Andino[1,2], **Keith Beven**[1,3], **Sven Halldin**[1,2], **Chong-Yu Xu**[1,4], **José Eduardo Reynolds**[1,2], **and Giuliano Di Baldassarre**[1,2]

[1]Department of Earth Sciences, Uppsala University, Villavägen 16, 752 36 Uppsala, Sweden
[2]Centre for Natural Disaster Science (CNDS), Uppsala University, Uppsala, Sweden
[3]Lancaster Environment Centre, Lancaster University, Lancaster LA1 4YQ, UK
[4]Department of Geosciences, University of Oslo, P.O. Box 1047, Blindern, 0316, Oslo, Norway

Correspondence to: Diana Fuentes-Andino (diana.fuentes@geo.uu.se)

Abstract. Studies for the prevention and mitigation of floods require information on discharge and extent of inundation, commonly unavailable or uncertain, especially during extreme events. This study was initiated by the devastating flood in Tegucigalpa, the capital of Honduras, when Hurricane Mitch struck the city. In this study we hypothesized that it is possible to estimate, in a trustworthy way considering large data uncertainties, this extreme 1998 flood discharge and the extent of the inundations that followed from a combination of models and post-event measured data. Post-event data collected in 2000 and 2001 were used to estimate discharge peaks, times of peak, and high-water marks. These data were used in combination with rain data from two gauges to drive and constrain a combination of well-known modelling tools: TOPMODEL, Muskingum–Cunge–Todini routing, and the LISFLOOD-FP hydraulic model. Simulations were performed within the generalized likelihood uncertainty estimation (GLUE) uncertainty-analysis framework. The model combination predicted peak discharge, times of peaks, and more than 90 % of the observed high-water marks within the uncertainty bounds of the evaluation data. This allowed an inundation likelihood map to be produced. Observed high-water marks could not be reproduced at a few locations on the floodplain. Identifications of these locations are useful to improve model set-up, model structure, or post-event data-estimation methods. Rainfall data were of central importance in simulating the times of peak and results would be improved by a better spatial assessment of rainfall, e.g. from radar data or a denser rain-gauge network. Our study demonstrated that it was possible, considering the uncertainty in the post-event data, to reasonably reproduce the extreme Mitch flood in Tegucigalpa in spite of no hydrometric gauging during the event. The method proposed here can be part of a Bayesian framework in which more events can be added into the analysis as they become available.

1 Introduction

Losses caused by natural hazards have a significant impact on the world economy, and floods account for around half of all disasters globally (UN/ISDR, 2016). Prevention and mitigation of floods require information on discharge and extent of inundation. Such information is commonly unavailable or uncertain, especially during extreme events when gauging equipment becomes insufficient or is lacking. Data scarcity is further aggravated in developing countries with weak infrastructure.

Nearly 11 000 people were killed in Central America during Hurricane Mitch because of extreme flooding, an estimated 2.7 million lost their homes, and flood damages were estimated to more than 6 billion USD (McCown et al., 1999). This study was initiated by the flood in Tegucigalpa, the capital city of Honduras, on 30–31 October 1998 when Mitch struck the city. The estimated 500-year return period rainfall produced by Mitch (JICA, 2002) caused significant damage to Tegucigalpa, where 1000 casualties were reported and approximately 40 % of its capital stock was damaged (Angel et al., 2004; JICA, 2002). In addition to these calamities, many of Honduras' hydrological archives were swept away from their premises at SANAA (Servicio Autónomo Nacional de Acueductos y Alcantarillados) which was located close to the main channel of the upper Choluteca River.

Simulations of water-level dynamics caused by disastrous events are needed for preparedness, to produce flood-inundation maps useful for urban planning, and to prioritize investments (Pappenberger et al., 2006; Schanze, 2006). Such simulations are also relevant to better comprehend the hydraulic mechanism of large flood events in order to improve model structure (Beven et al., 2011; Jarrett, 1990). However, given that simulations of extreme floods are generally associated with limited data availability and large uncertainties, the question arises as to whether it is possible to achieve simulations that can be useful for contingency planning and prevention.

When hydrometric measurements of discharge and water levels during an event are lacking or highly inaccurate, such information may be inferred from post-event surveys. These can be done through eye-witness accounts and field campaigns (Brandimarte and Di Baldassarre, 2012; Ciervo et al., 2015; Gaume and Borga, 2008; Horritt et al., 2010; JICA, 2002; Smith et al., 2002), sometimes in combination with additional methods such as searches into historical documentation and paleo-flood techniques (Mård Karlsson et al., 2009; Smith et al., 2012; Valyrakis et al., 2015). Such surveys have been useful to estimate hydrometric data of the floods. Pictures and movies can be used to identify locations, flow type, depth, flow velocity, and discharge at the time they were taken (e.g. Ciervo et al., 2015; Le Boursicaud et al., 2016). Post-event information of channel topography and maximum water level can be used to estimate maximum peak discharge (Dalrymple and Benson, 1968; Matthai, 1968).

Post-event-estimated maximum peak discharge can be used to produce probabilistic regional envelope curves (Castellarin, 2007; Gaume et al., 2009) and discharge series for flood-frequency analysis (Cœur and Lang, 2008). These provide design-flood estimates used for inundation mapping (e.g. Brandimarte and Di Baldassarre, 2012). However, an assessment of flood development in time is required for early-warning systems (Schanze, 2006). The development of a flood in time can be obtained through a strategically planned post-event survey of peak discharge and the associated time of the peak (e.g. Delrieu et al., 2005). Detailed hydrographs can also be obtained from rainfall time series in conjunction with post-event hydrometric data, by the use of a rainfall–runoff model (RRM). A RRM in turn can be coupled with a hydraulic model to estimate the water-level development along a floodplain (Bonnifait et al., 2009; JICA, 2002; Montanari et al., 2009; Pappenberger et al., 2005a). Results from hydraulic models can be validated against post-event-estimated peak discharge, time of the peak, maximum water level, and flood-extent data (e.g. Bonnifait et al., 2009; Brandimarte and Di Baldassarre, 2012; Horritt et al., 2010).

Post-event data have been used with deterministic calibration within hydraulic models (e.g. Horritt et al., 2010; JICA, 2002), and for coupling RRMs with hydraulic models (e.g. Ciervo et al., 2015). Using post-event data, Bonnifait et al. (2009) present a multi-variable assessment to find a group of best parameter sets for the TOPMODEL RRM and a 1-D hydraulic model. Borga et al. (2008) and Pappenberger et al. (2006) suggest that post-event data should be used within an uncertainty-analysis framework given their large uncertainties. Di Baldassarre et al. (2010) discussed the advantages of distributed uncertainty mapping, as first proposed by Romanowicz and Beven (1998), in comparison with deterministic mapping. Uncertainty-analysis techniques have been used to account for uncertainty in hydraulic models (Aronica et al., 1998; Bozzi et al., 2015; Brandimarte and Di Baldassarre, 2012; Pappenberger et al., 2005a, 2007) and for the coupling of a RRM with a hydraulic model (Montanari et al., 2009; Pappenberger et al., 2005a) using event-measured data.

Uncertainty-analysis techniques account for possible errors involved in the modelling process, e.g. errors in model parameters and input data, due to lack of knowledge of their true values, spatio-temporal variability, or inaccurate estimation, and errors related to limited knowledge of the behaviour of the real system, i.e. epistemic uncertainty (Beven, 2016, 2009). Thus, in uncertainty-analysis techniques, uncertainties can be associated with several sources that interact among them, in which each interaction is associated with a likelihood dependent on how well it fits the observations. The formal Bayesian approach is a widely used method for uncertainty analysis, with different set-ups available (e.g. Smith and Roberts, 1993). Bayesian techniques have been commonly applied in hydraulic and hydrological modelling (e.g. Hall et al., 2011; Renard et al., 2008) and can be used within a global sensitivity analysis (see summaries by Iooss and Lemaître, 2015, and Sarrazin et al., 2016) to assess the effect of each source of uncertainty on the output (e.g. Abily et al., 2016). An informal Bayesian approach is the generalized likelihood uncertainty estimation (GLUE) framework (Beven and Binley, 1992), which differs in the way likelihood is defined and in that it does not require prior knowledge on the correlations or distributions of the parameter errors, yet with GLUE it is possible to get posterior information in the parameter combinations. In this study we hypothesize that it is possible to reasonably estimate, considering the large uncertainties in the observations, the extreme 1998 flood discharge in Tegucigalpa and the extent of the inundations that followed, from a combination of models and post-event data. We are aware of works that use the combination of hydraulic models and RRMs to assess flood dynamics or others that use post-event data to calibrate either RRMs or hydraulic models, both deterministic and through uncertainty analyses. We are not aware of any previous study

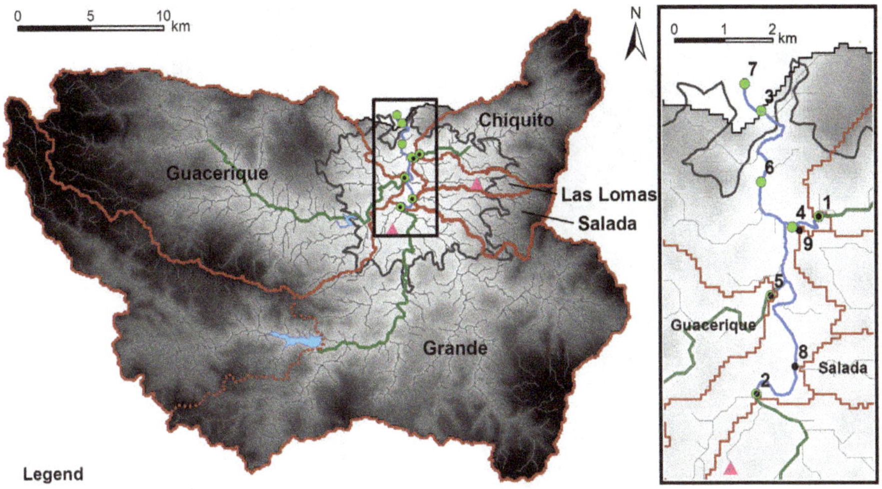

Figure 1. Study area and data location; topography data from the Shuttle Radar Topography Mission (SRTM).

combining a RRM, hydraulic modelling, and post-event data within an uncertainty-analysis framework to prove that reasonable estimation of an extreme flood is possible when hydrometric data are lacking. The methodology suggested in this paper integrates TOPMODEL (Beven and Kirkby, 1979; Kirkby, 1997), Muskingum–Cunge–Todini (MCT) (Todini, 2007) routing, and the LISFLOOD-FP (Neal et al., 2012a) hydraulic modelling tool in a GLUE framework.

2 Study area and data

2.1 Area description

The study area is the floodplain at Tegucigalpa, approximately 13 km of river length downstream from the upper part of the Choluteca River catchment. The area draining to the floodplain is around 811 km^2 and is composed of five sub-catchments: Grande River (448 km^2), Guacerique River (243 km^2), Chiquito River (71 km^2), Salada Creek (25 km^2), and Las Lomas Creek (12 km^2) (Fig. 1). Rainfall in the region is affected by high hurricane recurrence (Alvarado and Alfaro, 2003; Strobl, 2009) and convective activity. These two features in combination with the mountainous nature of the terrain (Amador et al., 2006) might lead to a high spatial variation of rainfall. Westerberg et al. (2010) found that daily precipitation has a high spatial variability and that bias in the estimations is likely due to insufficient gauge stations to measure in space and at different elevations. The land use and geology are relatively uniform in all sub-catchments. The land use is mainly composed of sparse coniferous forest at higher-elevation lands, and fallow, pastures, and urbanized areas in the low land (CIAT, 2007). The geology at the surface is mainly composed of tuff and limestone to a minor degree; the superficial aquifer is classified as poor to moderately productive (ING, 1996). The average basin slope estimated in the Grande River, Guacerique River, Chiquito River, Salada Creek, and Las Lomas Creek sub-catchments is 19.5, 18, 25, 17.5, and 11 % respectively. Two reservoirs operated by SANAA are established upstream of the Tegucigalpa floodplain: Concepción reservoir, located at the Grande River sub-catchment, and Los Laureles reservoir, located at the Guacerique River sub-catchment (Fig. 1).

2.2 Data

2.2.1 Topography

An airborne light-detection and ranging (lidar) survey in Tegucigalpa was conducted in 2000 by the University of Texas in cooperation with the US Geological Survey (USGS) during their survey in Honduras in response to Hurricane Mitch (Mastin, 2002). They generated a 1.5 m cell-resolution digital-terrain model (DTM) with an estimated vertical accuracy of 0.14 m (Fig. 2). These lidar data were used by Haile and Rientjes (2005) to investigate the effect of a digital elevation model (DEM) resolution on simulated flood extension using the SOBEK modelling tool. In 2001, JICA (2002) also conducted a topographic field survey as part of a flood/landslide-mitigation master plan and a total of 99 cross sections along the rivers in the floodplain at Tegucigalpa, surveyed at intervals of approximately 100 m, were

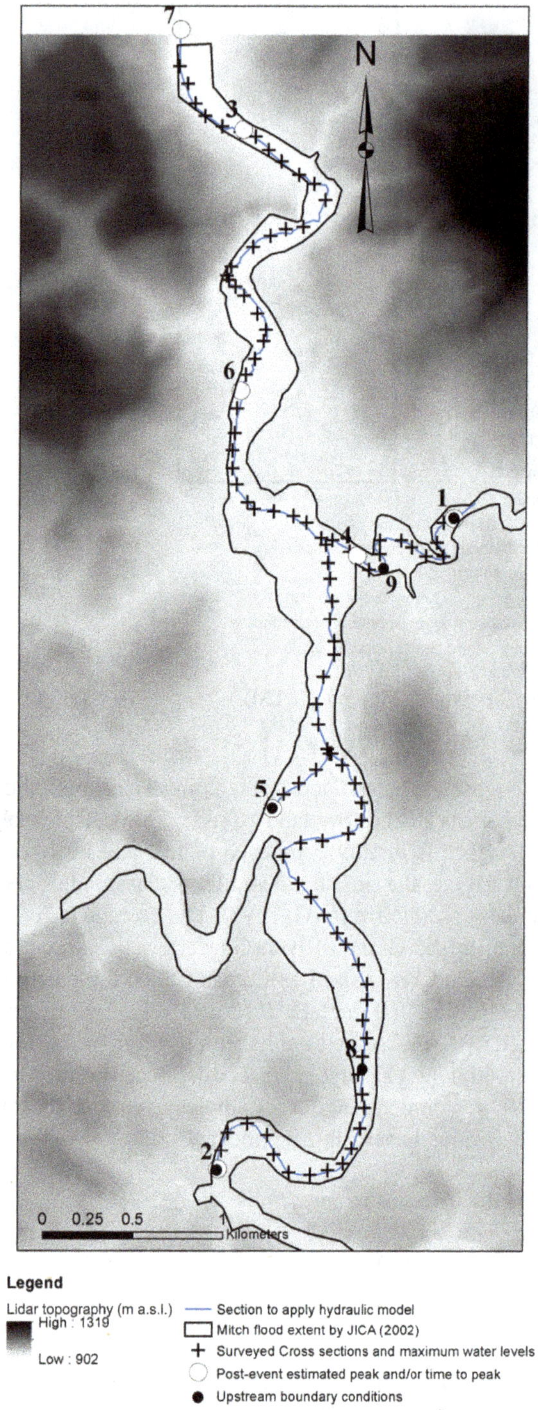

Figure 2. Geometry set-up for hydraulic simulation at the Tegucigalpa floodplain. Lidar data from Mastin (2002).

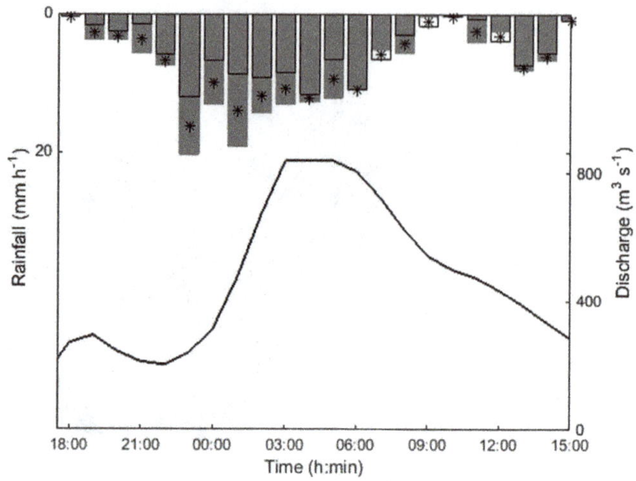

Figure 3. Hourly rainfall on 30–31 October 1998 at SMN station (grey bars), UNAH station (black outlined bars), average of the two stations (asterisks), and measured outflow at Concepción reservoir (continuous line).

used in this study (Fig. 2). In addition, orthographic pictures were taken at Tegucigalpa by JICA (2002).

The topography of the Tegucigalpa floodplain upstream sub-catchments was available from the 90 m spatial resolution Shuttle Radar Topography Mission (SRTM) data described by Reuter et al. (2007) (Fig. 1).

2.2.2 Precipitation

Upstream of the Tegucigalpa floodplain, two stations measured hourly rainfall during the Mitch event (Figs. 1 and 3). One of the stations is operated by Servicio Meteorológico Nacional (SMN, national weather service) and the other by the Universidad Nacional Autónoma de Honduras (UNAH).

2.2.3 Discharge

Discharge at three locations was estimated post-event by Smith et al. (2002) using the standard USGS techniques by Benson and Dalrymple (1967). The peaks at the Chiquito River and the Grande River (points 1 and 2 in Figs. 1 and 2 and Table 1) were estimated using the width-contraction analysis that uses the continuity and energy equations between a cross section approaching the contraction section under a bridge (Matthai, 1968). The peak at Choluteca (point 3) was estimated using the slope-area analysis, in which discharge is computed on the basis of the uniform-flow equation involving channel geometry, high-water marks, and roughness coefficients (Dalrymple and Benson, 1968). The measurements of discharge using the width-contraction analysis and the slope-area analysis can be associated with a 25 % error for unfavourable field-data conditions (Benson and Dalrymple, 1967), but up to 100 % overestimation might be associated with the slope-area analysis for slopes greater than 0.2 % (Jarrett, 1987).

A deterministic reproduction of the flood produced by Hurricane Mitch was done by JICA (2002) by setting a rainfall–runoff analysis using a linear reservoir model driven with hourly rainfall data from the SMN station. The produced hydrograph was used as input for the 1-D Mike 11 modelling tool (DHI, 2000) for unsteady flow conditions. In

Table 1. Post-event estimated peak discharge and time of peaks.

Location	Discharge ($m^3 s^{-1}$)	Time of peak (day month hh:min)	Source	Reference number (Figs. 1 and 2)
Chiquito River	167	31 Oct 00:00	Smith et al. (2002)	1
Grande River	2340	31 Oct 00:00–02:00	Smith et al. (2002)	2
Choluteca River	4360	31 Oct 00:30	Smith et al. (2002)	3
Chiquito River	436	–	JICA (2002)	4
Guacerique River	1177	30 Oct 23:00	JICA (2002)	5
Choluteca River	–	31 Oct 01:00	JICA (2002)	6
Choluteca River	3880	–	JICA (2002)	7

addition to the flood extent (Fig. 2), JICA (2002) reported the maximum peak discharge at the points 4, 5, and 7 in Figs. 1 and 2 and Table 1.

Controlled flow release through the spillway at the Concepción reservoir was conducted and recorded by SANAA during the Mitch event (Fig. 3). The outflow over Los Laureles dam was not recorded. However, SANAA reported that its gate was overtopped at 22:30 LT on 30 October, reaching a maximum of approximately 1200 $m^3 s^{-1}$ (JICA, 2002; Smith et al., 2002). Peak times in Table 1 except at point 5 were obtained by interviewing witnesses. The time of the peak at point 5 was estimated by propagating the peak reported at Los Laureles reservoir.

2.2.4 Maximum water levels

High-water marks during the Mitch flood were surveyed post-event by JICA (2002); the data were obtained by interviewing residents who experienced the event. The survey was carried out at the same locations where the topographic cross sections were made (Fig. 2).

3 Method

3.1 Consistency in the post-event measured data

An inspection of the consistency of the data was done prior to the analysis. The inspection was done by plotting the maximum water-level profile to detect possible outliers. The consistency in timing and magnitude along the river network for the post-event maximum peak discharge was also checked. The flood-wave peak and time of the peak were expected to be larger and later downstream from the river confluences respectively.

3.2 Uncertainty and evaluation function

To quantify the propagation of uncertainty, the GLUE method was used. The assumptions of more formal statistical approaches can not be justified in data-scarce cases with high epistemic uncertainties. Within the GLUE methodology, parameter sets were generated using a Monte Carlo technique, assuming a uniform prior distribution of the parameters.

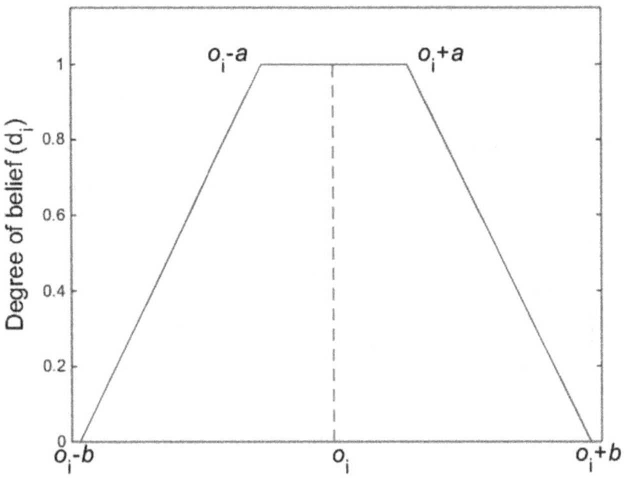

Figure 4. Fuzzy membership function for evaluation of model performance: a and b depend on the uncertainty associated with the evaluation (o_i).

Behavioural parameter sets, those that perform well in predicting the observations, were selected using a likelihood measure that reflected the performance of individual simulations with respect to one or several evaluation variables (o_i). Likelihoods were inferred by using the degree of belief (d_i) of a trapezoidal fuzzy membership function (Fig. 4), whose shape was chosen to account for uncertainties in the post-event estimated values, which are not considered crisp estimations. Thus the degree of belief for a difference smaller than a between the simulated and post-event estimated values is equal to 1, and it declines linearly to 0 for differences larger than b.

3.3 Modelling framework

The dynamic of the water level along the river channel and floodplain was reproduced with the sub-grid channel formulation of the LISFLOOD-FP hydrodynamic model (Neal

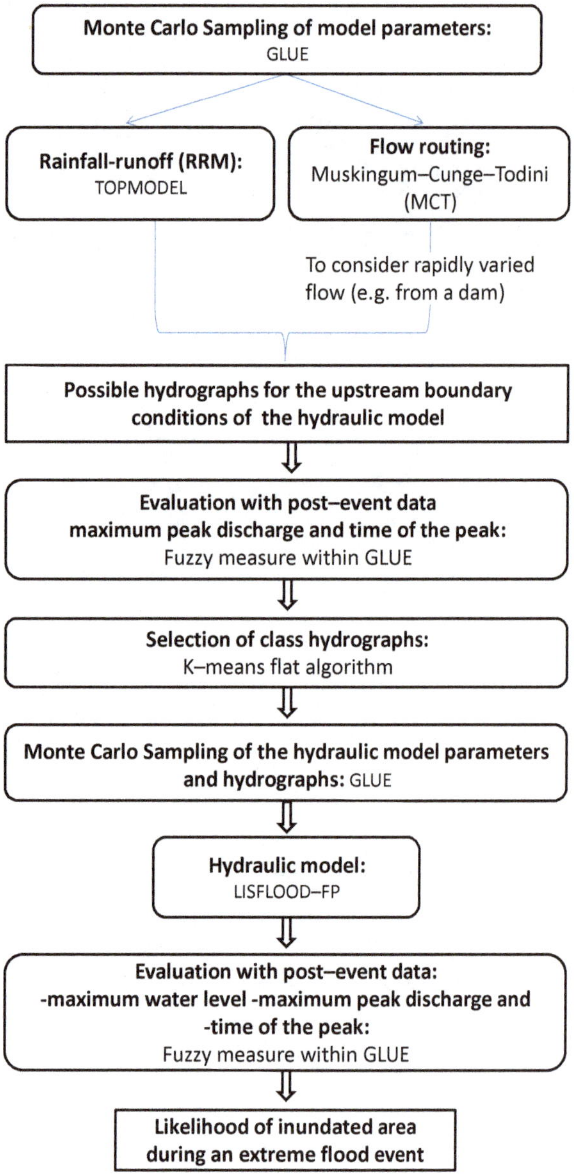

Figure 5. Scheme of the modelling framework used to reproduce an extreme flood event using post-event-estimated data to drive and constrain a combination of modelling tools within an uncertainty-analysis framework.

et al., 2012a). The model requires flow hydrographs as upstream boundary conditions, which were generated using the TOPMODEL RRM (Beven and Kirkby, 1979; Kirkby, 1997) as in Fuentes-Andino et al., (2017) (Appendix A) together with the Muskingum–Cunge–Todini (MCT) flood-routing approach (Todini, 2007) (Appendix B). A scheme of the modelling framework is shown in Fig. 5.

3.4 Representative hydrographs for the upstream boundary condition

Topographic information is a basis to set up TOPMODEL, which was one reason to select it in our mountainous catchment. Additionally, the version used here (Fuentes-Andino et al., 2017) has been shown to improve model prediction by considering the uncertainty associated with the spatially averaged estimation of rainfall. The mass-conservative version of the Muskingun–Cunge routing, the MCT, was incorporated to consider the sudden release of water from the Concepción reservoir, and it was chosen since a more complex routing could not be applied given the lack of data in the upstream area of the floodplain. The effect of Los Laureles dam on simulating the hydrograph of the Guacerique River sub-catchment was assumed to be negligible since the dam was overtopped long before the most intensive period of the storm.

The TOPMODEL and MCT combination assumes slope-dependent variable velocity at a hillslope, constant velocity at a normal channel, and a variable velocity (according to the diffusive wave model of the MCT) at the main channel (whose length was estimated to have a minimum drainage area equal to 65 km^2). For each sub-catchment, the main channel was sub-divided into reaches of approximately 2.5 km to execute the MCT routing. For the MCT routing at Grande River, the inflow for the most upstream reach was set equal to the outflow hydrograph from the reservoir, and for other sub-catchments, to be equal to the hydrograph draining to that reach using TOPMODEL. For the subsequent reaches, this inflow was estimated as the sum of the outflow from the MCT routing at the immediate upstream reach and the hydrograph produced by TOPMODEL in the area draining to that reach (excluding the area draining to the upstream reaches). The modelling time step was equal to 5 min, smaller than the estimated travel time of the flood wave along the reach, as required by the MCT routing.

For the TOPMODEL, a network width function for each reach was created using topography from the SRTM raster. Only two rain-gauge stations were available, which made it difficult to infer the spatial distribution of rainfall. However, rainfall registered at the two stations was similar; thus, rainfall was assumed to be spatially uniform and estimated as the average of the two time series. Given the large magnitude of the event, it was expected to be associated with little spatial variation.

Uncertainty in rainfall input was taken into account by a multiplier (R); in addition, uncertainty of six model parameters was considered: the rate of decline of transmissivity (m), horizontal transmissivity (T_o), time constant (t_d), land-use coefficient (l_u), flood-wave celerity (v_c), and maximum soil infiltration rate (i_{max}) (Appendix A). The MCT method required information of the river slope and the geometry of the cross sections (Appendix B). The former was approximated from SRTM data, while the latter was inferred

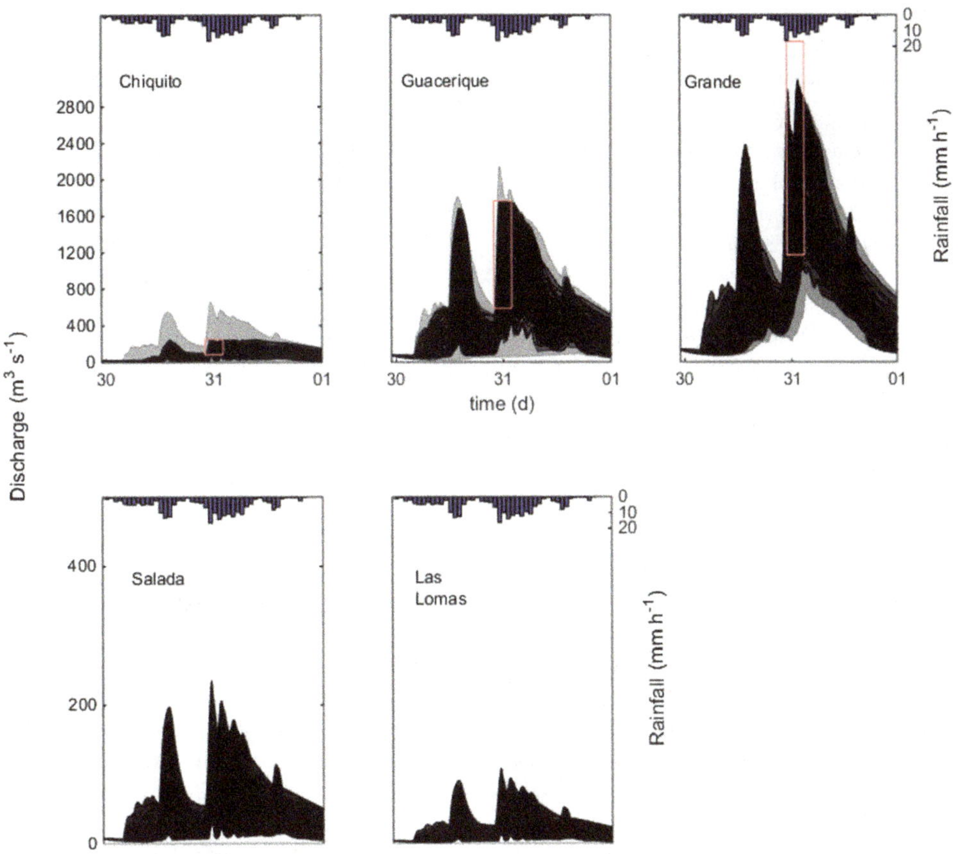

Figure 6. Precipitation (bars) and 100 class hydrographs chosen from the behavioural ones (black plots) for five sub-catchments upstream of the floodplain. Predictive range of the 100% probability limits for all hydrograph simulations (grey shaded area) and rectangles representing the fuzzy set to allow for uncertainty for peak discharge and time of the peak for the sub-catchments of the Chiquito, Guacerique, and Grande rivers.

here as a function of discharge using the Manning equation for a wide parabolic channel as in Tewolde and Smithers (2007), with the channel roughness coefficient (n_{cu}) assumed uniform along all the reaches to make the modelling system simple and, in view of the lack of data, to constrain localized values.

All parameters were sampled from uniform distributions with ranges considered large but possible in the literature (Table 2) and each generated parameter set was used to simulate the Chiquito, Grande, and Guacerique river sub-catchments (outlets at points 1, 2, and 5 in Figs. 1 and 2 and Table 1). A stopping criterion as in Pappenberger et al. (2005b) was used to decide the number of simulations required. For every 500 behavioural simulations added, a cumulative distribution function (CDF) of the predicted peak discharge and one of the time of the peak were estimated (evaluation variables; see Sect. 3.4.1). These estimated CDFs were compared with the previous one and the number of runs was considered sufficient when the addition of behavioural simulations did not change the CDF significantly (i.e. $P < 0.05$) using the Kuiper (1960) statistical test (Appendix C). This statistical test was considered suitable since it is sensitive to changes in the tail and to the median values of the distribution; therefore, it makes sure that the distributions did not change along the whole range of values.

Las Lomas Creek and Salada Creek (points 8 and 9 in Figs. 1 and 2) did not have data to constrain the simulations and, by proximity, the behavioural parameters found at both Grande and Chiquito were used to simulate them. This is expected to not greatly affect the system as the contributing areas for Las Lomas Creek and Salada Creek are relatively small in comparison to the three sub-catchments where post-event data were available (Fig. 1). In addition, these two areas were smaller than the threshold drainage area for applying MCT; therefore, only parameters from TOPMODEL were transferred to those sub-catchments.

3.4.1 Output evaluation

To decide on behavioural hydrographs for the Chiquito, Guacerique, and Grande river sub-catchments, the maximum peak and time of peak post-event observations, together with their associated uncertainty, were used (refer to points 1, 2, and 5 in Table 1). The assumed uncertainty range was $b =$

Table 2. Sampling parameter ranges to run the rainfall–runoff model.

Parameter	Abbreviation	Unit	Sampling range
Rainfall multiplier	R	(–)	0.4–2.0
Rate of decline of transmissivity	m	(m)	0.005–0.035
Horizontal transmissivity	T_o	($\mathrm{m^2\,h^{-1}}$)	0.001–20
Time constant	t_d	($\mathrm{m\,h^{-1}}$)	1–60
Land-use coefficient	l_u	($\mathrm{m\,s^{-1}}$)	0.04–0.2
Flood-wave celerity	v_c	($\mathrm{m\,s^{-1}}$)	1.0–3.5
Maximum soil infiltration rate	i_max	($\mathrm{m\,h^{-1}}$)	0.005–0.03
Main channel roughness coefficient	n_cu	($\mathrm{s\,m^{-1/3}}$)	0.001–0.08

$a = \pm 50\,\%$ of the peak flow for the peak magnitude and $b = a = \pm 2.5$ h for the time of peak (Fig. 4). For the evaluation of the hydrographs, a was set equal to b; thus, every hydrograph within the uncertainty bounds was considered behavioural and to have an equal degree of belief. The uncertainty in peak discharge at points 1 and 2 was chosen considering, and was assumed larger than, the value suggested in Benson and Dalrymple (1967). The discharge at point 5, although it was estimated by running a RRM by JICA (2002), was considered reliable for calibration since its magnitude was similar to the maximum peak outflow measured at Los Laureles dam, located in the same river and with nearly equally contributing upstream areas as in point 5 (Fig. 1). It was expected that 50 % of the flow uncertainty, as well as for points 1 and 2, was also reasonable at point 5. All times of peak came from the same source, i.e. witness accounts, and there was no additional information on their uncertainties; thus, we allowed up to 2.5 h uncertainty considering that the survey was carried out 2 years after the event and because of the expected difficulties in witnesses identifying the exact times when the peak occurred.

To reduce computational costs and avoid redundancy, 100 representative hydrographs (class hydrographs) were obtained for each sub-catchment by clustering the full behavioural ensemble. Clustering was done using the K-means flat algorithm also called Lloyd's algorithm, originally developed by Lloyd (2006), described in Madhulatha (2012), and with a tool available for use at Mathworks (2011). Following the K-means algorithm, the number of groups (K) to cluster an ensemble of data (here the behavioural hydrographs) were defined (here equal to 100). Then, a number of K hydrographs were randomly chosen from the ensemble to represent the cluster centroids. Each of the hydrographs in the ensemble was assigned to one of the centroid hydrographs according to the smallest distance, here taken as the sum of the absolute differences between hydrographs. Subsequently the centroid for each of the clusters was replaced with the hydrograph whose sum of distances from all hydrographs within the cluster is minimized; and then each hydrograph in the ensemble was assigned to the new centroid found. The procedure of moving centroids and assigning hydrographs to new centroids is repeated until there is no change in the clusters. To consider the extreme cases, the hydrograph from each cluster with the largest sum of the distances to all other centroid hydrographs was chosen.

3.5 Flood-wave propagation

The LISFLOOD-FP was used to propagate the flood waves along the channels and across the floodplain. Here the subgrid channel formulation following Neal et al. (2012a) was used, where the floodplain and the channel have a 2-D square grid representation and flow is conveyed using the local inertia formulation (de Almeida et al., 2012). Thus, the continuity equation (Eq. 1) and a simplified version of the momentum equation (where the convective-acceleration term was assumed negligible) (Eq. 2) were used to keep the continuity of mass and momentum respectively in each cell and between cells.

$$\frac{\partial h}{\partial t} + \frac{\partial Q_x}{\partial x} + \frac{\partial Q_y}{\partial y} = 0, \tag{1}$$

$$\frac{\partial Q_x}{\partial t} + gA\left(S_x + \frac{n^2 Q_x |Q_x|}{(R^{4/3})\,A^2}\right) = 0, \tag{2a}$$

$$\frac{\partial Q_y}{\partial t} + gA\left(S_y + \frac{n^2 Q_y |Q_y|}{(R^{4/3})\,A^2}\right) = 0, \tag{2b}$$

where Q_x and Q_y, and S_x and S_y are the volumetric flow rates and the slopes respectively in the x and y directions, h the water depth, t time, A the cross-sectional area of flow, g gravity, n the Manning coefficient, and R the hydraulic radius, taken as the cell cross-sectional area divided by the wetted perimeter.

Equations (1) and (2) are solved using an explicit forward difference scheme on a staggered grid (Bates et al., 2010) which requires fewer numerical operations (about an order of magnitude) than a full 2-D dynamic model (Neal et al., 2012b). The former numerical procedure was computationally more efficient than the latter and therefore more suitable for uncertainty analysis. In addition, the model-grid representation made it possible to obtain the discharge and water-level time series output at any grid along the channel or floodplain.

The basic input data for the LISFLOOD-FP are topography, hydrographs at the upstream boundary conditions, a downstream boundary condition, and Manning roughness coefficients. To use as topographic input to the model, the lidar data were aggregated to 21 m cell resolution, as a trade-off between high resolution and the speed of simulations. The surveyed cross sections and orthographic pictures from JICA (2002) were used to define channel depth and width respectively. Test simulations of this event were performed within the HEC-RAS 1-D hydraulic model (Brunner, 2001) considering the topography of the bridges, and preliminary results showed that bridges had a negligible effect on the overall flood profile. Thus, the geometry of bridges in the LISFLOOD-FP implementation was neglected by assuming a limited and localized impact on flood levels as in e.g. Castellarin et al. (2009), especially since the calibration data are associated with large uncertainties so that the localized effect of structures is not possible to detect (Fewtrell et al., 2011).

Uncertainty of the input hydrographs at each of the upstream boundary conditions was considered by sampling from the 100 class hydrographs. By assuming normal flow, the overall downstream valley slope, b_c, was used as the downstream boundary condition. This assumption was considered in view of the lack of hydrograph information at the downstream boundary; however, water-level predictions at the most downstream cross sections can be associated with larger uncertainties due to this assumption (Pappenberger et al., 2006). Besides b_c the channel-roughness coefficient, assumed uniform along all the channel length, n_c, and the floodplain-roughness coefficient uniform along all the floodplain, n_f, were also considered to be uncertain parameters. Ideally roughness coefficients would be allowed to vary spatially to reflect changes in channel and floodplain characteristics (e.g. one value per reach or per each side of the floodplain), but this would have led to an increased number of parameters in the hydraulic model when there was not enough information at each reach to constrain the local roughness.

Using a one-at-a-time (OAT) design for sensitivity analysis, the effect that uncertainty in the channel depth and channel width (through a multiplying factor) had on the outputs was explored, which led to the incorporation of the channel-width multiplier (w_f) in the uncertainty analysis. For the hydraulic simulations, a total of 130 000 parameter sets were sampled from a uniform distribution with ranges considered large but possible in the literature (Table 3) in the same way as for the RRM.

3.5.1 Output evaluation

Different degrees of belief (d_i) (Fig. 4) were obtained by comparing the simulations with the following evaluation data.

- One degree of belief value, d_1, as performance in predicting the maximum peak discharge value of point 3 (Figs. 1 and 2 and Table 1).
- Two degrees of belief values, d_{2-3}, as performance in predicting the time of the maximum peak discharge of points 3 and 6 (Figs. 1 and 2 and Table 1).
- Ninety-nine degrees of belief values, d_{4-102}, as performance in predicting maximum water levels along the main river and two tributaries (Fig. 2).

The fuzzy set values of a and b for evaluating the simulated peak discharge were set to 20 and 50 % of observed values respectively. Thus, for differences between observed and predicted peak discharge within 20 % of the observation, the degree of belief was assumed to be equal to 1, and decreased to 0 for differences larger than 50 %. These values were chosen taking into account those values suggested by Benson and Dalrymple (1967) and Jarrett (1987). The fuzzy set values of a and b for evaluating the time of the peak were set equal to 0.5 and 2.5 h respectively; thus, the degree of belief for differences between observed and predicted times of the peak smaller than 0.5 h was assumed to be equal to 1, and it decreased to 0 to allow for up to 2.5 h of difference, an error considered possible in the observations. And finally, the fuzzy set values of a and b for evaluating the water levels were set equal to 0.5 and 1.8 m respectively. Thus, 0.5 m was chosen to account for error in topography representation (Neal et al., 2009), and 1.8 m was chosen considering the magnitude of the observed water level and that 2 years after the event witnesses' memories might have been associated with large uncertainties.

A parameter set was considered behavioural if the degree of belief was larger than 0 for each of the 102 evaluation points. For every parameter set, a global score (GS) was calculated based on a weighted average of the degrees of belief obtained for each evaluation criterion.

$$\mathrm{GS} = \sum_{i=1}^{i=102} w_i d_i, \tag{3}$$

where w_i are the weights associated with the degrees of belief corresponding to the observations. The weight associated with the peak discharge and the two times of the peak data (d_{1-3}) were set equal to 0.1 each; thus, 0.7 was the weight corresponding to the sum of the degrees of belief associated with all the observed maximum water levels (d_{4-102}). A larger aggregated weight was given to predict the observed water marks in comparison to the peak discharge and times of the peaks to reflect the larger number of observed water marks (99) and because the focus was on predicting flood extent. The weights could be changed according to the purpose of the study, which might also result in different ensembles being behavioural for different purposes (Pappenberger et al., 2007).

Subsequently, likelihood values were obtained by scaling the global scores by a constant C, so they will sum to

Table 3. Sampling range of parameters to run the hydraulic model.

Quantity	Parameter	Abbreviation	Unit	Sampling range
1	Channel width factor	w_f	–	0.5–2.0
1	Slope for downstream boundary condition	b_c	%	0.005–0.03
1	Channel roughness coefficient	n_c	$s\,m^{-1/3}$	0.005–0.3
1	Floodplain roughness coefficient	n_f	$s\,m^{-1/3}$	0.005–0.3
5	Hydrograph for the upstream boundary condition (100 class hydrographs)	–	units	1–100

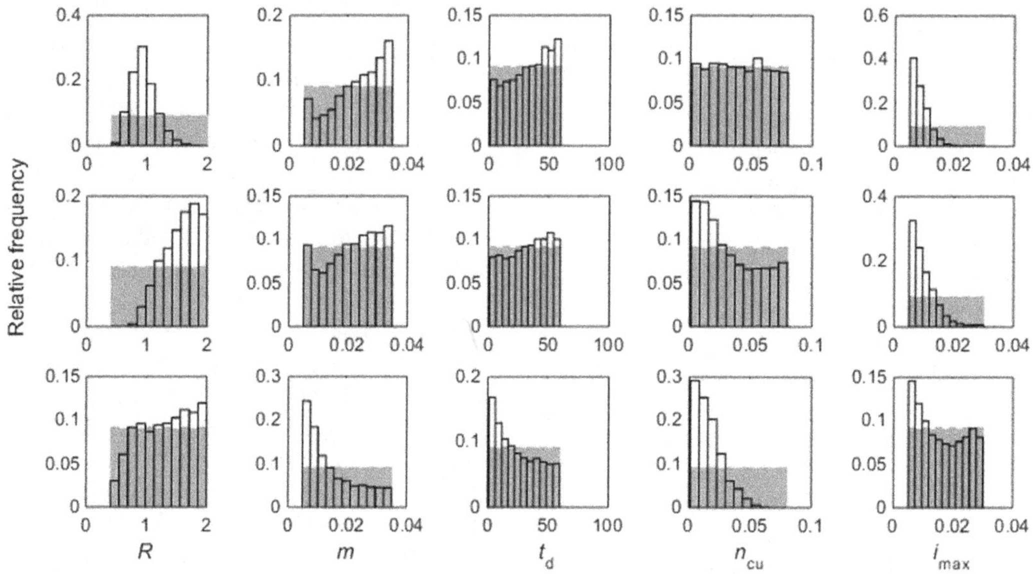

Figure 7. Prior (grey) and posterior (black outlined) relative frequency distribution for the most sensitive rainfall–runoff parameters: rainfall multiplier (R), rate of depletion (m), time factor (t_d), the main channel roughness coefficient (n_{cu}) and the maximum soil infiltration rate (i_{max}) for the Chiquito, Guacerique, and Grande catchments (first, second, and third rows respectively).

unity over all behavioural sets (Beven, 2009). Finally, the behavioural parameter sets were used to generate a fuzzy likelihood water-level profile and map of the maximum flood extension during the Mitch event as in Di Baldassarre et al. (2010).

4 Results

4.1 Consistency in the post-event measured data

From prior inspection of the data, it was found that information about the maximum peak discharge and time of the peak was consistent (i.e. in comparison to locations at the upstream reaches): discharge values and times of the peaks were larger and later at downstream locations after the confluences. A plot of the high-water marks showed sudden jumps at some observation points without any obvious physical explanation, but this is perhaps to be expected given the origin of those observations (witness accounts from memory). Thus, we did not eliminate any of the observations, but instead allowed an uncertainty range associated with all observation points.

4.2 Representative hydrographs for the upstream boundary condition

Behavioural hydrographs to use as the upstream boundary conditions of the hydraulic model were obtained for the sub-catchments of the Grande, Guacerique, and Chiquito rivers and, by using behavioural sets at the Grande and Chiquito river sub-catchments, at the Salada Creek and Las Lomas Creek sub-catchments (Fig. 6). The cumulative distribution function (CDF) of the predicted peak discharge and of the time of the peak of 2000, 8000, and 9000 behavioural simulation for sub-catchments of the Chiquito, Guacerique, and Grande rivers respectively did not change significantly by adding 500 behavioural simulations more. Thus a total of 3000, 9000, and 10 000 behavioural simulations, obtained from a total of 61 205, 60 237, and 60 833 samples respectively, were considered enough to infer 100 class hydrographs for the Chiquito, Guacerique, and Grande river sub-catchments respectively. When comparing the prior and pos-

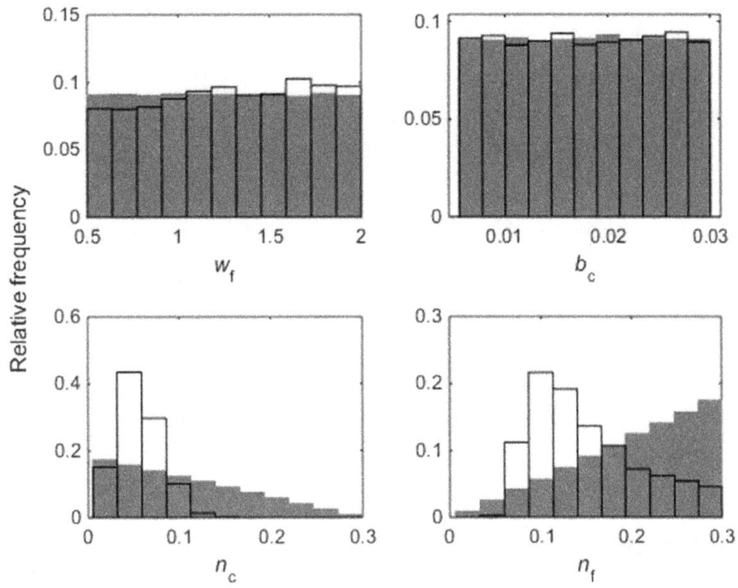

Figure 8. Prior and posterior relative frequency distribution (grey and black outlined bars respectively) of the LISFLOOD-FP parameters (width factor, slope for the downstream boundary condition, channel roughness coefficient, and floodplain roughness coefficient: w_f, b_c, n_c, and n_f respectively).

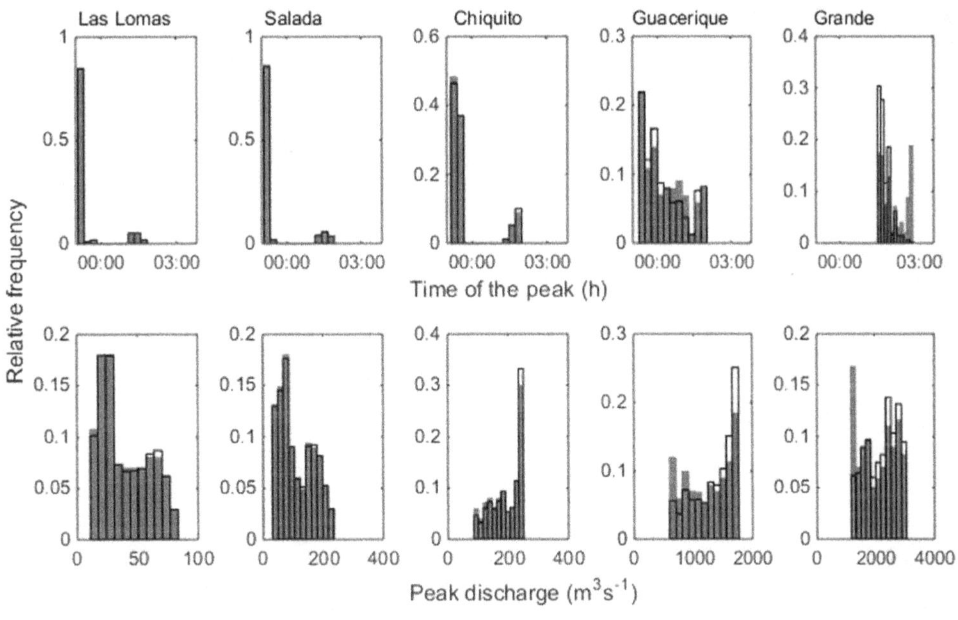

Figure 9. Prior and posterior relative frequency distribution (grey and black outlined bars respectively) of simulated maximum peak and time of the peak of input hydrographs for boundary conditions.

terior distributions of the rainfall–runoff model parameters, five out of eight parameters were sensitive: the rainfall multiplier (R), rate of depletion (m), time constant (t_d), main channel roughness coefficient (n_{cu}), and maximum soil infiltration rate (i_{max}) (Fig. 7).

4.3 Flood-wave propagation

There were no simulations for which all degrees of belief were larger than 0. Criteria d_{1-3} were fulfilled by 47 894 out of 130 000 total simulations, but some observed water marks (criteria d_{4-102}) were constantly and largely under- or over-predicted. To allow for special cases, i.e. larger error in the observations or in the hydraulic simulations, the constraints

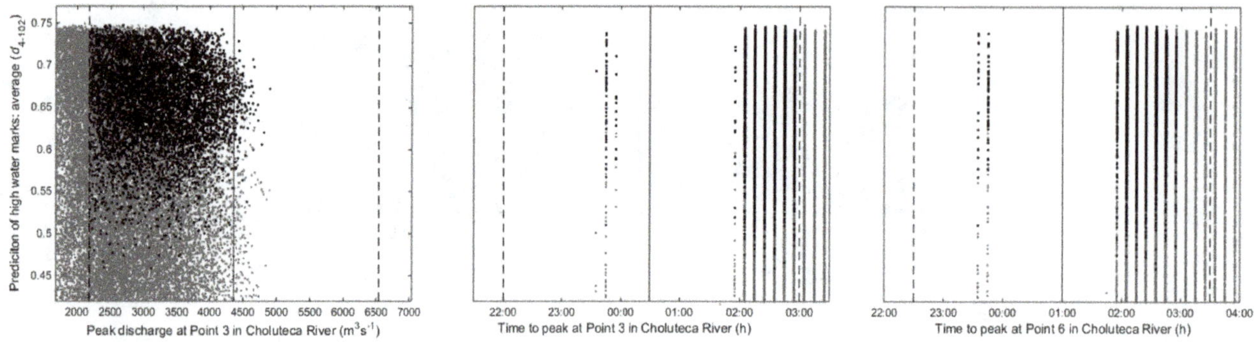

Figure 10. Performance of the model in predicting high-water marks, average (d_{4-102}), against predicted maximum peak discharge and two times of peak at the Choluteca River (reference points 3 and 6 at Figs. 1 and 2 and Table 1) for non-behavioural simulations (grey dots) and behavioural ones (black dots). Observed values and their limits of acceptability are plotted in continuous and dashed vertical lines respectively.

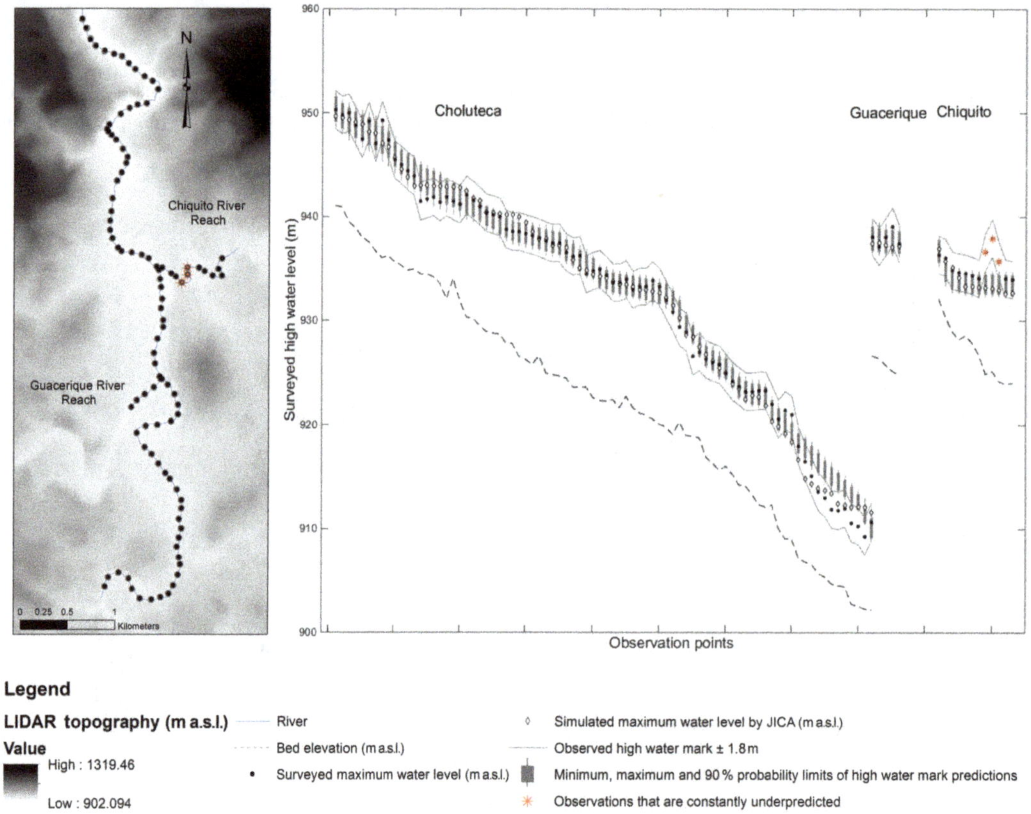

Figure 11. Likelihood of high-water marks during the Mitch event, considering uncertainty in model parameters, model input, and evaluation data to drive and constrain a combination of rainfall–runoff and hydraulic modelling tools.

were relaxed by allowing 10 % of observed water marks (10 out of 99 observations) to be outside the fuzzy bounds, i.e. the degree of belief was allowed to be equal to 0. By relaxing the constraints a total of 6357 parameter sets were found; the degrees of belief for those parameters varied between 0.001 and 1, 0.04 and 0.96, 0.29 and 0.79, and 0.46 and 0.75 (for d_1, d_2, d_3, and the average of d_{4-102} respectively), and the global score (GS) from 0.40 to 0.78.

Change in the posterior distributions of the parameters showed that the channel roughness coefficient and floodplain roughness coefficient were more sensitive than the channel width factor and the slope for the downstream boundary condition (Fig. 8). Changes in the posterior distribution of the peak and time of the peak showed that the model was unsurprisingly more sensitive to input hydrographs from the larger sub-catchments than from small sub-catchments (Fig. 9).

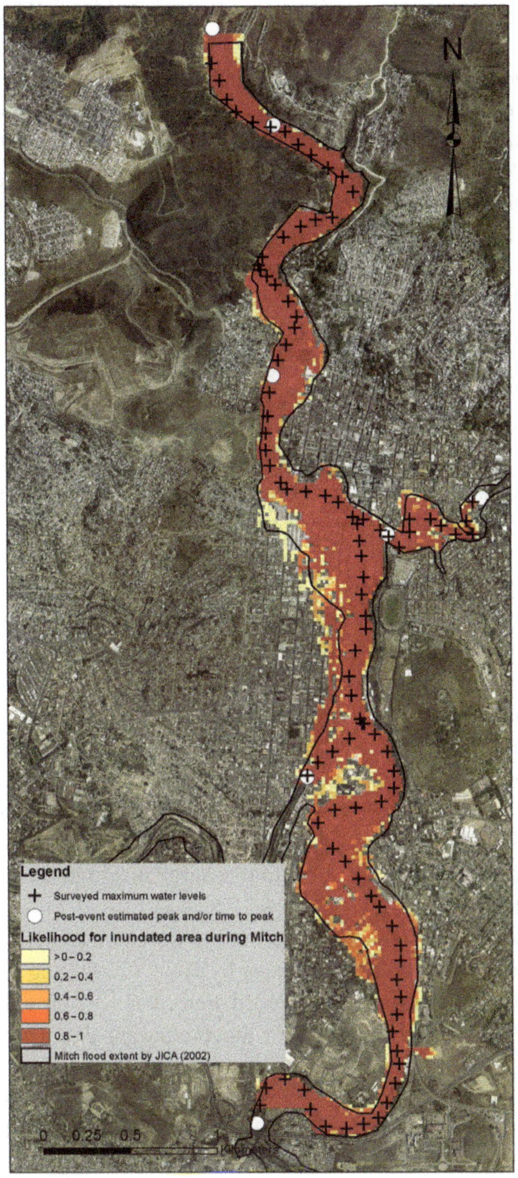

Figure 12. Likelihood of inundated area during the Mitch event on 30–31 October 1998, considering uncertainty in model parameters, model input, and evaluation data to drive and constrain a combination of rainfall–runoff and hydraulic modelling tools. The deterministic flood extent was obtained by digitalization of the flood extent in JICA (2002).

Flood-wave propagation of different input-hydrograph combinations led to prediction of two markedly different times of the peak at the floodplain, resulting in under- (over-) prediction when the earliest (latest) peak of input hydrograph combinations prevailed (Fig. 10).

There were three observed high-water marks in the Chiquito River reach that were constantly under-predicted and outside the uncertainty bounds of the observations (Fig. 11). The propagation from the water-level uncertainty to the flood extent was more evident in urban areas, where the flood extent varies more with changes in the water level due to the presence of structural features such as buildings (Fig. 12). From behavioural simulations, the 90 % confidence interval for prediction of the discharge at the floodplain outlet was 2708 to 4619 $m^3 s^{-1}$, encompassing the 3880 $m^3 s^{-1}$ value estimated in JICA (2002) (reference point 7 in Fig. 1 and Table 1). For reference point 4, at the Chiquito River, the 90 % confidence interval was 247 to 482 $m^3 s^{-1}$, also encompassing the 436 $m^3 s^{-1}$ value estimated in JICA (2002).

5 Discussion

A field campaign after a large flood event is an opportunity to collect information useful for flood forecasting and subsequent contingency planning in places where hydrometric measurements are lacking because of non-existing or broken gauges.

Our study demonstrated that it was possible, in a data-scarce situation, to reproduce an extreme flood event that was within the bounds of the uncertainty in the evaluation data. Our results support those of Bonnifait et al. (2009) and Ciervo et al. (2015) about the possibility of reproducing an extreme flood event by a suitable combination of RRM and hydraulic modelling tools with only event-based rainfall data and post-event hydrometric data. Here we additionally incorporated the GLUE methodology to account for expert knowledge of uncertainties in model parameters, rainfall input, and evaluation data. Thus, the combination of a RRM with a hydraulic modelling tool within an uncertainty framework as in Montanari et al. (2009) and Pappenberger et al. (2005a) proved to be useful also in the case with only post-event-estimated hydrometric data.

After considering the uncertainties and their interaction it was possible to identify behavioural parameter sets that were used to obtain a realistic probabilistic reproduction of the flood-water level (Fig. 11) and flood extension (Fig. 12). In comparison to the deterministic estimates made by JICA (2002) using different modelling tools, in this work it was possible to obtain predictive ranges of the water level that encompassed most of the observations. The flood extent here, associated with a likelihood at each flooded cell, generally extended beyond the extent of the JICA (2002) mapping.

The combination of TOPMODEL and MCT allowed us to estimate behavioural hydrographs for the Chiquito, Guacerique, and Grande sub-catchments. The simulations could be constrained (Fig. 6) in spite of the wide uncertainties in the data and the simplified assumption of the MCT routing for ungauged basins applied here. The rainfall multiplier (R), rate of depletion (m), time constant (t_d), main channel roughness coefficient (n_{cu}), and maximum soil infiltration rate (i_{max}) were more important in selecting the resulting hydrographs (Fig. 7), whereas horizontal transmissivity (T_o), land-use coefficient (l_u), and flood-wave celerity (v_c) were less sensitive.

The rainfall multipliers were sensitive and the means of their posterior distributions varied across sub-catchments (0.93, 1.5, and 1.3 for Chiquito, Guacerique, and Grande respectively) (Fig. 7), suggesting that the spatial average rainfall estimated from the two available gauges was overestimated at Chiquito and underestimated at the Guacerique and Grande sub-catchments. The Guacerique and Grande sub-catchments are larger and have a higher topographic elevation than the Chiquito sub-catchment. Underestimation of rainfall for these sub-catchments might be the result of lack of stations to represent the rainfall spatial pattern, highly variable in the area (Westerberg et al., 2010). Thus, a simplistic account of a space- and time-averaged rainfall multiplier as in Fuentes-Andino et al. (2017) was also useful here to account for bias estimation of the spatially averaged rainfall. The posterior distribution of the rainfall multiplier at the Chiquito and Guacerique sub-catchments clearly aggregated to different mean values. The sensitivity to the multiplier was different in the case of the Grande sub-catchment, which also showed a different posterior marginal distribution shape for the rate of depletion (m) and the time constant (t_d) (Fig. 7).

Different shapes of posterior marginal parameter distributions at the Grande River sub-catchment relative to the Guacerique and Chiquito river sub-catchments could be caused by parameter adjustment to fit the observations or by different hydrological processes going on in the different sub-catchments. The sudden release of water from the dam could also be a reason for these differences. The posterior marginal parameter distributions for the Grande River sub-catchment suggest that it has a shallower effective soil depth (low m) and a faster channel response in the MCT routing (low n_{cu}) than the other two sub-catchments. Hydrographs from a total of five sub-catchments (Fig. 6) from the TOPMODEL and MCT combination were used as upstream boundary conditions for the hydraulic simulations.

Even if more detailed post-event observations of flood extent might do better than water levels in constraining the LISFLOOD-FP (Fewtrell et al., 2011; Horritt and Bates, 2002), the modelling tool predicted the observed high-water marks, peaks, and times of peaks well. Behavioural simulations for which the degree of belief for the peak discharge, time of the peak, and at least 90 % of predicted high-water marks (89 out of 99 observations) were above 0 were identified.

The channel and floodplain roughness coefficients were the most important parameters for the hydraulic model (Fig. 8). As roughness coefficients directly affect the estimation of discharge and water level, the impact of their uncertainty has been shown previously in other studies (Dimitriadis et al., 2016; Pappenberger et al., 2005b; Warmink and Booij, 2015; Wohl, 1998). Here, uncertainty is expected to be particularly large as these coefficients interacted with uncertain post-event estimated discharge and high-water marks and also because they were assumed to be spatially aggregated due to data limitations. For example, a more localized calibration of such coefficients could have helped to tackle the problem of localized channel erosion during flood events common in the area (Guerrero et al., 2012). Given the assumed spatial representation of the roughness coefficients and the uncertainty they are associated with, they interacted with all other sources of uncertainty in a complex way that is difficult to separate. Such complex interactions are contained implicitly in the resulting ensemble of behavioural simulations (Beven, 2016).

The effect of the input hydrographs from the Grande River and Guacerique river sub-catchments on the resulting outputs is evident in Fig. 9. Thus, as in Dimitriadis et al. (2016), here the roughness coefficients and input flow were the most important sources of uncertainties. Two peaks in the input rainfall (Fig. 3) led to two main large peaks in the hydrographs as input boundary conditions (Figs. 6 and 9). The propagation of input hydrographs along the floodplain led to under- or over-prediction of the times of peak (Fig. 10). This suggests that the spatial pattern of rainfall was not well represented by the gauge average, as also suggested by the posterior distribution of rainfall multipliers in the RRM. Since rainfall data played an important role in predicting the times of peak, investment to improve the rainfall measurement system, e.g. radar estimates or a denser rain-gauge network, should be prioritized in the study area, especially because these data are easier to collect relative to discharge in a high-magnitude event.

Some observed high-water marks were constantly largely underpredicted in the estimates by JICA (2002) and outside the prediction bounds produced here, even when allowing for significant uncertainty in the evaluation data (Fig. 11). Inspection at the points that were constantly underpredicted showed that no man-made structure could have been the reason for such disagreement. Thus the problem of predicting at those locations could be caused by the inability of the hydraulic modelling tool to simulate the system under extreme conditions where effects such as sharp river bends might have an important local effect on the flow. However, a previous experiment using the 1-D HEC-RAS model on the same river also agreed with the results obtained here, and no localized effect in the under-predicted places was obtained. Another reason for the disagreement could be large errors in the post-event data.

In general, minor errors between prediction and observations in this work could be caused by a weak spatial representation of topography and roughness coefficient, i.e. special topographic details in a highly populated area with man-made structures that could not be captured by the DEM. However, those local features might not affect the general flood extent (Haile and Rientjes, 2005).

The peak discharge at point 3 (Figs. 1 and 2) was underpredicted by most of the simulations (Fig. 10). However, the high-water mark was over-estimated at that location

(Fig. 11). The reasons for this could be an over-estimation of the post-event peak discharge, or an under-estimation of the observed high-water mark, or the simplistic representation of the downstream boundary condition assumed.

A general under-prediction of the water level in the Chiquito River reach could be due to the low (perhaps under-estimated) post-event-estimated peak discharge; as in the comparison with the Grande and Guacerique sub-catchments, most of the hydrograph simulations for the former were rejected because the simulated peaks were larger than the evaluations (even considering the uncertainty) (Fig. 6). This could also be the reason for a lower rate of behavioural sets for the Chiquito River sub-catchment when comparing with the other two.

A detailed inspection of model structure, model set-up, and data at specific points where the modelling tools did not perform well even after considering possible uncertainties in the parameters, input, and evaluation data, could reveal areas for improvement.

This study was set up to demonstrate the use of post-event data and a combination of suitable RRM and hydraulic modelling tools with uncertainty analysis to reproduce an extreme flood in a data-scarce area. The behavioural ensemble found here depends on the uncertainties coming from the model structure (Dimitriadis et al., 2016), quality of the data (Pappenberger et al., 2006), topographic resolution (Haile and Rientjes, 2005), and spatial aggregation of the parameters (Beven, 1995). Considering the dependency with those sources of uncertainties and their interaction, the post-event data proved to be useful in reproducing the Hurricane Mitch flood event. High-water marks obtained from personal memories of an event are a good source of information. To decrease uncertainty of such information, institutions in charge of disaster prevention should be prepared to carry out such surveys soon after flood events when memory is fresh. In fact, soon after extreme events it is also possible to collect that information by surveying the marks left by the flood (e.g. Neal et al., 2009). Post-event-estimated peak discharge, though it is known to be associated with large uncertainties (Benson and Dalrymple, 1967; Jarrett, 1987), was a valuable source of information in this work. A higher spatial availability of flood peak discharge and time of the peak estimates would greatly benefit this methodology as it will allow a better quality control of individual estimates, to leave some of the estimates out for validation, and to estimate more localized patterns of roughness coefficients.

The use of this methodology can be done within a Bayesian framework in which the posterior distribution of the parameters is updated when more events become available. Data from more events could further reduce the predictive uncertainties and help us to learn from the flow behaviour at some localized areas where the errors were large. Post-event estimates in the future could likely also come from social-media information which is becoming gradually more available (Fraternali et al., 2012; Triglav-Čekada and Radovan, 2013).

The flood-hazard map presented here can be used by the committee in charge of disaster contingency and management in the city of Tegucigalpa (CODEM-DC) as a complement to the 5-, 10-, 25-, and 50-year return period hazard map produced in JICA (2002) and the the 50-year hazard map produced in Mastin (2002) and Mastin and Olsen (2002) for spatial planning and to prioritize investment. If real-time discharge measurements are available to calculate the initial saturation of a catchment, behavioural parameter sets updated from a range of events can be used for forecasting the flood extent as shown by Romanowicz and Beven (2003) and Montanari et al. (2009). In the absence of such measurements, a guess of the initial discharge may also work since it will not significantly affect the prediction for the intense period of the event. Furthermore, for that period, our methodology can give a better performance since calibration is done against discharge, time, and water level at the peak. It is also tempting to consider this methodology for forecasting fed both by an improved rain-gauge network and water-level information coming from social media.

6 Conclusions

In this study we tested the possibility of reproducing an extreme flood disaster in a data-scarce area, the devastating flood in Tegucigalpa triggered by Hurricane Mitch in 1998. It was possible to realistically reproduce this large ungauged flood event by using post-event hydrometric data in combination with rainfall data and various modelling tools, demonstrating the value of post-event field campaigns to constrain the uncertainties in estimates of hydrometric data, model parameters, and output. A methodology has been proposed where post-event-estimated data are used to drive and constrain a combination of rainfall–runoff and hydraulic modelling tools to reproduce floods within a GLUE uncertainty-analysis framework. Results of the flood extent proposed here were comparable to the deterministic mapping produced by JICA (2002) using different modelling tools. However, here more information was embedded as likelihoods of inundation associated with each cell in the floodplain.

Combining the TOPMODEL with the MCT routing to reproduce hydrographs in catchments with rapidly varied flow, e.g. release from a dam, resulted in hydrographs that were within the uncertain bounds of the observations. The predictive capability of the TOPMODEL and MCT combination warrants further exploration with more detailed and less uncertain event data. The rate and bias in the rejection of the hydrographs due to over-estimation indicated under-estimation of post-event-estimated discharge at one location. The propagation of estimated hydrographs through the 2-D hydraulic LISFLOOD-FP resulted in successful predictions of observed high-water marks, discharge peaks, and times of peaks within the uncertainty bounds for most of the evaluation variables. A few critical locations in the floodplain were identified where the model set-up could not reproduce the maximum water level. Locations of disagreement between simulations and evaluations, after considering all important sources of uncertainties, can provide information useful for improving model structure or post-event data-estimation methods. Results showed the importance that rainfall data have in simulating the times of peaks; thus, results would be improved by a better spatial assessment of rainfall. Improvements of this methodology can be done by using it within a Bayesian framework of updating the parameters' posterior distribution when more events become available. The methodology proposed here can be useful for planning, prioritizing investments, and flood forecasting.

Data availability. The lidar data on Tegucigalpa described in Mastin (2002) are available on request to the US Geological Survey (USGS). Post-event-estimated peak discharge obtained by the USGS is found in Smith et al. (2002). Post-event-estimated peak discharge obtained by JICA (2002) is found in http://libopac.jica.go.jp/images/report/P0000054205.html. The topography field survey and maximum water level survey described in JICA (2002) are found in http://libopac.jica.go.jp/images/report/P0000054208.html data provided by the Servicio Meteorológico Nacional (SMN, national weather service) and by the Universidad Nacional Autónoma de Honduras (UNAH), found in the Supplement. Data of the flow release at the Concepción reservoir provided by the Servicio Autónomo Nacional de Acueductos y Alcantarillados (SANAA) can be found in the Supplement.

Author contributions. The experiment was designed by DFA, KB, SH, CYX, and GDB. DFA carried out the experiment and performed the simulations. DFA prepared the manuscript with contributions from all co-authors.

Competing interests. The authors declare that they have no conflict of interest.

Acknowledgements. This research was carried out within the Universidad Nacional Autónoma de Honduras (UNAH) through agreement number 75000511–01 and the CNDS research school, supported by the Swedish International Development Cooperation Agency (Sida) through their contract with the International Science Programme (ISP) at Uppsala University (contract number: 54100006). The computations were performed on resources provided by SNIC through the Uppsala Multidisciplinary Center for Advanced Computational Science (UPPMAX) under project p2011010 and the High Performance Computing Center North (HPC2N) under project SNIC 2015/1-448. Thanks to the staff at the Servicio Meteorológico Nacional (SMN, national weather service), the Universidad Nacional Autónoma de Honduras (UNAH) and the Servicio Autónomo Nacional de Acueductos y Alcantarillados (SANAA) for their assistance in providing data for this study. Thanks to the School of Geographical Sciences at the University of Bristol for useful support regarding the LISFLOOD-FP model.

Edited by: Roger Moussa

References

Abily, M., Bertrand, N., Delestre, O., Gourbesville, P., and Duluc, C.-M.: Spatial global sensitivity analysis of high resolution classified topographic data use in 2-D urban flood modelling, Environ. Modell. Softw., 77, 183–195, https://doi.org/10.1016/j.envsoft.2015.12.002, 2016.

Alvarado, L. and Alfaro, E.: Frecuencia de los ciclones tropicales que afectaron a Costa Rica durante el siglo XX, Tópicos Meteorológicos y Oceanográficos, 10, 1–11, 2003.

Amador, J. A., Alfaro, E. J., Lizano, O. G., and Magaña, V. O.: Atmospheric forcing of the eastern tropical Pacific: a review, Prog. Oceanogr., 69, 101–142, https://doi.org/10.1016/j.pocean.2006.03.007, 2006.

Angel, S., Bartley, K., Derr, M., Malur, A., Mejía, J., Nuka, P., Perlin, M., Sahai, S., Torrens, M., and Vargas, M.: Rapid urbanization in Tegucigalpa, Honduras. Preparing for the doubling of the city's population in the next twenty-five years, Woodrow Wilson School of Public and International Affairs, Princenton, available at: http://ch.tool-alfa.com/LinkClick.aspx?fileticket=62r4HGSTAdw%3D&tabid=72&mid=421 (last access: 13 July 2017) 2004.

Aronica, G., Hankin, B., and Beven, K.: Uncertainty and equifinality in calibrating distributed roughness coefficients in a flood propagation model with limited data, Adv. Water Resour., 22, 349–365, https://doi.org/10.1016/S0309-1708(98)00017-7, 1998.

Bates, P. D., Horritt, M. S., and Fewtrell, T. J.: A simple inertial formulation of the shallow water equations for efficient two-dimensional flood inundation modelling, J. Hydrol., 387, 33–45, https://doi.org/10.1016/j.jhydrol.2010.03.027, 2010.

Benson, M. A. and Dalrymple, T.: General field and office procedures for indirect discharge measurements, in: Techniques of Water- Resources Investigations of the United States Geological Survey, available at: http://pubs.usgs.gov/twri/twri3-a1/html/pdf.html (last access: 13 July 2017) 1967.

Beven, K.: Linking parameters across scales: subgrid parameterizations and scale dependent hydrological models, Hydrol. Process., 9, 507–525, https://doi.org/10.1002/hyp.3360090504, 1995.

Beven, K.: TOPMODEL: a critique, Hydrol. Process., 11, 1069–1085, https://doi.org/10.1002/(SICI)1099-1085(199707)11:9<1069::AID-HYP545>3.0.CO;2-O, 1997.

Beven, K.: Rainfall–Runoff Modelling: the Primer, 2nd edn., John Wiley & Sons, Chichester, West Sussex; Hoboken, NJ, 2012.

Beven, K.: Facets of uncertainty: epistemic uncertainty, non-stationarity, likelihood, hypothesis testing, and communication, Hydrolog. Sci. J., 61, 1652–1665, https://doi.org/10.1080/02626667.2015.1031761, 2016.

Beven, K., Gilman, K., and Newson, M.: Flow and flow routing in uplands channel networks, Hydrol. Sci. Bull., 24, 303–325, 1979.

Beven, K., Leedal, D., McCarthy, S., Hunter, N. M., Keef, C., Bates, P. D., Neal, J., and Wicks, J.: Framework for assessing uncertainty in fluvial flood risk mapping, FRMRC Research Report SWP1.7, 2011.

Beven, K. J.: Environmental Modelling: an Uncertain Future? An Introduction to Techniques for Uncertainty Estimation in Environmental Prediction, Routledge, London, 2009.

Beven, K. J. and Binley, A.: The future of distributed models: model calibration and uncertainty prediction, Hydrol. Process., 6, 279–298, 1992.

Beven, K. J. and Kirkby, M. J.: A physically based, variable contributing area model of basin hydrology/Un modèle à base physique de zone d'appel variable de l'hydrologie du bassin versant, Hydrol. Sci. Bull., 24, 43–69, https://doi.org/10.1080/02626667909491834, 1979.

Bonnifait, L., Delrieu, G., Lay, M. L., Boudevillain, B., Masson, A., Belleudy, P., Gaume, E., and Saulnier, G.-M.: Distributed hydrologic and hydraulic modelling with radar rainfall input: reconstruction of the 8–9 September 2002 catastrophic flood event in the Gard region, France, Adv. Water Resour., 32, 1077–1089, https://doi.org/10.1016/j.advwatres.2009.03.007, 2009.

Borga, M., Gaume, E., Creutin, J. D., and Marchi, L.: Surveying flash floods: gauging the ungauged extremes, Hydrol. Process., 22, 3883–3885, https://doi.org/10.1002/hyp.7111, 2008.

Bozzi, S., Passoni, G., Bernardara, P., Goutal, N., and Arnaud, A.: Roughness and discharge uncertainty in 1-D water level calculations, Environ. Model. Assess., 20, 343–353, https://doi.org/10.1007/s10666-014-9430-6, 2015.

Brandimarte, L. and Di Baldassarre, G.: Uncertainty in design flood profiles derived by hydraulic modelling, Hydrol. Res., 43, 753–761, https://doi.org/10.2166/nh.2011.086, 2012.

Brunner, G.: HEC-RAS river analysis system, Hydraulic Reference Manual, available at: http://www.hec.usace.army.mil/software/hec-ras/documents/HEC-RAS_4.1_Reference_Manual.pdf (last access: 9 September 2014), 2001.

Castellarin, A.: Probabilistic envelope curves for design flood estimation at ungauged sites, Water Resour. Res., 43, W04406, https://doi.org/10.1029/2005WR004384, 2007.

Castellarin, A., Baldassarre, G. D., Bates, P. D., and Brath, A.: Optimal cross-sectional spacing in Preissmann Scheme 1-D hydrodynamic models, J. Hydraul. Eng., 135, 96–105, https://doi.org/10.1061/(ASCE)0733-9429(2009)135:2(96), 2009.

CIAT: Land Use in Honduras, International Center for tropical agriculture, Francisco Morazán, Honduras, 2007.

Ciervo, F., Papa, M. N., Medina, V., and Bateman, A.: Simulation of flash floods in ungauged basins using post-event surveys and numerical modelling, J. Flood Risk Manag., 8, 343–355, https://doi.org/10.1111/jfr3.12103, 2015.

Cœur, D. and Lang, M.: Use of documentary sources on past flood events for flood risk management and land planning, Comptes Rendus Geosci., 340, 644–650, https://doi.org/10.1016/j.crte.2008.03.001, 2008.

Dalrymple, T. and Benson, M. A.: Measurement of peak discharge by the slope-area method, in: Techniques of Water-Resources Investigations of the United States Geological Survey, available at: http://pubs.usgs.gov/twri/twri3-a2/pdf/twri_3-A2_a.pdf (last access: 13 July 2017), 1968.

de Almeida, G. A. M., Bates, P., Freer, J. E., and Souvignet, M.: Improving the stability of a simple formulation of the shallow water equations for 2-D flood modeling, Water Resour. Res., 48, W05528, https://doi.org/10.1029/2011WR011570, 2012.

Delrieu, G., Nicol, J., Yates, E., Kirstetter, P.-E., Creutin, J.-D., Anquetin, S., Obled, C., Saulnier, G.-M., Ducrocq, V., Gaume, E., Payrastre, O., Andrieu, H., Ayral, P.-A., Bouvier, C., Neppel, L., Livet, M., Lang, M., du-Châtelet, J. P., Walpersdorf, A., and Wobrock, W.: The catastrophic flash-flood event of 8–9 September 2002 in the Gard Region, France: a first case study for the Cévennes–Vivarais Mediterranean Hydrometeorological Observatory, J. Hydrometeorol., 6, 34–52, https://doi.org/10.1175/JHM-400.1, 2005.

DHI: A Modelling System for Rivers and Channels: reference Manual, Danish Hydraulic Institute, Hørsholm, Denmark, 2000.

Di Baldassarre, G., Schumann, G., Bates, P. D., Freer, J. E., and Beven, K. J.: Flood-plain mapping: a critical discussion of deterministic and probabilistic approaches, Hydrolog. Sci. J., 55, 364–376, https://doi.org/10.1080/02626661003683389, 2010.

Dimitriadis, P., Tegos, A., Oikonomou, A., Pagana, V., Koukouvinos, A., Mamassis, N., Koutsoyiannis, D., and Efstratiadis, A.: Comparative evaluation of 1-D and quasi-2-D hydraulic models based on benchmark and real-world applications for uncertainty assessment in flood mapping, J. Hydrol., 534, 478–492, https://doi.org/10.1016/j.jhydrol.2016.01.020, 2016.

Fewtrell, T. J., Neal, J. C., Bates, P. D., and Harrison, P. J.: Geometric and structural river channel complexity and the prediction of urban inundation, Hydrol. Process., 25, 3173–3186, https://doi.org/10.1002/hyp.8035, 2011.

Fraternali, P., Castelletti, A., Soncini-Sessa, R., Vaca Ruiz, C., and Rizzoli, A. E.: Putting humans in the loop: social computing for water resources management, Environ. Modell. Softw., 37, 68–77, https://doi.org/10.1016/j.envsoft.2012.03.002, 2012.

Fuentes-Andino, D., Beven, K., Kauffeldt, A., Xu, C.-Y., Halldin, S., and Baldassarre, G. D.: Event and model dependent rainfall adjustments to improve discharge predictions, Hydrolog. Sci. J., 62, 232–245, https://doi.org/10.1080/02626667.2016.1183775, 2017.

Gaume, E. and Borga, M.: Post-flood field investigations in upland catchments after major flash floods: proposal of a methodology and illustrations, J. Flood Risk Manag., 1, 175–189, https://doi.org/10.1111/j.1753-318X.2008.00023.x, 2008.

Gaume, E., Bain, V., Bernardara, P., Newinger, O., Barbuc, M., Bateman, A., Blaškovičová, L., Blöschl, G., Borga, M., Dumitrescu, A., Daliakopoulos, I., Garcia, J., Irimescu, A., Kohnova, S., Koutroulis, A., Marchi, L., Matreata, S., Medina, V., Preciso, E., Sempere-Torres, D., Stancalie, G., Szolgay, J., Tsanis, I., Velasco, D., and Viglione, A.: A compilation of data on European flash floods, J. Hydrol., 367, 70–78, https://doi.org/10.1016/j.jhydrol.2008.12.028, 2009.

Grimaldi, S., Petroselli, A., Alonso, G., and Nardi, F.: Flow time estimation with spatially variable hillslope velocity in ungauged basins, Adv. Water Resour., 33, 1216–1223, https://doi.org/10.1016/j.advwatres.2010.06.003, 2010.

Guerrero, J.-L., Westerberg, I. K., Halldin, S., Xu, C.-Y., and Lundin, L.-C.: Temporal variability in stage–discharge relationships, J. Hydrol., 446–447, 90–102, https://doi.org/10.1016/j.jhydrol.2012.04.031, 2012.

Haile, A. and Rientjes, T. H. M.: Effects of lidar DEM resolution in flood modelling: a model sensitivity study for the city of Tegucigalpa, Honduras, ISPRS WG III3 III4 V3 Workshop Laser Scanning 2005, Enschede, the Netherlands, 12–14 September, 6, 2005.

Hall, J. W., Manning, L. J., and Hankin, R. K. S.: Bayesian calibration of a flood inundation model using spatial data, Water Resour. Res., 47, W05529, https://doi.org/10.1029/2009WR008541, 2011.

Horritt, M. S. and Bates, P. D.: Evaluation of 1-D and 2-D numerical models for predicting river flood inundation, J. Hydrol., 268, 87–99, https://doi.org/10.1016/S0022-1694(02)00121-X, 2002.

Horritt, M. S., Bates, P. D., Fewtrell, T. J., Mason, D. C., and Wilson, M. D.: Modelling the hydraulics of the Carlisle 2005 flood event, Proc. Inst. Civ. Eng. – Water Manag., 163, 273–281, https://doi.org/10.1680/wama.2010.163.6.273, 2010.

ING: Mapa hydrogeológico de la zona Central de Honduras (The hydrogeological map of the center zone of Honduras), Francisco Morazán, Honduras, 1996.

Iooss, B. and Lemaître, P.: A review on global sensitivity analysis methods, in: Uncertainty Management in Simulation–Optimization of Complex Systems, edited by: Dellino, G. and Meloni, C., Springer US, Boston,Mass, USA, 101–122, 2015.

Jarrett, R.: Hydrologie and hydraulic research in mountain rivers, Water Resour. Bull., 26, 419–429, 1990.

Jarrett, R. D.: Errors in slope-area computations of peak discharges in mountain streams, J. Hydrol., 96, 53–67, https://doi.org/10.1016/0022-1694(87)90143-0, 1987.

JICA: On flood control and landslide prevention in Tegucigalpa metropolitan area of the republic of Honduras, Pacific consultants International and Nikken consultants, Tegucigalpa, Honduras, available at: http://libopac.jica.go.jp/ (last access: 20 January 2017), 2002.

Kirkby, M. J.: Tests of the random network model, and its application to basin hydrology, Earth Surf. Proces., 1, 197–212, https://doi.org/10.1002/esp.3290010302, 1976.

Kirkby, M. J.: TOPMODEL: a personal view, Hydrol. Process., 11, 1087–1097, https://doi.org/10.1002/(SICI)1099-1085(199707)11:9<1087::AID-HYP546>3.0.CO;2-P, 1997.

Kuiper, N. H.: Tests concerning random points on a circle, Indag. Math. Proc., 63, 38–47, https://doi.org/10.1016/S1385-7258(60)50006-0, 1960.

Le Boursicaud, R., Pénard, L., Hauet, A., Thollet, F., and Le Coz, J.: Gauging extreme floods on YouTube: application of LSPIV to home movies for the post-event determination of stream discharges, Hydrol. Process., 30, 90–105, https://doi.org/10.1002/hyp.10532, 2016.

Lloyd, S.: Least squares quantization in PCM, IEEE Trans. Inf. Theor., 28, 129–137, https://doi.org/10.1109/TIT.1982.1056489, 2006.

Madhulatha, T. S.: An overview on clustering methods, ArXiv12051117 Cs, available at: http://arxiv.org/abs/1205.1117 (last access: 18 July 2016), 2012.

Mård Karlsson, J., Skelton, A., Sandén, M., Ioualalen, M., Kaewbanjak, N., Pophet, N., Asavanant, J., and von Matern, A.: Reconstructions of the coastal impact of the 2004 Indian Ocean tsunami in the Khao Lak area, Thailand, J. Geophys. Res.-Oceans, 114, C10023, https://doi.org/10.1029/2009JC005516, 2009.

Mastin, M.: Flood-hazard mapping in Honduras in response to Hurricane Mitch, US Geological Survey, Tacoma, Washington, available at: http://pubs.usgs.gov/wri/wri014277/pdf/WRIR01-4277.pdf (last access: 15 January 2017), 2002.

Mastin, M. and Olsen, T.: Fifty-year flood-inundation maps for Tegucigalpa, Honduras, US Geological Survey, Tacoma, Washington, 2002.

Mathworks: MATLAB Documentation, MathWorks Nordic, available at: https://se.mathworks.com/help/matlab/ (last access: 4 January 2017), 2011.

Matthai, H. F.: Measurement of peak discharge at width contractions by indirect methods, in: Techniques of Water-Resources Investigations of the United States Geological Survey, available at: http://pubs.usgs.gov/twri/twri3-a4/pdf/twri_3-A4_a.pdf (last access: 13 July 2017), 1968.

McCown, S., Ross, T., and Lott, N.: Mitch: the deadliest Atlantic hurricane since 1780, Natl. Ocean. Atmospheric Adm. NOAA, available at: ftp://ftp.ncdc.noaa.gov/pub/data/extremeevents/specialreports/Hurricane-Mitch-1998.pdf (last access: 11 July 2017), 1999.

McDonnell, J. J. and Beven, K.: Debates – the future of hydrological sciences: a (common) path forward? A call to action aimed at understanding velocities, celerities and residence time distributions of the headwater hydrograph, Water Resour. Res., 50, 5342–5350, https://doi.org/10.1002/2013WR015141, 2014.

Montanari, M., Hostache, R., Matgen, P., Schumann, G., Pfister, L., and Hoffmann, L.: Calibration and sequential updating of a coupled hydrologic-hydraulic model using remote sensing-derived water stages, Hydrol. Earth Syst. Sci., 13, 367–380, https://doi.org/10.5194/hess-13-367-2009, 2009.

Neal, J., Schumann, G., and Bates, P.: A subgrid channel model for simulating river hydraulics and floodplain inundation over large and data sparse areas, Water Resour. Res., 48, W11506, https://doi.org/10.1029/2012WR012514, 2012a.

Neal, J., Villanueva, I., Wright, N., Willis, T., Fewtrell, T., and Bates, P.: How much physical complexity is needed to model flood inundation?, Hydrol. Process., 26, 2264–2282, https://doi.org/10.1002/hyp.8339, 2012b.

Neal, J. C., Bates, P. D., Fewtrell, T. J., Hunter, N. M., Wilson, M. D., and Horritt, M. S.: Distributed whole city water level measurements from the Carlisle 2005 urban flood event and comparison with hydraulic model simulations, J. Hydrol., 368, 42–55, https://doi.org/10.1016/j.jhydrol.2009.01.026, 2009.

Pappenberger, F., Beven, K. J., Hunter, N. M., Bates, P. D., Gouweleeuw, B. T., Thielen, J., and de Roo, A. P. J.: Cascading model uncertainty from medium range weather forecasts (10 days) through a rainfall-runoff model to flood inundation predictions within the European Flood Forecasting System (EFFS), Hydrol. Earth Syst. Sci., 9, 381–393, https://doi.org/10.5194/hess-9-381-2005, 2005a.

Pappenberger, F., Beven, K., Horritt, M., and Blazkova, S.: Uncertainty in the calibration of effective roughness parameters in HEC-RAS using inundation and downstream level observations, J. Hydrol., 302, 46–69, https://doi.org/10.1016/j.jhydrol.2004.06.036, 2005b.

Pappenberger, F., Matgen, P., Beven, K. J., Henry, J.-B., Pfister, L., and de Fraipont, P.: Influence of uncertain boundary conditions and model structure on flood inundation predictions, Adv. Water Resour., 29, 1430–1449, https://doi.org/10.1016/j.advwatres.2005.11.012, 2006.

Pappenberger, F., Beven, K., Frodsham, K., Romanowicz, R., and Matgen, P.: Grasping the unavoidable subjectivity in calibration of flood inundation models: a vulnerability weighted approach, J. Hydrol., 333, 275–287, https://doi.org/10.1016/j.jhydrol.2006.08.017, 2007.

Renard, B., Kuczera, G., Kavetski, D., Thyer, M., and Franks, S.: Bayesian total error analysis for hydrologic models: quantifying uncertainties arising from input, output and structural errors, Proc. Water, 2008, 608–619, 2008.

Reuter, H. I., Nelson, A., and Jarvis, A.: An evaluation of void-filling interpolation methods for SRTM data, Int. J. Geogr. Inf. Sci., 21, 983–1008, https://doi.org/10.1080/13658810601169899, 2007.

Romanowicz, R. and Beven, K.: Dynamic real-time prediction of flood inundation probabilities, Hydrolog. Sci. J., 43, 181–196, https://doi.org/10.1080/02626669809492117, 1998.

Romanowicz, R. and Beven, K.: Estimation of flood inundation probabilities as conditioned on event inundation maps, Water Resour. Res., 39, https://doi.org/10.1029/2001WR001056, 2003.

Sarrazin, F., Pianosi, F., and Wagener, T.: Global sensitivity analysis of environmental models: convergence and validation, Environ. Modell. Softw., 79, 135–152, https://doi.org/10.1016/j.envsoft.2016.02.005, 2016.

Schanze, J.: Flood risk management – a basic framework, in: Flood Risk Management: hazards, Vulnerability and Mitigation Measures, Springer Netherlands, Ostrov, Czech Republic, available at: http://www.springerlink.com/content/u27867381875884l/references/ (last access: 13 May 2016), 2006.

Smith, A. F. M. and Roberts, G. O.: Bayesian computation via the Gibbs Sampler and related Markov Chain Monte Carlo methods, J. Roy. Stat. Soc. B Met., 55, 3–23, 1993.

Smith, M., Phillips, J., and Spahr, N.: Hurricane Mitch: peak discharge for selected river reaches in Honduras, US Geological Survey, available at: http://pdf.usaid.gov/pdf_docs/Pnacp984.pdf (last access: 13 July 2017), 2002.

Smith, R. A. E., Bates, P. D., and Hayes, C.: Evaluation of a coastal flood inundation model using hard and soft data, Environ. Modell. Softw., 30, 35–46, https://doi.org/10.1016/j.envsoft.2011.11.008, 2012.

Strobl, E.: The macroeconomic impact of natural disasters in developing countries: evidence from Hurricane Strikes in the Central American and Caribbean region, Proceedings of the German Development Economics Conference, Frankfurt a. M. 2009, Verein für Socialpolitik, Research Committee Development Economics, available at: https://ideas.repec.org/p/zbw/gdec09/35.html (last access: 18 February 2017), 2009.

Surkan, A. J.: Synthetic hydrographs: effects of network geometry, Water Resour. Res., 5, 112–128, https://doi.org/10.1029/WR005i001p00112, 1969.

Tewolde, M. H. and Smithers, J. C.: Flood routing in ungauged catchments using Muskingum methods, Water SA, 32, 379–388, https://doi.org/10.4314/wsa.v32i3.5263, 2007.

Todini, E.: A mass conservative and water storage consistent variable parameter Muskingum–Cunge approach, Hydrol. Earth Syst. Sci., 11, 1645–1659, https://doi.org/10.5194/hess-11-1645-2007, 2007.

Triglav-Čekada, M. and Radovan, D.: Using volunteered geographical information to map the November 2012 floods in Slovenia, Nat. Hazards Earth Syst. Sci., 13, 2753–2762, https://doi.org/10.5194/nhess-13-2753-2013, 2013.

UN/ISDR: Disaster Statistics – UNISDR, available at: https://www.unisdr.org/we/inform/disaster-statistics (last access: 7 September 2016), 2016.

Valyrakis, M., Solley, M., and Koursari, E.: Flood risk modeling of urbanized estuarine areas under uncertainty: a case study for Whitesands, UK, Br. J. Environ. Clim. Change, 5, 147–161, https://doi.org/10.9734/BJECC/2015/12915, 2015.

Warmink, J. J. and Booij, M. J.: Uncertainty analysis in river modelling, in: Rivers – Physical, Fluvial and Environmental Processes, edited by: Rowiński, P. and Radecki-Pawlik, A., Springer International Publishing, Cham, Switzerland, 255–277, 2015.

Westerberg, I., Walther, A., Guerrero, J.-L., Coello, Z., Halldin, S., Xu, C.-Y., Chen, D., and Lundin, L.-C.: Precipitation data in a mountainous catchment in Honduras: quality assessment and spatiotemporal characteristics, Theor. Appl. Climatol., 101, 381–396, https://doi.org/10.1007/s00704-009-0222-x, 2010.

Wohl, E.: Uncertainty in flood estimates associated with roughness coefficient, J. Hydraul. Eng., 124, 219–223, https://doi.org/10.1061/(ASCE)0733-9429(1998)124:2(219), 1998.

Appendix A: Description of the TOPMODEL rainfall–runoff modelling tool

The TOPMODEL scheme in Fuentes-Andino et al. (2017) used here assumes a grid-cell distributed catchment. For any nth cell, the precipitation infiltrates first through the root zone storage, with capacity equal to the minimum value between a constant and the local initial deficit (D_n) in units of length (L). The rate of infiltration is the minimum between the precipitation rate at that time or a specified maximum rate ($i_{\max}$), in units of length divided by time (LT^{-1}), where the excess rainfall is routed as surface runoff. Once the maximum capacity of the root zone storage is reached, water is leaked towards the unsaturated zone storage ($S2_n$) which has a maximum capacity equal to D_n minus the root zone storage capacity. Once this capacity is exceeded, excess is again routed to the outlet as surface runoff. A rate $q_{v_n} = S2_n/(D_n \times t_d)$ (LT^{-1}) infiltrates from $S2_n$ towards a lumped subsurface storage, where t_d is a local residence factor in LT^{-1} units. Thus the catchment unsaturated zone recharge volume is estimated as the sum of all vertical flows:

$$Q_v = \sum \mathrm{ac}_n \times q_{v_n}, \tag{A1}$$

for ac_n equal to the area of the cell.

Following the TOPMODEL concept (Beven, 1997, 2012; Kirkby, 1997), the following assumptions are made: (a) the saturated zone is in equilibrium with a steady recharge rate from an upslope contributing area (a_n); (b) the effective hydraulic gradient is assumed to be equal to the local surface slope ($\tan\beta_n$); (c) a subsurface transmissivity profile is described by an exponential function, $q_n = T_o \tan\beta_n \mathrm{e}^{-D_n/m}$ ($\mathrm{L}^2\mathrm{T}^{-1}$), which takes the value T_o when the cell is saturated and has a rate of decline controlled by the parameter m. Following these assumptions, the downslope subsurface flow rates along the stream channel are summed to obtain the baseflow compounded volume in the catchment (Q_b):

$$Q_\mathrm{b} = \sum q_n = A\mathrm{e}^{-\gamma}\mathrm{e}^{-\overline{D}/m}, \tag{A2}$$

where γ is the average soil topographic index, $\gamma_n = \ln(a_n/(T_o \tan\beta_n))$, of all the cells within a catchment, and $\overline{D}$ is the catchment mean storage deficit.

Equation (A2) can be inverted to obtain an initial estimation of $\overline{D}$ by assuming an initial baseflow; then, an estimation of the local deficit (D_n) is done through Eq. (A3).

$$D_n = \overline{D} + m[\gamma - \gamma_n] \tag{A3}$$

Update of the catchment average storage deficit is done at each time step by subtracting the unsaturated zone recharge ($Q_{v_{t-1}}$) and adding the baseflow ($Q_{b_{t-1}}$) from the previous time step:

$$\overline{D}_t = \overline{D}_{t-1} + \frac{[Q_{b_{t-1}} - Q_{v_{t-1}}]}{A}. \tag{A4}$$

Excess rainfall and water excess after the unsaturated zone storage that has reached its maximum capacity are routed towards the outlet using the network width function concept (NWF) (Kirkby, 1976; Surkan, 1969) which takes into account the structure of the river network when estimating the travel time from the nth cell to the outlet following the direction of flow. An adaptation by Grimaldi et al. (2010) was used here which assumes a varying hillslope velocity ($v_{hj} = \mathrm{l}_u \cdot \sqrt{s_j}$) dependent on the slope of the cell following the direction of the flow (s_j) and the land-use coefficient, l_u, and keeping a constant celerity (Beven et al., 1979; McDonnell and Beven, 2014).

Thus, the time spent by a water particle on the surface to travel from the nth cell to the outlet is estimated:

$$\tau_n = \sum_{j=1}^{j=N}\left[\frac{l_\mathrm{h}}{v_{\mathrm{h}_j}}\right] + \frac{L_\mathrm{c}}{v_\mathrm{c}}, \tag{A5}$$

where, following the same path that the flow takes, there are a total of N cells with length l_h from the nth cell at a hillslope towards the junction at the channel. And L_c is the length from the junction towards the catchment outlet. Thus the final hydrograph at the outlet cell is equal to the sequence of compound runoff volume from cells arriving at the same time (estimated by Eq. A5) plus the groundwater contribution (A2) at those times.

Appendix B: Description of the Muskingum–Cunge–Todini (MCT) routing

The Muskingum–Cunge–Todini routing (MCT) (Todini, 2007) used in this work was carried out using guidelines in Tewolde and Smithers (2007) to overcome the lack of river cross-sectional data. Thus, to propagate a flood wave in a reach of length Δx, the following procedure was followed: an initial guess for the outflow at the $t+\Delta t$ step ($O_{t+\Delta t}$) in units $\mathrm{m}^3\mathrm{s}^{-1}$ is made using Eq. (B1) and assuming $O_t \approx I_t$ for the initial time step:

$$\hat{O}_{t+\Delta t} = O_t + (I_{t+\Delta t} - I_t). \tag{B1}$$

The reference discharge for the times $\tau = t$ and $\tau = t + \Delta t$, (Q_τ), is given in Eq. (B2):

$$Q_\tau = \frac{I_\tau + O_\tau}{2}, \tag{B2}$$

and the reference water level y_τ, hydraulic radius R_τ, average cross-sectional area velocity v_τ, celerity c_τ, and cross-sectional area A_τ in units of length, length, velocity, velocity, and area respectively are estimated using Manning's equation and some empirical relationships as in Tewolde and Smithers (2007) (Eqs. B3 to B7):

$$y_\tau = \left(\frac{Q_\tau \times n}{0.508 \times P_\tau \sqrt{S}}\right)^{3/5}, \tag{B3}$$

where $P_\tau = 4.75\sqrt{Q_\tau}$ is the wetted perimeter estimated for stable river channels, S the reach slope, and n the Manning roughness coefficient.

$$R_\tau = \frac{2y_\tau}{3}, \tag{B4}$$

where Eq. (B4) assumes a wide parabolic channel.

$$v_\tau = \frac{1}{n}(R_\tau)^{2/3}\sqrt{S}, \tag{B5}$$

$$c_\tau = 1.4 \times v_\tau, \tag{B6}$$

where a coefficient equal to 1.4 was chosen as the average between a parabolic channel and wide rectangular channel (1.2 and 1.6 respectively).

$$A_\tau = R_\tau \times W_\tau \tag{B7}$$

where W_τ is the top flow width, assumed to be approximately equal to the wetted perimeter (P_τ).

The specialization factor for correction of the Courant and Reynolds number, β_τ, following Todini (2007), is

$$\beta_\tau = \frac{c_\tau A_\tau}{Q_\tau}. \tag{B8}$$

Thus, the corrected Courant number, C_τ^*, is estimated as

$$C_\tau^* = \frac{c_\tau}{\beta_\tau}\frac{\Delta t}{\Delta x}, \tag{B9}$$

and the corrected Reynolds number, D_τ^*, as

$$D_\tau^* = \frac{Q_\tau}{\beta_\tau W_\tau S c_\tau \Delta x}, \tag{B10}$$

which yields the following MCT parameters:

$$C_1 = \frac{-1 + C_t^* + D_t^*}{1 + C_{t+\Delta t}^* + D_{t+\Delta t}^*},$$
$$C_2 = \frac{1 + C_t^* - D_t^*}{1 + C_{t+\Delta t}^* + D_{t+\Delta t}^*}\frac{C_{t+\Delta t}^*}{C_t^*}, \quad \text{and} \tag{B11}$$
$$C_3 = \frac{1 - C_t^* + D_t^*}{1 + C_{t+\Delta t}^* + D_{t+\Delta t}^*}\frac{C_{t+\Delta t}^*}{C_t^*},$$

and the outflow at a reach at time $t + \Delta t$ is estimated by Eq. (B12):

$$\hat{O}_{t+\Delta t} = C_1 I_{t+\Delta t} + C_2 I_t + C_3 O_t. \tag{B12}$$

All the estimations for the time $\tau = t + \Delta t$ are computed twice to eliminate the influence of the first guess $\hat{O}_{t+\Delta t}$ in Eq. (B1).

Appendix C: The Kuiper statistic test

The Kuiper statistic (V) (Kuiper, 1960) is estimated as the sum of the maximum negative and maximum positive distances (D_- and D_- respectively) between two cumulative distribution functions (S_{N1} and S_{N2}):

$$V = D_- + D_+ = \max[S_{N1} - S_{N2}] + \max[S_{N2} - S_{N1}]. \tag{C1}$$

The significance level (p) is estimated by the following equation:

$$p = 2\sum_{j=1}^{j=\infty}(4j^2\lambda^2 - 1)e^{-2j^2\lambda^2}, \tag{C2}$$

where

$$\lambda = V\left(\sqrt{N_e} + 0.155 + \frac{0.24}{\sqrt{N_e}}\right), \tag{C3}$$

where

$$N_e = N_1N_2/N_1 + N_2, \tag{C4}$$

for N_1 and N_2 equal to the number of data points for the first and second distributions.

PERMISSIONS

All chapters in this book were first published in HESS, by Copernicus Publications; hereby published with permission under the Creative Commons Attribution License or equivalent. Every chapter published in this book has been scrutinized by our experts. Their significance has been extensively debated. The topics covered herein carry significant findings which will fuel the growth of the discipline. They may even be implemented as practical applications or may be referred to as a beginning point for another development.

The contributors of this book come from diverse backgrounds, making this book a truly international effort. This book will bring forth new frontiers with its revolutionizing research information and detailed analysis of the nascent developments around the world.

We would like to thank all the contributing authors for lending their expertise to make the book truly unique. They have played a crucial role in the development of this book. Without their invaluable contributions this book wouldn't have been possible. They have made vital efforts to compile up to date information on the varied aspects of this subject to make this book a valuable addition to the collection of many professionals and students.

This book was conceptualized with the vision of imparting up-to-date information and advanced data in this field. To ensure the same, a matchless editorial board was set up. Every individual on the board went through rigorous rounds of assessment to prove their worth. After which they invested a large part of their time researching and compiling the most relevant data for our readers.

The editorial board has been involved in producing this book since its inception. They have spent rigorous hours researching and exploring the diverse topics which have resulted in the successful publishing of this book. They have passed on their knowledge of decades through this book. To expedite this challenging task, the publisher supported the team at every step. A small team of assistant editors was also appointed to further simplify the editing procedure and attain best results for the readers.

Apart from the editorial board, the designing team has also invested a significant amount of their time in understanding the subject and creating the most relevant covers. They scrutinized every image to scout for the most suitable representation of the subject and create an appropriate cover for the book.

The publishing team has been an ardent support to the editorial, designing and production team. Their endless efforts to recruit the best for this project, has resulted in the accomplishment of this book. They are a veteran in the field of academics and their pool of knowledge is as vast as their experience in printing. Their expertise and guidance has proved useful at every step. Their uncompromising quality standards have made this book an exceptional effort. Their encouragement from time to time has been an inspiration for everyone.

The publisher and the editorial board hope that this book will prove to be a valuable piece of knowledge for researchers, students, practitioners and scholars across the globe.

LIST OF CONTRIBUTORS

B. Mazzorana
Department of Hydraulic Engineering, Autonomous Province of Bolzano, Bolzano, Italy

S. Simoni
Mountain-eering S.r.l., Bolzano, Italy

C. Scherer
Obrist & Partner Engineering, Caldaro, Italy

B. Gems
Institute for Infrastructure Engineering, University of Innsbruck, Innsbruck, Austria

S. Fuchs
Institute of Mountain Risk Engineering, University of Natural Resources and Life Sciences, Vienna, Austria

M. Keiler
Institute of Geography, University of Bern, Bern, Switzerland

Guido Felder and Rolf Weingartner
University of Bern, Institute of Geography, Oeschger Centre for Climate Change Research, Mobiliar Lab for Natural Risks, Bern, 3012, Switzerland

Gemma Coxon, Jeffrey Neal, Jim Freer and Paul Bates
School of Geographical Sciences, University of Bristol, Bristol, BS8 1SS, UK

Niall Quinn
Fathom Ltd., Bristol, BS1 6QF, UK

Andreas Paul Zischg
University of Bern, Institute of Geography, Oeschger Centre for Climate Change Research, Mobiliar Lab for Natural Risks, Bern, 3012, Switzerland
School of Geographical Sciences, University of Bristol, Bristol, BS8 1SS, UK

Chiara Arrighi and Fabio Castelli
Department of Civil and Environmental Engineering, University of Florence, Via di S. Marta 3, 50139 Firenze, Italy

Hocine Oumeraci
Leichtweiß-Institute for Hydraulic Engineering and Water Resources, TU Braunschweig, Beethovenstrasse 51a, 38106 Braunschweig, Germany

Marie-claire ten Veldhuis
Delft University of Technology, Watermanagement Department, Delft, 2628CN, the Netherlands
Princeton University, Hydrometeorology Group, Princeton, NJ 08544, USA

Long Yang and James Smith
Princeton University, Hydrometeorology Group, Princeton, NJ 08544, USA

Shuguang Liu
UNEP-Tongji Institute of Environment for Sustainable Development Shanghai, Shanghai, 20002 China

Zhengzheng Zhou
Princeton University, Hydrometeorology Group, Princeton, NJ 08544, USA
3Tongji University, School of Ocean and Earth Science, Shanghai, 200092, China
UNEP-Tongji Institute of Environment for Sustainable Development Shanghai, Shanghai, 20002 China

Qiang Zhang and Peijun Shi
Key Laboratory of Environmental Change and Natural Disaster, Ministry of Education, Beijing Normal University, Beijing 100875, China
State Key Laboratory of Earth Surface Processes and Resource Ecology, Beijing Normal University, Beijing 100875, China
Faculty of Geographical Science, Academy of Disaster Reduction and Emergency Management, Beijing Normal University, Beijing 100875, China

Xihui Gu
Department of Atmospheric Science, School of Environmental Studies, China University of Geosciences, Wuhan 430074, China

Vijay P. Singh
Department of Biological and Agricultural Engineering and Zachry Department of Civil Engineering, Texas A&M University, College Station, Texas, USA

Peng Sun
College of Territory Resources and Tourism, Anhui Normal University, Anhui 241000, China

M. A. Somos-Valenzuela, D. C. McKinney and D. R. Rounce
Center for Research in Water Resources, University of Texas at Austin, Austin, Texas, USA

A. C. Byers
The Mountain Institute, Washington DC, USA

C. Portocarrero
Independent Consultant, Huaraz, Peru

D. Lamsal
Graduate School of Environmental Studies, Nagoya University, Japan

Juliana Delgado
The Nature Conservancy, Bogotá, Colombia

Héctor Angarita
The Nature Conservancy, Bogotá, Colombia Grupo de ecología y territorio, Facultad de estudios ambientales y rurales, Pontificia Universidad Javeriana, Bogotá, Colombia

Albertus J. Wickel and David Purkey
Stockholm Environment Institute US Center, Davis, California, USA

Jack Sieber
Stockholm Environment Institute US Center, Somerville, Massachusetts, USA

John Chavarro
Centro de Investigación en Ciencias y Recursos GeoAgroAmbientales CENIGAA, Neiva, Colombia

Javier A. Maldonado-Ocampo
Laboratorio de Ictiología, Unidad de Ecología y Sistemática (UNESIS), Departamento de Biología, Facultad de Ciencias, Pontificia Universidad Javeriana, Bogotá, Colombia

Guido A. Herrera-R
Laboratorio de Ictiología, Unidad de Ecología y Sistemática (UNESIS), Departamento de Biología, Facultad de Ciencias, Pontificia Universidad Javeriana, Bogotá, Colombia
Laboratoire Evolution et Diversité Biologiques (EDB), Paul Sabatier University, Toulouse III, France

Francis W. Zwiers
Pacific Climate Impacts Consortium, University of Victoria, Victoria, V8N 5L3, Canada

Charles L. Curry
Pacific Climate Impacts Consortium, University of Victoria, Victoria, V8N 5L3, Canada
School of Earth and Ocean Sciences, University of Victoria, Victoria, V8N 5L3, Canada

Ben T. Gouweleeuw, Christian Gruber, Frank Flechtner and Andreas Güntner
GFZ German Research Centre for Geosciences, Section 5.4 Hydrology, 14473 Potsdam, Germany

Animesh K. Gain
Christian Albrecht University Kiel, Institute of Geography, Ludewig-Meyn-Str. 14, 24098 Kiel, Germany

Andreas Kvas and Thorsten Mayer-Gürr
Graz University of Technology, Institute of Geodesy, 8010 Graz, Austria

Eleni Maria Michailidi and Baldassare Bacchi
DICATAM, Università degli Studi di Brescia, Via Branze 42, 25123 Brescia, Italy

J. Herget, T. Roggenkamp and M. Krell
Department of Geography, University of Bonn, Bonn, Germany

Dan Yu
State Key Laboratory of Water Resources and Hydropower Engineering Science, Wuhan University, Wuhan, 430072, China

Ping Xie
State Key Laboratory of Water Resources and Hydropower Engineering Science, Wuhan University, Wuhan, 430072, China
Collaborative Innovation Center for Territorial Sovereignty and Maritime Rights, Wuhan, 430072, China

Xiaohua Dong, Ji Liu, Yinghai Li, Tao Peng and Haibo Ma
College of Hydraulic & Environmental Engineering, China Three Gorges University, Yichang, 443002, China
Hubei Provincial Collaborative Innovation Center for Water Security, Wuhan, 430070, China

Xiaonong Hu
Institute of Groundwater and Earth Sciences, Jinan University, Guangzhou, 510632, China

Kai Wang and Shijin Xu
Hydrologic Bureau of Huaihe River Commission, Bengbu, 233001, China

Diana Fuentes-Andino, Sven Halldin, José Eduardo Reynolds and Giuliano Di Baldassarre
Department of Earth Sciences, Uppsala University, Villavägen 16, 752 36 Uppsala, Sweden
Centre for Natural Disaster Science (CNDS), Uppsala University, Uppsala, Sweden

Keith Beven
Department of Earth Sciences, Uppsala University, Villavägen 16, 752 36 Uppsala, Sweden
Lancaster Environment Centre, Lancaster University, Lancaster LA1 4YQ, UK

Chong-Yu Xu
Department of Earth Sciences, Uppsala University, Villavägen 16, 752 36 Uppsala, Sweden
Department of Geosciences, University of Oslo, Blindern, 0316, Oslo, Norway

Index

CPSIA information can be obtained
at www.ICGtesting.com
Printed in the USA
LVHW060159060222
710369LV00002B/79

9 781647 401306